Atlantic Spain and Portugal

Cabo Ortegal (Galicia) to Gibraltar

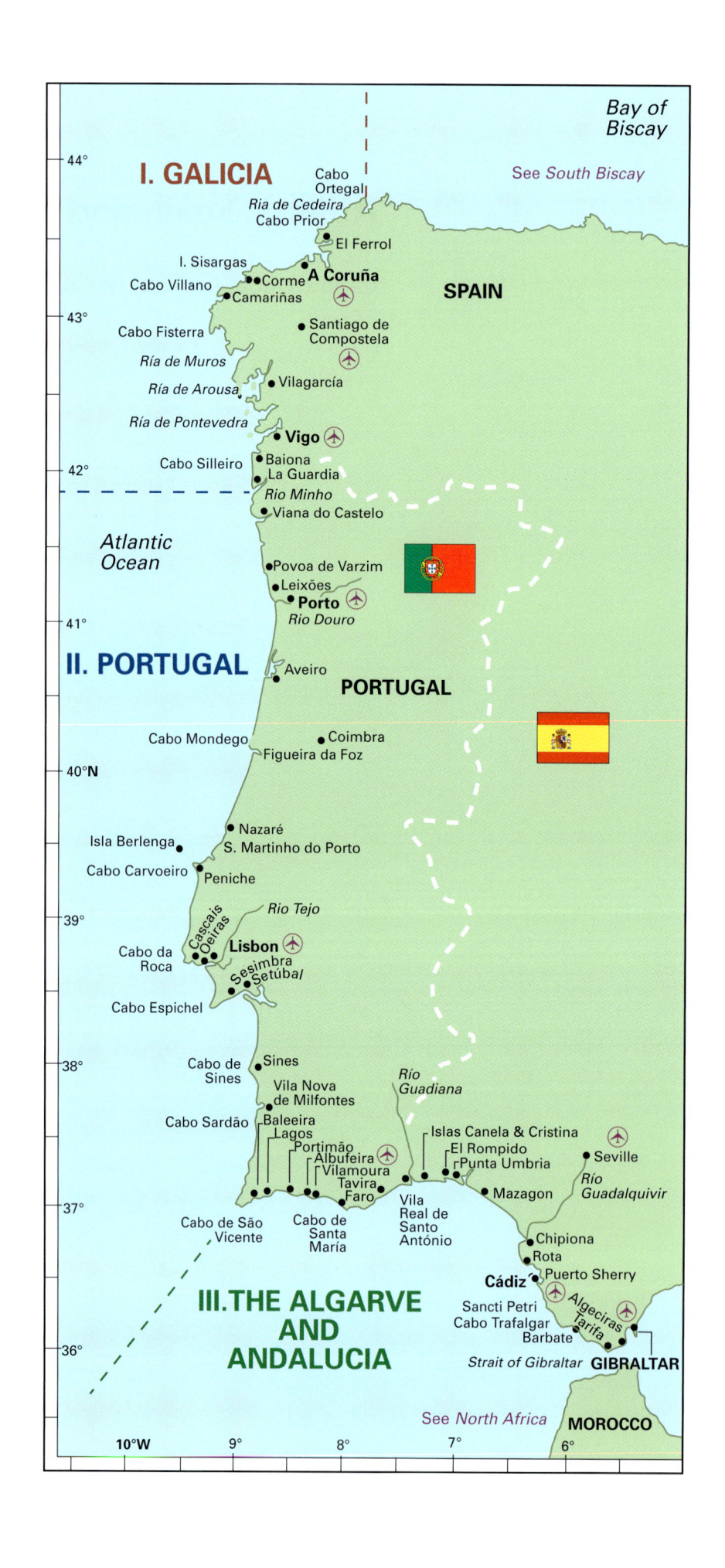

I. GALICIA
II. PORTUGAL
III. THE ALGARVE AND ANDALUCIA

Bay of Biscay
See *South Biscay*

Cabo Ortegal
Ria de Cedeira
Cabo Prior
El Ferrol
I. Sisargas
Corme
A Coruña
Cabo Villano
Camariñas
SPAIN
Cabo Fisterra
Santiago de Compostela
Ría de Muros
Ría de Arousa
Vilagarcía
Ría de Pontevedra
Vigo
Baiona
Cabo Silleiro
La Guardia
Rio Minho
Viana do Castelo

Atlantic Ocean

Povoa de Varzim
Leixões
Porto
Rio Douro
Aveiro
PORTUGAL
Cabo Mondego
Coimbra
Figueira da Foz

Nazaré
Isla Berlenga
S. Martinho do Porto
Cabo Carvoeiro
Peniche
Rio Tejo
Cascais
Oeiras
Lisbon
Cabo da Roca
Sesimbra
Setúbal
Cabo Espichel

Cabo de Sines
Sines
Vila Nova de Milfontes
Río Guadiana
Cabo Sardão
Baleeira
Lagos
Islas Canela & Cristina
Portimão
El Rompido
Albufeira
Punta Umbria
Vilamoura
Mazagon
Seville
Tavira
Río Guadalquivir
Faro
Vila Real de Santo António
Chipiona
Cabo de São Vicente
Cabo de Santa María
Rota
Cádiz
Puerto Sherry
Sancti Petri
Algeciras
Cabo Trafalgar
Tarifa
Barbate
Strait of Gibraltar
GIBRALTAR

See *North Africa*
MOROCCO

Atlantic Spain and Portugal

Cabo Ortegal (Galicia) to Gibraltar

ROYAL CRUISING CLUB PILOTAGE FOUNDATION

Henry Buchanan

Imray Laurie Norie & Wilson

Published by
Imray Laurie Norie & Wilson Ltd
Wych House The Broadway St Ives
Cambridgeshire PE27 5BT England
☎ +44 (0)1480 462114
Fax +44 (0) 1480 496109
Email ilnw@imray.com
www.imray.com
2019

© Text: RCC Pilotage Foundation 2019
© Plans: Imray Laurie Norie & Wilson Ltd 2019
© Aerial photographs not cited: Imray Laurie Norie and Wilson Ltd and Patrick Roach 2010
© Other photographs: As cited in caption

All rights reserved. No part of this publication may be reproduced, transmitted or used in any form by any means – graphic, electronic or mechanical, including photocopying, recording, taping or information storage and retrieval systems or otherwise – without the prior permission of the Publishers.

First edition 1988
Second edition 1990
Third edition 1995
Fourth edition 2000
Fifth edition 2006
Sixth edition 2010
Seventh edition 2015
Eighth edition 2019

ISBN 978 184623 964 9

British Library Cataloguing in Publication Data.
A catalogue record for this title is available from the British Library.

Reprinted 2022 in Croatia by Denona

Previous authors
Oz Robinson RCC
Anne Hammick RCC
Martin Walker RCC

UPDATES AND SUPPLEMENTS

Any mid-season updates or annual supplements are published as free downloads available from www.imray.com Printed copies are also available on request from the publishers.

FIND OUT MORE

For a wealth of further information, including passage planning guides and cruising logs for this area visit the Royal Cruising Club Pilotage Foundation website at www.rccpf.org.uk

FEEDBACK

The Royal Cruising Club Pilotage Foundation is a voluntary, charitable organisation. We welcome all feedback for updates and new information. If you notice any errors or omissions, please let us know at www.rccpf.org.uk

CAUTION

Whilst the Royal Cruising Club Pilotage Foundation, the author and the publishers have used reasonable endeavours to ensure the accuracy of the content of this book, it contains selected information and thus is not definitive. It does not contain all known information on the subject in hand and should not be relied on alone for navigational use: it should only be used in conjunction with official hydrographical data. This is particularly relevant to the plans, which should not be used for navigation. The Pilotage Foundation, the authors and the publishers believe that the information which they have included is a useful aid to prudent navigation, but the safety of a vessel depends ultimately on the judgment of the skipper, who should assess all information, published or unpublished. The information provided in this pilot book may be out of date and may be changed or updated without notice. The Pilotage Foundation cannot accept any liability for any error, omission or failure to update such information. To the extent permitted by law, the Pilotage Foundation, the author and the publishers do not accept liability for any loss and/or damage howsoever caused that may arise from reliance on information contained in these pages.

Positions and Waypoints
All positions and waypoints are to datum WGS 84. They are included to help in locating places, features and transits. Do not rely on them alone for safe navigation.

Bearings and Lights
Any bearings are given as °T and from seaward. The characteristics of lights may be changed during the lifetime of this book. They should be checked against the latest edition of the UK Admiralty *List of Lights*.

Contents

Foreword *vii*

Acknowledgements *viii*

Introduction *1*

I. Galicia
Cabo Ortegal to the Portuguese border *10*

    Ría de Cedeira to A Coruña *18*
    A Coruña to Laxe *36*
    Laxe to Cabo Fisterra (Finisterre) *44*
    Cabo Fisterra to Ría de Muros *52*
    Ría de Muros to Ría de Arousa *59*
    Ría de Arousa to Isla Ons *70*
    Isla Ons, Ría de Pontevedra to Islas Cies *99*
    Islas Cies and Ria de Vigo to Baiona *113*
    Baiona to the Portuguese border *124*

II. Portugal – the west coast
Foz do Minho to Cabo de São Vicente *130*

    Foz do Minho to Leixões *134*
    Porto to Figueira da Foz *152*
    Figueira da Foz to Cabo da Roca *168*
    Approaches to the Rio Tejo and Lisbon *184*
    Cabo Espichel to Cabo de São Vicente *208*

III. The Algarve and Andalucia
Cabo de São Vicente to Gibraltar *222*

    Cabo de São Vicente to Tavira *222*
    Río Guadiana to Río Guadalquivir *266*
    Río Guadalquivir to Cabo Trafalgar *302*
    Cabo Trafalgar to Gibraltar *320*

Appendix *341*
   I. Charts and books *341*
  II. Waypoints *342*
 III. Useful addresses *342*
 IV. Regulations, tax and VAT in Spain *342*
  V. Portugal and Andalucía online *343*
 VI. Glossary *344*
VII. Abbreviations used on the charts *349*

Index *350*

ROYAL CRUISING CLUB PILOTAGE FOUNDATION

The Royal Crusing Club Pilotage Foundation was formed as an independent charity in 1976 supported by a gift and permanent endowment made to the Royal Cruising Club by Dr Fred Ellis. The Foundation's charitable objective is 'to advance the education of the public in the science and practice of navigation'.

The Foundation is privileged to have been given the copyrights to books written by a number of distinguished authors and yachtsmen. These are kept as up to date as possible. New publications are also produced by the Foundation to cover a range of cruising areas. This is only made possible through the dedicated work of our authors and editors, all of whom are experienced sailors, who depend on a valuable supply of information from generous-minded yachtsmen and women from around the world.

Most of the management of the Foundation is done on a voluntary basis. In line with its charitable status, the Foundation distributes no profits. Any surpluses are used to finance new publications and to subsidise publications which cover some of the more remote areas of the world.

The Foundation works in close collaboration with three publishers – Imray Laurie Norie & Wilson, Bloomsbury (Adlard Coles Nautical) and On Board Publications. The Foundation also itself publishes guides and pilots, including web downloads, for areas where limited demand does not justify large print runs. Several books have been translated into French, Spanish, Italian and German and some books are now available as digital versions.

For further details about the Pilotage Foundation and its publications visit **www.rccpf.org.uk**

PUBLICATIONS OF THE ROYAL CRUISING CLUB PILOTAGE FOUNDATION

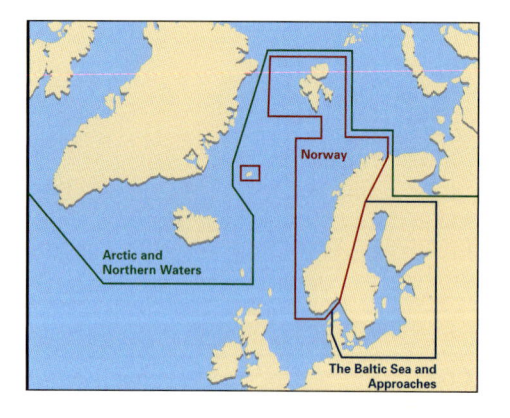

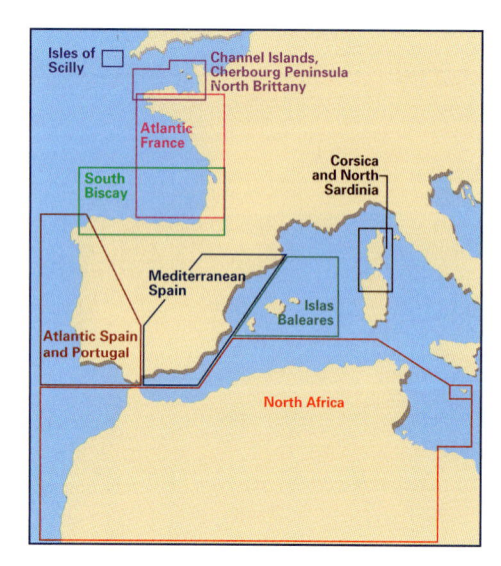

Imray
Arctic and Northern Waters
Norway
The Baltic Sea and Approaches
Channel Islands, Cherbourg Peninsula & North Brittany
Isles of Scilly
Atlantic France
South Biscay
Atlantic Islands
Atlantic Spain & Portugal
Mediterranean Spain
Islas Baleares
Corsica and North Sardinia
North Africa
Chile
Black Sea

Adlard Coles Nautical
Atlantic Crossing Guide
Pacific Crossing Guide

On Board Publications
South Atlantic Circuit
Havens and Anchorages for the South American Coast

The Royal Cruising Club Pilotage Foundation
Supplement to Falkland Island Shores
Cruising Guide to West Africa
Argentina
Brazil

Royal Cruising Club Pilotage Foundation Website
www.rccpf.org.uk
Supplements
Support files for books
Passage Planning Guides
ePilots - from the Arctic to the Antarctic Peninsula

PATRON OF THE ROYAL CRUISING CLUB PILOTAGE FOUNDATION

TRINITY HOUSE

The Royal Cruising Club Pilotage Foundation is privileged to have Trinity House as its Patron. Trinity House, established in 1514 under King Henry VIII, is a charity dedicated to safeguarding shipping and seafarers by providing education, support and welfare to the seafaring community as well as by delivering and monitoring reliable aids to navigation for the benefit and safety of all mariners. Proud of its long history and traditions in navigation and pilotage, Trinity House is nevertheless at the forefront of technological developments and works closely with other organisations around the world to improve aids to navigation and to optimise global navigation satellite systems and e-navigation. The ongoing safety of navigation and education of mariners are common goals of Trinity House and of the Pilotage Foundation.

To find out more go to www.trinityhouse.co.uk

Foreword to 8th edition

Atlantic Spain and Portugal was one of the Royal Cruising Club Pilotage Foundation's earliest publications with the first edition published in 1988. Over the following 30 years and through seven further editions it has been developed and expanded into the up-to-date and comprehensive cruising guide that is the 8th edition. With this, his second edition, Henry Buchanan has further refined and developed his previous work, applying his very extensive knowledge of the area.

The coastline covered by *Atlantic Spain and Portugal* stretches over 600 miles from the Rías of Galicia to the beaches of the Algarve, the estuaries of Andalucía and on the Punta Europa and the Strait of Gibraltar, offering a rich variety of terrain and cruising experiences.

Our thanks go to Henry Buchanan for another thoroughly researched and expertly compiled new edition and also to various contributors who have provided valuable input, especially members of the Irish Cruising Club. Thanks also to Jane Russell, the Pilotage Foundation's Editor in Chief, and the team at Imray for their expertise in bringing the new edition to publication, demonstrating the due level of clarity and authority that is associated with Pilotage Foundation publications.

The quality of this publication is in large part driven by the contributions from yachtsmen and women sailing these coasts and using this cruising guide. We welcome any reports and updates to navigational and other detail provided in this book via the Cruising Notes page on the Foundation's website (www.rccpf.org.uk). These reports will be posted on the website and consolidated into an annual supplement available at no charge www.imray.com and www.rccpf.org.uk.

Anthony Wells
Executive Director, Royal Cruising Club
Pilotage Foundation
March 2019

Preface

Welcome to this edition of the *Atlantic Spain and Portugal Pilot*. As a cruising yachtsman of 45 years it has been a rewarding experience to work on this book, very early versions of which were invaluable Foreign Port Information (FPI) Notes written by the members of the Royal Cruising Club (RCC). RCC authors have developed these Notes into the Pilot you see today, assisted by mariners of many nationalities who have freely contributed information to the benefit of all.

On the author's first cruise from Gibraltar to the UK in 1989 there were no modern marinas in Atlantic Spain and Portugal but a few yacht clubs, many fishing harbours and of course some useful anchorages. Subsequently, two further cruises along the entire coast both northwards and southwards, cruises to Galician waters and land visits to both Spain and Portugal have added greatly to the authors understanding of this fascinating coast and its people.

Updates for this edition include the following: For Galicia, pilotage information (including photographs) on the northern entrance to the Ría de Arousa and many anchorages have been generously donated by Geraldine Hennigan and Norman Kean following the Irish Cruising Club (ICC) cruise to the Rías Baixas in 2017.

In Portugal, the harbour at Nazaré on the west coast has been extensively researched with enormous help from Dody Stiller of the ketch *Tonga*, under major refit there using the expanding facilities and developing marina run by the Club Naval de Nazaré. Information on facilities in Lisbon has also been extensively revised including the update on marinas and the continuing development of a new boatyard at Algés.

Cruising the west coast of Portugal has been made safer by two recent initiatives by the Portuguese Marine. They have introduced a 'flag' system on their website to provide information on the status of access to harbours along the west Portuguese coast where Atlantic swell and fast flowing rivers can combine to cause a significant hazard. Also, following accidents along this coast, all ports have upgraded their services and keep a 24-hour-watch on VHF Ch16. Mariners are encouraged to call in on VHF Ch16 before attempting an entry to harbour. These 24-hour watches have been expressly installed with pleasure

ATLANTIC SPAIN AND PORTUGAL

craft in mind and provide information on the actual sea conditions at the entrance. Details on all these facilities are included in this edition.

Cruising yachtsmen and land visits by the author have provided useful updates to the Algarve and Atlantic Andalucian coasts. Safer navigation into harbours of the latter has been provided by the Agencia Pública de Puertos de Andalucia (APPA). The APPA website now provides invaluable bathymetric information for those harbours affected by silting and shifting sands that present such a challenge to safe navigation.

Safe cruising and have fun.

Henry Buchanan

Acknowledgements

The author remains grateful to the previous ground-breaking members of the Royal Cruising Club (RCC), but also to the growing number of mariners of many nationalities who have taken the trouble to send in their suggestions and comments.

These contributors are recognised with thanks in the annual supplement to this pilot, disseminated each spring online through the Pilotage Foundation and Imray websites. As the full list is now so long, only those individuals who have helped recently with production of this edition are included here. My apologies if anyone has been inadvertently omitted:

Special thanks must go to: Geraldine Hennigan and Norman Kean for their detailed pilotage information and photographs produced for the 2017 Irish Cruising Club (ICC) cruise to the Rías Baixas, Galicia. Also to Dody Stiller of the ketch *Tonga* at Nazaré who through her many contacts has provided invaluable insights to developments there and in west Portugal.

The other stalwarts are: Jose Manuel Lodeiro, Michael & Barbara Pollitt, Will Pedder, Chris & Katie Russell, Lars Gulbrandsen, Alberto Lagos, Arnulf Doerner, Willem Melching, Helen Norris, Carmela Núñez, Mike Gill, Richard Lassen, Madeleine Strobel, Helmut Heine, Mike & Devala Robinson, Tim Trafford, Philip Leith, Richard Waite, Steve Pickard, Gavin McLaren, Richard Salkeld, Ian Powolny, Peter Fabricius, William Maltby, Ana Morales and Javier Monjas.

All contributions are welcomed with heartfelt thanks. They enhance the content and accuracy of information. Please send in any new corrections and updates to info@rccpf.org.uk.

Finally, thanks go to Lucy Wilson and her team at Imray for producing yet another fine book.

Aldan, Ría de Pontevedra, Galicia
Geraldine Hennigan

Left
Lifeboat Nazare Portugal *Henry Buchanan*

Right
Dom Vasco da Gama at Sines, Portugal *Henry Buchanan*

Introduction

The character of the Atlantic coasts of Spain and Portugal varies widely between the cliffs and rocky shoreline north of Cabo Fisterra in Galicia, and the flat sandy lagoons of the Faro area in the Portuguese Algarve beyond Cabo São Vicente. Their attraction for the cruising yachtsman is equally variable. The aim of this book is to describe the cruising grounds, harbours and facilities of the area and the safety information available in terms of the weather, sea state and navigational hazards. It does not pretend to be a comprehensive guide and should not be used without the appropriate charts. Excellent travel guides are available for crews who wish to explore this intriguing and beautiful coastal region.

Local place names are used except for a few cities and towns, such as Lisbon and Seville, which are widely known by their anglicised form. In Galicia the Gallego form of the name is generally given. Gallego, an ancient language which falls somewhere between Castilian Spanish and Portuguese, remains in everyday use; while away from major routes, road signs rarely use Castilian Spanish. Other non-English words used will be found in the glossary.

Although Gibraltar is included in this book, as it remains an important refuge or staging post for those bound for the Mediterranean or heading south towards the Canaries and beyond, it has offered less to yachtsmen in recent years. Nearby La Línea across the border in Spain offers an attractive alternative.

The cruising grounds

In cruising terms, the Atlantic coast of Spain and Portugal described in this pilot falls naturally into three parts:

Part I Western Galicia: This includes the northwest facing rías and coast of Galicia between Cabo Ortegal and Cabo Fisterra, and the southwest facing rías, known as the Rías Bajas, and their outlying islands from Cabo Fisterra to the Portuguese border at the Rio Miño.

Part II The west coast of Portugal from the Spanish border south to Cabo de São Vicente.

Part III The south coast of Portugal and Spanish Andalucia trending eastward from Cabo de São Vicente to the Algarve, Atlantic Andalucia and Gibraltar.

Galicia

Northwest rías and coast

Some 12M southwest of Cabo Ortegal is a secure anchorage in the Ría de Cedeira that provides a welcome refuge after a long haul south across the Bay of Biscay. Sailing on south and west along this dramatic coastline, the rías of Ferrol, Ares and de Betanzos, and Coruña are reached that provide marinas and facilities, and cruising opportunities in their more sheltered waters. This part of Galicia is the most exposed to the Atlantic weather and swell, however, and the aptly named Costa da Morte between A Coruña and Cabo Fisterra should be respected. Cruising this challenging coast is for the adventurous and although good shelter, anchorages and marinas (Camariñas and Muxia) can be found in the Ría de Camariñas, the entrance is fully exposed to winds and seas from the northwest and may be inaccessible in rough weather.

Southwest rías (Rías Bajas) and offlying islands

Some consider this area to be the best cruising area in Galicia and spend weeks pottering about the ports and anchorages, taking advantage of good communications and safe harbours and marinas to explore inland. Less exposed to the Atlantic weather than the coast and rías to the north of Cabo Fisterra, the Rías Bajas have beaches, interesting towns, and opportunities for rock-hopping for those wishing to test their pilotage. There are many restaurants and hotels, while excellent Atlantic fish and local shellfish are readily available.

Offshore are the Isla Ons and Islas Cies, beautiful islands with sandy beaches now part of the National Park and subject to strict access regulations (see page 15–17).

This area suffers more from fog than the north western rías, and the Azores high pressure system in summer can, on occasion, produce a clear weather north easterly blow of Force 5–6 which may last for several days. But there is always shelter to be found within a short distance.

Atlantic Portugal

This coast is not a cruising paradise but it includes some remarkable places to visit, notably Porto and Lisbon for their history and interest, and Aveiro and the Rio Sado for their sandbanks and swamps. The coast itself is, on the whole, low, the hills are inland and in summer may be lost in the haze, and in places there are miles of featureless beach.

The harbours are commercial or fishing in origin, but most are making increasing concessions to yachts. Many have natural hazards of one sort or another in the entrance; Leixões, Nazaré and Sines are notable exceptions. The most common are bars that alter with the winter storms and which, although safe enough for freighters, can be dangerous for the smaller vessel if there is a swell running. The bars are associated with rivers, and conditions are generally worse on the ebb.

Another major feature of this region is the Portuguese trade winds. Many take advantage of these prevailing northerly winds to slide south past the coast as quickly as possible. Making the passage northwards can be tedious, even in summer, but it is possible to day sail north keeping an eye on the weather and, in particular, the swell.

Algarve and Andalucía

The southern coasts of Portugal and Spain offer easier cruising than the west coast. Having rounded the corner at Cabo de São Vicente, the influences of the Mediterranean and the Moors begin to show. Harbours are generally more frequent and better equipped and, with a couple of exceptions, are easier to enter than those on the Atlantic coast.

The Algarve is crowded, both summer and winter, and its harbours busy. The shallow lagoons of Faro and Olhão, the quiet Río Guadiana and the relatively busy Río Guadalquivir, are the best areas for wildlife.

A particular hazard of this coast is the tunny net, which can stretch several miles out to sea at right angles to the shoreline, and is strong enough to foul the propeller of a small coaster. Currently five or six are set annually. Details and locations are given in the text.

Sailing and navigation

Winds and climate

Weather systems
The northern part of the region is influenced by North Atlantic weather systems. In winter, fronts and occasionally secondary depressions may cross the area. Winds are variable but those between southwest and northwest are more common. In summer, land and sea breezes can be expected inshore but the influence of the Azores Highs tends to produce winds from the north; this northerly tendency starts about April and as summer progresses and latitude decreases these winds develop into the Portuguese trades. At the height of summer in the south of the region, the Portuguese trades remain dominant well offshore west of 20°W, while eastwards their influence is felt along the coast from Cabo de São Vicente towards Faro, often reinforced in the afternoons by the land effect. This influence wanes until, by Cádiz, summer afternoons may produce a westerly sea breeze. Cádiz can also be affected by a *levante* coming out of the Mediterranean. Towards the Strait of Gibraltar the winds tend to be either easterly or westerly, the former more common in summer and the latter in winter.

Gales
Gales are rare in the summer. The better known are the *levante* and *poniente*, the easterly and westerly gales of the Strait of Gibraltar, and the *nordeste pardo*, a cloudy northeaster of the Finisterre area. In theory the *vendavale*, a southwesterly blow in Galicia, is unlikely to occur in summer but exceptions do occur. Tarifa, protruding into the Strait of Gibraltar, will frequently experience very strong local winds and yachts should be prepared for this.

Rainfall
Galicia is the wet corner of Spain – it has much the same climatic feel as southwest England. To the south, whilst winters may be like June in the English Channel, in summer rainfall decreases and temperatures rise until, around Cádiz, Mediterranean levels are reached.

Fog
Sea temperatures in summer range from 17°C in Galicia to 21° at Gibraltar, and in winter from 12° to 14°. The chances of coastal fog along the west coast of the Iberian peninsula are greatest in July and August when incidence may rise as high as one day in 10. In the larger rías of southern Galicia it occasionally lasts for a week at a stretch in summer. It is much rarer along the southwest coast.

Swell
Atlantic swell is a factor to consider along the whole of this coast because the edge of the continental plate runs close to the shoreline and so there is not much shelf to dissipate the wave energy. There can be a lag of several days between wind and waves increasing and decreasing – sometimes there will be wind but flat seas, but also there can be no wind but big seas. Websites with swell predictions are useful to help plan a passage down the coast.

There are seasonal variations, and once Cabo de São Vincente has been rounded, heading south, there is less likely to be a problem. For safety and comfort it is imperative that swell forecasts are monitored. See 'Weather forecasts on the internet' (page 6) for some useful websites that show predicted swell direction and height over several days.

Currents and tides

Currents
Currents are much affected by recent winds and may set in any direction. The trend along the Atlantic coast is from north to south, though north of Finisterre there can be an easterly set into the Bay of Biscay. East of Cabo de São Vicente, the upper layers of the sea re-supply the Mediterranean with water lost through evaporation. The current sets towards the Strait at about 0·5kn at the western end, increasing to around 2kn through the Strait itself, to which a tidal element may have to be added – see page 322. However, prolonged easterly winds can produce a reverse current, which is said to set into the bays as far west as Cabo de São Vicente.

INTRODUCTION

Tidal streams
Information on tidal streams is confusing. Off the Rías Bajas the flood is supposed to run north and off Peniche, in Portugal, to the southeast. The only reasonably safe assumption is that the flood tide sets into the Galician rías and the ebb drains them. The same is generally true of a Portuguese rio, but this is less than a certainty and depends on the amount of water coming down the rio itself. The Rio Douro is a particular example of this. In the Strait of Gibraltar, tidal streams can exceed 3kn at springs.

Tide times
The standard ports for the area are A Coruña, Lisbon, Cádiz and Gibraltar and quoted time and height differences for other harbours are related to them. An excellent source of tidal information for those with internet access is the UK Hydrographic Office's user-friendly (and free) Easytide programme at www.ukho.gov.uk/easytide which gives daily tidal data for almost all major harbours and many minor ones. Imray's Tide Planner app works offline.

Tidal range

	A Coruña	Vigo	Lisbon	Faro	Cádiz	Gibraltar
Springs	3·3	2·9	3·3	2·0	2·0	0·9
Neaps	1·3	1·4	1·6	1·2	1·3	0·4

Lights and buoyage

All buoys and lights in this area adhere to the IALA A system, based on the direction of the main flood tide. In Portugal and Spain, heights of lights are measured from mean sea level. They therefore generally appear in Iberian publications as a metre or so higher than in British Admiralty publications.

The four-figure international numbering system has been used to identify lights in text and on plans. In addition to being shown on the plans, details of the main leading lights and, in Galicia, the outer breakwater light are given in the text. All bearings are given from seaward and refer to true north.

Charts

See Appendix I on page 341.
Current British Admiralty information is largely obtained from Spanish and Portuguese sources. The Spanish and Portuguese Hydrographic Offices issue their own charts (often to a much larger scale than Admiralty coverage and corrected by their own *Notices*) but they can be difficult to obtain outside the peninsula. *Notices to Mariners* to update Admiralty charts will be found on www.ukho.gov.uk; the Spanish and Portuguese equivalents – *Avisos* – on www.armada.mde.es/ihm and www.hidrografico.pt/hidrografico respectively.

Before departure Spanish and Portuguese charts (as well as fully corrected Admiralty publications) can be obtained through

Imray Laurie Norie & Wilson Ltd,
Wych House, The Broadway, St Ives,
Cambridgeshire, PE27 5BT, UK
✆ +44 (0)1480 462114
www.imray.com

In Spain Spanish charts can be ordered from
Instituto Hidrográfico de la Marina,
Plaza de San Severiano 3, DP 11007 Cádiz
✆ +34 956 599409.

In Galicia there are Spanish chart agents in A Coruña, Vilagarcía de Arousa and Vigo; in Andalucía in Huelva, Seville, Cádiz and Algeciras. A few marina offices are also willing to order charts for visiting yachts.

In Portugal only two companies, both in Lisbon, sell charts. Full contact details are given in the Facilities section for Lisbon.

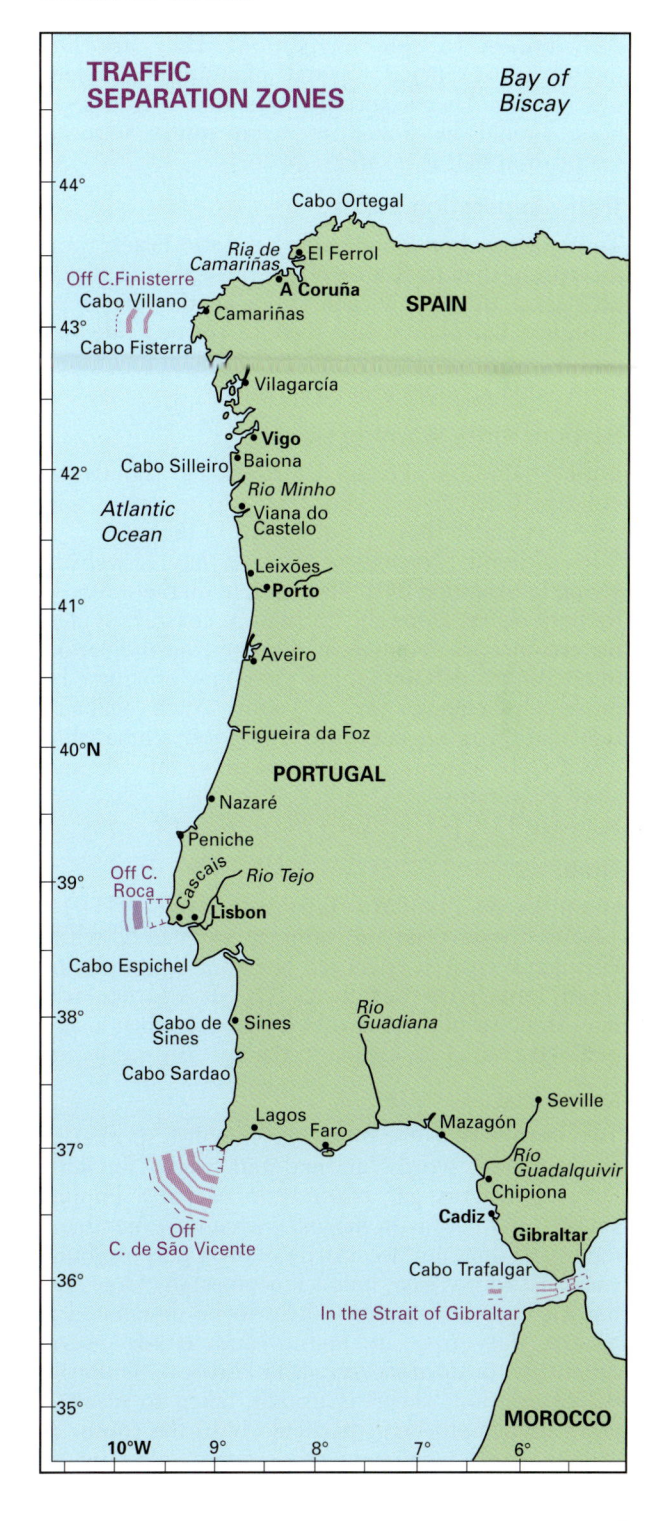

ATLANTIC SPAIN AND PORTUGAL

In Gibraltar fully corrected Admiralty charts and other publication are available from the Gibraltar Chart Agency – contact details are given under Gibraltar.

Horizontal chart datum and satellite derived positions

Most charts are now based on WGS84 datum and this is used for all positions in this book. However, some Portuguese charts are still to be converted and navigators are advised to check the chart datum if plotting satellite derived data. GPS positions have been derived from both paper and electronic charts, and observation in harbour. These are offered as an aid to rapid orientation within the book as well as a contribution to safe navigation. They are not intended to replace normal planning or visual observation. Unless specifically stated in the text, none should be linked to form routes without verification that it is safe to do so.

Traffic Separation Zones

Traffic Separation Zones exist off Cabo Fisterra, on the approaches to Ría de Vigo, off Cabo da Roca, off Cabo de São Vicente and in the Strait of Gibraltar. Each has a wide Inshore Traffic Zone and yachts are strongly advised to avoid crossing the main shipping lanes if at all possible.

Harbour entry warning signals

Both Spain and Portugal use visual signals to indicate whether a harbour is safe to enter, and where available these are described in the text.

In addition, Portuguese Marine has a website giving information by a 'Flag' system on the status of harbour access along the Portuguese coast. Provided for commercial shipping, it does give an indication of conditions pertaining, but these may of course be more challenging for a yacht. Such website information is no substitute for good seamanship and a close watch on weather, state of the tide and swell conditions.
See page 131, *II Portugal – the west coast*.

Time

Spain keeps Standard European Time (UT+1), advanced one hour in summer to UT+2, while Portugal keeps UT, advanced one hour in summer to UT+1. (effectively the same as BST). It is particularly important to allow for this difference when using tidal data based on Lisbon in the Spanish *rías bajas*.

Nomenclature

Two likely pitfalls for the unwary English speaker in Iberia are the words 'marina' and 'yacht'. In both Spain and Portugal *marina* or *marinha* implies simply 'marine' (as in *marina mercante* – merchant navy) and does not necessarily imply a purpose-built yacht harbour which, unless it is unusually large and has all facilities, is more likely to be designated a *puerto deportivo* in Spain, and either *porto desportivo* or *doca de recreio* in Portugal. Similarly, the description 'yacht' is usually taken to mean a good-sized motorboat, particularly in the south. A sailing boat of whatever size is a *barco de vela* or, in Portugal, a *barco à vela*.

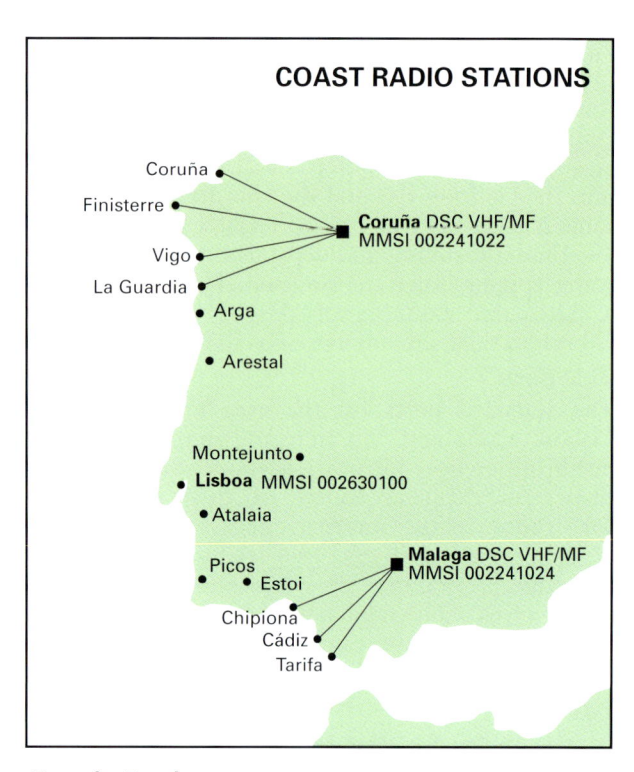

COAST RADIO STATIONS

Coruña
Finisterre
Vigo
La Guardia
Arga
Arestal
Montejunto
Lisboa MMSI 002630100
Atalaia
Picos
Estoi
Chipiona
Cádiz
Tarifa

Coruña DSC VHF/MF MMSI 002241022
Malaga DSC VHF/MF MMSI 002241024

Google Earth

Google Earth satellite photographs provide an interesting overview of the area. Google Maps can also be useful for planning passages. Be aware that the date shown on the photograph is not necessarily the date that it was taken and in many areas satellite photographs are several years old.

Coast radio stations

Details of coast radio stations will be found in the Admiralty Leisure publication *NP 289* and in the text. Locations are shown on the plan above, out-stations are controlled by A Coruña, Lisboa and Malaga. On receipt of traffic, Spanish coast radio stations will call vessels once on Ch 16; after that the vessel's call-sign will be included in scheduled MF traffic lists.

Weather forecasts

It should be noted that although marinas generally display weather information, yachts may find difficulty receiving official forecasts when in harbour or anchored in quiet bays. Yachts heading for the Mediterranean may later find that reception there can be erratic. Attention is therefore drawn to the use of weatherfax and RTTY messages from DWD and the usefulness of GRIB files.

Fog
Thick fog may descend along this coast with little warning. It may be localised and not mentioned in weather forecasts.

Navtex stations and forecast areas

(Spanish areas are shown on the diagram opposite)
France uses the same forecast areas for the Bay of Biscay plus Alborán.
Portugal uses the same Atlantic areas below 45°N.

INTRODUCTION

Navtex Schedules 518kHz
A	Corsen	
D	Coruña	
R	Monsanto	
G	Tarifa	
M	Casablanca (proposed)	

* Weather Bulletins
0000*, 0400, 0800, 1200*, 1600, 2000
0030, 0430, 0830*, 1230, 1630, 2030*
0250*, 0650*, 1050*, 1450*, 1850*, 2250*
0100, 0500, 0900*, 1300, 1700, 2100*

Navtex on 490kHz
E	Corsen	in French
W	Coruña	in Spanish
G	Monsanto	in Portuguese

Poor reception may be a problem in the Galician rías or in harbours throughout the area.

GALICIA
Radio Weather Bulletins* and Navigational Warnings

Coruña Finisterre	1698kHz and 1764kHz	0703*, 1303*, 1903*
Coruña	VHF Ch 26	0840*, 1240*, 2010*
Coruña MRSC	VHF Ch 10	0005*, 0205, 0405*, 0605 0805*, 1005, 1205*, 1405 1605*, 1805, 2005*, 2205
Finisterre	VHF Ch 22	0840*, 1240*, 2010*
Finisterre MRCC	VHF Ch 11	0033, 0233*, 0433, 0633* 0833, 1033*, 1233, 1433* 1633, 1833*, 2033, 2233*
Vigo	VHF Ch 65	0840*, 1240*, 2010*
Vigo MRSC	VHF Ch 10	0015*, 0215, 0415*, 0615 0815*, 1015, 1215*, 1415 1615*, 1815 2015*, 2215
La Guardia	VHF Ch 21	0840*, 1240*, 2040*

PORTUGAL
Radio Weather Bulletins and Navigational Warnings

Portugal coastal waters up to 20M offshore are in three zones:
Zona Norte	Rio Minho to Cabo Carvoeiro (40°N)
Zona Centro	Cabo Carvoeiro to Cabo São Vicente
Zona Sul	Cabo São Vicente to Rio Guadiana

Forecasts and navigational warnings: in Portuguese and English

RT(MF)	2657kHz	0905, 2105
VHF	Ch 11	0705, 0905, 1905, 2105 Norte & Centro 0805, 0905, 2005, 2105 Centro & Sul

ANDALUCIA
Radio Weather Bulletin* and Navigational Warnings

Huelva MRSC	VHF Ch 10	0315*, 0515*, 0715*, 1115*, 1515*, 1915*, 2315*
Chipiona Tarifa	1656kHz and 1704 kHz	0733*, 1233*, 1933*
Cádiz	VHF Ch 26	0833* 1133*, 2003, 2033*
Tarifa	VHF Ch 81	0733*, 0833*, 1233* 1933*, 2003*
Tarifa MRCC	VHF Ch 10, 67	Ev Hrs +15* On Receipt
Algeciras MRSC	VHF Ch 74	0315*, 0515*, 0715*, 1115*, 1515*, 1915*, 2314*

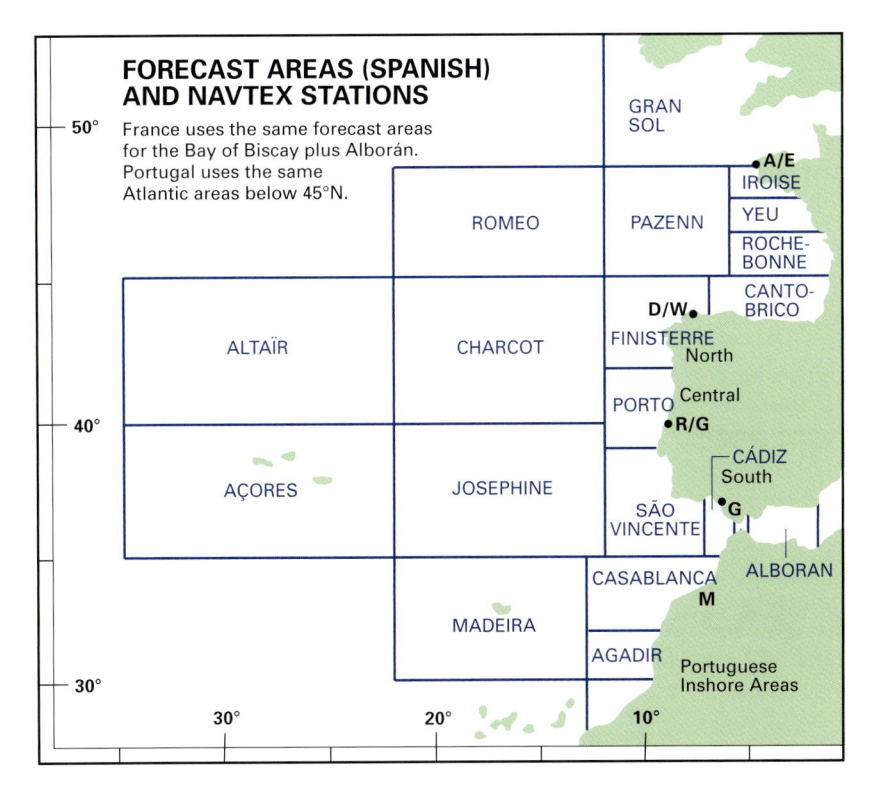

FORECAST AREAS (SPANISH) AND NAVTEX STATIONS

France uses the same forecast areas for the Bay of Biscay plus Alborán. Portugal uses the same Atlantic areas below 45°N.

Areas shown: GRAN SOL, ROMEO, PAZENN, IROISE (A/E), YEU, ROCHE-BONNE, ALTAÏR, CHARCOT, FINISTERRE (D/W), CANTO-BRICO, PORTO (R/G) – North, Central, AÇORES, JOSEPHINE, SÃO VICENTE (G), CÁDIZ South, ALBORAN, MADEIRA, CASABLANCA (M), AGADIR, Portuguese Inshore Areas

Weatherfax and RTTY

Northwood (RN) broadcasts a full set of UK Met Office charts out to five days ahead on 2618·5, 4610, 8040 and 11086·5kHz. (Schedule at 0236, surface analysis at three hourly intervals from 0300 to 2100 and 2300.)

Deutscher Wetterdienst broadcasts German weather charts on 3855, 7880, 13882·5kHz. (Schedule at 1111, surface analysis at 0430, 1050, 1600, 2200.)

DWD broadcasts forecasts using RTTY on 4583, 7646, and 10001·8kHz (in English at 0955 and 2155) 11039 and 14467·3kHz (in German at 0820, 1429, 2020). Alternatively, a dedicated receiver will record automatically – see 'weatherman' on www.nasamarine.com

Inmarsat

Broadcast times for weather for METAREA III are 1000 and 2200.

GRIB

This service enables arrow diagram forecasts for up to five days ahead, and other information to be obtained in email form (or by marine HF and HAM radio). The data are highly compressed so that a great deal of information can be acquired quickly, even using a mobile phone connected to laptop.

ATLANTIC SPAIN AND PORTUGAL

Gibraltar weather forecasts – VHF (FM)

LT	BFBS 1 Mon-Fri	Sat	Sun	BFBS2 Mon-Fri	Gibraltar BC Mon-Fri	Sat	Sun
0530					X	X	
0630					X	X	X
0730					X	X	X
0745	X						
0845	X	X	X				
0945		X	X				
1005	X						
1030					X		
1200				X			
1202	X	X					
1230					X	X	X
1602		X					
1605	X						

Also storm warnings on receipt 1438 AM
93·5 FM 89·4 FM 91·3 FM
97·8 FM 99·5 FM 92·6 FM
Includes high and low water times 100·5 FM

Weather forecasts online

Excellent weather-related information, including swell forecasts, can be found on the internet.

A guide to marine weather forecasts and how to use them is at
www.weather.mailasail.com/Franks-Weather.

Other useful websites are as follows:
www.metoffice.gov.uk	UK Met Office
www.inm.es	Spanish Met Office
www.meteo.pt	Portuguese Met Office
www.passageweather.com	
www.windguru.cz	
www.magicseaweed.com	(surf site)

Weather forecasts to be found ashore

Nearly all marina offices display a weather forecast and synoptic chart(s), usually updated daily; although often in the local language, the vocabulary is limited and can easily be deciphered.

For a more general indication of trends try the weather map in a local newspaper e.g. El País, Voz de Galicia or El Correo Galicia (Spain) or Jornal de Notícias or Público (Portugal).

Spanish television shows a useful synoptic chart with its land weather forecast every evening after the news at about 2120 weekdays, 1520 Saturday and 2020 Sunday.

Weather forecasts by radio

A variety of weather forecasts are available by radio, though relatively few in English. It should be noted that all times quoted for weather messages, navigational warnings and traffic lists are in Universal Time (UT) unless otherwise stated. This contrasts with harbour and marina radio schedules, which are generally governed by office hours and are therefore given in Local Time (LT).

BBC Radio 4

Shipping forecasts are broadcast on 198kHz (1515m) at 0048, 0520, 1201 and 1754. They consist of a gale warning summary, general synopsis, and sea-area forecasts on UK local time (BST in summer, UT in winter). The relevant areas are Biscay, Fitzroy and Trafalgar but the latter is only included in the 0048 forecast. While undoubtedly useful, particularly in Galicia, the areas covered are large, reception may be difficult, and forecasts may have little relevance to local conditions.

Radio France International

Weather information is broadcast at 1140 UT daily, (timed to fit the vagaries of programming and therefore not always punctual). The following receiving frequencies vary according to location: English Channel and Bay of Biscay 6175kHz; North Atlantic east of 50°W 11700, 15530, 17575kHz. Although in French, the format is straightforward: gale warnings, synopsis, development and 24 hour area forecasts.

Radio Nacional de España

Weather information is broadcast at 1000 and 1300 LT from: A Coruña 639kHz; Seville 684kHz.

Sociedad España de Radio

A programme containing information for commercial fishing operations, plus weather forecasts and sea conditions, is broadcast between 0600 and 0700 LT and again in condensed form at 2205 LT from: A Coruña 1080kHz; Vigo 1026kHz; Huelva 100·5MHz; Cádiz 1485kHz; Seville 792kHz.

Radiodifusão Portuguesa

Broadcasts a forecast for the coastal waters of Portugal at 1100 daily on the following frequencies: 650kHz, 666kHz, 720kHz, 1287kHz, 94·7MHz, 96·4MHz, 97·6MHz, 97·9MHz.

Practicalities

Entry and regulations

The impact of Brexit is not yet known. Under EU regulations, EU registered boats arriving in another EU country are not required to fly the Q flag unless they have come directly from a non-EU country (which could be Gibraltar), have non-EU nationals aboard, or are carrying dutiable goods. Yachts registered outside the EU should always fly the Q flag on arrival. All visiting yachts should fly the relevant national courtesy flag.

It should be noted that the Spanish Maritime Ensign, which should be flown as a courtesy flag, differs from the Spanish National Flag in that it does not have the crown in the centre.

Spain

On first arrival in the country check with immigration, most easily done via a yacht club or marina office. Ship's papers, insurance documents and passports should be to hand. It is also a requirement that at least one member of the crew has a VHF radio operator's certificate. At subsequent ports it is not necessary to seek out officialdom, though one may occasionally be approached for information. This relaxed attitude is more noticeable in Galicia than Andalucía, where smuggling is more common and there is greater public awareness of Gibraltar as a political issue. It should be noted that Spain requires all vessels over 6m to carry proof of

INTRODUCTION

third party insurance in Spanish. UK marine insurers are aware of this and will provide the appropriate certificate free of charge on request. Skippers should be aware that differing initial length of stay and visa requirements apply according to crew nationalities and also that anyone staying in Spain for more than 183 days in any 12-month period is liable to Spanish tax legislation. A note on this, and VAT, is included in Appendix IV. Officials may not recognize time spent in Gibraltar as being out of Spain.

Portugal
In theory, yachtsmen are still required to notify the authorities on arrival in every harbour, whether entering Portugal for the first time or from elsewhere within it – and to do so immediately upon coming ashore. This should not present problems at one of the increasing number of marinas. In general, produce passports, ship's papers (including proof of VAT status and insurance documents) complete a *Movimento de Embarcacoes de Recreio* form and state an intended departure date. In most harbours there is no requirement for formal outward clearance. Skippers should also carry an International Certificate of Competence or equivalent. In the UK this is administered by the Royal Yachting Association www.rya.org.uk/cruising or *Email* cruising@rya.org.uk. At least one crew member must have a VHF operator's certificate. There is no limitation on length of stay for a VAT paid or exempt yacht. However, visiting yachts spending more than 183 days a year in Portugal are liable to tax (see page 343 for details).

For anchoring in Algarve waters, a certificate showing payment of the light dues (a few euros per year) is required. The marinas do not sell them so a visit to a Port Captain's office is necessary.

Gibraltar
Although Gibraltar is a British Territory, it is not part of the EU. Fly the Q Flag on approach and clear customs at marinas. See page 336 for details.

Day signals / anchor lights
A number of skippers in both Spanish and Portuguese waters have faced an on the spot fine for not displaying a black ball or white light when at anchor and a cone when motor sailing. Yachts have also been fined for not flying a courtesy flag.

In Galicia, early morning in particular, small open boats anchored in shallow bays may be encountered flying Code flag A. Sometimes there is nobody aboard. On some of them there is an air pump aboard the boat, and it is connected to a (shellfish) diver by a long hose. It is a very bad idea to get between the boat and the diver. Often the diver's position is indicated by a small float, and a stream of bubbles.

Drugs
Drug running is a serious problem along the entire Iberian coast. The authorities may board yachts at any time, including on passage, though normally this is confined to 'interesting' yachts, with the names of others merely being noted down. In both countries, yachtsmen are asked to inform the authorities of any yacht that merits a particular interest – and presumably of any other goings-on which appear suspicious.

Laying up
Yachts can safely be left afloat, whether laid up or over-wintering, in most of the larger marinas described. It should be clear from the text when this is not the case.

Facilities, chandlery and repairs
In Galicia, the facilities for yachts are extensive and expanding, and travel lifts frequent. The harbour facilities available are included in the text, and a useful publication can be found at major marinas. The following websites are also useful:
www.marinasdegalicia.com and
www.portosdegalicia.com.

In the Portugal and Andalucía sections details are in the text, and for Andalucía the comprehensive website www.puertosdeandalucia.es can also be consulted.

Chandleries
Well-stocked yachting chandleries are not always easy to find in either Spain or Portugal, and by no means all marinas have one on site. Amongst the best are those at Sada, A Coruña, Vilagarcía de Arousa, Vigo and Baiona (Galicia). Viana do Castelo, Leixões, Cascais and Lisbon (Atlantic Portugal) Lagos, Portimão and Vilamoura (Algarve); Isla Christina, Punta Umbria, Chipiona, Seville, Puerto Sherry and Barbate (Andalucía). Gibraltar's chandleries are some of the best in Iberia, as well as being duty-free. Basic boat tackle is more widely available.

Repairs
There are numerous boatyards throughout all the regions, mainly geared to fishing and other commercial vessels but able to do basic work on yachts. However, for major repairs or other work reportedly good yards are currently located at Sada, Vilagarcía de Arousa and Vigo (Galicia); Lisbon and Seixal (Atlantic Portugal); Lagos, Portimão and Vilamoura (Algarve); El Rompido, Seville (Puerto Gelves) and Puerto Sherry (Andalucía); and, of course, Gibraltar. Note that if taking expensive electrical or mechanical equipment ashore for repair, particularly in Portugal, it is wise to first inform the *GNR–Brigada Fiscal*. Possession of a receipt will confirm that the equipment was bought elsewhere. With the availability of cheap flights it might be preferable to fly back to one's own country.

Fuel
Diesel is widely available (except to yachts visiting fishing harbours); petrol rather less so. In both countries fishermen have access to diesel at a lower rate of tax than do yachtsmen. Fuel supplies are generally clean, but it can do no harm to filter all fuel taken aboard as a matter of course. Credit cards are generally – but not always – accepted when paying for fuel and it is essential to confirm the local situation before going ahead.

Standard grade paraffin (*parafina*) is virtually unobtainable in much of Spain, though the more expensive medicinal grade is stocked by most pharmacies. In Portugal *petróleo para iluminãçao* (lamp oil) is widely available.

Drinking water

Water is available at all marinas and on many fuelling pontoons. It is usually included in the price of berthing. In those harbours where a piped supply is not available for yachts, a public tap can generally be found, when a good supply of five or 10-litre plastic cans will be useful. Though water quality throughout the peninsula is generally good, bottled water is widely available.

Bottled gas

Camping Gaz exchanges are widely available, usually from *ferreterías* (ironmongers), filling stations or supermarkets – in 2·7kg bottles identical to those used in the UK.

Getting other cylinders refilled is much more of a problem, particularly if the cylinder is more than five years old. Boats heading south for extended cruising might consider carrying the appropriate adaptor and regulator and buying local gas on arrival in Spain or elsewhere.

In Spain, if the gas bottle locker is at least 300mm in diameter by 595mm deep, a standard Spanish 12·5kg butane bottle can be accommodated. The Spanish bottle takes the same regulator as the Irish one, which is the push-on type, not the left-hand-thread British one. Bottles and regulators are not hard to find.

The website www.mylpg.eu lists all the gas stations in Europe that sell LPG, but not all will refill a stand-alone UK Calor cylinder.

The full set of European gas refilling adapters are available from www.lpggpl.co.uk see also GasBOAT solutions at www.whayward.com.

Calor Gas dealers in the UK can advise on installations and supply the necessary parts. www.calorgas.co.uk.

Electricity

Electricity is available on nearly all marina pontoons, generally via standard marina sockets, although adaptors should be carried to cope with the European domestic type socket. Mains electricity is 220 volt 50Hz; yachts equipped with 110 volt 60Hz equipment will require a transformer. (These are best bought before arrival; they are readily obtainable from builders merchants in the UK.)

Holding tanks

Since 2004 it has been compulsory for Spanish flagged vessels to fit holding tanks. Pump-out facilities are increasing and there is a determination to protect the water quality for both the fishing and tourist industries. Skippers should be aware that Spanish legislation on prevention of sewage does not permit sewage to be discharged in port areas, protected zones, rivers, or bays. Crumbled and disinfected sewage may be discharged from four miles off shore by vessels exceeding 4kn.

Marina charges

It is not practicable to list the varying rates at all the different marinas and harbours. Charges will often be based on length x beam and skippers should carry documentation which records both of these (SSR documentation does not).

Marina office hours (local time)

In Spain (both Galicia and Andalucía) it is normal for marina offices to be closed during the siesta period, any time between 1200 and 1700, though seldom for as long as this. In Portugal a shorter lunch break – often from 1230 until 1400 – is the norm. While the majority of marinas have 24-hour security, most offices are closed overnight, sometimes from as early as 1800.

While this latter can cause problems when wishing to leave, a firmly locked office is more likely to disrupt things on first arrival, particularly if an electronic card is needed to open an access gate to the pontoons. In Portugal, where marina offices are increasingly handling clearance procedures, it can also frustrate a quick shopping trip into town or a well-deserved meal ashore.

Sometimes security guards have authority to issue pass cards, often they do not. There is no guarantee that a guard will re-admit an unknown yachtsman to the marina pontoons, particularly if not carrying the yacht's papers and a passport or other identity document.

Security

Crime afloat is not a major problem in most areas. It is sensible to take much the same precautions as at home – to lock up if leaving the yacht unattended, to padlock the outboard to the dinghy, and to secure the dinghy (particularly if an inflatable) with chain or wire rather than line, both to the yacht and when left ashore.

General information

Embassies, consulates and national tourist offices are listed in Appendix III.

Websites relevant to Galicia are www.turgalicia.es www.marinasdegalicia.com www.portosdegalicia.com

Websites relevant to Portugal and Andalucía are listed in Appendix V.

Medical

No inoculations are required before visiting either Spain or Portugal. Minor ailments may best be treated by consulting a *farmacía* (often able to dispense drugs which in some other countries would be on prescription), or by contact with an English-speaking doctor established via the *farmacía*, marina office, tourist office or possibly a hotel. In Spain the emergency number is ☏091; in Portugal it is ☏112.

All EU nationals should carry a European Health Insurance Card (EHIC) issued in the UK by the NHS Business Services Authority, www.ehic.org.uk, ☏ 0300 3301350. This entitles one to free medical

INTRODUCTION

treatment under reciprocal agreements with the National Health Service. Private medical treatment is likely to be available but may be expensive.

Money
The unit of currency is the Euro. Major credit cards are widely used although it is wise to check this particularly before refuelling. Bank hours are normally 0830 to 1400 Mondays to Fridays with a few also open 0830 to 1300 on Saturdays; most banks have ATMs.

Mail
Nearly all marinas are willing to hold mail for visiting yachts but it is wise to check first. All mail should be clearly labelled with both the name of the recipient and the yacht, but avoiding honorifics such as Esq, which may cause confusion and misfiling. In Portugal it is technically illegal for uncollected mail to be held for more than five days without being returned, though most marinas will stretch this period. Far better to address an outer envelope directly to the marina office, with a short covering note asking for the envelope enclosed to be held pending the yacht's arrival.

Letters also may be sent *Posto Restante* to any post office in either country, though again they are likely to be returned if not collected promptly. In Spain they should be addressed with the surname of the recipient followed by *Lista de Correos* and the town and province. In Portugal, *Posta Restante* is used, and the collection counter labelled *Encomendas*. A passport is likely to be needed on collection. Post Offices are signed: in Spain PTT on a yellow background, in Portugal postal services are indicated by *Correios* on a red background.

Telephones
Country code numbers are: Spain ☎+34, Portugal ☎+351, Gibraltar ☎+350 (Gibraltar from Spain ☎9567).

Key to symbols used on the plans

	English	Portuguese	Spanish
	harbourmaster	diretor do porto/capitania	capitán de puerto/capitanía
	fuel (diesel, petrol)	gasoleo, gasolina	gasoil, gasolina
(25T)	travel-lift	pórtico elevador	pórtico elevado
	yacht club	club náutico, club naval	club náutico
	anchorage	fundeadouro	fondeadero
	visitors' moorings	amarradero,	ancladero
	slipway	carreira	varadero

Email
Internet connection facilities are widespread and marina WiFi is becoming increasingly available. Telephone numbers as well as email addresses and websites are listed for each harbour or marina.

Transport
In both Spain and Portugal almost every community has some form of public transport, if only one bus a day. Local buses and trains can provide a view of the interior not otherwise available without hiring a car, although the latter offer good value and the road network in Galicia is excellent.

There are rail connections to El Ferrol, A Coruña, Pontevedra, Vigo, Porto, Lisbon, Lagos, Faro, Tavira, Vila Real de Santo António, Huelva, Seville, Cádiz and Algeciras. Other towns may be served by branch lines. Long distance coaches are also popular, and on a par with the railways for cost.

International airports serve A Coruña, Santiago de Compostela, Vigo, Porto, Lisbon, Faro, Seville, Jerez de la Frontera and Gibraltar.

National holidays and fiestas
Fiestas are extremely popular throughout both Spain and Portugal, often celebrating the local saint's day or some historical event. Some local *fiestas* occurring during the sailing season are mentioned in the text.

Spain
1 January	New Year's Day
6 January	Epiphany
	Good Friday
	Easter Monday
1 May	May Day/Labour Day
(early/mid June)	Corpus Christi
24 June	Día de San Juan (the King's name saint)
25 July	Día de Santiago (celebrated throughout Northwest Spain as 'Galicia Day')
15 August	Feast of the Assumption
12 October	National Day
1 November	All Saints' Day
6 December	Constitution Day
8 December	Immaculate Conception
25 December	Christmas Day

When a national holiday falls on a Sunday, the autonomous region may either celebrate it the following day or use it to celebrate a regional festival.

Portugal
1 January	New Year's Day
	Good Friday
25 April	National or Liberty Day
1 May	Labour Day
(early/mid June)	Corpus Christi
10 June	Portugal Day (Camões Day)
15 August	Feast of the Assumption
5 October	Republic Day
1 November	All Saints' Day
1 December	Restoration of Independence Day
8 December	Feast of the Immaculate Conception
25 December	Christmas Day

ATLANTIC SPAIN AND PORTUGAL

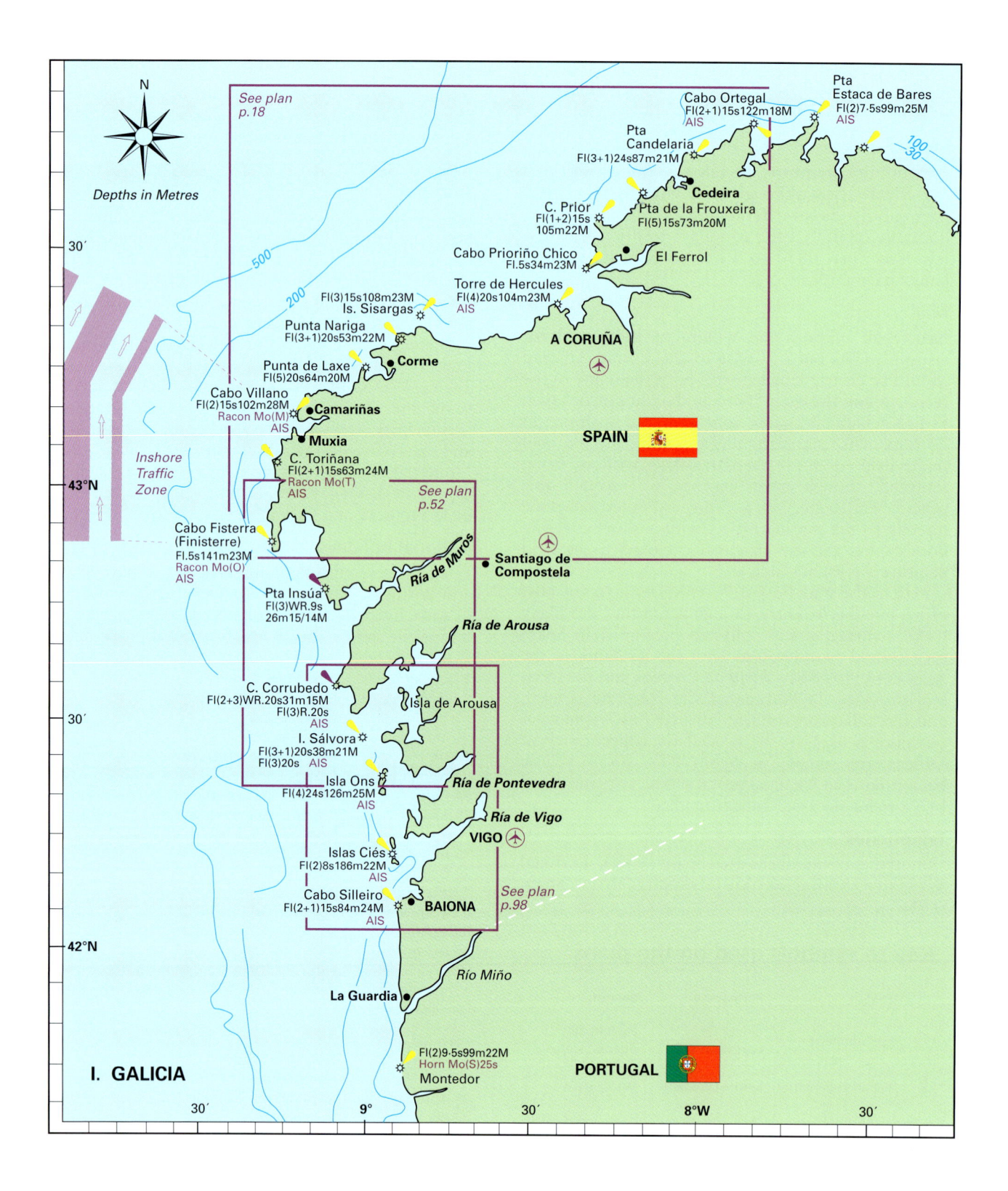

Positions Although a few official charts of this area have yet to be converted from Datum ED50, skippers should note that all positions in this book are to WGS84. Any numbered waypoints are shown in safe-water positions. In most cases this is on an approach line to a port, harbour or anchorage to indicate where pilotage may take over from GPS navigation. Waypoints and tracks between them should always be plotted and checked on an up-to-date chart before being used for navigation. Users are reminded that they are offered as an aid to navigation. All should be cross-checked against other sources of information and used in conjunction with eyeball navigation.

I. Galicia
Cabo Ortegal to the Portuguese border

The dramatic 'Aguillons' off Cabo Ortegal *Geraldine Hennigan*

Cabo Silleiro just N of the border with Portugal *Henry Buchanan*

GALICIA

Overview

This section of the pilot is written for the mariner crossing the Bay of Biscay and making landfall at Cabo Ortegal in Galicia before sailing on southwest and south to the border with Portugal. Cabo Ortegal is one of the highest coastal cliffs in Europe. The 'Aguillons' beneath it strike fear into any sailor. The first place of refuge is the anchorage in the Ría de Cedeira some 12M southwest of the Cape. Ría de Cedeira is the only one of the Rías Altas on the northwest coast of Galicia. The others are all east of Cabo Ortegal and any mariner sailing from this direction should consult *South Biscay* (Imray) for information.

The *rías* of Galicia offer varied cruising in a most attractive setting. They are well worth visiting in their own right, and changing crew there is straightforward via the airports at A Coruña, Santiago de Compostela and Vigo. The rías also offer a safe haven to yachtsmen on the haul south from northern European waters to the Mediterranean or before heading out into the Atlantic. There is challenging pilotage for those who relish it and there are good anchorages, and many welcoming marinas where boats may be safely secured while the crew explore ashore or leave for extended periods.

Steady development since the mid-1980s has benefited from the injection of significant EU infrastructure funding. The fishing fleets are of vital importance to the local economy and are well provided for; many now have their own robust, purpose-built marinas in their harbours. Good roads allow rapid travel around the area and, in their wake, have brought major construction of homes and hotels, particularly in the more southern rías. Some beaches are buoyed to protect swimmers, and anchorages are, therefore, moved further offshore.

The stretch of coast between Cabo Ortegal and Cabo Fisterra includes generally small rías with some exposed harbours. The coastline is often high and rugged in between. In the onshore winds and swell for which it is renowned, this coast becomes a dangerous lee shore and the Costa da Morte is aptly named. In settled weather, however, this area provides enjoyable cruising with access to marinas in the A Coruña area and at Camariñas and Muxia some 16·5M north of Cabo Fisterra.

South of Cabo Fisterra are the Rías Bajas and beyond the offshore dangers north of Ría de Muros, the four rías of Muros, Arousa, Pontevedra and Vigo offer more sheltered cruising with a variety of anchorages and harbours to visit. With few exceptions, the rías are wide and deep, and the hazards well marked, although this is not always the case further off the beaten track and, sometimes, close to harbours. Lights, buoys and beacons are generally well maintained.

For general background information on Galicia visit www.galiciaguide.com.

Hazards

Apart from the clearly marked Traffic Separation Zone which lies well off shore, the main hazards are the changeability of the weather and *viveros* (a widely-used term to describe the numerous rafts for cultivating mussels and clams in shallow water – although *bateas* is the correct name for the mussel rafts):

Weather

Forecasts are readily obtainable, but local conditions may change rapidly and it is advisable to have a contingency plan when visiting some of the more interesting anchorages. In the summer months, *rías*, which may start the day in brilliant summer conditions, can be plunged into lingering local mist making passage through the *viveros* somewhat challenging.

Viveros

The areas on the plans marked as *viveros* cannot be definitive; some show up clearly on the aerial photographs but, although many are well established and remain year after year, some may be removed and others established elsewhere. A few *viveros* will be found in the more northern *rías* but the majority are further south, with over 3,000 rafts said to be in Ría de Arousa alone.

The rafts are unlit, but steep-to. Their ropes and anchor chains go straight down and it is quite safe to give a *vivero* a berth of a boat's length or less. They do at least indicate deep water as they are normally moored in not less than 10m. Another positive aspect is that in large numbers *viveros* are, in effect, extensive floating breakwaters, and significantly reduce the wave heights in their lee.

It is usually possible to sail and anchor between them and inshore of them. However, although the outer perimeters of the rafts are usually marked by yellow buoys and often lit, they do offer a very significant obstacle, particularly at night. An idea of the scale and layout of the viveros may be gleaned from satellite images such as Google Earth.

Posts

Shallow waters may include numerous posts, many of these are only visible towards low water. They are dangerous to dinghies. Although their outer edge may be indicated by a solid pole, yellow with an × topmark, care should always be exercised when boating ashore from an anchored yacht.

Small fishing boats

In addition to the offshore fishing fleet and the *viveros* support boats, large groups of small fishing boats, some with a clam cage handle stretching up to 20m behind them, may be encountered hard at work or jostling to unload their catch. Life in this area revolves around the fishing fleets and they dominate the harbours. Skippers will wish to respect this when planning their local cruising routes and crews will enjoy the abundant fresh seafood which is obtainable everywhere.

OVERVIEW

Cabo Fisterra (Finisterre) *Henry Buchanan*

Swell
The exposed coastline is subject to large swells from the Atlantic, sometimes originating from storms hundreds of miles offshore. (See page 2.)

Winds
In summer the dominance of the Azores high pressure area, usually combined with low pressure over the Iberian peninsula, leads to prevailing northeasterlies in the northern part of the area, gaining a more northerly component south of Cabo Fisterra. However, land or sea breeze effects may dictate conditions locally, sometimes leading to a 180° shift in wind direction during the warmer parts of the day.

Gales are infrequent during the summer but may occur, notably the *nordeste pardo*, a cloudy northeaster of the Finisterre area. The southwesterly *vendavale* is also uncommon at this time of year.

In winter, Galicia's weather is largely determined by the passage of North Atlantic frontal systems bringing strong southwesterlies – probably the reason why the Bay of Biscay gained its fearsome reputation in the days of the square-riggers.

Visibility
The chances of coastal mist are greatest in July and August when the incidence may rise as high as one day in 10 or 12 (many yachtsmen would argue that this is conservative), with many more days of early morning mist which then disperses. In the *rías* Bajas visibility of less than 2M may occasionally last for a week at a stretch.

Currents
Off Cabo Ortegal currents may set easterly into the Bay of Biscay. South of Cabo Fisterra the general trend is southwards, seldom reaching more than 0·5kn.

Tides
Tidal predictions for north of Cabo Fisterra use A Coruña as the Standard Port; those for the *rías* Bajas use Lisbon. When calculating Spanish tides using Lisbon data, note that allowance has already been made for the difference in time zone (Spanish time being UT+1, Portuguese time UT, both advanced one hour in summer – see page 3).

If A Coruña tide tables are not available, as a very rough guide high water occurs at approximately 0510 and 1650 at springs ±20 minutes; and 1045 and 2330 at neaps ±50 minutes. The same figures for Lisbon are approximately 0410 and 1630 ±30 minutes, and 0920 and 2230 ±1 hour 10 minutes.

Ranges are near 3m at springs and 1·4m at neaps, but both time and height may be affected by wind, particularly in the *rías* Bajas south of Cabo Fisterra.

The flood stream sets north and northeast around the coast. Unlike some of the rios of Portugal and southern Spain, all Galicia's rías are fully tidal, certainly as far as a yacht is likely to penetrate.

Where no tidal data is given for an individual harbour it will be found under the preliminary notes for the ría as a whole.

Climate
Galicia is the wet corner of Spain – it has much the same climatic feel as southwest England, though on average is rather warmer. Mean air temperature varies from around 20°C in August to 9°C in January, sea temperature from 17°C in summer to 12°C in winter.

Islas Cies looking north to Cabo Fisterra (Finisterre) *Henry Buchanan*

GALICIA

ATLANTIC SPAIN AND PORTUGAL

GALICIA

An anchorage in the Ría de Arousa Geraldine Hennigan

Yacht clubs and marinas
There are two types of marina in Galicia, the commercial marinas and the ones owned and run by yacht clubs - *(Real) Club Nautico*; the *Real* (Royal) being a much sort after accolade. All Yacht Club marinas in Galicia have 10% of their berths kept free for visitors, and belong to the Clubs' Association - ASNAUGA.

It is courteous to recognise that the *(Real) Club Nauticos* are members' clubs which, while they remain welcoming to visitors, do expect a standard of behaviour (dress in the clubhouse etc) similar to a yacht club at home.

A discount on berthing fees of 15% can be obtained by buying a *Passporte* for a small sum. This is valid for two years and can be used at the following Galicia marinas: Marina Viveiro, Marina Sada, Marina Coruña, Marina Muxia, Marina Muros, Marina A Pobra do Caraminal, Marina Vilagarcia de Arousa, Nauta Sanxenxo, and Marina Davilo at Vigo.

Language
Galicia is a popular holiday area but few foreigners visit the *rías*. Although English and other languages are spoken in the major marina offices, visiting yachtsmen who do not speak Spanish should arm themselves with the necessary phrasebook.

Berthing costs
Contact details are provided for most ports so that applicable costs can be checked in advance if desired. Joining a *Passporte* system may provide discounts.

Facilities
Galicia is no longer a remote cruising area. The large number of fishing fleets means that emergency and basic technical and harbour support is widely available. For normal routine work or chandlery seek advice from the multilingual staff of the major marinas. A Coruña and Sada offer the most comprehensive support in the north: Portosin, Vilagarcia, Sanxenxo, Cangas, Punta Lagoa, Vigo, Baiona in the four southern rías. Easy refuelling places are indicated by * at the start of the sections. Water, food shops and restaurants are widely available.

Viveros (Bateas) mussel rafts. An ubiquitous hazard in the Rias Baixas *Geraldine Hennigan*

The compass rose of Celtic regions, set beneath the Torre de Hercules in A Coruña, highlights the connections between Galicia and the other Celtic nations *Jane Russell*

14 ATLANTIC SPAIN AND PORTUGAL

GALICIA ATLANTIC NATIONAL PARKS

The following website provides details of the islands, their bird life, flora and sealife:
www.magrama.gob.es/en/red-parques-nacionales/nuestros-parques/islas-atlanticas/

National Park Permits

Experience has shown that the best way to ensure the most trouble-free access to Galician national parks is to apply for a Navigation Permission permit by e-mail before sailing from home. Permits can be obtained, however, through the major marinas and by visiting Park offices. Through marinas there is normally a processing period of a few weeks, but with assistance (see Navigation Permission below) it is reported that this can be reduced to 3 hours. Visiting the actual Park office involves a delay of a few days between applying for and receiving the appropriate permit. However, once a permit has been obtained renewal is reported to be a straightforward process.

Each vessel/skipper combination is only given a cumulative limit of days within a year. For National Park spots it is about 10 full days, but half days are allowed for a lunch stop without staying overnight, for example. The system is reliant on having internet access because once the Navigation Permission has been granted it is still necessary to email in advance for an Anchoring Permission for the appropriate number of days when intending to visit a park area.

Notes from the National Park Authority

Contacts

Parque Nacional Maritimo Terrestre das Illas Atlanticas de Galicia
Edificio Cetmar (1ª planta), c/o Eduardo Cabello s/n, 36208
Bouzas - Vigo
✆ +34 886 21 80 90
Email fondeos.iatlanticas@xunta.es
www.iatlanticas.es

Navigation Permission

The Navigation Permission, required to obtain the Anchoring Permission, is biannual and allows navigating in National Park waters during the current year. In order to apply for it go to
www.iatlanticas.es > Anchoring > VERY IMPORTANT: fill in this form
Then either:
a. Send the completed form to the National Park bureau together with the requested documents or
b. With the help of a harbourmaster/marina office, the application form must be printed and filled out as it is not possible to do this online. Scan the completed form together with passport, vessel Registration document (e.g. SSR), and Certificate of Competence. Email to fondeos.iatlanticas@xunta.es with a short explanatory letter in Spanish, hopefully written by the Harbourmaster/Marina who should be requested to phone the Park HQ (Xunta) ✆ +34 886 21 80 90 to ensure that the email had been received and is adequate. Navigation Permission should come by email within 3 hours. Print the Permission in order to be able to show to an Island warden.

There is no need to send in a renewal application unless there are changes in vessel ownership, registration, name and personal data of the owner, in which case they must be declared.

Anchoring Permission

Make an application for Anchoring Permission online, even for same day visits (no need to apply through the Park Office).

- Go to www.iatlanticas.es
- Click on Anchoring Management
- Scroll down and enter a User ID (this is the vessel owner ID number – number, space, capital letter)
- Enter Password (this is the Navigation Permission number. You will be prompted to change the password for one of your own choice afterwards).
- This will also give you access to vessel and owner data.
- The drop-down menu in the lower part of the screen shows the archipelagos.
- Select one and give details of the number of passengers.
- Another drop-down menu displays the next seven calendar days, from which you can select three.

If your application is made between 15 September and 14 June, a thirty-day calendar will appear which allows you to choose up to a maximum of ten days.

Permissions can be downloaded from three to ten days before use. They are valid on a daily basis and must therefore be printed and carried onboard the vessel.

Park wardens will check boat names and number of people on board as logged in the application process.

Note that if a permit to anchor is booked at one of the islands, but plans are changed, the permit should be cancelled. If a check discovers that a permit had been given and not used, access to the website will be blocked for a fortnight. This is designed to stop boats making block bookings just in case they fancy a trip sometime.

There are some beautiful walks in the National Parks. This is on Route 1 to Monte Faro on Islas Cies, looking S *Jane Russell*

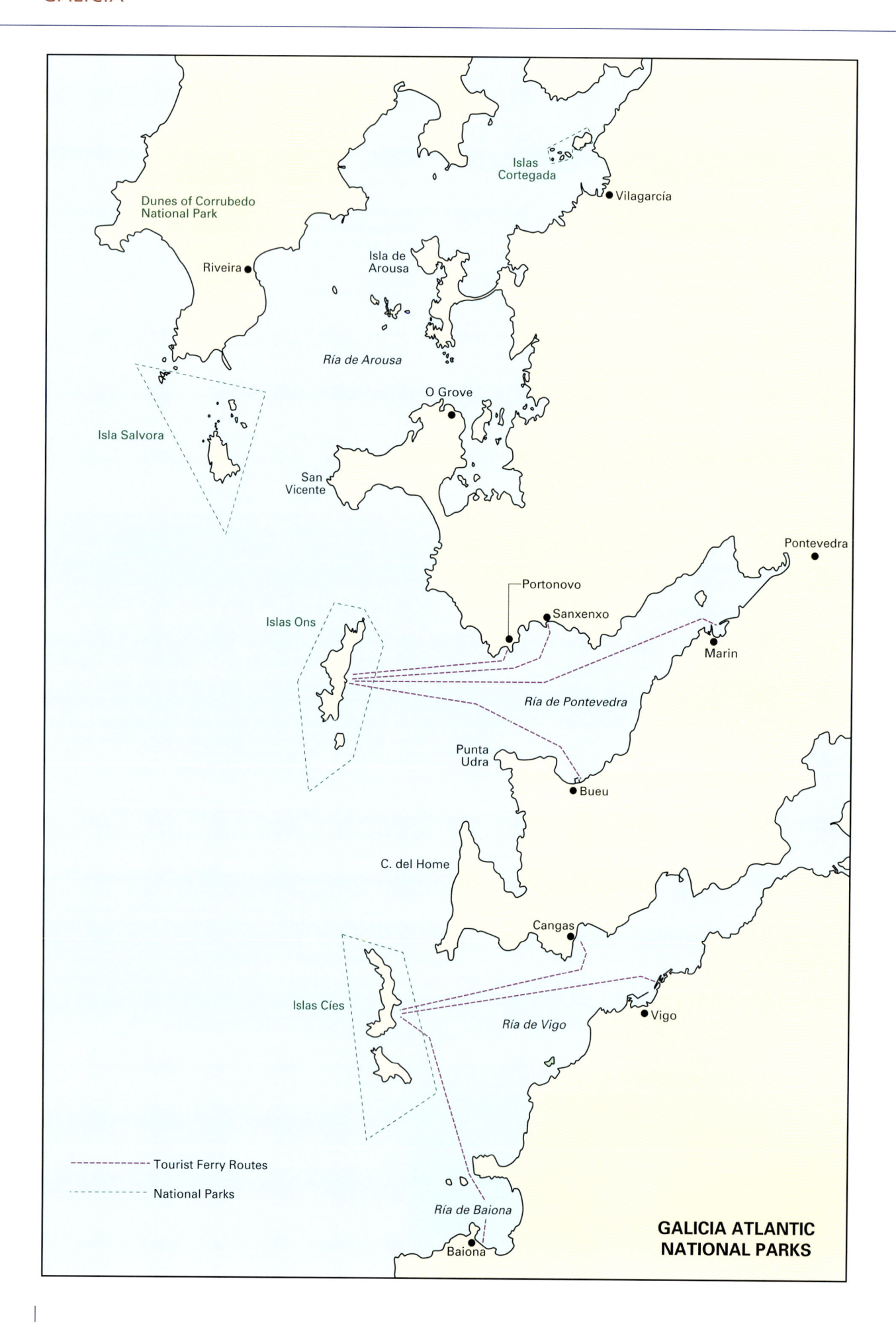

GALICIA

GALICIA ATLANTIC NATIONAL PARKS

16 ATLANTIC SPAIN AND PORTUGAL

GALICIA NATIONAL PARKS

Islas Cíes *page 112* Isla Ons *page 99*
Islas Cíes and Ons are well served by ferries and are popular for walking – routes are shown on the two plans below.

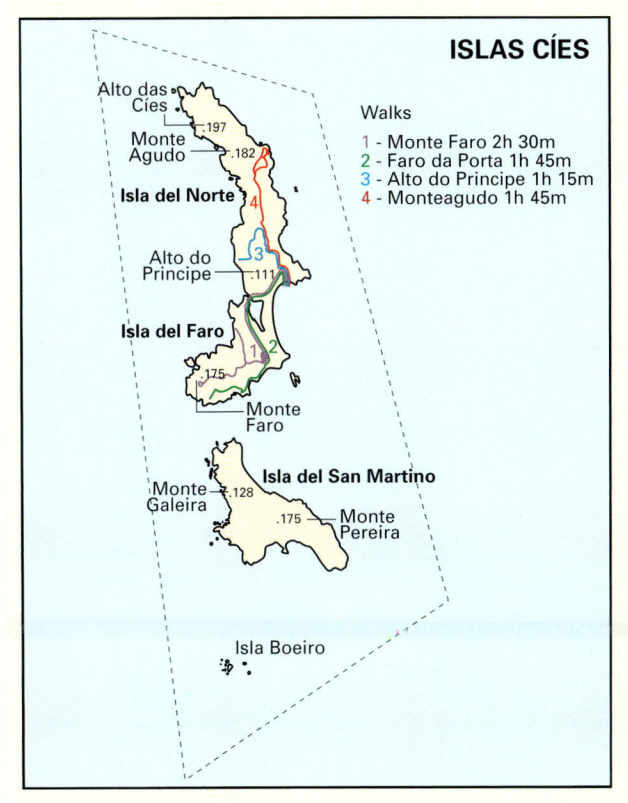

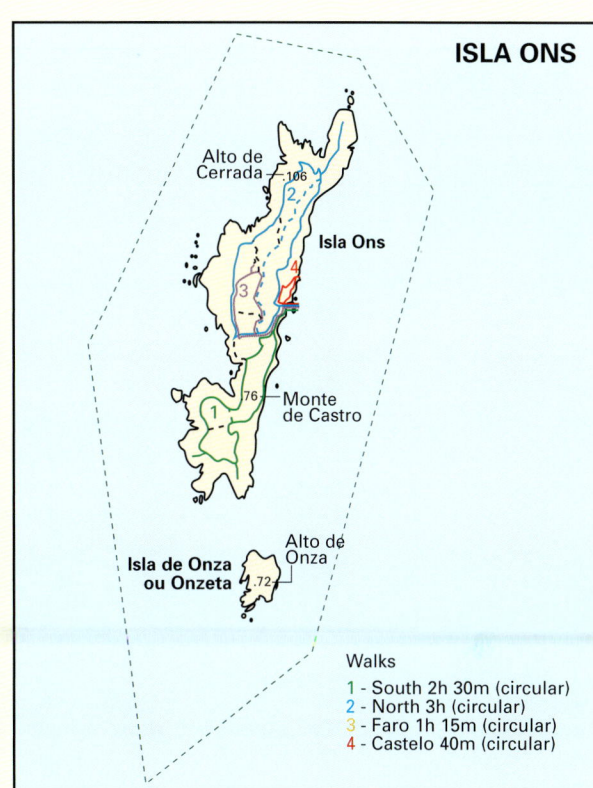

ISLAS CÍES

Alto das Cíes .197
Monte Agudo .182
Isla del Norte
Alto do Principe .111
Isla del Faro
.175
Monte Faro
Monte Galeira .128
Isla del San Martino
.175 Monte Pereira
Isla Boeiro

Walks
1 - Monte Faro 2h 30m
2 - Faro da Porta 1h 45m
3 - Alto do Principe 1h 15m
4 - Monteagudo 1h 45m

ISLA ONS

Alto de Cerrada .106
Isla Ons
Monte de Castro .76
Isla de Onza ou Onzeta
Alto de Onza .72

Walks
1 - South 2h 30m (circular)
2 - North 3h (circular)
3 - Faro 1h 15m (circular)
4 - Castelo 40m (circular)

Islas Sálvora *page 72* Islas Cortegada *page 86*
Sálvora and Islas Cortegada are not served by ferries and visits by yachtsmen are not encouraged.

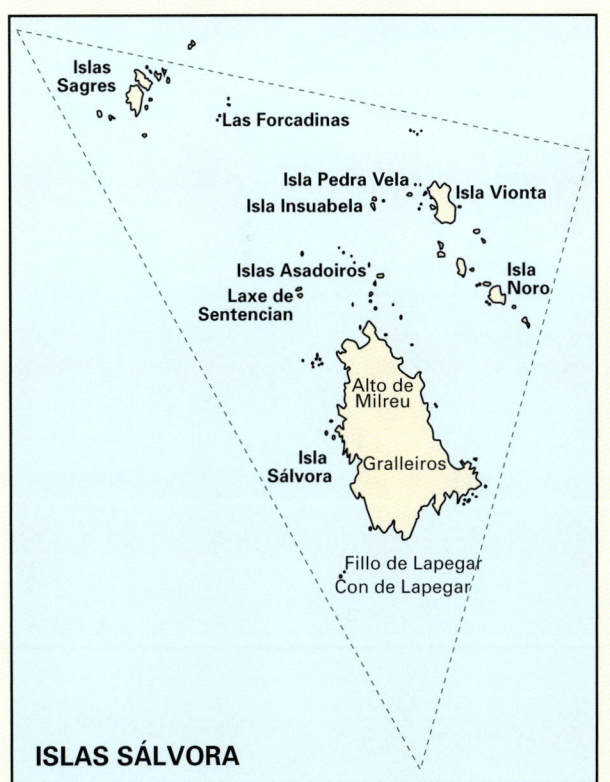

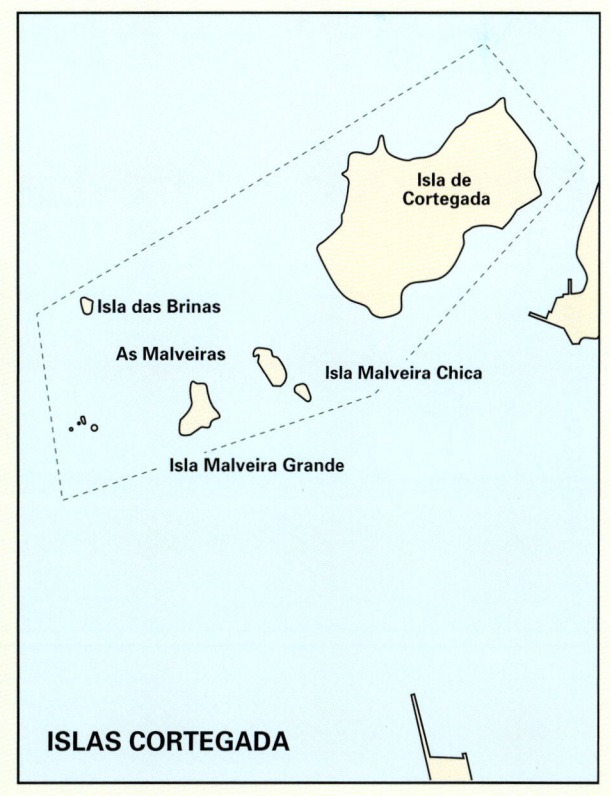

ISLAS SÁLVORA

Islas Sagres
Las Forcadinas
Isla Pedra Vela
Isla Insuabela
Isla Vionta
Islas Asadoiros
Laxe de Sentencian
Isla Noro
Alto de Milreu
Isla Sálvora
Gralleiros
Fillo de Lapegar
Con de Lapegar

ISLAS CORTEGADA

Isla de Cortegada
Isla das Brinas
As Malveiras
Isla Malveira Chica
Isla Malveira Grande

GALICIA

ATLANTIC SPAIN AND PORTUGAL 17

RÍA DE CEDEIRA TO CABO FISTERRA (FINISTERRE)

Ría de Cedeira to A Coruña

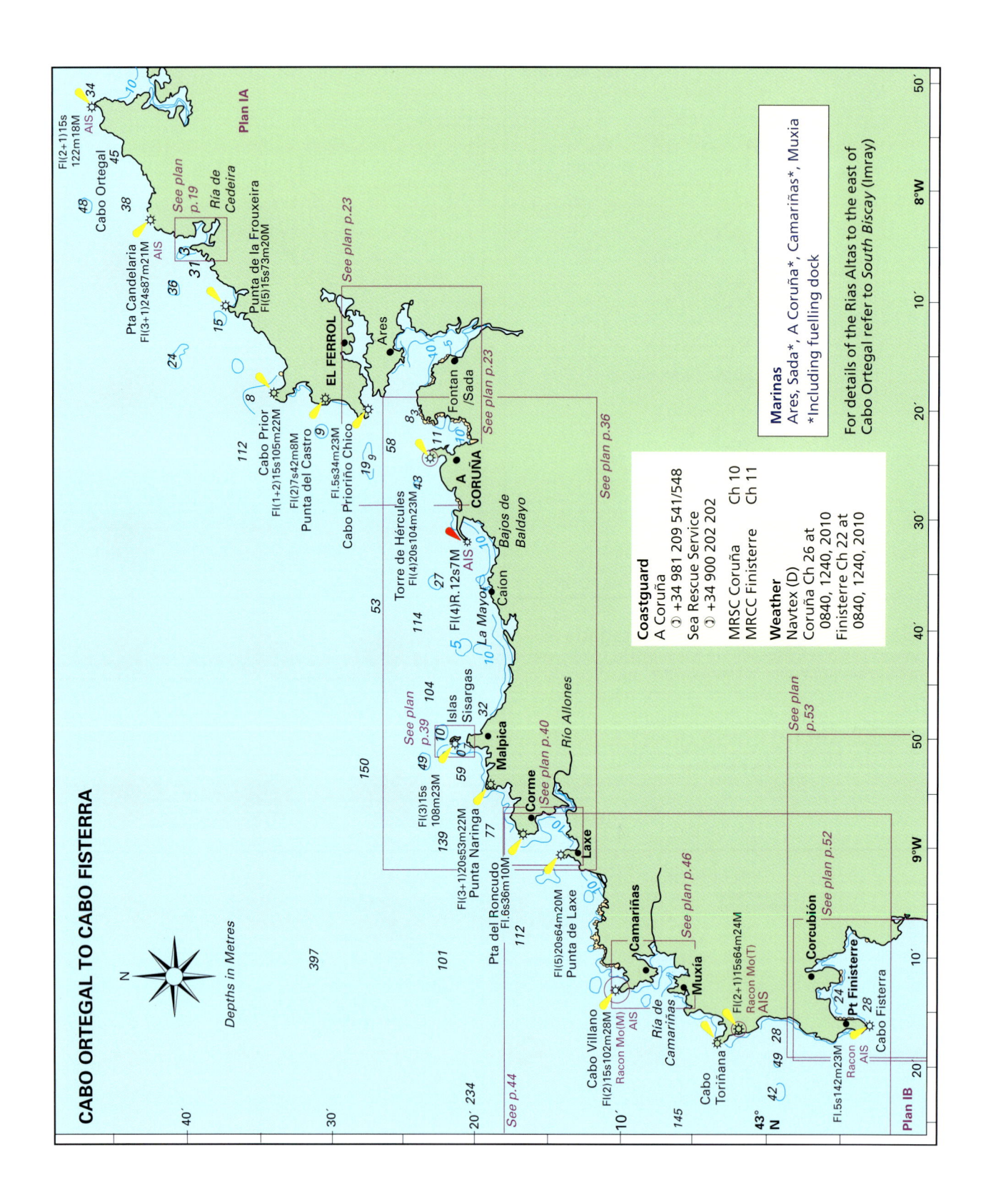

18   ATLANTIC SPAIN AND PORTUGAL

RÍA DE CEDEIRA

Cedeira

Location
43°40'·00N 08°04'·00W

Tides
HW A Coruña +0050
LW A Coruña +0050
Mean height of tide (m)
MHWS	MHWN	MLWN	MLWS
4·1	3·2	1·5	0·6

Warning
Offlying rocks off W entrance.
Shelter not too good in NW gale
Depth min 6m in approaches.

Communications
Try *Cedeira Practicos* on
VHF Ch 12

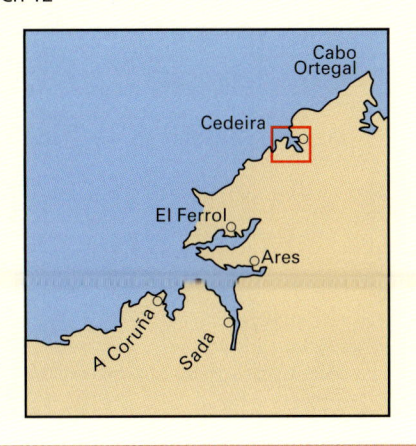

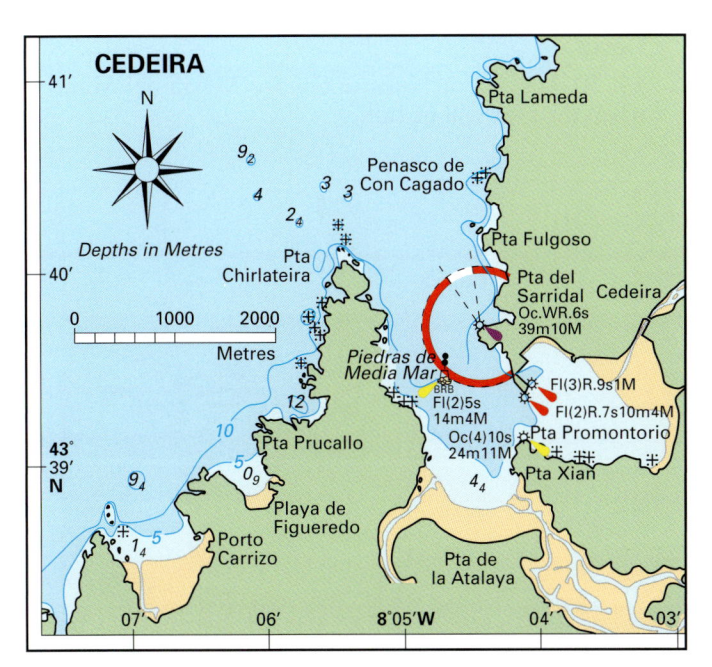

Beautiful ría behind an open bay conceals anchorage sheltered from Atlantic swell

The fishermen, although friendly, use all the facilities; watering, fuelling and provisioning entail some effort.

Approaches

By day or night
Give Punta Chirlateira a good 0·5M berth if coming from the west to avoid the offliers and approach the entrance from the north or northwest. The entrance to the Ría de Cedeira can be difficult to make out from seaward.

Entrance
Proceed down the bearing of 155° on Punta Promontorio (white hexagonal tower, Oc(4)10s) just open of Punta Sarridal (red round tower, Oc.WR.6s) in the white sector of the latter. Shortly after, the track passes into the west, red sector of Punta Sarridal which should be left at least 50m to port. Thence round the breakwater end (Fl(2)R.7s) and proceed to the anchorage.

Anchoring
In 2–4m to the southeast of the moorings, good holding in grey sand with weed patches and some detritus (mooring lines and fishing gear) on the seabed. A windy spot, the high hills funnel the wind giving the impression that it is much rougher outside. Generally well-protected from the Atlantic swell, which can be a problem on this coast, once you have turned in past the breakwater.

Moorings
None for visitors.

Berthing
The old quay can be used for embarking fuel and water, and landing; there is from 1·7–2·2m alongside the east half of the south side of it. There is one short pontoon with a gate at the top on the east end of the quay but it is for locals.

Ashore
Cedeira has always welcomed visiting yachtsmen but not done much for them. There is a travel-lift and some hard standing used by fishermen possibly usable in extremis.

Facilities
Daily weather updates – including Windguru – posted on Cruz Roja office near the dinghy landing on the old quay. Water from the old quay; garage (☏ +34 981 480 34 30) will deliver fuel here if more than 70 litres; 100-tonne travel-lift; shops are a good 0·5M walk but easier by dinghy near highwater; several restaurants in the village; ice from the new *lonja*; supermarket in Avienda de Castelao, close to Praza de Lopez Corton.

GALICIA

ATLANTIC SPAIN AND PORTUGAL 19

RÍA DE CEDEIRA TO CABO FISTERRA (FINISTERRE)

Cedeira looking east

Leisure
Good beaches round the ría and the Río Loira is worth a dinghy trip provided it is not breaking at the mouth. Visits to La Concepcion castle, the church of Nuestra Señora Maria del Mar and chapel of San Antonio are worthwhile.

Travel
Occasional local buses to El Ferrol and A Coruña; nearest airport at the latter (60km).

Fiesta
14–30 August for Nuestra Señora Maria del Mar, when the port will be full.

Cedeira looking northeast towards the old quay *Geraldine Hennigan*

RÍA DE CEDEIRA

GALICIA

Cedeira anchorage looking SW *Jane Russell*

Cedeira fishing harbour looking S over breakwater end towards the anchoring area and the light on Punta Promontorio *Jane Russell*

The entrance to Ría de Cedeira looking W. Breaking seas can be seen over rocks off Punta Chirlateira *Jane Russell*

You can dinghy into the centre of Cedeira, but not at low tide! *Jane Russell*

ATLANTIC SPAIN AND PORTUGAL   21

RÍA DE CEDEIRA TO CABO FISTERRA (FINISTERRE)

Punta del Frouxeira

Location
43°38'·54'N 08°10'·79W

An open anchorage

One of the few anchorages well-sheltered from the west behind the Punta in 2–10m, sand.

Punta del Frouseira looking southwest

Cabo Prior

Location
43°33'·01'N 08°20'·08W

The only shelter from the east between Cedeira and El Ferrol

A small bay 2M south of Cabo Prior in 2–8m on sand has good protection. The only anchorage in less than 10m lies east of Isla Blanca in 4m but stay two cables clear because of the dangerous rocks that surround it.

Cabo Prior looking northeast

22 ATLANTIC SPAIN AND PORTUGAL

GOLFO ARTABO

Approaches to Rías de Ferrol, de Ares, de Betanzos and A Coruña

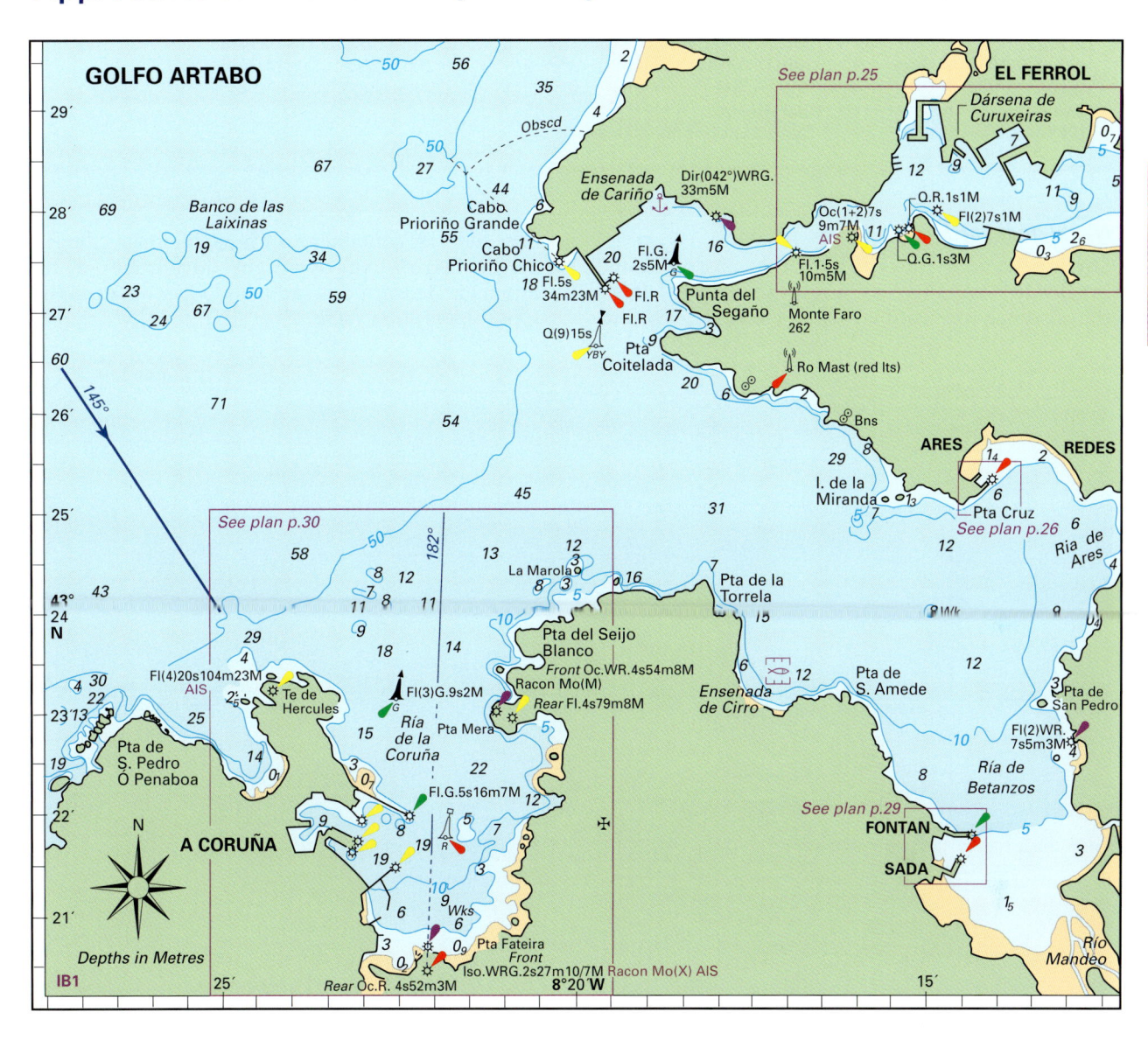

Tides
See A Coruña page 31

This group of rías in the Golfo Artabo include the major commercial and naval port of El Ferrol, the small friendly marina at Ares, and the major marinas at Sada and A Coruña.

Approach
In rough weather the sea breaks over two banks about 1M off the coast north of Cabo Prioriño – Bajos Tarracidos and Cabaleiro – and a third, Banco de las Laixinas some 2–4M west of that Cape. Under such conditions it is advisable to approach these rías from the west and remain well clear of Banco de las Laixinas. Clearing lines are shown on the plan.

Torre de Hercules, A Coruña *Henry Buchanan*

ATLANTIC SPAIN AND PORTUGAL   23

RÍA DE CEDEIRA TO CABO FISTERRA (FINISTERRE)

El Ferrol

Location
43°28'·00N 08°18'·00W

Tides
HW A Coruña +0005
LW A Coruña +0010

Mean height of tide (m)
MHWS	MHWN	MLWN	MLWS
4·2	2·8	1·6	0·3

Tidal stream
Up to 3 knots in the narrows

Warning
Keep clear of works and shipping in approaches

Naval dockyard

Stirring scenery starts behind the massive outer breakwater and there are a few facilities 4M from the entrance for visiting yachts. However, a brand new and vast container port now dominates the Ría de El Ferrol. An overnight anchorage in the Ensenada de Cariño is sadly no longer an attractive spot for a visiting yacht.

El Ferrol from the west with the forts of San Felipe to port and La Palma to starboard in the narrows

24   ATLANTIC SPAIN AND PORTUGAL

RÍA DE EL FERROL

Approach and entrance

By day or night

Approach on a track of 065° to clear the outer end of the new breakwater seen in the photograph to line up 045° in the white sector of San Cristobal light (white truncated tower Dir.WRG.33m5M). Before reaching Punta Segaño align the next marks on 085° (both white truncated towers front Pta de San Martin Fl.1s, rear Oc.4s) taking care to leave the starboard hand buoy and shallows off Pta del Segaño to starboard. Then follow the buoyed channel inwards and identify the entrance to Darsena de Curuxeiros beyond the RoRo berth (Fl(2)R.7s).

Berthing

The only yacht berths now are in Darsena de Curuxeiros (which is also busy with local ferries) and it will be a question of taking what is available, an alongside berth may be found here.

There are a number of small marinas:

The small marina at La Graña has been renovated and can accept the occasional visitor up to 12m in 4–6m but with only a few facilities. The moorings off it are often poorly anchored and the anchorage itself is subject to violent downdrafts in any W wind.

Marina Playa de Mugardos
43°27'·80N 08°15'·59W

Another marina with a good anchorage and some mooring buoys off it.

Anchoring

Temporary anchorages can be found in the following places:
To the east of Castillo de San Felipe
Ensenada de Baño
Off La Graña.

Ashore in El Ferrol

There is an excellent walkway around the northern defences to El Ferrol.

The outer mole at El Ferrol and the approach to the narrows

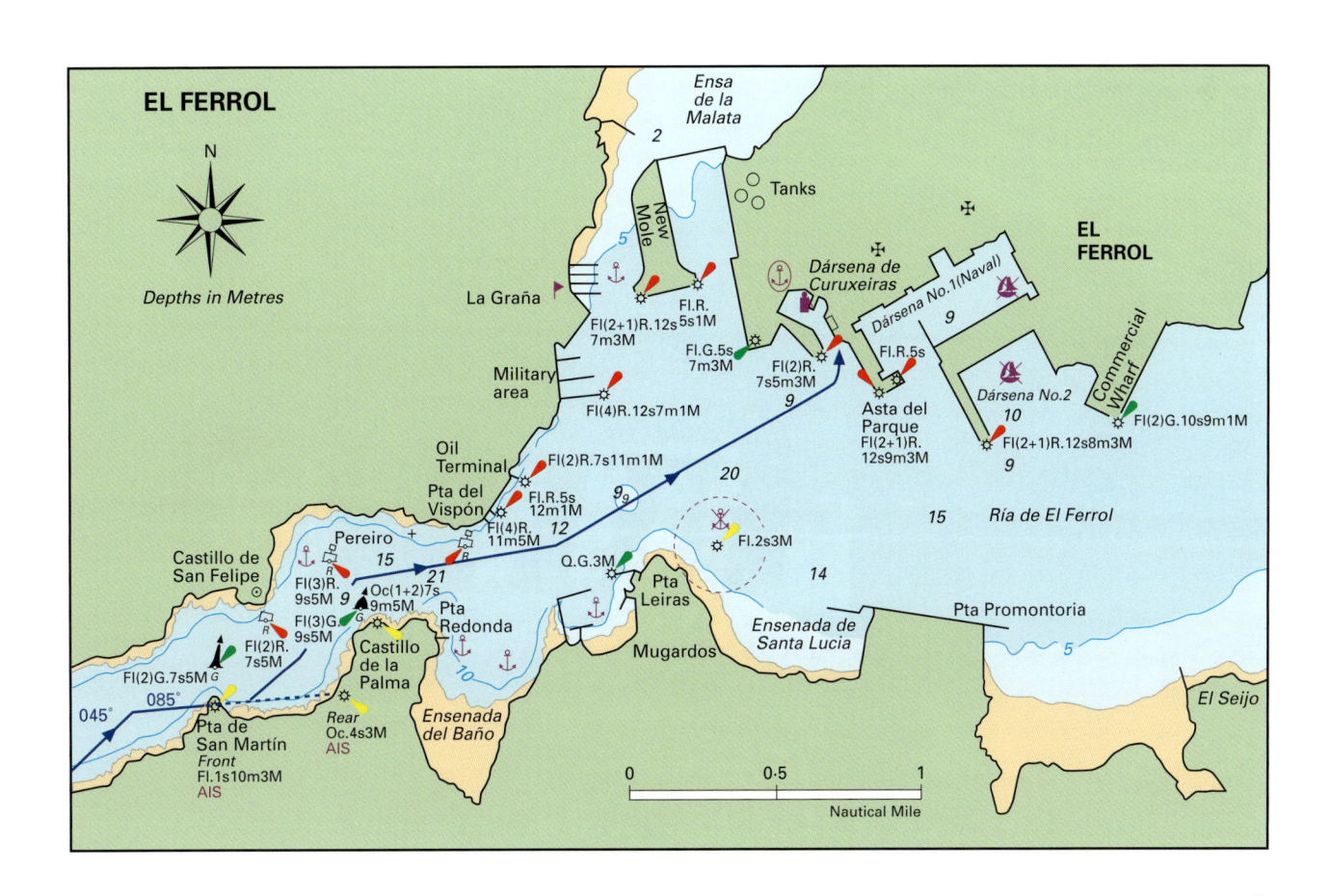

ATLANTIC SPAIN AND PORTUGAL   25

RÍA DE CEDEIRA TO CABO FISTERRA (FINISTERRE)

Ares Marina

Location
43°25'·35N 08°14'·33W

Tides
As for A Coruña (Standard Port)
Mean height of tide (m)
MHWS	MHWN	MLWN	MLWS
4·2	2·8	1·6	0·3

Communications
VHF Ch 09 (English spoken)
☎ +34 610 73 73 44 or +34 981 46 87 87
Email secretaria@nauticoares.com
www.nauticoares.com

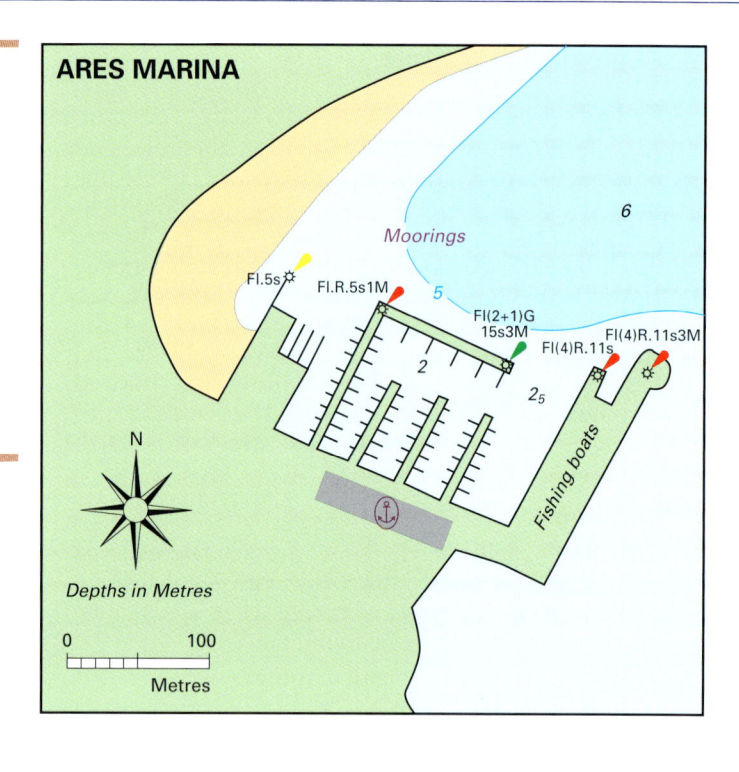

Ares Marina looking north-northeast

26   ATLANTIC SPAIN AND PORTUGAL

RÍAS DE ARES AND BETANZOS

Small marina with a great outlook onto sands, beach and town

Ares is a modern town and has the usual distractions of a seaside resort with good but crowded beaches. The town has a fiesta on the weekend of St James's day, with sailing and swimming races.

Approach and entrance by day or night

From the west in any swell, keep south of Bajo de Miranda with 3·7m over it lying to the southwest of Isla de Miranda and approx. 1M west of Ares breakwater (Fl(4)R.11s). The east end of the outer marina pontoon is lit Fl(2+1)G.15s. Berth here if not directed or call on Ch09 for a berth (0900–2200).

Beware of semi-submerged moorings in the bay.

Berthing

Ares Marina has the usual facilities, and there are 26 visitors' berths (yachts up to 14m) either on fingers on the south side of the outer pontoon or along the outside of that pontoon. Good protection is provided except in a NE wind. The minimum depth is 2-2·5m.

Access to the marina from the shore is via (normally) locked gates.

Moorings

All private.

Anchoring

The bay provides excellent anchorage in 2–3m to the east or northeast of the breakwater, well sheltered from the prevailing winds. The holding is good on sand. Anchor clear of the moorings wherever depth allows. For those at anchor, the best landing is on the slipway at the centre of the bay, which is at the centre of the village. Dinghies can be left afloat there. There is water at the root of this slipway, or water cans can be filled at the marina.

Facilities

Water and electricity on the pontoons; showers, laundry and toilets in the marina building; craneage available and a 35-tonne travel-lift; fuel at the moment only by cans from the garage who will deliver in quantity; repairs by arrangement.

Ares Marina building

Clubhouse and meteorological information in marina office. Cycle hire from here also.

There is a restaurant and café in the marina building.

Ashore there are the usual shops, a pharmacy and a good *ferreteria* (hardware shop), which sells Gaz, a few metres from the slipway. The best supermarket is about 400m away and can be reached by walking NE along the front and then leaving the park to the right.

There are many bars and restaurants along the front, and in the town.

Travel

Half-hourly bus service to El Ferrol (20 minutes) whence there are bus and rail connections to the rest of Spain. Nearest airports A Coruña (40 minutes) and Santiago de Compostela (one hour).

Ría de Ares

The ría extends eastward for three miles from Ares to Betanzos and the Río Eume. The north shore is now much obstructed by fish farms but the one at Ensenada de Redes has gone. Anchor outside moorings in 3–4m. Popular weekend spot for boats from Sada. Pretty houses in the village but not much else.

It may also be possible to anchor to the north of a farm between Isolete Mouron and Punta Modias with some shelter from the west but Spanish charts 4125 or 412A would be needed.

The ría shallows gradually up to the low railway bridge before Puentedueme town where there is 1m but no discernible channel.

Puentedueme is a historical town and worth a dinghy trip at most stages of the tide; the Castelo de Andrade perched over the town is worth a visit.

Ría de Betanzos

Río Mandeo may be entered to the south of Miño peninsula which lies 1M south-southeast of Sada. There is a small drying harbour on the south side of Miño. From here the río winds 4M to Betanzos, passing under a bridge with a clearance of approximately 20m. Spanish chart 412A is the only guide to the run of the channel and although excursion boats run up to the drying quay at Betanzos on the tide, it would be an adventurous stranger that tried it in a deep-draught yacht.

Betanzos is an ancient medieval city with many historical attractions including the 12th-century church of Santa Maria de Azogue, an excellent museum and many restaurants around the main square and waterfront.

RÍA DE CEDEIRA TO CABO FISTERRA (FINISTERRE)

Sada Marina (Fontán)

Location
43°21'·00N 08°14'·00W

Tides
As for A Coruña (Standard Port)
Mean height of tide (m)
MHWS	MHWN	MLWN	MLWS
4·2	2·8	1·6	0·3

Communications
VHF Marina Sada Ch 09
☎ +34 981 61 90 15
Email administracion@marinasada.com
(Manager) teijido@marinasada.com
www.marinasada.com
www.marinasdegalicia.com

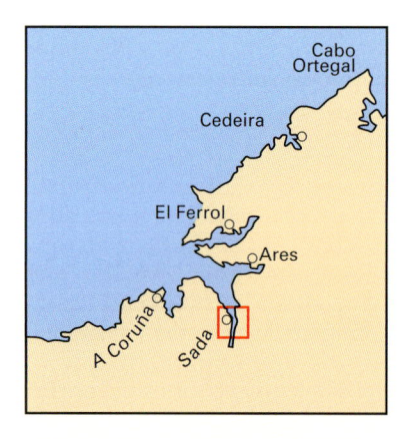

Large expanding marina with all facilities and security; a good place to lay up

The fishing harbour in Fontán and the marina at Sada have developed in parallel. Much progress has been made to the marina side in recent years and continues. The scope of the harbour was much enhanced by the removal of La Pulgeira rock and beacon in the middle of the harbour near the end of the pier for the local boats on the West side.

Approaches

By day or night

From off the entrance to El Ferrol there are no offlying dangers provided 0·5M is kept offshore and a track of 120° on Punta de San Pedro (Fl(2)WR.7s5m3M) maintained until the Sada breakwater (Fl(4)G.11s) is sighted and the way is clear to the entrance.

Entrance

Wide and straightforward except for anchored and possibly unlit boats. Sada marina lies to port on entry to the main harbour.

Berthing

A prior call on Ch 09 may get a berth allocated. Otherwise select a vacant one on the outer pontoons of the eastern breakwater and check with the office. An additional marina – Club Nautico de Sada – with 313 berths up to 22m fills the centre of the harbour. It has its own travel-lift.

Sada Marina looking north

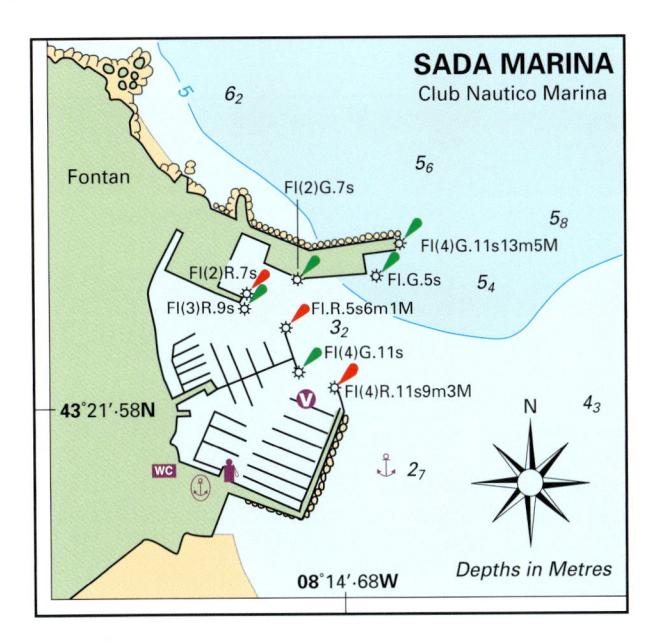

RÍAS DE ARES AND BETANZOS

Travel
Sada is off the main rail and motorway routes (but not by much) and buses run to Betanzos to connect. If laying up here, A Coruña airport, with direct flights to London Heathrow or to other destinations via Madrid, is only 15km, with Santiago de Compostela international airport 45 minutes along the motorway.

Ensenada de Cirro
Location
43°23'·31N 08°17'·92W

An alternative to the busy marinas hereabouts
Behind the extensive fish farm lies a small harbour with a West Country (UK) feel. Entirely given over to fishing, an anchorage may be found just off the beach (see plan page 23). An entry channel is marked by port and starboard markers but is encumbered by fishing rafts. Any route through the rafts can be used.

Ensenada de Cirro, harbour

Ensenada de Cirro © Google Earth

Moorings
None for visitors.

Anchoring
There are now moorings, which appear to be private, in the harbour entrance N and NNW of the S breakwater. Thus there is no longer room to anchor W of a line joining the breakwater heads. Anchorage is possible E of the S breakwater, but this is exposed to the predominant N–NE winds. The anchorage S of the S breakwater is shallow and there are many small craft moorings.

Ashore
There are good laying up facilities and security and this is probably the best place to overwinter along the coast.

Facilities
Water and electricity on the pontoons to which access is by card; diesel and petrol at the fuel berth; 32-tonne travel-lift; craneage up to 10-tonnes; heads and showers; repair facilities under cover if needed; chandlery; free WiFi. There are adequate shops within easy walking distance, a market and a large supermercado south of the marina.

Leisure
Sada is a popular seaside resort and there is the usual range of restaurants, shops, cafés and entertainments. Otherwise a dinghy trip up the Río Mondeo to the ancient town of Betanzos on the tide, or by one of the excursion boats that run up the river might amuse. See above for some details of Betanzos. There is a good beach at Playa de Sada.

Fiestas
16 July Feast of Our Lady of Mount Carmel
15–18 August St Roch.

GALICIA

ATLANTIC SPAIN AND PORTUGAL

RÍA DE CEDEIRA TO CABO FISTERRA (FINISTERRE)

Final approaches to Ría de la Coruña

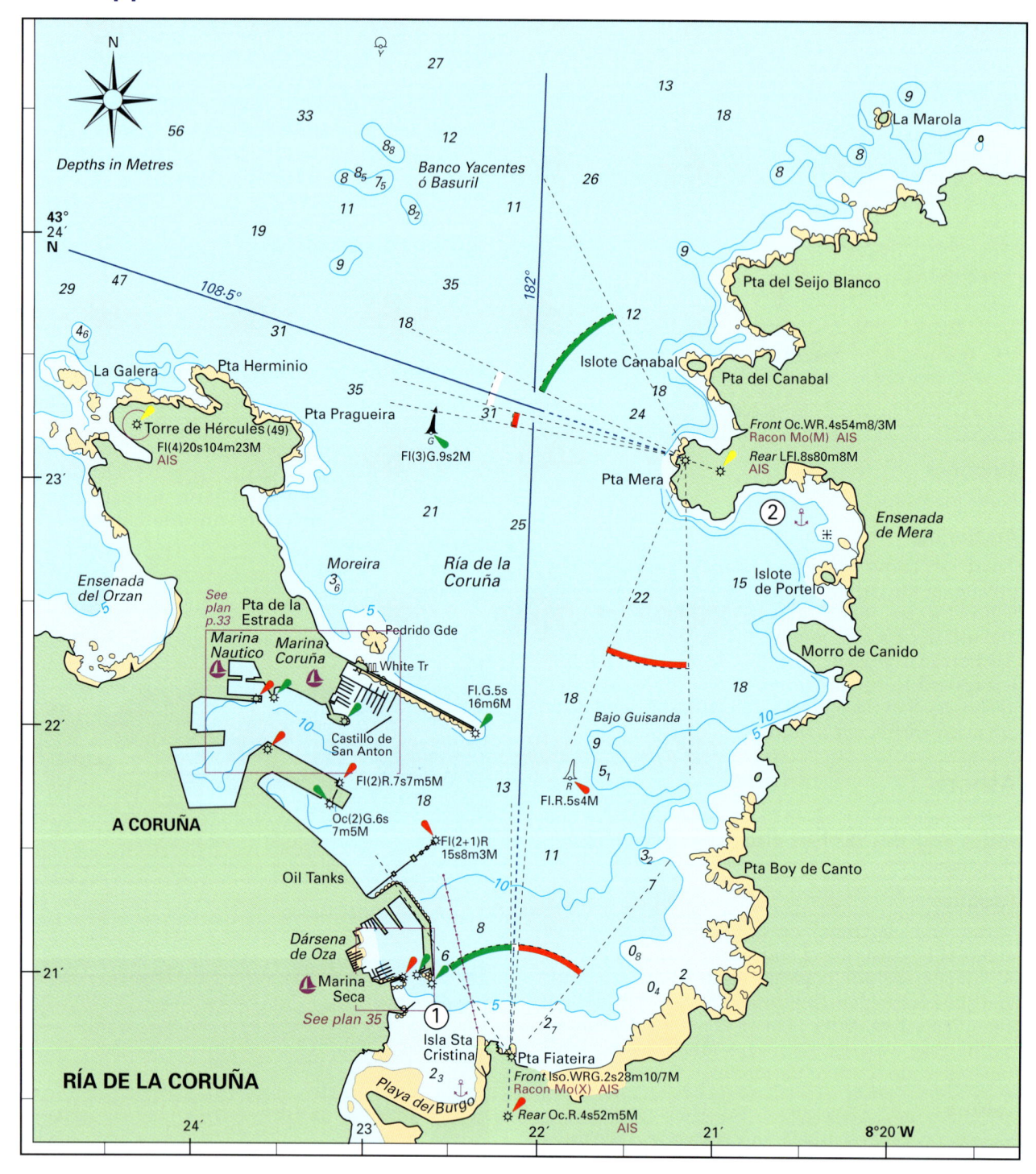

Lights
Pta Mera Ldg Lts 108°30′
Front Oc.WR.4s54m8/3M White 8-sided tower
Rear LFl.8s79m8M White 8-sided tower

Pta Fiateira LdgLts 182°
Front Iso.WRG.2s27m10/7M Red and white chequered square tower
Rear Oc.R.4s52m3M Red and white chequered square tower
Breakwater head 43°21′·9N 08°22′·47W Fl.G.5s16m6M Truncated conical tower

Torre de Hércules

Coruña breakwater tower

30 ATLANTIC SPAIN AND PORTUGAL

A CORUÑA

A Coruña (La Coruña)

Location
43°21'·9N 08°22'·47W
(Outer breakwater light)

Tides
Standard Port A Coruña
Heights in metres
MHWS	MHWN	MLWN	MLWS
3·8	2·8	1·5	0·5

Warning
Banco Yacentes must be avoided and the leading lines followed in heavy weather or swell

Communications
Port Control Ch 12
Marinas Ch 09

Navtex
518kHz (D) at 0030, 0430, 0830*, 1230, 1630, 2030*
(*weather only)
490kHz (W) (Spanish) at 0340, 0740, 1140, 1540, 1940, 2340

Weather bulletins
MF 1698kHz at 0703, 1303, 1903
VHF Ch 26 at 0840, 1240, 2010
MRSC Ch 10 at 0005, 0405, 0805, 1205, 1605, 2005

Navigational warnings
MF 1698kHz at 0703, 1903
VHF Ch 26 at 0840, 2010
MRSC Ch 10 at 0205, 0605, 1005, 1405, 1805, 2205

Primary working freqs
c/s Coruña Radio
Manual Ch 26 Tx 1698 Rx 2123
Autolink Ch 28 Tx 2806 Rx 3283
DSC Ch 70 2187·5kHz

A major city port with modern marina facilities

A Coruña is the major city of northern Galicia, offering good communications by road and air. It has a busy commercial port with welcoming marinas. The old city is picturesque with narrow paved streets, houses with characteristic glassed-in balconies, and numerous small restaurants and cafés. North of the town is the Torre de Hércules, begun by the Romans, and the oldest functioning lighthouse in the world.

The people of A Coruña erected a monument to their hero Lieutenant-General Sir John Moore who was killed leading the defence of A Coruña in the Peninsular War. The monument can be found in the beautiful memorial garden of St. Carlos (Jardin de San Carlos) that was built in 1843 and overlooks the bay and Castillo de San Anton. This balance of history is reassuring. The city's more prominent hero is Maria Pita whose statue gazes over the main square, Plaza Maria Pita, and the Town Hall. Maria Pita is honoured for her heroic part in the defense of A Coruña against the English 'pirate' Francis Drake in 1589.

Santiago de Compostela is an easy day trip away by train.

Approach

Caution

The only safe approach in heavy swell or storm conditions is on the Punta Mera leading line south of Banco Yacentes. The latter should be avoided in any seaway. Note also that the lit yellow buoy to the north of this bank is reported as small and difficult to identify.

For the outer approach refer to page 23.

From the north This is potentially dangerous in strong southwest or northwest winds. Pick up the Punta Fiateira leading line on 182°. The white tower on the mole will be conspicuous on this approach. After passing the outer mole turn onto 280° for Marina Coruña and Marina Nautico.

From the west This is the big ship route and the safest in bad weather. Pick up the Pta Mera leading line on 108°. Conspicuous to starboard will be the Torre de Hércules followed by the white tower on the mole. Once clear of the green channel mark Fl(3)G.9s the course may be altered towards the mole end or the Pta Fiateira leading line.

Berthing and anchorage

A Coruña offers visitors two main marinas:

Marina Coruña

Close south of the prominent tower on the breakwater, has a secondary marina for engineering services and lay-up facilities at Marina Seca. The latter has a waiting/service pontoon only.

Marina Nautico (RCN de A Coruña Marina)

Lies tucked in further west beyond Castillo de San Anton.

There is now less space to anchor behind the breakwater and the authorities may restrict or forbid this. The bottom is mud with patchy holding and foul in places so it is advisable to use a tripping line.

In gales from southwest through to northwest, swell is likely to be reflected around the Ría de la Coruña making Anchorages 1 and 2 (plan page 30) untenable and affecting visitor pontoons in the marinas. The resulting surge and snatch on mooring lines can be quite violent. Take precautions if leaving a boat unattended for some time. The locals use substantial steel springs as mooring points.

Maria Pita, heroine of the defense of A Coruña against Francis Drake *Jane Russell*

ATLANTIC SPAIN AND PORTUGAL

RÍA DE CEDEIRA TO CABO FISTERRA (FINISTERRE)

A Coruña from the north. Torre de Hercules at lower right

A Coruña marinas from the northwest

32 ATLANTIC SPAIN AND PORTUGAL

CORUÑA

Marina Nautico
43°22′N 8°23′·7W
VHF Ch 09 ☎ + 34 981 226 880
Email marina@rcncoruna.com www.rcncoruna.com
There is a video introduction to A Coruña and Marina Nautico at www.youtube.com/v/gcWpQuXFfts

The Marina Nautico is conveniently placed for the city facilities; it is owned by the Real Club Náutico (which is very formal) and includes 44 reserved visitors' berths, including four for vessels up to 30m. Call ahead on VHF Ch 09.

After rounding the breakwater, head towards Castillo de St Anton (on approximately 280°) and continue to the dock entrance about 300m beyond the Castillo. The three pontoons for visitors are immediately ahead on entering, and can be affected by swell entering the harbour. Forty-four berths are reserved for visitors including four for vessels to 30m.

Marina Nautico

Facilities
There is water and electricity on the pontoons; major repairs to hull, engine, electrics and electronics are possible; a 32-tonne travel-lift and craneage is available.

A modern wooden building houses the marina office at its east end and a bright taverna restaurant at the other while domestic facilities lie in between.

The tourist office is at the northwest corner of the marina, and there is an internet café off Plaza de Maria Pita just west of the Plaza.

Entrance to the marina seen from the office *Martin Walker*

RCN building from the north *Martin Walker*

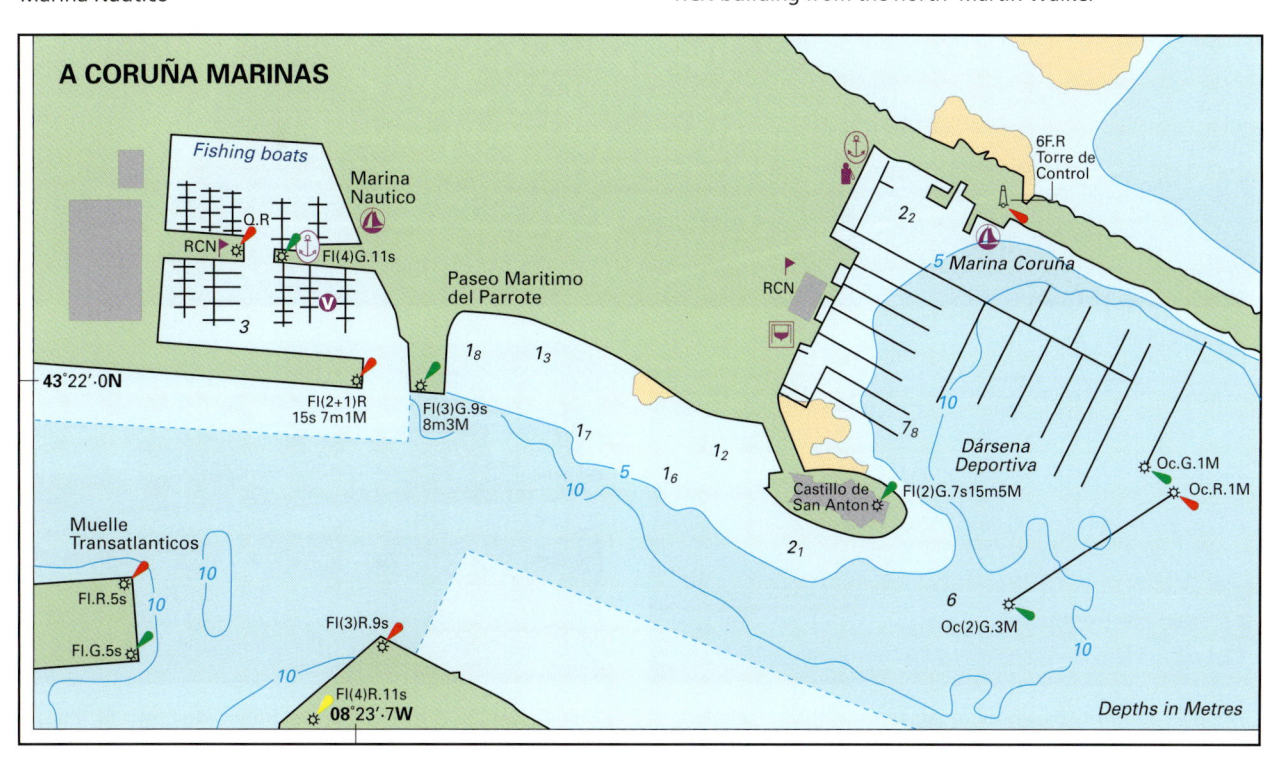

GALICIA

ATLANTIC SPAIN AND PORTUGAL 33

RÍA DE CEDEIRA TO CABO FISTERRA (FINISTERRE)

Marina Coruña
43°22′N 8°23′W
VHF Ch 09 ☏ +34 881 92 04 82
Email marinacoruna@marinacoruna.es
www.northwestmarinas.com
www.marinasdegalicia.com

This large marina has been built beneath the prominent tower on the harbour breakwater and is protected by two yellow striped wave breakers. Enter through the central gap marked by red and green lit posts. Substantial pontoons with finger berths run off a massive central pontoon. Call VHF Ch 09 on the approach.

Swell can make any of the berths here liable to quite severe snatching on the mooring lines. Use metal spring attachments to absorb the snatching if leaving the boat unattended for any length of time.

Facilities
There is water and electricity on the pontoons; fuel and pump out are available close to the office building; laundry; small grocery shop and chandlery; cash machine and WiFi; restaurant on site.

Electric buggies are available to those berthed a long way from the shore and facilities. The nearest supermarket is some 10 minutes' walk away.

The associate marina at Marina Seca, in the south of the Ría de la Coruna, provides engineering services and lay-up facilities. It has a waiting/service pontoon only.

After passing through the wave-breakers turn to starboard for fuel *Martin Walker*

Marina Coruña

The port authority may order boats to leave the anchorage
Martin Walker

Marina Coruña. Office, shop, restaurant, domestic facilities. Fuel and pump out *Martin Walker*

34   ATLANTIC SPAIN AND PORTUGAL

A CORUÑA

Marina Seca
43° 20'·87 N 8° 22'·59 W
Darsena Deportiva Faro de Oza s/n, 15006 A Coruña.
VHF Ch 09 +34 881 913 651
Email marinaseca@marinaseca.com
www.northwestmarinas.com

It should be noted that Marina Seca is a service marina only, with just one long pontoon at the northern side of the other four pontoons in the photograph. The latter are the property of a private fishing and ship repair enterprise that does not take visitors. The Marina Seca pontoon is a waiting/service pontoon only for use while repairs are being undertaken or a lift out arranged.

It is part of Marina Coruña in the Northwest Marinas group and is the main site for yacht work in A Coruña. There is a dry storage facility for small boats and most technical work can be undertaken. There is a small chandlery on site but domestic facilities are very limited and there are no shops nearby.

Marina Seca from the southeast *Northwest Marinas*

Arrivals berth, looking towards entrance from fuel dock
Martin Walker

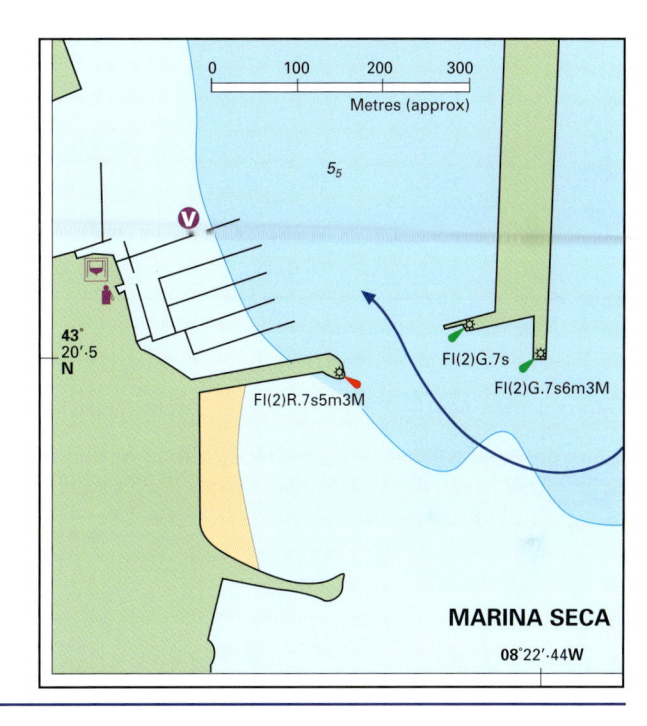

Alternative anchorages (see plan p.30)

1. **Playa del Burgo** 43°20'·7N 08°22'·6W
   Off the east end of the Playa del Burgo, partly sheltered by the Isla de Santa Cristina, in 2–3m with good holding over sand and weed. Dinghies can be left on the sandy beach. There is a small restaurant ashore and a supermarket one road further back. The ferry to A Coruña departs from the tiny pier every hour, and must not be impeded.

2. **Ensenada de Mera** 43°22'·8N 08°20'·4W
   In the Ensenada de Mera, protected from northwest clockwise to south. Beware the unmarked rock some distance from the mole, which only shows near low water. Anchor as moorings and depth permit in 3–4m over sand and weed, surrounded by a crescent of sandy beach (a line of closely spaced yellow buoys may define the swimming area). The village is very much a holiday resort, with restaurants and limited shopping plus a ferry to/from A Coruña.

Early morning in Playa del Burgo anchorage looking NNW
Lilian Duckworth

A misty Ensenada de Mera at low water springs.
The unmarked rock is just visible *Jane Russell*

GALICIA

ATLANTIC SPAIN AND PORTUGAL   35

RÍA DE CEDEIRA TO CABO FISTERRA (FINISTERRE)

A Coruña to Laxe (Lage)

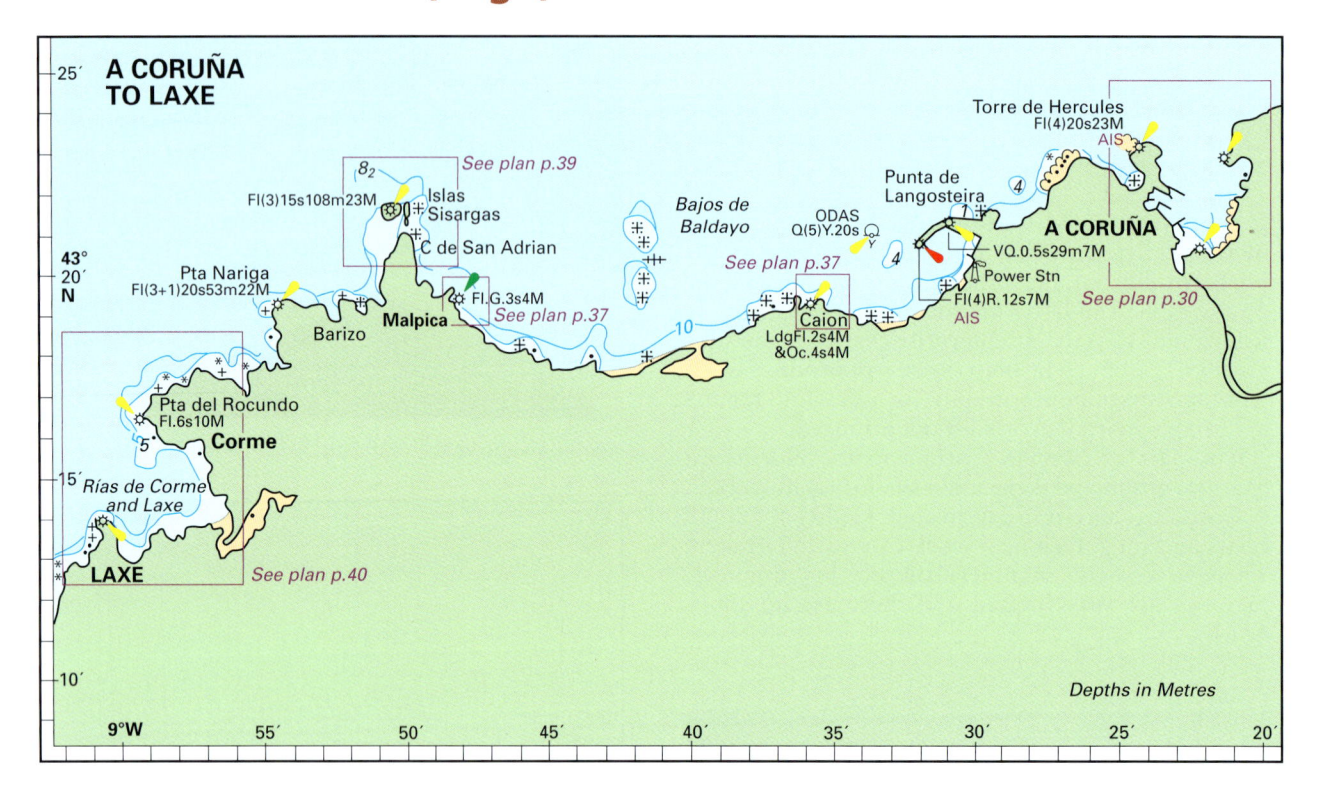

Lights
Torre de Hércules Fl(4)20s104m23M Square stone tower, 8-sided top
Sisargas Fl(3)15s108m23M 8-sided tower with white house
Pta Nariga Fl(3+1)20s53m22M Round tower on grey building
Pta del Roncondo Fl.6s36m10M White round tower

Tides
Standard Port A Coruña
Heights in metres

MHWS	MHWN	MLWN	MLWS
3·8	2·8	1·5	0·5

Industrial developments

A very large commercial harbour/gas terminal has been constructed approximately four miles west of A Coruña extending southwest from the coast at Punta Langosteira. This complex has at its northern extremity a quay 1·8M long with its end at approximately 43°20'·74N 08° 32'·00W. This point is also about 4M northeast of Caion. This area should be avoided by mariners.

Passage overview

This rugged coast continues to justify its name as Costa da Morte. Only in the most settled weather will yachtsmen wish to close the coast between A Coruña and Laxe. Most will choose to keep offshore. It would be unwise to go rock hopping without a large-scale chart. Heavy swell builds rapidly in a northerly wind. Malpica offers some protection but has extensive unmarked dangerous shallows to the east. There are shallows off Isla Sisargas with its massive lighthouse. Beyond that the wind farms start high above Pta Nariga and continue southwards.

The best goose barnacles are harvested along the Costa da Morte *Martin Walker*

36 ATLANTIC SPAIN AND PORTUGAL

MALPICA

Over the leading line for Caion - two white marks just visible on hillside

Caion 43°19'·2N 08°36'·1W

Strictly a fair weather spot; the tiny harbour of Caion is tucked to the east of Punta Insua de Caion and should be approached on the leading line on 147°. The harbour faces east with a high stone breakwater offering protection from north through west to south. Although lit, it should not be approached in darkness. It may be possible to lie alongside for a short period if the fishing boats are out and there is no swell.

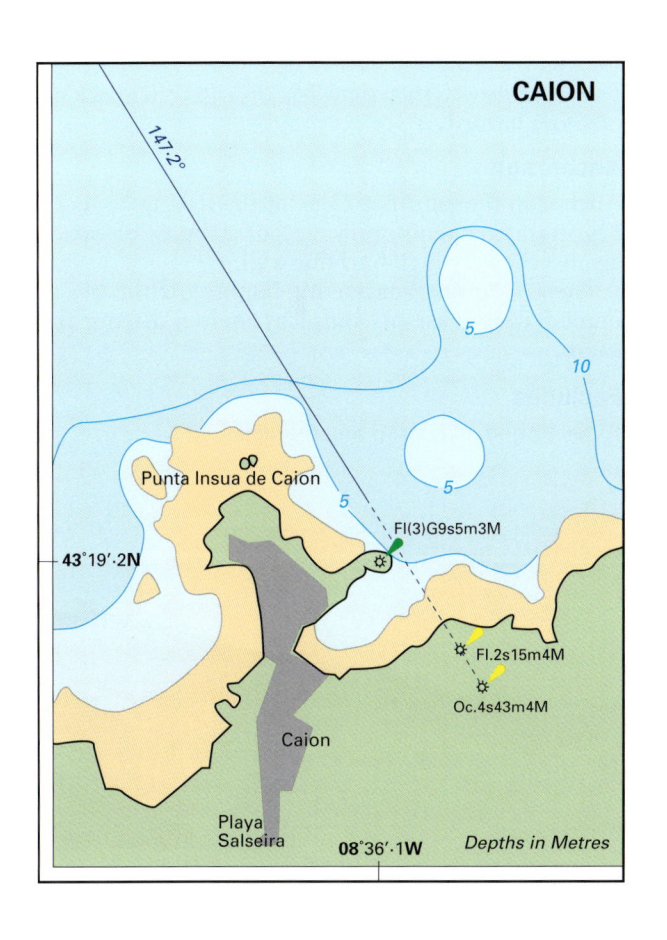

Malpica

Location
43°19'·31N 08°48'·12W

Light
Breakwater Fl.G.3s18m4M. Green column

A harbour devoted to fishing

Malpica is a fishing port on a rugged coastline, and a minor tourist outlet for A Coruña. The harbour is colourful and there are good beaches nearby. The 420m mole is backed by a high wall over which heavy spray breaks in gales. There is good protection from south through west and north and northeast but a swell builds rapidly in a northerly wind and a northeasterly swell may come some way round the corner of the mole. The main harbour is full of fishing boat moorings. A small, shallow inner

GALICIA

ATLANTIC SPAIN AND PORTUGAL

RÍA DE CEDEIRA TO CABO FISTERRA (FINISTERRE)

Malpica harbour looking southwest

harbour (with a launching ramp, 100-tonne travel lift and hardstanding) is not normally open to yachts, neither is the fuel station.

The town has everyday provisions and restaurants.

Approach

From the east The unmarked Bajos de Baldayo must be avoided. There is a fair-weather inside route about 0·7M offshore. Normally keep at least 5M off shore before turning southwest for the harbour.

Round the mole head well clear of the shore as there are reported to be unmarked rocks near the entrance.

From the west Other than Isla Sisargas there are no offshore hazards.

Anchorage

Anchor in the entrance clear of the fishing boats or negotiate the temporary use of a buoy or space against the very high harbour wall.

There is an alternative anchorage off the beach immediately west of Malpica, sheltered from the south.

Facilities

Expect none, except in an emergency.

The anchorage at Malpica. Harbour entrance to starboard
Geraldine Hennigan

38 ATLANTIC SPAIN AND PORTUGAL

ISLAS SISARGAS

Islas Sisargas

Location
43°21'·47N 08°50'·30W (landing)

The Islas Sisargas landing, in the cone between Sisarga Grande and Sisarga Chica (sometimes referred to as Sisarga Pequeña) is sheltered from the north. The gap between the two islands is very narrow, and virtually non-existent at low water. Anchor southeast of the stone quay in 3–4m: holding is variable over sand and rock. There are steps at the quay, and a track leading up to the lighthouse on the island's summit. The islands are a seabird reserve, and audible from a considerable distance. If walking ashore in June wear headgear as the herring gulls protect their young aggressively.

The Sisargas channel is hazardous. Both east and west winds can produce breakers and there are strong tidal streams. The approaches, which should not be attempted without large-scale charts (e.g. inset to Spanish 928), are as follows:

a. From the northwest, keep the left-hand edge of the Cabo de San Adrian in line with the left-hand edge of the prominent headland of Atalaya de Malpica on 133°.
b. From the southwest, keep to the south of La Carreira and Laxe de Barizo.
c. From the east, by following a leading bearing of 265° towards the rock Pedra do Lobo and changing towards Punta del Rostro when this bears 314°. The channel is about 400m wide; keep closer to Punta Pedro d'Areas than Isla Sisarga Chica (which has a rock, La Chan, awash some 250m to the south).

Alternative anchorages

Playa de Seaya SE of Cabo de San Adrián
43°19'·8N 08°49'·6W
Sheltered from the south and west.

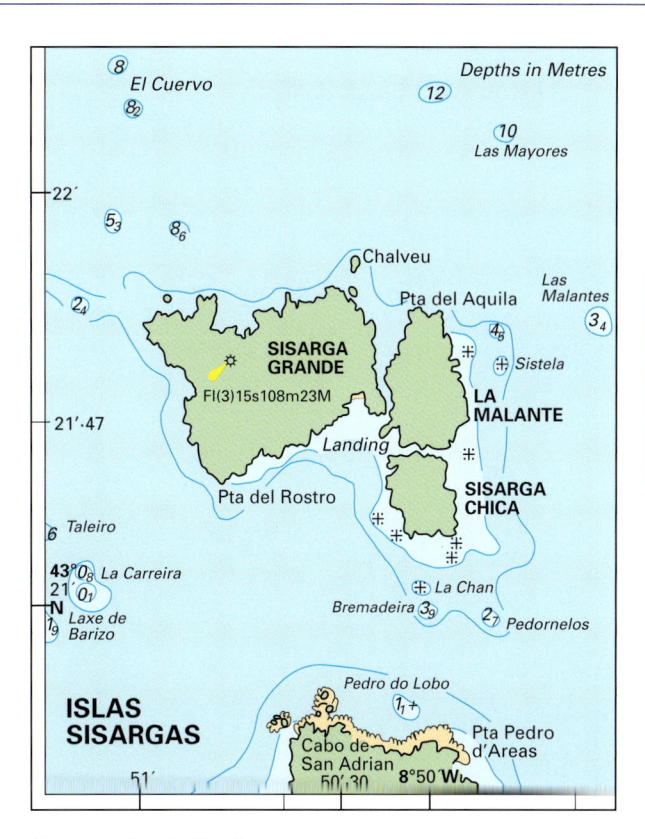

Ensenada de Barizo
(entrance 43°19'·2N 08°52'·85W)

The bay is 3M southwest of Isla Sisargas and is overlooked by cliffs and the Punta Nariga wind farm. A ledge runs out from the eastern headland leaving a usable width of about 250m in the entrance. The bay, which is open to the northwest and subject to swell from that quarter, opens out inside and provides shelter for small fishing vessels to lie to summer moorings, with more craned ashore. A concrete mole, slipway and green light structure lie in the southwest corner.

There is a fine sandy beach at the head of the bay, but otherwise the bottom is rock and sand.

Islas Sisargas - two yachts at anchor off the landing quay

GALICIA

ATLANTIC SPAIN AND PORTUGAL   39

RÍA DE CEDEIRA TO CABO FISTERRA (FINISTERRE)

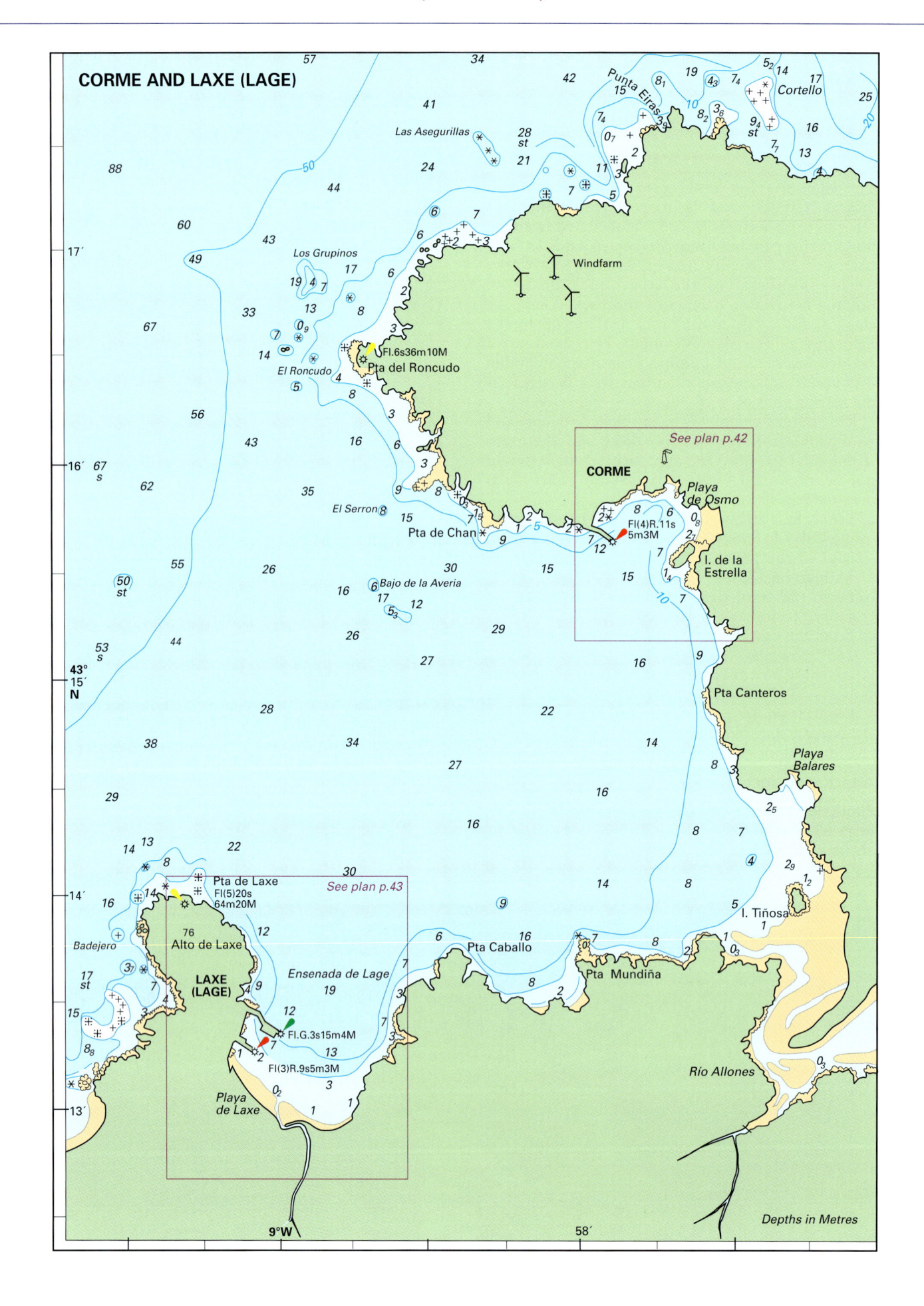

40 ATLANTIC SPAIN AND PORTUGAL

RÍA DE CORME Y LAXE

Ría de Corme y Laxe

Location
22°43'·15N 09°00'·63W (entrance)

Tides
Standard port A Coruña
Mean time differences
HW +0045; LW +0045
Heights in metres

MHWS	MHWN	MLWN	MLWS
3·7	2·8	1·5	0·5

Lights
Pta del Roncudo Fl.6s36m10M
Corme breakwater lt Fl(2)R.11s5m3M
Pta de Laxe Fl(5)20s64m20M

Warning
Note offlyers off Pta del Roncudo and Pta de Laxe; also note Bajo de la Avería to the southwest of Pta de Chan

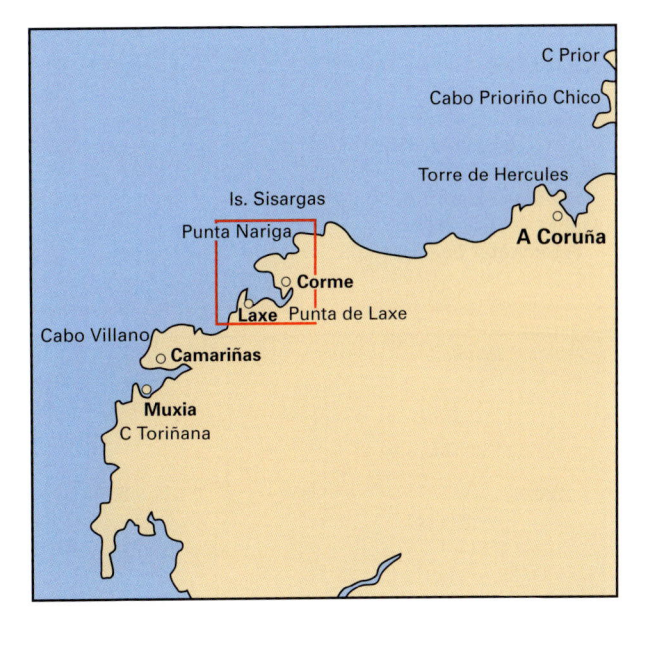

A pleasant ría

For many, the Ría de Corme y Laxe offers welcome anchorage following the 35M coastal passage from A Coruña. The two could hardly be more different with the busy city being exchanged for dramatic scenery, quiet beaches and the chance to explore, by dinghy, the beautiful Río Allones as it winds its way 5M up to the picturesque old bridge at Pontecesco.

If heading north, into prevailing north or northwest winds, then departure from here, rather than A Coruña, avoids giving away considerable ground to windward.

Laxe. Anchorage off the southerly breakwater *Roddy Innes*

Corme. Anchorage between *viveros* and the harbour *Martin Walker*

GALICIA

ATLANTIC SPAIN AND PORTUGAL 41

RÍA DE CEDEIRA TO CABO FISTERRA (FINISTERRE)

Corme

Location
43°15'·64N 08°57'·78W

Tides
See Ría box information on page 41

Light
Breakwater beacon Fl(2)R.5s12m3M Red Column

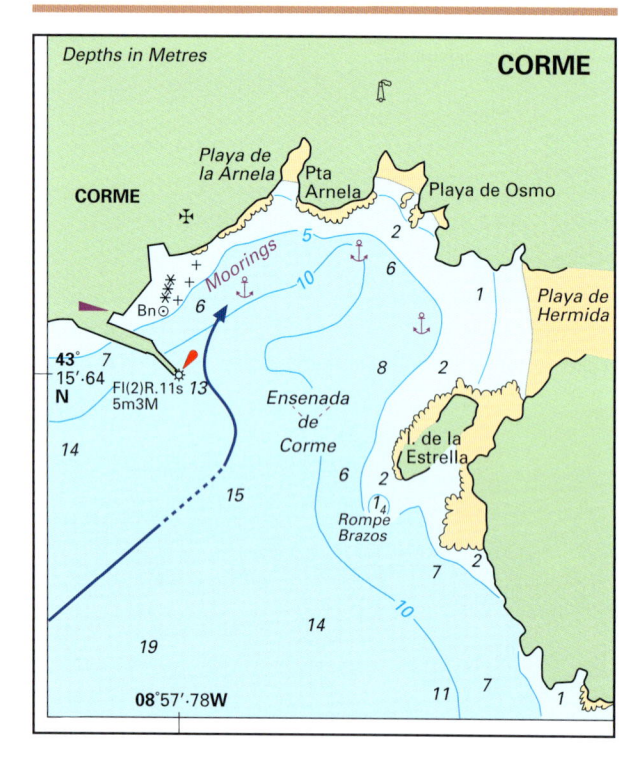

Most attractive anchorage off a fishing village

On entering this pleasant ría, the reason the surrounding hills are covered in wind farms becomes clear. There are very strong sea breezes here which reinforce the prevailing NE winds. The valley in Corme itself funnels the wind even more through the harbour. Corme remains, however, a small and picturesque fishing village and the anchorage is peaceful and delightful.

This is where the much sort after *Percebes* (Goose barnacles) are harvested by intrepid local people.

Energetic crews will enjoy the walk amidst wild granite scenery out to the lighthouse on Punta del Roncudo.

Approach

From the north Islas Sisargas, Pta Nariga and Pta del Roncudo (white round tower) are well marked. Round Pta del Roncudo with an offing of at least 1M. The recommended route is then to pass west and south of Bajo de la Aveiria (5m). In heavy weather the seas break on all the banks in the area. (See the plan on page 40.) The route in to the anchorage passes between the breakwater and a green buoy, that is now of a size that can be identified from seaward.

From the south Be guided by the advice in Approach for Laxe, see page 43.

Anchorage

Fishing boats use the inside of the breakwater, while the small area to the northeast is filled with moorings. There are rocks inshore of the moorings, marked by an unlit green beacon.

After passing another green buoy, anchor in 10m or less but weed can be a problem. Further round the bay off both Playa de Osmo and Playa de Hermida there is plenty of room and good holding. There are slipways where it is possible to leave a dinghy.

The anchorage is well sheltered other than from the south when Laxe (Lage) may be preferable. The removal of *viveros* has noy helped with swell reduction.

Facilities

There are limited facilities and none specifically for yachts. There is small village shopping, restaurants, hotels and a bank.

Corme from the south – anchor west or north of *viveros*

42   ATLANTIC SPAIN AND PORTUGAL

LAXE (LAGE)

Laxe (Lage)

Location
43°13'·37N 08°59'·97W

Tides
See Ría box information on page 41

Light
Breakwater beacon Fl.G.3s15m4M Green column

Communications
Club Náutico de Laxe
VHF Ch 09
Email náuticolaxe@hotmail.com

Limited facilities for yachts

Laxe (the common name) is a holiday resort around a fishing village with a small port. There is a long sandy beach to the south and the 14th-century church of Santiago de Lage overlooks the harbour. This is a popular area for sailing dinghies. There is a street market on Fridays. Good walks, impressive scenery.

Approach

From the north Be guided by the advice in Approach for Corme, see page 42.

From the south Keep 1M off the coast northeast of Cabo Villano, with its attendant windfarm (plan page 46). Keep out 500m or more rounding Pta de Laxe, and follow the coast around at that distance to pick up Laxe breakwater.

Anchorage

The 300m breakwater offers good shelter in most conditions, though swell may work in. In fair weather, and south or west winds, anchor off the beach near the south mole but clear of the harbour approach in 5m or less over sand. Small buoys may impede swinging room. This would become untenable in a north wind when Corme will provide better shelter. Fishing boats enter day and night, timber-loading ships berth along the north mole.

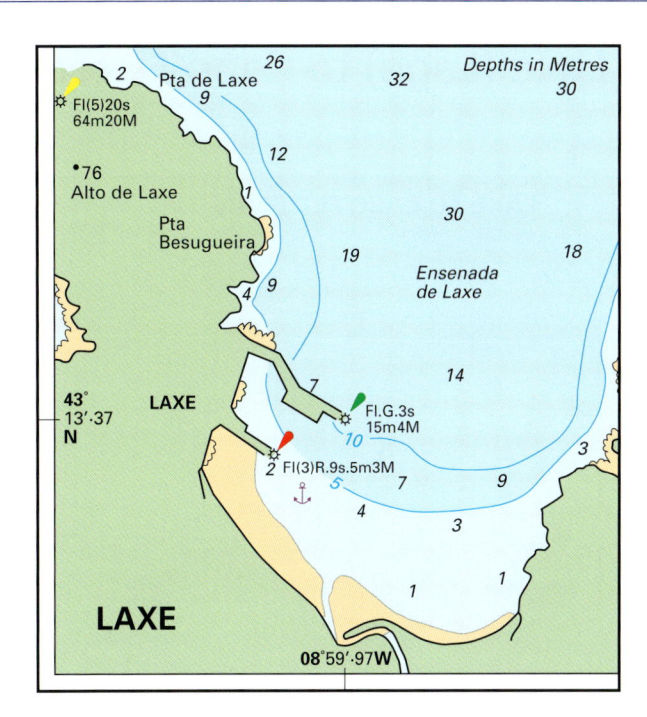

There are many small-craft moorings within the harbour, some trail floating lines.

Facilities

Water on the quay, shops, hardware store, banks, restaurants and bars.

Laxe - note the anchoring options

ATLANTIC SPAIN AND PORTUGAL

RÍA DE CEDEIRA TO CABO FISTERRA (FINISTERRE)

Laxe (Lage) to Cabo Fisterra (Finisterre)

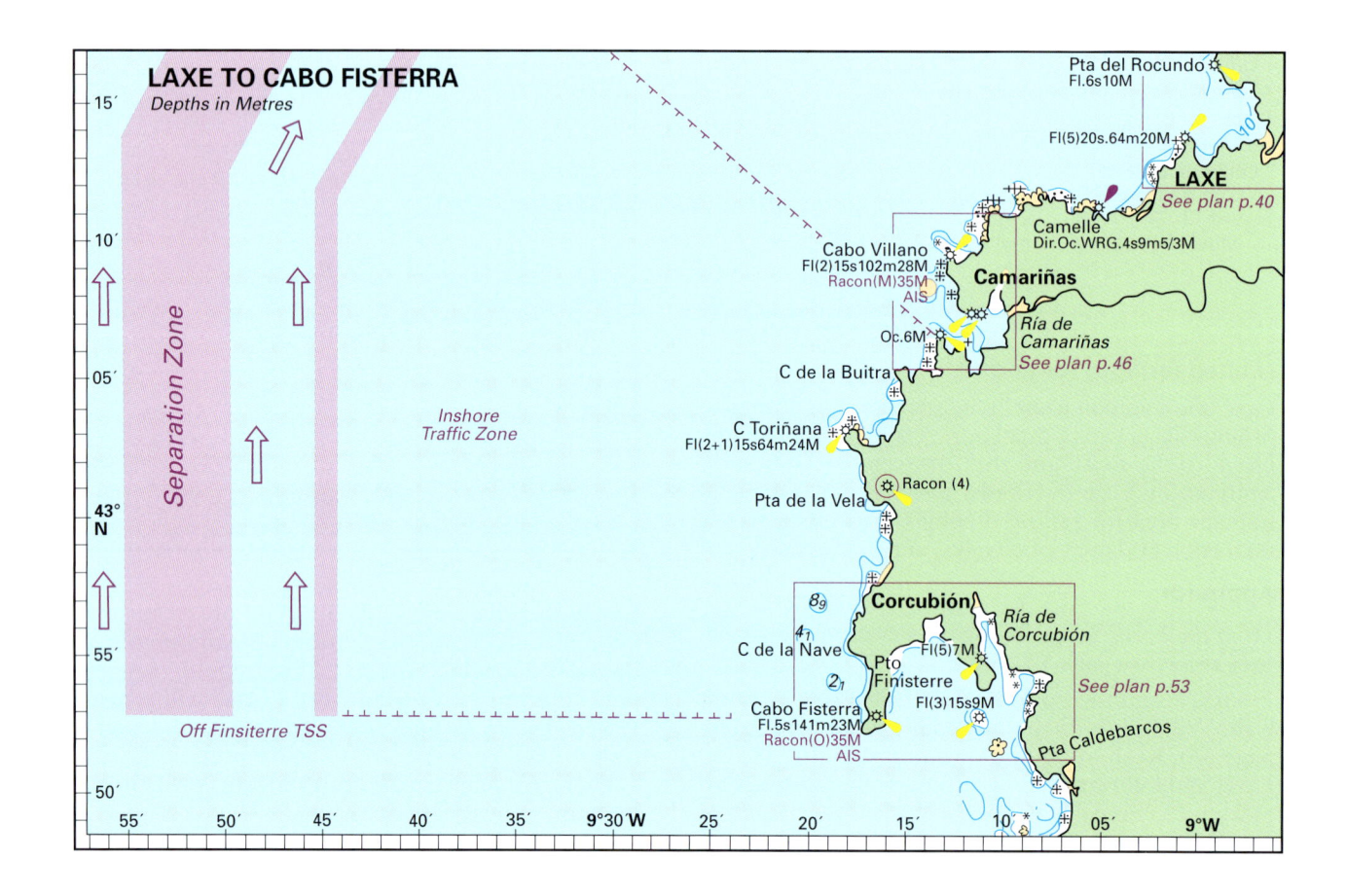

Lights
Pta del Rocundo Fl.6s36m10M White round tower
Punta Laxe Fl(5)20s64m20M
 White truncated conical tower
Cabo Villano Fl(2)15s102m28M
 8-sided tower, grey cupola
Pta de la Barca Oc.4s11m10M
 Grey truncated conical tower

Cabo Toriñana Fl(2+1)15s63m24M
 White round tower
Cabo Fisterra Fl.5s142m23M
 8-sided stone tower and white dwelling

Warning
A local magnetic anomaly has been reported within a radius of 13M of Cabo Toriñana

Laxe from the anchorage off the south mole, looking NW   *Jane Russell*

44   ATLANTIC SPAIN AND PORTUGAL

CAMELLE

Overview
The rugged Costa da Morte continues on to Cabo Fisterra from Laxe. Unless wishing to enter the delightful ría de Camariñas, for Camariñas and Muxia, the mariner should make passage well out to sea. If sailing between Corme/Laxe and Camariñas, do not cut the corner, avoid Camelle and stand well out towards. Stay away from Cabo Toriñana where, even on the calmest days, the Atlantic swell crashes on the outlying rocks off the lighthouse sitting on the edge of the barren peninsula.

Traffic Separation Zone
A very busy 19M wide Traffic Separation Zone (TSZ) lies off Cabo Fisterra. Yachts should use the Inshore Traffic Zone, also 19M wide, and only cross the TSZ at right angles in accordance with regulations.

Finisterre Vessel Traffic Services (Finisterre VTS)
The VTS monitors all traffic and will give advice to particular vessels and those nearby. It provides regular navigational and weather information - see page 51.
c/s Finisterre Traffic (Finisterre Trafico)
VHF Ch 11, 16 (74) ☏ +34 981 76 73 20 & 76 77 38

Camelle
Location
43°11'·34N 09°05'·19W
(outer breakwater green column)

No place for sailing yachts
Camelle is a small harbour lying between Laxe (Lage) and Camariñas. Any rock hopping, inquisitive yachtsman considering making this a lunchtime stop is strongly advised to remain well offshore. In winds from the north to west this is a dangerous lee shore.

Swell works into the outer harbour which is narrow and with isolated rocks inside the breakwater; the inner harbour is shallow, except by the quay but that lies beyond a criss-cross of mooring lines lying on and beneath the surface. The harbour is recorded here only as a place to avoid – unless coming by land to beachcomb in which case it has a charm of its own.

GALICIA

Camelle looking SE

ATLANTIC SPAIN AND PORTUGAL

RÍA DE CEDEIRA TO CABO FISTERRA (FINISTERRE)

46 ATLANTIC SPAIN AND PORTUGAL

APPROACHES TO RÍA DE CAMARIÑAS

Ría de Camariñas

Location
43°07'·28N 09°13'·00W

Tides
Standard port A Coruña
Mean time differences
HW +0005; LW −0005
Heights in metres
MHWS	MHWN	MLWN	MLWS
3·8	2·8	1·5	0·5

Lights
Cabo Villano Fl(2)15s102m28M
8-sided tower, grey cupola
Pta de la Barca Oc.4s11m10M
Grey truncated conical tower
Pta de Lago Oc(2)WRG.6s13m6-4M
White truncated conical tower

Warning
Note hazards of El Bujardo, Las Quebrantas, Bajo Peneiron and the shallows southwest of Monte Farelo, and further note the warning below regarding Leixon de Juanboy. The only sound signal in the area is on Cabo Villano.

West of the plan, and lying between the two leading lines shown, is the small but dangerous 5m shoal of Leixon de Juanboy – position 43°07'·48N 09°14'·97W.

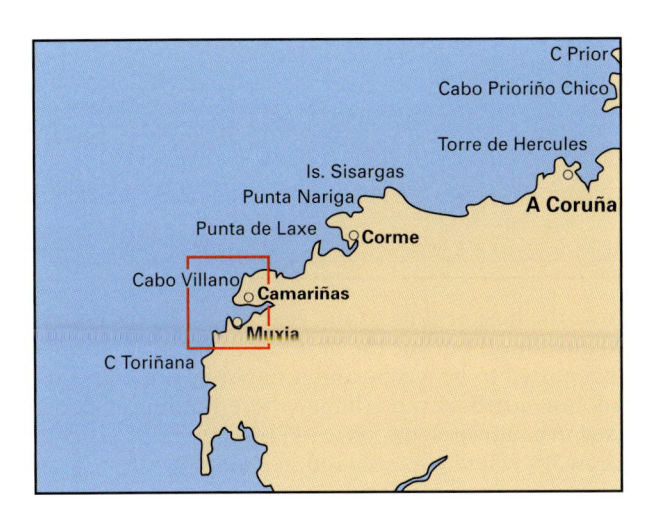

Cabo Vilano *Geraldine Hennigan*

Well placed, scenic and useful ría

Many would consider the Ría de Camariñas amongst Galicia's loveliest, with the added advantage that it contains anchorages protected from almost every direction. However, the entrance to the Ría is fully exposed to winds and seas from the northwest and may be inaccessible in rough weather. The two towns of Camariñas and Muxia meet the daily needs of the cruising yachtsman. Camariñas is a pleasant town which thrives on tourists and a well-established welcoming marina. Muxia's new southern curving mole has improved protection within the harbour and shields a new marina. Crews can dig for their shell-fish lunch on the beaches or walk through the unspoilt countryside.

Approach

Entry can be made by day and night although a first entry by night is not recommended.

From the north Keep well off Cabo Villano, with its wind farm, to avoid El Bujardo, a pinnacle rock awash at low tide. Either stay well off shore, to avoid Las Quebrantas, until Pta de Lago bears 108° (white sector) or come inside that bank.

From the southwest Keep well off Cape Toriñana and do not cut the corner around Pta de la Barca. Pick up the leading line on 079°40' and follow until Pta de Lago bears 108° (white sector). Alter on to 108° and maintain the line towards Pta de Lago until shaping course for Camariñas or Muxia.

Anchorages

The plan opposite shows anchorages around the ría:

Those to the north and east of Camariñas offer shelter from north or northeast winds and the chance to enjoy the fine beaches in solitude. Good holding has been reported here.

A settled weather anchorage off the mouth of the Río del Puente del Puerto offers the chance to take the dinghy 2M up the river to the town (of the same name) with its shops, restaurants, banks etc.

To the southeast of Camariñas there is a good settled weather anchorage, on sand, off the beach south of Pta. De Lago at about 43°06'·56N 09°10'·00W.

To the south, offering some shelter from southerly winds is a lonely anchorage just to the S of Pta de Choreate. The anchorage is at about 43° 05'·91N 09° 11'·73W, inside an isolated danger mark. The latter marked *viveros* that have been removed (2017). Depths are rather shallow, but a little deeper than the chart suggests as the beach is relatively steeply shelving. Landing here is tricky in a swell.

Anchorage south of Pta de Choreate, Ensenada de Merejo looking N *Tim Trafford*

GALICIA

ATLANTIC SPAIN AND PORTUGAL

RÍA DE CEDEIRA TO CABO FISTERRA (FINISTERRE)

Camariñas

Location
On the north side of the Ría de Camariñas
43°07'·47N 09°10'·70W

Tides
See Ría box information on page 47

Light
Breakwater beacon Fl.R.5s3M Red concrete beacon

Communications
Club Náutico de Camariñas
Peirao Novo s/n, 15123 – Camariñas
VHF Ch 09
☏ +34 981 737 130
cnc@cibergal.com   www.cncamarinas.com

Welcoming and efficient marina

Camariñas has an attractive harbour enclosed by a long breakwater which gives excellent shelter from all directions other than east and northeast. There was talk of building a mole extending southeast from Pta Insuela to improve protection from that quarter. Shelter from these winds can be found across the ría. The Club Náutico Camariñas has an active dinghy club and a long well-deserved reputation for making visiting yachtsmen welcome.

Approach

See page 47 for the outer approaches to the ría. Make the final approach when the Camariñas breakwater light comes well clear of Pta del Castillo, avoiding the shallows that extend south of the rear light on Pta del Castillo.

Berthing

Visiting yachts are usually berthed on substantial finger pontoons towards the outer ends. Catamarans and larger yachts use the T-ends. Very large yachts secure to the wall south of the marina.

There are 83 berths of which 60 are reserved for visitors up to 18m, in a depth of 3-5m. There is electricity and water available on the pontoons.

The berthing master's office is the small wooden hut at the top of the centre pontoon. The fuelling pontoon is immediately beneath that.

Camarinas looking N from anchorage off Cala de Vila
Jane Russell

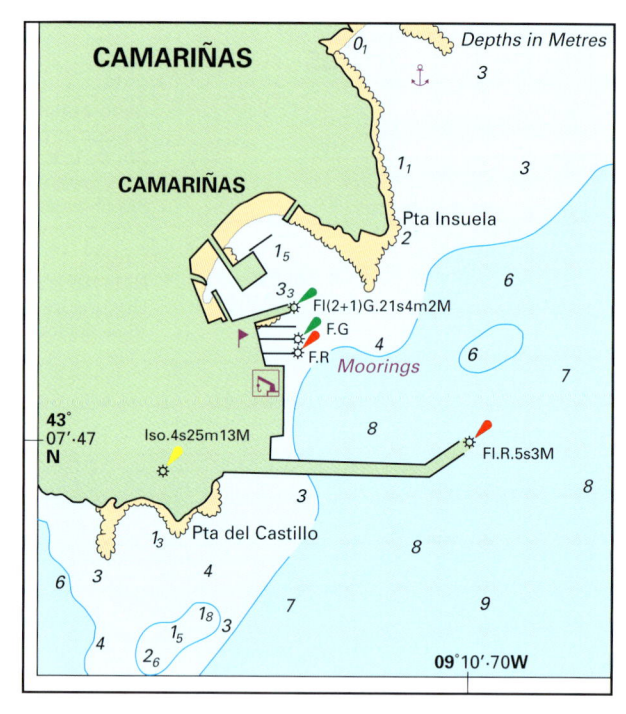

At the busiest time of the year it may be necessary to anchor off outside the moorings. The bottom here is reported to be weedy and it might be preferable to anchor north of the village where holding is good (see Anchorages on page 47). There are several slipways where you can land in a dinghy.

Facilities

The Club Náutico de Camariñas provides, or can arrange, most support facilities. It has a boat lift but no travel-lift. There are several walls in the old harbour where it might be possible to dry out. Fuel is available on site for normal top up; larger quantities will be readily arranged for delivery by tanker to the main quay – yachts would find this position bumpy in an east wind. Otherwise the nearest alongside fuel pumps are in A Coruña or Muros.

Apart from providing showers, the club has an excellent small bar/restaurant and two computers for visiting yachtsmen and WiFi. A same-day laundry service is available close to the marina.

The town of Camariñas has a market and shops for reprovisioning. Tourism is increasing and cafés and restaurants are close to the harbour.

CAMARIÑAS

Camariñas from north

Major refuels | Marina office, refuel, club with showers/bar/restaurant | Old harbour

Camariñas. Club Náutico Camariñas from the outer mole looking northwest   *Martin Walker*

ATLANTIC SPAIN AND PORTUGAL

RÍA DE CEDEIRA TO CABO FISTERRA (FINISTERRE)

Muxia (Mugia)

Location
43°06′·43N 09°12′·92W
On the south side of the Ría de Camariñas

Tides
See Ría box information on page 47

Lights
Breakwater beacon Fl(4)G.11s14m5M Concrete beacon, green top

Communications
Marina Muxía Marina Cataventos
Puerto deportivo Muxia S/N, 15124 Muxia A Coruña
VHF Ch 09
Marina Office ☏ +34 673 168 199
Manager +34 652 97 16 67
Admin ☏ +34 666 36 93 24
Email info@cataventos.net or info@marinamuxia.com
www.cataventos.net www.marinamuxia.com
www.marinasdegalicia.com

Fishing harbour with a marina in its south side

Muxía is a minor fishing harbour including a marina known as the Puerto Deportivo de Muxía. A few old buildings remain amidst the modern blocks as tourism is developed. The 17th-century church of La Virgen de la Barca on the northern point was destroyed by fire started by lightning on Christmas Day 2013. There is a clean sandy beach to the south of the harbour and fine views over the ría from Punta de la Barca.

Approach

See under Ría de Camariñas on page 47 and note warnings.

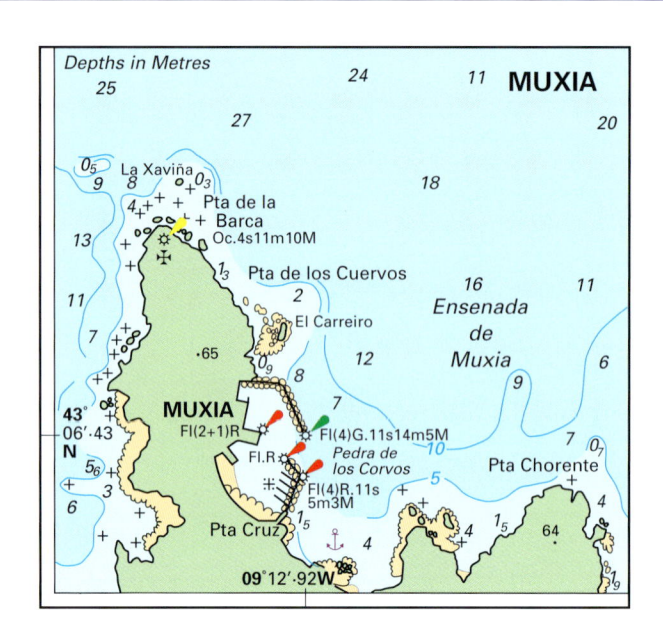

Berthing

A southern mole has been constructed and provides shelter to a marina boasting 232 berths, all on finger pontoons. There are plenty of transit berths, for yachts from 6m to 14m, in 2m to 3m of water.

Anchorage

Anchor on sand southeast of the outer mole. This is likely to be untenable in northerly winds.

Facilities

Water and electricity on the pontoons; showers; laundry; fuel by tanker truck; free WiFi; security; berthing assistance 0900-2400. Clemente, a skilled mechanic ☏ +34 648 901632 can attend to both electrical and mechanical problems.

Several small supermarkets, restaurants, bars, banks, a hardware store and post office are in the town.

Muxia from the hill above Pta de la Barca looking SE *Geraldine Hennigan*

CABO FISTERRA (FINISTERRE)

Cabo Fisterra (Finisterre)

Location
42°54′N 9°15′W

Tides
Standard port Lisbon
Mean time differences
HW +0105 ±0010; LW +0130 ±0010
(the above allows for the difference in time zones)
Heights in metres
MHWS	MHWN	MLWN	MLWS
3·3	2·6	1·2	0·5

Note
A considerable inshore set may be encountered south of Cabo Fisterra with a westerly wind and flood tide

Navtex
518kHz (D) at 0030, 0430, 0830*, 1230, 1630, 2030*
(*weather only)

Weather bulletins
MF 1764kHz at 0703, 1303, 1903
VHF Ch 22 at 0840, 1240, 2010
MRCC Ch 11 at 0233, 0633, 1033, 1433, 1833, 2233

Navigational warnings
MF 1764kHz at 0703, 1903
VHF Ch 22 at 0840, 2010
MRCC Ch 11 at 0033, 0433, 0833, 1233, 1633, 2033
AIS

Primary working frequencies
Manual Ch 22 Tx 1764 Rx 2108
Autolink Ch 27 Tx 2596 Rx 3280
DSC Ch 70 2187·5kHz. MMSI 992242117

GALICIA

Approach to Cabo Fisterra

It has been noticed that N or NE winds are considerably stronger between Cabo Vilano and Cabo Fisterra than NE or S of these two capes. This acceleration zone extends to about 5 miles offshore. Once a couple of miles S of Cabo Fisterra, the wind generally drops away.

Cabo Toriñana, the most western point of mainland Spain, looking south towards Cabo Fisterra (Finisterre) Jane Russell

Cabo Fisterra (Finisterre) lighthouse from the south. The harbour and anchorage visible east and north

ATLANTIC SPAIN AND PORTUGAL   51

CABO FISTERRA (FINISTERRE) TO ISLA ONS

Cabo Fisterra (Finisterre) to Ría de Muros

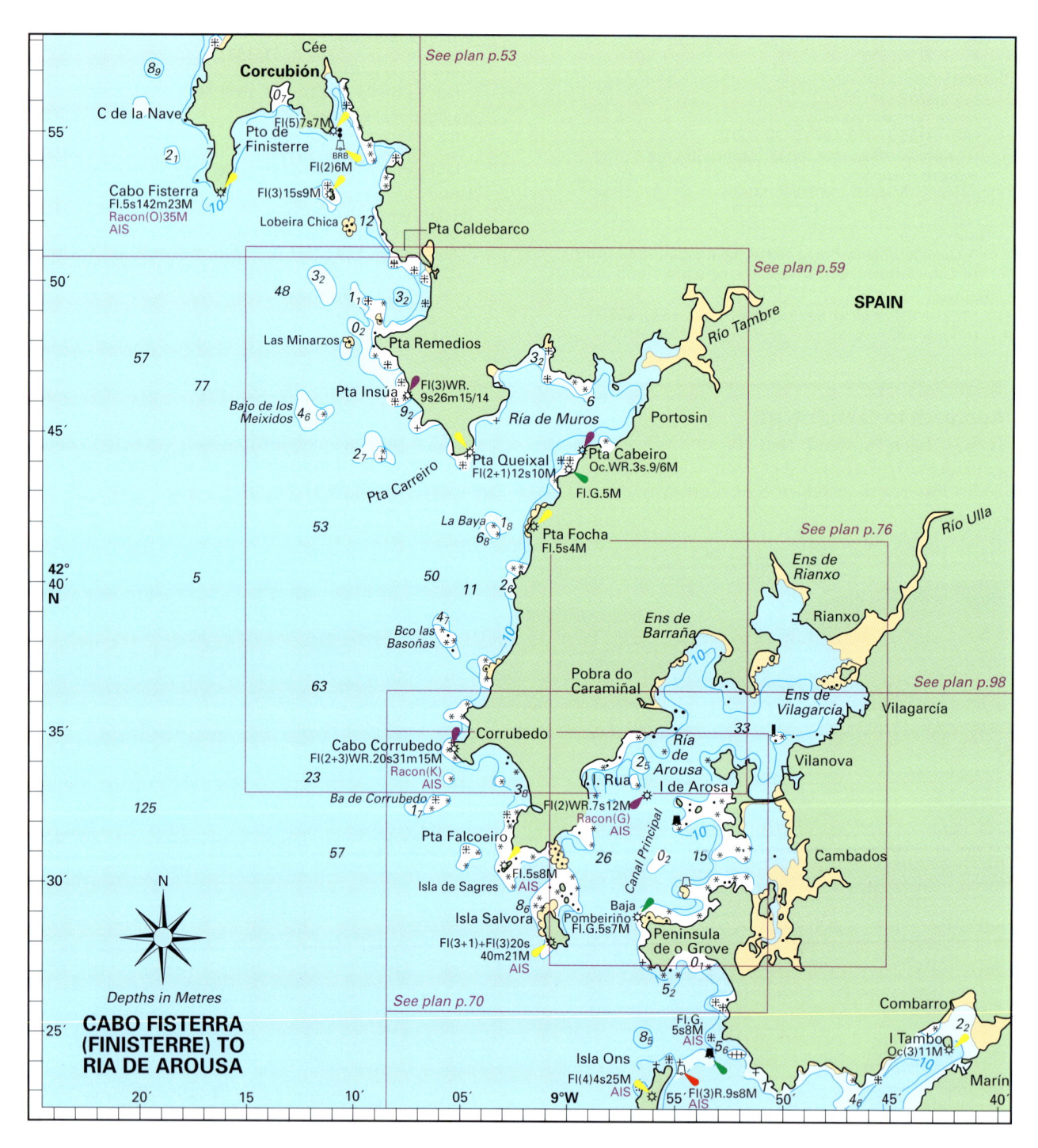

Coastguard
Fisterra ☎ +34 981 767 500

Sea Rescue Service
☎ +34 900 202 202 MRCC Finisterre Ch 11

Weather
Navtex (D)
Finisterre Ch 22 at 0840, 1240, 2919

Lights
Cabo Fisterra Fl.5s142m23M 8-sided stone tower and white dwelling
Carrumeiro Chico Fl(2)7s7m10M Black balls on black beacon, red bands
Cabo Cée Fl(5)13s26m10M 8-sided tower on red roofed white dwelling
Punta Insua Fl(3)WR.9s26m15/14M 6-sided tower, metal cupola and dwelling
Pta Queixal Fl(2+1)12s26m10M 6-sided tower and white dwelling
Pta Focha Fl.5s28m4M White tower and round building
Cabo Corrubedo Fl(2+3)WR.20s31m15M Round masonry tower, white cupola
Isla Sálvora Fl(3+1)20s39m21M White 8-sided tower, red band
Isla Ons Fl(4)24s126m25M 8-sided white tower on corner of building

52 ATLANTIC SPAIN AND PORTUGAL

SENO DE CORCUBÍON

GALICIA

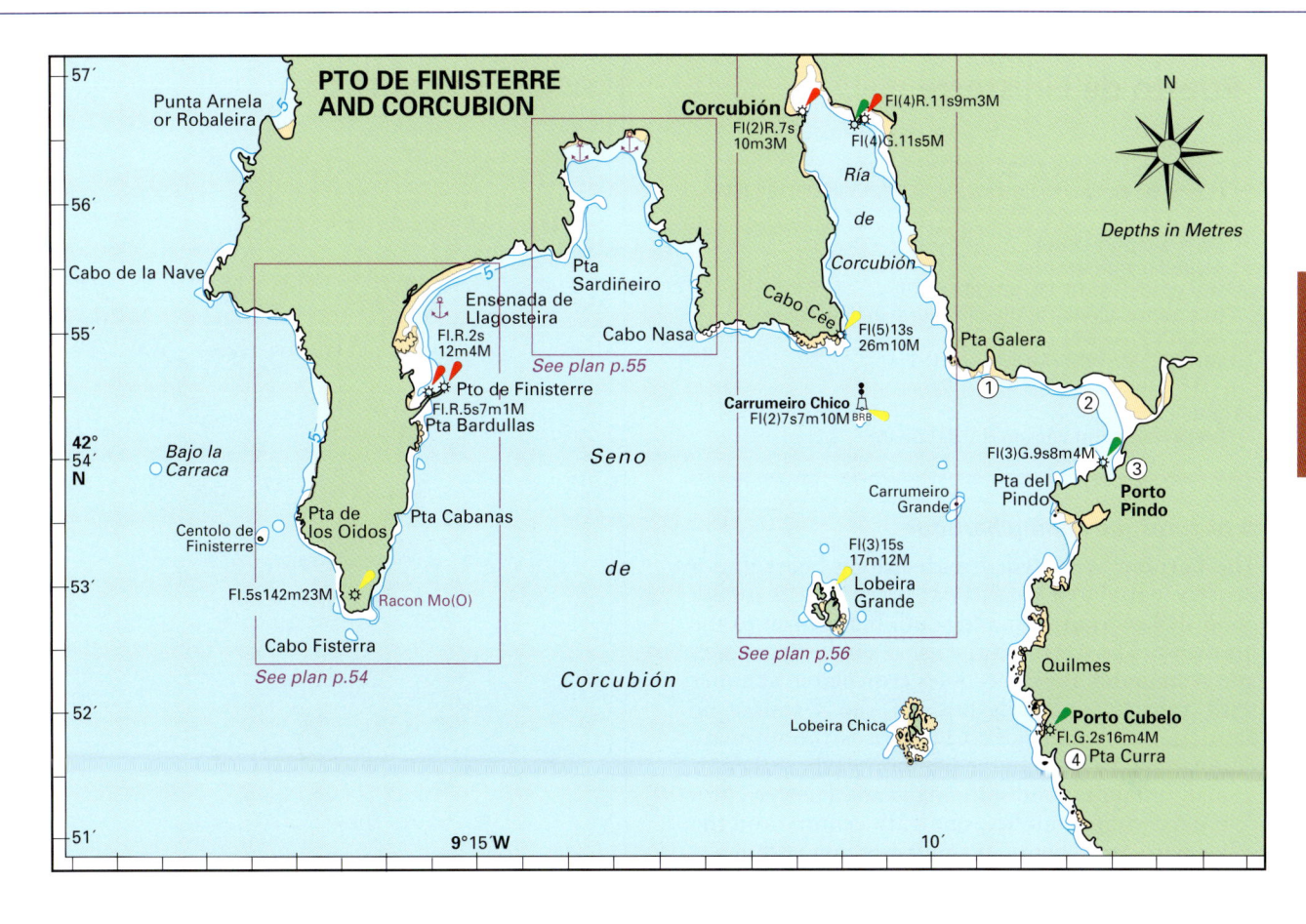

Puerto de Fisterra (Finisterre) from the northeast   *Henry Buchanan*

Looking NW from the anchorage in Ensenada de Llagosteira with porpoises in the foreground   *Henry Buchanan*

ATLANTIC SPAIN AND PORTUGAL   53

CABO FISTERRA (FINISTERRE) TO ISLA ONS

Puerto de Finisterre

Location
Cabo Fisterra light 42°52'·94N 09°16'·32W
Puerto de Finisterre breakwater 42°54'·56N 09°15'·36W

Tides
Standard port Lisbon
Mean time differences
HW +0105 ±0010; LW +0130 ±0010
(the above allows for the difference in time zones)
Heights in metres
MHWS	MHWN	MLWN	MLWS
3·3	2·6	1·2	0·5

Light
Breakwater end beacon Fl.R.4s12m4M

A picturesque fishing harbour

The harbour is crowded with fishing boats and a densely populated small boat marina. It provides good shelter from west and south but is open to the northeast. The town has the usual small shops, bars and restaurants but it becomes crowded in summer with tourists and pilgrims on the Camino de Santiago for whom Cabo Fisterra is the ultimate destination. Most go to the lighthouse where there is a small restaurant and stunning views. Finisterre has two interesting churches, one 12th century and the other Baroque. There is a small museum within the Castello San Carlos.

Rounding Finisterre and final approach

From the north See plans pages 52 and 53. The main options are either to keep 2M off and avoid the 2m patch Bajo La Carraca, 1M to the northwest of Centolo de Finisterre (an island some 20m high), or to come inside both – much will depend upon the weather. At the Cape there is a similar option: either pass more than 0·5M off or about 200m off in order to avoid El Turdeiro shoal – a large-scale chart is needed for the latter passage. Strong local winds are possible. Once round, keep at least 300m off until reaching Finisterre breakwater.

From the south Plan page 52. Give Punta Insúa a 5M offing to clear Bajo de los Meixidos and head straight for Finisterre mole. On a night approach, take the outside passages and keep at least 300m off the east coast of the Cape.

Anchorage and possible alongside moorings

Small yachts may find space to moor alongside the outer pontoon of the small boat marina but depths are shallow. A new pontoon (2017) with water and electricity has been built from the northwest corner of the fishing quay on the main breakwater, but this is really for local working boats only.

It is possible to anchor outside the new pontoon and behind the breakwater but beware foul ground close to the breakwater. The best option, and a popular anchorage, which provides protection from the summer northerly winds, is off the sandy beach of Ensenada de Llagosteira to the north. A dinghy dock is available in town.

Seno de Corcubión

The area northeast and east of Cabo Fisterra offers a variety of anchorages depending on the direction of the wind and, to the east, interesting pilotage for rock-hopping sailors armed with chart BA 3764.

Passage planning

Keep well west of Cabo Fisterra if making passage south to Muros or beyond. Otherwise refer to the section on Puerto de Finisterre for rounding the cape above.

Puerto de Finisterre from the southeast (photo predates new pontoon)

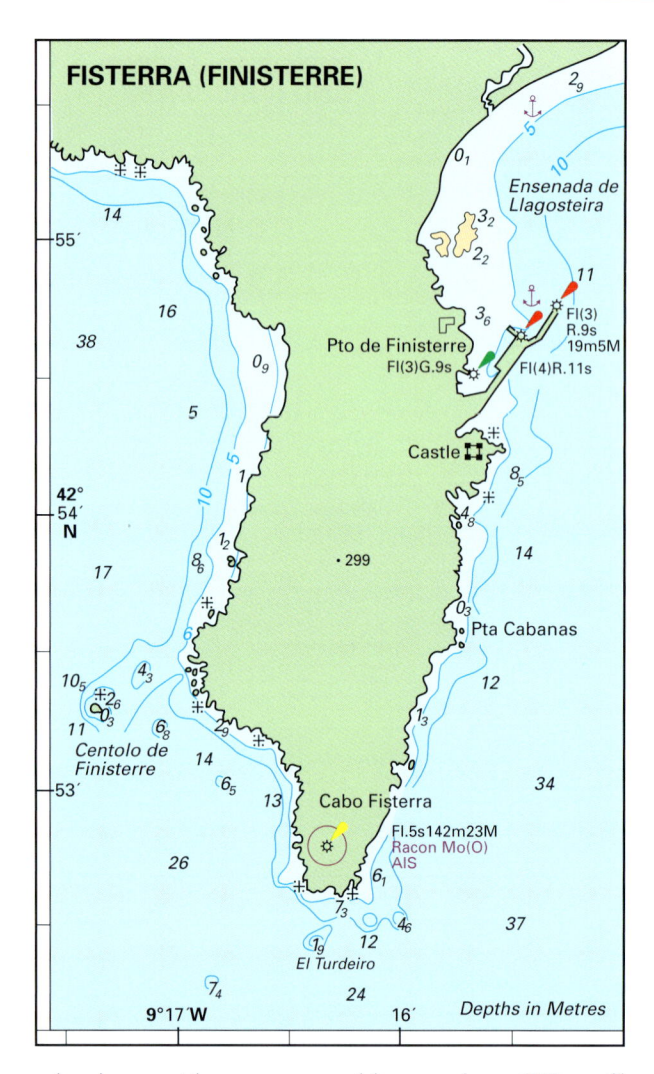

54 ATLANTIC SPAIN AND PORTUGAL

ENSENADA DEL SARDIÑEIRO

Ensenada del Sardiñeiro

Location
42°55·5N 09°13'·40W (entrance)

Tides
Standard port Lisbon
Mean time differences
HW +0105 ±0010; LW +0130 ±0010
(the above allows for the difference in time zones)
Heights in metres
MHWS	MHWN	MLWN	MLWS
3·3	2·6	1·2	0·5

An unspoilt anchorage

Although open to the south, this unspoilt anchorage provides good protection from west through north to east. Both Playa Sardiñeiro and Playa Esordi are good bathing beaches.

Approach

Approach is straightforward but care is required to avoid the shallow patch of La Eyra.

Ensenada del Sardiñeiro anchorage Roddy Innes

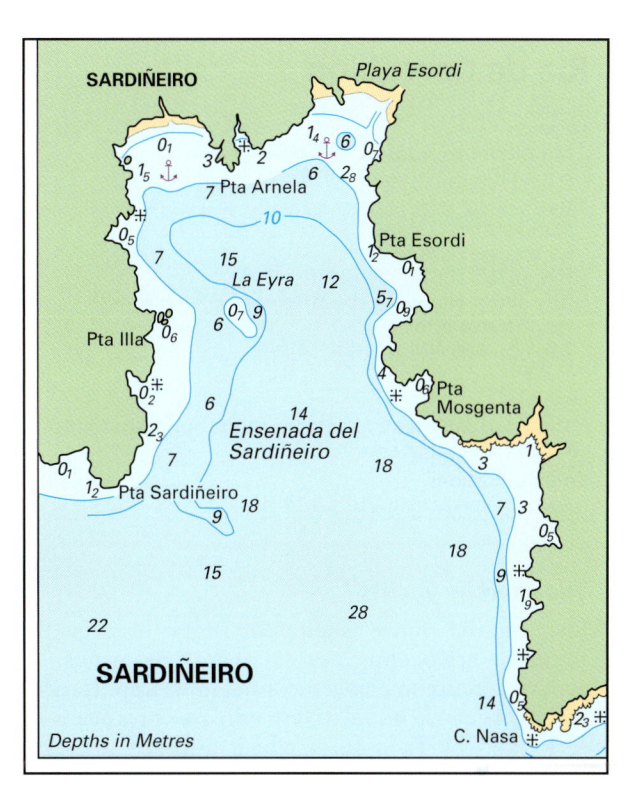

Anchorage

Anchor in either bay to suit conditions. Both have been recommended and offer good holding in sand; Playa Sardiñeiro generally has the least swell.

Facilities

The village, with supermarkets, restaurants and camp site, straddles the road between Corcubión and Finisterre.

Pta Arnela (centre) divides the two anchorages of Ensenada del Sardiñeiro, seen from the south

GALICIA

ATLANTIC SPAIN AND PORTUGAL

CABO FISTERRA (FINISTERRE) TO ISLA ONS

Ría de Corcubión

Location
Mouth of ría (⊕33) 42°54′·5N 09°10′·1W
Corcubión fish quay 42°56′·6N 09°11′·35W

Tides
Standard port Lisbon
Mean time differences
HW +0105 ±0010; LW +0130 ±0010
(the above allows for the difference in time zones)
Heights in metres
MHWS	MHWN	MLWN	MLWS
3·3	2·6	1·2	0·5

Warning
There are considerable hazards on the approach to the ría and south and east of it

Communications
Corcubión Practicos VHF Ch 14,16

Little used by yachts

Most of the more sheltered spots in Ría de Corcubión are occupied by small craft moorings. In the past Corcubión enjoyed considerable importance, not least because its relatively narrow entrance was overlooked by twin forts which allowed it to be defended in a way not possible in most other rías.

The picturesque small town, which is on the west bank of the ría, is a summer holiday resort with banks, shops, restaurants and bars.

Waterborne processions mark the fiesta of the Virgen del Carmen on 16 July (also at Muros and in many other harbours).

Cée, a larger and beautifully developed town at the head of the estuary, can be reached by dinghy, on foot or by bus. It has a major supermarket along with a good general market and excellent shops. In contrast, the large industrial works and dock on the east side of the ría appears very run down with dangerous sea work extensions to the docks south of Pta Fornelos surrounded by just a low floating barrier.

Approach

From the west See page 54 regarding rounding Cabo Fisterra (Finisterre).

From the south See plan on page 52. Give Punta Insúa an offing of at least 5M to clear Bajo de los Meixidos, or if using the inner passage, hold the course towards Cabo Fisterra (Finisterre) until the passage between Carrumeiro Chico and Islote Lobeira Grande can be approached from the southwest.

Anchorages

(See photograph page 57). The Corcubión fishing quay becomes uncomfortable as soon as wind builds up. Be prepared to anchor. Anchorages in the ría, none of which offer shelter from southerly winds, are:

1. In the small bay of Playa de Quenje. Inshore is occupied by moorings, but some shelter will still be gained outside them – even so it would be uncomfortable in winds from south through east to north. There is a restaurant on the beach fringing the bay, and considerable recent development to the south.
2. Southeast of the main quay in 8–10m is probably the best bet, as it has yet to be filled with moorings.
3. North of the main quay in 3–4m, between the many small-craft moorings and the shoal water to the north. Holding is poor. If not busy it might be possible to lie alongside briefly.
4. In the northeast corner of the ría between the commercial quay and Punta Fornelos. Depths shoal rapidly once within the 5m line. This anchorage provides shelter in strong north winds.

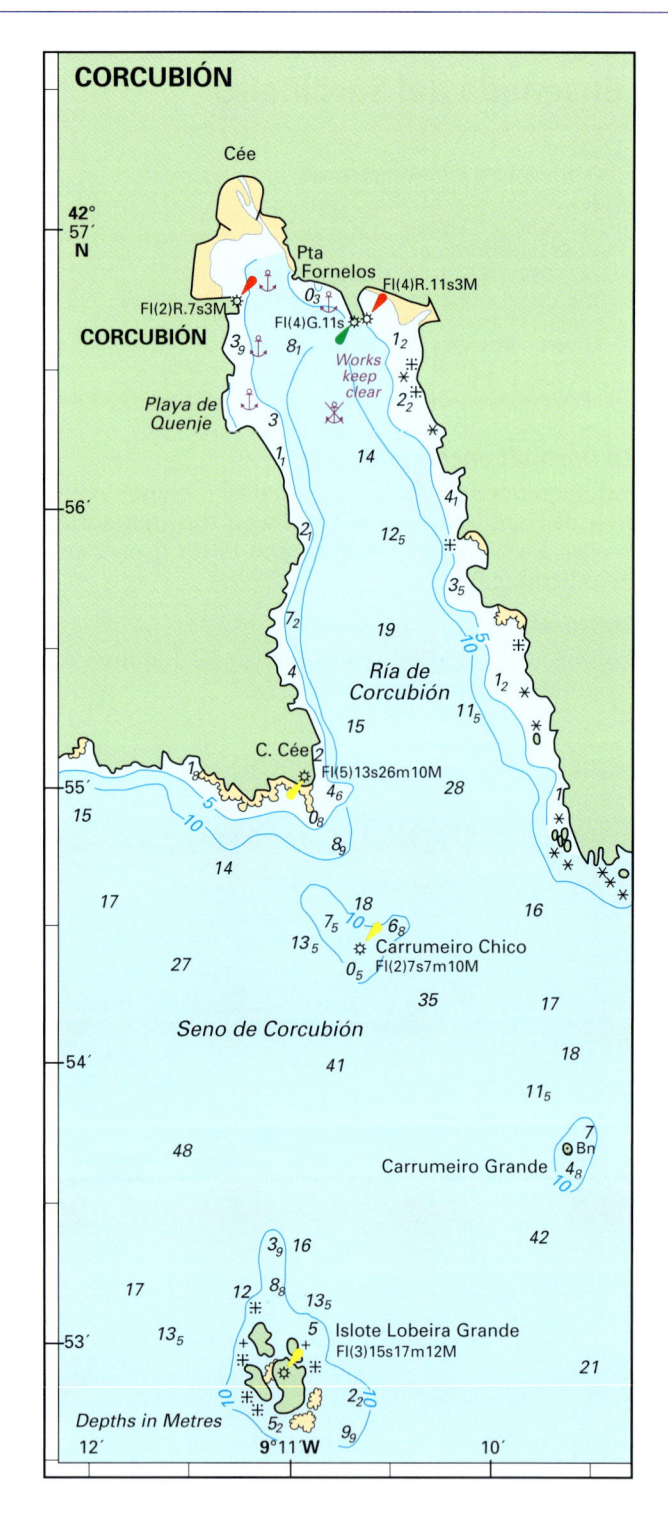

The bottom in all these anchorages is a mixture of rock and sand and the holding is variable.

RÍA DE CORCUBIÓN

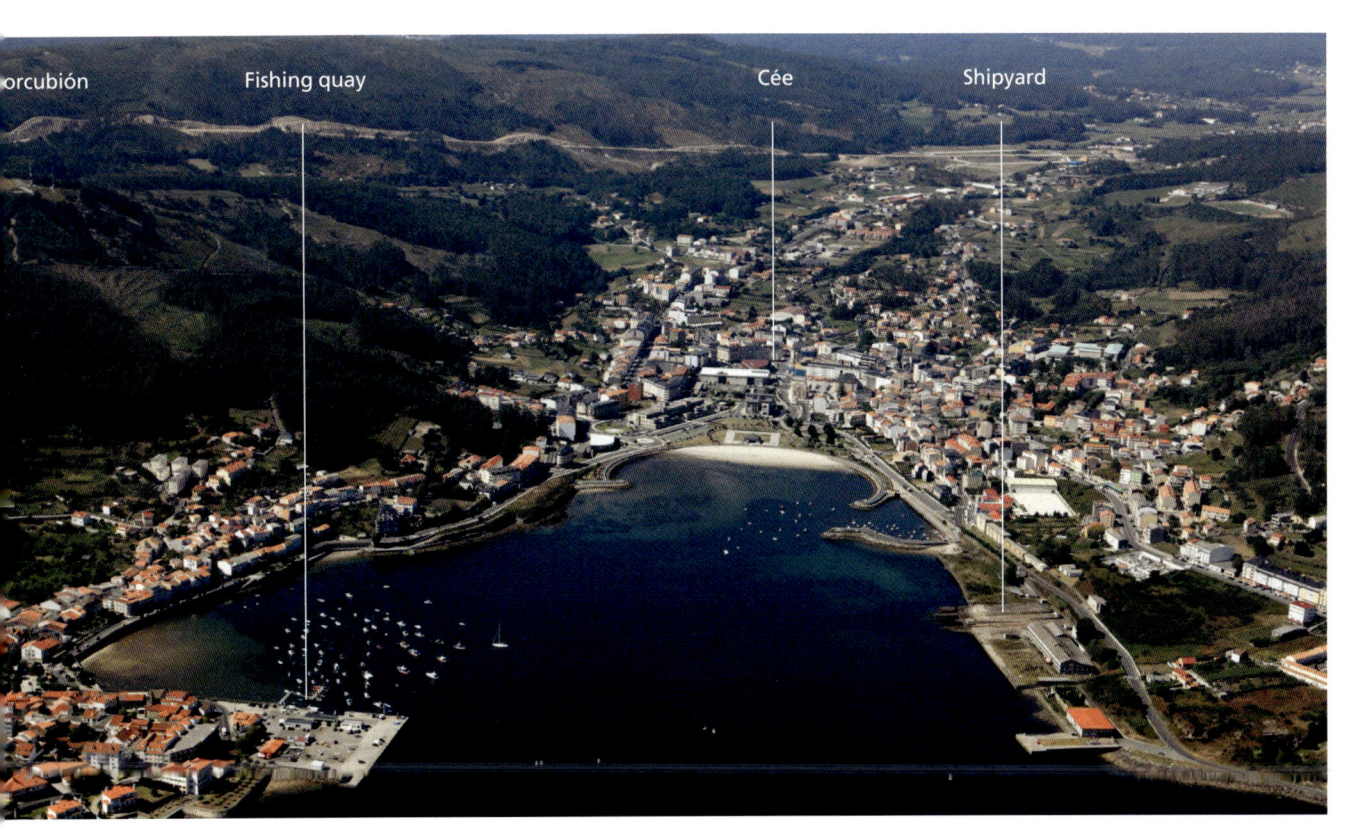

Corcubión and Cée

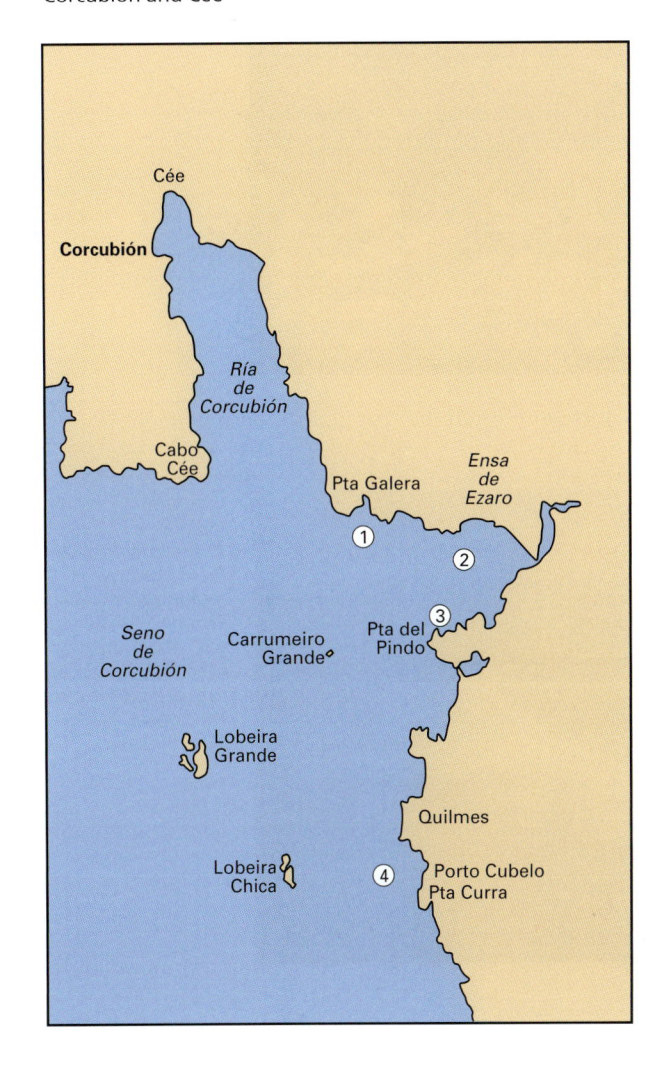

Anchorages between Ría Corcubión and Ría Muros

Yachts rarely visit the area surrounded by reefs and rocky outcrops off the coast heading south from Ría Corcubión. Given settled weather, chart 3764 and an escape plan, there are several anchorages worth visiting.

1. Off Playa Gures 42°54'·6N 09°08'·9W

Anchor in sand, avoiding the weed patches, with shelter from the north but with a possibility of squally winds.

2. Ensenada de Ezaro 42°54'N 09°08'W

This is a beautiful bay with fine beaches but totally exposed to the west. The rocky banks of Los Bois and El Asno might complicate a hasty departure.

3. Porto del Pindo Breakwater green column at 42°53'·81N 09°08'·04W

The harbour is open to the north but, with eyeball navigation on the approach, temporary space might be found near the head of the mole. The inner harbour is full of moorings. Pindo has restaurants and limited supplies.

4. Porto Cubelo Breakwater green column at 42°48'·45N 09°08'·13W

This harbour is best approached from the north/northeast to avoid the numerous rocks and reefs to the northwest and west. A short stop near the end of the breakwater, on a calm sunny day when eyeball navigation is possible, might be considered. Subject to fishing activities, short-term berthing may be found alongside the modern *lonja* (fish-handling building) but check depths. Limited facilities in the village about one mile away.

GALICIA

ATLANTIC SPAIN AND PORTUGAL   57

CABO FISTERRA (FINISTERRE) TO ISLA ONS

Anchorages between Ría Corcubión and Ría Muros *Above* Looking north over Pta del Pindo and the harbour (3) to Ensenada de Ezaro (2). Playa Gures (1) is just to the west *Below* Porto Cubelo (4)

Left View from the hill above Pt Carreiro at the entrance to Ría de Muros, looking NW to Cabo Fisterra (Finisterre) over the Canal de los Meixidos. Breaking seas are visible over the shoals
Jane Russell

58 ATLANTIC SPAIN AND PORTUGAL

Ría de Muros to Ría de Arousa

Approaches to Ría de Muros

Tides Standard port Lisbon
Mean time differences (at Muros)
HW +0100 ±0010; LW +0125 ±0010
(the above allows for the difference in time zones)
Heights in metres

MHWS	MHWN	MLWN	MLWS
3·5	2·7	1·3	0·5

Lights
Pta Queixal Fl(2+1)12s26m10M
Cabo Corrubedo Fl(2+3)WR.20s31m15M
Racon(K) AIS

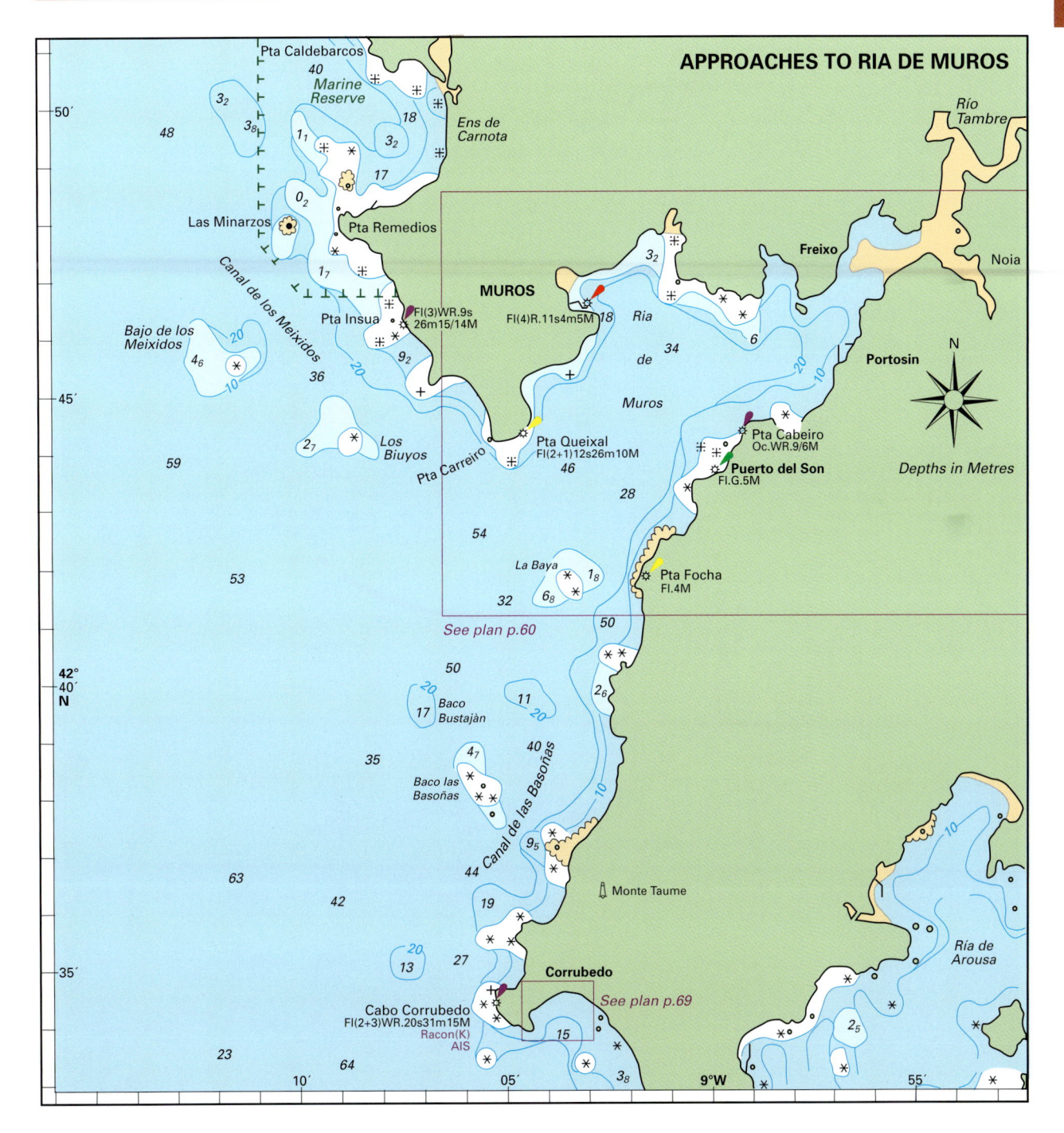

ATLANTIC SPAIN AND PORTUGAL

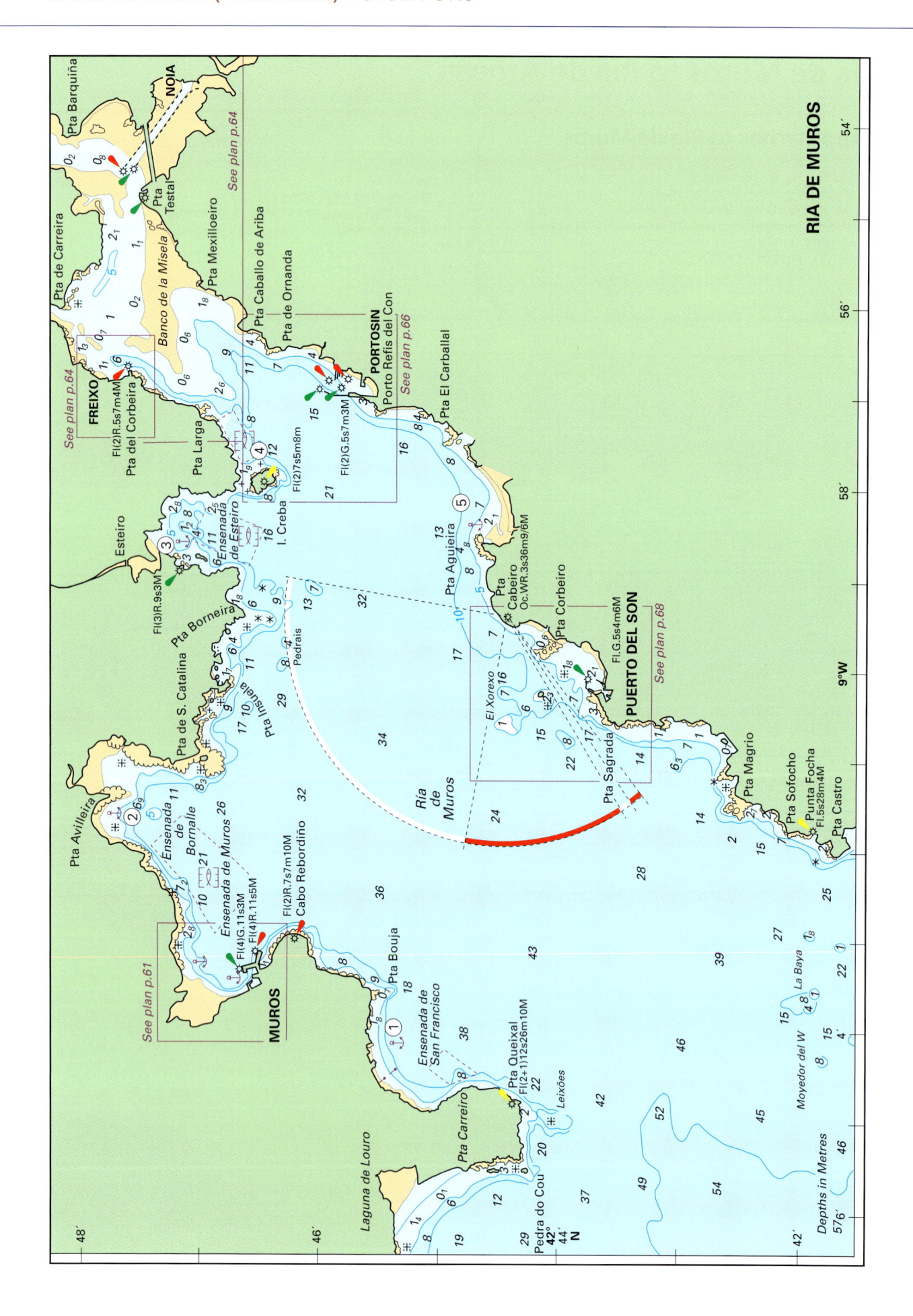

CABO FISTERRA (FINISTERRE) TO ISLA ONS

60 ATLANTIC SPAIN AND PORTUGAL

RÍA DE MUROS

A scenic ría

Ría Muros is the least developed of the rías. It has good anchorages, old towns and welcoming marinas at Portosin and Muros.

Approach

The safest approach, and in particular by night, is from the westsouthwest. Keep 5M off Pta Insúa or 3M off Cabo Corrubedo. In fair weather:

From the north Canal de Los Meixidos may be used. Do not cut inside the prominent rock off Pta Carreiro.

From the south Canal de Las Basoñas, the passage inside the banks, may be used.

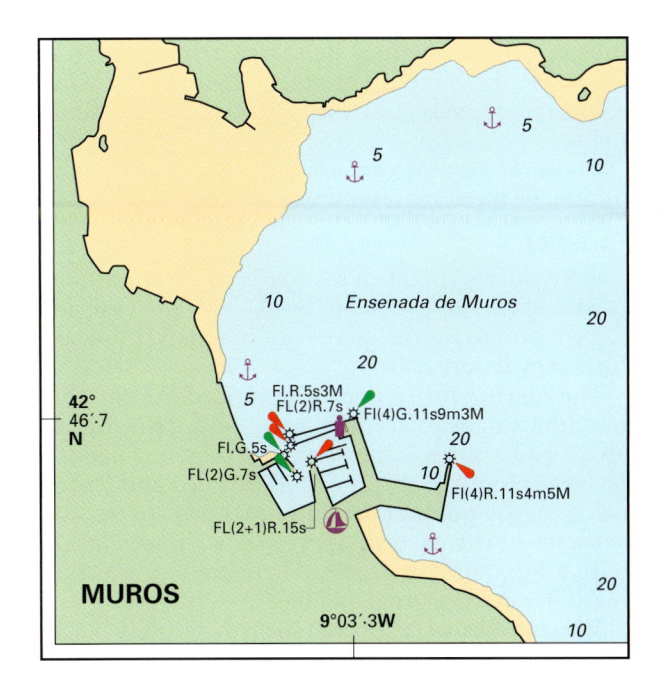

Muros

Location
42°46'·30N 09°03'·16W

Tides
See page 59

Lights
Breakwater beacon Fl(4)R.11s4m5M
White round tower

Communications
Puerto de Muros, S/N 15250, Muros, A Coruña
VHF Ch 09
☏ +34 981 82 76 60 *Mobile* +34 608 174 395
Email muport@muport.es
www.muport.es www.marinasdegalicia.com

A picturesque fishing town with a busy marina

The whole feeling of Galicia changes as the Lauro peninsula, past Pta Queixal, is rounded and the warmer, softer ría is entered with its immediate sense of increased shelter and temperature, tourism and prosperity. Inland, the fields of sweetcorn give way to massed vineyards.

Muros is a gorgeous old fishing town with many very old stone buildings dating back to the 18th century, narrow cobbled streets, flower baskets hanging from balconies, colonnaded pavements, covered and open-air markets, a Romanesque church and a number of friendly bars and restaurants. It has long been popular with cruising yachtsmen due to both its atmosphere and its facilities. Waterborne processions mark the fiesta of the Virgen del Carmen on 16 July, a practice which has spread throughout the area. The town is popular with tourists.

GALICIA

Muros marina looking north northwest *Henry Buchanan*

ATLANTIC SPAIN AND PORTUGAL **61**

CABO FISTERRA (FINISTERRE) TO ISLA ONS

Security at Muros marina. The Repsol pump at left is for fishing boats only *Henry Buchanan*

The marina fuel facility at Muros *Henry Buchanan*

Approach
Head northeast from the mouth of the ría until Cabo Rebordiño lighthouse comes into view, then steer to clear it by 200m. If approaching by night be aware that there are isolated unlit rafts inside 20m.

Berthing
The Marina in Muros is in full operation, with friendly staff reporting recent busy seasons when, on many occasions, they have had to turn visiting yachts away and ask them to anchor in the bay because the marina has been full to bursting.

Approach around the west end of both the wavebreaker and the fishing boat pontoon just inside the wavebreaker, and turn east for the finger pontoons. The end of the wavebreaker is off the slip on the east shore of Muros town, marked with a red post and light at its west end (nearest the shore). There are berths for boats from length 6m to 20m and beam of 3m to 6·75m. There are at least 50 berths that can take a 12·6m boat and a 15m yacht should have no problem finding a berth.

There is one security gate with key access. Note that Muros is the local headquarters of Spanish Customs.

Anchorage
Anchorage is in the Ensenada de Muros as shown on the Plan. In several areas the ground is foul with lobster pots and other debris. A tripping line is advisable. Holding is variable. Note that the wind sometimes funnels quite strongly off the surrounding hills.

Those at anchor can use the marina to dinghy ashore, or there are several sets of steps.

Facilities
The Repsol fuel pump at the west side of the harbour is strictly for use by fishing boats only. The east side Repsol pumps on the quay with pontoon below are for use by leisure craft.

The marina office is in a converted house (blue building opposite security gate) with two lounge areas, and a small kitchen/laundry room including a fridge. An outside sitting area is shielded and fenced off from the public. There are two private outside showers in the garden, as well as a shower inside with a loo, all 24hr access. There are two washing machines in the marina building.

WiFi is available in a special room in the office block, and to the pontoons but is weak at the outer edges.

Work and chandlery is geared generally to fishing boats but there is a good hardware store. There is a boat lift and 100-tonne travel lift and some space

Yacht entering Muros marina. Photo taken looking east *Henry Buchanan*

ATLANTIC SPAIN AND PORTUGAL

RÍA DE MUROS

ashore to over-winter. There is a tidal scrubbing berth at a quay some 600m north of the harbour, on hard sand with about 2·5m at high water springs. It is well sheltered other than from southwesterly swell but inspect for debris before use – alternatively the sand in Ensenada de Muros is hard and clean.

The town is well provided with shops of all kinds, banks, hotels, restaurants and pavement cafés. There are excellent ones by the harbour. There is a good produce market, plus a fish market on the quay. There is a Gadis supermarket 100m beyond the office and other supermarkets and a good hardware store will be found near the north end of the town, some distance away from the harbour. A good fridge engineer is available in town.

There is a free computer for use in the morning at the library. Also WiFi at the Aclan Bar and at the Theatro Restaurant in the Plaza on the bend in the road around the corner of the marina.

Anchorages in the Ría de Muros

1. **Ensenada de San Francisco** 42°45'·4N 09°04'·30W
   In strong northerly winds, the Ensenada de San Francisco 1·5M southwest of Muros provides good shelter. Anchor in the northern part of the bay in 7m or less with excellent holding over sand. Land on the beach, where there are shops and cafés.

   It has been reported that an anchor trapping pipe of some kind ran out into the bay from a point near the 'lollipop' lights on the road, terminating near the 10m line (see plan page 60). No more is known of its position or purpose.

2. **Ensenada de Bornalle** 42°47'·60N 09°01'·7W
   In the northwest corner of the Ensenada de Bornalle, nearly 2M northeast of Muros, in 5m or less. There is a good bathing beach and a freshwater stream, but holding is variable due to large patches of very dense weed. The massed ranks of *viveros* in the entrance to the bay give some protection from southwesterly swell.

The anchorage at Pta Testal   Roddy Innes

3. **Ensenada de Esteiro** 42°47'·20N 08°58'·50W
   About 4M east of Muros, well protected from west through north to east. The bay is effectively divided into two by a central rocky promontory (with shallow off-liers) and anchorage can be had on either side in 3–4m over sand and weed, avoiding the rock patches. There is a private quay on the west shore of the western arm and the entire surroundings are somewhat built up. Both arms of the bay shelter small but attractive beaches and there are normally some *viveros* moored in the entrance.

4. **Northeast of Isla Crebra** 42°46'·60N 08°57'·6W
   Lit at its southerly extreme (Fl(2)7·5m0M Metal post 3m) and easily identified by the red-roofed building on its summit. Anchor north of the Vella rocks and close NE of the island, in 2–4m, sheltered from southwest to north (see Portosin plan on page 66). This is an isolated anchorage in the ría, with no facilities and notices forbidding landing.

5. **Punta Aguiera** 42 44·62'N 08 58·26'W
   There is good holding E of Punta Aguiera which provides good shelter out of the swell in a strong S blow. Anchor in 5m on sand off the small boat channel through the swimming buoys off the beach. It is a picturesque anchorage in an area popular with fishermen, who might be found surrounding the yacht in the morning.

There are other anchoring possibilities at Freixo and in the approaches to Noia (see pages 64-65).

Ría de Muros, looking ENE up the ría towards Isla Crebra (top right) from the peak above Pta Carreiro. Ensenada de San Francisco anchorage is off the long beach on the left   Jane Russell

GALICIA

ATLANTIC SPAIN AND PORTUGAL

CABO FISTERRA (FINISTERRE) TO ISLA ONS

Approaches to Freixo and Noia

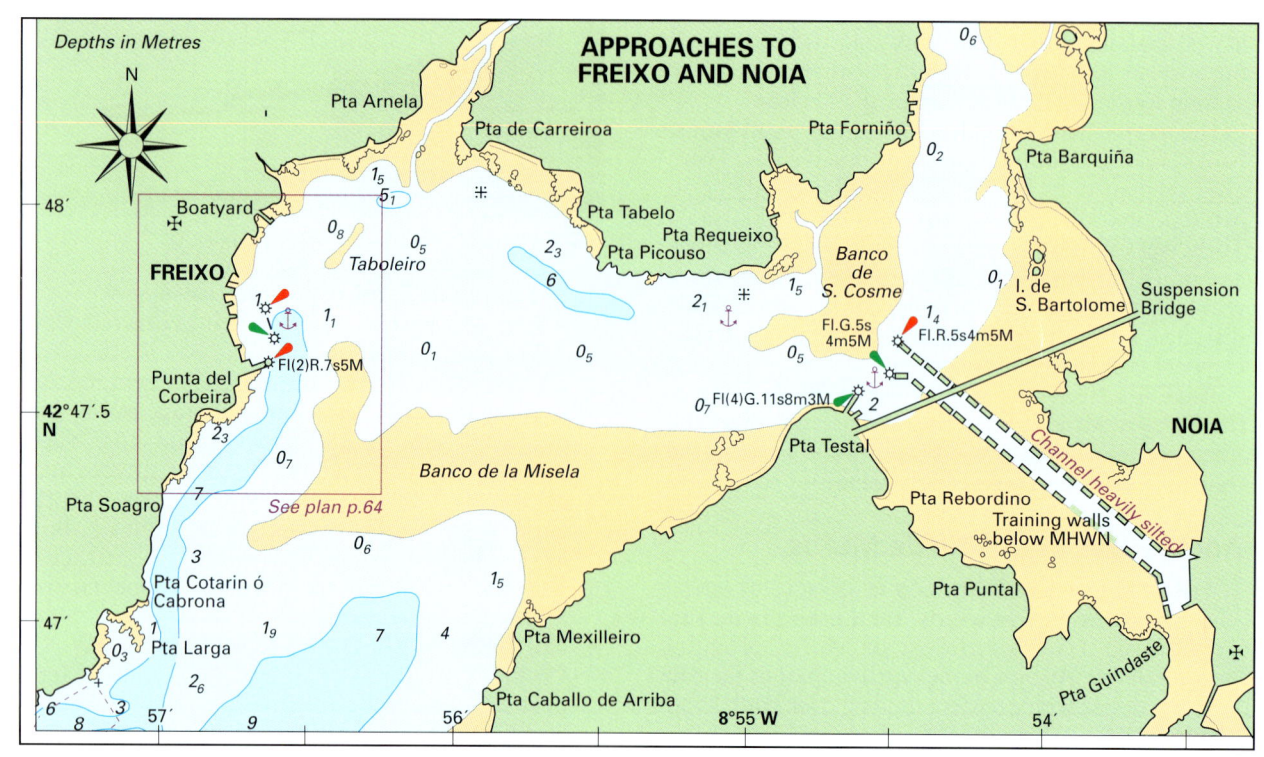

Freixo (Freijo)

Location
42°47'·62N 08°56'·62W

Tide
West winds may increase tidal heights in the upper parts of the ría by up to 0·6m, but tidal flow in general is weak.

Light
Breakwater beacon Fl(2)R.7s5M Red and white column
Wave breaker lights on thin posts (Green and BYB)

Straggling village with active boat yard

Freixo (Freijo) offers a sheltered anchorage and minor food shops and restaurants ashore. Yachts are also welcome on the outer pontoon but check depths carefully.

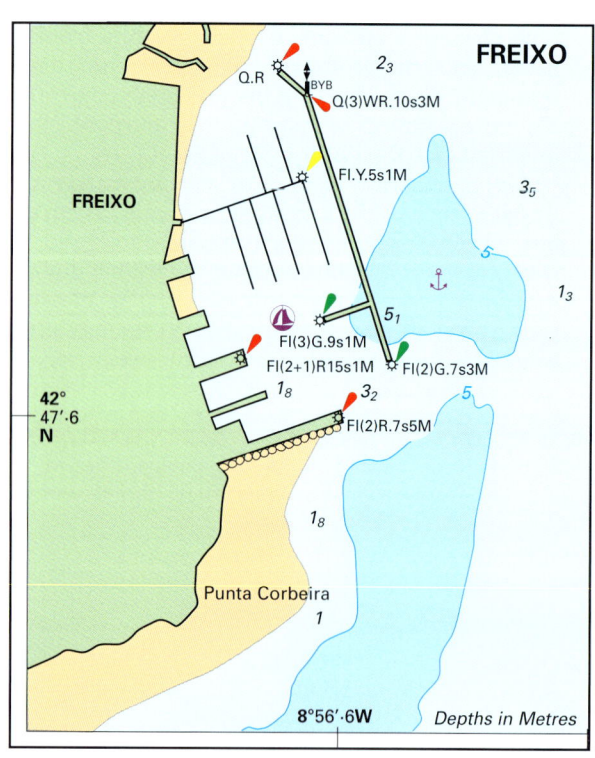

Approach (see plan and chart 1756)
The deep water shallows rapidly off Punta Larga. Pick up the channel as it follows the west bank past the reef extending from the point.

64 ATLANTIC SPAIN AND PORTUGAL

FREIXO AND NOIA

Caution
Watch the depth gauge north of Punta Corbeira, before you reach the southern harbour wall as the channel may have shifted. There is also a lot of diving activity in the area to watch out for (diving for shellfish it is believed), but divers down flags are usually used.

Anchorage
Anchor off the east side of the wavebreaker pontoon in 5m, mud.

Freixo from the south

Noia (Noya)

Location
Noia lies 1M southeast from Pta Testal between training walls at 42°47′N 08°53′·5W

Training wall
Beacons are red and white and green and white. Pta Testal beacon is green and white. All are lit.

Silting and suspension bridge restrict access to old town and port

The harbour and approaches to Noia are now severely silted but at high water it is still possible for a yacht drawing less than 2m to get within 1M of the town off Punta Testal. Then continue by dinghy, or land at the quay at Punta Testal and walk into town, a distance of about 2·5km (taxis are available in the main square for the return journey). Punta Testal is fringed by a clear sandy beach, where a yacht able to take the ground could dry out.

A very large suspension bridge across the estuary blocks access to Noia for yachts.

Approach
Leave Freixo after half flood, or as draught allows. From the 5m patch off Freixo head for Punta Tabelo until the 5–6m trench is reached. Follow the trench past Punta Picouso. When it starts to shoal, head just north of the tip of the Punta Testal sand, where red and green buoys mark the start of the channel within the training wall.

Anchorage
Anchor south of Pta Picouso or between the south training wall and Pta Testal molehead. The latter offers more shelter but is a holiday area, the water is shallower and there are many small boat moorings. There is little room for more than one visiting boat to anchor (see photograph page 63).

Facilities
All the domestic facilities of a bustling small town.

Looking towards the new suspension bridge from Noia Henning Dürr

ATLANTIC SPAIN AND PORTUGAL

CABO FISTERRA (FINISTERRE) TO ISLA ONS

Portosin

Location
42°45'·94N 08°56'·91W

Tides
Standard port Lisbon
Mean time differences (at Muros)
HW +0100 ±0010; LW +0125 ±0010
(the above allows for the difference in time zones)
Heights in metres
MHWS	MHWN	MLWN	MLWS
3·5	2·7	1·3	0·5

Light
Breakwater beacon Fl(3)G.9s Green round tower

Communications
Real Club Náutico Portosin
VHF Ch 09 ① +34 981 766 583 / +34 625 445 083
Email info@rcnportosin.com
www.rcnportosin.com

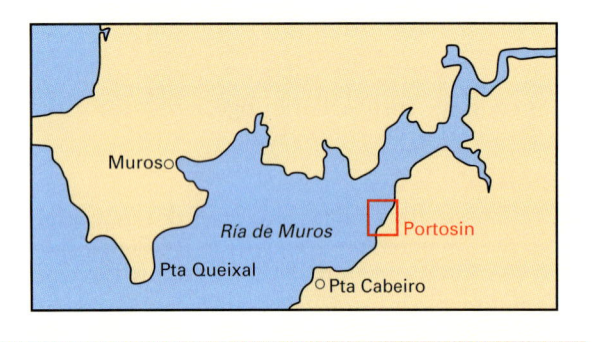

A welcoming and well run Real Club Náutico

The large harbour houses an established marina, the Real Club Náutico, which has long received unanimous praise from visitors. It is the closest marina for a visit to Santiago de Compostela and the use of the international airport there. A yacht can be left here for extended periods in safety. The marina has an attractive setting backed by wooded hills, and with a good beach nearby.

Approach

Head up the middle of the ría to the approach to the harbour which is on the south shore opposite Isla Crebra. The marina is to port on entering harbour.

Berthing

Call ahead and, unless a berth has been pre-arranged, visitors should secure to the first hammerhead marked 'Waiting'. Most berths are bows-on with finger pontoon or a mooring line provided astern; yachts up to 20m can be accommodated in depths of 2–5m. Shelter is good though some surge may be experienced in north easterlies.

Harbourmaster hours Winter Mon-Sun 0800-2100. Summer (1 June-30 September); Mon-Sun 0800-2200.

Office hours Winter Mon-Sat 1000-1900. Summer (1 June -30 September) Mon-Fri 0830-2000, Sat 1000-1900, Sun 1000-1400 and 1630-1900.

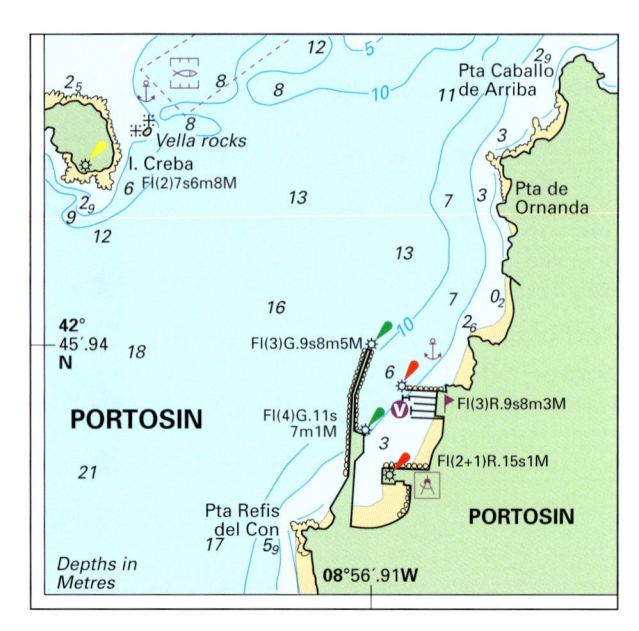

Anchorage

Yachts may anchor immediately north of the mole in 5–6m, sheltered from northeast through to south or southwest. Holding is reported to be good in sand.

Facilities

Facilities are very good within the marina, both for boat support and domestics. There is diesel on site, although access may be limited by depths at low tide. There is a travel-lift (32T), auxiliary crane, free use of bicycles, and a battery change service.

It has good showers and laundry facilities, the Club has WiFi, and there is a good bar and restaurant. Hire cars can be arranged from here and there is a bus service into Noia.

Ashore

Portosin has an excellent supermarket and there is a produce market on Saturdays.

At the head of the ría, the old town of Noia (declared an Area of Historical Importance) is a short bus-trip away. Noia offers supermarkets, an excellent covered market and a weekly general street market. Santiago de Compostela, its airport and the excellent 'Atlantic' motorway, are less than an hour away.

Galicia has excellent fish stalls *Roddy Innes*

ATLANTIC SPAIN AND PORTUGAL

PORTOSIN

Portosin harbour

Looking down Ría de Muros from Portosin *Henry Buchanan*

View into Portosin marina looking south-southwest *Henry Buchanan*

CABO FISTERRA (FINISTERRE) TO ISLA ONS

Puerto del Son

Location
42°43'·74N 09°00'·05W

Tides Standard port Lisbon
Mean time differences (at Muros)
HW +0100 ±0010; LW +0125 ±0010
(the above allows for the difference in time zones)
Heights in metres

MHWS	MHWN	MLWN	MLWS
3·5	2·7	1·3	0·5

Lights
Breakwater beacon Fl.G.5s7m3M Green and white round concrete tower
Pta Cabeiro Oc.WR.3s36m9/6M Grey truncated pyramidal tower

Warning
Final approaches from between the west and southwest and only with great care

Small fishing harbour

A yachtsman might find shelter here. The village has basic shops and there are good beaches nearby.

Approach

The safest route is from the southwest with Pta Cabeiro bearing 56·5° (the narrow-beam red sector of the light) until the end of Puerto del Son breakwater bears 170°.

Anchorage

Anchor in the outer harbour clear of the approach channel to the fishermen's quays. In quiet periods it may be possible to lie alongside the quay for a short while.

Facilities

Water on the quay, shop, restaurants, post office but little else.

Puerto del Son

68   ATLANTIC SPAIN AND PORTUGAL

RÍA DE MUROS

Corrubedo

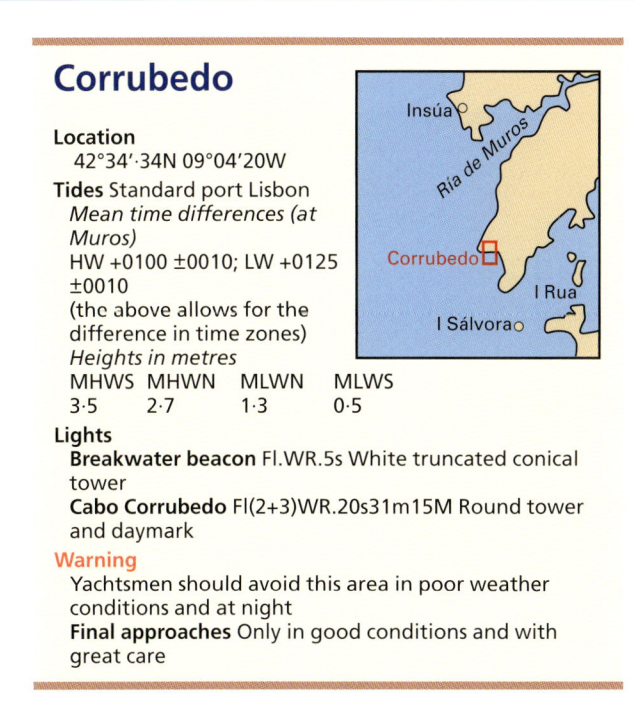

Location
42°34'·34N 09°04'20W

Tides Standard port Lisbon
Mean time differences (at Muros)
HW +0100 ±0010; LW +0125 ±0010
(the above allows for the difference in time zones)
Heights in metres

MHWS	MHWN	MLWN	MLWS
3·5	2·7	1·3	0·5

Lights
Breakwater beacon Fl.WR.5s White truncated conical tower
Cabo Corrubedo Fl(2+3)WR.20s31m15M Round tower and daymark

Warning
Yachtsmen should avoid this area in poor weather conditions and at night
Final approaches Only in good conditions and with great care

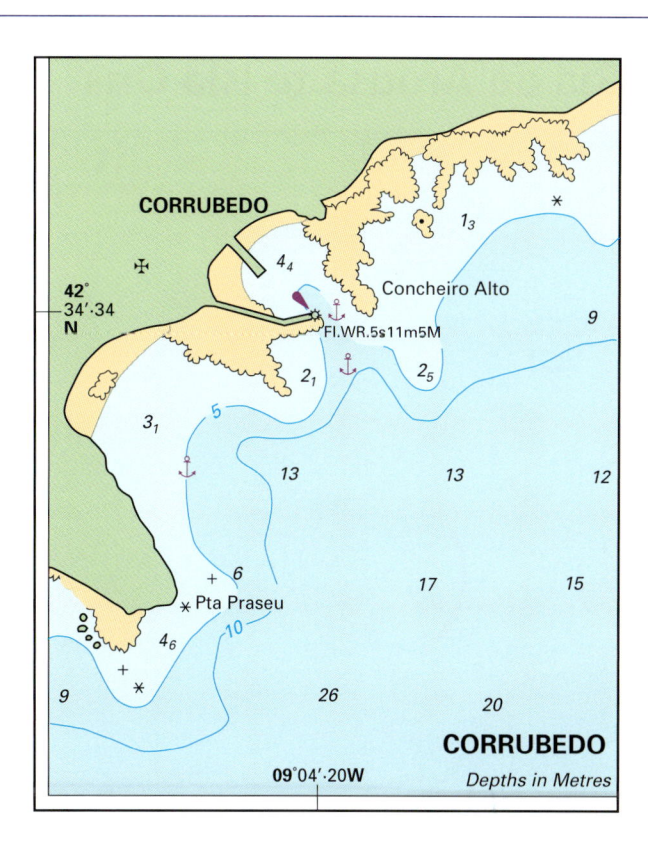

A small fishing harbour offering little space or protection

Corrubedo should be visited in fair weather only and using chart 1734. The approaches should only be attempted in calm weather and daylight. If a southerly develops it would be necessary to clear out. There are basic shops and restaurants ashore. To the east lies the Dunes National Park with vast sand dunes and nature trails.

Approach

From Ría de Muros Keep 200m off the rocky ledges of Pta Posalgueiro and inside the Bajo la Marosa, and shape a course on approximately 100° to keep outside the 10m line while rounding Punta Praseu and its offlying rocks. Then approach Corrubedo in the white sector of the breakwater light bearing north before manoeuvring to the desired anchorage.

From Ría de Arousa Approach Corrubedo in the white sector of the breakwater light bearing north before manoeuvring to the desired anchorage.

Anchorage

The bay to the southwest of the harbour may offer more room and greater comfort than the harbour itself but note the swell in the picture.

Corrubedo from the south

ATLANTIC SPAIN AND PORTUGAL   69

GALICIA

CABO FISTERRA (FINISTERRE) TO ISLA ONS

Ría de Arousa to Isla Ons

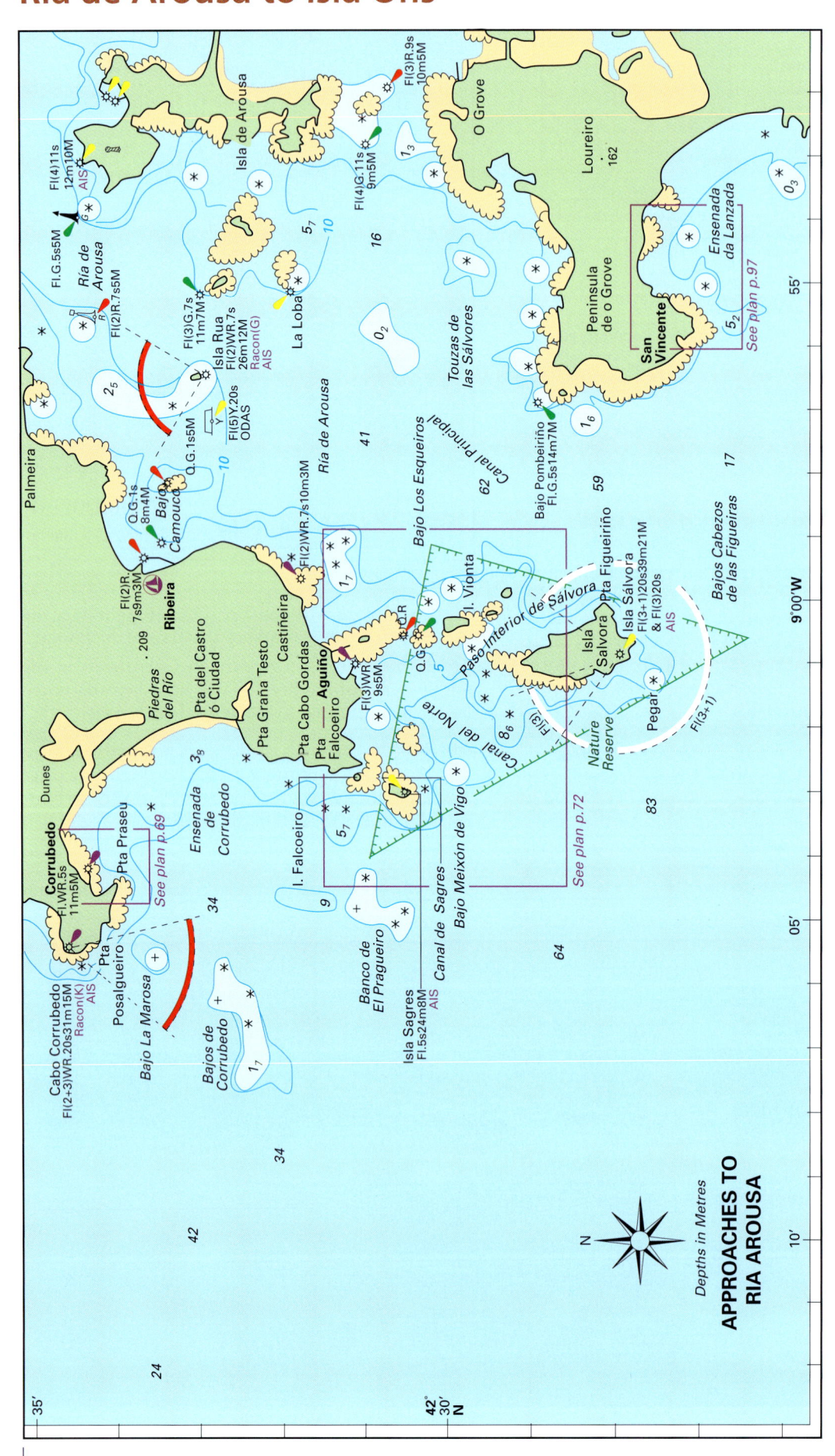

Lights
Isla Sagres Fl.5s24m8M Column
Isla Sálvora Fl(3+1)20s39m21M+Fl(3)20s White 8-sided tower, red band
Bajo Pombeiriño Fl.G.5s15m7M White truncated conical tower, green band

APPROACHES TO RÍA AROUSA
Depths in Metres

70 ATLANTIC SPAIN AND PORTUGAL

Passages into Ría de Arousa

Passage via the Canal Principal
The easiest and safest approach to the ría, particularly at night or in poor conditions, is from the south through the Canal Principal. This leads between Isla Sálvora and Pombeiriño, at the northwest point of the Península de o Grove. Isla Rúa light, that is some 7M into the ría, can be seen from well out to sea, and from offshore is safe to approach on a bearing of between 010° and 025°.

Coming from the north on passage, clear Cabo Corrubedo by 5M to avoid the dangers of Bajos de Corrubedo. When past them, steer to round Isla Sálvora giving the lighthouse a berth of 1M to avoid the Pegar rock group and enter by the Canal Principal.

Passages between Isla Salvora and Aguino at the North entrance to the Ría de Arousa
In good visibility and settled conditions there are alternative routes into the Ría de Arousa, but all require eyeball navigation: visual pilotage is essential for safe transit. There is at least 6m in all of the channels at LAT. Navigational aids number only three: a beacon on the Islas Sagres, and two marking the Paso del Carreiro – a stone tower (white with green top) on the Piedras del Sargo on the south side, and a slimmer perch (white with red top), new in 2016 and replacing a port hand buoy, on Pentones de Centolleira on the north.

Charts
BA1768 Ría de Arousa (or its Spanish counterpart) is essential for an overall view. The detail chart BA1734 (or the Spanish 415B) is useful but not essential. The charts, paper or electronic, appear to be quite accurate here. The Canal de Sagres has not been surveyed since 1905 but the Paso Interior was done in 2005.

Warning
Strong and unpredictable currents can run strongly through the channels which should not be attempted in less than perfect weather or at night. The waypoints provided should only be used for reference and orientation at sea and must not be linked for direct routing without plotting. Visual pilotage is vital for safe transit of these passages.

Anchorage in the Ría de Arousa *Geraldine Hennigan*

CABO FISTERRA (FINISTERRE) TO ISLA ONS

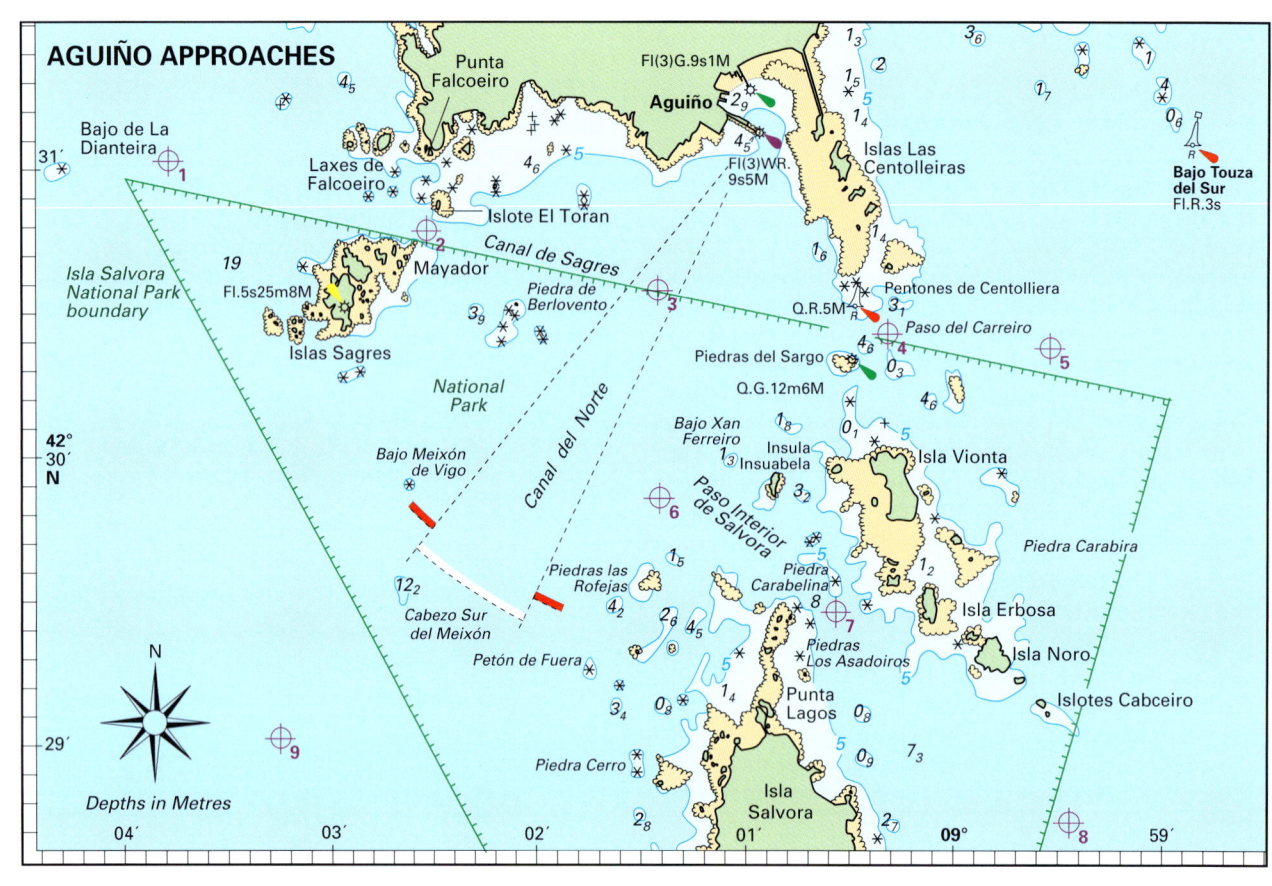

⊕1 42°30'·95N 09°03'·85W 0·6M WNW Islas Sagres
⊕2 42°30·77N 09°02·50W 0·09M S Islote El Toran
⊕3 42°30·55N 09°01'·40W 0·7M WSW Aguiño
⊕4 42°30·44N 09°00·40W 0·12M NNE Piedras del Sargo tower
⊕5 42°30'·4N 08°59'·5W 0·72M E Piedras del Sargo
⊕6 42°29'·9N 09°01'·4W W App Passo Sálvora
⊕7 42°29·50N 09°00·60W 0·08M S Piedra Carabelina
⊕8 42°28·81N 08°58·32W
⊕9 42°28'·9N 09°03'W App Canal del Norte

Passage A

The visual passage through the Canal de Sagres and the Paso de Carreiro is guided by:

⊕1, ⊕2, ⊕3 and ⊕4 moving from west to east. Approaching from the north on a heading of approximately 172° from Corrubedo, continue south avoiding the Banco El Pragueiro (see plan page 70) until turning for the Canal de Sagres in the vicinity of ⊕1. From ⊕1, head towards the Pentones de Centolleira perch (red and white) which should bear about 100°. This course passes about 80m north of the visible Mayador rocks and 150m south of the submerged rocks off Pta Falcoeiro. Continue on 100° via ⊕2 and ⊕3 towards ⊕4 in the Paso de Carreiro which, seen from the Canal de Sagres, is roughly midway between the Piedras del Sargo tower (green and white) to starboard, and the Pentones de Centolleira perch (red and white) to port.

Passage B

A visual passage from the Canal de Sagres and through the Paso Interior de Salvora is guided by: ⊕1, ⊕2, ⊕3, and then ⊕6, ⊕7 and ⊕8 moving from north to south. See the photographs for Passage B and the guidance given with each of them to help with navigation.

This route was once described as being suited to local fishermen or devoted rock-hoppers – take care!

Anchorage in the Sálvora group

The National Park website identifies only two permitted anchorages in the whole Sálvora group: Praia do Castelo and Praia do Almacén, which are pretty much the same place - the bay with the island's pier, at the SE end.

The charming, snug Isla Salvora group anchorage is at the SE corner of Isla Salvora. Enter from the NE into the cove behind a small jetty (no berthing), heading for the mermaid statue. Leave to port the prominent drying rock at the jetty end. Anchor in 2m on sand. There is just room for one yacht to swing.

Otherwise anchor N of the pier in 5 to 10m. There are uncharted rocks in the bay behind the pier. An anchoring permit is required. There is access from the jetty by a track to the lighthouse at the southern tip of island.

The pier at the Isla Sálvora anchorage *Geraldine Hennigan*

72 ATLANTIC SPAIN AND PORTUGAL

PASSAGES INTO RÍA DE AROUSA

Key views on Passage A

Laxes de Falcoeiro   *Mayador Rocks*

This shows the principal hazard of the drying Laxes de Falcoeiro with water breaking on it. The view is taken with the vessel on a southeasterly heading before turning to port in the vicinity of ⊕1 on the approach to the Canal de Sagres going west to east. The Laxes de Falcoeiro must be left to port *Geraldine Hennigan*

El Toran

This is a view on the Canal de Sagres looking north from ⊕2 on a west to east passage. The rocky outcrop of Islote El Toran is abeam (note factory on the mainland) *Geraldine Hennigan*

Looking south from the Canal de Sagres over the Islas Sagres *Geraldine Hennigan*

Pentones de Centolliera   *Piedras del Sargo*

This view shows the Paso de Carreiro seen from the Canal de Sagres. ⊕4 is roughly midway between the Piedras del Sargo tower (green and white) to starboard, and the Pentones de Centolleira perch (red and white) to port *Geraldine Hennigan*

GALICIA

ATLANTIC SPAIN AND PORTUGAL   **73**

CABO FISTERRA (FINISTERRE) TO ISLA ONS

Key views on Passage B

This view does not show the whole passage of the Paso Interior de Salvora but two prominent features useful for orientation. The humpback Isla Insuabela is on the left and the conspicuous pyramidal Isla Noro is on the right, both will be left to port. The vessel is on a southeasterly course heading for ⊕7 at the narrowest point of the Paso Interior de Salvora. At this point the drying Piedra Carabelina will be to the NE and the mainly above water Piedras Los Asadoiros to the SW *Geraldine Hennigan*

This is Isla Insuabela, looking NE from between ⊕6 and ⊕7 on the Paso Interior de Salvora *Geraldine Hennigan*

This is a view of the mainly above water Piedras Los Asadoiros with the Isla Salvora beyond. Be aware that the drying rocks extend more than a cable to the N and SE of these above water heads *Geraldine Hennigan*

View of the Isla Noro the Paso Interior de Salvora where it widens out at its southern end
Geraldine Hennigan

Looking NW up the Paso Interior de Salvora with Isla Salvora to the left and Isla Noro to the right at the start of a north-going passage *Geraldine Hennigan*

74   ATLANTIC SPAIN AND PORTUGAL

AGUIÑO

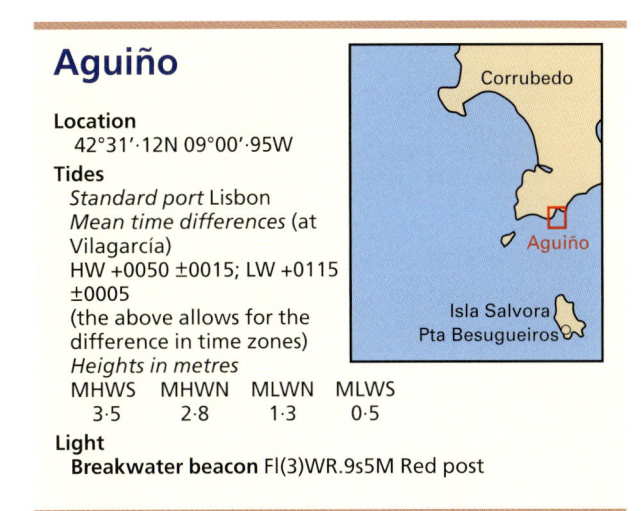

Aguiño

Location
42°31'·12N 09°00'·95W

Tides
Standard port Lisbon
Mean time differences (at Vilagarcía)
HW +0050 ±0015; LW +0115 ±0005
(the above allows for the difference in time zones)
Heights in metres

MHWS	MHWN	MLWN	MLWS
3·5	2·8	1·3	0·5

Light
Breakwater beacon Fl(3)WR.9s5M Red post

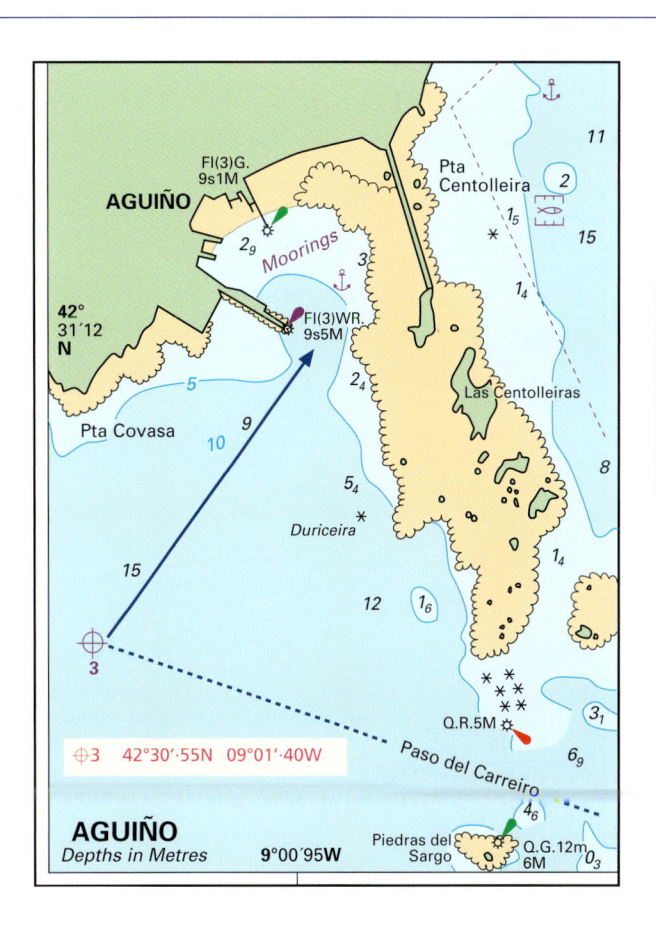

Fishing harbour

Aguiño is dedicated to fishing – primarily for shellfish. It lies at the head of numerous reefs and islands which form a National Park.

Approach

The deepwater, lit approach to Aguiño is via the Canal del Norte (⊕9 and ⊕3). See plan on page 72.

Anchorage

The Las Centolleiras reef continues to be filled in to form a causeway protecting the harbour from the east. As a result the harbour is reasonably sheltered, though the entrance is exposed to the southwest. The best anchorage is occupied by smallcraft moorings. Anchor about 150m north or northeast of the breakwater as space allows in 2–4m over sand, keeping clear of the approach to the fishermen's quay on the inside of the breakwater.

Aguiño fishing harbour. A seafood paradise
Geraldine Hennigan

Aguiño

ATLANTIC SPAIN AND PORTUGAL 75

CABO FISTERRA (FINISTERRE) TO ISLA ONS

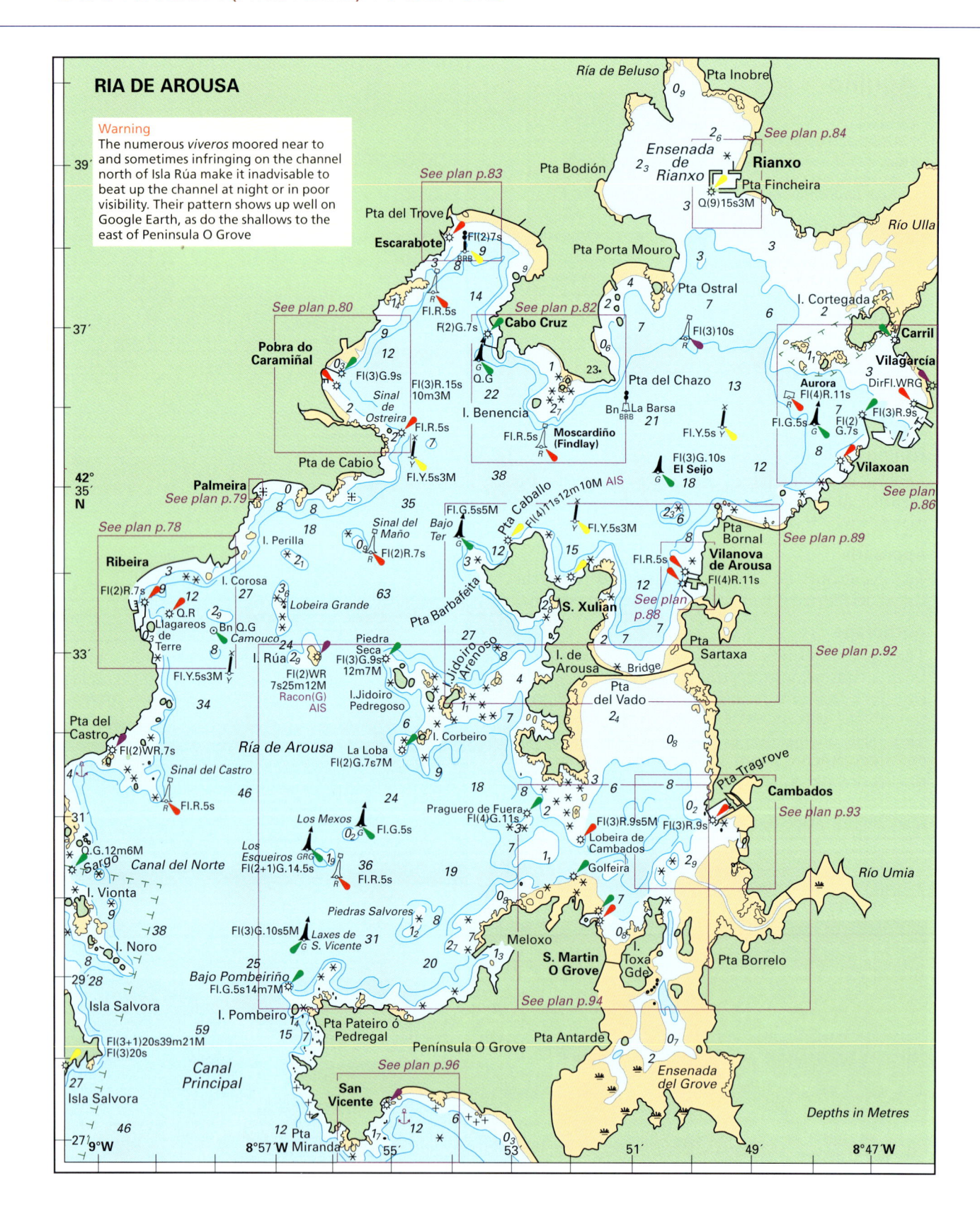

RIA DE AROUSA

Warning
The numerous *viveros* moored near to and sometimes infringing on the channel north of Isla Rúa make it inadvisable to beat up the channel at night or in poor visibility. Their pattern shows up well on Google Earth, as do the shallows to the east of Península O Grove.

76   ATLANTIC SPAIN AND PORTUGAL

RÍA DE AROUSA

Ría de Arousa

Tides
Standard port Lisbon
Mean time differences (at Vilagarcía)
HW +0050 ±0015; LW +0115 ±0005
(the above allows for the difference in time zones)
Heights in metres
MHWS	MHWN	MLWN	MLWS
3·5	2·8	1·3	0·5

Lights
Isla Sálvora Fl(3+1)20s39m21M White 8-sided tower, red band
Bajo Pombeiriño Fl.G.5s14m7M White truncated conical tower, green band
Piedras del Sargo Q.G.12m6M White truncated conical tower, green band
Bajo La Loba Fl(2)G.7s9m7M Green and White truncated conical tower.
Isla Rúa Fl(2)WR.7s12M. AIS Round masonry tower and dwelling
Bajo Piedra Seca Fl(3)G.9s11m7M White truncated conical tower, green band
Punta del Caballo, Isla Arousa Fl(4)11s12m10M 8-sided masonry tower, red and white dwelling
Bajo Sinal de Ostreira Fl.R.5s9m5M Red and White truncated conical tower.

The largest Galician ría

The largest of the Galician rías and perhaps the most attractive for cruising, Ría de Arousa has many pleasant anchorages to explore and some interesting challenges in the way of pilotage. Not surprisingly it is also very popular with the Spanish, both afloat and on the many beaches. Food and other basics may be obtained in most of the small harbours on its shores, though the widest choice is undoubtedly to be had at Vilagarcía de Arousa, an otherwise unappealing town.

The variety of anchorages is such that shelter from any wind direction can be found relatively easily. The simplest harbours to enter in darkness are Santa Uxia de Riveira, Pobra do Caramiñal and Vilagarcía de Arousa – night approaches to other places would be easier with local knowledge, not least because of the dangers posed by unlit *viveros*, of which the Ría Arousa is particularly full.

In addition to the harbours detailed in the following pages, a number of nominal *puertos* exist, usually consisting of a short breakwater (sometimes lit) behind which small fishing vessels lie on moorings. Few can be approached by a keel yacht at all states of the tide. Similarly, not all the possible anchorages in this large ría can be described, though an attempt has been made to include those most popular.

Pombeiriño light with Aguiño in the distance looking NW from O Grove *Martin Walker*

A Galician shellfish harvest *Martin Walker*

ATLANTIC SPAIN AND PORTUGAL

GALICIA

CABO FISTERRA (FINISTERRE) TO ISLA ONS

Ribeira (Sta Uxia de Ribeira)

Location
42°33'·75N 08°59'·26W

Tides
Standard port Lisbon
Mean time differences (at Vilagarcía)
HW +0050 ±0015; LW +0115 ±0005
(the above allows for the difference in time zones)
Heights in metres

MHWS	MHWN	MLWN	MLWS
3·5	2·8	1·3	0·5

Light
Marina breakwater beacon Fl(2+1)G.15s3M GRG pillar
See plan for main harbour lights

Communications
Club Náutico Deportivo de Ribeira
VHF Ch 09 ☎ +34 981 874 739 +34 648 187 170
Email secretaria@nauticoribeira.com
www.nauticoriveira.com

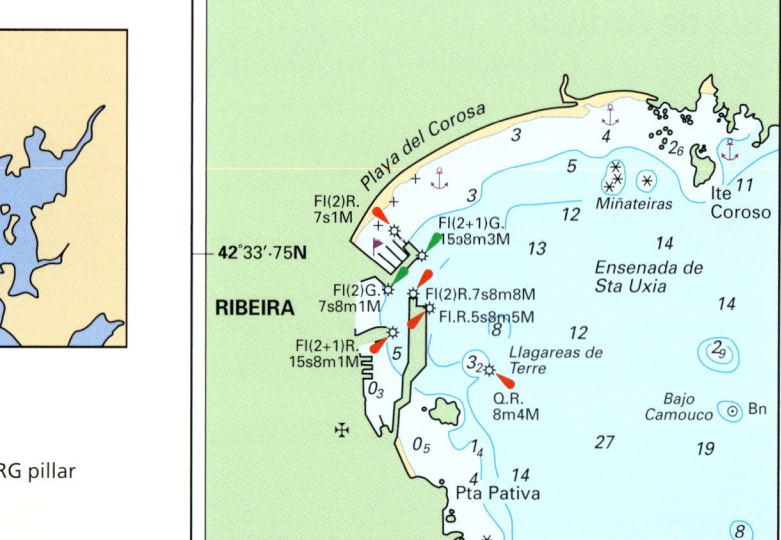

Ribeira with marina to the north of the main port

78 ATLANTIC SPAIN AND PORTUGAL

RIBEIRA

Small club marina next to large commercial harbour

The main harbour caters for coasters, fishing boats and small local boats. It is well marked and has a substantial breakwater. Yachts go to the marina immediately to the north which offers shelter.

Approach

Ribeira lies in the bay to the west of the prominent Isla Rúa. Approach is straightforward. Head up the ría towards Isla Rúa until clear of Bajo Touza del Sur to the southeast of Castineira. As the bay opens, identify the harbour wall, and off-lying red topped tower of Llagareos de Terre Q.R, before closing the marina breakwater.

Berthing and anchorage

This small club marina has become crowded in recent years, with all pontoon berths occupied by local boats, even in low season. Visitors may be directed to lie bow-to on one of the inner pontoons in the northern part of the marina where depths are at least 5m. Boats of up to 16m can be accommodated. The outer pontoon is likely to be untenable in a northeaster, and access to power and water on this pontoon is limited.

Anchorage is possible off Playa del Corosa to the northeast of the marina in 3–5m over sand and mud.

Ribeira Marina looking east Geraldine Hennigan

Approach the anchorage on a course of 325° towards the wooded headland with the caravans, leaving Llagareas de Terre to port and Bajo Camonco to starboard. The shallows are generally obvious.

Facilities

The Club Náutico Deportivo de Ribeira is welcoming with good facilities and a pleasant restaurant.

Fuel and technical support can be found in the local area. The marina is close to the large town with a wide choice of restaurants and all normal facilities. There is a good supermarket reasonably close by, plus a produce and fish market.

Anchorages to the northeast of Ribeira

1. **Northeast of Isolote Coroso**
   42°33'·95N 08°58'·05W
   In 3-4m over sand, surrounded by smooth, pinkish boulders. Approach only in good light. Use chart 1755.

2. **Ensenada de Palmeira** 42°34'·90N 08°57'·04W
   Use chart 1734 or 1764. There are isolated rocks shown in the east of part of the bay. Immediately west is the small village and harbour of Palmeira. It has little space and the shallow approach should be checked by dinghy before considering entering above half tide for minor provisions or a meal ashore. On the outer breakwater is one of a number of monuments seen on this coast to the many people who have emigrated from Galicia.

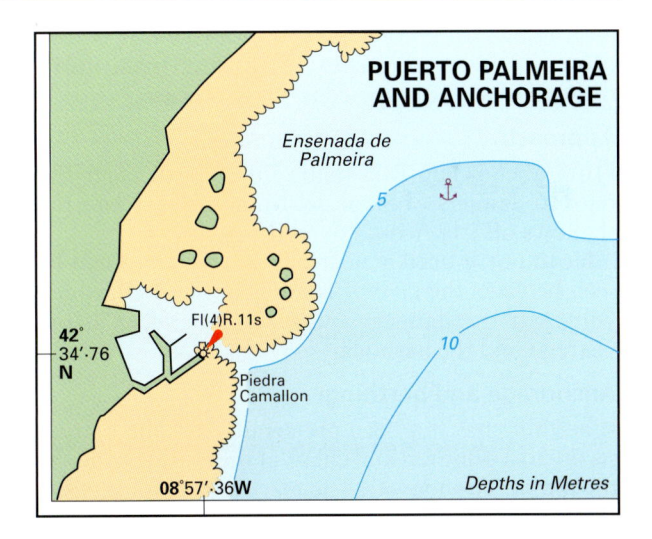

Approach to Islote Coroso Geraldine Hennigan

Monument to emigrants pointing west, Palmeira Martin Walker

ATLANTIC SPAIN AND PORTUGAL

CABO FISTERRA (FINISTERRE) TO ISLA ONS

A Pobra do Caramiñal

Location
42°36'·25N 08°56'·00W

Tides
Standard port Lisbon
Mean time differences (at Vilagarcía)
HW +0050 ±0015; LW +0115 ±0005
(the above allows for the difference in time zones)
Heights in metres

MHWS	MHWN	MLWN	MLWS
3·5	2·8	1·3	0·5

Lights
Harbour breakwater Fl(3)G.9s9m5M White and green round tower
Marina mole head Fl(2+1)R.15s3M White and red round tower (low red green red pillar at pontoon head)

Communications
Club Náutico do Caramiñal
VHF Ch 09 ☎ +34 981 832 504
Email info@cncaraminal
www.nauticocaraminal.es   www.marinasdegalicia.com

Well-liked marina and a town with good restaurants

Yachtsmen welcome the substantial pontoons at Pobra (as it is known locally) which provides normal marina facilities alongside a useful town. It is well protected by the big ship breakwater from north through west, but exposed to the southeast.

Approach

From abeam Isla Rúa maintain 030° to clear the buoyed dangers of Sinal del Maño to port and the shallows off Isla Arousa to starboard.

Head north until a clear passage to Pobra can be seen between the *viveros* heading about 285° which will clear the dangers and *viveros* between Islote Ostreira and the harbour.

Anchorage and berthing

If berthing has not been pre-arranged in the marina secure to a pontoon and check at the marina office at the top of the gangway. The marina itself is excellent and the staff friendly and helpful.

Yachts may anchor off the beach clear of the marina entrance where there is good holding. Landing by dinghy is available at the large slipway south of the marina where there is a water tap, or in the marina itself.

Facilities

There are a total of 281 marina berths, with 27 reserved for visitors. The wide, spacious berths are bows-to with two mooring lines aft. There is electricity and water on the pontoons.

There is a 40-tonne travel-lift, administered by the club, and several workshops to be found in the port. By notifying the *capitanía*, the fuel station in town will bring fuel to the pontoons next day.

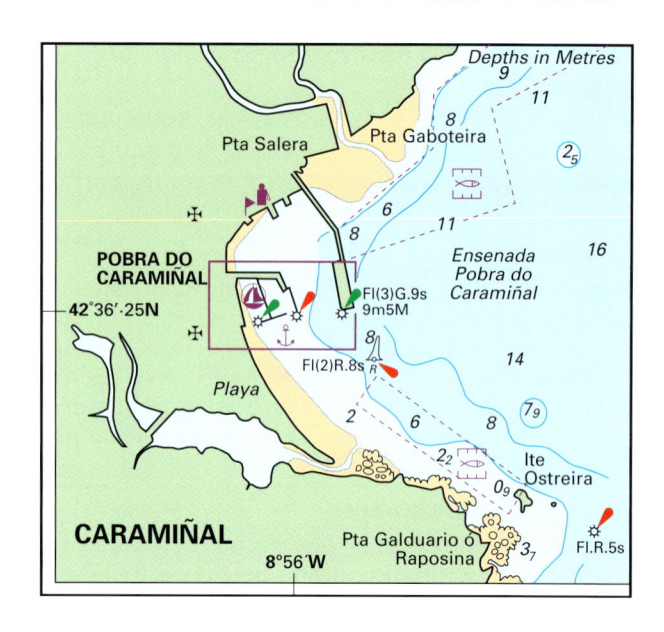

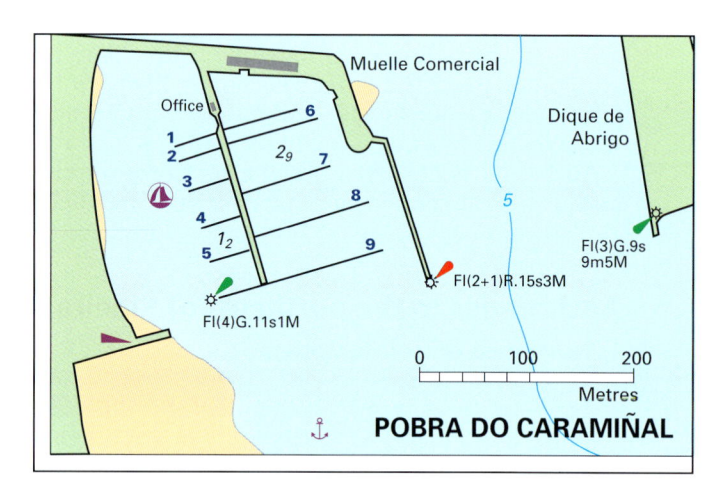

Otherwise there is a fuel station for cars at about the point stated on the chartlet with an additional pump for vessels. However, this is up against a wall and involves climbing a ladder as there is no pontoon. A tidal gauge at the site would suggest that access is restricted at low water.

The town is vibrant and there are evening street markets. There is an excellent fresh produce market. There are two excellent supermarkets (Gadis and Eroski) in the refurbished building overlooking the anchorage.

Alternative anchorage

Southeast of Pobra towards Islote Ostreira inside the *viveros* in 3–5m.

Rowing for Glory, Pobra Do Caramiñal *Geraldine Hennigan*

POBRA DO CARAMIÑAL

Pobra do Caramiñal. Works yard, including travel-lift and chandlery, is on the northern quay

Marina from the outer breakwater across a mussel boat inbound from a day at the *viveros Martin Walker*

GALICIA

ATLANTIC SPAIN AND PORTUGAL

CABO FISTERRA (FINISTERRE) TO ISLA ONS

Puerto de Cruz

Location
42°36'·89N 08°53'·43W

Tides
Standard port Lisbon
Mean time differences (at Vilagarcía)
HW +0050 ±0015; LW +0115 ±0005
(the above allows for the difference in time zones)
Heights in metres

MHWS	MHWN	MLWN	MLWS
3·5	2·8	1·3	0·5

Light
Breakwater beacon Fl(2)G.4s1M White and green round tower

Communications
Club Nautico de Boiro - Marina Cabo de Cruz
Ensenada de Corbiño S/N Boiro, Cabo de Cruz 15939
A Coruña, Spain
VHF Ch 09 ☎ +34 622 884 846
Email info@nauticoboiro.com www.nauticoboiro.com

A busy fishing harbour with a young marina

A fishing village in an attractive setting with harbour moles enclosing a large harbour outside the original one. Puerto de Cruz remains dedicated to the fishing industry but a marina has been built in the northern part of this outer harbour.

The harbour gives shelter from all winds while the open bays to the southeast provide shelter from west through north to east. The village depends on the cultivation and canning of mussels for its livelihood, and there are many *viveros* close offshore.

Approach

There is much foul ground to the southeast of Cabo Cruz, and the safe approach lies west of the distinctive humped Isla Benencia (about 0·7M southeast of Cabo Cruz), 16m high with a rocky ridge and a reef extending south-southwest from its southern tip.

Head north up the ría keeping west of Isla Benencia. Entry to the harbour complex is from the west.

82 ATLANTIC SPAIN AND PORTUGAL

PUERTO DE CRUZ

Puerto de Cruz - the marina is to port on entry

Club Nautico Marina Cabo de Cruz *Geraldine Hennigan*

Caution
There is a wave breaker extending south from the inner end of the northern breakwater.

Berthing
200 berths, including 30 for visitors, from 6 to 22m. Depth in the marina 2m to 5m. Water and electricity on pontoons. Video surveillance service 24/7 and magnetic card access to the pontoons.

Facilities
Showers and WC, laundry, fuel, WiFi, restaurant, bicycle rental.

The village has a small supermarket, restaurants and a bank.

Alternative anchorages

Northwest of Cabo Cruz
Playa Barrana (Escarabote)
42° 38'·18N 08° 53'·82W
(see plan page 76 but use chart 1764)

Holding is good in 3m over mud and sand. The bay is exposed from the southeast through to southwest although a line of viveros offshore lend added shelter. A temporary alongside berth may be available on the long outer pontoon at the harbour. Small yachts might anchor near the harbour mouth.

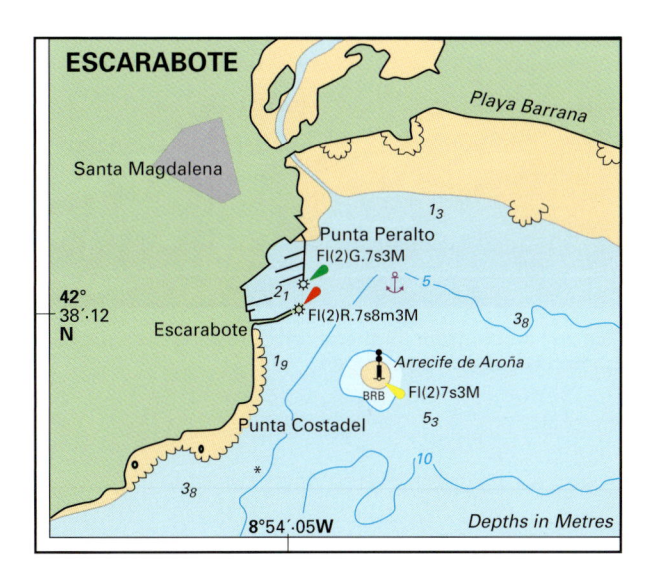

East of Cabo Cruz

1. **South Bay** 42°36'·74N 08°53'·05W
   Anchor in the centre of the bay clear of the fishing boat moorings in 5m over sand and weed, exposed to southeast round to southwest. There are rocks in the eastern part of the bay off Punta Pineirón.

2. **Playa de Carregeros** 42°36'·38N 08°52'·55
   Anchor in the angle between the southeast end of the beach and Isla Benencia with its associated reef, in 2–3m over sand. There is reasonable clearance between the island and an isolated half-tide rock to the northeast, but approach should only be made in flat conditions and good light. The reef (largely exposed at low tide) and the closely-packed viveros give some shelter from the south.

3. **Playa Lobeiro Grande/ Ladeiro do Chazo**
   42°36'·84N 08°51'·29W

4. **Mañons, the bay between Las Hermanas and Punta Ostral** 42°37'·39N 08°51'·045W
   Both 3 and 4 are described as very pleasant, quiet and sheltered spots to anchor.

The long outer pontoon at Escarabote *Geraldine Hennigan*

GALICIA

ATLANTIC SPAIN AND PORTUGAL

CABO FISTERRA (FINISTERRE) TO ISLA ONS

Rianxo (Rianjo)

Location
42°39'·00N 08°49'·40W

Tides
Standard port Lisbon
Mean time differences (at Vilagarcía)
HW +0050 ±0015; LW +0115 ±0005
(the above allows for the difference in time zones)
Heights in metres
MHWS	MHWN	MLWN	MLWS
3·5	2·8	1·3	0·5

Lights
Breakwater elbow Q(9)15s3M ✠ card bn
Entrance beacons Fl(3)G Green pillar
Fl(3)R.11s Metal post

Communications
Club Náutico de Rianxo
☎ +34 981 866 107 Mobile +34 609 833 433
Email info@nauticorianxo.com
www.nauticorianxo.com

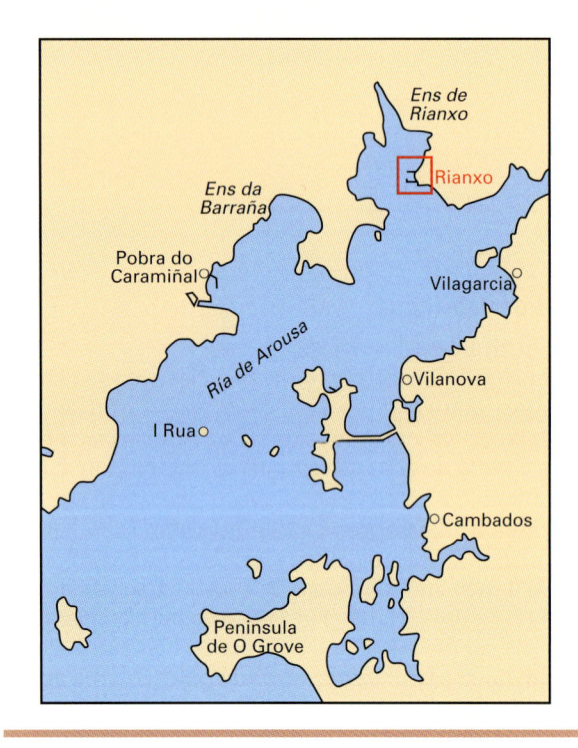

A protected fishing harbour with facilities for yachts

The majority of the harbour remains in active use by the fishing fleet but limited berthing may be available on the yacht pontoons.

A sardine festival is celebrated in June, while in September the week-long fiesta of Santa Maria de Guadaloupe takes place, with entertainment every evening culminating in an all-night event.

The historic town of Padrón lies 16km away by road. Called Iris Flavia by the Romans, it was important in the middle ages and still displays the stone post to which, legend claims, the boat bearing the remains of St James the Great was moored in the headwaters of the ría. The relics were subsequently lost and rediscovered before coming to rest at what is now Santiago de Compostela.

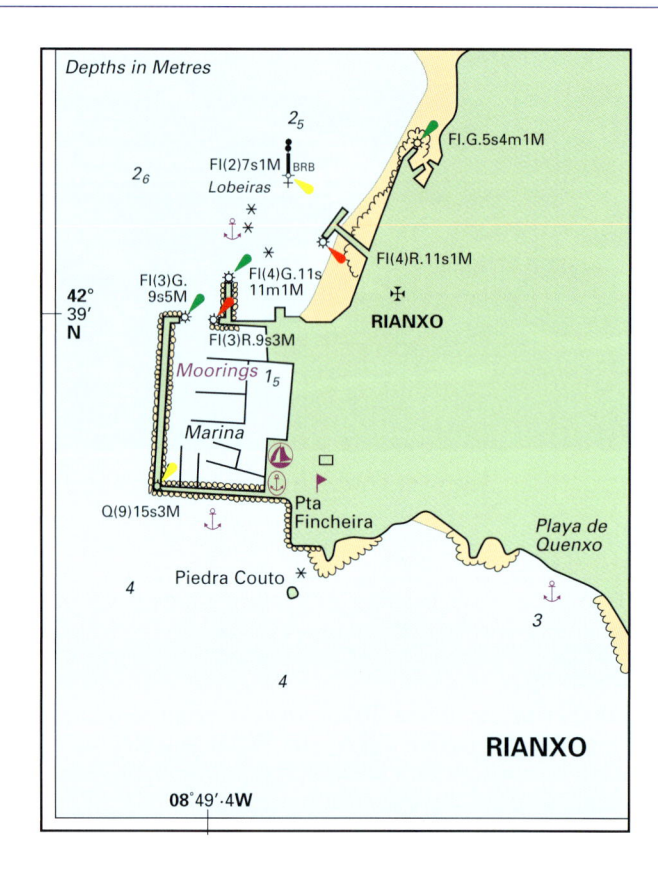

Approach

Come up the centre of the ría and continue past Pta Porta Mouro from where a clear but watchful approach can be made through the mass of *viveros*. Head north and follow the mole around to the entrance on the north side. A west cardinal beacon is on the southwest corner of the harbour.

Rianxo harbour from southeast corner looking over marina pontoons *Geraldine Hennigan*

84   ATLANTIC SPAIN AND PORTUGAL

RIANXO

Rianxo from the south

Berthing and anchorage
Proceed with care on entering harbour as many fishing boats lie to moorings and depths are reported to range from 4–2m. Secure to the marina pontoons and seek advice from the security box at the gangway to the pontoons.

Anchoring is not permitted in the harbour but is possible north of the entrance and west of the Lobeiras rocks.

Facilities
There is adequate technical and domestic support available within, or close to, the harbour and the small club is welcoming. The town offers all the normal facilities of a small town, including a good fish market.

West cardinal beacon on breakwater southwest corner
Martin Walker

GALICIA

ATLANTIC SPAIN AND PORTUGAL

CABO FISTERRA (FINISTERRE) TO ISLA ONS

Vilagarcía (Villagarcía de Arousa)

Location
42°36'·04N 8°46'·20W

Tides
Standard port Lisbon
Mean time differences (at Vilagarcía)
HW +0050 ±0015; LW +0115 ±0005
(the above allows for the difference in time zones)
Heights in metres
MHWS	MHWN	MLWN	MLWS
3·5	2·8	1·3	0·5

Lights
Muelle head Iso.2s2m10M Round masonry tower
Marina entrance beacons 3-sided towers, red and green, flashing Q.R and Q.G

Communications
Marina Vilagarcía
VHF Ch 09 ☎ +34 986 500 088
Email marinavilagarcia@marinavilagarcia.com
www.marinavilagarcia.com www.marinasdegalicia.com

An efficient and welcoming marina

Vilagarcía Marina is self-contained within the arms of the commercial port and is run pleasantly and efficiently by the port authority. The staff are particularly helpful and will arrange lift out, technical support and will also handle travel and hotel services. There is a pleasant Club de Mar on the outer mole. Yachts may safely be left here while visiting Santiago de Compostela or else laid up. Vilagarcía is a good place for crew change or re-provisioning.

Approach

Approach up the centre of the ría. From abeam Isla Rúa follow a track of 030° to clear the northeast hazards of Isla de Arousa and then 075° between the vast *viveros* fields.

Berthing

Do not anchor in the harbour. Call ahead by radio and be prepared to turn immediately to starboard after passing through the narrow marina entrance. Unless ordered to the fuel jetty, expect to secure to finger pontoons (the outer pontoon near the entrance is reported to be untenable in strong northerly winds).

Facilities

Vilagarcía is a good marina with technical support facilities available, a 35-tonne travel lift and a fuel berth for diesel and petrol.

The modern office building includes a restaurant and showers. Weather forecasts are posted daily in the marina office.

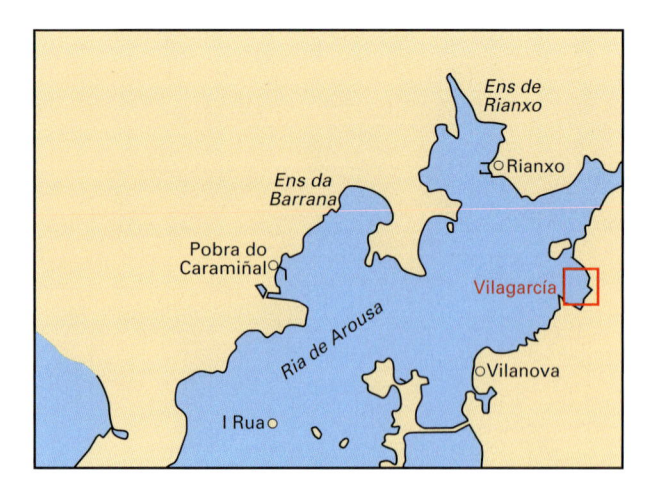

Vilagarcía marina *Martin Walker*

Entrance to Vilagarcía marina *Roddy Innes*

86 ATLANTIC SPAIN AND PORTUGAL

VILAGARCIA

Approach to Vilagarcía Marina (Green buoy, Vilagarcía Marina)

Alternative anchorages

1. **Vilaxoan (Villajuan)** 42°35'·41N 08°47'·47W
   Small fishing harbour southwest of Vilagarcía. (See plan opposite.) It may be possible to anchor in the shelter of the breakwater or moor alongside the inner quay.

2. **South of Carril** 42°36'·7N 08°46'·85W
   Small harbour close north of Vilagarcía. Approach from the southwest and keep clear of the El Porron beacon (yellow lattice metal tower). Keep well clear of the lines of stakes which mark the shell-fish beds. Most are covered at high tide. Their outer limits tend to be marked with a yellow beacon with an x topmark. Anchor south of the Bahia de Tierra beacon (white tower red band). Enter the harbour only by dinghy. Isla Cortegada, and the small islands to the southwest are a National Park (see page 17) and a permit is required before landing to walk around or across the island. There is an excellent, and expensive, fish restaurant close to the harbour.

Vilaxoan looking SE

Carril looking SE. Anchor and take the dinghy to harbour (Bahia de Teierra beacon)

GALICIA

ATLANTIC SPAIN AND PORTUGAL 87

CABO FISTERRA (FINISTERRE) TO ISLA ONS

Vilanova Marina

Location
42°33'·97N 08°50'·04W

Tides
Standard port Lisbon
Mean time differences (at Vilagarcía)
HW +0050 ±0015; LW +0115 ±0005
(the above allows for the difference in time zones)
Heights in metres

MHWS	MHWN	MLWN	MLWS
3·5	2·8	1·3	0·5

Lights
Harbour entrance
Mole heads carry green and white and red and white pillars and lights.

Communications
☎ +34 938 105 611
www.marinaarousa.es

A pleasant modern marina

This is a welcoming marina and has received praise for its helpful attitude and facilities. Known as El Puerto Deportivo de Vilanova de Arousa it is the northern part of the Marina Arousa harbour.

Approaches to Vilanova

From just west of El Seijo green buoy, turn south and follow the passage 1·5M through the *viveros* until Vilanova bears east. Turn to port and head for the main entrance.

Berthing

Visitors' berths for up to 16m yachts are on finger pontoons on the west outer end of the centre pontoon. Larger yachts up to 20m use the three hammerheads. There is water and electricity on the pontoons.

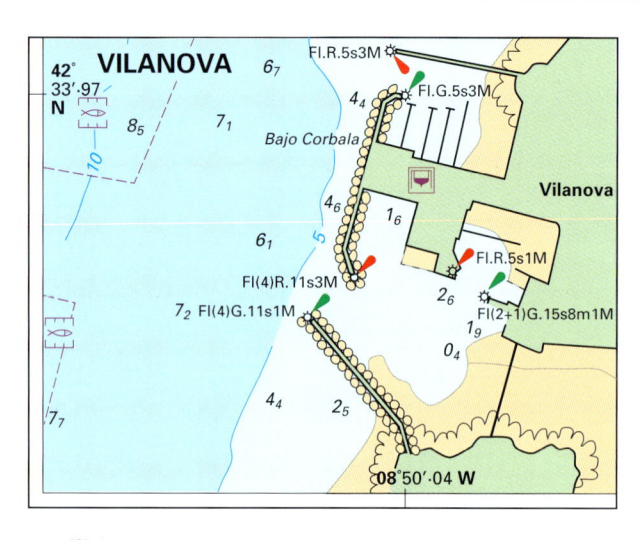

Facilities

A travel-lift (35 tonne) and large lay-up ashore area is available. A fuelling berth is not available.

The marina has a well-stocked chandlery, and engineering and electrical work can be undertaken.

There is a small restaurant on site and good shopping facilities in town, a Friday market and a bus service to Vilagarcia.

Vilanova Marina looking northeast *Geraldine Hennigan*

Vilanova

88   ATLANTIC SPAIN AND PORTUGAL

ISLA DE AROUSA

Isla de Arousa

Location
42°34'N 08°52'W

Tides
Standard port Lisbon
Mean time differences (at Vilagarcía)
HW +0050 ±0015; LW +0115 ±0005
(the above allows for the difference in time zones)
Heights in metres
MHWS	MHWN	MLWN	MLWS
3·5	2·8	1·3	0·5

Boatyard, anchorages, good beaches, dense fishing activity

The Isla de Arousa comprises two islands connected by an isthmus on which the pretty holiday and fishing village of San Xulian (San Julian) sits with its picturesque narrow winding streets. There is a good supermarket south of the pier. It is connected to the mainland by the long El Vado bridge which is conspicuous from the north. The west coast has a number of islets and sections of this coast require very careful navigation. The northern approach is clear until closing the shore. The *viveros* are numerous, as are their support boats, but there are clear routes around and between them.

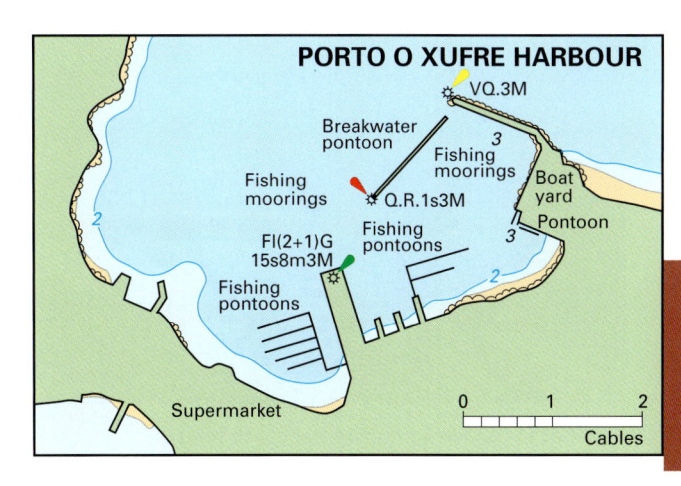

Varadoiro do Xufre boatyard
42°34'·05N 08°51'·9W

The much acclaimed boatyard of Varadoiro do Xufre is at the NE corner of the Ensenada Norte de San Xulian (see plan). The yard's tall shed and tower crane are conspicuous from seaward. There is 3m at LAT all the way in to the yard's working pontoon. The shed has 22m overhead clearance inside. There are no visitor pontoons, just 3 moorings. A family business run by Nito Dieguez, the level of service is outstanding. This is a good place for repair and maintenance, lifting in and out (8 metres max beam) and overwintering, all at attractive prices. The travelhoist can lift 180 tonnes. A courtesy car is available for customers' (self drive) use.

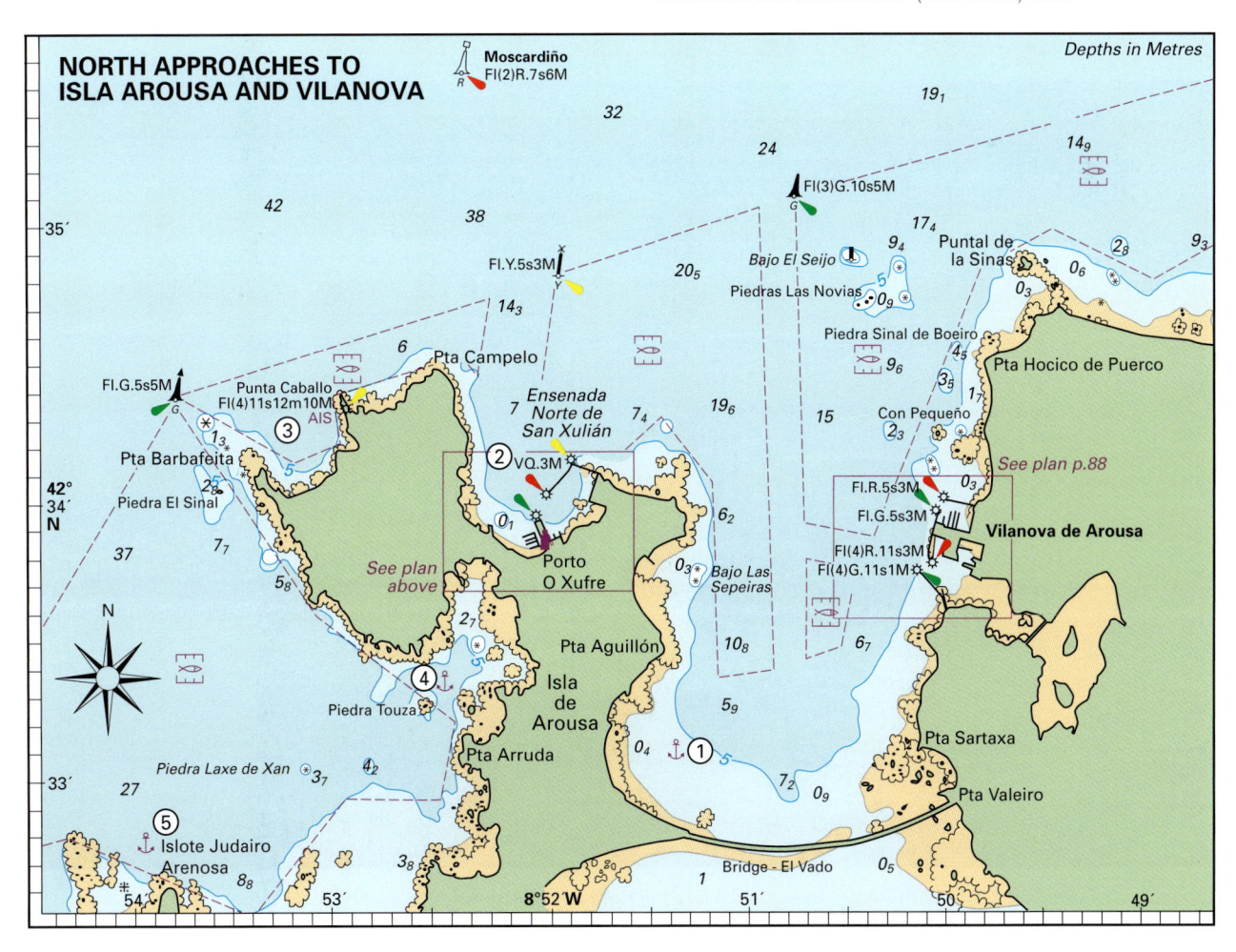

ATLANTIC SPAIN AND PORTUGAL

GALICIA

CABO FISTERRA (FINISTERRE) TO ISLA ONS

Fara de Pta Caballo lighthouse is set back from giant granite rocks *Geraldine Hennigan*

The boatyard at Xufre, Isla de Arosa *Geraldine Hennigan*

Isla de Arousa anchorages

1. The large bay to the north of the bridge between Isla de Arousa and the mainland shoals gradually towards the shores and the bridge. It has fine beaches. Anchor in 2-4m.
2. **Ensenada Norte de San Xulian**
   42°34'·2N 08°52'·1W
   The friendly, bustling little harbour of Porto O Xufre has a small boat marina and many moored fishing boats. Finding space to anchor (in sand/mud/stones) will be difficult. Enquire for a fisherman's mooring; those without pickup lines are generally not in use. Fuel is available on the jetty where sports boats, fishing boats and cars squeeze in as best they can.
3. **Southwest of Pta Caballo off the beach**
   42°34'·15N 08°53'·22W
   A long sandy beach generally clear of the fishing fleet. Approach from the north to anchor in 5–10m clear of the shoreline rocks.
4. **Ensenada Sur de San Xulian**
   42°33'·38N 08°52'·56W
   A small natural harbour, guarded by rocks and filled with small boats. Under good light one might work in and find space to anchor outside the moorings. This is a quiet harbour with shoreside restaurants, and calm compared to the main port just the other-side of the isthmus to the north. There is good shelter except from the southwest. The church carillon of bells ring *Ave Maria* at midday.

Looking east over San Xulian with Anchorages 2 and 4 left and right of the isthmus. The route through the *viveros* to Vilanova – central on the far shore – can be seen. Vilagarcía is at top left

90   ATLANTIC SPAIN AND PORTUGAL

ISLA DE AROUSA

Islote Jidoiro Arenoso anchorage   Geraldine Hennigan

5. **Islote Jidoiro Arenoso**
A lunch stop, but not overnight anchorage, is available in 8-10m, close N and NW of Punta Laño, the N point of Islote Jidoiro Arenoso, with its very conspicuous sandy beach. But beware, the area is rather badly charted. An approach steering SW, with the beacon tower on Bajo La Loba bearing 220° over the rocks, and the island beach kept half a cable to port, leads to the anchorage; but do not venture past the N tip of the island as it shallows very suddenly.

Approaching from Bajo Piedra Seca beacon NW of Pedregoso, stay close to, or between, the numerous viveros to avoid the drying rocks between the beacon and the anchorage.

Looking east over O Grove with Isla Toxa Grande middle right (anchorages beyond) and Cambados at top

ATLANTIC SPAIN AND PORTUGAL   91

CABO FISTERRA (FINISTERRE) TO ISLA ONS

The approach to Cambados, Isla Toxa and O Grove

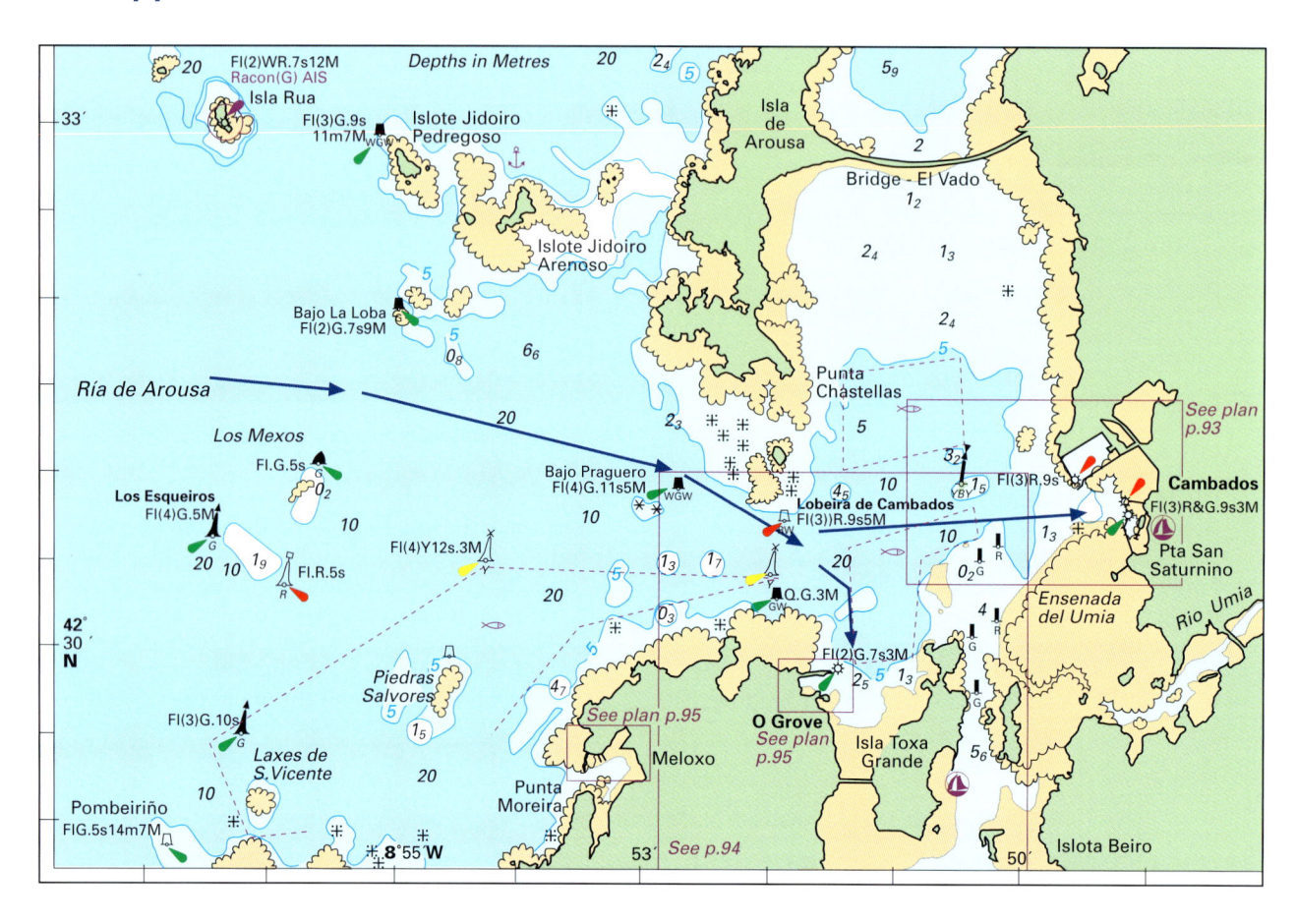

Location
Centred on 42°30'·5N 08°51'·2W

Tides
Standard port Lisbon
Mean time differences (at Vilagarcía)
HW +0050 ±0015; LW +0115 ±0005
(the above allows for the difference in time zones)
Heights in metres
MHWS	MHWN	MLWN	MLWS
3·5	2·8	1·3	0·5

Lights
Bajo La Loba Fl(2)G.7s9m7M Grey truncated conical tower, green top
Bajo Praguero Fl(4)G.11s9m5M White truncated conical tower, green band
Bajo Lobeira de Cambados, Fl(3)R.9s10m5M White truncated conical tower, red top
Bajo Golfeira Q.G.10m3M White truncated conical tower, green top

A chance to stray from the beaten track

O Grove is popular with tourists in season and numerous tripper boats operate from here.

Cambados is a sophisticated old town with limited mooring facilities for yachtsmen.

Toxa (Isla Toxa Grande) is for the smart set and offers pleasant anchorages.

Approach

The area south of Isla de Arousa and north of the Peninsula O Grove and approaching Cambados has numerous shallows, rocks and fields of *viveros*, but it is well marked.

From a point approximately 1·5M south of Isla Rúa, head east and pass midway between La Loba and Los Mexos. Both are clearly marked dangers. Leave Bajos Praguero beacon to starboard and Lobeira de Cambados beacon to port.

For Cambados Track between *viveros* on about 075° towards the breakwater, leaving 1·5m shoal patch marked by a W cardinal, to port.

For the Toxa anchorages head almost to Cambados before working south through the shallows.

For O Grove from Lobeira de Cambados beacon Head southeast to the line of *viveros* which run down to O Grove harbour. Do not cut the corner, rocks protrude well beyond the line between Golfeira and the harbour.

ATLANTIC SPAIN AND PORTUGAL

CAMBADOS

Cambados (Puerto de Tragove and Cambados old harbour)

(See also plan page 76)

Location
42°30'·91N 08°49'·58W

Tides
Standard port Lisbon
Mean time differences (at Vilagarcía)
HW +0050 ±0015; LW +0115 ±0005
(the above allows for the difference in time zones)
Heights in metres
MHWS	MHWN	MLWN	MLWS
3·5	2·8	1·3	0·5

Light
Breakwater Fl(3)G.9s Green round tower

Attractive old town, shallow harbours

The modern harbour (Puerto de Tragove) is large but shallow and supports the major mussel industry. The old harbour (Cambados-San Tome) is small and shallow but has fuel.

Cambados is a small town with an attractive and historic central square and imposing buildings. It is the home of O Albariño, considered by many to be Galicia's best wine. A *sardiñada* (sardine festival) is held on 25 July (Galicia Day) and a wine festival on the first Sunday in August.

Approach
See page 92.

Anchorage and berthing

Main Harbour (Tragove Marina) The harbour shallows rapidly from the major fishing boat pontoon. Only the outer sides of the yacht pontoon should be considered; inside is very rocky. Lying to anchor, facing the harbour mouth, with stern to the pontoon offers greatest depth. Anchoring may be possible behind the fishing boats depending on the random moorings and the busy boat traffic.

Old Harbour (Cambados Marina) This is small, attractive harbour, well placed for the town but now (2017) has less than 1 metre due to silting. Approach and enter with caution, and check at the fuel dock for mooring opportunities. A yacht drawing 1·8m would be able to lie alongside a fishing boat just beyond the fuel berth, at neaps.

Cambados Marina. Fuel dock to starboard
Geraldine Hennigan

Cambados harbours from the west

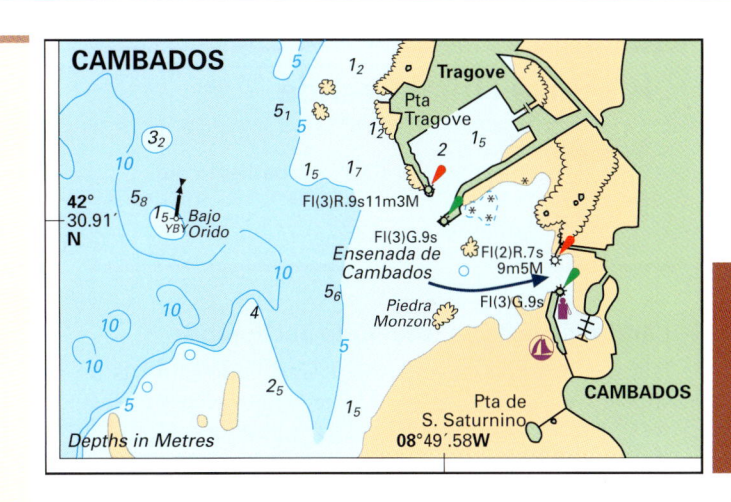

GALICIA

ATLANTIC SPAIN AND PORTUGAL   93

CABO FISTERRA (FINISTERRE) TO ISLA ONS

Isla Toxa (Toja) Grande

Warning
Silting has been reported in the approaches to the anchorages

Careful navigation leading to anchorages

Isla Toxa Grande is south of Cambados and is a smart, well groomed island. The bridge access to the west crosses over drying sands; the anchorages all lie to the east.

Approach to anchorages (and berthing)

Warning The routes across sandbanks should only be made on a rising tide. Viveros may well impede the route.

From Cambados From Cambados harbour head southwest for 0·4M into deeper water before tracking south for 0·25M to the east of the Meana del Norte rocky shoal. Then track 0·3M on 240° before turning south through the passage between Isla Toxa Grande and Isla Toxa Pequeña.

Eyeball the route to avoid shallows and kelp. There were unlit red and green boys reported laid here in 2018 indicating a channel. These are thought to start at the East end of the viveiro area to the northeast of Punta Cabreiròn. Anchor in 3–5m over sand where indicated in the chartlet.

New pontoons (2018) have been added to the Club Nautico Isla de la Toja (CNIT) jetty where it may be possible to berth (42°29'·3/N 08°50'·55W) ☏+34 986 960 726 www.clubnauticoisladelatoja.es.

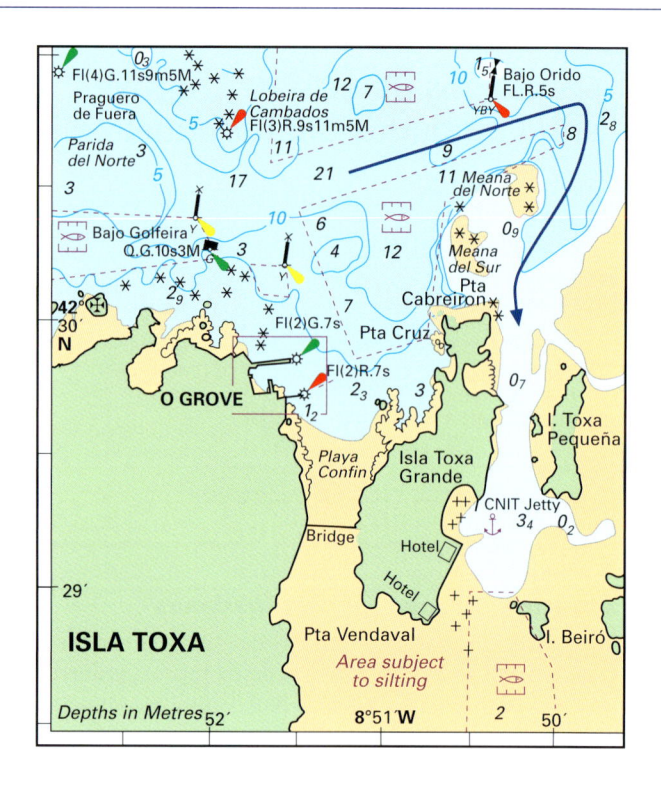

From just south of Lobeira de Cambados Make a course of approximately 107° for 1·25M to pass between the Meana del Sur rocky shoal and Pta Cabreiron. Again, eyeball the route to avoid shallows and kelp. On no account attempt to pass inside the rock off Pta Cabreiron. Then turn south, as above, through the passage between Isla Toxa Grande and Isla Toxa Pequeña for the anchorages and CNIT jetty.

Anchorages of Isla Grande Toxa – O Grove at top left
Inset Showing extension to Club Nautico Isla de la Toja (CNIT) jetty

94   ATLANTIC SPAIN AND PORTUGAL

ISLA TOXA AND PUERTO O GROVE

Puerto O Grove (San Martin del Grove)

(See photo page 91)

Location
42°29'·88N 08°51'·52W

Tides
Standard port Lisbon
Mean time differences (at Vilagarcía)
HW +0050 ±0015; LW +0115 ±0005
(the above allows for the difference in time zones)
Heights in metres

MHWS	MHWN	MLWN	MLWS
3·5	2·8	1·3	0·5

Light
Breakwater Fl(2)G.7s Green round tower

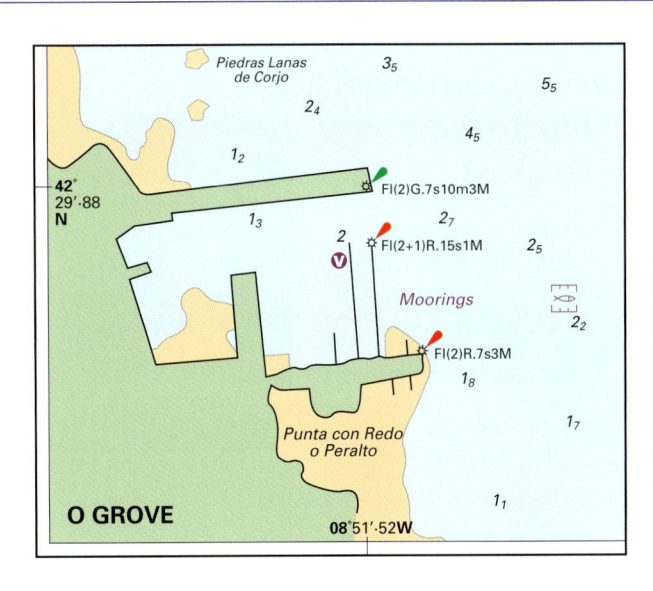

A shallow fishing and tripper boat harbour

O Grove is a major holiday resort and the shallow fishing harbour has been developed for fast tripper boats to visit the offlying islands.

Mooring and anchorage

There is a small pontoon within the harbour or berth alongside the north breakwater. There is little room for shallow-draught boats to anchor in the harbour itself, and very limited space outside as the water shoals rapidly immediately south of the harbour. Pick up a mooring buoy outside the harbour but do not leave the boat unattended for long.

Facilities

Water on the quay, usual shops and many restaurants. A seafood festival takes place at O Grove on 14 September.

Porto de Meloxo (Melojo) 42°29'·32N 08°53'·51W

(Breakwater end with red light) is a fishing harbour on the west side of the northern arm of Peninsula O Grove. It is exposed to the west. The harbour is full of fishing boats on moorings. It might be possible to negotiate to borrow a mooring or anchor outside, although the harbour and the small village appears to have little to offer the yachtsman.

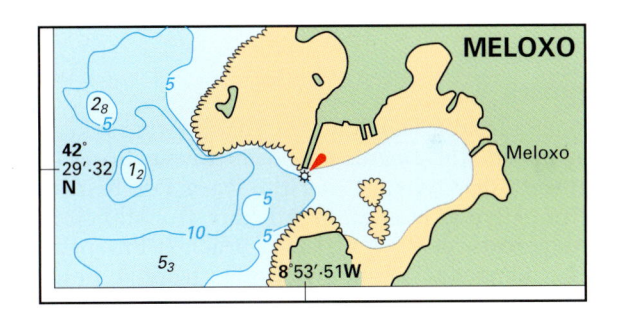

Meloxo is devoted to the fishing fleet *Martin Walker*

ATLANTIC SPAIN AND PORTUGAL   95

CABO FISTERRA (FINISTERRE) TO ISLA ONS

San Vicente del Mar (Porto Piedras Negras)

Location
42°27'·47N 08°55'·06W

Tides
Standard port Lisbon
Mean time differences (at Vilagarcía)
HW +0050 ±0015; LW +0115 ±0005
(the above allows for the difference in time zones)
Heights in metres

MHWS	MHWN	MLWN	MLWS
3·5	2·8	1·3	0·5

Lights
Breakwater beacon Fl(4)WR.11s5m4/3M Red post
Approach buoys Fl(2)G.9s Green buoy
Fl(3)R.9s Red buoy

Communications
VHF Ch 09 ☎ Office +34 986 738 325
Marineros +34 986 738 430
Email administracion@cnsvicente.org
www.cnsvicente.org

A small, smart marina with good facilities

There is little outside the marina except houses, hotels and a small supermarket. This is a place to relax, enjoy the stunning walk to Pta Miranda or visit the beach.

Approach

If coming from Carol Principal, Ría de Arousa, keep clear outside the *viveros* of the northwest shores of Peninsula de O Grove and the Roca Pombeirino beacon. Keep at least 800m offshore around before heading towards the long sandy beach at Ensenada de La Lanzada. Punta Muranda, from a point midway the red and green buoys Peda Seca and Siral de Balea, head direct to the harbour.

Caution

An uncharted rock exists in the Ensenada de la Lanzada 0·35m ENE of the breakwater end at Piedras Negras (San Vicente). It is more or less on the low water mark of a beach charted as uniformly sandy. Be very cautious of those dark patches of weed on the bottom. Some of them are made of granite.

Berthing and anchoring

There are 134 berths, 10 reserved for visitors for boats 6-12m in 4m depth.

The pontoons are very small for a 12m yacht, otherwise anchor off the beach as close to the rocks as you dare.

Facilities

Electricity and Water on the pontoons. Fuel available, good showers, a small bread shop and supermarket. WiFi - ask at the Yacht Club.

The Board Walk going north is a must with many cafes and restaurants plus the benefit of coves and sandy beaches.

San Vicente from the south

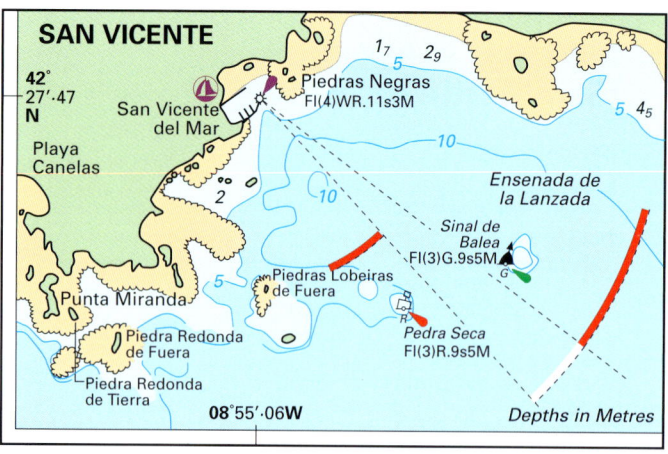

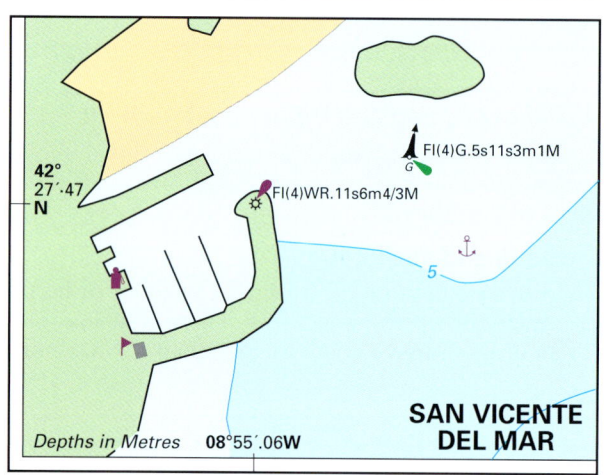

Pedras Negras harbour looking southwest *Geraldine Hennigan*

96 ATLANTIC SPAIN AND PORTUGAL

SAN VICENTE DEL MAR

Santiago de Compostela

The airport at Santiago de Compostela is useful for crew changes in Galicia, but the city is a delight to visit in its own right.

The cathedral holds the shrine of the apostle Saint James the Great which is the focus of a network of pilgrims' ways or pilgrimages known as the Camino de Santiago. The pilgrimage to Santiago has never ceased from the time of the discovery of St. James' remains in 812 AD, and many today follow its routes as a form of spiritual path or retreat for their spiritual growth.

The main pilgrimage route to Santiago follows an earlier Roman trade route, which continues to the Atlantic coast of Galicia, ending at Cabo Fisterra (Finisterre).

The fiesta of St James (celebrated throughout the province on Galicia Day) takes place on 25 July with associated cultural events for a week or so on either side.

The Cathedral at Santiago de Compostela *Henry Buchanan*

St Jean Pied de Port, a key stop on the pilgrims route to Santiago *Henry Buchanan*

The dedicated end the Camino at Cabo Fisterra (Finisterre) *Henry Buchanan*

GALICIA

ATLANTIC SPAIN AND PORTUGAL

ISLA ONS TO THE PORTUGUESE BORDER

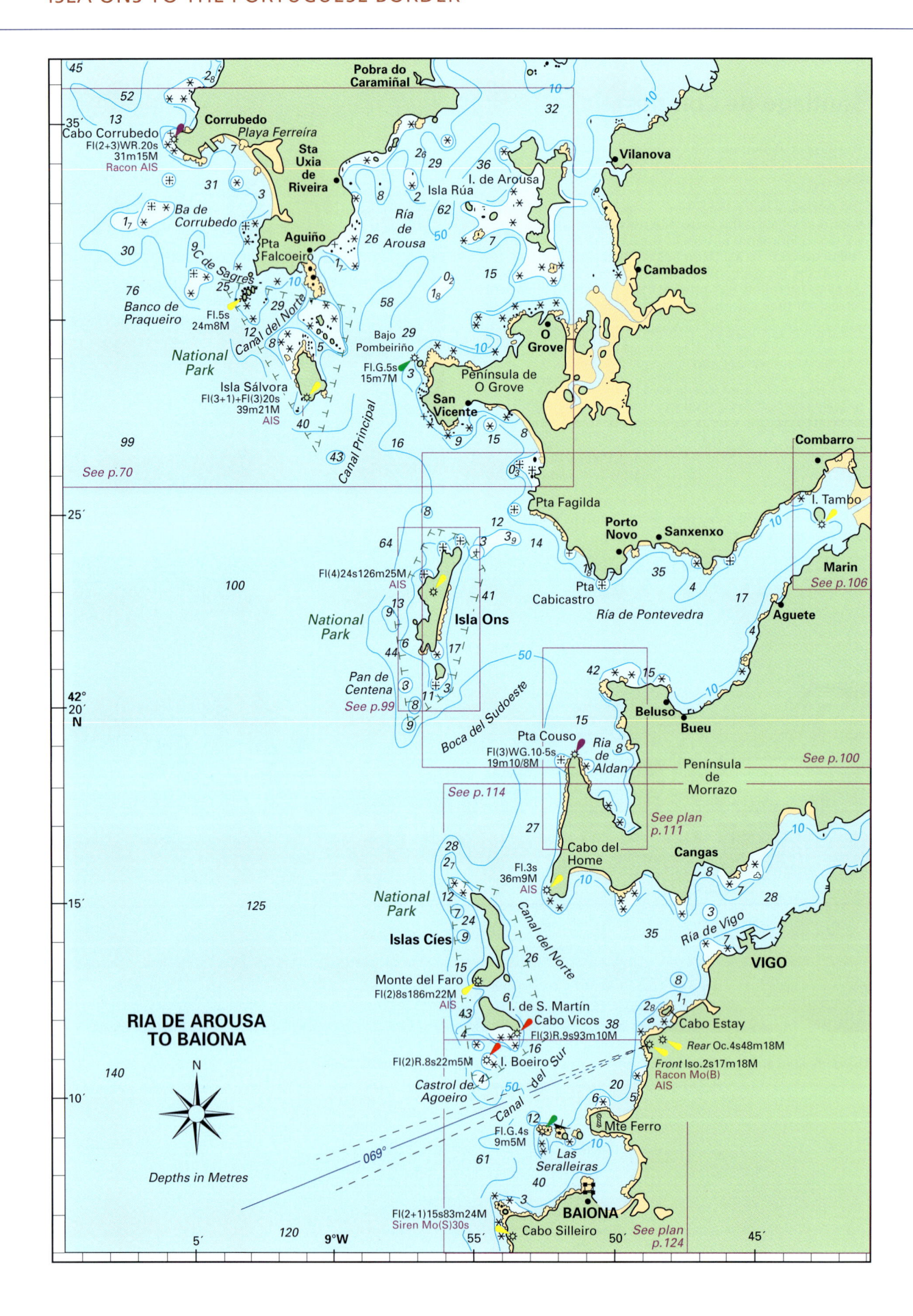

98 ATLANTIC SPAIN AND PORTUGAL

Isla Ons, Ría de Pontevedra to Islas Cies

Isla Ons

See pages 15–17
Location
42°22'·62N 08°55'·77W
Communications
See Notes on National Parks' Permits p15
Lights
Isla Sálvora Fl(3+1)20s39m21M White 8-sided tower, red band
Isla Ons Fl(4)24s126m25M 8-sided white tower on corner of building
Monte del Faro Fl(2)8s185m22M Tower and dwelling
Cabo Silleiro Fl(2+1)15s83m24M White 8-sided tower, red bands on white dwelling

National Park, limited anchorages

Visiting yachts require a permit to visit, anchor or dive around Isla Ons – see page 15 – National Parks' Permits.

Isla Ons helps protect the Ría de Pontevedra from westerly seas and winds. It is a rugged and attractive island with few permanent inhabitants. It is much visited by campers in the summer, tripper boats from Ría de Arousa and Ría de Pontevedra, and regular ferries from Porto Novo, Sanxenxo and Marin. All land at Almacén. Shelter is limited on the east coast which offers the only normal anchorages. Landing is forbidden on the small southern island of Onza (Onceta) which is a bird sanctuary.

Approach
See Ría de Pontevedra page 100 and close the island from the east.

Anchorages
Anchorages should be vacated if the wind gains an easterly component.

1. **Almacén** 42°22'·62N 08°55'·77W
   The mole at Almacén is not a good place to lie. There is little room and frequent ferries. Just north of the mole are 13 blue visitor buoys and 3 red buoys. Some buoys may have dragged as some spaces are barely sufficient for a 10m yacht. These buoys tend to become vacant after 1800. South of the mole are 3 yellow buoys, probably for the use of ferries.

   If picking up a blue buoy and requiring a lift ashore Hostal Casa Checho can be contacted on ☏+34 629 71 81 04 or +34 639 56 35 72. This is the first restaurant on the left when stepping ashore. At the head of the slip is a tourist office and 500m beyond a first aid station. There is a campsite at Almacén.

   Reefs extend north and south of the entrance but it is possible to anchor east-northeast of the mole head in 12m or more over rock and weed.

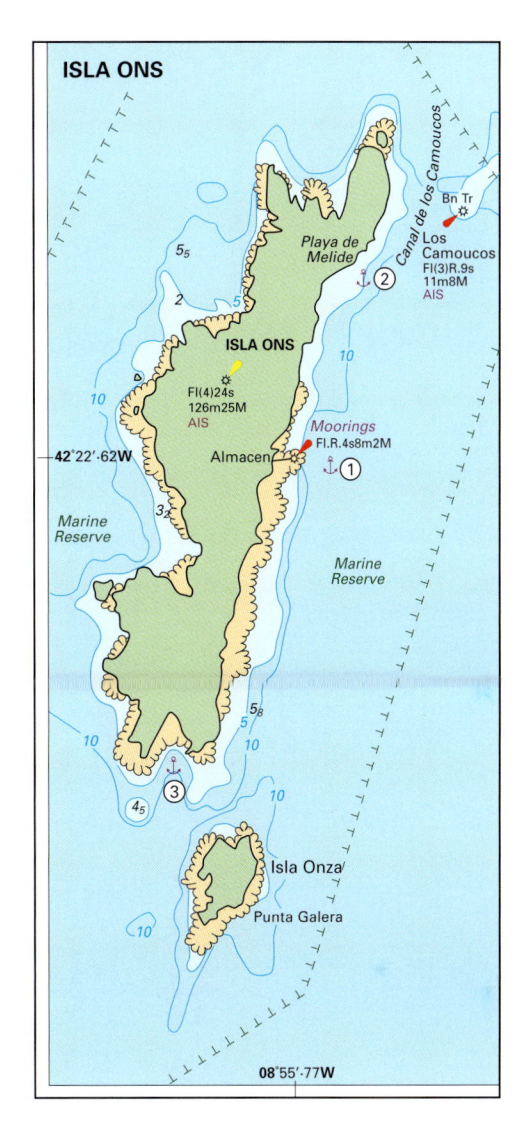

2. **Playa de Melide** 42°23'·33N 08°55'·43W
   The beach is about 1M north of Almacén mole. Anchor in 4m over sand, rock and weed. The anchorage is sheltered from north through west to southwest. The beach is favoured by nudists.

3. **Southern Bay** 42°21'·23N 08°56'·47W
   A short stay possibility in a light northerly is the small bay between Punta Fedoranto and Punta Rab d'Egua on the south coast.

Isla Ons E coast Almacén just in view   William and Sarah Maltby

ISLA ONS TO THE PORTUGUESE BORDER

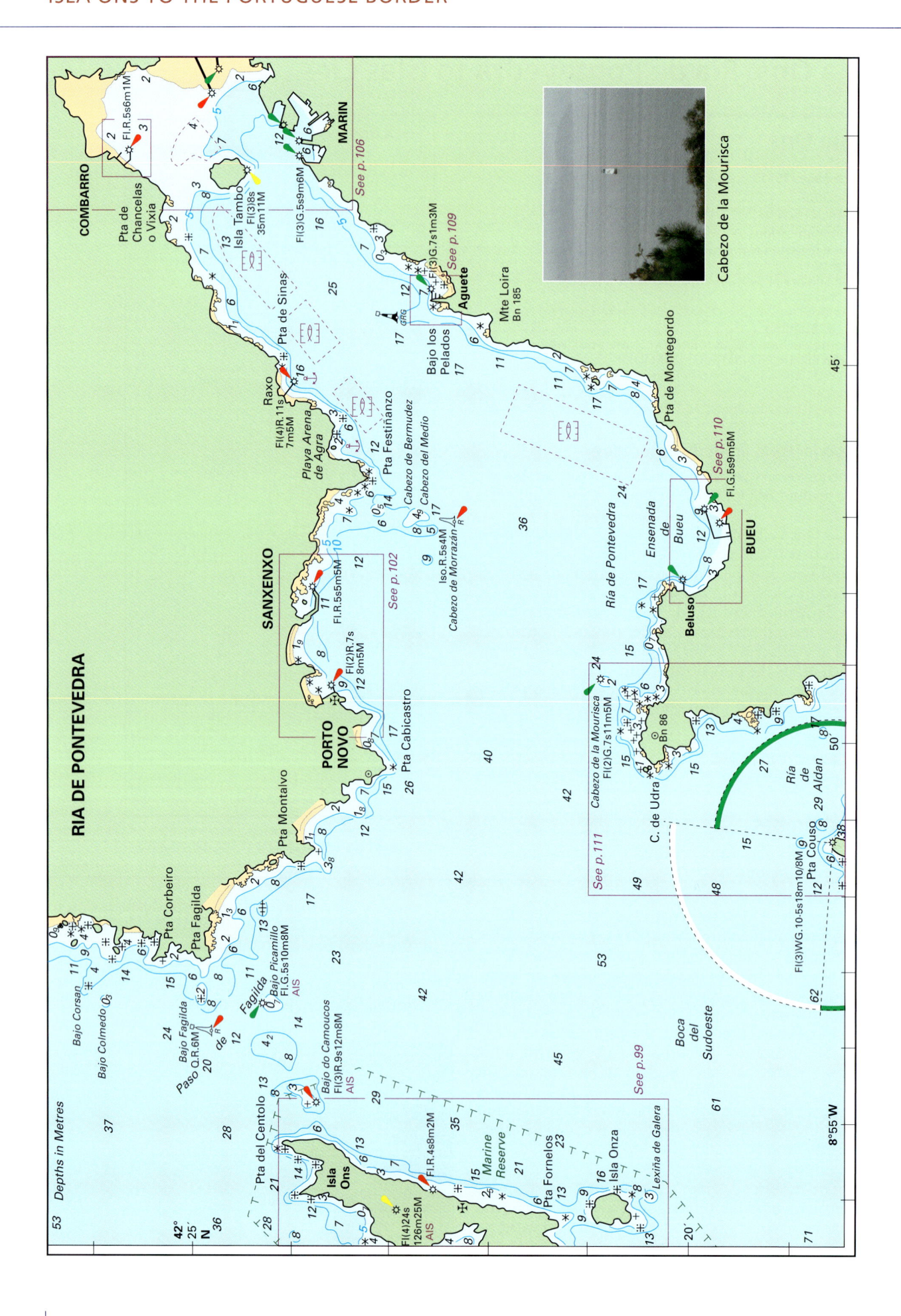

RÍA DE PONTEVEDRA

Approaches to Ría de Pontevedra

Location
42°22'N 08°53'W

Tides
Standard port Lisbon
Mean time differences (at Marín)
HW +0100 ±0010; LW +0125 ±0005
(the above allows for the difference in time zones)
Heights in metres
MHWS	MHWN	MLWN	MLWS
3·3	2·6	1·2	0·5

Coastguard
Vigo ☎ +34 981 297 403
Sea Rescue Service ☎ +34 900 202 202
MRCC Finisterre Ch 11
MRSC Vigo Ch 10

Navtex
518kHz (D) at 0030, 0730, 0830*1230, 1630, 2030*
(*weather only)

Weather bulletins VHF
Vigo Ch 65 at 0840, 1240, 2010
MRSC Vigo Ch 10 at 0015, 0415, 0815, 1215, 1615, 2015

Navigational warnings VHF
Vigo Ch 65 at 0840, 2010
MRSC Ch 10 at 0215, 0615, 1015, 1415, 1815, 2215

Primary working freqs
c/s Coruña Radio
Vigo Manual Ch 65
Autolink Ch 62 Tx 2596 Rx 3280
DSC Ch 70 2187·5kHz

Lights (opposite page)
Isla Ons Fl(4)24s126m25M 8-sided white tower on corner of building
Los Camoucos Fl(3)R.9s11m8M Red and white tower
Bajo Picamillo Fl.G.5s10m8M Green and white tower
Isla Tambo Fl(3)8s34m11M Round tower, on truncated conical base
Bajo Cabezo de la Mourisca Fl(2)G.7s11m5M Green and white tower
Punta Couso Fl(3)WG.10·5s19m10/8M White truncated conical tower, green top

A ría much developed in recent years

The fast road to Sanxenxo continues to bring development in its wake, both with tourism and the upgrading of harbour facilities. These include Porto Novo, Sanxenxo which is a major marina and Combarro, on the northern shore towards the head of the ría. This attractive old village is worth visiting by sea or land, preferably for a leisurely lunch in one of its numerous restaurants. Pontevedra itself lies upriver and is reachable only by small yacht. The Spanish Naval College has its home and marina at Marin but this is not open to visiting yachts.

Approach

From the north or Ría de Arousa approach through Paso de Fagilda marked by a red buoy Bajo Fagilda in the north and a beacon on Bajo Picamillo in the south.

From the southwest The main channel is through Boca del Sudoeste between Isla Ons and the mainland.

From the south and Ría de Vigo is through Canal del Norte between Islas Cíes and the mainland.

Note The entrance to the ría proper lies between the unmarked Punta Cabicastro, which has a rock off it, and Cabo de Udra which is surrounded by foul ground (see plan opposite).

Caution

A storm in February 2017 destroyed the beacon that was marking Bajo Picamillo. In March 2017 a green lattice buoy with radar reflector and a light was stationed 250m ENE of the rock. The light has a range of 8M and height of 5m. The rock itself is now marked by a virtual AIS beacon.

GALICIA

Approach to Ría de Pontevedra from the north with Punta Fagilda left

ATLANTIC SPAIN AND PORTUGAL

ISLA ONS TO THE PORTUGUESE BORDER

Approach to Porto Novo and Sanxenxo

Location
42°23'·5N 08°48'·7W (between ports)

Tides
Standard port Lisbon
Mean time differences (at Marín)
HW +0100 ±0010; LW +0125 ±0005
(the above allows for the difference in time zones)
Heights in metres
MHWS	MHWN	MLWN	MLWS
3·3	2·6	1·2	0·5

Marinas in a major holiday area

The VRG (Via Rapida Galicia) connects the Sanxenxo area to the main Motorway Atlantic and the cities of Santiago de Compostela and the rest of Galicia. Holidaymakers and business firms pour down this road making this part of Galicia both thriving and developing. The yachtsman can now choose between seeking space at the club marina of Port Novo, making use of the vast Sanxenxo marina or anchoring in between them off Playa de Silgar.

Approach

Approach from the west or south is straightforward, giving headlands an offing of at least 200m. From the east, shallows extend up to 600m southwest off Pta Festiñanzo towards the Cabezo de Morrazan port hand buoy. In settled weather and good visibility a yacht may safely pass about midway between the buoy and the shore.

Be aware of the ferries, to the ría and the outlying islands, which operate from a small pontoon on the very end of the main breakwater at Sanxenxo.

Playa Silgar anchorage between Porto Novo and Sanxenxo
Martin Walker

Looking west over Sanxenxo and Playa de Silgar beyond

102 ATLANTIC SPAIN AND PORTUGAL

PORTO NOVO

Porto Novo

Location
42°23'·64N 08°49'·12W

Tides
Standard port Lisbon
Mean time differences (at Marín)
HW +0100 ±0010; LW +0125 ±0005
(the above allows for the difference in time zones)
Heights in metres
MHWS	MHWN	MLWN	MLWS
3·3	2·6	1·2	0·5

Light
Marina breakwater beacon Fl(3)R.7s3M Red tower

Communications
Club Nautico Portonovo
VHF Ch 09 ☏ +34 986 723 266
www.nauticoportonovo.com
Email administracion@nauticoportonovo.com

Attractive fishing harbour with club marina

Porto Novo is a fishing village and holiday resort with an easy approach.

The Club Náutico de Portonovo has a small club house with a restaurant and bar, with facilities at the end of the inner quay from which sprout the boat pontoons.

Approach
See pages 98 and 100.

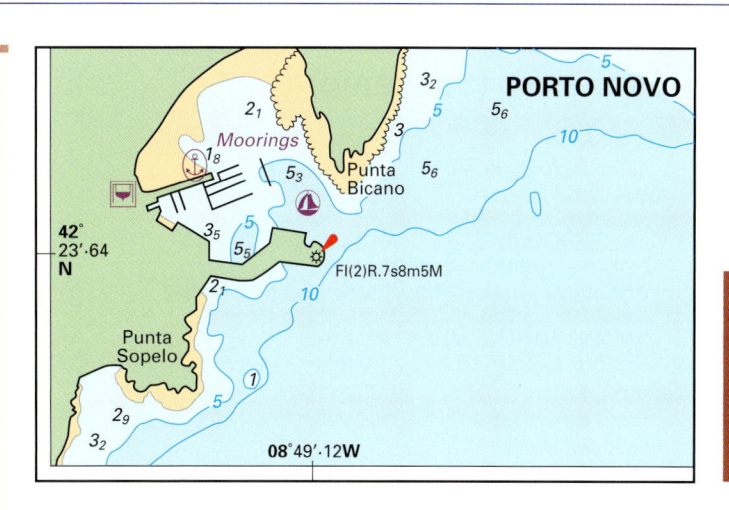

Berthing
There are 106 Club Náutico berths on finger pontoons for vessels of 6 to 20m with maximum draught 4m. On arrival, secure to an outer pontoon and seek a berth. There is no anchoring in the harbour.

Facilities
Porto Novo has a new (2017) floating breakwater which protects the marina from E and SE. This has considerably improved comfort on the outer hammerheads.

Electricity and water on the pontoons, 110-tonne travel-lift. Showers and laundry, WiFi, bar and restaurants.

Nearby are further bars and restaurants, shops and a supermarket and a fine beach.

The new breakwater at Porto Novo
Geraldine Hennigan

Porto Novo from southeast

GALICIA

ATLANTIC SPAIN AND PORTUGAL 103

ISLA ONS TO THE PORTUGUESE BORDER

Sanxenxo (Sangenjo)

Location
42°23'·80N 08°48'·06W

Tides
Standard port Lisbon
Mean time differences (at Marín)
HW +0100 ±0010; LW +0125 ±0005
(the above allows for the difference in time zones)
Heights in metres
MHWS	MHWN	MLWN	MLWS
3·3	2·6	1·2	0·5

Light
Breakwater beacon Fl.R.5s Red and white round tower

Communications
Nauta Sanxenxo
Avda. Augusto Gonzalez Besada, s/n 36960 Sanxenxo (Pontevedra)
VHF Ch 09 ☎ +34 986 720 517
Email nauta@sanxenxo.org www.sanxenxo.org
www.marinasdegalicia.com

An easily accessible major marina (pronounced Sanshensho)

Sanxenxo Marina has three main areas: The mole head - with fuel dock, lift, workshops and ferry pontoon. The central quay - orange roofs with the harbour office, domestic facilities, shops and restaurants. The western end - the prominent RCN Club house and a large covered carpark.

Approach
Straightforward – see pages 98–100.

Berthing
The marina has 379 berths to take boats of 8m-44m in length. Water depths vary from 3·5m to 7·5m. Call ahead for a berth, or alternatively proceed between the two parts of the marina towards the central mole and the arrivals pontoon. At crowded times it may be necessary to moor initially along the extended fuel pontoon but it is a very long walk from here to the office marina facilities.

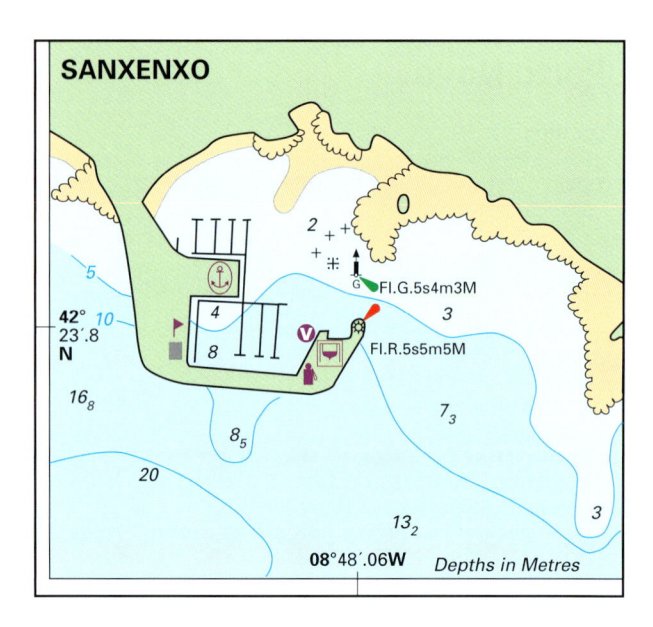

Office hours are 0930 to 1330 and 1600 to 2000. The marina staff are friendly and helpful. Access to the Nauta Sanxenxo pontoons is by key card. Anchoring is not allowed in the harbour.

Facilities
Electricity and water at the berths; fuel berth; 64 tonne travel lift; camping gas; showers; WiFi; shops and numerous restaurants close to the marina. There is a major Froiz supermarket about a mile away at the roundabout leading to the highway out of town.

Anchoring
The anchorage off the Playa de Silgar in the bay between Sanxenxo and Porto Novo has a sandy bottom with good holding. The beach is protected by a line of yellow buoys, but 5m water depth can be found outside. The anchorage is subject to any swell from the southwest.

Sanxenxo fuel dock and technical area *Martin Walker*

104 ATLANTIC SPAIN AND PORTUGAL

SANXENXO

Sanxenxo looking north

Alternative anchorages

1. There is a lovely anchorage off the Playa Arena de Adra (42°23'·56N 08°46'·16W) to the east of Sanxenxo and tucked into the NE of the wooded Punta Festiñanzo. It is well enough charted as long as care is taken close to shore.
2. 2·6M east of Sanxenxo it is also possible to anchor off Raxó. Anchor outside the local boat moorings.

Raxó bay looking NE towards Isla Tambo and Marin *Martin Walker*

GALICIA

ATLANTIC SPAIN AND PORTUGAL

ISLA ONS TO THE PORTUGUESE BORDER

Combarro

Location
42°25'·62N 08°42'·22W

Tides
Standard port Lisbon
Mean time differences (at Marín)
HW +0100 ±0010; LW +0125 ±0005
(the above allows for the difference in time zones)
Heights in metres

MHWS	MHWN	MLWN	MLWS
3·3	2·6	1·2	0·5

Lights
Marina breakwater beacon
Fl(2)R.9s5M Red round tower

Communications
Edificio de Capitania 36993 Combarro – Poio (Pontevedra)
VHF Ch 09, 10
☎ +34 986 778 415 or
+34 607 427 726 (24h)
Mobile +34 695 955 750
Email comercial@combarromar.com
www.combarromar.com

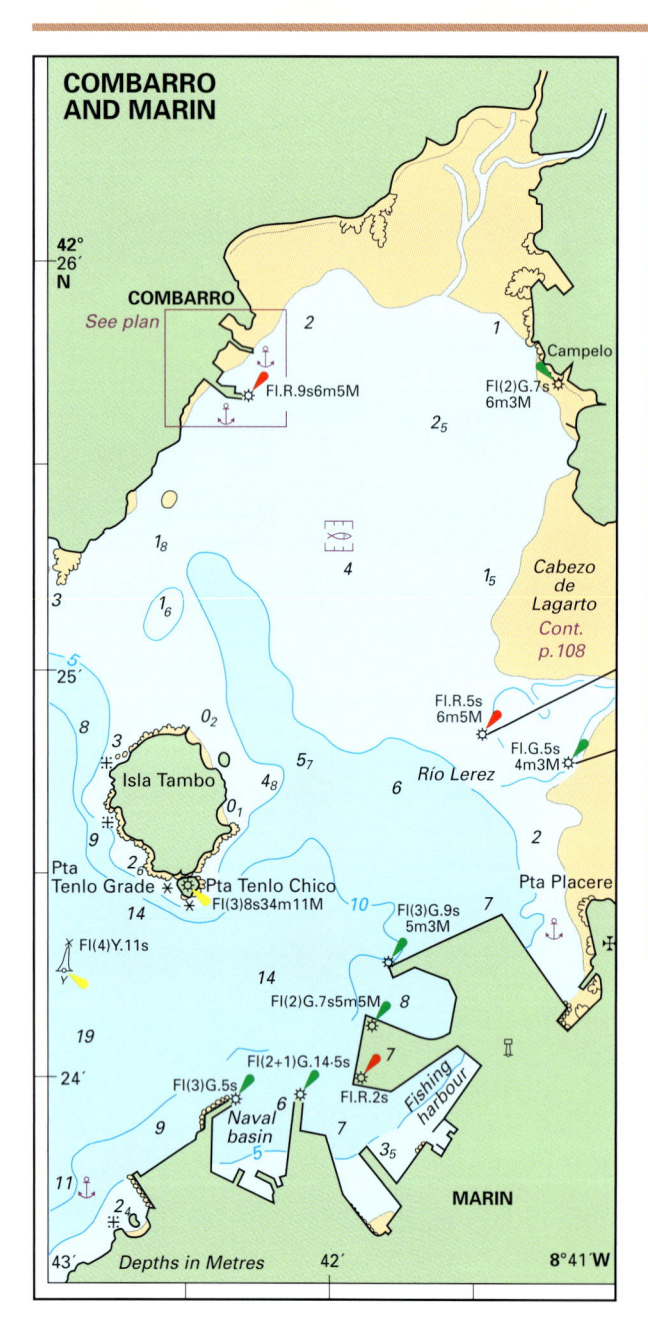

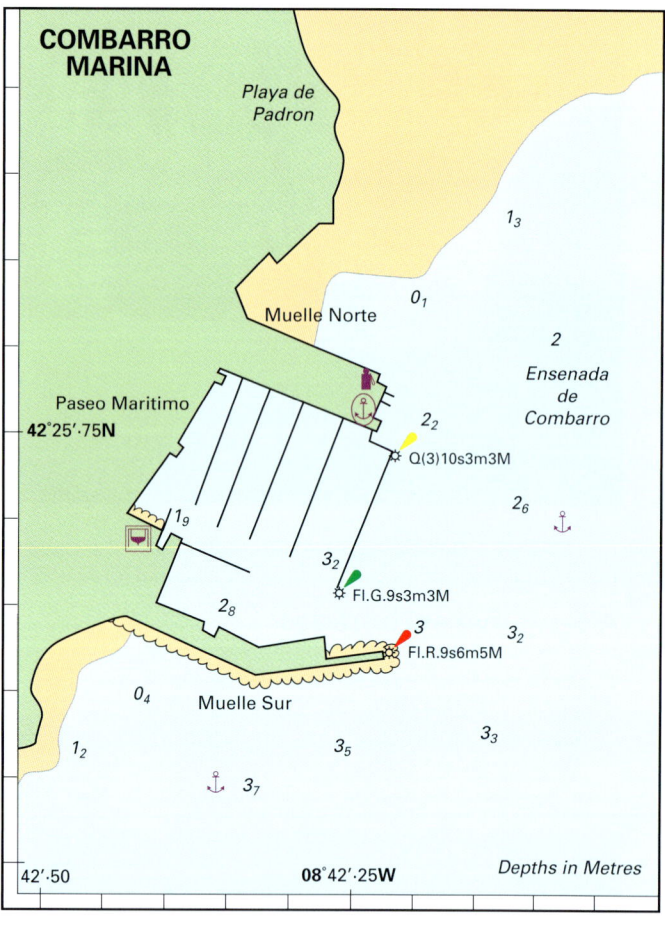

Modern marina, anchorage, gem of a village

It would be a shame to visit this part of Galicia and miss seeing Combarro. This restored old fishing village, of massive granite and surrounded by vineyards, is very picturesque; numerous restaurants serve excellent seafood. In addition to the attractions of the old village, all routine shops are available plus a morning fruit market in the square.

Approach and berthing

The best approach is from east of Isla Tambo around or between the *viveros*. Call VHF Ch 09 for a berth. The marina has 335 berths for boat lengths from 6m to 16m. The maximum water depth of 3m is at the inside of the outer pontoon. Visitors also berth on the outside of this pontoon.

106 ATLANTIC SPAIN AND PORTUGAL

COMBARRO

Left Combarro looking north; haul out, repair and chandlery around top left hard-standing. Red office block has domestic facilities and restaurant. Numerous restaurants from the root of the north quay, around the square and in the old village to the right

Below Approaching Combarro marina looking NW *Jane Russell*

GALICIA

Facilities
Full service marina. Water and electricity at the berths. 50-tonne travel-lift. Fuel and pump-out pontoons are outside the marina alongside the red office building. 24hr security. WiFi.

Small town shopping and numerous restaurants nearby. There is a bus service to Pontevedra.

Anchorage
Anchor off the marina, clear of *vivero* rafts and away from the entrance. Seaweed can be a problem when anchored off, but when dug in holding is good in sand and mud.

Combarro maize stores on waterfront
William and Sarah Maltby

ATLANTIC SPAIN AND PORTUGAL

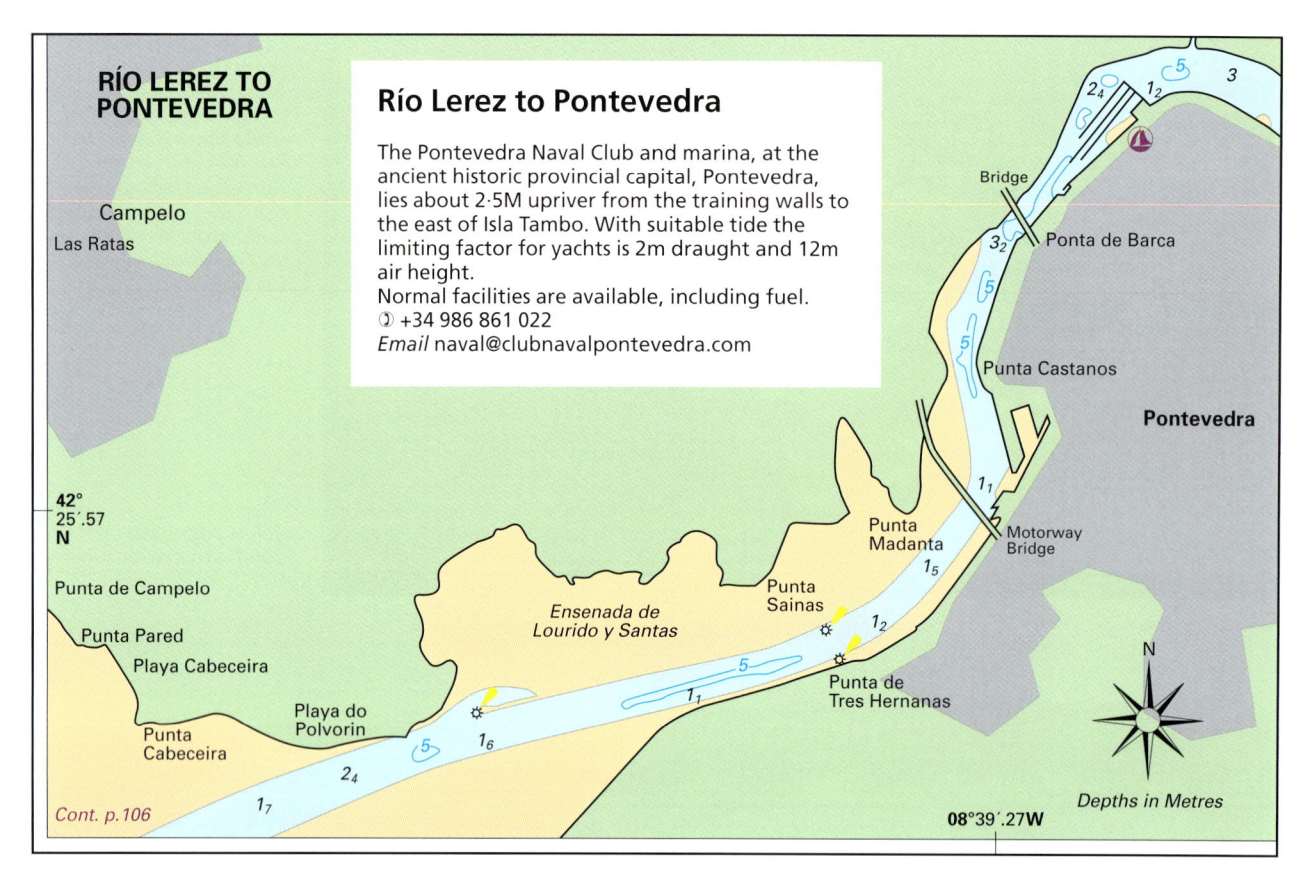

ISLA ONS TO THE PORTUGUESE BORDER

RÍO LEREZ TO PONTEVEDRA

Río Lerez to Pontevedra

The Pontevedra Naval Club and marina, at the ancient historic provincial capital, Pontevedra, lies about 2·5M upriver from the training walls to the east of Isla Tambo. With suitable tide the limiting factor for yachts is 2m draught and 12m air height.
Normal facilities are available, including fuel.
☏ +34 986 861 022
Email naval@clubnavalpontevedra.com

Marin

(See plan page 106)
Location
42°24′N 08°42′W

Traditional craft passing Isla Tambo, Marin behind in the distance
David Russell

Isla Tambo Lt looking SW
William and Sarah Maltby

Consider only as a port of refuge

Marin is a commercial fishing and naval port and the home of the Spanish Naval College. The west basin (with its marina) and offlying Isla Tambo are restricted military areas. Two other pontoon areas are for small local boats only.

Anchorages

Shelter from strong southerlies might be sought off Playa Placere (42°24′·5N 08°41′·4W) before the shallows which protrude immediately north of that area. In other winds, anchoring in the lee of Isla Tambo might be more satisfactory. Note from charts 1732 and 1733, that a cable runs from the yellow lightbuoy to the southwest of Isla Tambo to Pta Placere.

Marin, looking northeast with the Naval College in the foreground

108 ATLANTIC SPAIN AND PORTUGAL

AGUETE

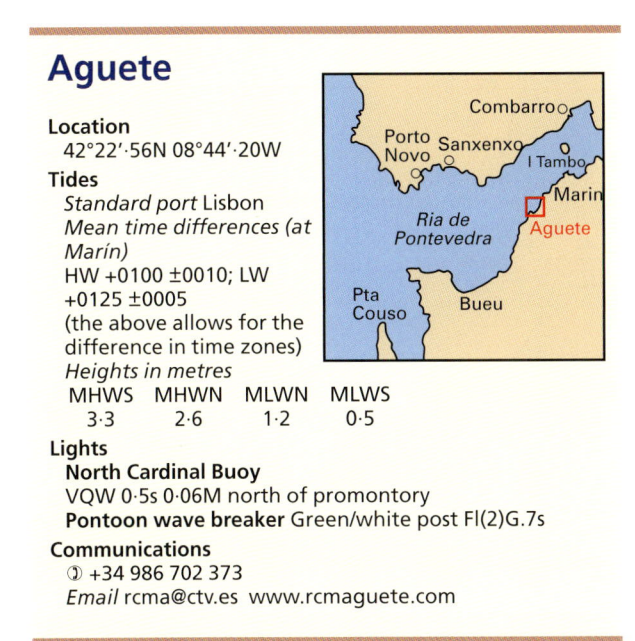

Aguete

Location
42°22'·56N 08°44'·20W

Tides
Standard port Lisbon
Mean time differences (at Marín)
HW +0100 ±0010; LW +0125 ±0005
(the above allows for the difference in time zones)
Heights in metres

MHWS	MHWN	MLWN	MLWS
3·3	2·6	1·2	0·5

Lights
North Cardinal Buoy VQW 0·5s 0·06M north of promontory
Pontoon wave breaker Green/white post Fl(2)G.7s

Communications
☎ +34 986 702 373
Email rcma@ctv.es www.rcmaguete.com

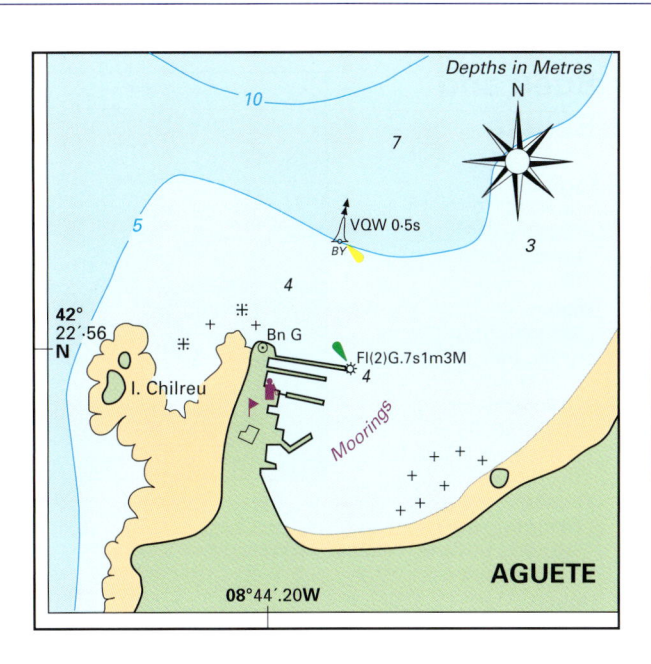

Small club marina

Aguete has been an active recreational marina for Marín since 1974 and is situated in an attractive bay with steep hill behind. The Real Club de Mar de Aguete welcomes visitors and has an attractive clubhouse, with restaurant, overlooking the harbour.

Aguete is one of the many harbours in Galicia to celebrate the fiesta of the Virgen del Carmen on 16 July with a waterborne procession. A lifesize statue of the Virgin is taken on a tour of the harbour in the club launch accompanied by local craft of all sizes decked out with flags and bunting.

Approach

A preferred channel-to-port lateral mark (GRG) (Fl(2+1)G.12s) at 42° 23'·03N 8° 44'·44W 0·5M to the NNW of the breakwater marks the northern edge of the Bajo Los Pelados in the approach to Aguete. A North Cardinal Buoy (VQW 0·5s) marks the edge of the rocky shoal which extends north of the promontory Punta de Aguete.

Berthing and anchoring

The outer separated pontoons act as a wave breaker. Berth on the first pontoon behind the wave breaker or anchor off the beach clear of the moorings. Even in calm weather, some swell from passing boats works in as the harbour and moorings are fully exposed to the north.

Facilities

Fuel available.

Aguete from the north – North Cardinal Buoy is bottom right

now a cardinal

ATLANTIC SPAIN AND PORTUGAL

ISLA ONS TO THE PORTUGUESE BORDER

Bueu and Beluso

Location
Bueu 42°19′·79N
08°47′·01W
Beluso 42°20′·01N
08°47′·90W

Tides
Standard port Lisbon
Mean time differences (at Marín)
HW +0100 ±0010; LW +0125 ±0005
(the above allows for the difference in time zones)
Heights in metres

MHWS	MHWN	MLWN	MLWS
3·3	2·6	1·2	0·5

Lights
Breakwater Bueu Fl.G.5s5M Green column
Breakwater Beluso Fl(3)G.11s3M Green column

Communications (Beluso)
☏ +34 981 545 794
Email portosdeportivos@portosdegalicia.com
www.portosdegalicia.com

Busy fishing harbour/small marina

Bueu is a small fishing and market town with shops, restaurants, market and good beaches. 0·6M west is the small marina of Beluso with one nearby restaurant.

Approach

Straightforward from the north down a wide fairway between *viveros* to offlying rocks of Isolote El Caballo de Bueu to the west. There is a clear route inside the *viveros* between the two harbours.

Berthing and anchorage

No space is reserved for yachts in Bueu (though inquire at the harbour office if requiring lifting with the 100-tonne travel lift there). There may be room to anchor outside the harbour mouth and small moorings in 4–6m over mud. Try the first pontoon in Beluso, borrow a mooring there, or anchor midway between harbours in 3–5m over sand and mud.

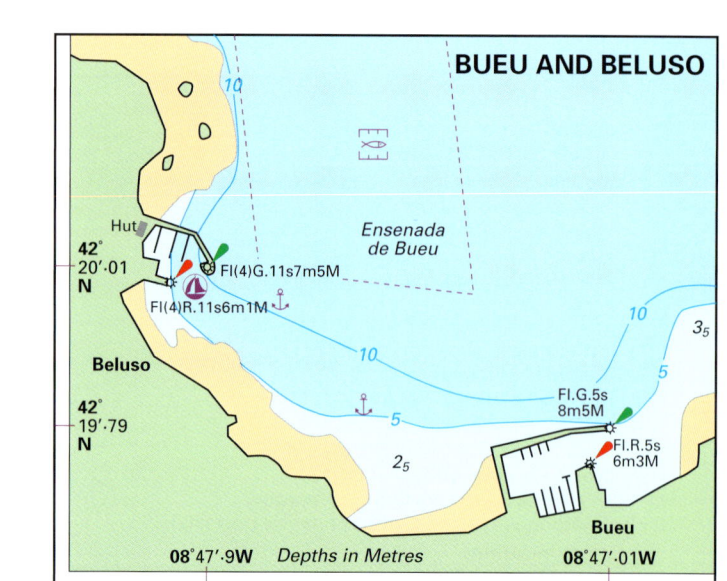

Bueu harbour with travel lift in southwest corner

Beluso – best to anchor off

110 ATLANTIC SPAIN AND PORTUGAL

ALDAN

Ría de Aldan Anchorages

Location
42°19'·6N 08°51'·2W

Tides
See Ría box information on page 101

Overview

The Ría de Aldan, between Punta Couso and Cabo de Udra is worth a visit, in suitable conditions, for its rocky shores and small secluded beaches. It should be avoided if winds build from the north or northwest. However, the bottom is quite weedy with sea lettuce, so make sure the anchor is well set.

There are numerous *viveros* lining the west side of the ría but space should be found inside them. The eastern side of the bay is deeper and somewhat prone to swell.

Inside the ría there are several chartered shoals and rocks along both shorelines and a large scale chart is advised.

Approach

From the north Cabo de Udra is foul. Passage between Cabezo de la Mourisca beacon and the shore is inadvisable.

From the south The rocks and islets offlying Pta Couso should be given a wide berth.

Anchorages

Anchor in one of the small bays on the west side of the ría, but beware the offlying rocks. The rock at 42°16'·82N 8°49'·77W in the southwest corner of the bay (dries about 1·4m) is particularly dangerous and hazards a boat heading out to sea from the anchorage.

In the southeast corner, towards the head of the bay, an anchorage may be found off the ramp in 10m mud. The short mole at Aldan (42°16'·95N 08°49'·37W red beacon) offers little protection for yachts. The best landing is on the E side of the harbour at steps, or at the base of the large slipway, where there are ladders.

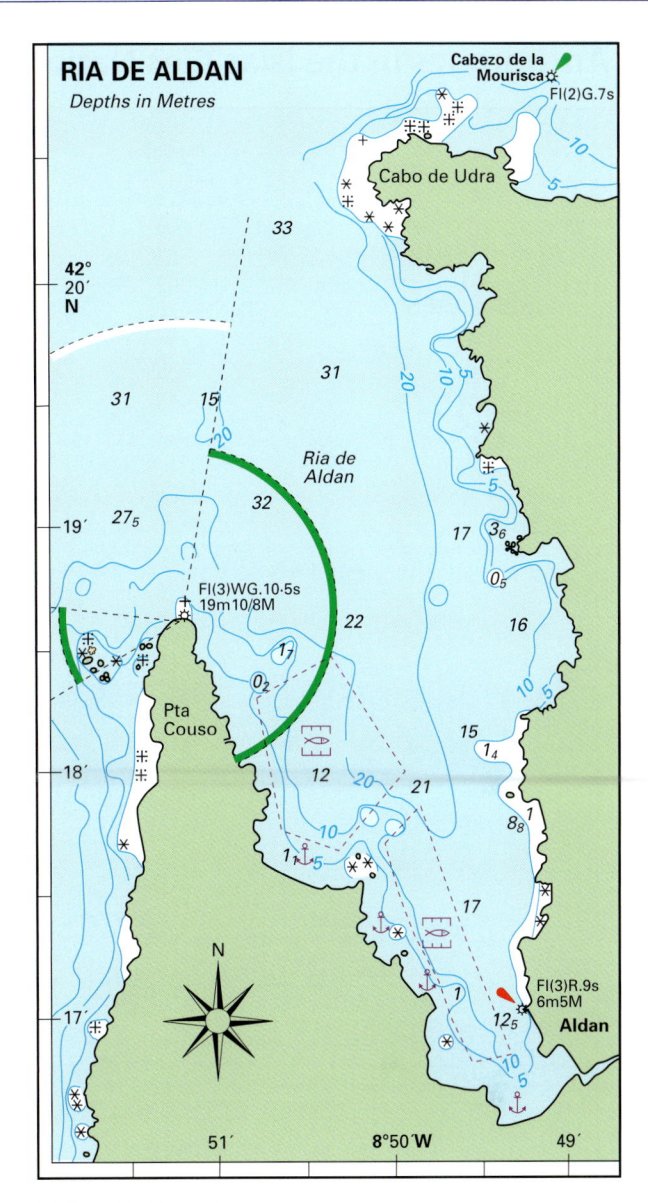

Aldan Peninsula

There are good walks through the woods on the peninsula up ancient, steep, stone-paved tracks. Aldan village is a charming spot where locally produced wines are available at the supermarket.

The head of Ría de Aldan looking south

ISLA ONS TO THE PORTUGUESE BORDER

Anchorages in the Islas Cies National Park

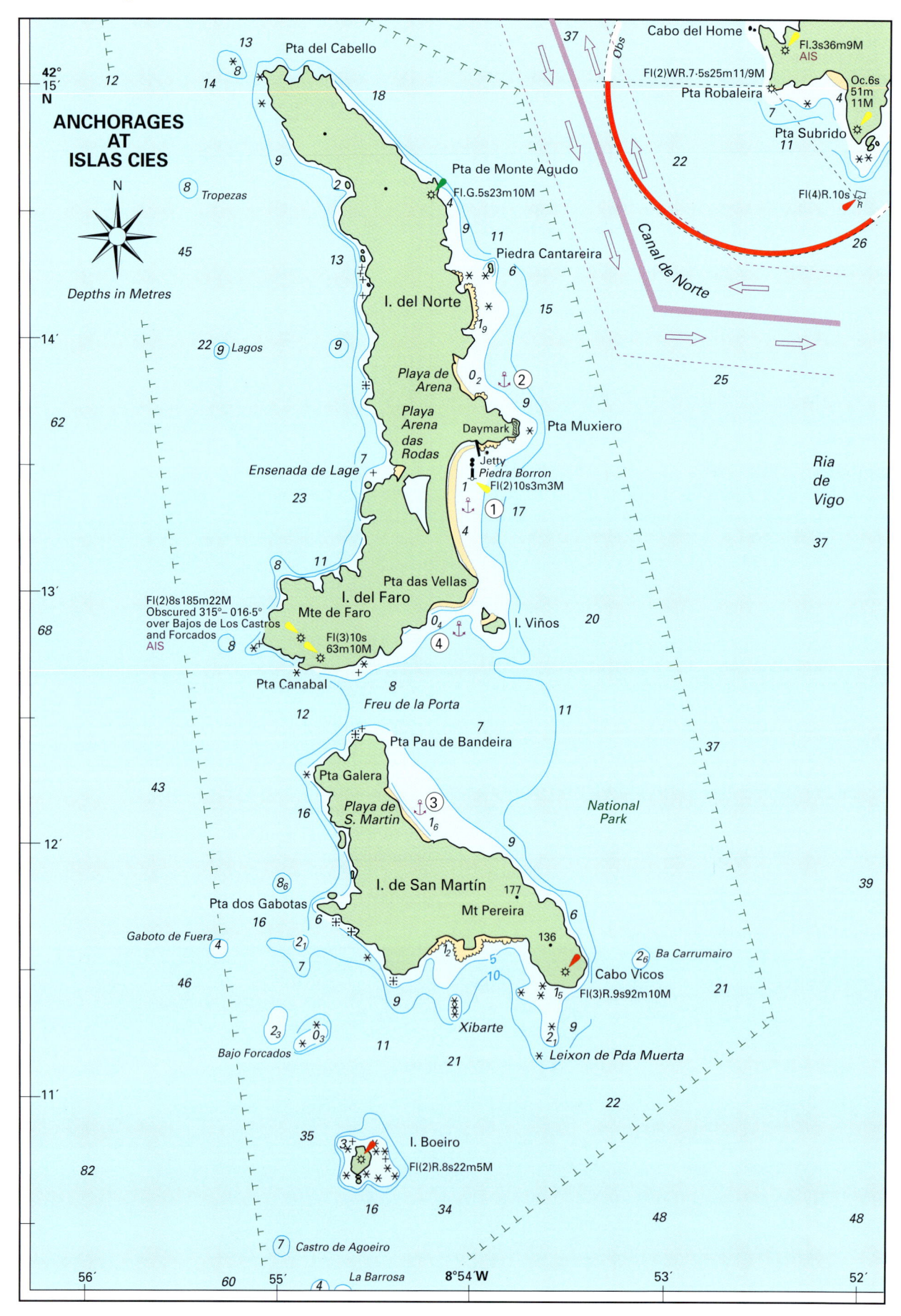

Islas Cíes and Ría de Vigo to Baiona

Islas Cíes

See National Parks pages 15–17
Location
42°13'·00N 08°54'·00W
Tides
Standard port Lisbon
Mean time differences (at Vigo)
HW +0050 ±0010; LW +0115 ±0010
(the above allows for the difference in time zones)
Heights in metres
MHWS	MHWN	MLWN	MLWS
3·4	2·7	1·3	0·5

Daymark
42°13'·65N 08°53'·78W
Communications
See Notes on National Parks' Permits page 15

National Park; a nature reserve with good anchorages

Visiting yachts require a permit to visit, anchor or dive around Isla Cíes – see page 15. It is strongly advised that these permits are arranged well before visiting, even before leaving home. The Islas Cíes are mountainous, wooded and very attractive. The whole area is a Nature Park, and in addition a large part of Isla del Norte, Isla del Faro and all of Isla de San Martín are bird sanctuaries (mostly herring gulls, lesser black-backed gulls and shags, plus a few guillemots) where access is forbidden. However, there are good tracks on Isla del Norte and Isla del Faro, which are linked by a narrow sandy isthmus, and it is worth studying the map displayed at the northern end of Playa Arena das Rodas. There are stunning views from the lighthouse with the evening sun.

There are no cars on the islands and few permanent inhabitants, but in summer many campers and day visitors come by ferry from Vigo, Baiona and Cangas to enjoy the clean sandy beaches so time a visit for midweek if possible. In terms of their surroundings the anchorages, which are on the east side of the islands, are amongst the best in the rías, but all are open to the east.

Islas Cies anchorages from the north. See also photo on p.15

Approach

Monte del Faro is easily identified, standing on the highest point of the central island, Isla del Faro, as is the long beach lining the isthmus between Isla del Faro and Isla del Norte. Be aware that when approaching the north end and also down the east side of the islands there may be marked acceleration in winds.

Anchorages

1. **Playa Arena das Rodas** 42°13'·36N 08°53'·89W
Anchor over sand, rock and weed towards the middle of the beach as depth allows. Piedra Borron, a submerged rock some 20m across, lies about 200m south of the stone jetty. It shows at low water and is marked by a beacon (tall black pole, two balls, light). Avoid anchoring too close to the mole, which is in constant use by tourist ferries. It is possible for a shallow-draught boat to anchor inshore of the rocks, though in summer the beach itself is buoyed-off for swimming. Good anchorage, clear of both rocks and ferries, is to be found with the western white tower on Cabo del Home framed in the centre of a cleft in the rocks at the end of Punta Muxiero. Holding is good in sand.

2. **Playa de Arena** 42°13'·93N 08°53'·89W
In southerlies, anchor in the bay north of Punta Muxiero and its daymark.

3. **Isla de San Martin** 42°12'·23N 08°54'·18W
In south to northwest conditions, better anchorage is to be had on the north coast of Isla de San Martín off the Playa de San Martín, in 3–5m over rock and sand. This is a particularly quiet and attractive spot although without access to facilities of any kind. The island is a bird sanctuary where landing is forbidden.

4. **Isla Viños** 42°12'·88N 08°54'·09W
In east winds some shelter may be found in a small bay on the south coast of the Isla del Faro immediately west, and in the lee, of Isla Viños. It is occasionally used by fishing boats and there is not much room. The Monte Faro jetty some 600m to the west is used by fishing boats and the occasional ferry, and yachts are not welcome.

Facilities

A few restaurants and a small supermarket at Playa Arena das Rodos and a good visitors' centre above the campsite.

ISLA ONS TO THE PORTUGUESE BORDER

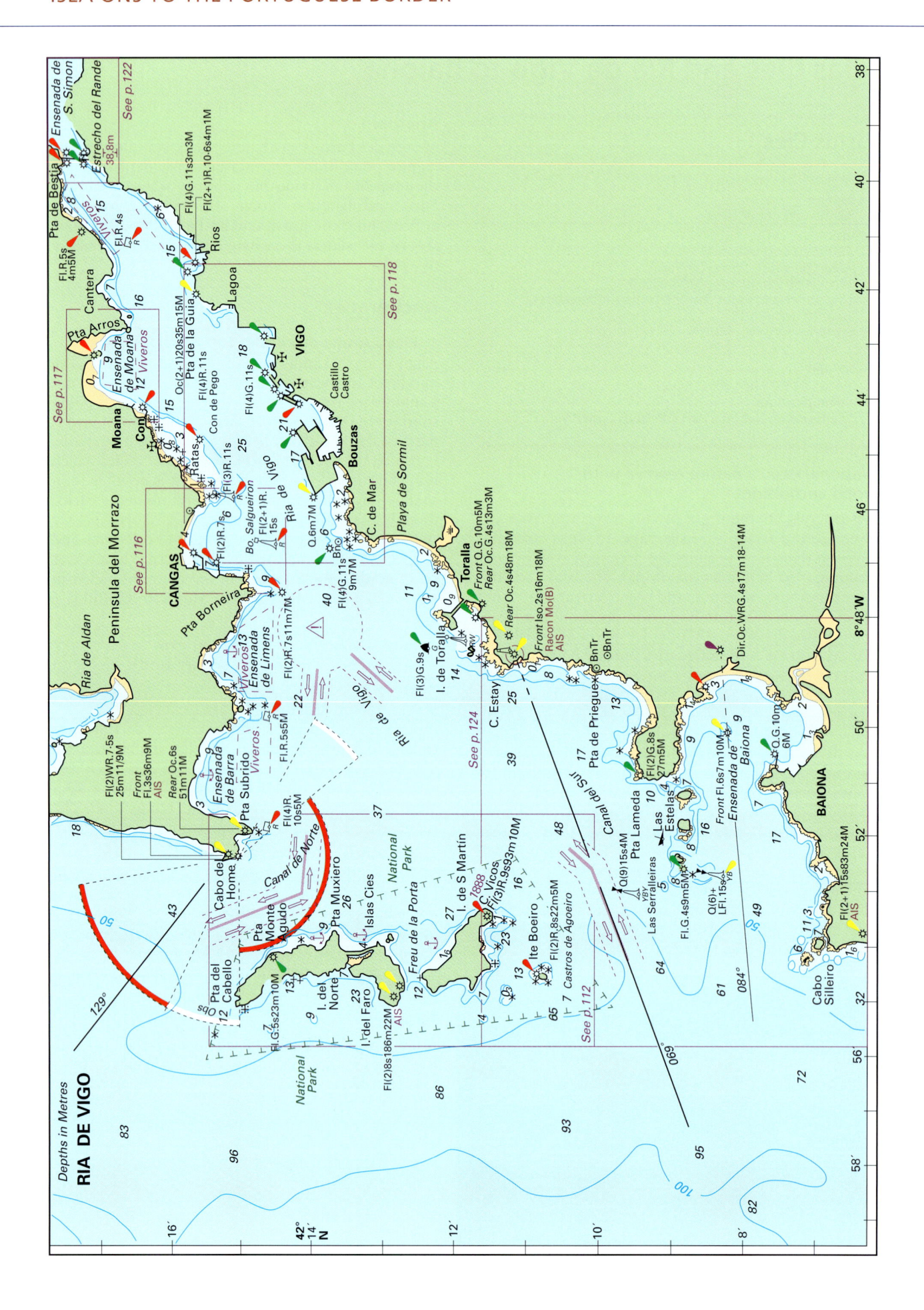

RÍA DE VIGO

Ría de Vigo

Tides
Standard port Lisbon
Mean time differences (at Vigo)
HW +0050 ±0010; LW +0115 ±0010
(the above allows for the difference in time zones)
Heights in metres
MHWS	MHWN	MLWN	MLWS
3·4	2·7	1·3	0·5

Approach lights (opposite page)

Canal de Norte
Cabo del Home Fl(2)WR.7·5s25m11/9M Red round tower
Ldg Lts 129° *Front* Fl.3s36m9M White round tower
Punta Subrido *Rear* Oc.6s51m11M White round tower
Monte Agudo Fl.G.5s23m10M White round tower with white wall

Canal del Sur
Cabo Estay Ldg Lts 069°20′ *Front* Iso.2s16m18M White 4-sided tower, red bands
Cabo Estay *Rear* Oc.4s48m18M Red truncated pyramidal tower, white bands

Vigo Narrows
Bajo Borneira No.6 Fl(2)R.7s11m7M Red and white tower
Bajo Tofiño No.3 Fl(4)G.11s9m7M Red and white tower

Baiona approaches
Cabezo de San Juan Ldg Lts 084° Fl.6s7m10M White truncated conical tower
Playa de Panxón *Rear* Dir.Oc.WRG.4s18m9m White truncated tower on 8-sided base

Islas Cíes
Monte Faro Fl(2)8s185m22M Tower and dwelling

Warning
Ría de Vigo and Ensenada de Baiona are separated by the Islas Las Estelas and Isolas Serralleiras with their off lying, extensive and dangerous reefs and individual rocks. North/south passage between islands is not recommended without local knowledge, or in fair weather and using Spanish chart 4167.

Note A traffic separation scheme operates through Canal de Norte and Canal del Sur. There are sound signals on Cabo Silleiro and Cabo Estay.

A partly industrial ría but with good marinas and attractive anchorages

The Islas Cíes shelter Ría de Vigo from the worst of the Atlantic swell. Industrial dockland Vigo dominates the upper part of the ría on the south side and its suburbs and dormitory towns spread down both sides. With them come harbours, ferries and marinas. There is peace as well, both in Ensenada de San Simón beyond the giant Rande Suspension bridge, or off the lovely beaches west of Cangas. Buoys or beacons mark the shallows off most headlands on both sides of the ría.

Approach

From the north or the northern rías Canal de Norte is well marked and free from dangers. (If coming from seaward note the dangers extending well north of Isla del Norte (Islas Cíes), if approaching from Ría de Pontevedra do not cut the corner off Pta Couso). Pick up the line of red buoys after clearing Cabo del Home and Pta Subrido to head up ría.

From the west or south Canal del Sur is marked by the Cabo Estay leading lights 069° on the TSS centre line. Keep to the southern side of the TSS.

From Baiona (See plan on page 124). In fair weather and towards high tide, Canal de la Porta, between Monte Ferro and the easternmost of the three Estelas Islands, may be used. There is a 0·9m patch in the middle of this channel and a separate 1·6m patch about 0·1M further northwest. Favour the west side, use Spanish chart 4167 and then keep 1M clear of the headland, and Cabo Estay, before heading up Ría de Vigo.

Anchorages

1. **Ensenada de Barra** 42° 15′·56N 08°51′·32W or 42°15′·46N and 08° 50′·51W
   Anchor off the delightful beach but note that this is a popular nudist beach on weekends and holidays. Ensenada de Barra offers a good anchorage in 6m over sand and weed, open southwest to east.

2. **Ensenada de Limens** This beautiful bay between Cangas and the Ensenada de Barra offers splendid shelter from winds with any north in them, and has a lovely beach. However, it is quite badly charted, so approach with due care. There is a very obvious drying rock close to the beach in the centre of the bay, but a group of boulders, awash at LAT, lurk just offshore of it and must be guarded against. The highest head is in position 42°15′·45N 008°48′·75W. Facilities ashore are limited to a friendly little bar at the campsite.

GALICIA

Anchorage in Ensenada de Limens *Geraldine Hennigan*

Ensenada de Barra anchorage looking E up Ría de Vigo *Jane Russell*

ATLANTIC SPAIN AND PORTUGAL

ISLA ONS TO THE PORTUGUESE BORDER

Cangas

Location
42°15'·63N 08°46'·95W

Tides
Standard port Lisbon
Mean time differences (at Vigo)
HW +0050 ±0010; LW +0115 ±0010
(the above allows for the difference in time zones)
Heights in metres

MHWS	MHWN	MLWN	MLWS
3·4	2·7	1·3	0·5

Light
Outer breakwater beacon Fl(2)R.7s3M
Red round tower

Communications
Club Náutico de Rodeira
VHF Ch 06 ☎ +34 986 304 246 or +34 671 660 105
Email club@nauticorodeira.com
www.nauticorodeira.com

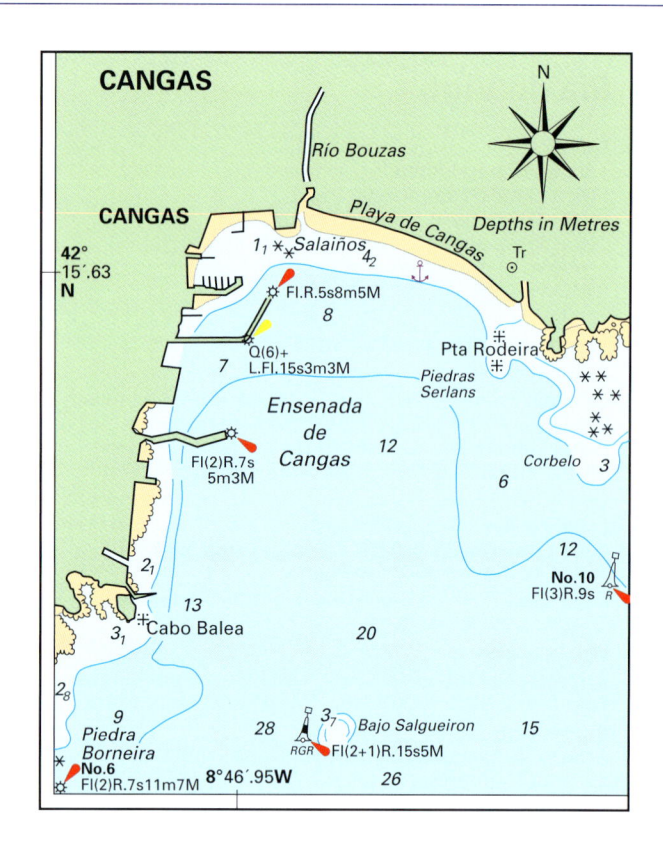

Cheerful welcome from a modern marina

Cangas has a small, friendly marina alongside an attractive town with fishing and some industry. There are regular ferries to Vigo.

Approach

Buoys mark the extent of the rocks off the headlands to east and west. Approach to Cangas is straightforward between Piedra Barneira and Bajo Salgueiron or between the No.10 buoy off headland and Bajo Salgreion.

Anchorage and berthing

On rounding the breakwater there are three sections to the harbour, fishing boats to main harbour left, ferries to the right hand pier and yachts to the marina in the middle harbour. There are 269 berths for boats up to 20m length. The minimum depth is 2m. An anchorage is available off Playa de Cangas in 5–6m over sand.

Facilities

Electricity and water, Fuel; 64 tonne travel lift; WiFi; security.

The domestic facilities (including washing machine) and restaurant are in the end of the main blue roofed building on the centre mole. The main club house is next to the Shell fuel station immediately outside the harbour road entrance. There is a seafront market on Friday. There is a chandler just outside the marina - Ibericamar ☎+34 986 303 972 or +34 678 553 303 www.ibericamar.es.

Cangas from the south

CANGAS AND MOAÑA

Moaña

Location
42°16'·68N 08°43'·99W

Communications
VHF Ch 09   +34 986 31 11 40
Email info@moanamar.es   www.moanamar.es

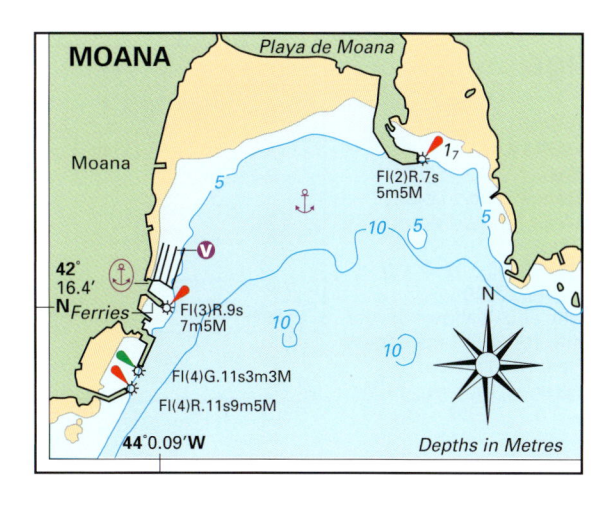

A small marina with easy access to Vigo via the adjacent ferry jetty

Moana is spelt 'Moaña' and is pronounced 'Mowannia', not 'Mowanna'.

There is an hourly ferry service to Vigo with all the advantages of a small seaside town with easy access to a big city, should it be needed.

Approach
Approach the northeast entrance through the *viveros*. The arrivals pontoon is to starboard beyond the outer pontoon with visitors' berths close to the entrance.

Berthing
Depths in the marina get down to just over two metres at LW at the pontoon berths furthest away from the entrance, but otherwise there is plenty of water. The marina can take boats of lengths from 8m to 16m and is well organised, with a *marineiro* on duty all day and into the evening.

Facilities
There is good WiFi connectivity at the pontoons. A Carrefour supermarket is within walking/cycling distance. The marina office has bikes for hire.

Anchorage
Anchor outside the marina in mud and sand.

Moaña town band   *Geraldine Hennigan*

Moaña marina and anchorage from the south

ATLANTIC SPAIN AND PORTUGAL

GALICIA

ISLA ONS TO THE PORTUGUESE BORDER

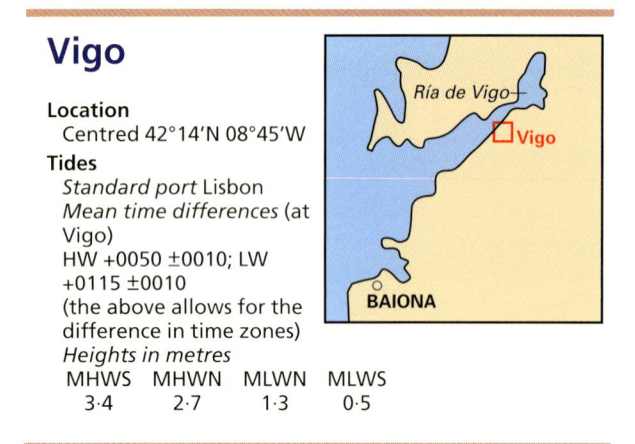

Vigo

Location
Centred 42°14'N 08°45'W

Tides
Standard port Lisbon
Mean time differences (at Vigo)
HW +0050 ±0010; LW +0115 ±0010
(the above allows for the difference in time zones)
Heights in metres

MHWS	MHWN	MLWN	MLWS
3·4	2·7	1·3	0·5

A lively, modern maritime city

Vigo has an ancient history and strong maritime connections. Its wharfs stretch for two miles handling cargo, deep-sea fishing and cruise ships as well as building coasters and fishing vessels.

Marinas

There are three marinas in the main waterfront dock area of Vigo that will accept visiting yachts. A fourth, Punta Lagoa, is to the northeast of the docks under the wooded Monte de la Guia. Other marinas can be seen, particularly by Bouzas bridge, but they are generally private or rather shallow.

Facilities

Any repair work is possible in Vigo. In addition to the facilities at the marinas, the long established Astilleros Lagos boatyard in Darsena de Bouzas continues to offer major technical support and repair.

Astilleros Lagos Avda. Eduardo Cabello 2, 36208 Vigo, Spain
☎ +34 986 232 626
www.astilleroslagos.es
Email astillero@astilleroslagos.com

Astilleros Lagos boatyard, Vigo
William and Sarah Maltby

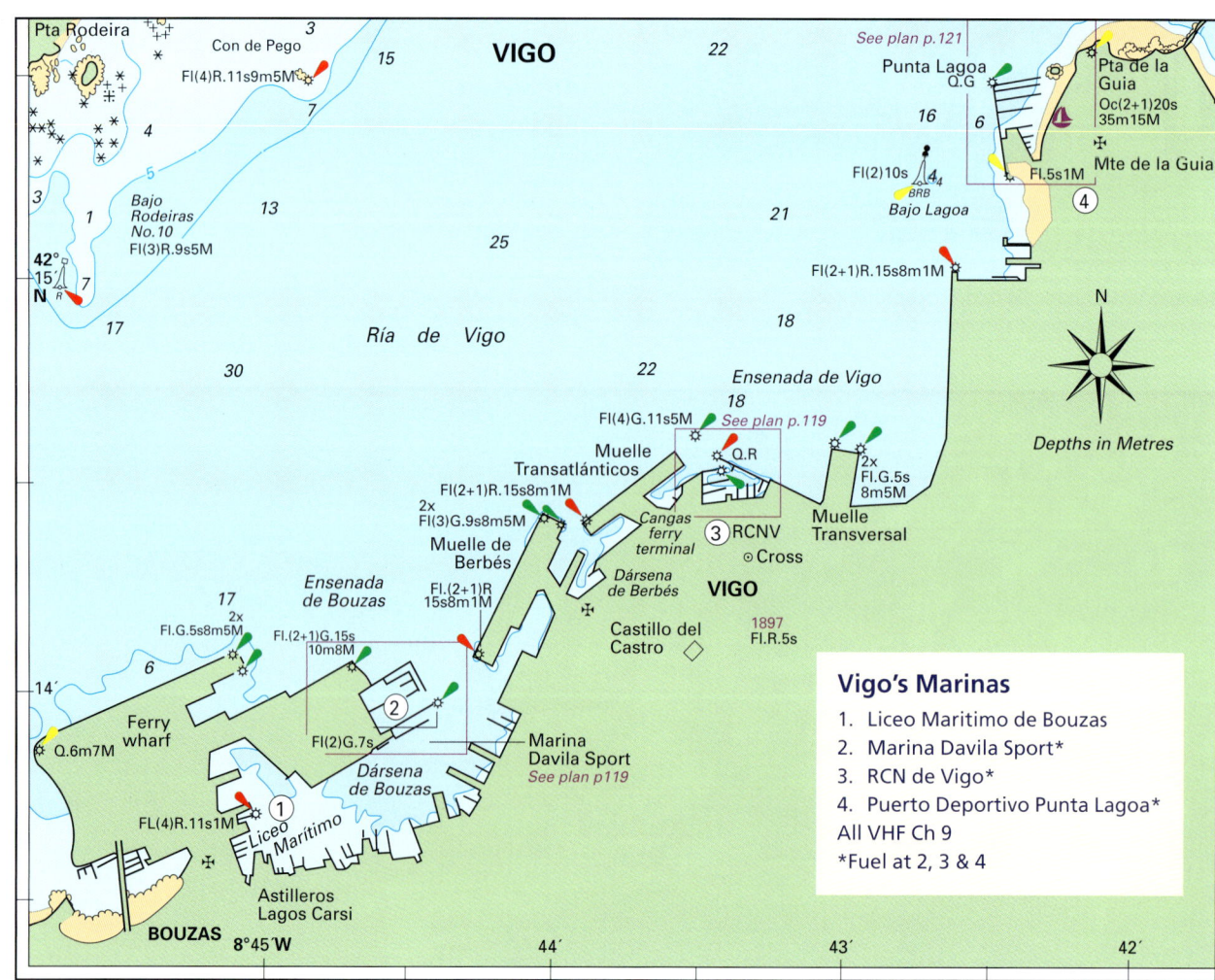

Vigo's Marinas

1. Liceo Maritimo de Bouzas
2. Marina Davila Sport*
3. RCN de Vigo*
4. Puerto Deportivo Punta Lagoa*

All VHF Ch 9

*Fuel at 2, 3 & 4

118 ATLANTIC SPAIN AND PORTUGAL

VIGO

Darsena de Bouzas

1. **Liceo Maritimo** 42°13'·70N 08°44'·95W
   A long established marina, close to the noise and dust of shipyards and some way from town. There are 277 finger berths from 6m to 12m. WiFi available.
   ☎ +34 986 232 442
   Email info@liceobouzas.com
   www.liceobouzas.com

2. **Marina Davila Sport** 42°13'·9N 08°44'·5W
   This marina was built for megayachts with all the facilities that entails. It is north of the main southwest/northeast mole in the Dársena de Bouzas and protected by a wavebreaker pontoon. The marina offers good shelter as well as modern technical and shore-side layup facilities, but is a very long way from town.
   ☎ +34 986 244 612
   Email marina@davilasport.es
   www.davilasport.com www.marinasdegalicia.com
   VHF Ch 09

Facilities at Marina Davila Sport

Electricity and water Available on the finger pontoons
Fuel The easily accessible fuel dock and travel lift (inside a long pontoon) are south of the southern mole in the shelter of Dársena de Bouzas.
Ship lift There is a 70 tonne travel lift.
Chandlery Jose Betanoz in the village for a well-stocked chandlery.
Travel The Marina is a walk of 20 minutes from the shops and supermarkets, but bicycles are provided free of charge making it a 5 minute trip. For major provisioning the El Campo mega supermarket is 10 minutes on a bicycle.
   The marineros will order taxis for anywhere and car hire is available in central Vigo.
Internet WiFi is provided free of charge.
Laundry The *lavanderia* is no longer operational. Washing has to be left with the marina office who arrange for it to be collected, washed and returned - usually within 24 hours.
Gas The marina will organize a round trip cab ride to the local *ferreteria* to exchange gas bottles.
National Park Permits The marina office will arrange these permits.
Restaurants An excellent restaurant is above the office and offers superb views up and down the ría.

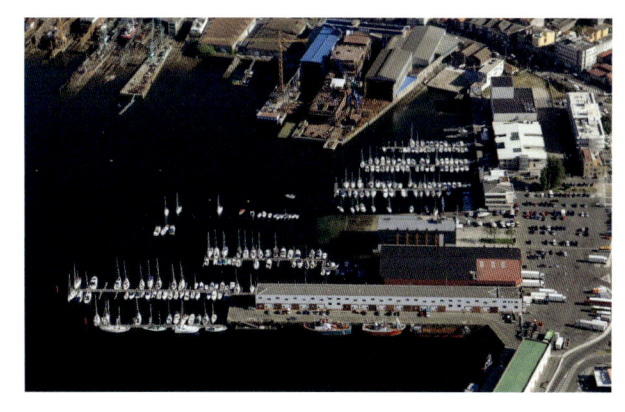

Liceo Marina

Convenient refuelling on the outer fuel berth at Davila Sport

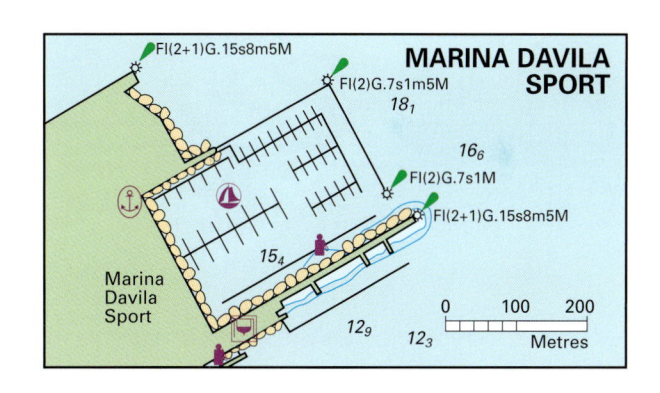

Marina Davila Sport looking east

GALICIA

ATLANTIC SPAIN AND PORTUGAL   119

ISLA ONS TO THE PORTUGUESE BORDER

East of Muelle Transatlanticos

3. Real Club Náutico de Vigo 42°14'·57N 08°43'·43W
 ☎ +34 986 44 96 94
 Berthing reservations: ☎+34 902 104 762
 www.rcnauticovigo.com info@rcnauticovigo.com
 VHF Ch 09

Approach

Approach square on, heading south, but beware ferries emerging from starboard. If conditions allow secure to the reception/fuel pontoon immediately in the entrance (see photo) and seek instructions.

Berthing

The entrance to the original berthing area, bow/stern-to mooring, is immediately to port on entry, but a marina extension has been built to the southwest entrance (see photo). The RCNV is a very congested marina with little space to manoeuvre. The main basin to the east has 320 berths for 8m (53) to 22m (5) boats. The smaller basin to the west past the ferry terminal can only take boats up to 10m on finger pontoons. Minimum depth 2m, 12m in the entrance.

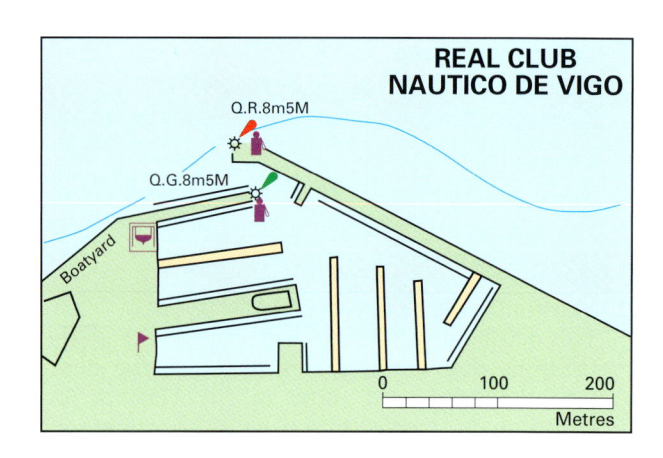

Facilities

Water and electricity on pontoons.
Travel-lift 32 tonne; fuel; WiFi

There are good facilities on site and easy access to the city.

RCN de Vigo Marina (note that the marina extension to the right of the picture (west) is not shown)

Looking southwest to the RCNV marina extension from the reception pontoon *Henry Buchanan*

Looking east into the main berthing area entrance from the reception pontoon
Henry Buchanan

120 ATLANTIC SPAIN AND PORTUGAL

PUNTA LAGOA

Puerto Deportivo Punta Lagoa

Location
42°15'·55N 08°42'·30W Close west of Islote Cabron

Tides
Standard port Lisbon
Mean time differences (at Vigo)
HW +0050 ±0010; LW +0115 ±0010
(the above allows for the difference in time zones)
Heights in metres
MHWS	MHWN	MLWN	MLWS
3·4	2·7	1·3	0·5

Lights
Pta de la Guia Oc(2+1)20s35m15M
White round masonry tower
Breakwater 42°15'·52N 08°42'·45W Q.G.3M Green post
Entrance Green post

Communications
VHF Ch 09 *Callsign* Punta Lagoa
☎ +34 986 374 305
www.marinapuntalagoa.com
Email info@marinapuntalagoa.com

A snug and friendly marina

Punta Lagoa marina is just north of Vigo and nestles between the wooded slopes of the prominent Monte de la Guia and a long breakwater stretching out north from the old Punta Lagoa commercial area. It offers good protection from swell and is a comfortable place to berth a boat with good security. There are magnificent views down the ría from here across the full frontage of Vigo and out to the Islas Cíes.

Approach

Punta de la Guia is high, tree-clad and prominent as it juts out into the ría beyond all the docks and industry of the city of Vigo. Turn south into the marina leaving the Islote Cabron and a line of posts to port against the shoreline.

Puerto Deportivo Punta Lagoa looking southwest towards the Islas Cies   Henry Buchanan

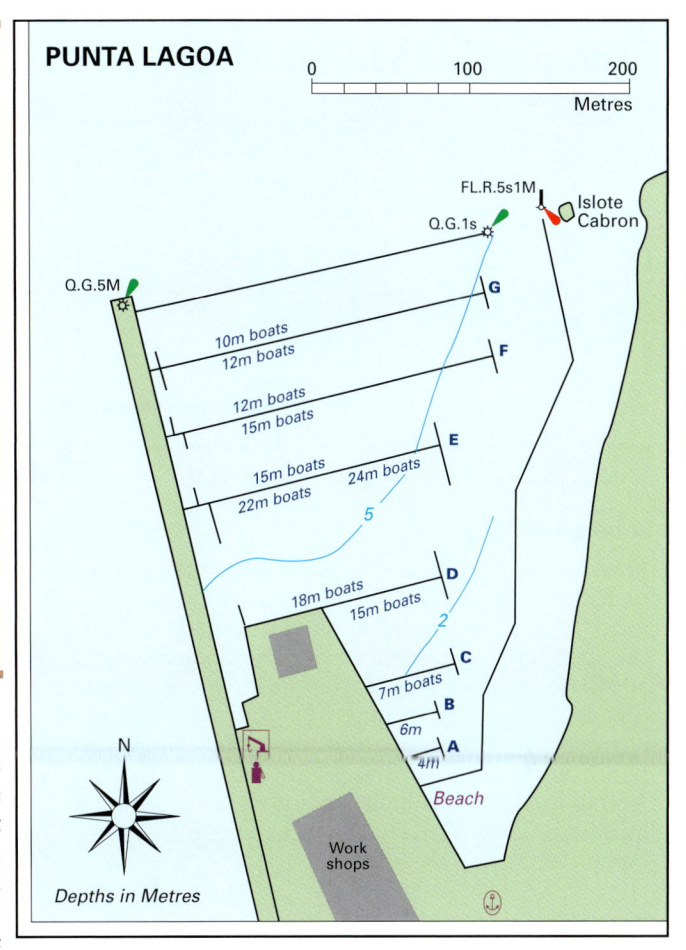

Berthing

There are a total of 300 moorings on finger pontoons for boats of between 6m(27) and 39m(1). Depths reduce from some 4m in the entrance to 3 meters in the inner harbour at low water, but 2m beyond pontoon D.

Facilities

Electricity and water On the pontoons.
Fuel Diesel and petrol pumps.
Travel-lift 2 Travel-lifts of 110 and 50 tonnes and a fixed crane.
Security 24 hours a day security with a hut on the breakwater and at the marina road entrance gate.
Pump out Greywater and sewage.
Showers and WC These left a little to be desired in 2013 unless access was achieved to the cafe/bar/restaurant that had been shut down over a local planning dispute. Hopefully this will have been resolved.
Travel Being a little out of Vigo it is a twenty minutes' walk up a steep hill to shops and public transport in Guia, but good for fitness. There are numerous buses into Vigo from Guia, the No 17 has a stop nearest to the marina. The office or guard (24 hrs) at the main gate can order taxis.
   The airport at Vigo is 15 minutes away by bus or taxi.
Engineering services There are engineering services on site managed by Yatesport (www.yatesport.com.es) or contracted in from Vigo yards. Yatesport have mechanical, rigging, electronics, carpentry, GRP expertise, but no longer build boats.
Internet WiFi in the marina.

ATLANTIC SPAIN AND PORTUGAL

ISLA ONS TO THE PORTUGUESE BORDER

Ensenada de San Simón

Location
42°17'·3N 08°39'·6W
Bridge

A beautiful bay

Ensenada de San Simón is a pretty bay at the top end of Ría de Vigo, and is little visited by other than local yachts. It tends to be shallow, particularly in the northern part, but offers several anchorages, adequate facilities and peace. The stream runs hard through the high bridge (38·8m) crossing the narrows leading into the bay and there are significant circular streams within the bay itself. San Adrian is a hive of fishing activity, particularly in the mornings when refrigerated trucks wait to load vast quantities of mussels.

Puerto Deportivo San Adrián

42°18'·05N 08°39'·14W (Entrance)

If an overnight berth can be negotiated it is well worth a visit to this picturesque, quiet spot in a welcoming marina.

☏ + 34 986 67 38 07 +34 618 82 63 30

From the west Isla de San Simón is above the left-hand bridge tower. Anchorage 1 is beyond the cranes to the right; Anchorage 2 is south of the islands

122   ATLANTIC SPAIN AND PORTUGAL

ENSENADA DE SAN SIMON

Berthing
This is a club marina with privately owned berths, so visiting boats should berth temporarily on the north side of the long gangway up to the gate. There are 204 berths from 6m(78) to 18m(2), beam 2·5m to 3m. Berthing is free whilst dining at the superb and well-priced restaurant but the berth is on the outside of the marina without electricity or water. There is a charge for an overnight stay and an overnight berth inside the marina will need to be found.

If berthing alongside, favour the pontoon parallel to land to avoid being pinned by wind and tide. The inside berths avoid the worst of the wash from fishing boats.

Facilities
Electricity and water; 24hr security; good showers/toilets; WiFi. There is a small shop about 1km towards Pontevedra.

San Adrián marina and clubhouse looking SW
Geraldine Hennigan

Club Náutico de Cobres
There is a second marina, Club Náutico de Cobres, close north of the pier at 42°19'·08N 08°38'·91W and inside the Islote Don Pedro. Access to this is only via a card controlled gate.
☎ +34 610 013 133
Email cncobres@gmail.com.
www.nauticocobres.es

Anchorages
The following are suggested anchorages:
1. On the south shore beyond the cranes off Punta Soutelo, before the shallows, in 3–4m mud. Beware the shallows extending off the mouth of the Ría de Redondela, and the training walls, which cover at half tide.
2. The S tip of Isla de San Simón off two stone crosses or southwest of the reef which extends south from the island. Anchor clear of the beacon at the latter in 3m mud or work in between moorings towards the sand shore. There is a restaurant on the spit of beach, and a bakery and shop 400m inland, or take the dinghy to the small harbour of Cesantes (there are food shops but up a steep hill).
3. South of Pta Pereiro with its pontoons shielded in shallow water behind Islote Pedro.
4. Muelle de San Adrián de Cobres 42°18'·14N 08°39'·27W village mole, red beacon. Anchor off the pier in 4m. The best place to land for those at anchor is at the slipway between the two marinas.

GALICIA

From the northeast San Adrián Anchorage 4 off quay, and San Adrián Marina. Punta Lagoa marina is beyond the prominent tree-clad hill on the left down the ría

ATLANTIC SPAIN AND PORTUGAL

ISLA ONS TO THE PORTUGUESE BORDER

Baiona to the Portuguese border

Lights
Canal del Sur Ldg Lts 069°20′
Cabo Estay *Front* Iso.2s17m18M Red truncated pyramid tower red bands
Cabo Estay *Rear* Oc.4s49m18M as above

Baiona approach Ldg Lts 084°
Cabezo de san Juan *Front* Fl.6s7m10M
 White truncated conical tower
Playa de Panxón *Rear* Dir.Oc.WRG.4s18m9M
 White truncated tower on 8-sided base
Cabo Silleiro Fl(2+1)15s84m24M White 8-sided tower, red bands, on dwelling

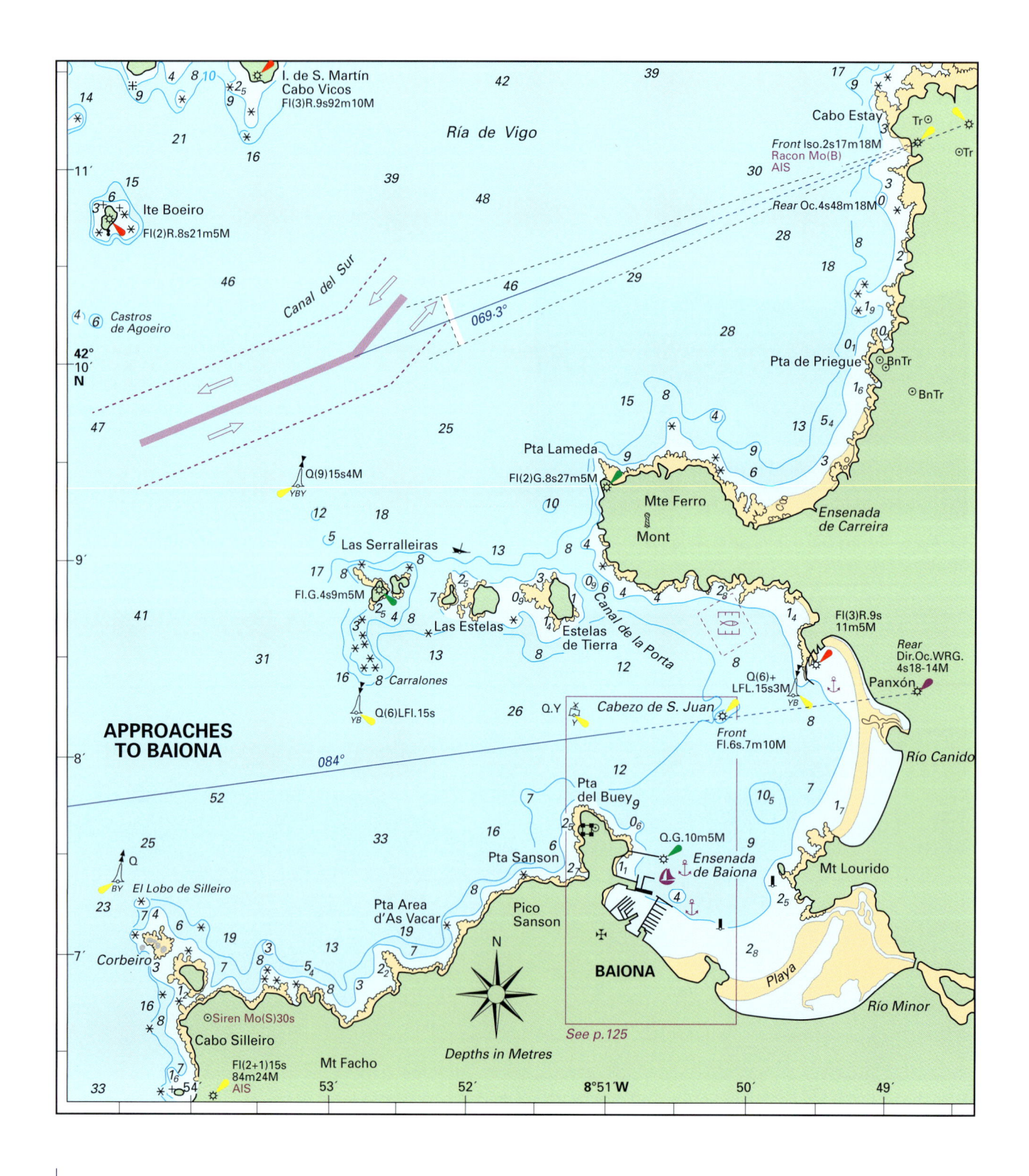

BAIONA

Baiona (Bayona)

Location
42°07'·47N 08°50'·55W

Tides
Standard port Lisbon
Mean time differences
HW +0045 ±0010; LW +0110 ±0010
(the above allows for the difference in time zones)
Heights in metres
MHWS	MHWN	MLWN	MLWS
3·5	2·7	1·3	0·5

Light
Breakwater beacon Q.G.5M Green and white tower

Communications
Monte Real Club de Yates
VHF Ch 06 or 71 Monte Real Club de Yates
☎ +34 986 385 000
Email secretaria@mrcyb.com www.mrcyb.es
Porto Deportivo Baiona
VHF Ch 09 Baiona Sport Harbour
☎ +34 986 38 51 07
Email puertobaiona@puertobaiona.com
www.puertobaiona.com

First European harbour to hear that Columbus had discovered America

Baiona is easily approached by day or night and is an excellent port of call whether arriving from transatlantic passage, working north or heading south. It offers the chance to relax, to wait out inclement weather and to re-provision. It is generally well protected except from strong winds with an easterly component, although prevailing northerlies also bring a swell into the harbour, the more marked beyond the protection of the main breakwater running out from Monte Real. Anchorage can be found in the southeast of the bay beyond the two marinas.

The town is attractive and thriving as a tourist resort, with well protected beaches and a secure place in history as Columbus' first mainland landfall in 1493 after returning from the New World. This is commemorated by a replica of the Pinta permanently berthed in the harbour. The old part of the town is surprisingly un-commercialised compared to the tourist shops along the front, and a cool place to take a leisurely stroll on a hot day. Medieval walls surround the Parador Conde do Gondomar on the northern headland, commanding the harbour and its approaches, and there are pleasant walks among the pine forests beyond, where stands the enormous statue of the Virgen de la

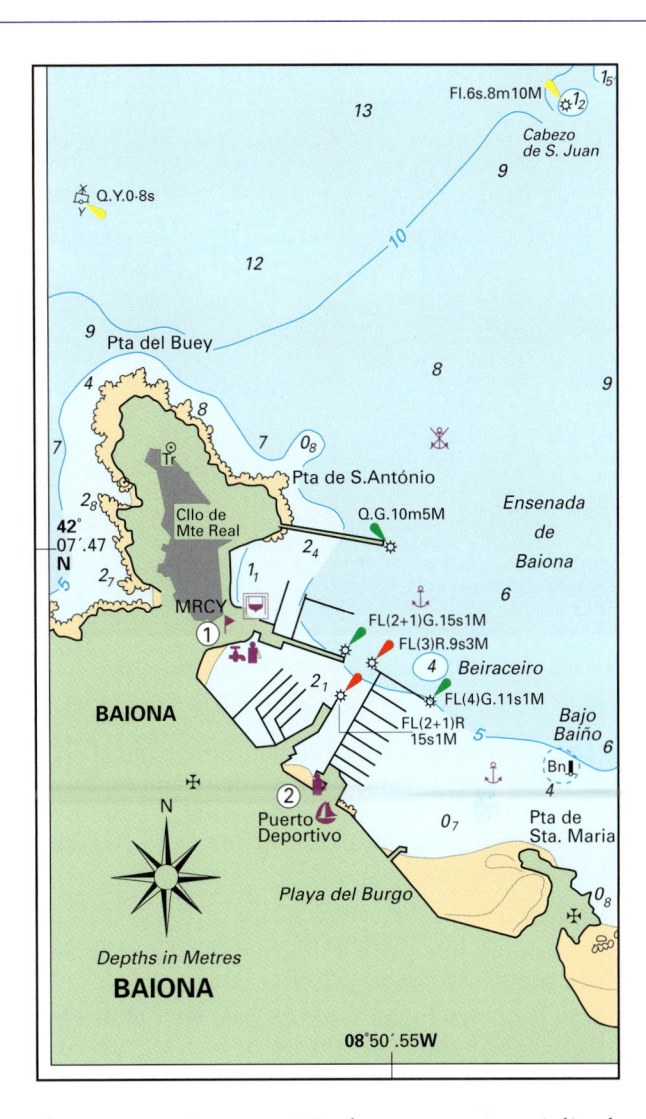

Looking NNW from Pta del Buey across Las Estelas in the approaches to Baiona. Islas Cies beyond *Jane Russell*

ATLANTIC SPAIN AND PORTUGAL

ISLA ONS TO THE PORTUGUESE BORDER

Baiona – Puerto Deportivo and MRCY from the north

Roca. WiFi in Baiona is difficult to find and signals are weak. Cafe Erizana on the waterfront, half way between the two main marinas provides the best service, but is also available at the Gold Bar, and Parador cafés.

Approach
The leading line of 084° through Cabezo de San Juan and Panjón keeps you clear of dangers.

From the north In fair weather keep west of 08°57′W to clear the hazards northwest of Islas Cíes, before setting heading for Cabo Silleiro and then turning into Ensenada de Baiona keeping well clear of Las Serralleiras. With an Atlantic swell running it can be quite a boisterous ride in to Pta del Buey, but everything starts to calm down as you close the end of the breakwater.

From Ría de Vigo With settled weather and with good visibility Canal de la Porta may be used (but see warning on page 115). Otherwise take a route around the outside of the dangers of Las Serralleiras and the Las Estelas group of islands and rocks.

From the south Stay off shore, coming no closer than 2M off Cabo Silleiro before turning onto the approach towards Pta del Buey.

Go aboard the Pinta and discover how Columbus' men lived
David Russell

Caution
For about 10M south of Cape Silleiro there is a multitude of unmarked fishing pot floats inshore without flags, plastic and mostly coloured grey or black.

Berthing

1. Monte Real Club de Yates 42°07′·20N 08°50′·40W

The MRCY is a long established club in a superb situation on the harbour ramparts of the headland. The old defensive walls tower above it and house the Parador hotel.

There are 222 berths for boats up to 40m and maximum draught 6m on two long pontoons, one with fingers, one without (pick a rope up from the pontoon, walk it out to the bow, or stern, to tie it off). It is more expensive for a boat on a finger berth if one is available. The best approach on arriving at the MRCY is to secure to the hammerhead marked 'Transitos' and wait to be allocated a berth by the staff.

Office and domestic facilities are on the lower level beneath the restaurant.

Facilities
Communications Marina Baiona, Recinto del Parador s/n 36300, Baiona (Pontevedra), Noelia, Estévez Calvar. ☎+34 986 38 50 00
  Email secretaria@mrcyb.com www.mrcyb.es
Restaurant The club restaurant
  (*Email* restaurante@mrcyb.com ☎+34 986 356 226) provides good food and an excellent view over the harbour. Visitors are welcome and are expected to match the dress code of members.
Services Water and electricity
Fuel Available 24 hours at the MRCY from the inside of the most westerly pontoon, in front of the clubhouse. There is a helpful team of Club Bosuns
Engineering Repair shop
Travelift 17 tonne
Internet WiFi available

ATLANTIC SPAIN AND PORTUGAL

BAIONA

Looking SE: MRCY pontoons in foreground, Puerto Deportivo beyond *Henry Buchanan*

MRCY Baiona marina berths (to the right) and Yacht Club looking N *MRCY*

2. Puerto Deportivo de Baiona, Baiona Sports Harbour

This marina is popular with visiting yachts and a little closer to town than the MRCY, but the planned shoreside development has stalled and the facilities are provided in portacabins (see photo below). A concrete wave breaker connects to the long feeder pontoon that has finger pontoons branching off it. There are 370 berths for vessels of up to 40m in length.

Facilities
Services Water and electricity
Fuel Diesel and petrol
Travelift 50 tonne

PD de Baiona facilities' buildings – office to the left
Henry Buchanan

Technical Services Ronautica, Avenida Monte Real s/n 36300 Baiona (Pontevedra)Spain.
☎ +34 986 385 104
Email patricia@ronautica.com www.ronautica.com

Anchoring

The best anchorage close to Baiona is between the Puerto Deportivo Marina and the Bajo Baiño. However, the space to anchor is decreasing as moorings, many of them disused, steadily encroach east from the marina towards the isolated danger beacon. In addition there are several semi-submerged derelict moorings in the anchorage area and reportedly semi-submerged remains, including a complete bathing platform which, it is said, can be seen at low water.

Neither marina in Baiona permits the dinghies of anchored yachts to use them. One alternative is to use one of three sets of steps to the southeast along the sea wall which allow easy access into Baiona. The steps nearest the Marina Deportivo are congested with local boats, the second less so, but the third set is likely to be the best bet. Watch the depth at LW. Another alternative is to use the long 'Pinta' pontoon or take the dinghy to the beach.

Anchorage to the northeast of the bay

(See plan page 124)

42°08′·5N 08°49′·4W

In settled or easterly conditions it is possible to anchor off the small town of Panjón (Panxón) on the eastern side of the Ensenada de Baiona, with some protection from northwest round to south. The short stone mole (Fl(3)R.9s12m5M Red column 7m) shelters a small harbour packed with moorings, but it provides convenient steps ashore while the Club Náutico de Panjón at its root has showers, a restaurant and bar. South of the harbour is a long sandy beach, the Playa de América. Basic shopping is available in the town, which is dominated by a spectacular church.

ISLA ONS TO THE PORTUGUESE BORDER

La Guardia

Location
41°54'·04N 08°52'·90W

Tides
Standard port Lisbon
Mean time differences
HW +0050 ±0010; LW +0115 ±0010
(the above allows for the difference in time zones)
Heights in metres
MHWS	MHWN	MLWN	MLWS
3·3	2·6	1·2	0·4

Lights
North breakwater Fl(2)R.7s5M
Red truncated conical tower
Cabo Silleiro Fl(2+1)15s84m24M

Navtex
518kHz (D) at 0030, 0630, 0830*, 1230, 1630, 2030*
(*weather only)

Weather bulletins VHF
Vigo Ch 65
La Guardia Ch 21 at 0840, 1240, 2010
Vigo MRSC Ch 10 at 0015, 0415, 0815, 1215, 1615, 2015

Navigational warnings VHF
Vigo Ch 65
La Guardia Ch 21 at 0840, 2010
MRSC Vigo Ch 10 at 0215, 0615, 1015, 1415, 1815, 2215

Primary working frequencies
c/s Coruña Radio
Manual: Vigo Ch 65; La Guardia Ch 21
Autolink: Vigo Ch 62 Tx 2596 Rx 3280
DSC Ch 70 2187·5kHz

A harbour of limited use to yachtsmen

A border town and centre of seafood gastronomy in an attractive setting, La Guardia has more shops, restaurants, hotels and banks than might be expected. It is a busy fishing port with few opportunities to anchor in the harbour, and despite a mole partially closing the entrance from the north heavy swells from the west can set in. A visit in settled conditions can be rewarding, but be prepared to leave at once if conditions deteriorate.

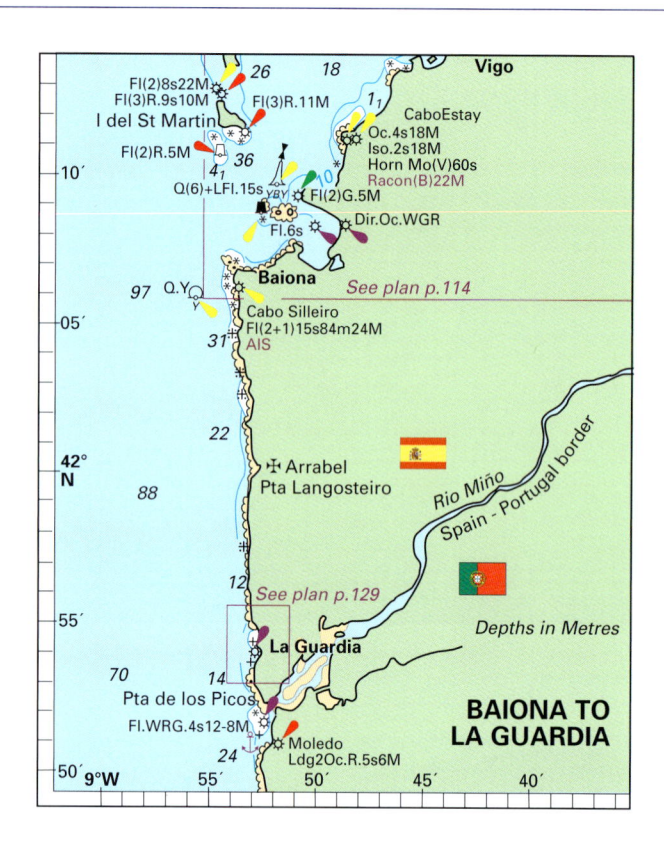

Monte de Santa Tecla, which rises steeply behind the town, repays the effort of the 350m climb. Near the summit is a remarkable Roman-Celtic hut settlement, though somewhat over-restored, and beyond this a series of large stone crosses leads to a tiny church, a restaurant and a hotel. In clear weather there are magnificent views south to the Río Miño, and Portugal, and as far north as the Islas Cíes.

Several fiestas take place in La Guardia during the course of the year, including that of the Virgen del Carmen on 16 July, and those of Monte de Santa Tecla during the second week of August.

The hazards off Cabo Silleiro

Mte Ferro Islas Cíes — Les Serralleiras — Monte Ferro — Baiona Parador — Cabo Silleiro lighthouse

128 ATLANTIC SPAIN AND PORTUGAL

LA GUARDIA

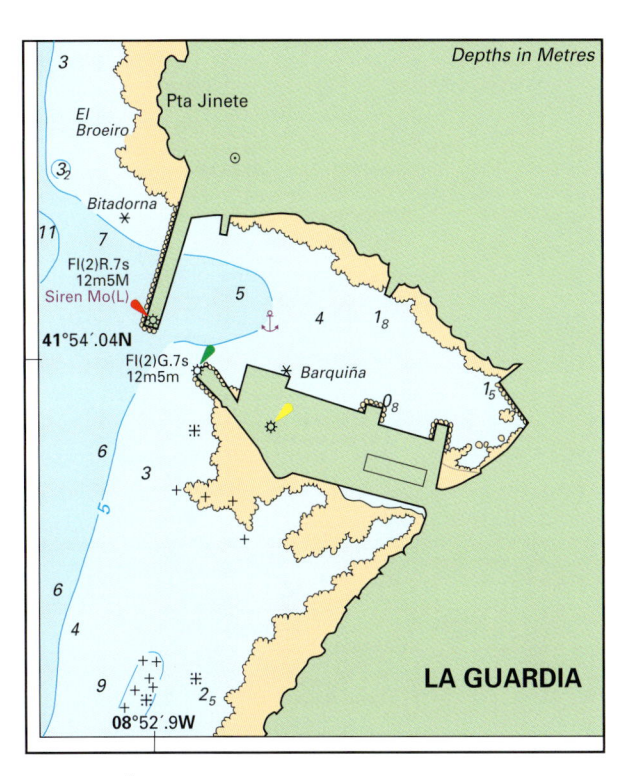

Approach

From the north The coast south from Baiona or Cabo Silleiro holds nothing for the yachtsman but potential hazards. Rocks awash extend up to 0·7M to the northwest of Cabo Silleiro. Swell builds up to crash on what is generally a lee shore and fog can obscure the shoreline although the tops of the hills behind may be in the clear. Straggling buildings run along the coast road as far as the village of Arrabel with its ancient church.

Stay at least a mile offshore until La Guardia has been identified close north of Monte de Santa Tecla. There are two chimneys on the coast just north of La Guardia.

Caution

For about 10M south of Cape Silleiro there is a multitude of unmarked fishing pot floats inshore without flags, plastic and mostly coloured grey or black.

From the south. Keep at least 1M off. Conical Monte de Santa Tecla stands out prominently with a clutch of stone buildings and radio aerials on the summit – and the two chimneys near the shore.

Do not approach La Guardia at night, in thick foggy weather, or if there is any noticeable swell.

Entrance

Make final approach from the west. The gap between the two moleheads is no more than 70m wide: enter on approximately 105°, staying near the centre as neither wall goes down sheer. Favour the north side of the harbour once inside, and keep well outside a line drawn from the molehead to the corner of the inner wharf in order to clear Barquiña, a rocky shoal some 20m outside this line.

Depths shoal from 8m at the entrance to 0·5m off the quay at the head of the harbour, and on either side it shoals rapidly.

Anchorage and mooring

Very little space remains in which to anchor, as the centre of the harbour is taken up by closely packed fishing boat moorings, while to the south the fairway to the quay must not be obstructed. North of the moorings the water is shallow with an uneven, rocky floor likely to foul an anchor – should it hold at all.

Enlist the help of local fishermen, who may be able to advise if a mooring is free. It is essential to ask (preferably attempting some Spanish) rather than to help oneself.

La Guardia from the west

GALICIA

ATLANTIC SPAIN AND PORTUGAL

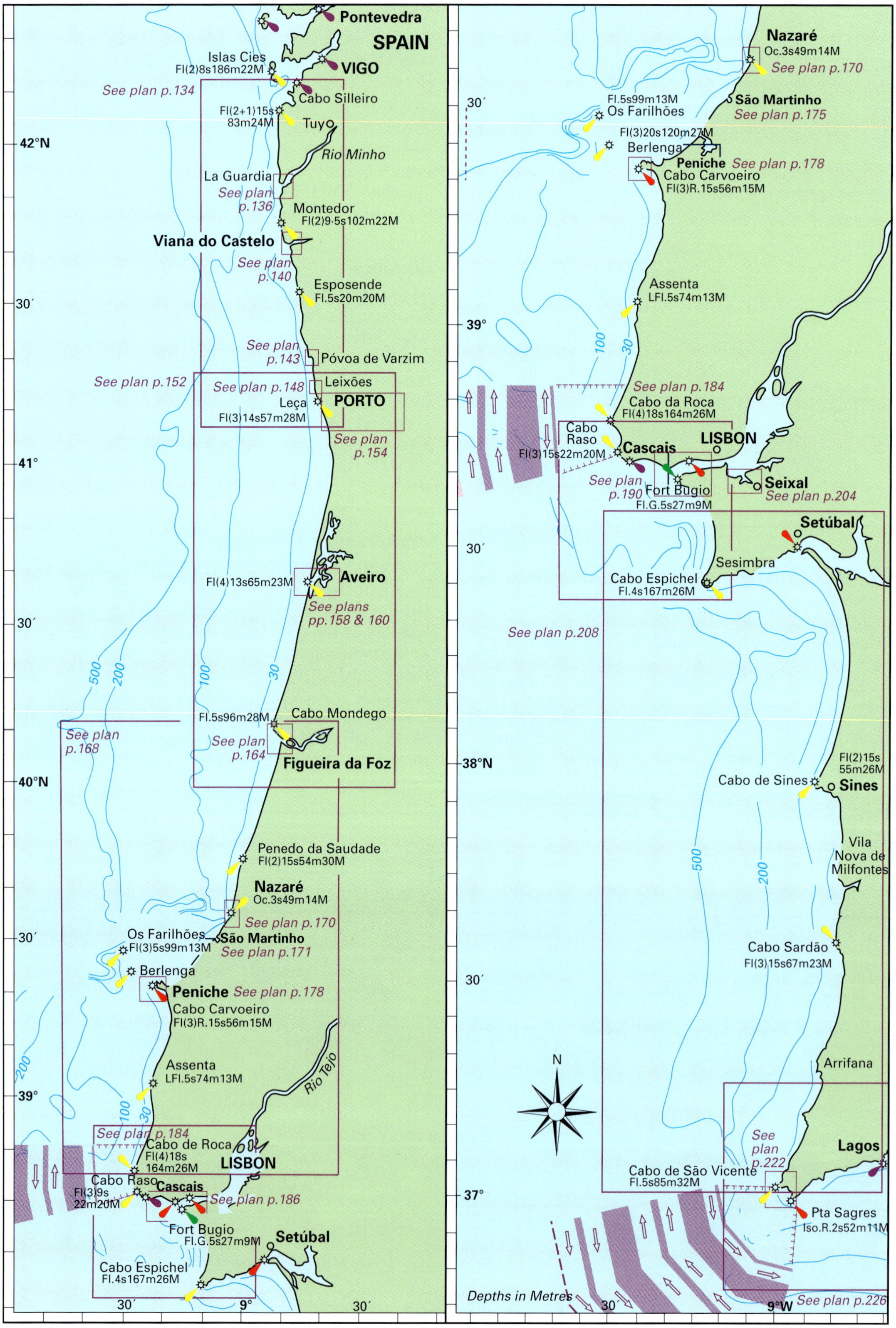

Pontevedra
SPAIN
Islas Cies
Fl(2)8s186m22M
VIGO
See plan p.134
Cabo Silleiro
Fl(2+1)15s
83m24M
Tuy
42°N
Rio Minho
La Guardia
See plan p.136
Montedor
Fl(2)9·5s102m22M
Viana do Castelo
See plan p.140
Esposende
Fl.5s20m20M
30´
See plan p.143
Póvoa de Varzim
See plan p.152
See plan p.148
Leixões
Leça
PORTO
Fl(3)14s57m28M
See plan p.154
41°
Fl(4)13s65m23M
Aveiro
See plans pp.158 & 160
30´
500
200
100
30
Fl.5s96m28M
Cabo Mondego
See plan p.168
See plan p.164
Figueira da Foz
40°N
Penedo da Saudade
Fl(2)15s54m30M
Nazaré
Oc.3s49m14M
See plan p.170
30´
Os Farilhões
Fl(3)5s99m13M
São Martinho
See plan p.171
Berlenga
Peniche
See plan p.178
Cabo Carvoeiro
Fl(3)R.15s56m15M
200
Assenta
LFl.5s74m13M
Rio Tejo
39°
100
30
See plan p.184
Cabo de Roca
Fl(4)18s
164m26M
LISBON
Cabo Raso
Fl(3)9s
22m20M
Cascais
See plan p.186
Fort Bugio
Fl.G.5s27m9M
Setúbal
Cabo Espichel
Fl.4s167m26M
30´
9°
30´
Nazaré
Oc.3s49m14M
See plan p.170
30´
Fl.5s99m13M
Os Farilhões
São Martinho
See plan p.175
Fl(3)20s120m27M
Berlenga
Peniche
See plan p.178
Cabo Carvoeiro
Fl(3)R.15s56m15M
Assenta
LFl.5s74m13M
39°
100
30
See plan p.184
Cabo da Roca
Fl(4)18s164m26M
Cabo Raso
LISBON
Fl(3)15s22m20M
Cascais
See plan p.190
Fort Bugio
Fl.G.5s27m9M
Seixal
See plan p.204
Setúbal
30´
Sesimbra
Cabo Espichel
Fl.4s167m26M
See plan p.208
38°N
Fl(2)15s
55m26M
Cabo de Sines
Sines
Vila Nova de Milfontes
500
200
Cabo Sardão
Fl(3)15s67m23M
30´
N
Arrifana
See plan p.222
Lagos
Cabo de São Vicente
Fl.5s85m32M
37°
Pta Sagres
Iso.R.2s52m11M
Depths in Metres
30´
9°W
See plan p.226

Portugal – the west coast
Foz do Minho to Cabo de São Vicente

Viana do Castelo (Montedor) in the north of the region *Henry Buchanan*

Cabo São Vicente in the south – the springboard for the great Portuguese Discoveries

ATLANTIC SPAIN AND PORTUGAL   *131*

PORTUGAL – THE WEST COAST

Overview

In the past many yachtsmen viewed the west coast of Portugal as best avoided, or to be skirted at some distance offshore en route to the Algarve or beyond. This was their loss, as it has much to offer including pockets of stunning scenery, busy wildlife habitats and a mass of history. The increased accuracy of weather and swell forecasts has played its part, since west-facing entrances can become dangerous in onshore swell, while the almost universal use of GPS has reassured navigators on the long stretches of the coast which are low and featureless and in summer may be lost in the haze.

Facilities for yachts have hugely improved with some provision for visiting yachts in almost every harbour.

However, local yacht ownership has also increased and, in most places, it is wise to telephone ahead to check that a berth will be available. Berthing is no longer the relatively cheap option it once was, a situation compounded by there being relatively few all-weather anchorages. A useful overview of some, but not all of the marinas in Portugal is given at www.portaldomar.pt click on Recreational Boating > Marinas and Harbours.

A 'long stay' yacht tax is applied to all foreign-registered yachts kept anywhere in Portugal, either ashore or afloat, for a continuous period of more than 183 days in any tax year. There is then a 30-day period, within which the tax must be paid.

In Portugal, the calendar year is the tax year. This means that if a yacht arrives in Portugal after 2nd July, it cannot become liable in that tax year. If it is in Portugal on 1 January, it would only become liable for the tax on 4 July (and the tax must then be paid by 3 August). Therefore, the standard 9-month winter contract avoids this tax.

Boats with an engine of less than 20Kw (26·82HP) or registered before 1986, are exempt from the tax. There is no requirement to register or to claim this exemption. From 2008, 'Boat Tax' became based on engine power only. It uses kilowatts as the measure. Collection is in the hands of the local *GNR–Brigada Fiscal*, and though non-payment can in theory lead to a fine of around €150 it is often poorly publicised. A certificate and receipt are issued on payment, valid for one year from the date of arrival in Portuguese waters (including the Azores and Madeira).

> **SWELL**
> Swell along this coast has its origins in low pressure storm systems which may have been centred way out in the Atlantic. It is seldom absent. In many ways it poses a greater danger than the wind, not least because it is extremely easy to underestimate its extent while still in deep water and be taken by surprise by its height and power on closing the coast. In winter it can come from anywhere between southwest and northwest; in summer it is more likely to come from northwest, with heavy swell occurring about 10% of the time. Monitor swell forecasts (see page 2).

A few harbours have hazards of one sort or another on their approach, most commonly a bar which alters with the winter storms and can be dangerous if there is a swell running, particularly if it meets an ebbing tidal stream. Even though most river mouths are now dredged and no longer pose a threat in terms of depth – those of the Rio Minho in the north and Vila Nova de Milfontes in the south being notable exceptions – nearly all can be dangerous in heavy weather, and on average at least one yacht is lost (or at least capsized) each year while attempting to enter a harbour on the Portuguese Atlantic coast in the wrong conditions.

Hazards – lobster and fish pots

Clusters of fish pots may be met with at intervals all along the Portuguese coast and particularly around the approaches to harbours. Others are laid well out to sea in surprising depths, and although most are reasonable well marked with flags, a minority rely on dark coloured plastic containers or even branches.

Winds

In April the prevailing northerly Portuguese trades – the *nortada* – begin to set in, generally blowing at around 15–25kn (Force 4–6), and becoming more firmly established from north to south as the season advances. In winter, fronts and occasionally secondary depressions may cross the area. Summer gales are unusual – in winter, onshore gales can close some harbours for days.

Particular mention should be made of the strength of the afternoon sea breezes. From early summer onwards these start to blow at around 1200 each day, regularly reaching 25kn (Force 6) and occasionally 30kn (Force 7) and continuing to blow until sundown. Typically they pick up from the east, swinging north and increasing during the afternoon. For this reason passages north, particularly in smaller yachts or if lightly crewed, are most easily made in short daily hops between dawn and midday with afternoons spent in harbour.

However it should be stressed that while these are the typical conditions, others can and do override them from time to time. In particular, September will occasionally see southwesterly winds gusting to 35kn (Force 8) blow without respite for a week or more, in which case the only prudent course is to stay put.

Winds are frequently stronger in river mouths and in the lee of headlands (due to the katabatic effects) and allowance should be made for this if entering under sail.

Visibility

Poor visibility (less than 2M) can occur any time of year but there is a steep increase in its incidence (from 3% to 10%) 60M either side of Lisbon in July and an increase of approximately the same order further north in August and September. By October, all areas have returned to the 2–4% level. Coastal fog can occur at any time but generally comes with light onshore winds.

OVERVIEW

Shelter
Many Portuguese harbours provide excellent shelter once inside, but in strong onshore winds only Leixões, Nazaré, Peniche, Cascais, Lisbon and Sines are likely to be safe to enter. In really strong winds even these can become dangerous.

Harbour entry warning signals
Portuguese Marine has a website that uses a 'flag' system to give information on the status of access to harbours along the Portuguese coast. Although provided for commercial shipping, it does give an indication of conditions pertaining. These may of course be more challenging for a yacht, so the website is no substitute for good seamanship and a close watch on the weather, state of the tide and swell conditions. This is especially necessary at harbour entrances with tides on the ebb where large standing waves can form. More advice on this is in the information for each harbour in the following pages. The website is in Portuguese but the 'flags' have the following meanings:
Red entrance is closed;
Yellow there are restrictions on entry (move the cursor over the flag for more information);
Green the harbour is open.
www.amn.pt/DGAM/Capitanias/Paginas/Estado-das-Barras.aspx

Also, following accidents along this coast, all ports have upgraded their services and keep a 24-hour watch on VHF Ch 16 (in Nazaré this is provided by the Policia Maritima outside the Port Captain's office hours). Pleasure craft are encouraged to call in on VHF Ch 16 before attempting an entry to harbour. These 24-hour watches have been expressly installed with pleasure craft in mind and will provide information on the actual sea conditions at the entrance. Accident investigators have learnt that harbour entry warning signals are often very difficult to make out.

Currents
The set of the current depends upon the recent dominant wind, but the basic trend is from north to south. Its speed averages about 0·5 knot, though this can double in summer when the *nortada* has been blowing for some time.

Tactics making a passage north
The choice of whether to head offshore or head up the coast is largely down to timing. With time available it is possible to day sail nearly the whole way and have a great cruise.

Favourable windows are more likely to be found in the Spring (May – June). Later in the summer the Portuguese trades - *nortada* - usually fill in and dominate wind and swell. But there are still periods of calm when excellent progress can be made under motor. Sometimes SW winds can occur but usually only for short periods.

Close inshore between Cabo de São Vicente and Lisbon, and Peniche and Baiona, a reduction in the current has been experienced. The problem with any tactic to take advantage of this is that, even to some distance offshore, the Portuguese lay thousands of fishing pots, most of which are inadequately marked and unlit. In daylight a very good look out should be kept, and motoring close-in at night is definitely risky.

Tides
Tidal predictions throughout Portugal use Lisbon as the Standard Port, Volume 2 of the Admiralty *Tide Tables: The Atlantic and Indian Oceans including tidal stream predictions (NP 202)*, published annually, covering the entire coastline. Alternatively, consult the UK Hydrographic Office's *EasyTide* at www.ukho.gov.uk/easytide. Predictions for the current day and the next consecutive six days are available free of charge. Predictions and additional information for past or future dates can be obtained at a small charge.

Imray's Tide Planner app also offers predictions and can be used offline. Download on the App Store/Google Play.

The mean tidal range at Lisbon is 3·3m at springs and 1·6m at neaps, but both height and time of tide along the coast can be affected by wind. Offshore tidal streams are very weak and surprisingly little is known about them – at Cabo Carvoeiro it is said to flood to the southeast, roughly the opposite to the stream off Galicia, but it is not known where the change takes place.

Climate
Rain occurs mainly between November and March, with cloud following the same pattern. Cool in winter, warm in summer, cooler in the north, warmer in the south. July averages for Lisbon are 14–36°C with 57% humidity; in January 3–16°C with 75% humidity.

Maritime radio stations and weather/navigational services
Many Portuguese Maritime radio stations and those broadcasting weather and navigational information are situated between, rather than at, ports or harbours. Details will be found under the nearest harbour to the station. All Maritime radio stations are remotely controlled from Lisbon. Broadcast times are quoted in UT, but all other times (office hours etc) are given in LT.

FOZ DO MINHO TO LEIXÕES

Foz do Minho to Leixões

Principal lights
Cabo Silleiro Fl(2+1)15s83m24M AIS
  White 8-sided tower, red bands on dwelling
Montedor Fl(2)9·5s99m22M
  Horn Mo 'S' (···)25s 800m WSW
  Square masonry tower and building 28m
Esposende Fl.5s19m20M Horn 20s 100m S
  Red tower on white base and building 15m
Leça Fl(3)14s58m28M
  White tower, narrow grey bands, red lantern 46m

The long white sand beach south of the Rio Minho
Anne Hammick

Romaria Festa parade at Viana do Castelo
Henry Buchanan

Entrance to Vila do Conde *James Peto*

134 ATLANTIC SPAIN AND PORTUGAL

FOZ DO MINHO

Foz do Minho

Tides
  Standard port Lisbon
  Mean time differences (at La Guardia)
  HW –0010 ±0010; LW +0015 ±0010
  Heights in metres
  MHWS MHWN MLWN MLWS
  3·3   2·6   1·2   0·4

Principal lights
  Fort Insua Fl.WRG.4s17m12/8/9M
    357°-W-204°-G-270°-R-357°
    White conical tower on square base 7m
  Ldg Lts 100°
    Front Moledo Oc.R.5s12m6M
    White, red and yellow column on beach 3m
    Rear 25m from front Oc.R.5s15m6M
    White, red and yellow column behind beach 7·5m
  Piedra Cabrón (Bajo de las Oliveiras)
    Fl(2)5s3M Black beacon, red band, ⁞ topmark

Warning
  Night entry not feasible, though in calm conditions it might be possible to anchor in the entrance

Communications
  Maritime radio station
  Arga (41°48'·4N 8°41'·6W)
  Remotely controlled from Lisbon)
  Manual – VHF Ch 16, 24, 25, 28. Autolink – VHF Ch 83.

Attractive river with anchorages for the intrepid navigator

The Rio Minho (or Río Miño) forms part of the boundary between Spain and Portugal. It gives its name to Portugal's northern province, where the hilly landscape with its numerous villages and their vines, eucalyptus and fruit trees is as pretty as its produce is good. The Minho valley itself is particularly attractive, though increasingly built-up near its mouth. With local knowledge and a current large-scale chart, a yacht of modest draught can navigate a considerable distance up the river. Dinghies, multihulls and monohulls able to take the ground can penetrate as far as Valença on the Portuguese shore, and Túy (Tui) on the Spanish side, where there are bridges with an estimated clearance of 15m.

However, the dangers in navigating the Foz do Minho cannot be over-estimated. The river mouth (*Foz*) is continually changing in shape, particularly regarding the position of the deep channel. Local knowledge should be consulted if at all possible before entering.

Approach

North of the entrance to the Rio Minho the approach is dominated by the 350m Monte de Santa Tecla, topped by grey stone buildings and two tall aerials. On the mountain's western flank lies a conspicuous factory with two tall chimneys.

South of the entrance a narrow strip of land fronted by a wide sandy beach separates the sea from hills which rise to some 700m about 8km inland, while the entrance itself is guarded by the low-lying Insua Nova with its stone fortress.

The approach to the mouth of the Rio Minho

ATLANTIC SPAIN AND PORTUGAL

PORTUGAL – THE WEST COAST

FOZ DO MINHO TO LEIXÕES

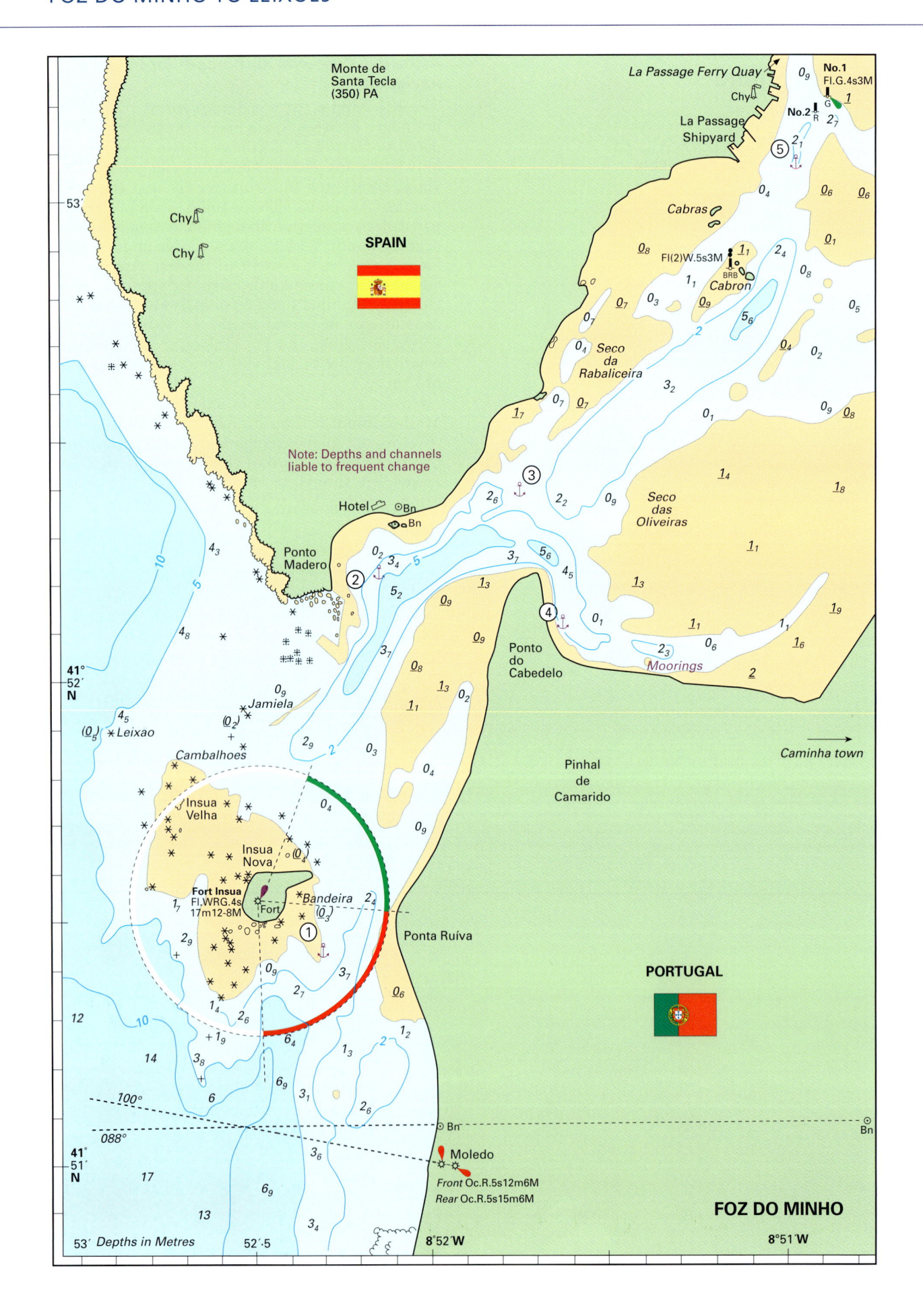

FOZ DO MINHO

Entrance
The entrance is difficult and can be dangerous, and has claimed more than one yacht as well as innumerable local craft. The Rio Minho is little visited by yachts, and it is essential that it should only be attempted in very settled weather and in the absence of any significant swell. These conditions are rare, but if they arise the river can be entered. Once inside, should westerly winds or swell get up a yacht can remain trapped for days, though well protected. There are many rocks, shoals and banks in the approaches and the river itself, the sands shift, and the currents run hard in the narrow entrance, particularly after rain. Once in the channel there are no buoys or other channel markers.

Entrance from the west
The western entrance should only be attempted with a GPS chart plotter and some very careful pre-planning, and preferably when the entrance is being used by fishing boats. A possible route on 090° passes about 40m north of the Jamiela drying rock. Along this transit the least depth shown on the chart is 1·3m (at chart datum) but this has been found in practice to be only 0·2m (at chart datum). Hence the advice of fair weather and no swell, and to this should be added 'and on the last third of the flood'. The depths found indicated that the chart cannot be relied on and this has been confirmed on the passage up river to La Passage. The charts give a general indication of where the channel is, but only a general indication as it shifts continuously.

Entrance from the south
If possible enter before half flood, when Bandeira rock, 150m east of Insua Nova, should be visible. At the same time some protection will be offered by the rocky shoals which largely block the western entrance. Follow the Moledo leading line in on 100°, noting that although the Moledo leading marks are lit, a night approach is out of the question. The nearby pair of beacons on 088°, see plan, may also be useful but the rear beacon, nearly a mile inland, is difficult to identify.

When the east side of Insua Nova bears 000°, turn onto approximately 015° and, if feasible, anchor about 250m southeast of the fort (anchorage 1) and reconnoitre by dinghy before pushing on. Pass as close to the island as Bandeira rock allows. The sandbank off Ponta Ruíva opposite is growing westwards by the year, yet remains very steep-to and in the least swell is likely to be indicated by breaking water. Beyond, the sandbank west of Ponto do Cabadelo is extending inexorably southwest requiring a dog leg to the northwest towards the Jamiela Cambalhoes rocks before turning northeast into the channel.

Beyond the entrance channel
If heading towards Caminha town and anchorage 4 turn to the southeast giving the sandbank off the Ponto do Cabedelo a wide berth. Thereafter the channel lies approximately 200m off the southern shore before shoaling as the shore turns northeast.

If continuing north-northeast favour the north shore towards anchorages 3 and 5. Beyond anchorage 3 leave to port the Cabras (goat) rocks, awash at high tide, marked with an isolated danger beacon at 41°52'·8N 8°51'·1W. Some 0·5M north of this in a direct line between the ferry terminals at Composantos and Caminha on the Spanish and Portuguese sides, there are three pairs of port and starboard beacons. Each pair is about 40m apart and some are lit.

Anchorages near the Foz
1. Temporary anchorage is possible 250m southeast of the fort on Insua Nova. Holding is good over clean sand, protected from west through north to southeast, but it is too exposed for an overnight stay in all but the very calmest conditions.

Entrance to the Rio Minho from Monte de Santa Tecla *Gavin McLaren*

FOZ DO MINHO TO LEIXÕES

2. South of the hotel on the Spanish side of the entrance, protected from the west by Ponto Madero, in 2–3m.
3. This anchorage in 2-3m is pleasant with room for several yachts anchored clear of the moorings. The stream runs hard, but not quite as hard as at La Passage (anchorage 5). It is very uncomfortable in wind against flood tide when strong NE winds blow. There is a pontoon where dinghies can be left although, around spring tides, this pontoon dries at low water.

    On the Spanish side near anchorage 3 is a busy beach with a restaurant, café and bars nearby. Ashore, the shop at the campsite is small and sells only basic groceries. It is about a half hour's walk into the modest town, where there is a market, tourist office and the usual shops.
4. Off the southern shore, east of Ponta do Cabedelo. This is a delightful anchorage with good holding and plenty of depth to moor inside, near the designated moorings full of small fishing boats.

    On the Portuguese shore near Caminha, a restaurant and a campsite with a small general store will be found near the anchorage. Caminha itself (within walking distance) has a post office, shops, a market, banks, restaurants and several public telephones. Taxis are available, with bus and train services to Valença, Vigo and Porto.
5. Abeam of the La Passage shipyard, but keeping clear of the dredged ferry channel, indicated by beacons. The holding is excellent but needs to be as the stream runs like a millrace. A yacht has recorded a virtual distance of 20M anchored overnight. At La Passage it is possible to land at steps north of the ferry pier.

    On the Spanish side near the anchorage there is a small shipyard building trawlers at La Passage. There are no facilities of any sort in the village, only some holiday homes and an active tennis club. There are no shops, cafés or restaurants and many derelict buildings.

Adjacent temporary anchorage

41°49′N 08°52′·2W (approach)

Ancora, with its small stone fort and miniature harbour, lies just over 2M south of Foz de Minho entrance. There is no room to seek protection inside the tiny harbour – even local craft are hauled high up a wide concrete apron – but in the right conditions anchoring is possible in 2–3m just off the breakwater. However, even if the morning breeze is offshore, by lunchtime the *nortada* may well make the anchorage untenable and the yacht should never be left unattended.

If intent on exploration, remain at least 0·5M offshore until the harbour has been identified, then pick up the leading marks on 071° (two red and white posts on white pyramid bases). The cross on the hill above is almost in line. Although lit, Fl(2)R.5s12m9M and Fl(2)G.5s7m6M, on no account should the coast be closed in darkness.

The town has shops and restaurants.

The mouth of the Rio Minho from the southwest. On the right is the small harbour at Ancora, about 3M south of the Foz do Minho

VIANA DO CASTELO

Viana do Castelo

Location
41°40'·34N 8°50'·43W (entrance)

Tides
Standard port Lisbon
Mean time differences (at La Guardia)
HW –0010 ±0010; LW +0015 ±0005
Heights in metres
MHWS   MHWN   MLWN   MLWS
3·5   2·7   1·4   0·5

Principal lights
Outer breakwater Fl.R.3s18m9M
  White tower, red bands 10m
Fishing harbour Ldg Lts 012° *Front* Castelo de Santiago Iso.R.4s16m5M 241°-vis-151° Red tower with white stripes, in corner of castle, white lantern 6m
Rear **Senhora da Agonia** 400m from front Oc.R.6s33m5M 005°-vis-020° Red tower with white stripes, beside prominent church, white lantern 9m
Note The above lights lead from the main channel into the fishing harbour and should NOT be followed through the entrance itself
East (inner) breakwater Fl.G.3s10m9M White tower, green bands 6m
Sectored entrance light Oc.WRG.4s18m8–6M 350°-G-005°-W-010°-R-025°-obscd-350°
Fishing harbour, port side Q.R.6m3M White column, red bands 2m
Fishing harbour, starboard side Q.G.4m4M Green column, white bands 2m

Communications
  Port Authority
  VHF Ch 11, 16 (call *Capimarviana*) (0900–1200, 1400–1700
  ☎ +351 258 359500 *Fax* +351 258 359535
  Email ipn@ipnorte.pt
  www.ipnorte.pt
  weekdays only)
  Viana Marina
  VHF Ch 12. Footbridge operation: VHF Ch 9 or 16
  ☎ +351 258 359 546
  Email marina@apvc.pt
  www.apvc.pt

Left The elegant front leading light on the corner of the Castelo de Santiago at Viana do Castelo *Anne Hammick*

Centre A float in the Romaria Festa parade – Viana do Castelo *Henry Buchanan*

Right This magnificent spectacle of song and dance with parades and fireworks display should not be missed *Henry Buchanan*

An old and attractive town with commercial harbour and a small marina on the north bank of the river

Known to the Romans and situated on the banks of the Lethe – the river of forgetfulness – in the 15th century it gained importance as the one of the main ports from which Portuguese explorers set sail. As a result, in the 16th century, the town grew rich from trade with Brazil and from cod fishing on the Newfoundland Banks.

Viana do Castelo is a pleasant town whose citizens built the beautiful grey granite and white stucco houses that make the old town so attractive today. It has good facilities including several supermarkets and the usual shops, bars and restaurants. It is on the right scale for a visiting yacht. The hospital ship, *Gil Eannes*, which acted as a mother ship to the fishing fleet on the Grand Banks in the 1860s and '70s, has been enthusiastically restored. There are many memorabilia and photographs of the cod fishery and a visit is recommended. She is berthed at the top end of the fishing dock, within easy walking distance of the marina.

A Rio style carnival takes place here every February, but one of the major festivals of the Minho area is the *Romaria* dedicated to Nossa Senhora da Agonía which takes place in Viana do Castelo over the weekend nearest to 20 August. It includes impressive floats, displays of local crafts, carnival giants (*gigantones*), local music and a magnificent fireworks display.

Approach

If coastal sailing, note that hazards lie close offshore both north and south of Viana do Castelo – for peace of mind keep outside the 20m line.

The major lights are Montedor to the north, Senhora da Agonia at Viana itself, and Esposende. There are a pair of leading lights at Neiva, 3·5M to the south, which are not relevant to Viana.

Entrance

From the north take a wide swing eastwards at least 500m south of the outer breakwater. At night, do not turn into the harbour until within the white sector of the entrance light (see plan), to pass up the centre of the buoyed channel.

From the south head in from the 20m line with the radio aerial on Faro de Anha bearing around 080° until within the white sector, then proceed as above.

ATLANTIC SPAIN AND PORTUGAL

FOZ DO MINHO TO LEIXÕES

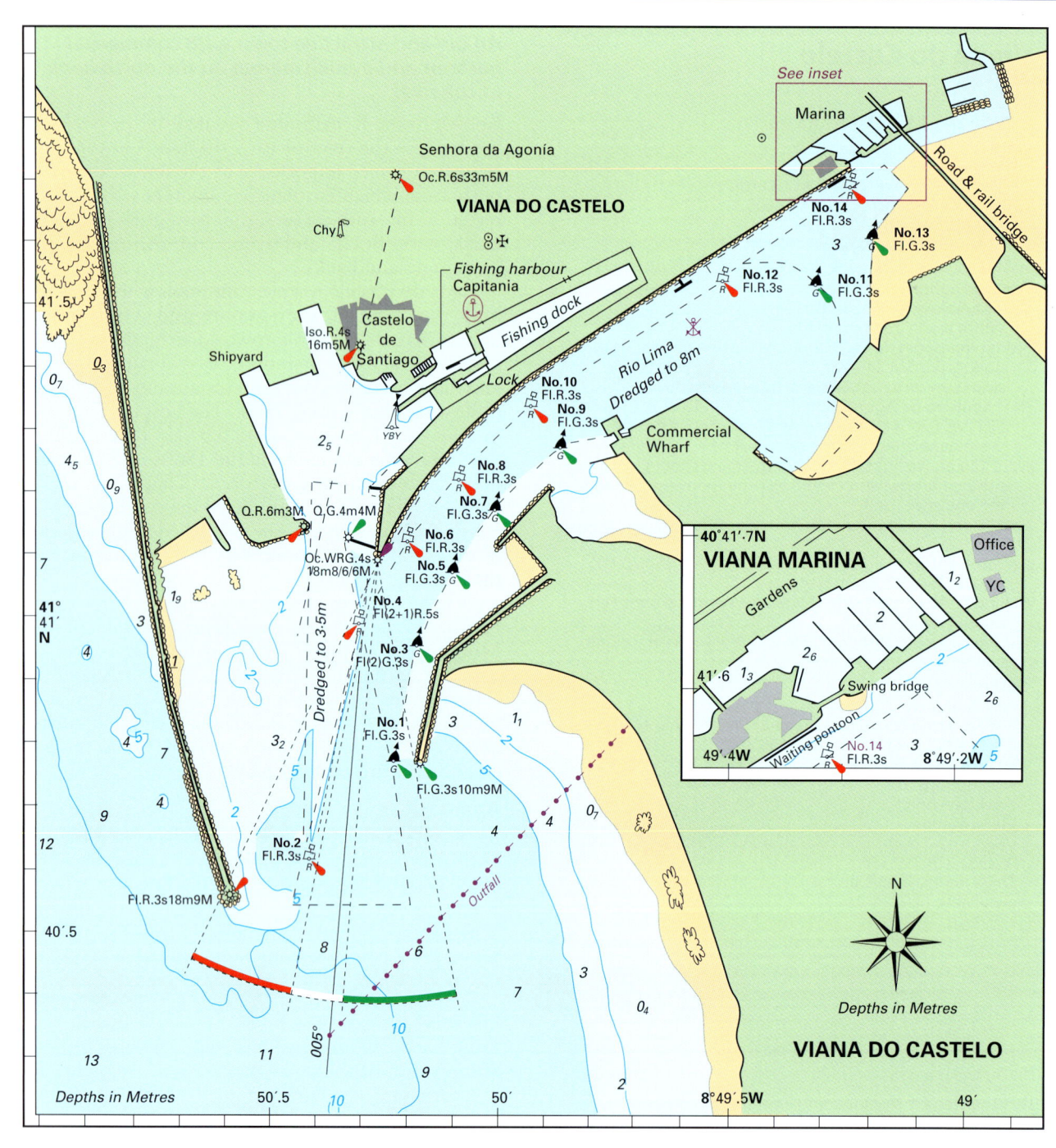

The entrance is kept dredged to 8m, making it safe in all but the severest weather or swell.

Leaving the entrance to the shipyard and fishing harbour to port, follow the buoyed channel northeast, past the commercial wharf on the starboard hand, to the marina on the north bank. This is just short of the road and rail bridge and marked by the swinging 'gate' of a cantilevered footbridge across the entrance. The footbridge has no visible lights when viewed from the west and it is hard to detect, both during the day and at night, against the background of the old road/train bridge of Rio Lima. Ten buoys are shown as marking the channel between the fishing dock and marina entrance, though it appears rare for all to be in place and working at any given time. Thus while night entry is perfectly feasible it should be undertaken with some caution.

Beyond the commercial wharf depths decrease from 8m to 3m, shoaling to less than 2·5m in the marina approach. Beware strong cross-currents at the marina entrance on both the flood and the ebb.

Caution

On the ebb at night, fishermen deploy drift nets across the entire width of the river, marked by faint white lights and a brighter white light at each end.

Berthing

Viana Marina lies about 1·5M upriver from the entrance, with its eastern end beneath the two-tier road and rail bridge (designed by Gustaf Eiffel of Tower fame). The old town is a short walk away

VIANA DO CASTELO

The south-facing entrance to Viana do Castelo

through public gardens which contain a children's playground.

The staff are helpful and will try to find a visitor a suitable place. Beware of the very strong streams running through the marina entrance and around the berths close to it. The direction and set of these are not obviously related to the times of local high and low water and there are strong eddies within the marina itself. This coupled with the strong flow in the river, which appears to be always seaward, even on the flood, merits more than usual caution when berthing here.

Just downstream of the marina the 'waiting pontoon' will take four normal sized yachts, more if rafted, and is more of a marina overflow than a waiting berth. This pontoon (and those in the marina itself) have water and electricity, but is a substantial walk from the marina office and facilities although significantly closer to town than the main part of the marina.

Beyond this is a swinging 'gate', of a cantilevered footbridge guarding the entrance. This is controlled

Entrance to Viana Marina showing the swinging footbridge (open) and waiting pontoon just downstream to port *Henry Buchanan*

by the marina staff, who can be contacted on VHF Ch 9 or 16. The 'gate' has, on occasions, been stuck open projecting out into the river. When this happens, care is needed to avoid being swept onto it by the strong stream in the river.

Within the marina space is limited. The only reasonable pontoon with fingers sometimes available to visitors is the first on the right when entering. However, this is mostly taken up with resident boats and sometimes the fuel berth is occupied. Visitors will normally berth bows or stern-

Viana Marina looking northeast

ATLANTIC SPAIN AND PORTUGAL

PORTUGAL – THE WEST COAST

FOZ DO MINHO TO LEIXÕES

to on the pontoon to port on entering. This is only a single pontoon, oriented NNE/SSW. Hauling off lines are tailed to the pontoon and there is room for about six yachts. The wall on the left has substantial vertical fendering and a large yacht could lie directly on it.

Anchoring

Although anchoring in the river is prohibited, a visiting yacht has been seen anchored immediately south of No 11 buoy. There appears to be plenty of room to anchor in this area in depths of 4-8m, well clear of the channel. The SW/NW orientated wharves in the area marked 'Commercial Wharf' are used by big ships, which need room to swing. The wharf shown directly south of No11 buoy is abandoned and there are disused mooring buoys off it. However, anchoring in this area may be possible, particularly if the marina and waiting pontoon are full. Anchoring in the bight SW of the commercial wharf is prohibited, and a yacht anchored here in 2018 was abruptly told to leave.

Facilities

Boatyard No boatyard at the marina, but extensive shipyards west of the fishing dock where commercial vessels, as well as GRP and timber fishing boats, are built. In an emergency there is little doubt that yacht repairs in most materials could be undertaken. Enquire at the marina office.

Travel-lift Not as such, but the marina has a mobile crane capable of lifting at least 20 tonnes, with larger ones available in the new commercial harbour on the south bank of the river. Yachts of suitable underwater shape may also use the tidal grid.

Engineers Costa & Rego Lda, ℡ 258 806140, situated between the river and the old commercial basin, are precision engineers and machinists. They can arrange engine repairs and will copy any unobtainable metal parts.

Next to them will be found Mechanica Magalhães (run by two brothers, it is sometimes referred to as Magalhães & Magalhães Lda), ℡ 258 823950, mobile 93 8344 797. Neither speak much English but the marina staff are happy to translate if necessary.

Finally Manuel Carvalhosa & Ca Lda, ℡258 832133, *mobile* 96 9024 743, has been recommended as 'fast, efficient and reliable' for work on diesel engines/electrics/fabrication/ welding etc.

Electronic and radio repairs Arrange through the marina office, who may well suggest Engineering Pires, mobile 91 7540 233.

Sail repairs Minor repairs may also be done locally (enquire at the marina office). For anything major try Pires de Lima in Porto (see page 149).

Chandlery A good range will be found at Angelo Silva Lda, ℡ 258 801465
www.marinehardware.en.ecplaza.net
Email geral@nautigas.pt
Overlooking the old commercial basin. Items not in stock can be ordered from a wide variety of suppliers. Ferraz & Ferraz Lda just beyond sells some chandlery in addition to all kinds of fishing tackle.

A chandlery is planned for the large building where the marina office is situated.

Water On the pontoons.

Showers Immaculate showers and toilets at the back of the block housing the marina office. The latter are open to all, the former accessed by key obtained from the marina office.

Launderette A washer and a dryer are provided in both the men's and the ladies' ablutions areas. There are several commercial launderettes in the town.

Electricity On the pontoons.

Fuel There is no longer fuel available at the marina entrance. Diesel and petrol from a filling station just beyond the road/rail bridge.

Bottled gas Camping Gaz is readily available. Angelo Silva Lda (see Chandlery above) can arrange for other bottles to be refilled, but allow a minimum of 24 hours.

Clube náutico Small but friendly *clube náutico* at the east end of the marina basin, which welcomes visiting yachtsmen.

Weather forecast At the marina office.

Banks Several in the town, nearly all with cash dispensers.

Shops/provisioning Good shopping of all kinds in the town, including several supermarkets, with a hypermarket about 1·5km inland.

Produce market Fish and produce market daily, plus open-air general market on Friday near the Castelo de Santiago at the seaward end of the town.

Cafés, restaurants and hotels A wide choice in and around the town. The *Clube Náutico* has a café/bar overlooking the marina which also serves light meals. It is open every day 1000–0200.

Medical services Hospital etc in the town.

Communications

Post office In the town.

Mailing address The marina office will hold mail for visiting yachts – c/o Instituto Portuário do Norte, Marina de Viana do Castelo, Rua da Lima, 4900-405 Viana do Castelo, Portugal. It is important that the envelope carries the name of the yacht in addition to that of the addressee.

Internet There is no WiFi at the marina or the waiting pontoon but several terminals in the nearby youth hostel (the rather boxy building) just upstream of the two-tier bridge. There are facilities in the café by the harbour office, and on the Rua General Luis do Rêgo (open 0900–1900 weekdays, 0900–1800 Saturday, closed Sunday) which also has printers.

Public telephones In the entrance to the *clube náutico* and elsewhere.

Car hire/taxis In the town. Taxis can be ordered from the marina office.

Buses and trains To Porto, Vigo and beyond.

Air services International airport at Porto some 50km away.

Not feasible – Esposende

Esposende (41°32'·5N 8°47'·5W), just under 10M south of Viana do Castelo, should be mentioned in passing – literally. A long sandbank blocks the mouth of the Rio Cávado, leaving a very shallow entrance some 50m wide which gives onto an equally shallow lagoon where a few small boats are moored. Shoals and isolated rocks (the Cavalos de Fão and Baixo da Foz) extend up to 1·5M offshore opposite the lighthouse. Give it a wide berth.

Póvoa de Varzim

Location
41°22'·15N 8°46'·14W (entrance)

Tides
Standard port Lisbon
Mean time differences
HW –0010 ±0010; LW +0015 ±0005
Heights in metres
MHWS	MHWN	MLWN	MLWS
3·5	2·7	1·4	0·5

Principal harbour lights
North breakwater Fl.R.3s14m12M
 White tower, red bands 5m Siren 40s
Note The breakwater projects some distance beyond the light structure
South breakwater LFl.G.6s13m4M
 White post, green bands 4m

Night entry
Straightforward, though care must be taken to observe the small, unlit, starboard hand buoys

Maritime radio station
Apúlia – *Digital Selective Calling* (MF)
MMSI 002630200 (planned)

Communications
Marina da Póvoa
VHF Ch 09, 12,16 (0900–1200, 1400–1700)
☎ +351 252 688121
Email clubenavalpovoense@mail.telepac.pt
www.clubenavalpovoense.com

Small, friendly marina in busy fishing harbour

Coming in from the sea, the view of Póvoa de Varzim's newer high-rise buildings belies the largely 18th-century town which lies to the east and south. This is a holiday resort close to Portugal's second city, and it has good beaches. Hotels and a casino front the beach, but the harbour still boasts an active fishing fleet and the Marina da Póvoa has gained a well-deserved reputation for friendly and efficient service. A colourful *romaria* is held on 15 August each year to commemorate those lost at sea, while the Museu Municipal de Etnografica e História on Rua do Visconde de Azevedo often has interesting displays relating to local fishing and other maritime pursuits in its handsome 18th-century headquarters.

South of Póvoa, at Rio Mau, lies the church of São Christovao completed in 1151, with some excellent carvings from this period. Two kilometres further on the same road, a left hand turn leads to Rates, where the 13th-century church of São Pedro de Rates is one of the best examples of Romanesque architecture in Portugal, boasting a magnificent rose window and some gracefully sculpted statues of saints.

The semi-circular harbour at Póvoa de Varzim, seen from a little west of south. The Marina da Póvoa can been seen on the right, with the fishing boat berths beyond

FOZ DO MINHO TO LEIXÕES

Approach

The coast between Viana do Castelo and Esposende has offlying dangers and should be given 2M clearance. From Esposende southwards there are sandy beaches and rocks with further isolated hazards all the way to Leixões. For relaxed sailing, keep outside the 20m contour, but even then fishing floats remain a hazard.

It has been reported that the (floating) wind turbine at an offshore alternative energy generation site, just inside the 50m contour about 6·8nm NNW of Povoa de Varzim, has been removed along with the 4 cardinal buoys that used to mark the exclusion zone. Continue to navigate with caution in this area because Povoa de Varzim is a centre for renewable energy where an experimental wave generator was once trialed. Something else may pop up anytime.

A distinctive white apartment block stands a short distance north of the harbour. The latter may be identified by its tower, reminiscent of an airport control tower, which also serves as an excellent landmark. A range of fish-handling buildings stand behind it.

Entrance

If approaching from the north, swing wide of the breakwater end and its associated breaking water, and note that it is also foul up to 30m off on the south side. Approach heading north-northeast towards the spur which projects at right angles from the north breakwater, giving the latter a 50m offing. When the southern breakwater head has been cleared, turn to starboard for the marina or anchorage, leaving the line of small, unlit, green buoys (which mark shoals on the inside of the breakwater) well to starboard and the (unlit) west cardinal buoy (believed to mark a rock) to port. Depth unknown.

The harbour is well protected from the northwest, but the entrance may be rough if the swell is heavy and, even in moderate conditions, breaking water can be expected off the breakwater end.

In bad weather the harbour can be closed in which case the following marks/signals are displayed from the radar tower at the root of the west breakwater:

By day A black cylinder
By night Red, green, red vertical lights.

These signals are reported difficult to see in bad weather so refer to the advice given in Harbour entry warning signals on page 133.

Beware: Alternative energy trial site (turbine removed 2017)
Henry Buchanan

The friendly and well-run Marina da Póvoa

144   ATLANTIC SPAIN AND PORTUGAL

PÓVOA DE VARZIM

Berthing
The Marina da Póvoa offers 241 berths on its six pontoons. There are about 50 berths for yachts of 10m or more with depth of at least 2·4m, and four berths for yachts of up to 18m with depth of at least 3m.

The marina lies in the shelter of the south breakwater, and even in gale force west-northwesterlies experiences remarkably little movement inside, although a vigorous chop comes across the harbour in fresh northerlies. All berths are provided with finger pontoons of appropriate length.

On arrival yachts should berth on the short hammerhead by the marina office. Office hours are 0900–2000 daily in summer, 0900–1230 and 1400–1730 in winter, with a night watchman providing 24 hour security.

Anchorage
Anchoring is permitted within the harbour provided neither the marina approach nor the many fishing boat movements to and from the north breakwater are impeded. There is room for several yachts to anchor between the buoys and the shore, or between the westerly cardinal buoy and the marina in about 2-2·5m in mud and sand. Depths shoal gradually at some distance from the shore. There is debris on the bottom so a trip line is recommended.

Formalities
If berthed in the marina (or anchored), visit the marina office taking passports, ship's papers and insurance documents. There are no forms to complete but copies of passports and boat's papers are needed. It is also not necessary to clear out from each port in Portugal as details are kept in computer systems which most ports have access to. If a change of crew is made, however, the authorities need to be informed for safety reasons.

Facilities
Boatyard Several businesses operate within the marina's secure area – ask at the office. There is a large area of open space fronting the marina, part of which is designated for use as hardstanding. A small covered workshop has been provided in the central marina building, next to the main gate.
Travel-lift A 32-tonne capacity hoist operates in the southern part of the secure area.
Engineers, electronic and radio repairs All skills available amongst those who service the fishing fleet – enquire at the marina office. A professional diver is also available.
Sail repairs Nothing nearby – try Pires de Lima in Porto (see page 153).
Chandlery Náutica Vaga, tucked away behind the old fort opposite the fishing harbour, has only limited stock. For anything major contact Angelo Silva Lda in Viana do Castelo or Nautileça in Leixões (see pages 139 and 149 respectively).
Water On the pontoons.
Showers In the central marina building.
Launderette In the central marina building.
Electricity At every berth.

Fuel No fuel at the marina, the original plan to install pumps on the reception pontoon having been shelved indefinitely. However diesel can be obtained in the fishing harbour (no minimum quantity) and small quantities of petrol, for outboards or generators, from the marina office.
Bottled gas Camping Gaz exchanges are readily available in the town, and Calor Gas bottles can be refilled. Ask at the office for directions.
Clube naval The Clube Naval Povoense, established 1904, has large premises overlooking the south breakwater, where members' dinghies and jet-skis are stored on the ground floor with a bar and restaurant above. Visiting yachtsmen are made particularly welcome. WiFi available.
Weather forecast 48-hour forecast posted daily outside the marina office.
Banks In the town, about ten minutes' walk.
Shops/provisioning Good range in the town, with a large supermarket about 2km distant.
Produce market In the town.
Cafés, restaurants and hotels Wide variety in the town, as well as a restaurant at the *clube naval*.
Medical services Well equipped first aid post in the marina's central building, with doctors and a hospital in the town.

Communications
Post offices In the town.
Mailing address By courier: Marina da Povoa, Porto de Abrigo da Povoa de Varzim, Mollhe Sul, 4490 Povoa de Varzim, Portugal.
By post: Club Naval Povoense, Rua da Ponte No 2, 4490 523 Povoa de Varzim, Portugal.
The *Clube Naval* will hold mail for visiting yachts – c/o Marina da Póvoa, Rua da Ponte No.2, Apartado 24, 4491 Póvoa de Varzim, Portugal. It is important that the envelope carries the name of the yacht in addition to that of the addressee.
Internet There is good WiFi on the marina pontoons and further access points in the town.
Public telephones At the marina's central building, with cards available from the office.
Car hire/taxis In the town. A taxi can be ordered via the marina office. Bicycles (some with small trailers) can be hired from an office at the root of the main breakwater.
Buses and trains To Porto, Viana do Castelo etc. The metro is fully open and there is an hourly express service into Porto and to near the airport (1hr). Several yachtsmen have also recommended the 'direct' bus as a convenient way to visit the city.
Air services International airport at Porto some 20km away. The metro provides easy access for crew changes.

Harbour closed. Povoa de Varzim in bad weather
James and Karin Lott

FOZ DO MINHO TO LEIXÕES

Vila do Conde

Location
41°20'·1N 8°44'·88W (entrance)

Tides
Standard port Lisbon
Mean time differences
HW –0010 ±0010; LW +0015 ±0005
Heights in metres
MHWS	MHWN	MLWN	MLWS
3·5	2·7	1·4	0·5

Principal lights
Breakwater Fl.R.4s8m9M Siren 30s
  Red column, white bands 8m
Outer Ldg Lts 079°
  Front **Azurara** Iso.G.4s9m6M
  White post, red bands 7m, at rear of beach
  Rear 370m from front Iso.G.4s26m6M
  Square white tower, red bands and ▲ 6m
Inner Ldg Lts 357° *Front* Barra Oc.R.3s6m6M
  White column, red bands 3m
  Rear 86m from front Oc.R.3s7m6M
  White column, red bands 5m

Warning
Night entry not feasible without local knowledge

Communications
Capimarviconde VHF Ch 11, 16 (0900–1200, 1400–1700 Monday–Friday).

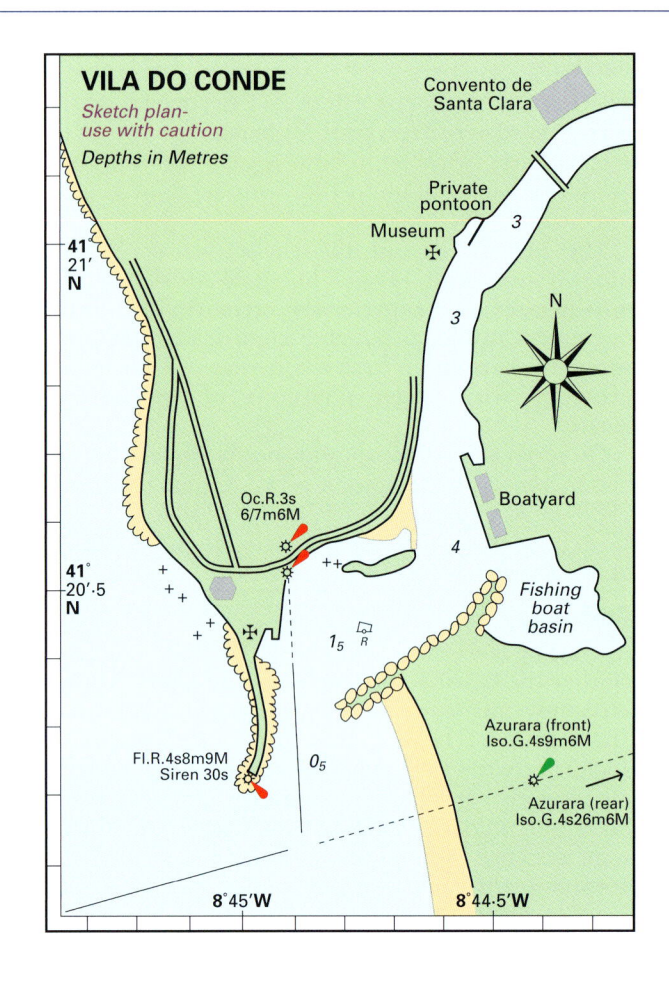

Looking into Vila do Conde from the south, with the white bulk of the Convento de Santa Clara clearly visible just left of centre

146 ATLANTIC SPAIN AND PORTUGAL

VILA DO CONDE

Pontoon, Convento de Santa Clara and road bridge looking upstream *James Peto*

Narrow river offering possible berth and anchorage

A small harbour only suitable for entry in calm weather, in daylight, and towards high tide. The town enjoyed its boom years as a shipbuilding centre during Portugal's Age of Discovery in the 15th and 16th centuries. The old fishing village, renowned for its lace, is dominated by the imposing Convento de Santa Clara. Traces of the old shipyard can still be made out, though now supplanted by the impressive building and repair yard overlooking the fishing basin. Lace-making is kept alive today at the Escola de Rendas (Lace-making School) installed on the premises of the town's Lace Museum on Rua de São Bento.

Five kilometres inland at the confluence of the rivers Ave and Este there is the pre-Roman site of Bagunte.

Approach and entrance

The entrance lies at the southern end of the line of high-rise blocks strung out along the beach between Póvoa and Vila do Conde. The low breakwater is some 350m long and has a small chapel dedicated to Senhora da Gaia at its root.

From offshore the outer leading marks, on 079°, clear the mole but are difficult to identify from offshore. The inner pair, on 357°, lead over the bar – which may shoal to 0·5m at low water springs – but as the bar shifts these do not always indicate best water.

Once round the eastern (inner) mole the channel swings to pass south of a small, L-shaped sandbank, marked by a single red buoy. A sizeable fishing boat basin, not available to yachts, lies to the east of the bend.

Tidal streams in the relatively narrow entrance can run strongly on both ebb and flood. It is advisable to enter the river at the end of the flood.

Berthing

There is a pontoon in the river just downstream of the road bridge (see photograph). It is private but it is reported to be possible to berth for a night against a vessel of suitable size, or in a gap on the basis that the owner may return. There is a gate at the end of the pontoon.

Anchorage

Anchor just short of the road bridge in 3–4m, taking care to buoy the anchor as the bottom is mainly foul. On the north bank there is an unusual fortified church with an almost Moorish white dome, while the entire area is overshadowed by the vast bulk of the Convento de Santa Clara.

Facilities and communications

Food shops, banks, and restaurants are all available as well as a lively produce market on Fridays. There is a post office and public telephones sited throughout the town. The metro and regular bus service provide transport north to Póvoa de Varzim and south to Porto.

FOZ DO MINHO TO LEIXÕES

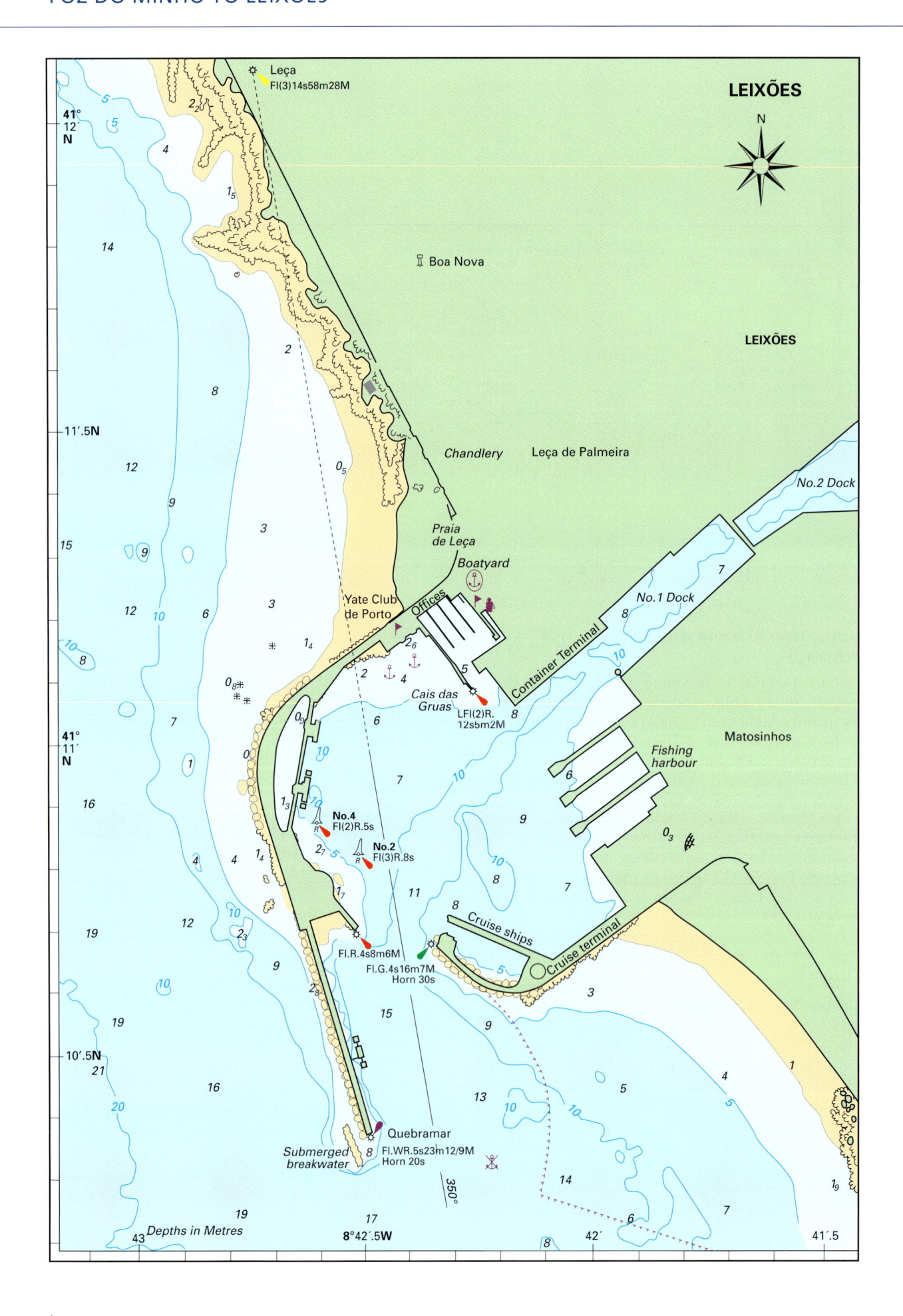

LEIXÕES

Leça
Fl(3)14s58m28M

Boa Nova

LEIXÕES

Chandlery   Leça de Palmeira

No.2 Dock

Praia de Leça
Boatyard

Yate Club de Porto   Offices

No.1 Dock

Cais das Gruas
LFl(2)R.12s5m2M

Container Terminal

Fishing harbour

Matosinhos

No.4 Fl(2)R.5s
No.2 Fl(3)R.8s

Cruise ships
Cruise terminal

Fl.R.4s8m6M
Fl.G.4s16m7M Horn 30s

Quebramar
Fl.WR.5s23m12/9M Horn 20s

Submerged breakwater

350°

Depths in Metres
8°42´.5W   42´   41´.5

148   ATLANTIC SPAIN AND PORTUGAL

LEIXÕES

Leixões

Location
41°10'·2N 8°42'·35W (entrance)

Tides
Standard port Lisbon
Mean time differences
HW −0015 ±0010; LW +0005 ±0005
Heights in metres

MHWS	MHWN	MLWN	MLWS
3·5	2·7	1·3	0·5

Principal lights
Leça
  Fl(3)14s58m28M White tower, narrow grey bands 46m
West breakwater head (Quebramar)
  Fl.WR.5s23m12/9M 001°-R-180°-W-001°
  Horn 20s Grey tower 10m
West breakwater spur
  Fl.R.4s8m6M Red lantern 4m
South breakwater
  Fl.G.4s16m7M 328°-vis-285° Horn 30s
  Hexagonal tower, green lantern 10m

Marina mole (Cais das Gruas)
  LFl(2)R.12s4m2M White post, red bands 3m

Night entry
Straightforward – the entrance is wide and the harbour well-lit. However it might be wise to anchor until daylight rather than enter the crowded marina

Weather bulletins and navigational warnings
Weather bulletins in Portuguese only, from the Rio Minho to Cabo de São Vicente to 20 miles offshore, are broadcast on VHF Ch 11 at 0705 and 1905 UT.
Navigational warnings in Portuguese and English within 200 miles offshore: VHF Ch 11 at 0705, 1905 UT

Communications
Marina Porto Atlântico
VHF Ch 09, 16 (0900–1230 & 1400–2000 daily 16 June–15 September, otherwise 0900–1230 & 1400–1830 Monday–Saturday).
① +351 229 964895
Email info@marinaportoatlantico.net
www.marinaportoatlantico.net (with English translation)

The large harbour at Leixões with the marina tucked in the north corner by the beach

The striking cruise ship terminal building on the eastern breakwater *Vysotsky (Wikimedia)*

ATLANTIC SPAIN AND PORTUGAL

FOZ DO MINHO TO LEIXÕES

A secure marina and adjacent anchorage which can be entered in all weather conditions

Leixões (pronounced '*layshoinsh*'), with its wide entrance, is by far the best port of refuge on this stretch of the coast and can be entered in almost any weather. During westerly gales the swell at the entrance may be heavy, but it decreases rapidly once inside. The busy commercial port is centred on oil, fishing and general trade, while the Marina Porto Atlântico in its north corner was one of the first yacht harbours to be established on the Portuguese Atlantic coast. The marina provides good shelter and is an excellent base from which to explore the fascinating city of Porto, easily accessible by bus, taxi or *metro*. Those cruising with small children may be interested to know that the infant school on the road which runs north past the marina allows visiting youngsters to use the play area in its grounds.

Perhaps inevitably, bearing in mind its position in the corner of a commercial harbour, with a refinery nearby, the marina sometimes suffers from poor water quality, but effective measures have been made to overcome this.

Approach

Compared to the coastline further north, the area around Leixões is somewhat featureless. The oil refinery 1·5M north is a good mark by day or night, with the powerful Leça light lying between it and the harbour.

A spherical yellow outfall buoy (Fl.Y.4s6M Horn 30s) and a yellow tanker discharge 'superbuoy' (Fl(3)15s6M Horn (3)30s) lie 2·2M northwest of the west breakwater at 41°12′·5N 8°44′·7W and 41°12′·2N 8°45′W respectively. If in the vicinity after dark, note that both have occasionally been reported as unlit, and that other unlit yellow buoys have been reported nearby. A prohibited zone extends 1000m in all directions from the superbuoy, which is located about 1·6M offshore and well outside the 20m depth contour.

Harbour regulations state that vessels must give the outside of the west breakwater a berth of at least 1M, but few fishing boats appear to observe this. There are, however, shoals up to 200m off the seaward side of this breakwater as well as obstructions off its end. There are fewer hazards if approaching from the south, though several lit yellow buoys may be encountered within 1M of the shore. The buildings of Porto can be seen from a good distance, with the entrance to Leixões 2M northwest.

Entrance

The breakwater light may be difficult to identify against shore lights, but from south of the harbour Leça light on 350° leads between the breakwater spur and the eastern breakwater on which there is a striking cruise ship terminal building. Once past the inner end of the eastern breakwater, the marina entrance will become visible. Floating debris can be a hazard when crossing the harbour, and it is also best to avoid entry in the early evening when the many fishing trawlers are heading out to sea.

Between the eastern mole and the cruise ship terminal a number of piles have been put in place with pontoons. These have water and electricity points but are probably intended for use by local craft. The striking building nearby is the cruise ship terminal.

Berthing

The three yacht clubs and the Marina Porto Atlântico are all located around the old fishing harbour at the north corner of the main harbour, behind a short mole (the Cais das Gruas). The narrow entrance (less than 50m wide) faces southeast, but even so considerable surge may work in during strong southwesterlies. Boats berthed near the entrance will obviously bear the brunt.

The marina, which has been dredged to 5m, can berth about 240 boats alongside narrow finger pontoons. It is crowded with local craft, but it is claimed that space can always be found for a visitor, even if this means rafting up at the reception berth.

The waiting/welcome pontoon is on the port side just after the turn into the marina, hard against the mole. The marina office and showers are at the root of the mole, through the self-closing and card accessed gate. Office hours are 0900–1230 and 1400–1830 daily from 16/6 until 15/9, closing all day Sunday outside the high season. The marina personnel have been consistently praised for their helpfulness and efficiency, and all office staff (though not all the *marineros*) speak good English.

Anchorage

A designated public anchorage exists just off the yacht club, outside the marina, in the angle formed between the marina mole and the western breakwater, in 5m or more. Holding, particularly near the mole, is reported to be good over mud. There is a single ladder on the outside of the marina mole at which a dinghy might be left (though note the 3m spring range). The short pontoon belonging to the Yate Clube de Porto is closed off by security gates from early evening. It is normally possible to leave a dinghy in the marina, in which case a small charge is made.

Leixões fuel berth looking southeast *James Peto*

150   ATLANTIC SPAIN AND PORTUGAL

Formalities

Visit the marina office equipped with passports, ship's papers, and insurance documents whether berthed in the marina or anchored off. There are no forms to complete but copies of passports and boat's papers are taken. There is also no need to clear out from each port in Portugal as details are kept in computer systems which most ports have access to. If a change of crew is made, however, the authorities need to be informed, for safety reasons.

Facilities

Boatyard The boatyard next to the marina is able to handle repairs in GRP, wood, steel and aluminium. The WOW chandlery (see below) will arrange engine, electrical, sail, rigging services.

Travel-lift No travel-lift, but 6·3-tonne capacity crane at the boatyard. The nearest large (i.e. 32-tonne capacity) travel-lift is at Póvoa de Varzim, 12M north.

Engineers, electronic and radio repairs Inboard and outboard engine specialists, and electrical and electronic workshops, are all available, though geared more to commercial vessels than yachts. Ask at the marina office. Lisbon-based NautiRadar Lda (see page 199) has a local agent, Antonio Rocha ☎ 229 381 391.

Sailmaker The Pires de Lima loft, Rua Joaquim Vieira Moutinho 35, 1160 Santa Cruz de Bispo, ☎229 952 218
  Email ukportugal@mail.telepac.pt, is situated a taxi-ride away near the airport. Sails are both made and repaired.

Chandlery There is a new (2018) chandlery next to the marina office called Walk on Wind (WOW). Open 0900-1300 and 1430-1830 and contactable by phone on Sunday. ☎+351 925 862 030 or *Mob* +351 963 237 060. It is small but has useful stock and is willing to order and ship (e.g. to a future port) most other items.

Charts Portuguese charts and other publications may be available from 'Sailing', at Traversa des Laranjeiras 34, Foz do Douro, 4100 Porto, ☎226 179 936

Liferaft servicing Can be arranged via the Walk on Wind chandlery, see above.

The Marina Porto Atlântico at Leixões looking east. The anchorage is in the clear area in the foreground

Water On the pontoons.

Showers At the marina – free if occupying a berth, but charged for if anchored off. The Yate Clube de Porto also has showers, which it may be possible to use by arrangement.

Laundry Full laundry service through the WOW chandlery.

Electricity On the pontoons.

Fuel The fuel berth is on the NE side of the marina. A rock is apparently just off the NE end of the fuel pontoon. The pontoons have been doubled up from the SE end to the fuel area so that there is a step in the end which is best avoided. Going in forward, it is quite difficult to reverse out and there is very little room to do a U-turn, especially as water depths are limited. It is suggested that the fuel berth is best approached going astern and after half tide, feeling the way in. It would be prudent to walk round from the waiting pontoon to check first. The fuel berth is open from 1000 to 1830 subject to there being enough water.

Bottled gas Through the WOW chandlery. Also, cylinders taken to the Petrogal refinery about 2km north of the marina will be exchanged or refilled as necessary.

Clube náuticos The Yate Clube de Porto, the Clube Vela Atlântico and the Clube Náutico de Leça all overlook the harbour and marina.

Weather forecast Posted daily at the marina office.

Banks In Leça da Palmeira (about 1km away), Matosinhos and Porto.

Shops/provisioning Good shopping locally, and a very wide choice in Porto.

Produce market In Matosinhos, a taxi-ride away – or at least for the return, if heavy laden.

Cafés, restaurants and hotels There is a good selection of simple restaurants and cafes just across the road from the port entrance. The Yate Clube de Porto has a formal restaurant as well as a very pleasant terrace bar. Otherwise, there are many in Leça da Palmeira, but nearly all at some distance from the harbour.

Medical services In Leça da Palmeira, with a large modern hospital in Porto.

Communications

Post offices In Leça da Palmeira, Matosinhos and Porto.

Mailing address The marina office will hold mail for visiting yachts – c/o Marina Porto Atlântico, Molhe Norte de Leixões, 4450-718 Leça da Palmeira, Portugal. It is important that the envelope carries the name of the yacht in addition to that of the addressee.

Internet access A public computer terminal is installed in the marina office. Good WiFi is available.

Car hire/taxis Both can be arranged via the marina office, though there is a good chance of flagging down a taxi on the main road outside the harbour gates.

Buses Number 507 runs into Porto (a city not to be missed) every 15/20 minutes. A convenient bus stop will be found on the main road just outside the harbour gates.

Trains Stations at Leça da Palmeira and Porto, both of which can be reached by bus. The metro line links Matosinhos to the city centre. Unlike most of its fellows, much of the line is above ground and a good part of that runs, tram-like, along city streets, making it scenic as well as practical.

Air services Porto International Airport lies about 6km northeast of the harbour and is reachable by metro. The WOW chandlery (see above) will arrange a shuttle to the airport.

PORTO TO FIGUEIRA DA FOZ

Porto to Figueira da Foz

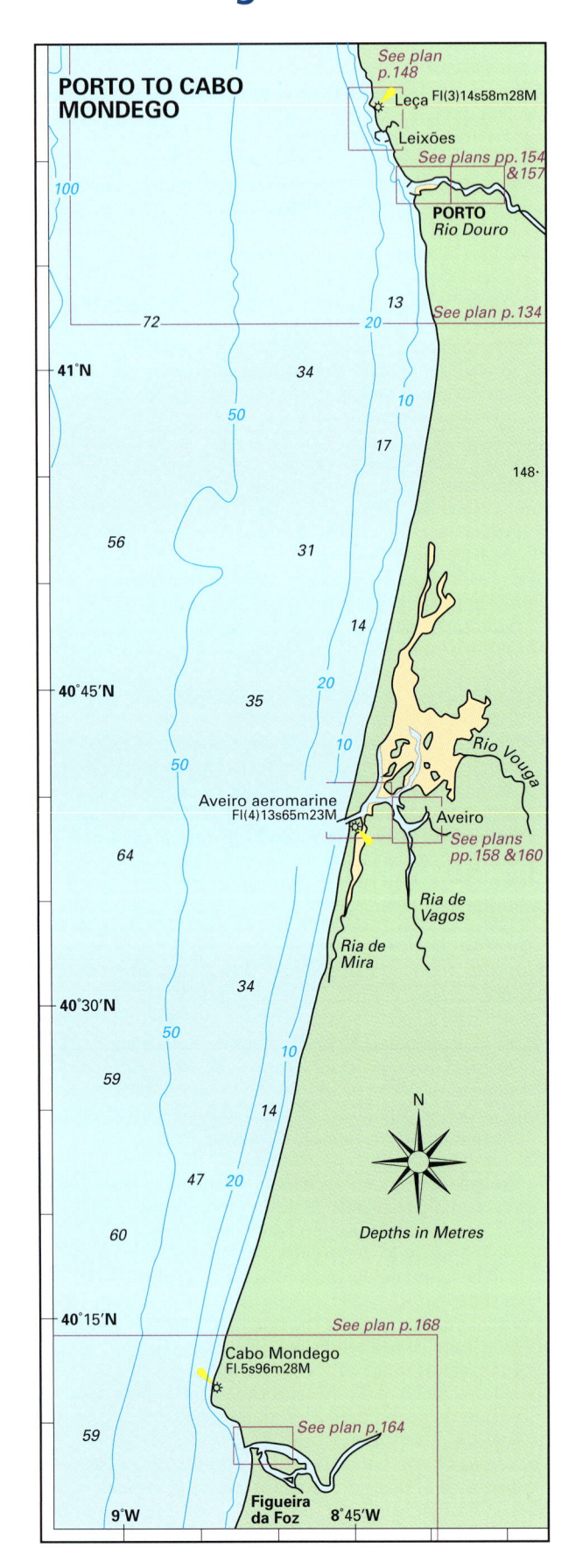

PRINCIPAL LIGHTS
Leça Fl(3)14s58m28M
  White tower, narrow grey bands 46m
Aveiro Fl(4)13s65m23M
  Red tower, white bands and building 62m
Cabo Mondego Fl.5s96m28M Horn 30s
  Square white tower and building, red cupola 15m

Rio Douro tide gauge at Cantareira mole *Jane Russell*

Typical coastline off Aveiro *Henry Buchanan*

The Marina at Figueira de Foz *Henry Buchanan*

152 ATLANTIC SPAIN AND PORTUGAL

PORTO

Porto and the Rio Douro

Location
 41°08'·54N 8°41'W

Tides
 Standard port Lisbon
 Mean time differences (at entrance)
 HW 0000 ±0010; LW +0020 ±0005
 Heights in metres
 MHWS   MHWN   MLWN   MLWS
 3·2   2·5   1·3   0·5
 Mean time differences (at Porto)
 HW 0000; LW +0040
 Heights in metres
 MHWS   MHWN   MLWN   MLWS
 3·3   2·6   1·3   0·5

Principal lights
 Molhe N (new north breakwater Lt)
  Fl.R.5s21m9M Red and White banded column
 Molhe S (new south breakwater Lt)
  Fl.G.5s17m6M Green and White banded column
 Leading Lights 059°
  Front Barra Foz horizontal red/white beacon Oc.Y.5s16m6M
  Rear Barra Foz horizontal red/white beacon Oc.Y.5s37m6M

Warning
 Night entry not feasible – divert to Leixões instead

Harbour communications
 Douro Marina, Rua de Praia, 4405 – 780 Vila Nova de Gaia, Portugal 41°08'·58N 008°39'·03W
 VHF Ch 9 ① +351 220 907 300 or +351 918 501 474 (mobile)
 Email info@douromarina.com www.douromarina.com

A fascinating old city on the Rio Douro

Extensive works involving the building of breakwaters and the erection of new lights and marks have improved the approach to the Rio Douro which used to be a famously testing entrance. The second city of Portugal, Porto rises magnificently above the gorge at the mouth of the Douro. Its historic involvement with the rest of Europe, the Americas and the East makes a fascinating tale. The reverberations remain in its architecture, its customs and its behaviour, as well as in its present commercial life.

Although there are few buildings of great historical significance, as a working city with a long and fascinating history (the bishopric is of very

Leading lights 059° at entrance to Rio Douro
Gavin McLaren

The Rio Douro looking east into Porto *Douro Marina*

PORTUGAL – THE WEST COAST

ATLANTIC SPAIN AND PORTUGAL   153

PORTO TO FIGUEIRA DA FOZ

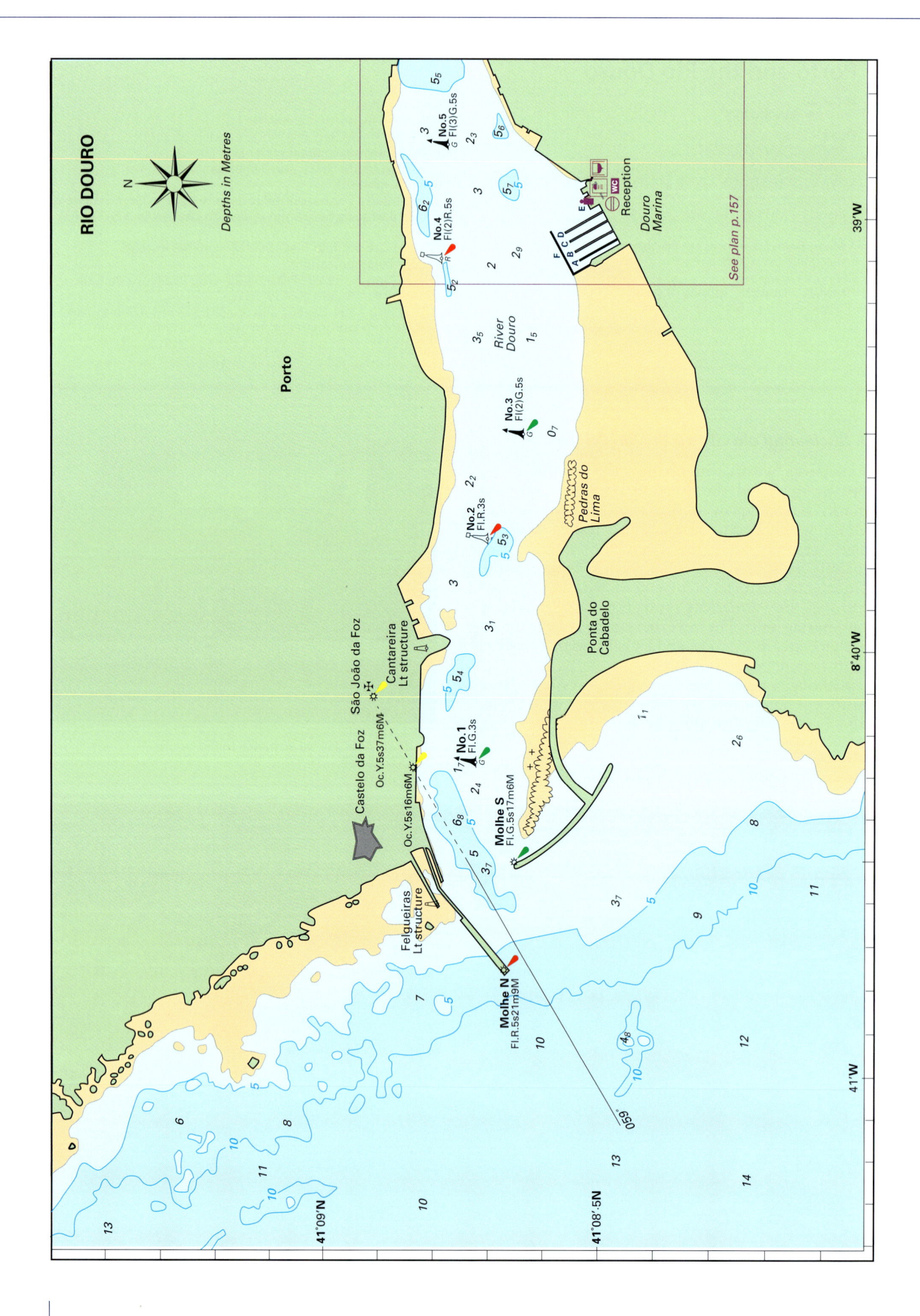

RIO DOURO

Depths in Metres

Porto

River Douro

Douro Marina
Reception
See plan p.157

No.5 Fl(3)G.5s
No.4 Fl(2)R.5s
No.3 Fl(2)G.5s
No.2 Fl.R.3s
No.1 Fl.G.3s

Pedras do Lima
Ponta do Cabadelo

São João da Foz
Cantareira Lt structure
Castelo da Foz
Oc.Y.5s37m6M
Oc.Y.5s16m6M

Felgueiras Lt structure

Molhe S Fl.G.5s17m6M
Molhe N Fl.R.5s21m9M

059°

154 ATLANTIC SPAIN AND PORTUGAL

PORTO

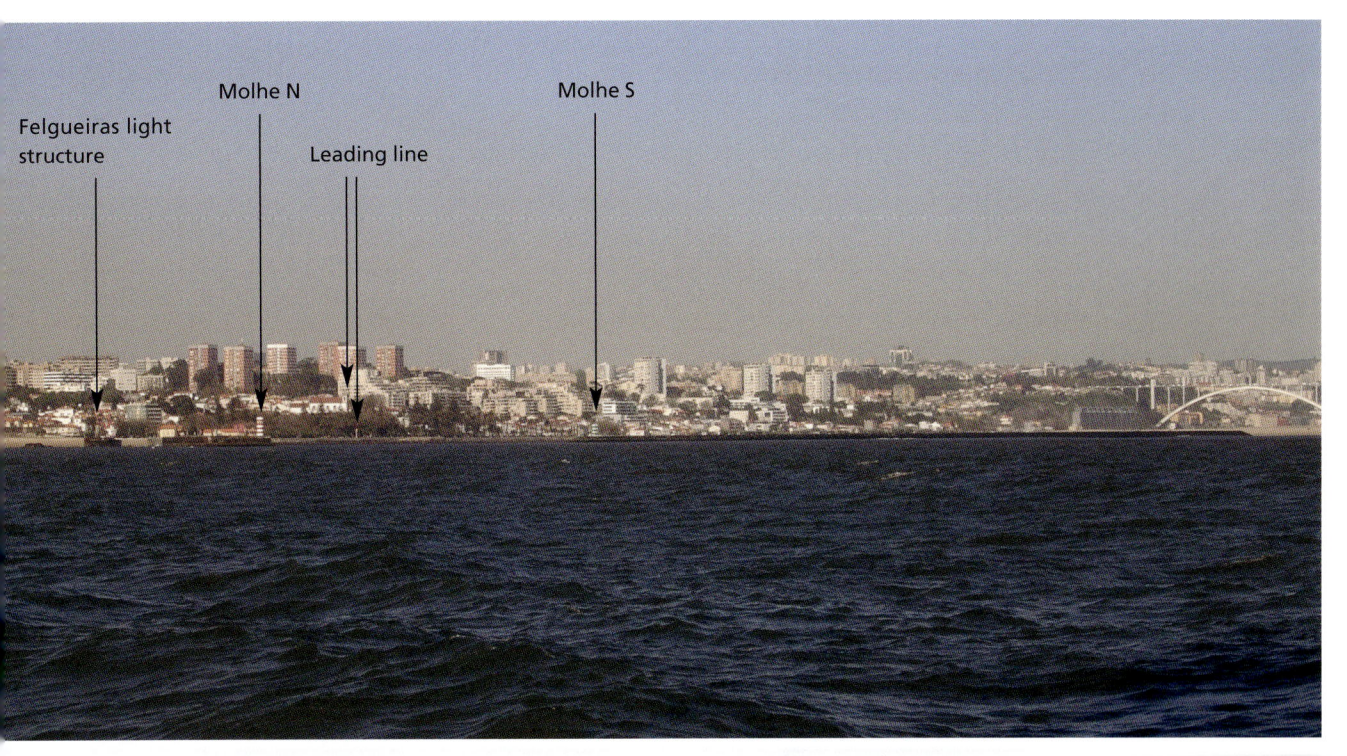

Entrance to the Rio Douro from seaward – Leading Line just open to starboard *Henry Buchanan*

ancient origin), it is a delightful town through which to wander, although a certain fitness is needed to cope with the city's hills. The cathedral area deserves to be explored, and the densely populated quarter of Barredo, which appears not to have changed since medieval times. The riverside quarter of Ribeira is also delightful, with narrow streets, typical houses and attractive life-style. It has been restored and now includes fashionable restaurants and bars. Equally lively and colourful is the market of Bolhão. More elegant shops can be seen nearby in the Baixa (down-town). There are continuous reminders of the town's long-standing and prosperous connection with the wine trade which flourished in the 18th century, after the English merchants began to lace the best Douro wines with brandy. A highlight of any visit to the city must be a trip to one or more of the port warehouses at Vila Nova de Gaia, on the south bank opposite the Cais da Estiva, for a guided tour and tasting.

Approach

The low hills along the coast between Leixões and Porto extend south beyond the mouth (*foz*) of the Rio Douro. Further south the foreshore is flat, with sandy beaches and marshes behind, and from that direction the buildings on the hill immediately north of the Rio Douro are conspicuous.

Entrance

The bar across the entrance is dangerous in strong onshore winds or when there is heavy swell, with a 6-7 knot current on the spring ebb which may be even stronger after rain. In winter, storms may close the entrance for weeks. See Harbour entry warning signals, page 133. To add to the challenge both the narrows and the 'bag' inside are frequently crowded with dozens of small, open boats lying at anchor whilst their owners fish. It hardly needs saying that entry should only be attempted in daylight and settled weather, preferably on the last third of the flood.

The leading line through the breakwaters into the Rio Douro has been established on a transit of 059°, marked by a red/white horizontally striped beacon at the front and a window in the tower of the little church (São João da Foz) at the rear. The forward light is 12m high and the rear light 37m high. The characteristics of both are Oc(1)Y.5s. Once inside, favour the northern shore towards Cantareira point rounding SHB No.1. The bar is claimed to carry at least 3m at MLWS, but this figure fluctuates from year to year. Cantareira mole has a rocky shoal off its southeast tip and should be given a wide berth before rounding PHB No.2 a little further in. Skirt close to No.2 buoy to keep well clear of the opposing Ponta do Cabadelo, a long sandspit which has been extending north and east.

Once in the Rio Douro, the channel as far as the Ponte de Arrábida (60·5m clearance) is well-buoyed and should present no problems. Beyond the bridge there are only two more buoys, but at least 6m should be found in mid-channel up to the Ponte Dom Luís I (8·8m).

ATLANTIC SPAIN AND PORTUGAL   155

PORTO TO FIGUEIRA DA FOZ

Douro Marina looking westward Douro Marina

DOURO MARINA

working with the port authority to have this area dredged. It should be noted that the marina normally meets visitors' boats with a rib as a courtesy service and this service is always available if a skipper has any concerns about the depth of the channel.

Douro Marina has much to recommend it. The staff are outstandingly helpful and speak good English. The facilities are first class. There is at least 2m in the marina itself where there are 300 berths, 60 of them for visitors, and boats up to 30m can be accommodated. It has a pontoon reserved for catamarans and applies the same prices as a monohull meaning that rates are calculated by the length and not by the beam.

Berthing
Navigate the channel into the Rio Douro and, when port-hand buoy No.4 bears north, steer 161° towards the marina entrance, a distance of about 0·3M. The depth in this access channel is 3·5m, but there is a small area outside and upstream of the channel that is shallow. Douro Marina has been

Formalities
Visit the marina office equipped with passports, ship's papers and insurance documents. There are no forms to complete but copies of passports and boat's papers are taken. There is also no need to clear out from each port in Portugal as details are kept in computer systems which most ports have access to.

Douro Marina from north shore. No 4 port hand buoy in foreground Jane Russell

156 ATLANTIC SPAIN AND PORTUGAL

PORTO

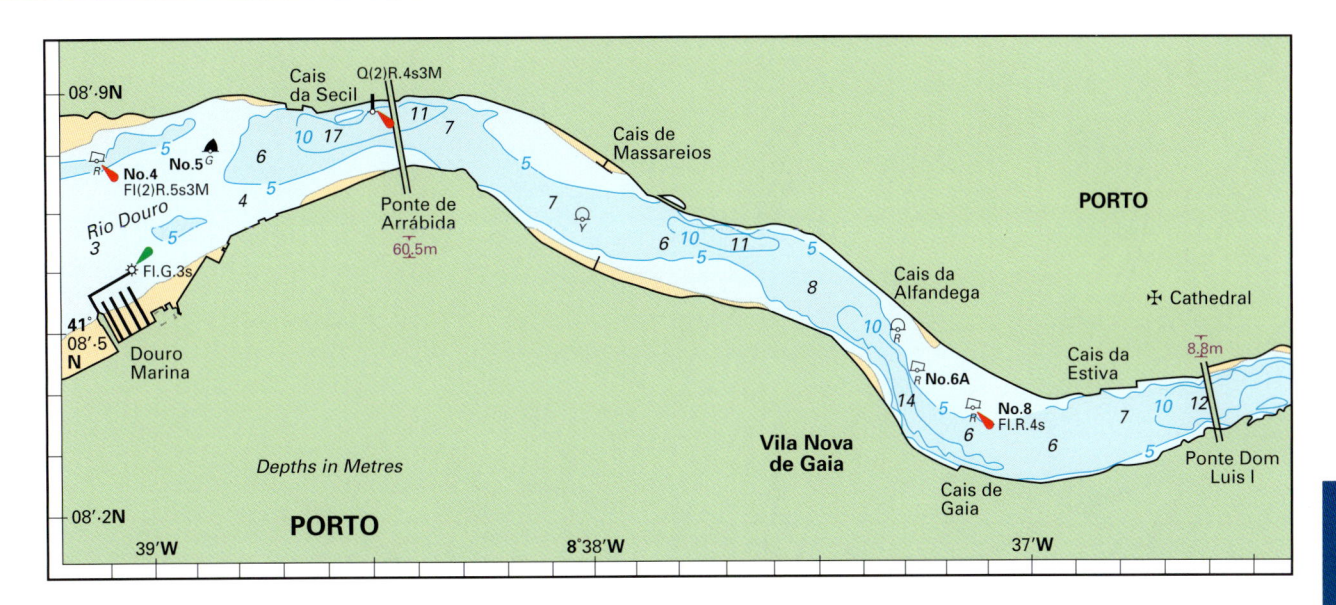

If a change of crew is made, however, the authorities need to be informed, for safety reasons.

Facilities
Security 24hr security. Access to the pontoons is via a swipe card system.
Boatyard There is a workshop for maintenance and repair of boats with brand expertise available such as Volvo, Yanmar, Dupon Marina Paint and International Paint.
Travel-lift 75 ton, Crane 3·2 ton, and a ramp.
Engineers Electronic and radio repairs. Enquire at the marina office.
Diving Diver available at the marina.
Sailmaker/sail repairs Sails in need of repair are normally sent to Lisbon for attention. Ask at the marina office.
Chandlery There is a small, helpful chandlery at the marina.
Water On the pontoons.
Showers Within the marina facilities.
Launderette The launderette is small, with only a single washer and drier. For the days when the laundry in the marina is overwhelmed, there is a large, much used, communal laundry area.
Electricity On the pontoons.
Fuel Diesel and petrol at the reception/fuel pontoon.
Bottled gas Enquire at the marina office.
Weather forecast Posted daily outside the marina office.
Banks ATM at the marina.
Shops/provisioning There is a paper shop in the marina and good shopping of all types in Porto. The village of (São Pedro Da) Afurada is close N of the marina. There are modest shops, sufficient for everyday needs, café/bars and simple restaurants. There is a fish market in the mornings from Tuesday to Saturday, and a general market on Saturdays only. About 15 min walk up the hill is a shopping centre with a large Continente supermarket.
 The very large El Corte Ingles department store chain has a supermarket some 4km away. They will send a free car to the marina to collect visitors and return them with their shopping.
Cafés, restaurants There are café-bars and restaurants at the marina. There is a traditional street barbecue restaurant a short walk from the marina in the village of Taberna Sao Pedro.
Medical services In Porto.

Communications
Post office In Porto.
Mailing address Marina Douro Rua da Praia, 430, 4400-554 Vila Nova de Gaia, Portugal. It is important that the envelope carries the name of the yacht in addition to that of the addressee.
Internet WiFi in the marina.
Fax service ☏+351 220 907 309
Car/bicycle hire Rent-a-car and Rent-a-bike at the marina.
Transport A ferry runs from the village to the Porto side at about ½ hour intervals. There is a good bus service from just outside the marina to the city centre. There is a cycle path along the bank of the Rio Douro.
Airport Douro Marina is 15km far from the international airport of Porto.

Upriver
Motorboats, or yachts with masts which can be lowered, can explore as far as Barca de Alva, 200km upstream, following cruise boats into the large locks. The approaches require care and 6kn of boat speed in some conditions.

The upper reaches of the Rio Douro are particularly attractive, and if unable to venture by yacht it could be worth jumping ship to spend a few days aboard one of the many hotel-boats which ply the river.

Not feasible – Lagoa de Esmoriz

The Lagoa de Esmoriz (40°57'·6N 8°39'·5W), close south of Espinho and some 11M south of Porto, bears more than a passing resemblance to Esposende – but on an even smaller scale. Sail on by.

PORTO TO FIGUEIRA DA FOZ

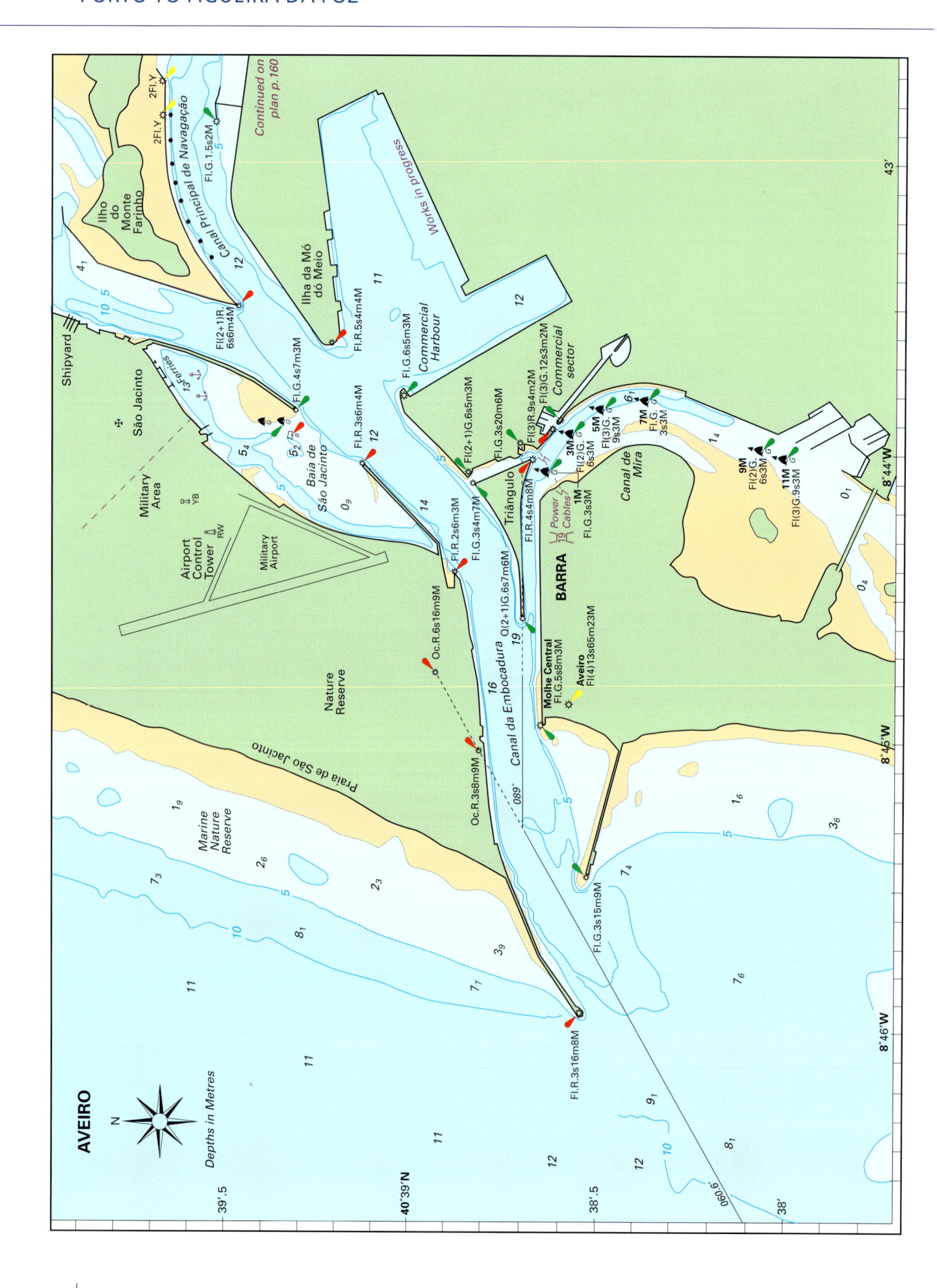

Ria de Aveiro

Location
40° 38'·36N 8°46'·09W (entrance)

Tides
Standard port Lisbon
Mean time differences (at entrance)
HW +0005 ±0005; LW +0010 ±005
Heights in metres
MHWS	MHWN	MLWN	MLWS
3·2	2·6	1·4	0·7

Principal lights
Aveiro Fl(4)13s66m23M Red tower, white bands and building 62m
North breakwater Fl.R.3s12m8M Horn 15s White tower, red bands 6m
South breakwater Fl.G.3s17m9M White tower, green bands 12m (20m from outer end)
Outer Ldg Lts 085° *Front* South breakwater
  Rear 850m from front Fl.G.4s54m9M 065·4°-vis°-105·4° Shares tower with Aveiro (above), at 50m
Entrance channel north side
  Fl.R.2s7m3M Red tower 4m
Entrance Ldg Lts 066° *Front* Oc.R.3s8m9M 060·6°-vis-070·6° Red column 4m
  Rear 440m from front Oc.R.6s16m9M 060·6°-vis-070·6° Red column 13m
South inner mole LFl.G.5s9m3M White tower, green bands 4m
Triangle – west corner Fl(2+1)G.6s8m6M Green tower, red band 4m
Inner Ldg Lts 089°
  Front **Triangle – west corner** (above)
  Rear **Fuerte de Barra** 870m from front Fl.G.3s21m6M 084·5°-vis°-094·5° White tower 19m
Monte Farinha Red tower, green band Fl(2+1)R.6s4M

Plus numerous lit and unlit beacons and buoys on the Canal Principal de Navegação, leading to the Canal das Pirâmides lock – see plan on page 160.

Warning
Night entry not recommended, even in light conditions. Although the entrance is well lit this does not extend to any of the yacht berths or anchorages

Communications
Capimaraveiro VHF Ch 11, 16 (0900–1200, 1400–1700 Monday–Friday)
Associação Aveirense de Vela de Cruzeiro (AVELA)
☏ +351 234 422 142, *Email* avela@avela.pt
www.avela.pt (in Portuguese only). VHF Ch9.
Maritime radio station
Arestal (40°46'·8N 8°21'4W)
Remotely controlled from Lisbon)
Manual – VHF Ch 16, 24, 25, 26. *Autolink* – VHF Ch 85.

Windswept channels and lagoons, inside a potentially dangerous entrance

The Aveiro estuary is made up of salt marshes and sand spits, low-lying and often deceptive. The ría has been developed as an oil, timber and general port but it is possible to escape into unspoilt, almost desolate, surroundings. The fishing port of Aveiro, some 12km from the entrance, was an ancient bishopric and the town prospered from the salt trade and fishing off Newfoundland, until a storm in the 16th century effectively closed the entrance. It was re-opened early in the 19th century and Aveiro recovered its prosperity. With its humpbacked bridges the slightly Dutch air to the town is reinforced by the range and quantities of food originating here. Today it combines modern business and industry with reminders of the past, and is one of the more attractive towns along the coast. The historic Feira de Março takes place from late March to late April featuring many folk and rock concerts, but the Festa da Ría in mid-Summer with its historic heritage of painted boats – moliceiros – is probably more appropriate for the nautically minded. The town is known for its general merrymaking during the festival. The Festas do Sao Paio in early September features a traditional boat race on the northern lagoon. A useful website provides nautical information for the Ria de Aveiro www.riadeaveiro.pt/nautic

Approach

If coastal sailing from the north, from the Rio Douro to Espinho the coast is backed by low hills some 7km inland and has isolated rocks inshore. South from Espinho one continuous beach backed by sand dunes and lagoons – known locally as the *Costa de Prata* or 'silver coast' – stretches for over 50M to Cabo Mondego, with the Barra de Aveiro rather less than halfway down its length. A dangerous wreck lies just over 2M southwest of the entrance at approximately 40°36'·7N 8°47'W.

Entrance

This is one of the harbours which should only be entered in settled weather and with little or no swell. The potential dangers of the entrance should not be underestimated. It is notable that, even in the summer, the Portuguese Navtex from Monsanto frequently reports Aveiro is closed due to swell. Winds from between northwest and southwest can quickly produce a vicious sea, at its worst on the ebb tide – which may reach 8kn in the entrance at springs following heavy rain. The ebb runs for about seven hours and the flood for five, the best time to enter or leave being shortly before high water.

The northern breakwater to Aviero has been extended and provided useful shelter in its lee to a yacht arriving in a 35kn northwester about 1·5 hours before high water, encountering overfalls before being swept up the channel at over 9kn. If coming from the north, give the end of the north breakwater a wide berth, as shoals often build around its tip, while least depths, and hence the worst seas, are also to be found in this area.

There is one leading line for the outer entrance on 060° consisting of two red columns which are hard to pick out. A leading line on 089° inside the entrance is intended mainly for commercial traffic heading for the Canal de Mira.

PORTO TO FIGUEIRA DA FOZ

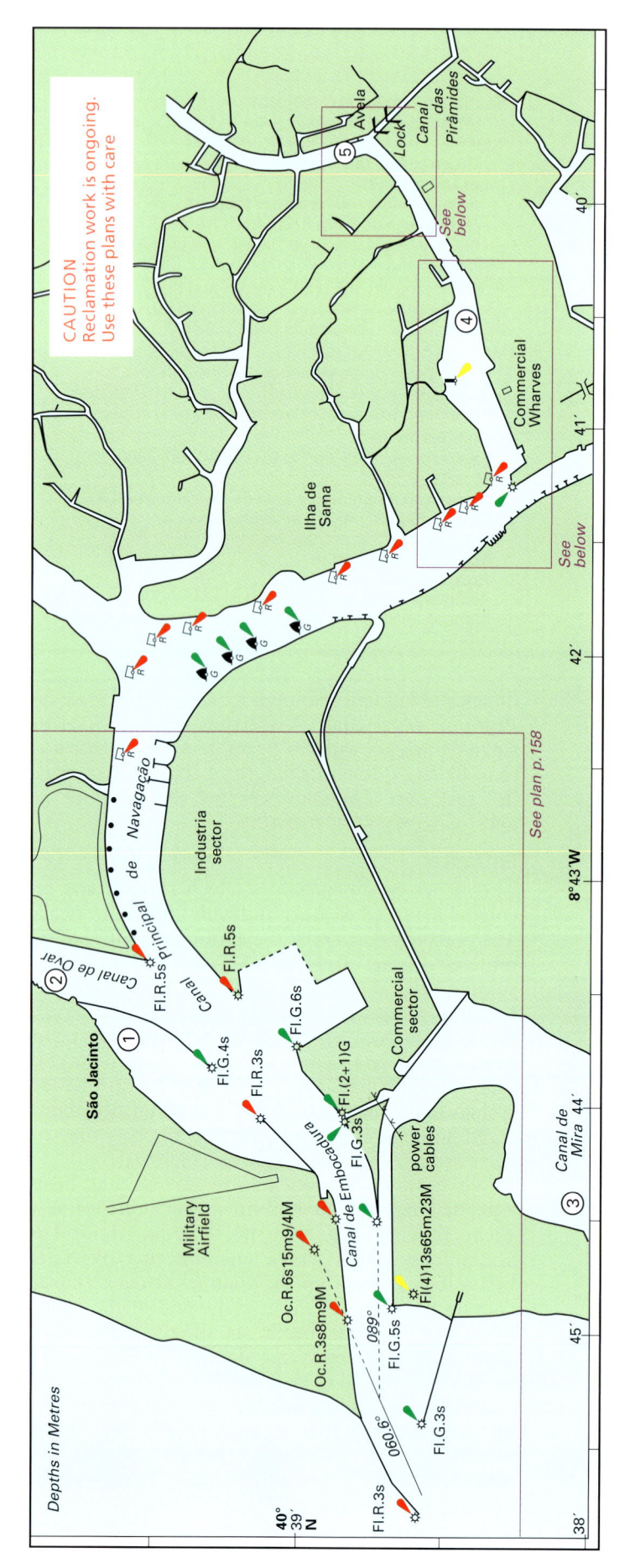

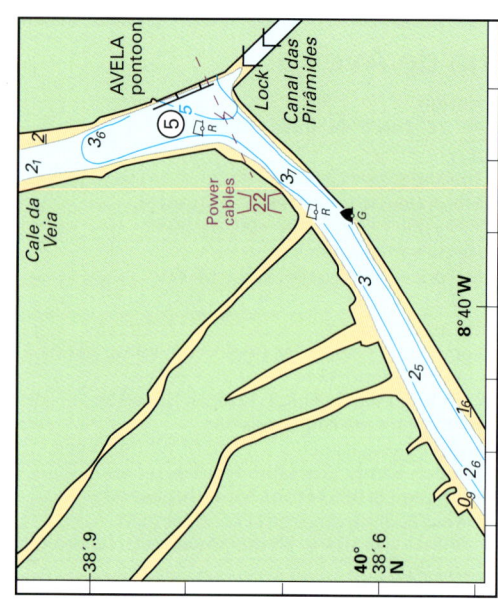

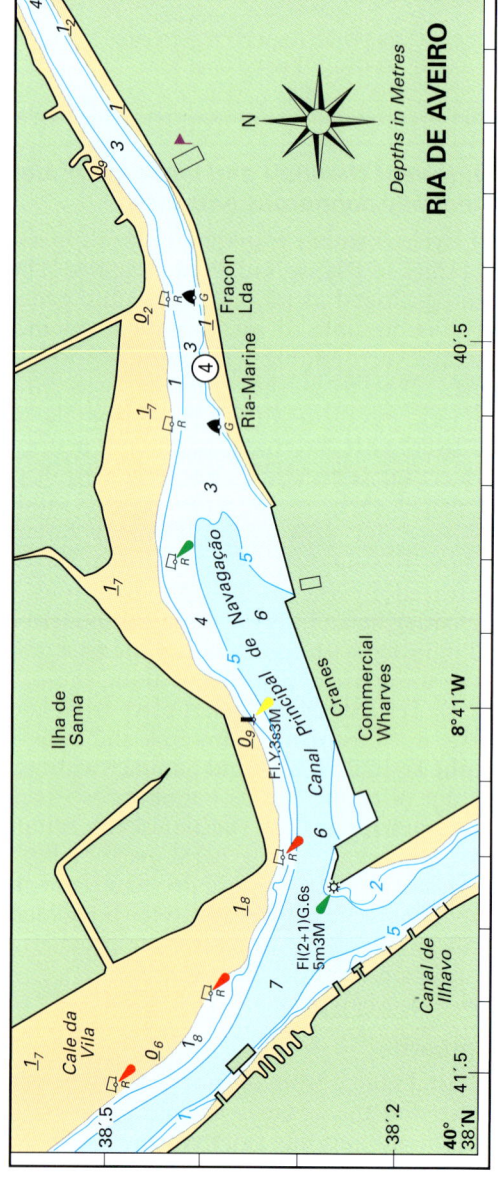

RIA DE AVEIRO

160 ATLANTIC SPAIN AND PORTUGAL

RIA DE AVEIRO

The potentially dangerous entrance to the Ria de Aveiro looking east-northeast. Note that the north breakwater was extended in 2013 after this photograph was taken. Yachts can just be seen anchored in Baía de São Jacinto, top left

Once inside the protection of the river mouth the tide may still run strongly, but there should never be less than 7m depths and frequently much more. Leave the Triângulo (islet) to starboard and continue up the Canal de Embocadura. The channel buoys are usually well maintained.

Anchorages and berthing
(see plans on pages 158 and 160)

There are very limited facilities for yachts, and the two small marinas in the Canal de Mira to the south (see plan) are not only shallow, but inaccessible to most cruising yachts due to the 8–10m power cables which cross the Canal at its northern end.

1. São Jacinto is very much a holiday town, with numerous cafés and restaurants, small shops, a post office and several public telephones. This is a good place to stay, weather permitting, to visit both Aveiro, which is a must to visit, and to catch the train to Coimbra. The ferry is co-ordinated with the bus in both directions which goes to the rail station, all within an hour.

   There is nothing specifically for yachts, though a small shipyard lies just to the north. There is a nature reserve along the beach to the west but the large military area, including the airfield, is off limits.

   Anchorage will be found in the Baía de São Jacinto, about 1·5M northeast of the river mouth, but the bay has become busy in recent years. Local moorings now occupy the north end of the bay, behind which are steps and a broad slipway. The ferry pier carries prominent 'no mooring' notices, and though it might be possible to land by dinghy at the small craft pontoon beyond, there is no possibility of lying alongside, even for a few minutes.

   The continual movement of small pleasure fishing boats is disturbing and getting ashore difficult as the pontoon is crowded with dinghies and any remaining space taken up by people fishing with rod and line that festoon the water front.

   The entrance to the Baía de São Jacinto is shallow although there are good depths once inside, but it is essential to observe the buoyage – currently red and green buoys to port and starboard on entering, with a further green buoy marking the western edge of the north shoal. The outer moles are both lit (F.R and F.G), but movement after dark is not recommended. Strong currents with unpredictable eddies run across and into the entrance on both the flood and the ebb.

   If the inner buoy is not in place and no local craft are on hand to offer a lead in, after passing between the entrance buoys, head for a conspicuous yellow and black water tower on approximately 330°. Remain on this bearing until past the shallowest part of the bar (0·5–1m at datum). When the Military Base pier (often with small military craft alongside) bears 015°, head in towards it, following the shore in 5–6m towards the ferry pier.

   Anchor south of the moorings in 7–10m. The bottom is somewhat uneven, with holding poor in places and excellent in others. One yacht has reported holding absolutely firm while laid over by gusts exceeding 50kn, while another tried five times to hold, only to be told later that a minimum of 50m of chain should have been veered. In the latter case the yacht was waved over to the ferry pontoon and secured against an old ferry in 'perfect peace'.

   An alternative used by another yacht that could not get its anchor to hold was to go to the southwest corner of the harbour although care is needed as the channel to that part is quite narrow, but there is over 3m depth.

2. It is also possible to anchor further north in the Canal de Ovar, a lagoon separated from the sea by a sandbank carrying the access road to São Jacinto. Navigation is tricky and a detailed chart is required. The advice is to go in (and out) through the dog-leg just north of the training wall off São Jacinto at slack high water to avoid being pushed around while manoeuvring through the

ATLANTIC SPAIN AND PORTUGAL

PORTO TO FIGUEIRA DA FOZ

Anchored at 40°41·039'N 08°43·012'W in the Canal de Ovar *Tim Good*

sand banks. Tidal currents weaken beyond São Jacinto, and though relatively shallow (2·5–3m) where the Canal is wide, the narrow stretches contain pools with 5-9m. A yacht has recently (2018) anchored at 40°41·039'N 08°43·012'W in 6-9m with good holding (see photo) to enjoy the wetlands, flamingoes and the Nature Reserve in peace.

3. Space may be found for a small visiting yacht at the Marina da Costa Nova on the Canal Mira, but air height is restricted to an estimated 8–10m by the power cables already mentioned. The channel is indicated by buoys and posts.
4. Yachts have in the past anchored in the Canal Principal de Navagação, a buoyed channel carrying 3–4m and leading to the town of Aveiro (see plan overleaf). However tidal currents are strong and it would be difficult to find swinging room without impeding local traffic. The Clube Naval de Aveiro and neighbouring Sporting Clube de Aveiro have no more than 1m at their quays – local smallcraft are craned ashore when not in use – but for short periods it may be possible to lie alongside the jetty at either the Ría-Marine or Fracon yards – see under Facilities, below.

The entrance to São Jacinto *James Peto*

Berthing at any of the fishermen's or commercial quays is strongly discouraged.

5. Space may be found alongside the 200m pontoon installed at the AVELA (the Associação Aveirense de Vela de Cruzeiro) Club marina (40°38·80'N 08°39·77'W) in the Canal de Veia, close to the Canal das Pirâmides lock. Though privately owned, visiting yachts are most welcome. Water and electricity are installed on the pontoon with alongside depths understood to be 4m.
VHF Ch9 ☏+351 234 422 142
Email avela@avela.pt www.avela.pt

Club rooms are at the end of a long building, just opposite the ramp from the pontoon. Shower and toilet facilities are available and AVELA provides a key for the security gate on the ramp.

Power cables with a reported air height of 22m crossing the Canal just downstream of the pontoon will restrict larger yachts from reaching the AVELA Club marina.

It is possible to anchor above the power cables and beyond the Avela pontoon in a position 40°38'·964N 08°39'·887W. Mooring with two anchors with 50m out on each leg, up and down stream reduces the sheering about in the strong currents.

162 ATLANTIC SPAIN AND PORTUGAL

RIA DE AVEIRO

The AVELA pontoon, close north of the Canal das Pirâmides Lock *James Peto*

As yachts are no longer permitted to use the Canal das Pirâmides, which runs through the centre of the old town of Aveiro, a good option is to take the dinghy for what would otherwise be a long hot walk to Aveiro. The town is charming and there are all the shops and facilities one would expect from a regional centre. This is a good place to spend a few days, relax and stock up in perfect shelter. The Canal is administered by the Associação Turistica Vigilância, with the lock reported to open for one hour either side of high water and on demand at other times – most often for small tourist vessels with which a dinghy could double up (the lock measures 18m by 5m). Strong tidal eddies may be encountered at the entrance.

Formalities

The *GNR–Brigada Fiscal* and possibly the *Polícia Marítima* may visit if anchored in the Baía de São Jacinto or moored at the AVELA pontoon.

Facilities

Boatyard Fracon Lda ☎ 234 422297
Email fracon@fracon.p www.fracon.pt on the Canal Principal de Navegação can handle repairs in all materials including GRP in large covered workshops. Staff are helpful with some English and German spoken, and security appears to be good. There is plenty of outdoor hardstanding for potential winter lay-up.

Ria-Marine Lda, ☎ +351 234 384049/426686, just downstream of Fracon, can handle work on yachts of all sizes in GRP, wood and steel. Little or no English is spoken. In the mid 1990s the yard was given responsibility for rebuilding Portugal's last surviving East Indiaman, the *D Fernando II e Glória*, for the Lisbon Maritime Museum, a commission which they carried out to a high standard.

Travel-lift Not as such, but Fracon has a 10-tonne capacity crane and can arrange for a 30 tonner to visit, and also has a marine railway (unsuitable for deep keels). Ría-Marine can haul yachts of all sizes by crane or on one of their two marine railways.

Engineers, mechanics, electricians At both Fracon and Ría-Marine as well as Quatro-Ventos (see *Chandlery*, below).

Sail repairs Can be organised via Quatro-Ventos, below.

Chandlery Good range at Quatro-Ventos, 230 Avenida Fernandes Lavrador, Praia da Barra (accessible by ferry from the São Jacinto anchorage),
☎ +351 243 394654
Email quatro-ventos@quatro-ventos.com,
www.quatro-ventos.com. Owner Augusto Pereir (who also runs a sailing school and is an agent for Bénéteau) is reported to be helpful and efficient, and to speak fluent English and French. He can arrange for maintenance and repairs to anything from engines to sails etc.

Charts Portuguese charts and other publications may be available from Bolivar, on Rua da Aviação Naval 51, 3810 Aveiro.

Water On the AVELA pontoon, or by can from the Clube Naval de Aveiro or one of the boatyards.

Showers May be available at the Clube Naval de Aveiro or at one of the yards.

Electricity On the AVELA pontoon, though see above.

Fuel By can from a filling station in Aveiro. In an emergency it might be possible to buy a few litres from Fracon's own supply, but they are not officially licensed to sell retail.

Clube naval The Clube Naval de Aveiro and the Sporting Clube de Aveiro both have premises on the Canal Principal de Navegação, but only the former appears to be open regularly.

Banks In Aveiro.

Shops/provisioning Good shopping in Aveiro, but a much more restricted choice in São Jacinto.

Cafés, restaurants and hotels Wide choice in Aveiro, with plenty of cafés and restaurants (but apparently no hotels) in São Jacinto.

Medical services In Aveiro.

Communications

Post offices In both Aveiro and São Jacinto
Telephones Public telephones in both towns.
Car hire/taxis In Aveiro.
Ferries Regular ferries from the pier at São Jacinto across the Canal de Embocadura to Barra, on the south side of the estuary, and tourist excursions downstream from Aveiro via the Canal das Pirâmides.
Trains Direct rail link to Porto, amongst other destinations.
Air services Porto International Airport lies about 70km to the north.

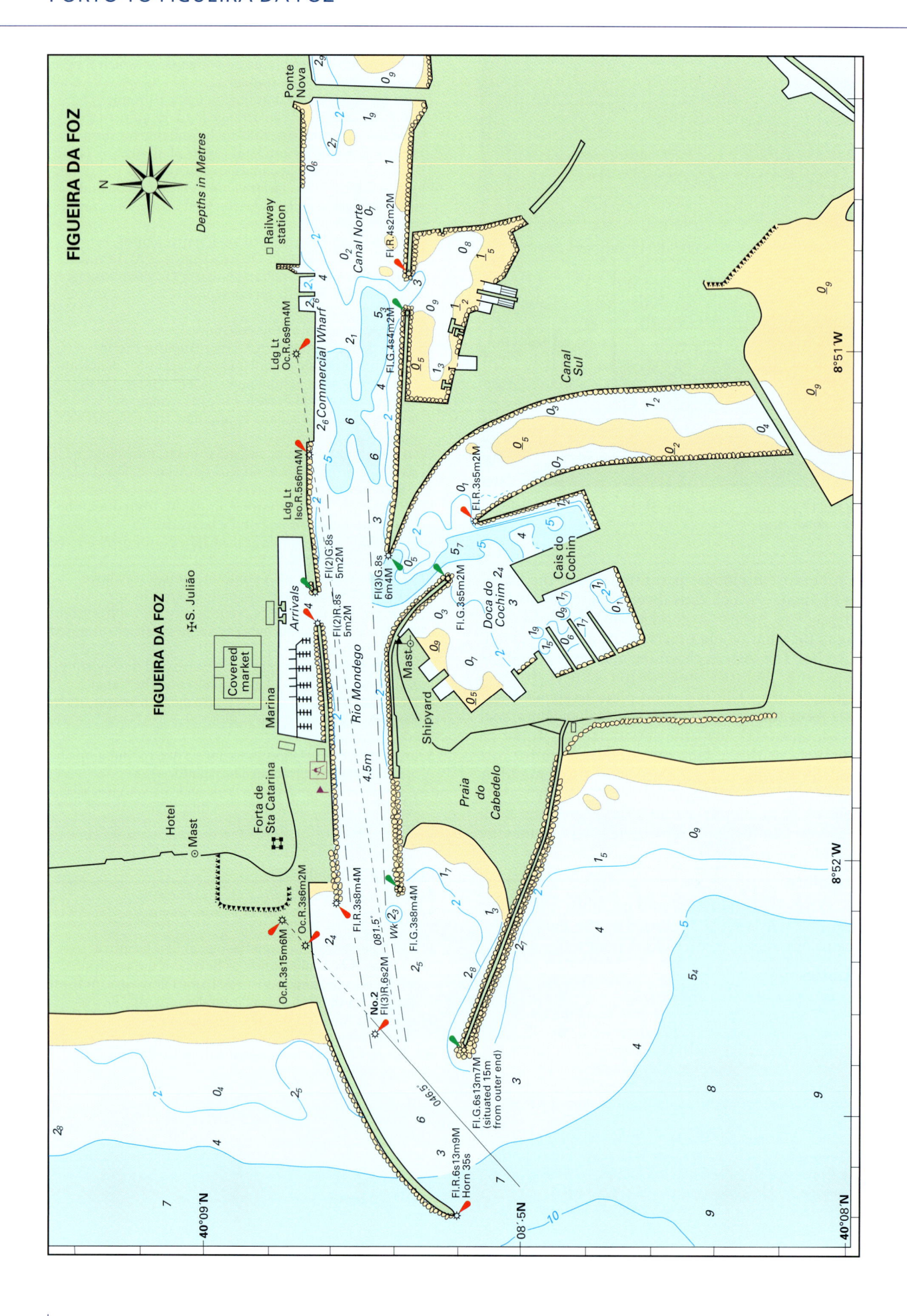

PORTO TO FIGUEIRA DA FOZ

164　ATLANTIC SPAIN AND PORTUGAL

Figueira da Foz

Location
40°08'·50N 8°52'·65W (entrance)

Tides
Standard port Lisbon
Mean time differences
HW −0010 minutes ±0010; LW +0015 minutes ±0005
Heights in metres
MHWS	MHWN	MLWN	MLWS
3·5	2·6	1·3	0·6

Principal lights
North breakwater Fl.R.6s13m9M Horn 35s
  White tower, red bands 9m
South breakwater Fl.G.6s13m7M
  White tower, green bands 7m (15m from outer end)
Ldg Lts *Front* Oc.R.3s6m6M. Red-White horizontal striped stone pylon.
Rear Oc.R.3s15m6M. Red-White horizontal striped stone pylon.
North inner mole Fl.R.3s8m4M
  Red tower, white bands 4m
South inner mole Fl.G.3s8m4M
  Green tower, white bands 5m
Marina, west mole Fl(2).R.8s5m2M Red column 3m
Marina, east mole Fl(2).G.8s5m2M Green column 3m
Confluência Fl(3)G.8s6m4M
  Green tower, red band 4m

Warning/Notes
Night entry straightforward other than in heavy onshore swell. The marina entrance is well lit with the reception/fuel berth opposite. However anchored smallcraft may be encountered in the entrance – see below

Communications
Instituto Portuário e dos Transportes Marítimos (IPTM)
VHF Ch 11, 16 ☎ +351 233 402910
Email geral.ffoz@imarpor.pt
Marina da Figueira da Foz VHF Ch 11, 16
☎ +351 233 402918

Attractive old town with small marina opposite a large commercial port

Figueira da Foz is on the north bank of the Mondego, the longest river to rise in Portugal. Although a modern town, depending largely on ship-building and tourism for its income, a large part of the attractive old town remains. Figueira da Foz saw action during the Peninsula War, with Wellington landing here in August 1808. The Casa do Paco has an interesting wall covered in Dutch tiles, and nearby is the Gulbenkian Museu do Dr Santo Rocha, an interesting archaeological museum with a marine section.

The city of Coimbra, some 48km upstream, is worth visiting by bus or train. Coimbra is the successor to the city of Conimbriga, the heart of Roman Portugal and was briefly the capital of Portugal in the 12th century. The university, in the upper part of the town, transferred there from Lisbon in 1320 and has played a major role in Portuguese life ever since. The university library (built as a direct legacy of Portugal's great age of exploration) is magnificent and the old city, including the crenellated 12th-century cathedral, is memorable. In the lower part of the town the church of Santa Cruz (containing medieval royal tombs) is not only significant historically, but was a British Army HQ during the Peninsula War.

Also in the upper part of the town, the fortress-like old Cathedral is a one of the finest Romanesque buildings in Portugal. Behind the cathedral is the old Bishop's Palace now the Museum of Machado de Castro containing some fine late medieval paintings and sculpture and subterranean passages dating back to Roman times. Although these are the highlights of Coimbra, the city is full of surprises and justifies time spent wandering its narrow streets.

Approach

Figueira da Foz lies 2·5M south of Cabo Mondego which at a distance, from both north and south, can be mistaken for an island. The shore to the south of the town forms a continuous low, sandy, beach backed by one of the largest coniferous forests in Europe. The major mark to the south is Penedo da Saudade, 25M distant.

Note that there is a concentration of fishing floats between Cabo Mondego and the harbour.

The pale grey suspension bridge 1·5M upriver from the entrance is conspicuous.

Entrance

Regular dredging of the previously shallow bar has greatly improved the entrance and a minimum of 5m should be found at all times. However, in strong onshore winds it can be dangerous as waves frequently break all the way across the gap. At springs the ebb can run at up to 7kns, particularly if there has been heavy rain inland, though this rate is unlikely to be reached during the summer.

Danger signals are displayed if necessary from Forte de Santa Catarina (on the north side of the entrance) as follows:
  GRGR / 2 black balls diagonally = no entrance or exit
  GRG / 1 black ball = no entrance <35m
  GRG / 1 black ball at half mast = no entrance <11m
  GRG flashing = no entrance or exit >12m.

These signals, which are near some strong sodium lights and difficult to see from offshore, are mandatory and instructions may also be given by radio. If no signals are displayed the entrance is considered to be safe, at least for large commercial vessels.

Also, refer to the advice given in Harbour entry warning signals on page 133.

Care must be taken to avoid the many local fishermen who anchor in the main channel apparently at random, peacefully line-fishing from small rowing boats and motor vessels. Although most either depart before dusk or show lights, this should not be relied upon. It is reported that nets are sometimes strung across the river, in which case a yacht will be guided through the gaps by hand signals.

PORTO TO FIGUEIRA DA FOZ

Berthing

The entrance to the Marina da Figueira da Foz lies on the port hand about 0·7M inside the river mouth. Beware of cross-currents, particularly on the ebb. Opposite the entrance, secure to the reception pontoon which has the marina office behind it open 0830–1230 and 1400–2200 daily.

The marina consists of a single long pontoon from which seven spurs run southward. All are fitted with individual finger pontoons and the two easternmost, some 36 berths, are reserved for visitors, though more will be fitted in elsewhere if necessary. Though easy to access, both eastern spurs are reported to suffer from strong cross-currents that can be the opposite to that experienced at the reception berth! There is a swell on the ebb.

This area is nominally dredged to 4·5m and able to take yachts of up to 25m LOA, though some would consider this optimistic.

A problem is that until a footbridge is built between the visitor pontoons and the marina office, it is a long walk between the two.

Formalities

Visit the marina office equipped with passports, ship's papers and insurance documents. There are no forms to complete but copies of passports and boat's papers are taken. There is also no need to clear out from each port as details are kept in computer systems which most ports have access to. If a change of crew is made, however, the authorities need to be informed, for safety reasons.

Reception, fuel pontoons and marina offices
Henry Buchanan

Facilities

Boatyard Not as such, though there are several concerns which could handle minor work. Papiro, ☎ +351 233 411849, at the west end of the basin advertises GRP work, including osmosis treatment, but appears fairly small.

There is a wide concrete slipway in the southwest corner of the basin where yachts of medium draught can dry out for scrubbing. A pressure washer (with operator) can be hired – enquire at the marine office. As with all such facilities it would plainly be wise to inspect thoroughly at low water before committing oneself.

Travel-lift None at present, though it is possible that a 50-tonne lift may be installed in the commercial area on the south side of the river. Enquire at the marina office.

Engineers, electronic and radio repairs Available in the commercial harbour – enquire at the marina office.

Sailmaker/sail repairs Sails in need of repair are normally sent to Lisbon for attention – ask at the marina office.

Looking east-northeast past the outer breakwaters at Figueira da Foz, with the marina at centre and the impressive Ponte Nova on the right

ATLANTIC SPAIN AND PORTUGAL

FIGUEIRA DA FOZ

The Marina da Figueira da Foz, with the town's park and the double-gabled covered market behind

Chandlery Limited stocks at Figueira Iates at the west end of the basin. Papiro (see above) stocks a full range of International Paints including antifouling, thinners etc.
Water On the pontoons, with a generous number of long hoses.
Showers In the marina office building.
Launderette Next to the showers in the marina office building.
Electricity On the pontoons.
Fuel Diesel and petrol on the fuel pontoon open during office hours.
Bottled gas Camping Gaz from Alavanca (which also stocks an enormous range of tools), on the road leading east from the marina basin.
Clube náutico The Clube Náutico de Figueira da Foz has a small clubhouse at the west end of the marina. The children's play area behind the building is a particularly nice touch.
Weather forecast Posted daily outside the marina office.
Banks In the town.
Shops/provisioning Good shopping of all types in the town. The nearest supermarket (open 0730) will be found across the road and slightly west from the marina gate, up a small side street.
Produce market The impressive covered market opposite the marina is amongst the best of its genre, and sells consumables of all types, clothing, souvenirs etc.
Cafés, restaurants and hotels A small café is adjacent to the marina office building. The Clube Náutico has a pleasant bar/restaurant with indoor and outdoor tables. There are others across the road from the marina entrance, and many in the town proper.

Communications

Post office Just off the square of public gardens which face the yacht basin.
Mailing address The marina office will hold mail for visiting yachts – c/o Instituto Portuário do Centro, AP 2008–3080, Figueira da Foz, Portugal. It is important that the envelope carries the name of the yacht in addition to that of the addressee.
Internet Several possibilities, including WebSymbol on Rua dos Bombeiros, which also sells computer equipment and expendables.
Public telephones At the post office.
Car hire/taxis In the town.
Buses and trains In the town. The station is less than 0·5km east of the marina.

Harbour entrance Figueira da Foz. Leading marks almost in line with the right hand edge of rectangular building to the right of the blue skyscraper *Henry Buchanan*

Leading line

ATLANTIC SPAIN AND PORTUGAL   167

PORTUGAL – THE WEST COAST

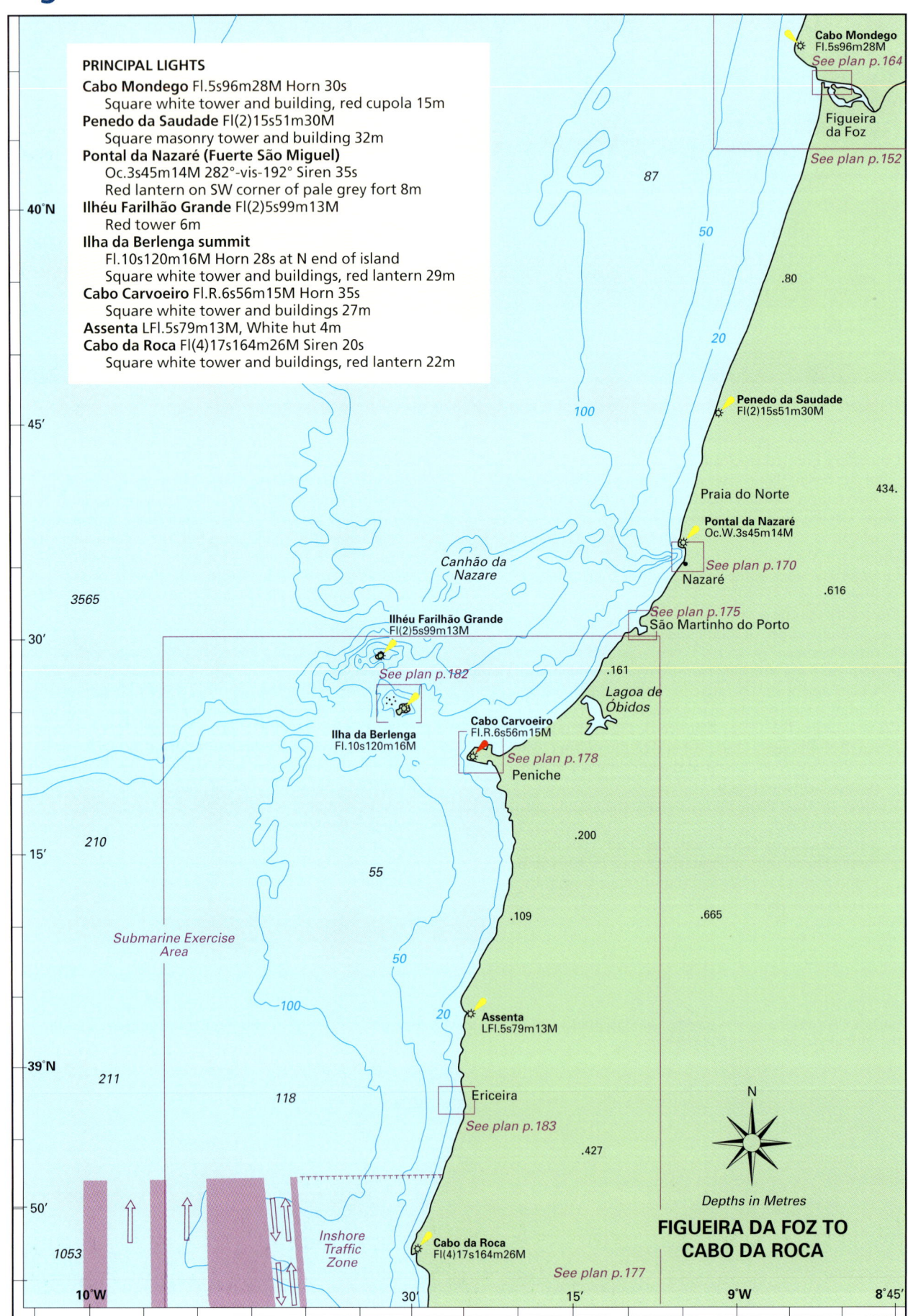

Figueira da Foz to Cabo da Roca

PRINCIPAL LIGHTS

Cabo Mondego Fl.5s96m28M Horn 30s
  Square white tower and building, red cupola 15m
Penedo da Saudade Fl(2)15s51m30M
  Square masonry tower and building 32m
Pontal da Nazaré (Fuerte São Miguel)
  Oc.3s45m14M 282°-vis-192° Siren 35s
  Red lantern on SW corner of pale grey fort 8m
Ilhéu Farilhão Grande Fl(2)5s99m13M
  Red tower 6m
Ilha da Berlenga summit
  Fl.10s120m16M Horn 28s at N end of island
  Square white tower and buildings, red lantern 29m
Cabo Carvoeiro Fl.R.6s56m15M Horn 35s
  Square white tower and buildings 27m
Assenta LFl.5s79m13M, White hut 4m
Cabo da Roca Fl(4)17s164m26M Siren 20s
  Square white tower and buildings, red lantern 22m

Depths in Metres

FIGUEIRA DA FOZ TO CABO DA ROCA

168 ATLANTIC SPAIN AND PORTUGAL

NAZARÉ

Nazaré

Location
39°35'·48N 9°04'·74W (entrance)

Tides
Standard port Lisbon
Mean time differences
HW −0020 ±0010 LW 0000 ±0005
Heights in metres
MHWS	MHWN	MLWN	MLWS
3·3	2·6	1·3	0·6

Principal lights
North breakwater LFl.R.5s14m9M
   White tower, red bands 7m
South breakwater LFl.G.5s14m8M
   White tower, green bands 7m

Notes
Night entry straightforward, though the small marina is crowded and it may be necessary to raft up to a fishing boat until daylight.

Communications
Clube Naval da Nazaré
VHF Ch09 ☏+351 262 560 422, *Mobile* +351 917 500 851.
www.cnnazare.pt
Email Secretariat: geral@cnnazare.pt
CNN Marina: marina@cnnazare.pt
Docapesca Portos E Lotas S.A. Nazaré
Email jorge.loarvo@docapesca.pt ☏ +351 262 569 098
Mobile +351 965 072 594
Nazaré Harbour Authority
☏+351 262 569 090 (general)
☏+351 916 001 260 (main security gate)
☏+351 918 498 031 (policia maritima)
☏+351 262 561 255 (capitania in town)

A major Portuguese fishing harbour with safe all-weather entry from the south

The harbour is a purpose-built, well-sheltered fishing port with no hazards on the approach. Indeed it is claimed that Nazaré's harbour is never closed, even in conditions in which it would be foolhardy to attempt any of those further north other than Leixões. This is due to the Canhão da Nazaré, a deep trench which runs close offshore and markedly reduces swell to the south of the trench and the entrance to the harbour. However, from the perspective of a sailing yacht this promised calming effect may not at times be very apparent, particularly if approaching from the north. To the north of the trench it is a different story.

The Portuguese Hydrographic Institute has been working to understand how the waves become so huge close-inshore at the Praia do Norte just north of Nazaré. They owe their size to the shape of the local seabed at the end point of a 230km submarine canyon, the longest in Europe. At its deepest point it plunges down three times as far as the Grand Canyon. Thanks to the canyon's funnelling effect, winter swells from the Atlantic crash with abnormal speed into its headboard, less than a mile offshore, instead of slowing gradually as the continental shelf's shallower waters would otherwise force them to do. This is where a new world record for the tallest wave ever surfed, at about 25m (80ft), was claimed in 2017. The canyon markedly reduces swell on its south side, as described above, although the prudent mariner would wish to avoid the conditions that generate such extremes.

The harbour, including the Porto de Recreio da Nazaré is administered by Docapesca Portos E Lotas S.A. Previous visitors to Nazaré will know that the yacht pontoons to the southwest of the basin used to

View out of Nazaré harbour over the dog-leg entrance
Henry Buchanan

ATLANTIC SPAIN AND PORTUGAL

FIGUEIRA DA FOZ TO CABO DA ROCA

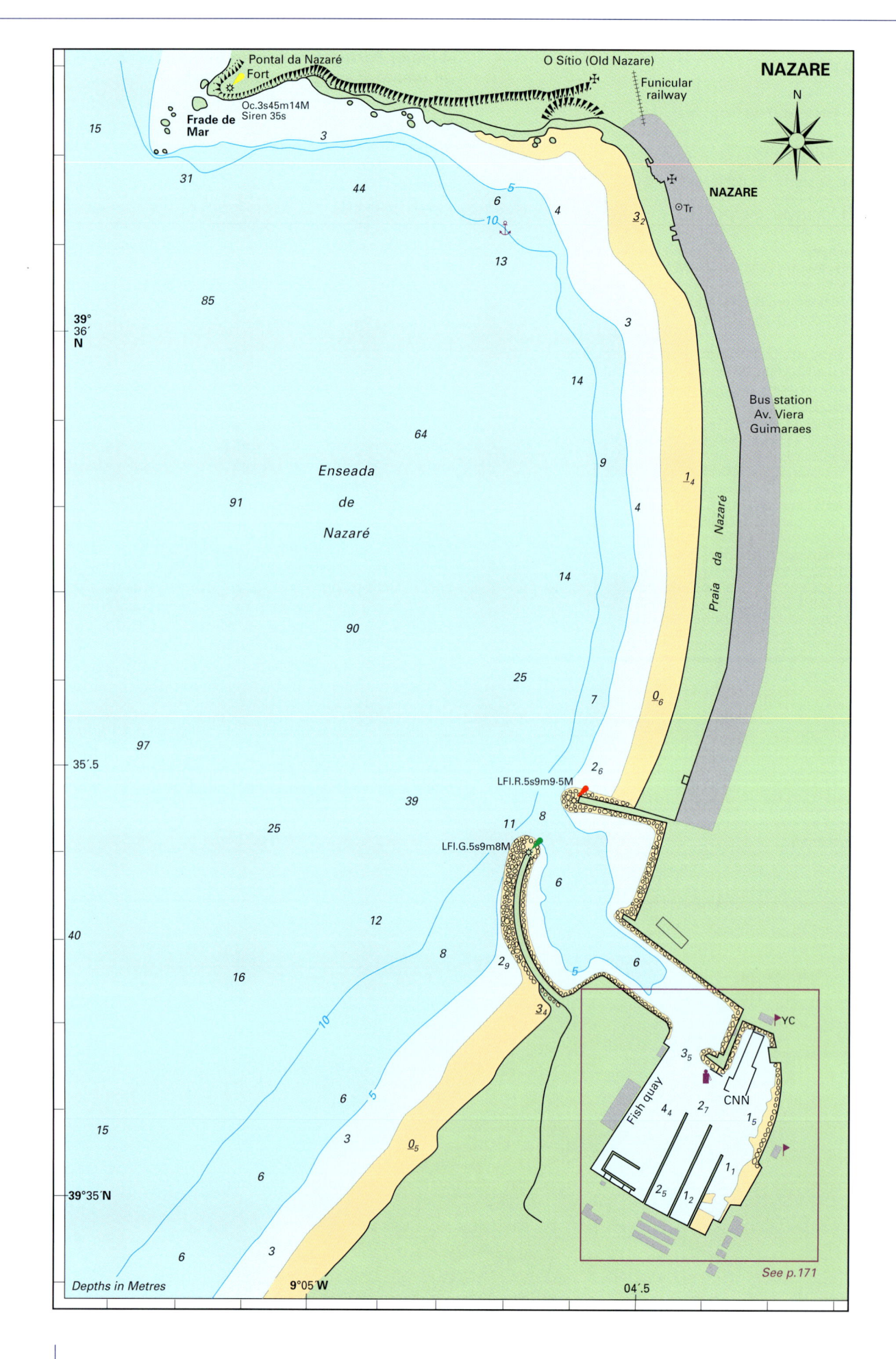

NAZARÉ

Nazaré harbour, Marina and approaches looking northwest towards Old Nazaré (Old Sítio) *Tobias Ilsanker*

be managed by Docapesca, but this has been taken on by the Clube Naval Da Nazaré which already welcomes visitors to its facility at the northeast of the basin.

Nazaré is a most useful port of refuge where the authorities are increasing the facilities available by encouraging new Enterprises such as the BOAT Marina Shop that is expanding its chandlery business and establishing a sail loft, amongst other things, in 2018. Other boatyard services are increasing too and details can be found in the 'facilities' section below.

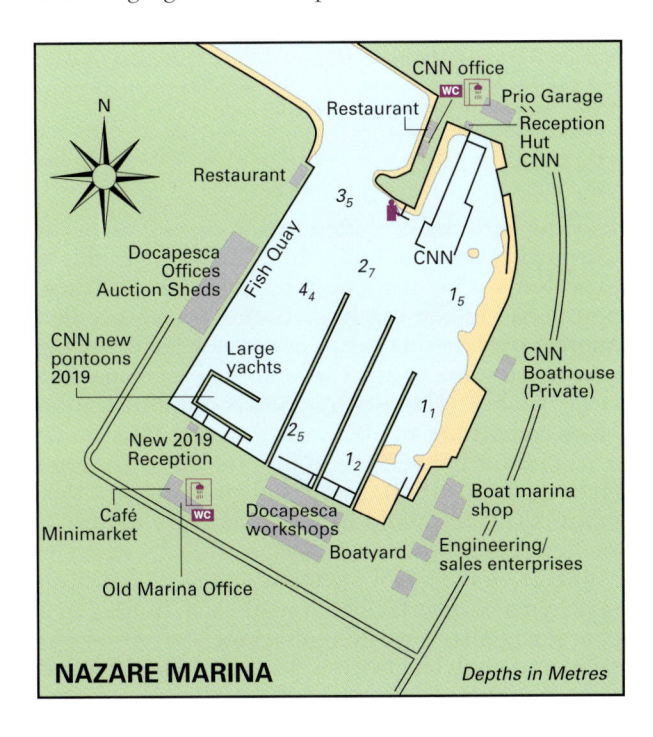

Nazaré is one of the most famous fishing villages in Portugal, lacking the architectural jewels of other towns but relying instead on its traditions for atmosphere. The Caldeirada à Nazarena is a rich fish-based stew typical of the area. The festival of Nossa Senhora da Nazre Romaria (8 September) is a major festival with a religious procession, bullfights and folk dancing. Old Nazaré (O Sítio), whose citizens claim Phoenician origin, occupies a fine position on the rocky promontory above the main part of the town and is accessible by funicular railway.

Possibly the most compelling reason to visit Nazaré, however, is as a base from which to visit a number of Portugal's most famous cultural and devotional sites, including Fatima, Tomar, Obidos, Alcobaça and Caldas da Rainha, all of which can be reached by public transport. However the top 'must see' is undoubtedly the early 15th-century abbey of Batalha (Battle Abbey) one of Europe's greatest Gothic masterpieces and a World Heritage Site. The slightly tortuous 60-minute bus journey via Leiria will be amply rewarded.

ATLANTIC SPAIN AND PORTUGAL   171

FIGUEIRA DA FOZ TO CABO DA ROCA

Existing PdeRN office, showers and WCs between the two pillars Henry Buchanan

Approach
The low-lying beach which reaches from Figueira da Foz to the light at Penedo da Saudade gives way to a more broken coastline backed by low hills leading south to the Pontal da Nazaré, with a light on the wall of its fort, São Miguel. The point has rocks 200m offshore to the southwest, but within a further 60m the bottom drops to 50m or more. If approaching from this direction it is worth standing on until the harbour entrance bears 120° before turning, to avoid concentrations of pot buoys in the northeast part of the bay.

The coast 4M south of Nazaré loses its sand dunes and becomes rocky. South of São Martinho, towards the Lagoa de Obidos, there is a rugged stretch of higher coast. South of this the coast is again a sandy beach, here backed by cliffs, as far as Cabo Carvoeiro. Fishing nets may be laid on a line parallel to and up to 4M off this stretch of shore. On final approach from the south, particularly in thick weather, note that the Canhão da Nazaré underwater canyon trends north of east into the Enseada da Nazaré, and that its 100m line comes within 600m of the shore.

CNN pontoon, reception, administration block beyond Henry Buchanan

Entrance
Entrance is straightforward between the moles, but watch out for fishing boats travelling at speed. In any swell the entrance appears somewhat daunting but turning to starboard through the dog leg brings you into calmer water very quickly.

Berthing
The berthing facilities for yachts at Nazaré are expected to be reorganized and greatly improved from the beginning of 2019. At that time the existing Porto de Recreio da Nazaré (PdeRN) marina on the southwest of the basin will be refurbished with new pontoons and become administered by the Clube Naval da Nazaré (CNN) that already has facilities at the northeast of the basin. In recent years visitors to Nazaré calling on VHF Ch 09 have been answered by the CNN staff. This will now become the normal procedure by agreement between CNN and the Docapesca. The CNN staff will direct yachts to either the increased number of pontoons at the northeast of the basin or the new pontoons at the southwest of the basin where depths are said to be of 3m throughout. At the time of writing it is not known whether the existing Porto de Recreio da Nazaré marina office, showers and WCs will continue to be used, or whether a new reception facility will be sited adjacent to the refurbished pontoons.

Security throughout the entire port area is said to be good though relaxed, with a watchman permanently on duty at the main gate into the fishing harbour, and CCTV surveillance for the whole port area. Access to the fishing-boat jetties has been improved in that all the nets have been removed, the ladders replaced and the lights repaired, but the walls are high. There is no water or electricity available here.

Clube Naval da Nazaré (CNN)
Clube Naval da Nazaré, Pavilhao Nautico do Clube Naval da Nazaré, Porto de Abrigo da Nazaré, 2450-075 Nazaré
☎ +351 262 560 422 *Mobile* +351 917 500 851
Email Secretariat: geral@cnnazare.pt
www.cnnazare.pt

CNN Marina
VHF Ch09 *Email* marina@cnnazare.pt

Existing berthing is limited to 4/5 visiting yachts at the northeast of the basin. In 2019 however this is expected to be increased by provision of new pontoons here, and a large but as yet unspecified number of alongside berths at the new facility at the southwest of the basin. The latter will accommodate large yachts. The existing CNN administration block comprising an office, showers and WCs are by a restaurant/bar. Office hours are 0900 to 2000 (June to September), and 0900 to 1900 all other months. There should be someone there to meet a yacht during these hours. Water and electricity is available on the CNN pontoons and there is a clean male/female toilet facility, one of each, housed in a container. Also a washing machine - no drier, but wind and sun! The town is a short walk (10 mins) from the CNN.

NAZARÉ

The staff are pleasant, efficient and effective at their jobs and speak English. Yacht paperwork will be completed by them.

The Clube Navale da Nazaré is keen to build the business and there are plans to replace the administration block with a new building on the quay leading to the Prio garage fuel pontoon. This would house the administration, toilet block, and laundry.

Anchorage

Anchoring is not permitted in the harbour or its approaches. However, in settled weather it is possible to anchor, best protected from the northerly swell, under the cliffs at Sitio on a plateau with good holding at 39°36′·121N 009°04′·704W. But beware the orange buoys with floating lines ashore just to the southeast and note this is also a popular spot for the friendly local fishermen. If anchored off the beach you may be asked to move by the Policía Marítima.

Facilities

Nazaré is actively developing its yachting and boating facilities to be a harbour of choice on the west coast of Portugal. The purpose built harbour is home to an important fishing enterprise (Docapesca Portos E Lotas S.A) and is happy to share its extensive facilities ashore with recreational sailors. In addition to the facilities initially established for the fishing fleet various enterprises have been encouraged to base themselves in the confines of the harbour. All these facilities are described as follows:

Travel-lift 80-tonne capacity hoist, backed by a large area of concrete hard-standing which serves both fishing boats and yachts. Electricity is laid on and owners are free both to work on their own boats and to live aboard whilst ashore.

Boatyard This is inside the main gate to the port area, and able to handle mechanical jobs, repairs in GRP, steel, wood, and painting etc:

1. Silvia of Silvia Artigos do Mar
   ☎+351 967 223 507 or +351 262 560 304
   Email silviaartigosparaomar@gmail.com
   Silvia provides boat propping; antifouling services; polishing; cleaning inside and out; guardianship; boat insurance and registration services; fishing material and nets etc.
2. Alec Lammas of Nazaré Nautica
   ☎+351-914 096 959
   Email nazarenautica@gmail.com
   Alec provides welding expertise, general engineering and DIY facilities. He is a pioneer in the development of electric propulsion for yachts. He has concessions from Lynch Motors of England (www.lynchmotors.co.uk) and works with a battery management company in Lisbon, Portugal on systems' design.
3. Alberto Mendes in the boatyard-area is a general mechanic for outboard engines and is also an authorized Honda Dealer ☎+351 930 512 107.
4. Joao (Planusnautica) is a specialist in GRP construction.
   ☎+351 262 551 224, *Mob* +351 915 859 590, +351 926 936 544, *Email* planusnautica@gmail.com
5. Miguel Costa of Atlantic Marine ☎ +351 967 030 602
   www.atlanticmarine.pt
   Email miguel.costa@atlanticmarine.pt
   Miguel is an agent for Yamaha Marine, Yachting Veneziani (boat paints and antifouling), and Zappata Racing (flyboards, hoverboards etc). He hires equipment to wave surfers at the Praia do Norte.
6. Jose Manuel Machado Codinha is a welder and handyman with a lathe *Mob* +351 963 951 474.
7. BOAT Marina Shop (BMS) run by Christophe Agostinho ☎+351 262 560 139
   Mob +351 939 644 625
   Email boatmarinashop@gmail.com
   Shop: ☎+351 262 560 139
   BMS Boat Marina Unipessoal, Lda, Porto de abrigo da Nazaré, Cx.postal n.° 28, 2450-075 Nazaré. BMS is a rapidly expanding business that will provide a large chandlery, a sail loft for sail repairs, GRP services, cleaning and painting, engineering services, work in wood, yachting clothing, and brokerage for small boats. BMS is an agent for Suzuki.

Fuel Diesel and petrol pumps are on the short hammerhead to port on entering the harbour basin. They are operated by the Prio service station (0600 to 2300) nearby and are separate to the Clube Naval da Nazaré. Use the intercom at the gate off the pontoon and ask the service station staff to open it. It is best to have two people to fuel a boat as one can be on the

Looking southwards from O Sítio towards Nazare harbour entrance *Jane Russell*

FIGUEIRA DA FOZ TO CABO DA ROCA

CNN Marina Office and restaurant beyond *Henry Buchanan*

self-service fuel pontoon while the other is arranging the fueling and payment at the service station. It is about 250m between the two.
Launderette Elena of the Mini Mercado Lena (formerly Estrelinha) offers a laundry service (washing or washing and drying). There is another launderette and two coin-operated launderettes in town.
Bottled gas Camping gas is available at the Mini Mercado Lena.
Weather forecast Posted daily in the Mini Mercado Lena and on the notice board next to the ISN (lifeboat) building.
Banks There is an ATM machine in the Prio service station in the northeast corner of the port. There are several banks in town.
Shops/provisioning The well-stocked mini-market next to the old Porto de Recreio da Nazaré marina office provides fresh bread several times a day. The Mini Mercado Lena can also obtain larger quantities of produce from the supermarkets in town. There is good general shopping in Nazaré town and several supermarkets. The Ulmar is on Avenida Viera Guimares, and Mini Preco and Pingo Doce are furtherup the same street to the left. Continente and Lidl are up in O'Sitio, the upper town reached by bus or via the funicular railway.
Produce market Good market in the town, open 0700–1300 daily in summer, closed Mondays in winter. A large open market is held every Friday just behind the public library and central bus station.

Cafés, restaurants and hotels There are two restaurants in the port area. The restaurant and bar behind the fishmarket close to the tower on the western side of the basin, open Monday to Friday 0900–2200 (and on request): ☏ +351 967 223 507 or +351 917 682 276, *Email* tapasaquilda@gmail.com. The Restaurant Marina Bar on the northeastern side of the basin close to the Clube Naval da Nazaré is closed on Tuesdays, otherwise open 1200–1500 and 1900–2200, ☏ +351 933 452 547; Mini Mercado Lena is also operated as a bar with snacks, coffee, drinks and a terrace. There are many restaurants, cafés, bars and hotels in town.
Medical services In Nazaré.

Communications
There is a Post Office in Nazaré.
Internet access Mini Mercado Lena offers free WiFi access, as does the restaurant and bar behind the fishmarket. Most restaurants and bars in town offer free WiFi.
Buses An excellent and reliable express-bus service connects Nazaré with all major towns in Portugal, e.g. Lisboa just 90 minutes away with five services daily. www.rede-expressos.pt.

Batalha, a top 'must-see' in Portugal *Jane Russell*

The Prio garage fuel pontoon *Henry Buchanan*

SÃO MARTINHO DO PORTO

São Martinho do Porto

Location
39°30'·76N 9°08'·9W (entrance)

Tides
Standard port Lisbon
Mean time differences
HW –0020 ±0010 LW 0000 ±0005
Heights in metres
MHWS   MHWN   MLWN   MLWS
3·3   2·6   1·3   0·6

Principal lights
Ponta do Santo António LFl.R.6s32m9M Siren 60s
  White tower, red, bands
  Obscured on a bearing of more than 165°
Ldg Lts 145° *Front* Carreira do Sul Iso.R.1·5s10m9M
  White column, red bands 6m
Rear 129m from front Oc.R.6s12m9·5M
  White column, red bands, on square white base 8m

Warning
Night entry not feasible without local knowledge

Shallow but attractive fair-weather anchorage

Once a small fishing port but now a growing tourist town, São Martinho do Porto has a most attractive setting. The sea has widened a breach in the hard cliffs and excavated a crescent-shaped bay out of the softer rock behind. A foot tunnel runs through the cliff just short of the Ponta de Santo António, debouching onto a rocky shore where the unwary can get soaked.

Even though many of the buildings are new and most along the seafront are of four or five storeys, the town is surprisingly attractive with an almost Mediterranean feel to its architecture, pavement cafés, and tourist shops. The shallow, sheltered waters of the bay ensure warmer than average swimming temperatures.

Approach and entrance

The bay is shallow and should ideally only be entered in calm, settled weather. However, on advice from English speaking local fishermen it would appear that whilst in strong winds the entrance has to be treated with caution, if entering or leaving near the top of the tide then no problems should be experienced.

Once inside there is little movement even when breaking crests fill the entrance, but leaving in such weather would be impossible.

If coastal sailing, much of that written about Nazaré, page 172, also applies. On closing São Martinho, keep outside the enclosing headlands until the entrance is clearly seen. In particular, beware the rocks 300m off the unlit Ponta do Facho. This promontory, if one is close inshore to the northeast, masks Ponta do Santo António and its light, 0·5M to the south.

The leading marks, on 145°, consist of two red and white banded columns 9m and 11m in height, which may be difficult to pick out against the sand and scrub background. Use them for the approach, but enter midway between Ponta do Santo António and Ponta Santana. Several dozen small white buoys are scattered across and just inside the entrance, presumably marking fish pots but posing an obvious hazard to propellers.

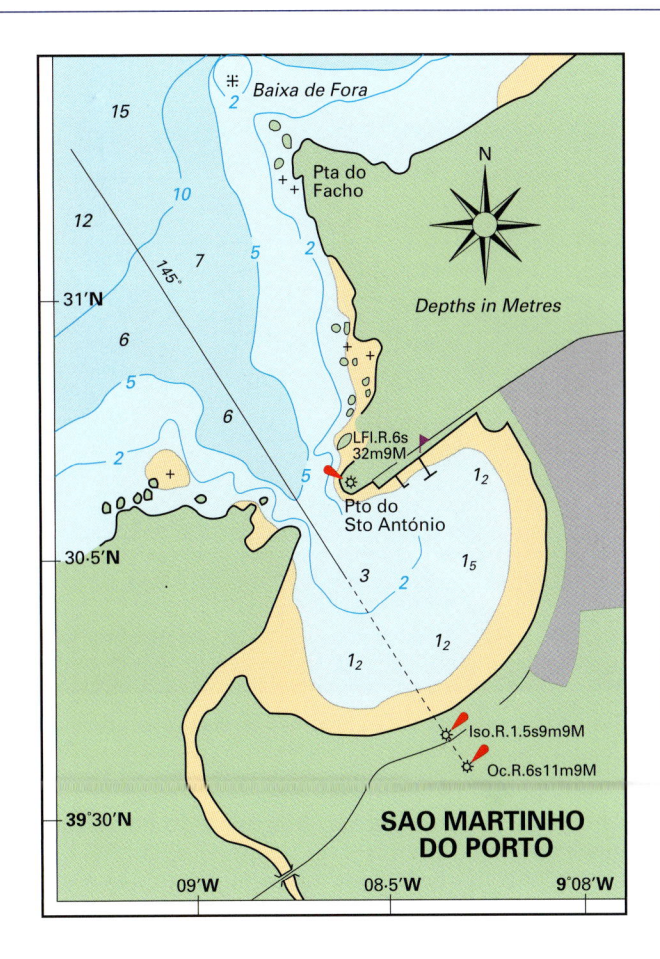

In even moderate weather, though the anchorage may be tenable a boat can be trapped by the swell at the exit. If the fishermen leave *en masse* it may be wise to follow.

Anchorage

Anchor outside the moorings in the northeast part of the harbour in about 2m over sand. The quay leading round from Ponta de Santo António has no more than this at its head, shoaling towards the town, and has underwater projections in places. There are two short jetties where one could land by dinghy, but there seems little point when the alternative is a clean, sandy beach.

Formalities

Call at the Policía Marítima office at the northeast corner of the beach (easily identified by its mast and lights) with passports, ship's papers and the documentation for the last port of call. A small anchoring tax will be asked for.

ATLANTIC SPAIN AND PORTUGAL   175

FIGUEIRA DA FOZ TO CABO DA ROCA

The narrow entrance to São Martinho do Porto's semicircular bay

Facilities and communications

The Clube Náutico de São Martinho do Porto has newly enlarged premises on the north quay. Water could doubtless be had for the asking, but there is no fuel available.

The town has reasonable shopping, banks, restaurants, bars etc., together with a post office and telephones. There is an excellent 'Union Jack Shop' behind the *Police Maritima* which sells English items not normally found, such as bacon, marmalade etc, but, more to the point, has an extensive book exchange and can provide good local advice.

Just beyond is the new Tourist Office which is very good and helpful for bus travel to Batalha etc., and has a lift at the back of the building to the higher levels. Frequent bus services are available but the tourist office does not recommend the railway.

The new *Intermarche* supermarket is adjacent to the bus-stops, and 15 minutes' walk from the pontoon where a dinghy can be left.

There are a number of good and relatively inexpensive restaurants there. WiFi in *Martinho* is excellent and the *Turismo* has a free to use computer.

In summary, this is a good place to stay, especially for those with children or who like warm seas and excellent beaches with showers etc.

Not feasible – Lagõa de Obidos

The Lagõa de Obidos (39°26′N 9°14′W), just south of Foz de Arelho and about halfway between São Martinho do Porto and Cabo Carvoeiro, may appear a possibility. However the mouth is almost totally blocked by sandbars and the tide runs swiftly through the gaps. Unlike the rather similar Esposende, there are no offlying hazards.

Looking southeast across the shallow bay at São Martinho do Porto from Ponta do Santo António Anne Hammick

PENICHE TO CASCAIS

Peniche to Cascais, including Ilha da Berlenga

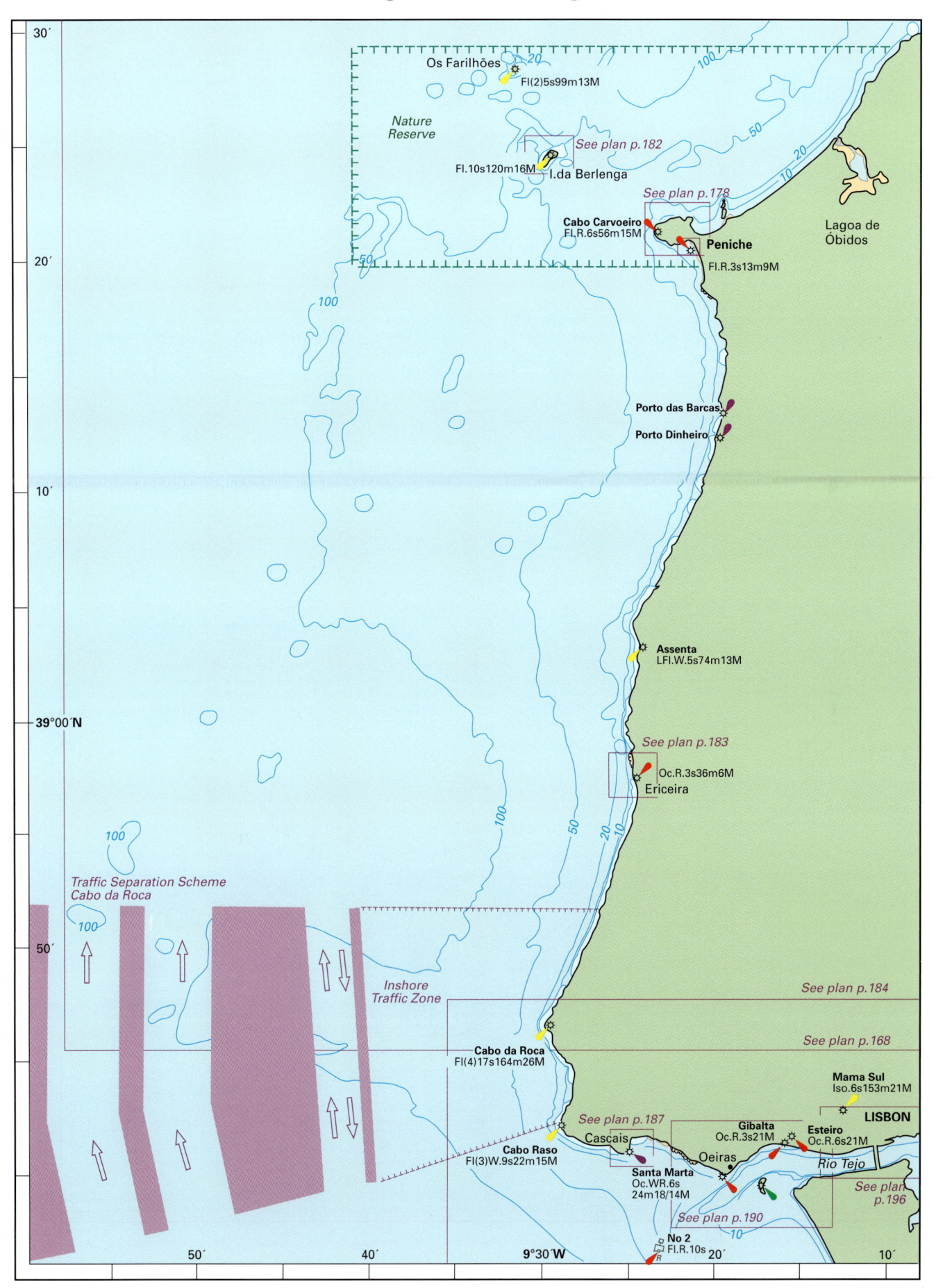

- Os Farilhões — Fl(2)5s99m13M
- I. da Berlenga — Fl.10s120m16M
- Nature Reserve
- See plan p.182
- See plan p.178
- Cabo Carvoeiro — Fl.R.6s56m15M
- Peniche — Fl.R.3s13m9M
- Lagoa de Óbidos
- Porto das Barcas
- Porto Dinheiro
- Assenta — LFl.W.5s74m13M
- See plan p.183
- Ericeira — Oc.R.3s36m6M
- Traffic Separation Scheme Cabo da Roca
- Inshore Traffic Zone
- Cabo da Roca — Fl(4)17s164m26M
- See plan p.184
- See plan p.168
- Mama Sul — Iso.6s153m21M
- See plan p.187
- Cascais
- Gibalta — Oc.R.3s21M
- Esteiro — Oc.R.6s21M
- LISBON
- Cabo Raso — Fl(3)W.9s22m15M
- Santa Marta — Oc.WR.6s 24m18/14M
- Oeiras
- Rio Tejo
- See plan p.196
- See plan p.190
- No 2 — Fl.R.10s

PORTUGAL – THE WEST COAST

ATLANTIC SPAIN AND PORTUGAL 177

FIGUEIRA DA FOZ TO CABO DA ROCA

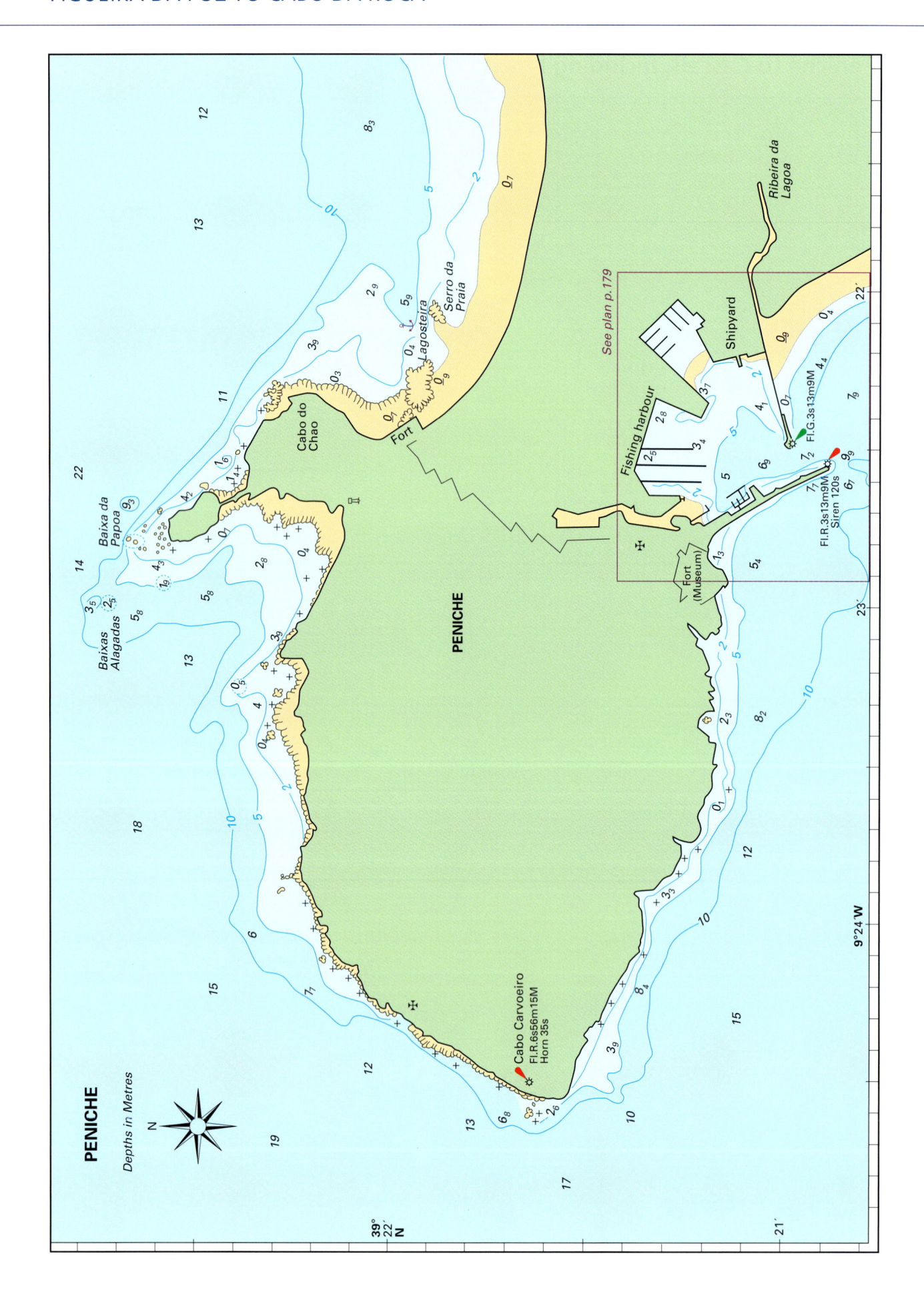

Peniche

Location
39°20'·82N 9°22'·4W (entrance)

Tides
Standard port Lisbon
Mean time differences
HW −0025 ±0010; LW 0000 ±0005
Heights in metres
MHWS	MHWN	MLWN	MLWS
3·5	2·7	1·3	0·6

Principal lights
West breakwater Fl.R.3s13m9M Siren 120s
  White tower, red bands 8m
East breakwater Fl.G.3s13m9M
  White tower, green bands 8m

Warning/Notes
Well lit, and without problems other than in strong southerlies. However space at the marina is often limited.

Maritime radio station
Montejunto (39°10'·5N 9°03'·5W)
Remotely controlled from Lisbon)
Manual – VHF Ch 16, 24, 25, 27. *Autolink* – VHF Ch 86.

Harbour communications
Port Authority
VHF Ch 11, 16 (call *Capimarpeniche*) (0900–1200, 1400–1700 weekdays only)
☎ +351 262 781109
Email japcpen@mail.telepac.pt
Marina da Ribeira
VHF Ch 11, 16 ☎ +351 262 781153

Busy fishing harbour with small yacht marina

Possibly settled by Phoenicians, and the scene of a landing in 1589 by an English force, Peniche today is an important fishing port with a large harbour. The town is of greater interest than many along this coast and the museum in the 16th-century Fortaleza, later converted into a political prison, is particularly recommended. Until the 15th century Peniche was effectively an island, and the defensive walls which protected its shoreward side still run unbroken from north to south.

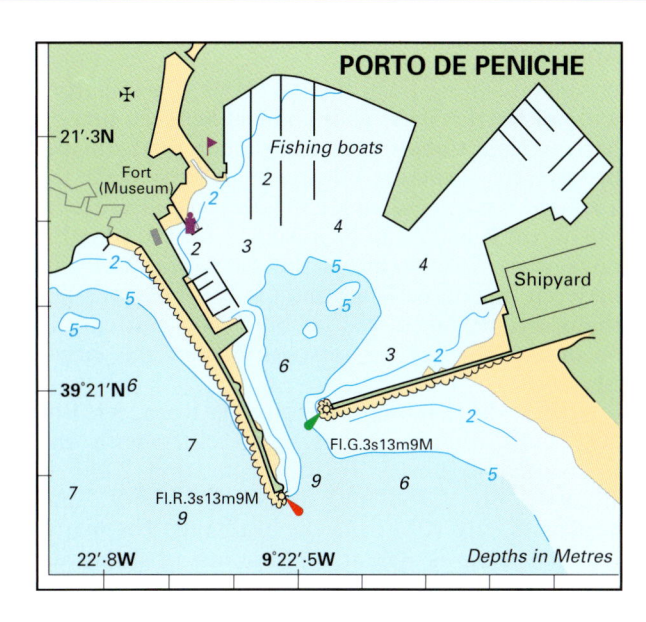

The port is large and well sheltered from the prevailing northerlies with an easy entrance, but it is not picturesque, though the comings and goings of the fishing fleet certainly add interest (and wash), as do the Ilha da Berlenga tourist ferries. The festival of Nossa Senhora da Boa Viagem takes place over the first weekend in August and includes harbour processions and blessing of the fishing fleet.

Peniche looking north, with the small Marina da Ribeira tucked behind the breakwater on the left

FIGUEIRA DA FOZ TO CABO DA ROCA

Approach
If coastal sailing from the north, most navigators will opt for the 5·5M wide channel between Ilha da Berlenga and Cabo Carvoeiro, though tidal streams between the islands and the mainland may make for a rough passage. When seen from some distance to the north, Peniche can be mistaken for the island it once was. Also viable is the narrower, 3M gap between Ilha da Berlenga and Os Farilhões, though there are offlying rocks on both side and care is needed as the current sets south onto the larger island.

From Cabo Carvoeiro to Cabo da Roca, 33M to the south, the coast has steep cliffs with the occasional beach. A Traffic Separation Zone is situated off Cabo da Roca, 7M wide and approximately 10M from the headland. The major light en route is Assenta, 1M south of Ponta da Lamparoeira.

Entrance
On final approach from the west around Cabo Carvoeiro, the east breakwater light appears to the north of the west breakwater light. Approach the west breakwater within 50–100m and turn in. The entrance is a little over 100m wide.

Peniche is a busy fishing port for vessels both large and small, and a greater than usual concentration of fish pots should be anticipated within 10–15M of the entrance. Some are well marked but the majority are not – be warned!

Berthing and formalities
Visiting yachts should secure to the long outer pontoon which shelters the marina proper, choosing a berth as space allows. Five or six yachts can moor in line ahead on the outside, rafting up from then on, while a few lucky ones may find places on the inside, though note that the northernmost inside berth is reserved for the *GNR–Brigada Fiscal* vessel. All berths alongside finger pontoons are private. At least 5m should be found throughout.

The marina is reasonably well protected, particularly at its northern end, though may suffer from swell in winds out of the south. More of a problem is the constant wash from fishing boats approaching and leaving their three long jetties to the northeast, at all hours of the day and night and almost invariably at speed, despite the 3kn limit prominently displayed on the eastern breakwater end. Generous fendering is therefore essential, and particular care should be taken that masts are staggered to avoid rigging becoming entangled should two boats roll together.

The marina office shares premises at the root of the breakwater with the Ilha da Berlenga ferry booking offices, and is normally open 0700–0745, 0930–1200 and 1600–1830 weekdays, 0700–1200 and 1600–1800 weekends and holidays. If arriving outside these hours the skipper should in theory either walk round to the Instituto Portuário do Centro office at the main port gate, or call them on ☏ 262 781153, but it is unlikely that any English will be spoken. It may be simpler to await the arrival of a marina official or security guard, who amongst other things will issue a card to work the electronic gate. *GNR–Brigada Fiscal* and *Polícia Marítima* officials may also visit.

If going ashore before a card is issued it is essential for someone to remain inside the gate to let others back in. Even the most agile would have a tough time getting around the guard wires. Transactions with the marina are cash only, credit and debit cards are not accepted.

Anchorage
Anchoring is allowed in the harbour on the starboard side of the entrance inside the east breakwater. There is no requirement to pay for anchoring in Peniche harbour, though payment can be made to use the showers, WiFi and facilities of the marina at half the marina rate.

In winds from the northern quadrant good holding over sand in reasonably comfortable conditions can be found south (outside) of the east breakwater.

Facilities
Boatyard Several boatyards with marine railways operate near the root of the east breakwater, backed by mechanical, electrical and electronic engineering workshops. Though more accustomed to fishing boats, in an emergency yachts can also be hauled – at a price.

Electronic and radio repairs Estêvão Alexandre Henriques Lda, ☏ 262 085536 Email estevaoah@netvisao.pt www.estevaoah.com two streets back from the harbour on Rua José Estêvão, sell and repair marine electronics of all kinds. Most of their trade comes from the fishing fleet but the engineers (some of whom speak English) are happy to visit yachts.

Chandlery Estêvão Alexandre Henriques Lda (see above) stock a limited amount of general chandlery and are willing to order.

Water On the pontoons.

Fish drying outside a house in Peniche *Anne Hammick*

PENICHE

Showers Two toilet/shower cubicles behind the marina office.
Launderette Next to the above – one washer but no dryer.
Electricity On the pontoons.
Fuel Diesel and petrol pumps at the head of the jetty opposite the marina office, administered by the Clube Naval de Peniche (see below). Long hoses run down to the berth, which has black fendering and is frequently occupied by small fishing boats. Fuel is available during office hours only (which vary) so check well in advance. Payment must be made in cash.
Bottled gas Camping Gaz available in the town, but no refills.
Clube naval The Clube Naval de Peniche has its headquarters in the small fort near the root of the west breakwater, beyond the red-doored lifeboat house.
Weather forecast Posted daily on the back of the large display board near the Ilha da Berlenga ferry offices, but generally in Portuguese text only (ie no synoptic chart). An English translation may be available from the marina office.
Banks In the town, nearly all with cash dispensers.
Shops/provisioning Good provisioning and general shopping, including a large supermarket in a new housing development northeast of the harbour.
Produce market In the town.
Cafés, restaurants and hotels Many, though sadly the tradition of grilling sardines on charcoal braziers by the roadside appears to have succumbed to modern hygiene regulations.
Medical services Hospital etc in the town.

Communications

Post office In the town.
Mailing address The marina office will hold mail for visiting yachts – c/o Instituto Portuário e dos Transportes Marítimos, Porto de Pesca de Peniche, 2520 Peniche, Portugal. It is important that the envelope carries the name of the yacht in addition to that of the addressee.
Internet There is no WiFi at the marina but it is available in many bars and at the *On Line* Cybercafé on Rua Antonio Cervantes (very close to the harbour).
Public telephones Kiosks on the root of the breakwater and elsewhere.
Car hire/taxis In the town. Taxis can be ordered via the marina office.
Buses Regular bus service to Lisbon (about 1hour 45 minutes) and elsewhere – a visit to the mediaeval walled town of Obidos is particularly recommended.
Ferries Tourist ferries to Ilha da Berlenga – and not a bad way to visit if one wishes to explore without the responsibility of a yacht at anchor (see below).
Air services International airport at Lisbon.

Adjacent anchorages

Peniche do Cima 39°21'·95N 9°22'W In settled and sometimes on the north side of the peninsula southeast of Cabo do Chao. There are leading marks on 215° but they appear to lead straight onto a rocky shoal. Keep well east, sounding in to anchor close to the above position in 5–6m over sand. The entire bay is open to the north, and any northwesterly swell will also work around the corner.

Looking northwest over the anchorage at Peniche de Cima

FIGUEIRA DA FOZ TO CABO DA ROCA

Ilha da Berlenga from the southeast, with the Ilhas Medas and Ilhas Estelas clearly visible behind

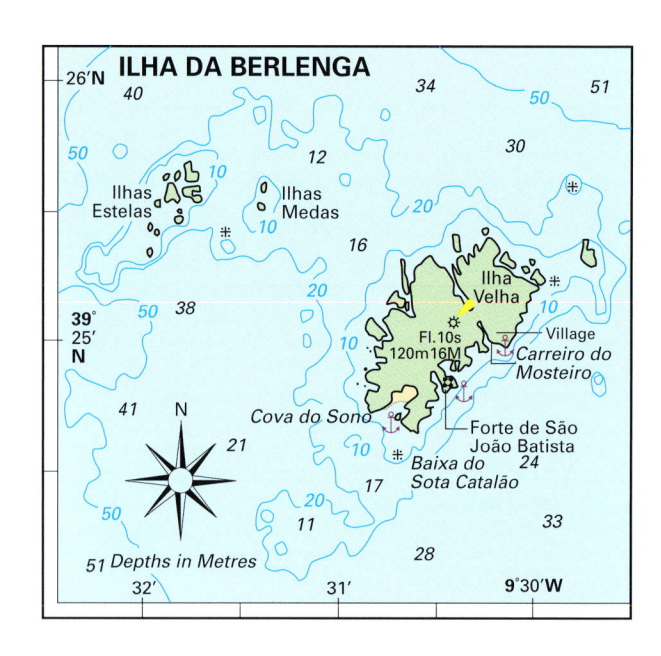

Ilha da Berlenga 39°24'·63N 9°30'·25W remains desolate and largely unspoilt, despite the numerous tourist boats which ply from Peniche. The entire island, together with its offlying rocks and the seabed out to the 3m contour, is a nature reserve frequented by seabirds including gulls, puffins and cormorants. For this reason parts of the island are off-limits to visitors – many of whom in any case appear unwilling to venture far from the landing quay at Carreiro do Mosteiro. (For those who enjoy their wildlife small but inquisitive, a small investment of damp bread will swiftly entice the resident lizards out of their crevasses, while walkers should watch out for their kamikaze brethren who dash across paths almost underfoot.)

Approach from the southeast or south in order to avoid off-lying rocks which fringe the island in all other directions, making for either Carreiro do Mosteiro or Carreiro da Fortaleza – in which stands the distinctive Forte de São João Batista – on the

The centre part of the Ilha da Berlenga with, from left to right, Forte de São João Batista, the island's 29m lighthouse, and the inlet and village of Carreiro do Mosteiro

182 ATLANTIC SPAIN AND PORTUGAL

southeast coast or Cova do Sono to the southwest (taking care to avoid the offlying Baixo do Sota Catalão). All three anchorages call for careful 'eyeball' pilotage in good light, made easier by the crystal clear water.

Both Carreiro do Mosteiro and Carreiro da Fortaleza have beaches at their heads, and in the former landing can also be made by dinghy at the stone quay used by the tourist ferries. It would be unwise to leave the yacht unattended for long in any but the calmest conditions, but a short tour by dinghy will be amply rewarded, viewing the impressive Forte de São João Baptista – built in 1502 by monks, tired of their undefended monastery being ransacked by pirates – and exploring the natural tunnels and caves. Once ashore, the small settlement of Bairro dos Pescadores overlooking the quay offers a café/restaurant and a small shop, the latter apparently selling little beyond ice cream.

The second possible anchorage, in the entrance to Cova do Sono in 8–10m over sand and rock, is somewhat better protected and has been used overnight in settled weather. However, although it is possible to land on the surrounding boulders, only a mountaineer – and one willing to ignore the bylaws which forbid roaming off the marked paths – could attain the island's virtually flat summit.

All official paths start and end at the quay in Carreiro do Mosteiro, but if intent on seeing the island in detail – and unless the crew is large enough to leave a person aboard at all times – it might be better to visit by ferry from Peniche, where several companies compete for business at the root of the main quay. A single day will be long enough to cover all the approved paths, but it is also possible to stay overnight, either in chalets or on the approved campsite – enquire at the tourist office in Peniche.

The Ilhéus dos Farilhões, some 4M north-northwest of Ilha da Berlenga, offer no feasible anchorages.

Ericeira 38°57'·72N 9°25'·4W

6M south of Assenta light and 11·5M north of Cabo da Roca, Ericeira offers a possible daytime anchorage in calm, settled weather. However the single breakwater provides absolutely no shelter from onshore winds or swell, and local craft are kept ashore on the wide slipway – not for nothing is the area popular with surfers from all over Europe. No large scale chart is currently available for the area, which is admitted to be poorly surveyed. Though lit, approach after dark would be most unwise.

Close the land keeping well clear of the breakwater head, which lost its outer section to a winter storm and has yet to be rebuilt. Although the outer block shows at all states of the tide, underwater rubble lies scattered in all directions. Best anchorage is to be found in the entrance to the bay, south of the breakwater head, in 5–6m over rock and sand. There is little depth off the small quay, though it has steps convenient for landing by dinghy.

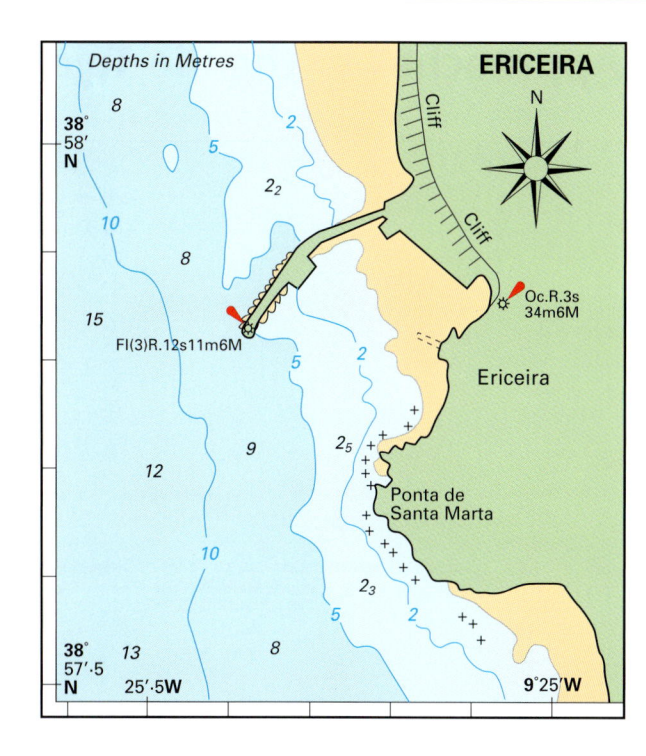

Once a clifftop village – though now dwarfed by the inevitable high-rise buildings – the old town centre has nevertheless retained much of its character and is renowned for its shellfish restaurants. The Clube Naval de Ericeira has a small clubhouse below the cliffs and there are several beach cafés, while the town itself offers the usual banks, shops, post office etc.

In 1910 Portugal's last king, Dom Manuel II, chose Ericeira as his port of departure after a military revolt and following the assassination of his father and elder brother. One can only wonder whether it was the little harbour's apparent unsuitability which prompted his choice.

The small, exposed harbour at Ericeira looking east

Approaches to the Rio Tejo and Lisbon

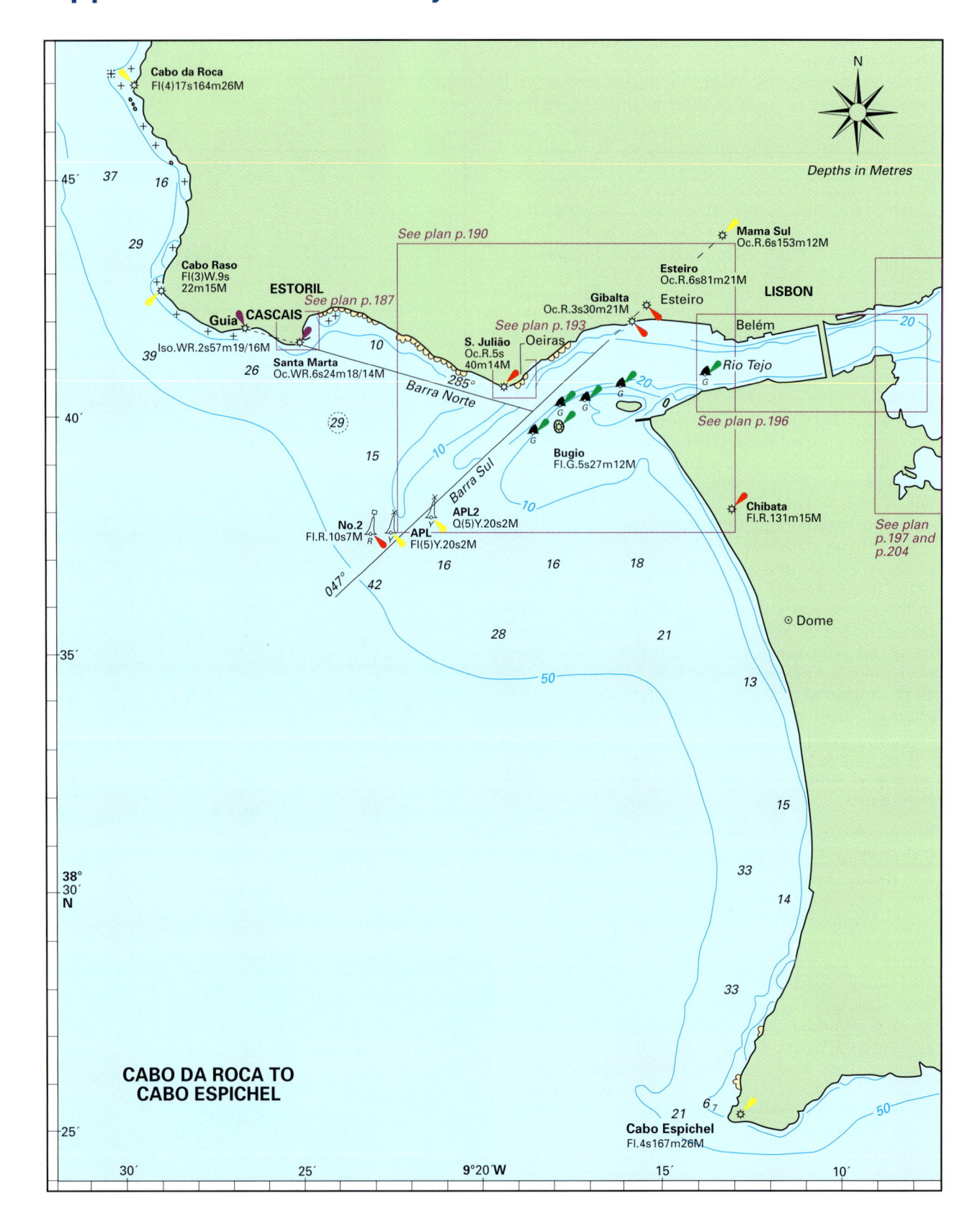

184 ATLANTIC SPAIN AND PORTUGAL

RIO TEJO ESTUARY

Approaches to the Rio Tejo and Lisbon

Principal lights
Cabo da Roca Fl(4)17s165m26M Siren 20s
  Square white tower and buildings, red lantern 22m
Cabo Raso, Forte de São Brás Fl(3)9s22m15M
  324°-vis-189°
  Red tower on white fort 13m
Guía Iso.WR.2s58m19/16M
  326°-W-092°, 278°-R-292°
  Grey and white octagonal tower and building 28m
Santa Marta Oc.WR.6s24m18/14M
  233°-R-334°-W-098°
  Square white tower, two blue bands, red lantern 20m
Punta de Rana Iso.WR.3s18m9M Tower 12m
Forte de São Julião Oc.R.5s40m14M
  Square grey tower, red lantern 24m
Forte Bugio Fl.G.5s28m12M Horn Mo 'B'(–···)30s
  Grey tower on centre of round grey fort, red lantern 14m
Barra do Sul Ldg Lts 047°
  Front **Gibalta** Oc.R.3s31m21M 039·5°-vis-054·5°
  White tower, vertical red ribs and lantern, floodlit red 21m
  Centre **Esteiro** 762m from front Oc.R.6s78m21M
  039·5°-vis-054·5° Racon Mo 'Q'(– –··)
  Square white tower, two red bands 15m
  Rear **Mama Sul** 4,636m from front Iso.6s153m21M 045·5°-vis-048·5° Platform (MAMA below summit)
Cabo Espichel Fl.4s167m26M
  Horn 31s 67m SW
  White hexagonal tower and building 32m

Communications
Maritime radio station
Lisbon (38°44'·1N 9°11'·3W) *Digital Selective Calling*
MMSI 002630100
MF Transmits on 2182, 2582, 2693, 2780kHz
Receives 2182kHz
VHF Manual – Ch 16, 23, 25, 26. *Autolink* – VHF Ch 83
Navtex
Monsanto Identification letters 'R' and 'G'
Transmits on 518kHz in English; 490kHz in Portuguese
Weather bulletins and navigational warnings for Galicia, Portugal and Andalucía: English – 0250, 0650, 1050, 1450, 1850, 2250 UT; Portuguese – 0100, 0500, 0900, 1300, 1700, 2100 UT
Weather bulletins and navigational warnings
Algés (38°44'N 9°11'W)
Weather bulletins in Portuguese and English for Galicia, Portugal and Andalucía: 2657kHz and VHF Ch11 at 0905, 2105 UT
Navigational warnings in Portuguese and English within 200 miles offshore: 2657 kHz and VHF Ch 11 at 1905, 2105 UT

Approach

From the north, keep 1M off the high cliffs of Cabo da Roca off which there is a Traffic Separation Zone 7M wide and approximately 10M from the headland.

From the south, Cabo Espichel is clear of offlying hazards, though all three headlands can produce nasty seas in wind over tide conditions.

See continuation into the Rio Tejo after Cascais page 191.

Cabo da Roca, with its prominent lighthouse and associated buildings, seen from the south

Approaching Cabo da Roca from the north *David Russell*

ATLANTIC SPAIN AND PORTUGAL

APPROACHES TO THE RIO TEJO AND LISBON

Cascais

Location
38°41'·65N 9°24'·75W (entrance)

Tides
Standard port Lisbon
Mean time differences
HW –0035 ±0010; LW –0010 ±0005
Heights in metres
MHWS	MHWN	MLWN	MLWS
3·5	2·7	1·5	0·7

Principal lights
Santa Marta Oc.WR.6s25m18/14M Horn 10s White tower, blue bands, red cupola 233°-R-334°-W-098°
Praia da Ribeira Oc.R.4s7m6M 251°-vis-309°
   White metal column, red bands 4·5m
Albatroz Oc.R.6s13m5M
   Lantern on verandah of Hotel Albatroz 6m
Marina southeast breakwater Fl(3)R.4s6m6M
   Red post, white bands, on concrete base 3m
Marina north mole Fl(2)G.5s4m3M
   Green post, white bands 5m

Notes
Night entry should not present problems in any but the strongest onshore conditions

Communications
Marina de Cascais Casa de S. Bernardo, 2750-800 Cascais.
Management offices: ☏+351 214 824 800
Email info@marinacascais.pt www.marinacascais.pt
Marina reception: Winter 0900–1800 and summer 0900–2000. VHF Ch09 ☏ +351 214 824 857.
Email reception@marinacascais.pt

Large marina with good facilities and shelter

A traditional fishing village, which flourished in the 14th century, when it was a port on the way into Lisbon. In the second half of the 19th century, it became a very fashionable summer resort when the king of Portugal converted the Fortaleza da Cidadela into the summer residence of the Portuguese monarchy. The festival of Our Lady of Seafarers has reproductions of saints carried through the town's streets and onto fishing boats. There is also bull-running, music, fireworks and lots of food.

It is a good 20 minutes' walk from the marina into the town centre, though buses run regularly from the main gate. Alternatively, a walkway has been completed along the walls above the Clube Naval de Cascais, giving excellent views and cutting the time considerably. An unexpected bonus is the very pleasant leafy park right opposite the marina's landward gates, complete with children's playground (a supervised indoor adventure play area is provided in the marina itself). There is also a small maritime museum nearby.

Approach

If coastal sailing from the north, between Cabo da Roca and Santa Marta there are steep rocky cliffs and fishing nets may be laid at least 0·5M offshore.

From the south, the track between Cabo Espichel and Cascais lies along 331°, leaving the Rio Tejo Fairway Buoy No.2 about 1M to port and thus crossing the Barra Sul at close to a right-angle. Considerable traffic should be anticipated at this point, and it is not a route to choose in poor visibility unless radar is carried. If approaching from the south at night, the light on São Julião will probably be picked up before that on Santa Marta. The bright shore lights may mask fishing boats, another time when radar will be useful.

Large yacht berths from the helipad. Office to the left
Henry Buchanan

Fuel and reception pontoon, office
Henry Buchanan

Looking N over the anchorage from the helipad (no landing on the beach beyond) *Henry Buchanan*

186   ATLANTIC SPAIN AND PORTUGAL

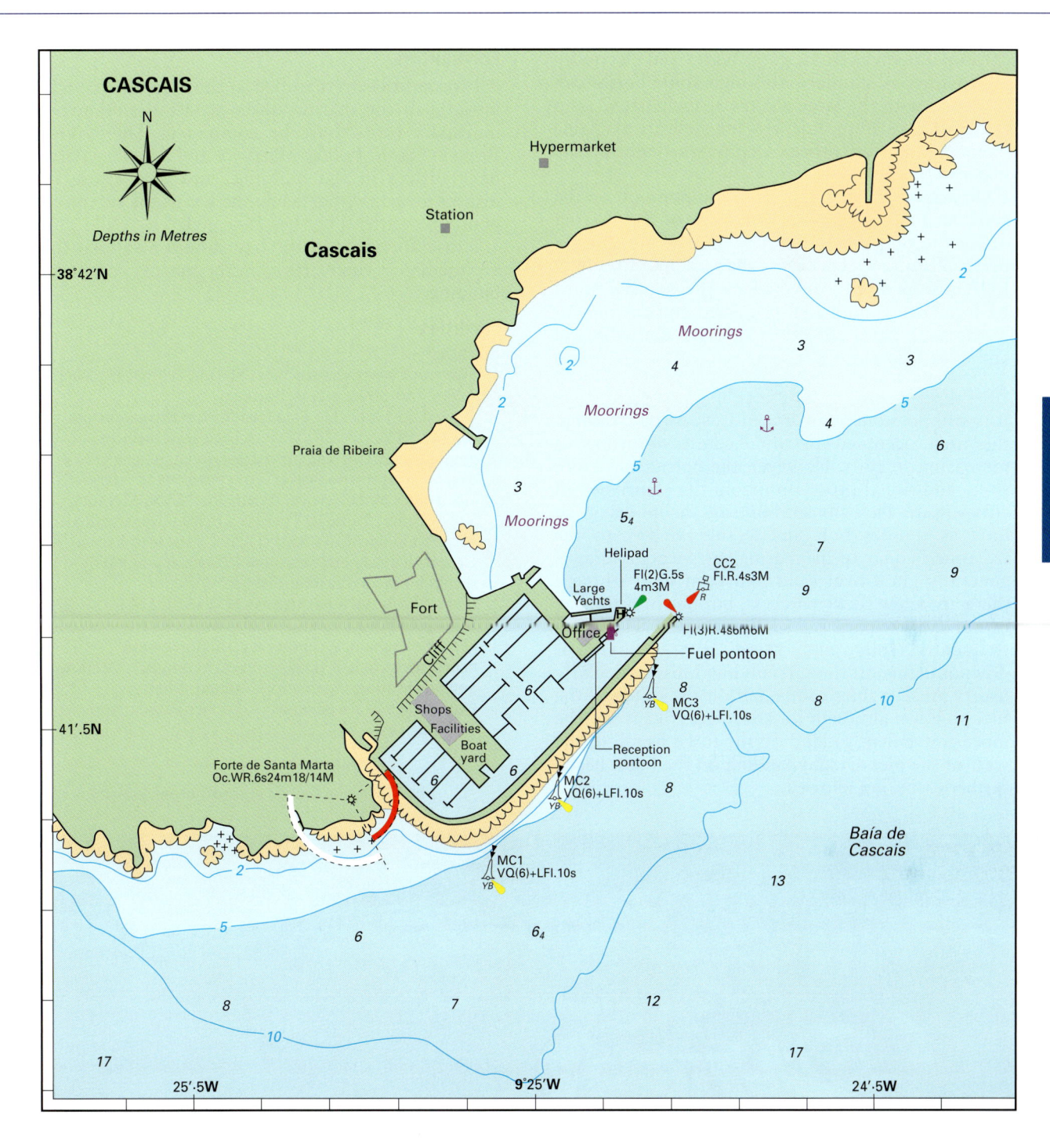

CASCAIS

Entrance
The bay is entered between the Cidadela de Cascais, prominently situated on the headland 300m behind the Marina de Cascais, and the Forte de Santo António da Barra, 1·5M to the east. Three south cardinal buoys and a single red can buoy are positioned some 100m from the marina's main breakwater to keep yachts off a second, submerged wall which lies some distance outside the visible one.

Berthing
A reception berth and fuel pontoon will be found on the starboard hand on entry, immediately below the marina office. Hours are from 0900–2000 from May to September inclusive, 0900–1800 during the rest of the year. Large yachts, those over 40m or so, berth on a pontoon outside the north mole, just inside the helipad, where they lie stern-to (with buoys provided) in a least depth of 7m. All 638 berths inside the marina are alongside finger pontoons (with thoughtfully rounded ends), with access to each main walkway controlled by the usual

ATLANTIC SPAIN AND PORTUGAL 187

card-operated electronic gate. Water and electricity is provided as standard although some berths are provided with the large electrical sockets (32 amp rather than 16 amp). Adapters for these are available from the marina office. Depths throughout the marina are in excess of 6m.

On arrival, berth at the reception pontoon on the starboard side under the windows of the marina office to complete formalities and be allocated a berth. Visiting yachts of less than about 14m (46ft) LOA are generally directed to the southwestern basin, which is both well-protected and convenient to the main gate. The office staff are multi-lingual and most helpful.

Anchorage

It is still possible to anchor in Cascais bay, though the area occupied by small craft moorings is increasing steadily. However, the marina provides some additional protection from the southwest to compensate. Pick any spot outside the moorings so long as it does not impede the fairway to the fishermen's quay or the marina entrance. Holding is generally good over sand and light mud (though there are a few rocky patches), but much of the bay is foul and a tripline is a wise precaution. The bay is frequently rolly and there may be violent downdraughts off the surrounding hills particularly overnight. Dinghies can be left on the inside of the fuel pontoon although for shopping trips it may be more convenient to land on the town beach to the west of the pier. Dinghy landing on the main beach further east is not allowed.

Formalities

All formalities are handled in the reception block, initially in the marina office where the standard multipart form must be completed. The *GNR–Brigada Fiscal*, *Polícia Marítima* and *Alfândega* also have offices in the building, and may chose to inspect a yacht either while she lies at the reception pontoon or after a berth is allocated.

Those anchored in the bay should also visit the authorities at their offices in the marina reception building.

Facilities

Boatyard
1. *Wavetech* www.wavetech.pt. Marina de Cascais, Loja 128, 2750-800 Cascais, Portugal.
   ☎+351 214 847 025 *Email* joaofortuna@wavetech.pt
   ☎+351 919 209 726. Wavetech services include: engine, generator and air-con servicing; painting; carpentry and wood care; GRP; gardienage; marine electronics and electrics. Agents for MAN, Mercury, Volvo Penta, Yanmar. There is a helpful rigger called Jorge Rainha (*Mob* +351 917 500 730) who lives in Cascais works partly through Wavetech and partly through his own firm in Lisbon.
2. *Yacht Works* www.yachtworks.pt ☎+351 214 601 388 *Email* info@yachtworks.pt Yacht Works services include: general mechanics, repowering, maintenance, generators, electrical, electronics, hydraulics, cleaning, and antifouling. Agents for: Yanmar, Mercury, Cummings, Mase generators, Fischer Pamda, and Yamaha.

The Marina de Cascais and anchorage looking north

CASCAIS

The anchorage at Cascais looking south. Dinghy landing is not permitted on this beach *Jane Russell*

3. *TECNI-MARINE* Marina de Cascais, Loja 121/129, 2750-800 Cascais, Portugal. Ⓣ +351 214 834 39
   Email geralcascais@tecnimarine.com.
   João Pedro Lopes Ⓣ+351 912 269 413.
   joaopedro@tecnimarine.com. Agents for: MAN, CAT, MTU, Volvo Penta, Lombardini Marine, Vitrifrigo, Hempel, Nautix, Furuno, and Idromar watermakers.

Travel-lift 70-tonne capacity lift in the boatyard area, with pressure hoses, etc. Book at the marina office. Maximum beam is currently 6·5m, but there are plans to increase this.

Engineers, mechanics, electronic and radio repairs All available via Wavetech, Yacht Works and TECNI_MARINE who are all authorised dealers for a number of international suppliers.

Sailmaker North Sails in the Marina: Marina de Cascais, Loja 27B, 2750-800 Cascais.
   Vicente Pinheiro de Melo ⓉⓉ+351 916 857 896. *Email* vicente.pinheiro@northsails.com.

Chandlery Sabor a Bordo: Marina de Cascais, Loja 33-34, 2750-800 Cascais, Portugal. Accastillage Diffusion: ⓉⓉ+351 214 835 557. *Email* ad-cascais@marine.pt. Management: Domingos João Mota Carvalho ⓉⓉ+351 966 392 387. *Mob* +351 969 778 026. Nautical Shop: *Email* saborabordo@marine.pt. In addition there is a good hardware/tool shop in the town.

Water On all pontoons.

Showers Three shower blocks, two in the central part of the complex and one at the reception building.

Launderette In the reception building (a longish walk from the southern basin). A 24-hour service wash is available if required.

Electricity On all pontoons, with plugs etc available at the marina office (deposit required).

Fuel The fuel pontoon is next to the reception pontoon under the marina office building. The Cepsa Gas Station facility is managed by Sabor a Bordo (see Chandlery above). ⓉⓉ+351 962 143 719 *Email* docais@marine.pt. Open marina office hours, with credit cards accepted. Fuel can also be obtained out of hours (2000-0900) through the marina office on payment of a surcharge. The out-of-hours *Mob* +351 966 392 387.

Bottled gas Camping Gaz cylinders can be exchanged at both the Sabor a Bordo chandlery and the fuel pontoon.
   Clube naval The Clube Naval de Cascais has premises immediately north of the marina, but there is no direct access.

Weather forecast Posted daily in the marina office.

Boatyard with supporting businesses beyond *Henry Buchanan*

Banks At least one automatic card machine in the marina complex, with banks in Cascais.

Shops/provisioning: Excellent grocery and other shopping can be found in Cascais itself.

Produce market In Cascais, plus fish sold on the beach in the late afternoon. A general market is held every Wednesday and every second Sunday.

Cafés, restaurants and hotels More than a dozen restaurants and cafés in the marina complex, with plenty more of all three in the town.

Medical services First aid centre at the marina office, with full medical facilities in the town.

Communications

Post office In Cascais.

Mailing address The marina office will hold mail for visiting yachts – c/o Marina de Cascais, Casa de S. Bernardo, 2750–800 Cascais, Portugal. It is important that the envelope carries the name of the yacht in addition to that of the addressee.

Internet WiFi is available throughout the Marina. Access details should be requested at reception.

Car hire/taxis Can be arranged through the marina office.

Buses Buses into Cascais from outside the main entrance.

Trains Frequent trains from Cascais to Lisbon's Cais do Sodré station, close to the city centre. The journey, via Estoril and Belém, takes about 30 minutes.

Air services Lisbon International Airport is less than an hour away by train and taxi.

APPROACHES TO THE RIO TEJO AND LISBON

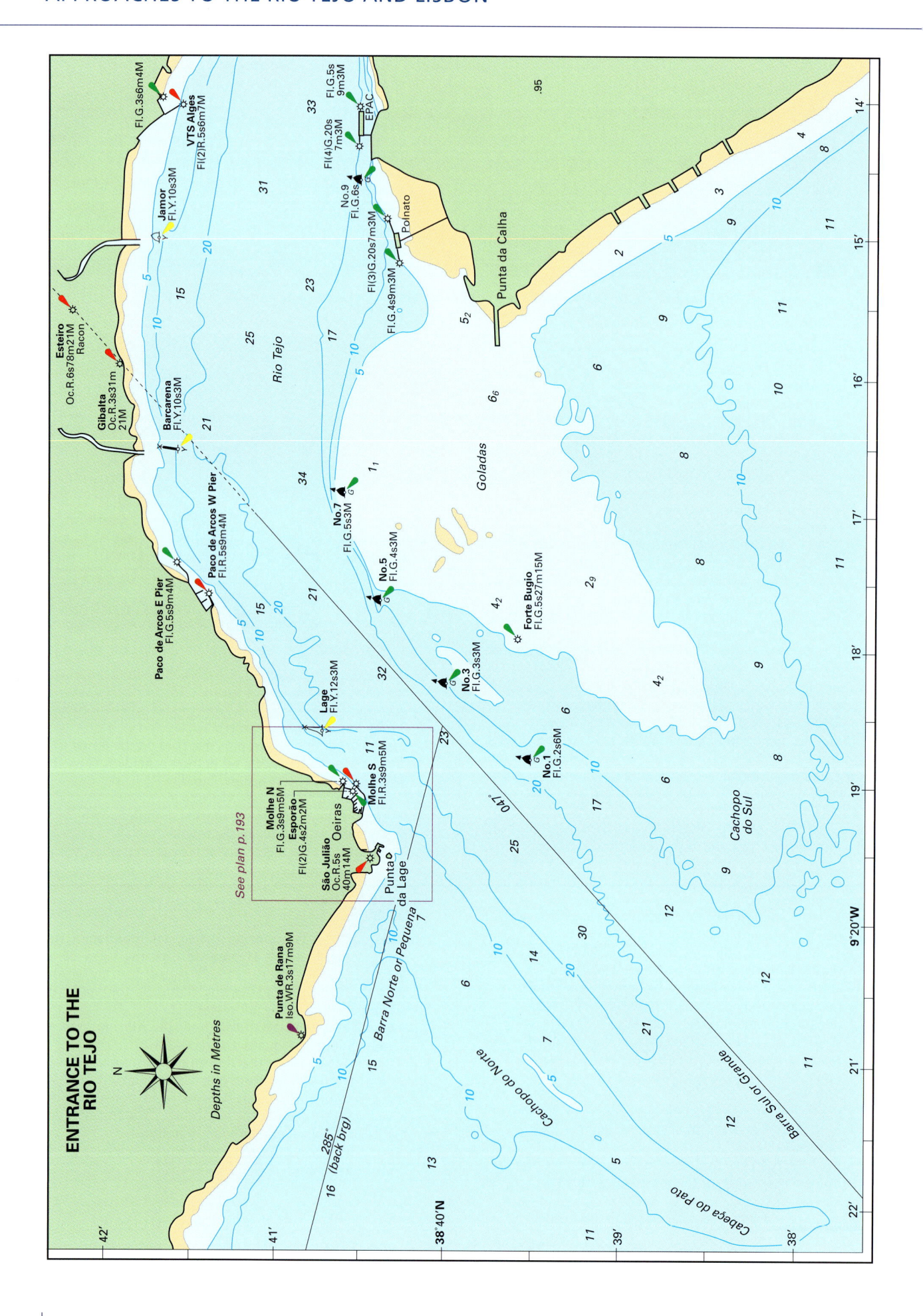

ENTRANCE TO THE RIO TEJO

The Rio Tejo

Approach
If heading for Oeiras or Lisbon the choice is between the main Barra Sul (or Grande) and the shallower but less defined Barra Norte (or Pequena). Depths of the Cachope do Norte, which separates the two channels, shoal to less than 5m and seas may break even in low swell. As the greatest danger to a well-navigated yacht is probably from shipping, the northern route on 105° (or a back bearing of 285°) on Santa Marta and Guia lights may be the best choice, particularly in poor visibility if not equipped with radar (see plans opposite and on p.180). At night however, shore lights tend to hide fishing boats which often display inadequate navigation lights or sometimes none at all.

If approaching from offshore or from the south the Barra Sul will be more direct, joining near Fairway Buoy No.2 and following the leading line on 047° (see plan page 184). It is also the safest route if any swell is running. Note, however, that shipping may approach from any direction, joining the Barra Sul well inside Fairway Buoy No.2 or crossing en route to the designated ship anchorage which lies directly between Fairway Buoy No.2 and Cascais. Tidal streams in the Barra Sul can attain 3kn at springs – more on the ebb after heavy rain – creating heavy seas during strong southwesterlies.

Entrance
The Rio Tejo is entered between Punta de Lage (Fort de São Julião) on the northern shore and Fort Bugio to the southeast, and yachts are advised to remain on, or slightly north of, the leading line as traffic dictates until well up to Gibalta before turning upriver. Tidal streams reach 2 or 3kn either way at springs, not always running parallel to the shore, but are somewhat less powerful near the northern bank. This should be given an offing of at least 300m until the unmistakable Tôrre de Belém has been passed, but beyond that can be approached within 100m in good depths. The Ponte 25 de Abril suspension bridge has a clearance of 70m – unlikely to worry any yacht! – but spare a glance for the towering statue of Christ near its southern end.

Forte Bugio, on the south side of the mouth of the Rio Tejo. Not very long ago it was surrounded by drying banks at all states of the tide

Looking northeast into the wide mouth of the Rio Tejo. The marina at Oeiras can be seen on the left and Forte Bugio and its associated shoals at right of centre

ATLANTIC SPAIN AND PORTUGAL

PORTUGAL – THE WEST COAST

APPROACHES TO THE RIO TEJO AND LISBON

Oeiras

Location
38°40'·6N 9°18'·76W (Oeiras entrance)

Tides
Standard port Lisbon
Mean time differences
HW –0020 ±0500; LW –0005 ±0500
Heights in metres
MHWS MHWN MLWN MLWS
3·7   2·9   1·4   0·6

Principal lights
South mole Fl.R.3s9m5M
  White tower, red bands, 5m
North mole Fl.G.3s9m5M
  White tower, green bands, 4m
Inner mole Fl(2)G.4s2m2M

Notes
Night entry feasible with care in light weather, but best avoided in stronger onshore winds

Communications
Puerto de Recreio Oeiras VHF Ch 09
① +351 214 401510
Email porto.recreio@oeirasviva.pt www.oeirasviva.pt
www.oeirasmarina.oeirasviva.pt

A marina conveniently close west of Lisbon

While for many the chief attraction of Oeiras will undoubtedly be its proximity to Lisbon (door-to-door in 40 minutes or so, less if a taxi is taken to the station) the marina is flanked by an outstanding beach and large sports complex including swimming pools. There are cafés and restaurants onsite. The Marina staff offer a free taxi service in their own vehicle to both the local Pingo Doce supermarket (and back) and the train station.

The old town centre is pleasant, and there are several attractions in the vicinity, including the palace of Sebastião José de Carvalho e Melo, later Marquês de Pombal. It can get very crowded during the popular arts and music festival in July.

Puerto de Recreio Oeiras looking west

Approach
For outer approaches see Approaches to the Rio Tejo and Lisbon, pages 184 and 191.

If coastal sailing from Cascais, no more than 5M to the west, the Barra Norte (or Pequena) is the logical choice of approach – see plan on page 184. After rounding Punta de Lage and the prominent Fort de São Julião, steer by eye until the marina entrance is open before rounding to port.

Entrance
Beware of strong currents (3kns at springs) across the entrance. The marina entrance is narrow with a pronounced dog-leg, difficult for less manœuvrable yachts and almost impossible under sail other than for the very skilled. The (well-fendered) reception/fuel berth is starboard-to on the west side of the inner mole. At least 5m will be found in the entrance and 3m at the reception berth.

The inner mole, it should be said, appears almost 100% efficient in preventing surge entering the marina, even in established easterlies.

Berthing
A marina official will often meet a yacht at the reception berth, otherwise walk up to the office near the root of the spur. It shares premises with a helpful Turismo desk and is open 0800–2200 from May - September and 0800–1800 from October - April, with security staff on duty at other times. The Staff are multilingual. Security is via the usual card-operated gates. If arriving after hours be sure to leave someone inside to operate the gate (via a button 10m or so down the walkway) if no official is to be found.

Visitors are normally berthed on the first three pontoons, with larger yachts near the root of the inner mole. Twenty-three of the 274 slots are reserved for visitors (defined as a stay of less than 30 days), all able to accommodate 10m or more overall in a minimum of 2m. Four of the nine berths able to take yachts of 15–20m are also currently reserved for visitors. All berths are alongside finger pontoons.

Formalities
Visit the marina office equipped with passports, ship's papers and insurance documents. There are no forms to complete but copies of passports and boat's papers are taken. There is also no need to clear out from each port as details are kept in computer systems which most ports have access to. If a change of crew is made, however, the authorities need to be informed for safety reasons. Should any officials wish to visit the yacht, most probable if either boat or crew are of non-EU origin, it is their responsibility to make the first move.

Facilities
The Puerto de Recreio Oeiras does not aspire to provide shoreside facilities for a yacht with serious problems, but these are near at hand in Cascais, Lisbon and Seixal.

Boatyard/travel-lift Not provided although a 7 tonne crane is available for small boats.
Engineers/electronics Kilinautica, Loja Nautica e pesca, Marina de Oeiras, Loja C8 ✆+351 211 131 545 www.kilinautica.pt *Email* kilinauticapesca@gmail.com Head office near airport: ✆+351 915 372 837 A company dedicated to general repairs in Recreational Boats. Agents for Mercury, MerCruiser, Mercury Diesel, Cummins, Mariner, Quicksilver, Valiant, Black Fin and Bayliner.
Chandlery Some available on site. Otherwise Lisbon's excellent chandleries are close at hand.
Sail repair/rigging West Coast Lisbon Sailing Centre (RYA Training Centre), Porto de Recreio de Oeiras, Loja C9 ✆+351 915 759 600 or +351 210 995 320 www.westcoast.pt *Email* info@westcoast.pt. Can provide sail repair and rigging services.
Water On the pontoons.
Electricity On the pontoons.
Fuel Diesel and petrol at the reception berth, nominally 24 hours per day. Credit cards are accepted.
Bottled gas Available through West Coast Lisbon Sailing Centre.
Showers In the reception block, with further toilets by the shops and cafés.
Launderette Available on site.
Weather forecast Posted daily at the marina office.
Banks In the town, about 20 minutes on foot.
Shops/provisioning Pingo Doce supermarket is a 15 minute walk but the marina office can provide free transport.
Cafés, restaurants, bars and hotels Several cafés, restaurants and bars are in the marina complex, and there are numerous hotels nearby. Overlooking the beach west of the marina is the unusual Carruagem Bar in an old (and very plush) railway carriage.
Medical services First aid centre in reception, with full services in the town.

Communications

Post office In the town centre, about 20 minutes on foot.
Mailing address The marina office will hold mail for visiting yachts – c/o Puerto de Recreio de Oeiras, Estrada Marginal – Praia da Torre, 2780-267 Oeiras, Portugal. It is important that the envelope carries the name of the yacht in addition to that of the addressee.

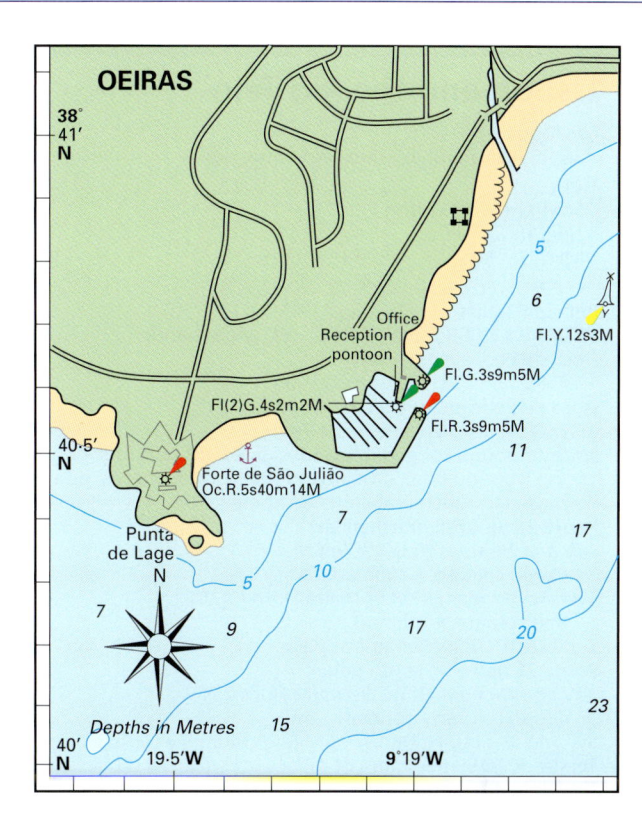

Internet WiFi is available throughout the marina.
Car hire/taxis Can be arranged through the marina office.
Trains Frequent (and cheap) trains to Lisbon's Cais do Sodré station, close to the city centre. Closest station is Santo Amaro, about 15 minutes on foot. Walk east along the seafront promenade, crossing the busy road (N2) via the underpass (the road itself is dangerous to cross!) which is part way along the beach, beyond the river estuary. Santo Amaro station is 100m or so north of the underpass. The journey takes about 20 minutes. Oeiras station is a little further and is best reached by car.
Air services Lisbon International Airport is less than an hour away by train and taxi.

Looking towards the reception pontoon beyond yellow bin on the pontoon
Henry Buchanan

APPROACHES TO THE RIO TEJO AND LISBON

Lisbon and the Rio Tejo

Location
38°40'·05N 9°18'·9W (Rio Tejo entrance)

Tides
Standard port Lisbon
Heights in metres
MHWS	MHWN	MLWN	MLWS
3·8	3·0	1·4	0·5

Principal lights
VTS Algés Fl(2)R.5s6m7M Red post, white bands
Doca de Pedroucos, west mole
  Fl.R.2s9m4·5M Metal mast 7m
Doca de Pedroucos, east mole
  Fl.G.2s9m4·5M Metal mast 7m
Note Although some publications give light details for both the Doca do Bom Sucesso and the Doca de Belém, neither have had functional lights for some years
Ponte 25 de Abril, north pillar
NW and NE sides Fl(3)G.9s7m6M
  Green column, ▲ topmark, 2m
SW and SE sides Fl(3)R.9s7m6M Horn (2)25s
  Red column, ■ topmark, 2m
Top Fl.R.10s189m Summit of pillar
Ponte 25 de Abril, south pillar
NW and NE sides Fl(3)G.9s7m6M Horn 25s
  Green column ▲ topmark, 2m
SW and SE sides Fl(3)R.9s7m6M Red column, ■ topmark, 2m
Top Iso.R.2s189m Summit of pillar
Both pillars NW and SW lights 000°-vis-180°
  NE and SE lights: 180°-vis-000°
Lisnave, Dolphin, Fl.G.2s3m3M Column with red and white bands
Doca da Marinha, W side F.R.10m2M Post 7m
Doca da Marinha, E side F.G.10m2M Post 7m
Seca (Seixal), north bank Fl.G.3s7m5M Green column 5m
Pilar (Seixal), south pillar Fl.R.3s5m6M
  Red and white pillar on concrete plinth 2m
Plus many other lights throughout the harbour and further upriver

Warning
Night entry probably best avoided if new to the area, though perfectly feasible in all normal conditions. Tides run strongly at springs

Communications
Lisboa Port Control VHF Watch: Ch 12, 13, 16, Working: 64 (call *Lisbon Control*) (24 hours)
☏ +351 213 922026 (for leisure craft berthing instructions)
Email admin.junqueira@porto-de-lisboa.pt
Administração do Porto de Lisboa (APL) VHF Ch 12 (0900–1300, 1400–1800 daily)
☏ +351 213 611000
Email geral@portodelisboa.pt
www.portodelisboa.com *(the same site as the above, in Portuguese only, and mainly about the commercial port)
Tagus Yacht Center – see Seixal, page 206
Marinas
Doca de Bom Sucesso VHF Ch12/74
☏ +351 213 922 080
Email doca.bomsucesso@portodelisboa.pt
Doca de Belém VHF Ch12/74
☏ +351 213 922 203
Email doca.belem@portodelisboa.pt.
Doca de Santo Amaro VHF Ch12/74
☏ +351 213 922 011/2
Email doca.stamaro@portodelisboa.pt
Doca de Alcântara VHF Ch12/74
☏ +351 213 922 048/58
Email doca.alcantara@portodelisboa.pt
Marina Parque das Nações VHF CH 09 (call sign: Marina Parque das Nações). ☏+351 218 949 066
www.marinaparquedasnacoes.pt
Email info@marinaparquedasnacoes.pt

Lisbon from the S bank. VTS tower far left, APL Marina docks on N bank opposite *Shutterstock*

Tôrre de Belém & Monument to the Discoveries beyond *William Maltby*

The world famous Lisbon Oceanarium in the Parque de Nações *Alvesgaspar*

Lisbon – a famous, maritime capital city with many facilities for yachts (but crowded)

An ancient city remarkable for its slightly dilapidated beauty and the reverberations of its maritime past – its people, its way of life and its architecture all show influences far removed from Europe. Its roots can be traced back to the Romans and very probably the Phoenicians and it has been the capital of Portugal since its very bloody reconquest by the Crusaders from the Moors in 1147. Throughout the Middle Ages it was one of Europe's busiest ports and it later owed its wealth to its trade in slaves. Much of the city was rebuilt after a serious earthquake and fire in November 1755 in which more than 40,000 people died.

Perhaps the most memorable parts of Lisbon are in the Belém area to the west of the city. These include the fairytale Tôrre de Belém and the Museu de Marinha (maritime museum) housed in the western wing of the impressive Mosterio dos Jerónimos. The Jeronimos Monastery is symbolic of Portugal's power and wealth during the Age of Discovery. King Manuel I built it in 1502 on the site of a hermitage founded by Prince Henry the Navigator. Vasco da Gama and his crew spent their last night in Portugal in prayer here before leaving for India and their historic voyage. Built to commemorate this voyage, Vasco da Gama's tomb is probably the most significant tomb in the monastery.

While wandering around Lisbon, it is impossible not to be constantly reminded of and impressed by Portugal's pioneering role in the voyages of discovery. This can be traced back to the early part of the 13th century when King Diniz set out to improve Portugal's emerging navy. In 1341, three vessels sailed from Lisbon and explored the Canary Islands and became what was the first official expedition by a European state to discover the lands beyond Europe. Portuguese captains soon became the best in Europe, using what was then the latest maritime technology and cartography.

The revitalised Alcantara docks have been transformed from their commercial past as warehouses into shops, offices, restaurants and nightclubs, and are buzzing with the attendant and inevitable noise. However, unlike the Doca de Santo Amaro where wooden decking literally overhangs the marina, the Doca de Alcântara has a relatively wide paved area between buildings and basin.

The Lisbon Festival of the Seas in August each year is meant as a celebration of Portugal's seafaring traditions. It does include some nautical events among the many other manifestations of the Portuguese way of life.

Cafés, restaurants and hotels are an essential part of life in Lisbon, but no visit to Lisbon is complete without sampling bars and restaurants featuring live Fado singing.

The monument to the Discoveries, with the masts of yachts in the Doca de Belém behind *David Russell*

APPROACHES TO THE RIO TEJO AND LISBON

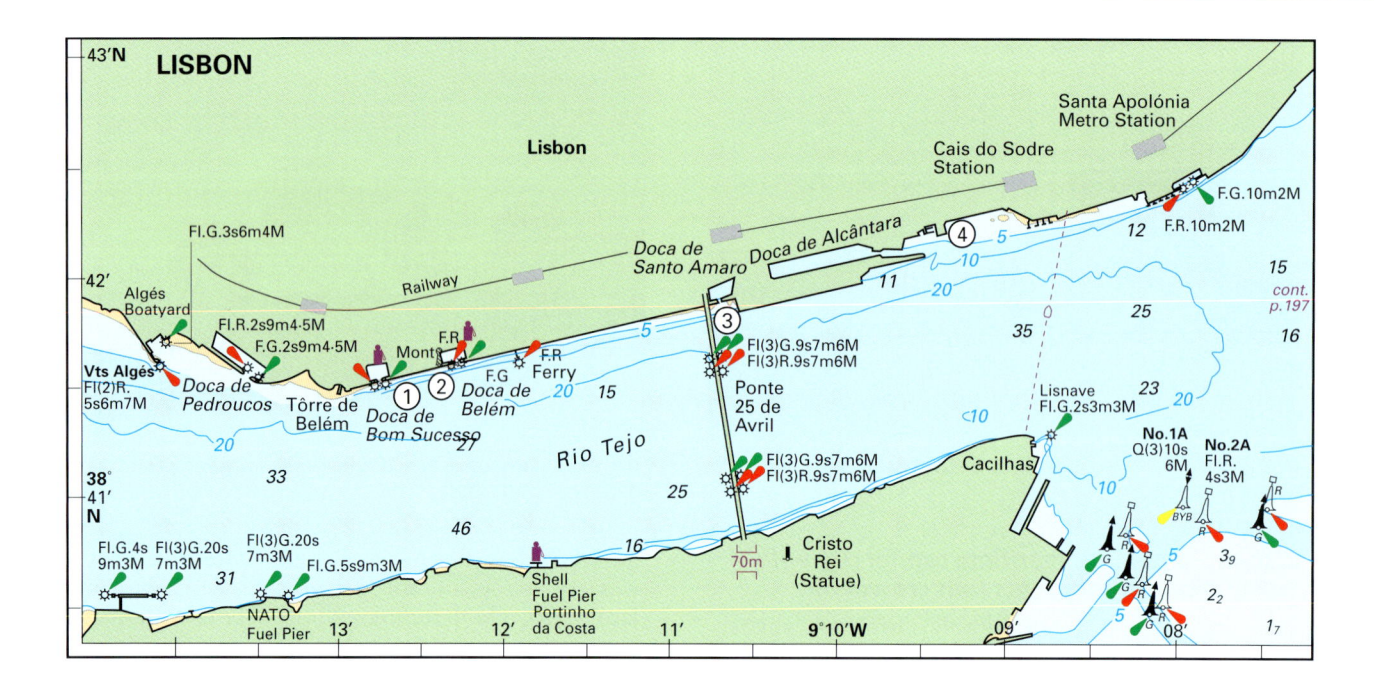

Berthing

There are five operational marinas in Lisbon, all on the north bank of the Rio Tejo. Two lie between the Tôrre de Belém and the Ponte 25 de Abril, two immediately above the bridge and the fifth, further upriver just downstream of the Ponte Vasco de Gama bridge.

The first four marinas are all run by the Administração do Porto de Lisboa (APL) and thus share characteristics such as good security with card-operated access gates, and similar working hours and price structure. All are popular with local yachtsmen, but space for a visitor can usually be found somewhere, though it is strongly advised to make contact before arrival. Apart from other considerations, none of the APL marinas have reception pontoons. Standard office hours are 0900–1300 and 1400–1800 daily throughout the year. Fluent English is spoken at both the main office at the Doca de Santo Amaro and at the individual marina offices:
www.portodelisboa.pt
Email geral@portodelisboa.pt

The fifth marina, Marina Parque das Nações (ex MarinaExpo), is run by the Parque Expo Group with all the facilities of a modern marina.

Note that the current in the river runs swiftly and that, with the possible exception of the Doca de Alcântara, all the marina entrances can have awkward crosscurrents at the entrance. Not only will these set the yacht sideways, they may also tend to slew her round during those seconds when the bow is in the stationary water of the entrance and the stern still in the moving river.

Formalities

At all the marinas it is only necessary to complete a standard form at the office, copies of which are distributed to the *GNR–Brigada Fiscal*, *Polícia Marítima* and *Alfândega* (customs). Whether any or all chose to visit will be based on the yacht and crew's nationalities and her last port of call.

APL Marinas

1. **Doca do Bom Sucesso** –
   VHF Ch12/74 ☎+351 213 922 080
   Email doca.bomsucesso@portodelisboa.pt
   Reception 0900-1300/1400-1800

   This a short distance upstream from the (floodlit) Tôrre de Belém. Once the marina to which foreign yachts were directed, it is now crowded with local yachts and unlikely to have space for a visitor unless a long-term berth-holder is known to be absent. The 163 berths (all with finger pontoons) are limited to 12m length overall, maximum draft 1·5m (2·5m depth at entrance). Fuel is available, the fuel pontoon being in the northeast corner of the basin with the office and showers nearby. There is very little room to manoeuvre.

2. **Doca de Belém**
   VHF Ch12/74 ☎+351 213 922 203
   Email doca.belem@portodelisboa.pt
   Reception 0900-1300/1400-1800

   This is 700m east of the Doca do Bom Sucesso and immediately beyond the prominent Padrão dos Descobrimentos (Monument to the Discoveries) which resembles a ship's prow.

   Again, the 194 berths are reserved for residents and, as in the Doca do Bom Sucesso, there is unlikely to be room for a visiting yacht except on a very temporary basis. Previously rather shallow, dredging has now ensured depths of 2m

LISBON

thriving boatyard (see *Facilities*, below). A welcome and imaginative touch, when new workshops were being built for boatyard contractors, was to place a café/restaurant on their roofs ensuring both cool breezes and interesting views.

3. **Doca de Santo Amaro**
   VHF Ch12/74   ℡+351 213 922 011/2
   Email doca.stamaro@portodelisboa.pt
   Reception 0900-1300/1400-1800

This is 150m beyond the Ponte de 25 Avril suspension bridge and dredged to a nominal 3m, though reported to carry considerably less than this over a very soft bottom. Second largest of the four with 331 berths all equipped with finger pontoons. It is nevertheless crowded with local craft though a visiting yacht can sometimes be squeezed in. The entrance is narrow and unlit, but there is a convenient pontoon just inside on the port hand (though short on mooring cleats as it is not technically a reception pontoon but the property of the local rowing club). The marina office, labelled APL Docas de Recreio, is at the northeast end of the basin at the east end of the row of cafés and restaurants.

The real drawback to the Doca de Santo Amaro, should space be available at all, is that it is not quiet. Traffic passing over the bridge sounds like a swarm of bees and could become irritating in time, but more importantly the area has become a popular centre for Lisbon nightlife with the bars and restaurants overlooking the basin remaining lively until 0400 or beyond. Of course more energetic crews may well consider this a plus.

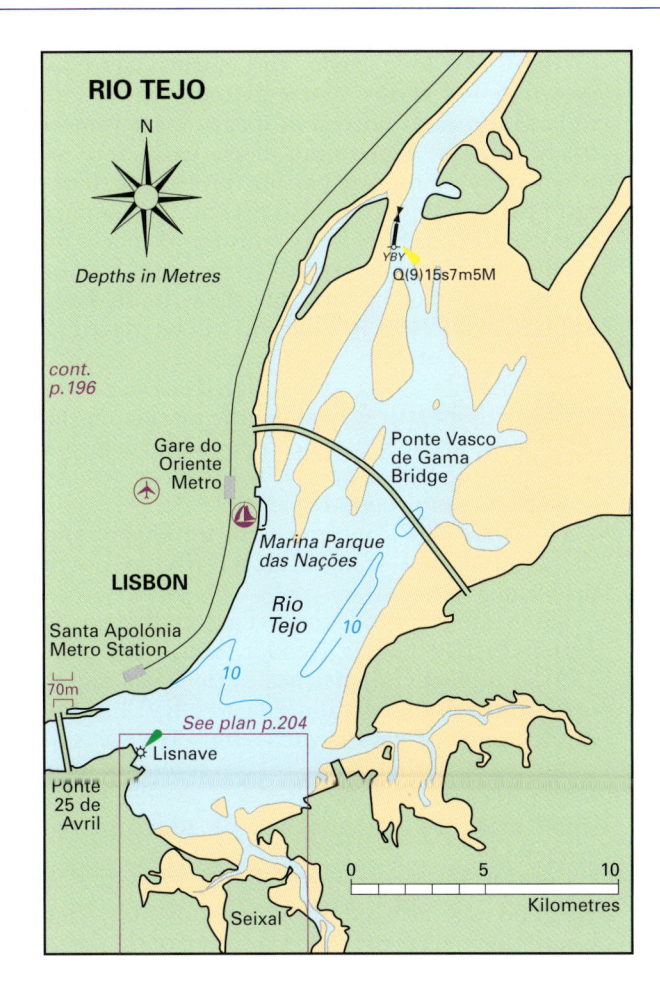

throughout (3m at the entrance). The marina office lies at the northeast corner of the basin with showers etc in the same block, both adjacent to a

Lisbon's Doca de Belém and Doca do Bom Sucesso looking a little north of west, with the Padrão dos Descobrimentos (Monument to the Discoveries) prominent in the centre. At far right is the Mosterio dos Jerónimos, which houses the extensive Museu de Marinha (maritime museum). Jutting out to sea at far left is the fairytale Tôrre de Belém

ATLANTIC SPAIN AND PORTUGAL   PORTUGAL – THE WEST COAST

APPROACHES TO THE RIO TEJO AND LISBON

The Doca de Santo Amaro close east of the Ponte de 25 Abril suspension bridge

4. **Doca de Alcântara**
   VHF Ch12/74   +351 213 922 048/58
   Email doca.alcantara@portodelisboa.pt
   Reception 0800-1300/1400-1900

   The control booth (when manned) operates on VHF Ch68 or ☏+351 213 92 20 90. This is a much larger basin than any of the others, entered about 1M upstream of the suspension bridge via an entry channel which, rather surprisingly, is not lit. A pedestrian bridge, or Ponte Móvel, which crosses the entrance, is normally left open for boats to pass through from 1900-0700. From 0730-1900 opening times are every half hour on the hour, and at half past the hour. Closing is signalled by lights and a horn. The bridge is positioned well inside the entrance proper, and though a waiting pontoon is not provided there are normally plenty of moored vessels alongside which a yacht could lie for a short time.

   Depths in the basin are 10m (7m at the entrance). Originally concentrated at the west end of the 0·5M long basin, the marina has now grown to 442 berths on ten pontoons and is said to have spread as far east as it can. Space is most likely to be at a premium in the early autumn when many visitors are passing through, yet long-term berth-holders are also present. In summer many of the latter are away cruising. Yachts of up to 30m are normally berthed in the basin bow or stern-to with pick up lines, but the seriously large are expected to stay outside and will be treated as the ships they are.

   The marina office and related services are situated about half way along the marina on the north side, inside a gated compound for which a security code is needed and which provides the only access to the pontoons.

   The Doca de Alcântara is a peaceful spot and the distant hum from bridge traffic is not a problem.

   The restored Portuguese East Indiaman *D Fernando II e Glória* (rebuilt Aveiro see page 159), is permanently berthed in the basin and is open to the public. In addition APORVELA, the Associação Portuguesa de Treino de Vela (sail training association), already keep several of their recreated caravels in the basin. It is possible that a small maritime museum will be added to the attractions.

5. **Doca de Pedroucous**
   No good and included for information only. This basin, just east of the Algés boatyard, was equipped with pontoons to host the Volvo Ocean Race stopover here in 2015. A race village was last set up here in 2017 for the Volvo Race yachts that year but the site is badly run down with no facilities ashore. It appears that APL who own the site do not want to maintain it and have been unable to find a business to lease it to. A problem is that the entrance is wide upon to big seas riding up the Tejo estuary that bounce waves around inside the basin.

Entry to the Doca de Alcântara at its east end is through a relatively narrow passage crossed by a pedestrian bridge

198   ATLANTIC SPAIN AND PORTUGAL

LISBON

View looking east into Doca de Alcântara Marina
Henry Buchanan

Doca de Alcântara office/facilities in gated compound, north side
Henry Buchanan

APL Marinas   Facilities

Many harbours have their 'Mr Fixit', in this case a gentleman known as Carlos, *Mobile* +351 91 9868 807, has been consistently recommended as able to either handle or at least advise on almost anything. A yachtsman himself, he is well aware of what visitors may need. Carlos speaks several languages including fluent English.

Boatyard Next to the Doca de Belém and administered by APL, with all work carried out by sub-contractors who have to satisfy APL of their competence. There is a large area of secure hard-standing where owners can, if they wish, do their own work and are generally permitted to live on board while the boat is ashore (though this must be confirmed with APL on an individual basis). It would also be a possible venue for winter lay-up.

If professional services are required the best place to start is undoubtedly Técniates Yacht Services: ☏+351 213 623 362 or +351 213 649 147
Email tecniates.volvo@mail.sapo.pt They have premises near the east end of the row of office/workshops and have been highly praised by more than one visiting skipper. As well as being an agent for Volvo Penta they can also handle repairs in GRP and timber, painting, osmosis treatment etc. Where a job is outside their sphere they can generally recommend a suitable contractor.

Travel-lift The 20-tonne capacity lift at the Doca de Belém is operated by Técniates Yacht Services (see above) though owned by APL, and bookings must be made at the marina office. Due to depth restrictions it can operate only about six hours in twelve, but urgent cases are given priority. Yachts are generally placed in cradles backed up by additional props.

Engineers Técniates Yacht Services at the Doca de Belém (see above) are Volvo Penta agents/engineers and may be willing to tackle more general problems. Otherwise they will advise who best to contact. See also Tagus Yacht Center, page 203.

Electronic and radio repairs NautiRadar Lda, Central Services at: Rua António de Saldanha, 65 | 1400-020 Lisboa. Showroom: Av. Brasília, Edifício de Apoio à Náutica de Recreio, módulo 4 Doca de Belém | 1300-598 Lisboa ☏ +351 213 005 050 *Mob* +351 932 340 070
Email geral@nautiradar.pt comercial@nautiradar.pt. GPS coordinates: 38° 41'43·15N 09°12'8·23W. They sell and repair radar, autopilots, GPS, generators etc and stock both whole units and spares for all the familiar names including Raytheon, Garmin, Mastervolt etc. Open 0900–1300 and 1400–1800 weekdays, closed weekends.

Sailmaker/sail repairs Vela-Rio at Rua Dom João de Castro, 15-B Santo André, 2830-186 Barreiro, Lisboa. *Email* info@vela-rio.pt ☏ +351 212 155 994 *Mob* +351 967 150 068 (TMN) or +351 969 376 895 (Optimus), They are on the south side of the Rio Tejo east of Seixal. Vela-Rio make and repairs sails and will also handle general canvas work such as sprayhoods and awnings.

Chandleries Lisbon is well served for chandleries, with five in the Cais do Sodré/Doca de Alcântara/Parque das Nações areas alone. All are short on display space with much more stock in store, so if you don't see what you want it is well worth asking. Among them are:

J Garraio & Ca Lda: Avenida 24 de Julho 2, 1200–478 Lisboa, opposite the Cais do Sodré station. ☏ +351 213 473 081 www.jgarraio.pt at 0900–1230 and 1400–1900 weekdays, 0900–1230 Saturday. Particularly strong on pilot books and charts (Admiralty and Imray) in both Portuguese and English, but also with some general stock.

Luíz Godinho Lda: Avenida 24 de Julho n°1 F/G, 1200–478 Lisboa, in the next block to J Garraio & Ca Lda. Office ☏ +351 968 100 081 Store ☏ +351 213 017 753 www.lgl.pt *Email* lgl@lgl.pt 0900–1800 weekdays, 0900–1300 Saturday. They are a conventional yacht chandler with good stocks of rope, chain, rigging wire and terminals (plus a swage machine) and other hardware, but few electronics and no books.

Marítima: Doca de Santo Amaro, 1350–353 Lisboa at the west end of the Doca de Santo Amaro, right

ATLANTIC SPAIN AND PORTUGAL

APPROACHES TO THE RIO TEJO AND LISBON

Marina Parque das Nações looking north-northwest

under the suspension bridge ℡+351 213 979 598 *Email* raul@maritimaonline.com 1000–1930 Monday to Saturday. They have a good range of clothing and boots, as well as hardware (including windlasses), teak fittings, paint, rope and galley ware.

General hardware Rua da Boavista, which runs behind the main produce market, contains a number of small hardware shops and is a good bet for non-standard items. In particular, plugs for the Doca de Alcântara electricity supply are available there.

Charts Surprisingly, only one company on the Atlantic coast of Portugal is licensed to sell Portuguese charts and that is J Garraio & Ca Lda. It may be worth noting that, whilst Admiralty charts are not cheap, Portuguese charts are even more expensive, even when bought in Lisbon (though there is some variation based on size and publication date) and are unlikely to be corrected to date. Charts can also be purchased directly from the Instituto Hidgrográfico in Lisbon.

Liferaft servicing NautiStar (Cascais) can arrange for servicing of most makes. Alternatively contact Orey-Técnica Naval e Industrial Lda at Polígono Industrial Lezíria Park, Armazém n° 2 - E.N. 10 625-445 Forte da Casa, Lisboa ℡+351 213 610 890 www.oreytecnica.com *Email* orey-tecnica@orey.com 38°52'·35N 09°03·21W. They supply and service liferafts as well as other safety equipment including flares, lifebuoys etc.

Water On the pontoons in all the APL marinas.

Showers At all the APL marinas, though in busy periods the six provided at the Doca de Alcântara are hardly adequate for its size.

Launderette No machines at any of the APL marinas, but many in the surrounding city.

Electricity On the pontoons in all the APL marinas.

Fuel Diesel and petrol pumps at both the Doca do Bom Sucesso and the Doca de Belém (the latter is more accessible, with depths of at least 2m), operational during office hours (0900–1300 and 1400–1800 daily). In summer they may stay open later, but this should be confirmed beforehand. Credit cards including VISA are accepted.

Bottled gas Camping Gaz exchanges at Marítima (see above) and elsewhere. Butane and propane refills can be organised by NautiStar (see above) as well as by the "Mr Fixit" Carlos (see above), who can also arrange for diving bottles to be recharged.

Clube naval The Associação Naval de Lisboa has premises next to the Doca de Belém, where visiting yachtsmen are made welcome.

Weather forecast Posted daily at all the marina offices.

Banks All over Lisbon, almost invariably with at least one cash dispenser outside. Banks are normally open 0830–1200 and 1345–1430, weekdays only.

Shops/provisioning Absolutely everything available, as befits a capital city. Most convenient for provisioning if in the Doca de Santo Amaro/Alcântara complex is the large Pingo Doce supermarket reached via a pedestrian tunnel under the road and railway (ask at the marina office for directions).

Produce market Impressive, air-conditioned produce market almost opposite the Cais do Sodré station east of the Doca de Alcântara (and thus very close to the Garraio chandlery), open 0600–1400 and 1500–1900. A vast area of fruit and vegetables is surrounded by flowers, eggs, meat and fish, all meticulously clean and with much ice in evidence.

Cafés, restaurants and hotels Many and varied, at all prices. Some bars and restaurants feature live Fado singing.

Medical services If berthed in an APL marina one has access to the Administração do Porto de Lisboa's own Medical Centre, close to the Doca de Santo Amaro/Alcântara complex. More extensive medical services of all kinds are available in the city.

Communications

Post office Large post office just west of the Praça Comerçio, plus many others.

Mailing address Mail for a yacht hoping to stay in one of APL's marinas is best sent to the head office: Administração do Porto de Lisboa SA, Gare Marítima de Alcântara 1350-355 Lisboa, Portugal. www.portodelisboa.pt *Email* geral@portodelisboa.pt ℡ +351 213 611 000. It is important that the envelope carries the name of the yacht in addition to that of the addressee.

Internet Many possibilities throughout the city. The Tourist Office on Praça dos Restauradores can supply a current list. The online Lisbon Guide at www.lisbon-guide.info carries a listing in its Essential Information section.

Car hire Many companies in the city, though APL receive a discount from AVIS which they pass on to the hirer. But be warned the city driving can be manic. At the very least, pay the extra charge for collision damage waiver.

Taxis No shortage. Taxis can generally be ordered via the marina office.

Buses/trams The city's well-organised bus and tram service is particularly useful near the waterfront, linking all four APL marinas with the city centre. Tickets covering travel by bus, tram, elevador and metro (see below) can be bought individually, by the day, or for longer periods, the latter often representing a considerable saving.

LISBON

Marina Parque de Nações. From L to R: Fuel pontoon; travel-lift; marina building; waiting pontoon; exit lock (entry off R) *Henry Buchanan*

Marina Parque de Nações. Inside the basin looking east
Henry Buchanan

Trains and Metro Regular and frequent rail service from the Cais do Sodré station to Cascais and other points west. Most other trains depart from Rossio station at the south end of the Avenida da Liberdade.

Lisbon's metro was given a facelift for the 1998 Expo, making it the quickest way to reach city destinations away from the waterfront. However finding a city centre station can be a real challenge. They tend to be very poorly signed.

Ferries Frequent ferries across the Rio Tejo to Cacilhas, from which one can get a bus up to the prominent statue of Christ near the south end of the 25 de Abril suspension bridge, as well as to Seixal and Montijo.

Air services Lisbon International airport is in the northeast part of the city served by the Red metro line running from San Sebastião station to the Airport.

Estuario do Tejo

Marina Parque das Nações (ex MarinaExpo)
38°45'·22N 09°05'·33W
VHF Ch9 ✆+351 218 949 066
www.marinaparquedasnacoes.pt
Email info@marinaparquedasnacoes.pt
Office reception hours are 0900 -1930 in summer, 0900-1900 in winter.

See Rio Tejo plan, page 197.

The Marina is located in the heart of the Estuário do Tejo, one of the most interesting areas of the Rio Tejo. It was built for Expo '98 (1998 Lisbon World Exposition). The theme of the fair was 'The Oceans, a Heritage for the Future', chosen in part to commemorate 500 years of Portuguese discoveries. The shoreside infrastructure is impressive as befits an Expo Site with wide shaded boulevards, entertainment, restaurants and cafés. The world renowned Oceanarium, a huge aquarium (see photo, page 195), is nearby providing an experience that is not to be missed. To a large extent the Parque das Nações is self-contained with impressive modern architecture, and although it is over seven miles from the centre of the city buses and trains provide frequent access to the historic old city of Lisbon.

Visiting yachtsmen have reported that the welcome here is outstanding, with a full information pack not only being provided but explained too. Discounts are offered to members of most of the better known cruising and sailing associations. If planning to stay for more than two weeks it is as cheap to stay for a month.

Silting, however, has been a major challenge since the marina was built and the Parque Expo Group has made a massive effort since 1998 to keep the marina fully operational. Redesigned with a lock entrance system that was commissioned in 2009 it, sadly, continued to suffer from silting (but reduced). In the summer of 2018 the silting that occurs in the middle of the marina had restricted the number of useable berths available from 400 to 250. The next full dredge to 2·5m will take place in April 2019 (taking 3 weeks), and from then on an annual dredge should keep the marina operational.

Entrance and berthing

The approach and entrance are straightforward, but require care as the streams in the Rio Tejo and within the marina entrance run hard. It is advisable to arrive two hours either side of high water and preferably near or at slack water, and to consult the marina in advance (VHF Ch 09). The locks (sluices) are open during the day from 0830 (early morning opening on demand) to approximately 1 hour after LW when they are closed for the night. This is nominally 2100 but detailed times are promulgated in the marina office. The entrance sluice gates are controlled by traffic lights, and are 9·5m wide. Catamarans are advised to wait for slack water at the waiting pontoon in the outer entrance pool near the office building (see photograph). Approaching from downstream turn boldly to port onto about

APPROACHES TO THE RIO TEJO AND LISBON

The 17km Ponte Vasco de Gama. The bridge at De Xira some 7km further north is the effective head of navigation for most yachts.

250° immediately after passing CR5 starboard hand buoy and pass between the lit breakwater heads into the entrance pool outside the southern basin. Keep well to port and, as soon as the entrance channel (the river side, right hand of the two) begins to open to view, turn hard to starboard and straighten up for the entrance.

Go through the locks (sluices) maintaining a fair speed. This is an occasion when a slow approach is less safe, as it is easy for a boat's bow to be in the still water of the entrance whilst the stern is still in the stream outside. Once through the entrance channel there is space to stop and manoeuvre into the allocated berth.

The marina will provide a RIB to guide a yachtsman through into the marina.

If arriving unannounced, or after dark when the locks will probably be shut, berth at the waiting pontoon.

There is a total of 400 berths with some for boats of up to 25m in length. The dredged depth in the basin is 2·5m, but 2m dredged depth should be the taken as a working assumption. The depth of the sill at the sluices is 2·4m.

This is described as a good place to leave a yacht to overwinter, being very close to the airport, very secure and, of course, totally enclosed by the locks.

Facilities

Boatyard A fully equipped boatyard with hardstanding managed by the operator: Estaleiro Naval de Lisboa ☎ +351 914 592 231
Email estaleironavallisboa@gmail.com. Their office is in the marina building.

Travel-lift 32-tonne travel-lift managed by the Boatyard operator: Estaleiro Naval de Lisboa ☎+351 914 592 231
Email estaleironavallisboa@gmail.com. 3-tonne crane via reception.

Fuel Fuel pontoon on the south side of the outer marina entrance. Open 0900 to 1800. Credit cards accepted.

Waste disposal Pump out facility on the fuel pontoon.

Security 24h/day with access by electronic card (deposit 20 Euros)

Weather Posted every day at reception.
Electricity and water At the pontoons.
Gas The marina can organise gas bottle refills.
Chandlery A small selection in the marina office but a huge hardware store called AKI which is 1·5km away.
Launderette There are washing and drying machines available.
Shops There is a large supermarket nearby which will deliver directly to the boat.
Banks To be found along the Alameda dos Oceanos and D.Joao II Avenue.
Shops/provisioning A Large supermarket at Vasco da Gama Shopping Centre which delivers to the boat. Pingo Doce supermarket at Av. Fernando Pessoa (0830-2130). Small grocery stores in the Rua das Musas. Market every Saturday (0900-1400) on the north side of the Parque das Nações near the Vasco da Gama Tower. A small convenience store at the Repsol service station (24hr).
Cafés/restaurants There are several cafés, bars and restaurants.

Communications

Mailing address Marina Parque das Nações, Edificio da Capitania, Passeio de Neptuno, 1990-193 LISBOA, Portugal. It is important that the envelope carries the name of the yacht in addition to that of the addresee.
Internet WiFi available in the marina.
Buses Frequent buses into central Lisbon and the best way to get there as the railway/metro involves several changes. Bus 781 from the Gás Portugal stop near the Marina to the Lisbon train/metro station Cais Sodré (trains out to Cascaisfrom here).
Metro/rail/airport The Gare do Oriente is a magnificent building and communications hub. The Red Line Metro is only 3 stops from Lisbon International Airport (5km by road).

LISBON

Looking into the Algés boatyard from the VTS Tower *Algés Boatyard*

VTS tower, Algés *Gavin McLaren*

Stand-alone boatyards in Lisbon, Seixal

Centro Náutico de Algés
Torre VTS 1495-165 Algés – Lisboa. www.cnalges.com
Email geral@cnalges.pt

The site is immediately upstream of the prominent VTS Tower (Maritime Traffic Control Centre Tower) and is shown in the photograph above.
The Sopramar boatyard, well known from Lagos on the Algarve now runs this rapidly developing boatyard at Algés, Lisbon. The Chairman of the Board of Directors for Soprama, Hugo Henriques, can be contacted on *Mob* +351 963 488 510 +351 213 032 440 *Email* hugo@sopromar.com.

The manager of the Algés boatyard is Joaquim Mendes de Brito who can be contacted on ☏+351 213 032 440 *Email* jmendesbrito@cnalges.pt.

There are plans and funding in place for a 1600m² new facilities building that is due to start at the end of 2018 and complete in June 2019.
Travel-lift 50 tonnes.
Services The boatyard can provide the following services: Storage, chandlery, engineering, painting, polishing, osmosis treatment, electronics, power electrical equipment, GRP and gelcoat work, carpentry, steel fabrication, rigging, bow-stern thruster work, watermaker servicing. Sail repair and servicing can be subcontracted.

Boat owners are allowed to do their own work and live onboard.
Showers and WC These are provided on site and will be upgraded in the new building.
Restaurant/café Are to be included in the new building also. There are good restaurants in Algés.
Shops/provisioning Algés, nearby, is good for provisioning stores and shops.
Transport The yard is about a kilometre from the nearest train station Algés on the Cais do Sodré to Cascais coastal line which is the fastest way into Lisbon.

Tagus Yacht Centre Seixal (south of the river)
Details of the well-equipped Tagus Yacht Center near Seixal on the south bank of the Rio Tejo above the Ponte 25 de Avril can be found on page 205 in the section on Seixal. It boasts a 70-tonne capacity hoist with about 7m width, operable at all states of the tide.

Alternative anchorages and moorings

There are two areas where anchoring can be made:
1. The first of these is beyond the impressive Vasco da Gama motorway bridge to the north where the main channel carries 5m. This widens into the Mar de Palha (literally 'Sea of Straw', or reeds). Large-scale Portuguese charts or electronic charts will be required for this area. Alandra is the effective limit for yachts working up the Rio Tejo as the bridge above (De Xira on plan) has only 10m clearance.
2. The second area for anchoring is to the southeast of Lisbon in the Canal do Montijo, and to a very limited extent at Seixal in the Canal do Judeu. Space in the latter has been taken for visitor moorings and a short stay pontoon, but find the details in pages 205-207. There are high speed ferry links between Seixal and Lisbon.

APPROACHES TO THE RIO TEJO AND LISBON

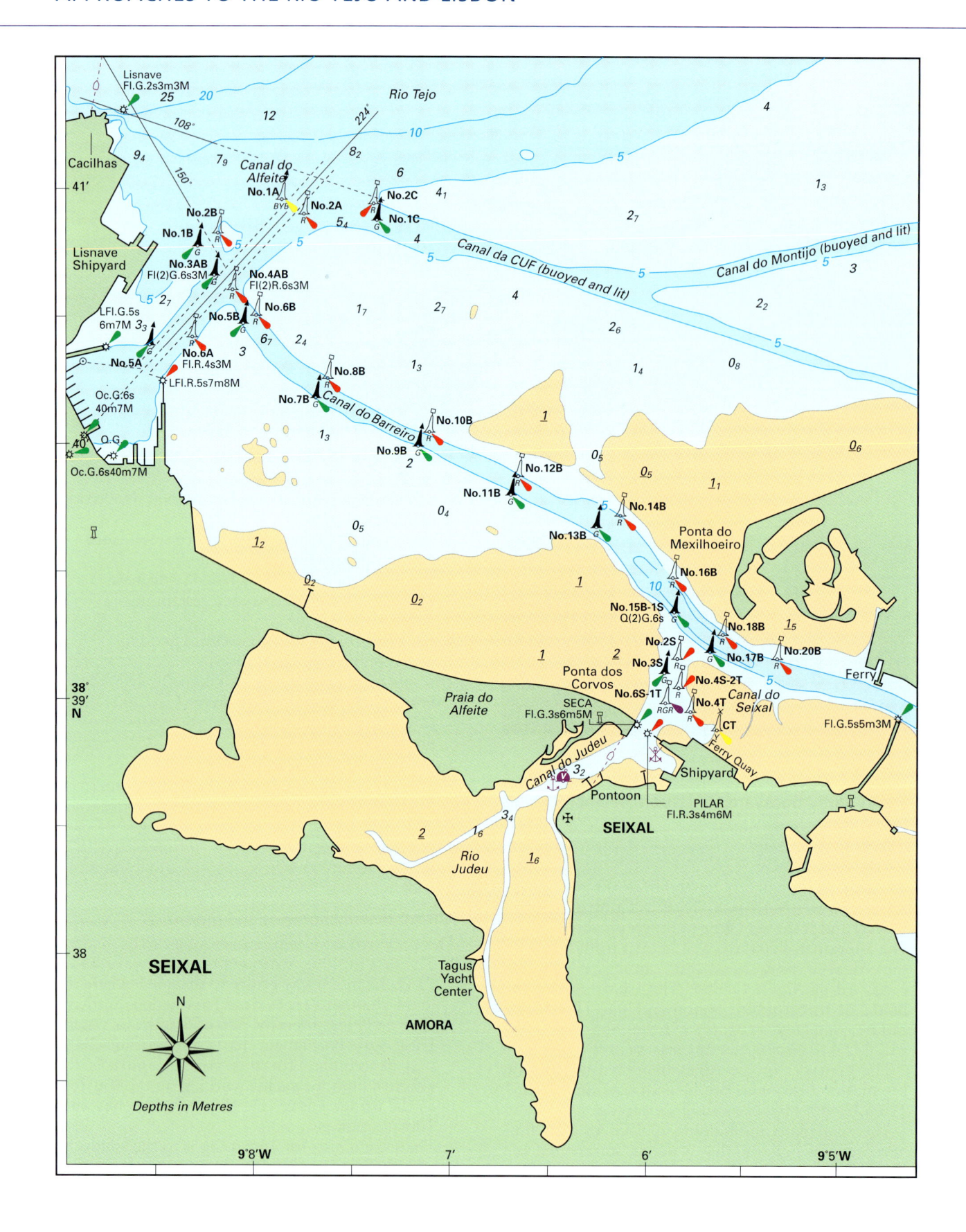

SEIXAL (LISBON)

Seixal

Location
38°38'·9N 09°06'W (entrance)

Principal lights
Lisnave, Dolphin, Fl.G.2s3m3M Column with red and white bands
Buoy No 3AB Fl(2)G.6s3M Reflector Radar
Buoy No 4AB Fl(2)R.6s3M Reflector Radar
Buoy No 15B-1S Q(2)G.6s3M Reflector Radar
Seca (Seixal), north bank Fl.G.3s6m5M Green column 5m
Pilar (Seixal), south pillar Fl.R.3s4m6M
Red and white pillar on concrete plinth 2m

Communications
Tagus Yacht Center ☎ +351 212 221 112 or +351 212 276 400. *Mobile* +351 932 199 450 or +351 968 451 327 or +351 913 837 721 www.tagusyachtcenter.com
Email info@tagusyachtcenter.com
(note the spelling of 'center')

Limited but quiet anchorage and mooring with impressive, full-service boatyard

There are two main reasons for visiting Seixal, which has the facilities expected of a small suburban town. One is to enjoy tranquil mooring, within easy reach of Lisbon by ferry. The other is to visit the Tagus Yacht Center, an enterprise which looks set to meet the maintenance needs of all but the very largest cruising yachts.

Approach (Canal do Barreiro)

Round Ponta de Cacilhas and the Lisnave Light, on the south bank of the Rio Tejo 1·5M east of the suspension bridge, and head 150° past the prominent Lisnave shipyard to cross the Canal do Alfeite near buoys No.3AB and No.4AB. Continue down the Canal do Barreiro, which is well buoyed but has quite heavy ferry traffic, some of it at high speeds. Buoy No.15B-1S marks the junction of the Canal do Barreiro with the Canal do Seixal which leads to the relatively narrow entrance to the Canal do Judeu.

Pass between buoys No.2S (R) and No.3S (G), then between the Pilar (Seixal) (red and white column on an old bridge support) leaving it firmly to port, and the Seca (Seixal) green post on the battlement, and pass through the narrow entrance at 38°38'·90N 9°06'·00W.

At least 2·5m should be found throughout the approach and entrance. Streams run hard, particularly at the entrance to the harbour. Beware of the high speed ferries which berth close southeast outside the entrance.

Berthing and mooring

Once inside there are many moorings. There are about eight for visitors on the northwest side of the channel in the vicinity of 38°38'·6N 9°06'·6W. Boats sheer around on these and the plastic buoys bump the bow.

There is a pontoon where a dinghy can be left (approx. 38°38'·7N 9°06'·3W). It might be possible to lie alongside there for a short while. Both water and electricity are connected. Mooring fees are payable at the harbour/tourist office. VHF Ch 09 ☎ +351 919 306 580.

A dinghy can still be secured on the old town quay ramp outside the pontoon security gates for no charge, but avoid landing a dinghy on their pontoon unless you want to use their facilities and pay. Do not impede the small ferry to Praia do Alfeite.

Anchorage

It is possible for a small boat to find space to anchor southwest of the visitor's moorings and a larger yacht might do so at neaps, particularly with two anchors laid out. It should be noted that no

The short stay pontoon at Seixal *Jane Russell*

APPROACHES TO THE RIO TEJO AND LISBON

Entrance to the Canal do Judeu at Seixal looking southwest. The isolated block in the centre, an old bridge support, must be left to port on entry

anchoring is allowed anywhere in the apparently suitable area just inside the entrance to the lagoon. Large barges are towed in and turned to go to the shipyard at the southeast of that first basin. The advised anchorage is where marked, just beyond the trot of moorings on the north side of the channel, but the anchoring space is much reduced as a result of the buoys being laid.

The area is surprisingly peaceful despite its proximity to the city and there is relatively little traffic (the ferry berth is outside the entrance). There is currently no charge for anchoring.

Shore facilities

Seixal has an attractive waterfront with a small sandy beach. All the usual shops will be found, as well as cafés, restaurants, a post office and public telephones. There is a Tide Mill museum at the west end of the lagoon and a maritime museum on the east bank, south of the town. The beautiful local sailing barges are linked to the maritime museum.

A high speedferry connects the town with Lisbon's Cais Terreiro do Paço, running every 25 minutes between 0610 and 2330 and taking about 15 minutes for the trip.

The short stay pontoon at Seixal with the Canal do Judeu beyond and Lisbon in the far distance *Jane Russell*

Boatyard: Tagus Yacht Centre

The Tagus Yacht Centre (TYC) 38°38'·1N 9°06'·8W
An excellent place to haul out ☎ +351 212 221 112 or +351 212 276 400 *Mobile* +351 932 199 450 or +351 968 451 327 or +351 913 837 721
Email info@tagusyachtcenter.com (note the spelling of 'center') www.tagusyachtcenter.com.

It is a friendly, family run, traditional yard and has all the necessary skills to carry out any work, including Awlgrip painting and major engine, rig or other repairs.

Staff are friendly and prices reasonable. Office hours are normally 0800–1200 and 1300–1700 weekdays only.

The 'floating dock' is no longer functional but the travel lift will manage 35 tonnes which can operate at all states of the tide. The yard is reached via a buoyed channel, marked 'Welcome to TYC', which is approximately 40m wide and dredged to 7m. The approach to the travel lift involves a tight last minute turn and it would be wise to explore by dinghy first. There is a small waiting pontoon close to the travel lift which will take a 13m boat, and there is water and shore power on it.

206   ATLANTIC SPAIN AND PORTUGAL

SEIXAL (LISBON)

Traditional vessel off Seixal *Jane Russell*

Almost any yacht-related task can be tackled, from straightforward painting to creating unobtainable parts from scratch (for which the shipyard's extensive machine-shop is utilised). Repairs can be carried out in GRP, wood and all types of metal, a large team of engineers have experience of virtually all makes of engine, and electricians and electronics experts can be called in from the shipyard as required.

Ashore there are the usual facilities. Rather primitive, but quite adequate, toilets and showers and a washing machine. There are no leisure facilities e.g. bar or restaurant in the yard. Within easy walking distance is a substantial supermarket and a village with the usual small shops, bars and cafés.

TYC would be good place to lay up a yacht for the winter and many cruisers do. Although the yard expects to handle major work, owners are welcome to carry out other tasks while their boat is ashore and can live aboard if they wish. If coming by land, the 113 bus from the Seixal ferry terminal passes close to the yard.

Other service facilities

Navegador, further upstream from the Tagus Yacht Center is reported to have good hardstanding and painting facilities.
Email felisberto.carlos@navegador.com.pt
☎ +351 212 277 913.
They do not, however, allow living onboard or DIY.
Sailmaker/sail repairs Vela-Rio at Rua Dom João de Castro, 15-B Santo André, 2830-186 Barreiro, Lisboa. *Email* info@vela-rio.pt ☎+351 212 155 994 *Mob* +351 967 150 068 (TMN) or +351 969 376 895 (Optimus), They are on the south side of the Rio Tejo east of Seixal. Vela-Rio make and repairs sails and will also handle general canvas work such as sprayhoods and awnings.

Canal do Montijo anchorages

From the Lisnave Lt (see plan page 204) head 108° into the buoyed Canal da CUF (Companhia União Fabril). The Canal do Montijo (also buoyed) leads off at 073° just over 1M from the entrance of the Canal da CUF. At high water it appears to be a large bay, but at low water mud and sandbanks define the channel accurately. The airfield on the low headland to the north is military, and landing is prohibited.

Montijo itself is not particularly attractive and has little room, but there are pleasant anchorages to be found by soundings along the channel or its southern offshoots. A current copy of either Admiralty 3222 or Portuguese 26305 is essential. There are no facilities.

Approaching Seixal looking SW down the Canal do Judeu with the town to port and moorings to starboard *Jane Russell*

CABO ESPICHEL TO CABO DE SÃO VICENTE

Cabo Espichel to Cabo de São Vicente

PRINCIPAL LIGHTS
Cabo Espichel Fl.4s167m26M
  Horn 31s 460m SW
  White hexagonal tower and building 32m
Forte do Cavalo Oc.5s32m14M
  Red tower 7m
Pinheiro da Cruz Fl.3s66m9M
  White column, red bands
Cabo de Sines Fl(2).15s55m26M
  001°-obscd-003° and 004°-obscd-007°
  White tower and building 28m
Milfontes (Rio Mira) Fl.3s22m10M
  White lantern on hut 5m
Cabo Sardão Fl(3)15s67m23M
  Square white tower and red-roofed
  building 17m
Cabo de São Vicente Fl.5s85m32M Aero
  Off-white tower, red top, and building 28m
Pta de Sagres Iso.R.4s52m11M
  Tower on a building mounted with a lantern
  and red cupola

One of the few remaining double-ended trading vessels which used to ply the Sado estuary under sail. Most now take tourists on river trips *Anne Hammick*

Approaching Sesimbra from Cabo Espichel *Jane Russell*

Arrifana bay from offshore *Henry Buchanan*

208 ATLANTIC SPAIN AND PORTUGAL

SESIMBRA

Sesimbra

Location
38°26'·3N 9°06'·2W (entrance)

Tides
Standard port Lisbon
Mean time differences
HW –0035 ±0010; LW –0015 ±0005

Heights in metres
MHWS	MHWN	MLWN	MLWS
3·4	2·6	1·4	0·6

Principal lights
Forte do Cavalo Oc.5s32m14M Red tower 7m
Ldg Lts 003° *Front* LFl.R.5s8m7M
  Red lantern on SW turret of fortress 10m
  Rear 34m from front LFl.R.5s16m6M
  Red lantern on NW turret of fortress 17m
Note These lights do NOT lead into the harbour but to a point on the shore about 0·5M to the east. Two sets of three lights in line (Fl.R and Fl.W), and one set of two lights in line (Fl.W) close east of Sesimbra mark a submarine cable area and again are NOT leading lights.
Breakwater head Fl.R.3s13m8M
  White tower, red bands 7m

Warning
Night entry straightforward in most conditions, though it would be wise to anchor until daylight rather than to attempt berthing alongside.

Communications
Marina de Sesimbra (run by the Clube Naval de Sesimbra) VHF Ch9, 12, 16 (0900-1200, 1400-1900)
① +351 212 233 451, +351 212 281 039
Email secnaval.sesimbra@mail.telepac.pt
www.naval-sesimbra.pt (in Portuguese only)

Busy fishing harbour sheltering a small, club-run marina

The town of Sesimbra lies 2km from its harbour, which despite the growing numbers of visitors is still dominated by the fishing industry. On the hill behind the town, on the site of a Moorish fortress captured in 1165, is the restored medieval castle built in the 13th century. Its five towers and walls protect the 12th-century church of Santa Maria. There are wonderful views from here. The town has always been popular with Portuguese royalty; the diminutive 17th-century fortress of Sao Teodosio was built by Joao IV to protect the port from pirates.

The harbour is very much a working port, with brightly painted fishing boats clustered alongside a newly expanded unloading wharf. It is well protected by a 900m breakwater and, despite having limited space for visiting yachts, makes an interesting port of call for those not overly concerned about a lack of marina comforts.

Sesimbra harbour from the south

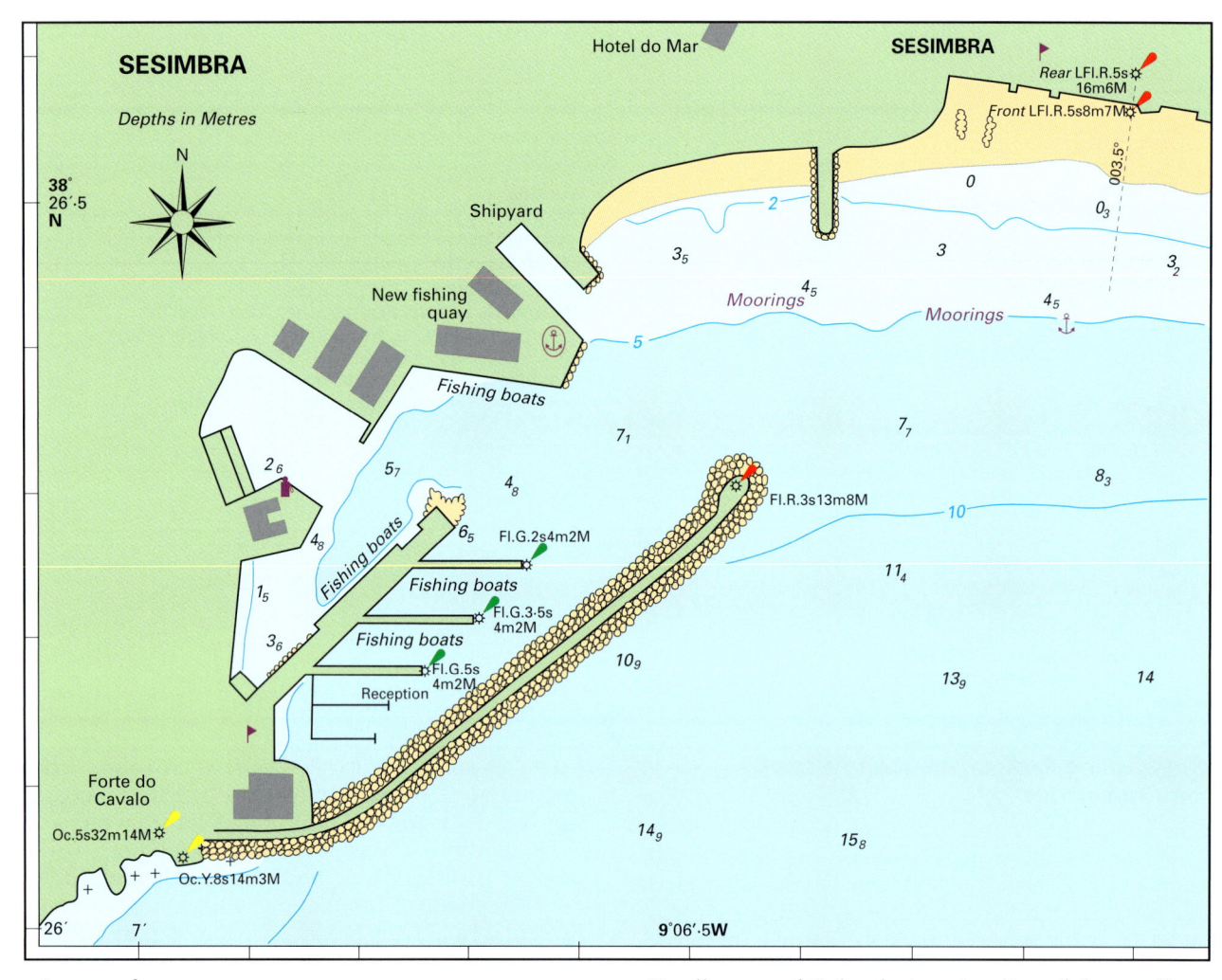

CABO ESPICHEL TO CABO DE SÃO VICENTE

Approach
The major mark from north or south is Cabo Espichel. The bluff trending east from Cabo Espichel rises from 160m near the cape to 500m towards Setúbal. Forte do Cavalo, 6·5M east of Cabo Espichel, marks the landward end of the outer harbour mole. If coastal sailing, the coast between the two should be given an offing of at least 0·5M. After rounding Cabo Espichel there is still some southing to be made to get round Ponta da Pombeira.

Note that the 'Leading Lights' at Sesimbra do NOT lead into the harbour but to a point on the shore about 0·5M to the east! Other Lights that can confuse a navigator are as follows:

Running up the hillside immediately east of Sesimbra are two sets of three lights in line: both sets flash 2·5s front, 3s centre, 3·5s rear, with a range of 2M; the western set on 030° flashes red and the eastern, on 003°, white. A third set of two white lights flashing 2·5s front and 3·5s rear, on 058°, are between the other two sets of three lights. They mark submarine cables and anchoring within their limits is prohibited. In addition, three outfalls lie within a 0·5M radius of the breakwater head to its southwest and southeast. Each is marked by a yellow post, × topmark on land, plus a nearby yellow spherical buoy, also × topmark. The pairs are lit, Fl.Y.8s3M, Fl.Y.6s3M and Fl.Y.4s3M respectively.

Finally, east of Cabo de Ares is a line of three yellow buoys with × topmarks (all Q(5)Y.10s2M). It would appear that they define the seaward extent of coastal water within which navigation is prohibited.

Entrance
The entrance is straightforward, though it would be unwise to cut the outer molehead too closely in case of fishing vessels exiting at speed.

Berthing
The small (130 berth) marina run by the Clube Naval de Sesimbra is full to capacity with local boats. If local yachts are away and berths are empty, perhaps room could be found but it would obviously be wise to make contact before arrival.

A clubhouse has been built at the extreme southwest end of the harbour, overlooking the marina.

Anchorage
Sesimbra is an extremely busy fishing port and there is nowhere inside the harbour that a visiting yacht can conveniently anchor. Local yachts and smallcraft lie on moorings off the beach between the shipyard and the short east mole, and the only possible anchorage is to the east of them in 5–6m, exposed to the south and southeast. Holding is variable over kelp and rock with sand patches – the excellent

sandy beach fronting the harbour and town is at least partially man-made.

Sesimbra has a deserved reputation for strong local northerlies which get up in the late afternoon and die in the small hours – lay ground tackle accordingly.

Formalities

The *Polícia Marítima* have premises on the new fishing wharf and there is a *GNR–Brigada Fiscal* office in the town. In theory it is the skipper's duty to seek them out immediately on arrival, but in view of the walk involved it would be worth checking at the *Clube Naval* whether this is still considered necessary. Alternatively one or both may come to the yacht.

Facilities

Boatyard Fast Boats Repair Lda ☎ +351 212 686 540 or +351 917 519 360 Email fastboats@iol.pt www.fboatrepair.com in the Zona Técnica da Marina, Doca de Sesimbra, 2970 Sesimbra, advertise their services for all kinds of maintenance and repair to wood and GRP, including painting and antifouling.
Travel-lift Not as such, though there are several cranes in the fishing quay.
Engineers, mechanics, electronic and radio repairs Available, though more used to working on fishing vessels. Enquire at the *Clube Naval*.
Water On the pontoons, and from a tap near the fuel pumps.
Showers At the *clube naval*.
Electricity On the pontoons.
Fuel Diesel and petrol are available from pumps on the old fishing quay (see plan) via long hoses. However depths alongside have not been verified and it would be wise to check by dinghy first – in any case, the wall is high and a visit at high water would make good sense.
Bottled gas Camping Gaz exchanges at several hardware stores in the town (a longish walk), but no refills.
Weather forecast Displayed daily outside the *Clube Naval*.
Banks In the town.

Shops/provisioning/produce market In the town.
Cafés, restaurants and hotels No shortage. Many of the former specialise in seafood, including an outdoor café opposite the new fishing quay.
Medical services In Sesimbra.

Communications

Post office In the town.
Telephones There does not appear to be a kiosk in the harbour area though there are plenty in the town.
Internet access Several cybercafés in Sesimbra.
Car hire/taxis In the town.
Buses Bus station near the market (about an hour to Lisbon), with minibuses running a frequent service into town from a stop at the root of the fishing mole.

Adjacent anchorages

1. An unnamed bay 1·5M east of Cabo de Ares (3·5M east of Sesimbra), which has an offlying rock requiring at least 0·5M clearance, over sand off a pleasant beach. The bottom shoals steadily towards the shore at the west end of the beach. It was reported in 2007, however, that the cliffs had collapsed onto the beach so this spot may no longer be such an attractive place to anchor.
2. Portinho de Arrábida 38°28'·6N 8°58'·7W (see plan on page 213), a wooded bay backed by high cliffs some 6M east of Sesimbra. While very scenic, and with good holding, in the evenings it is prone to very heavy downdrafts of wind from the mountains. There is sometimes 25–30kn of wind in the anchorage, whereas 3 miles offshore, there could be only 5–10kn! Some would say the anchorage is for lunchtime stops only. However, although being fully open to the south, a surprising number of small craft lie on summer moorings in the western part of the bay.

The approach from the west is complicated by a drying sandbank, the Baixo de Alpertuche, off Forte Arrábida. Keep 0·4M offshore until lightbeacon No.2 bears 090°, before altering to 033° to clear Forte Arrábida by 150–200m. This should give a least depth of 2·2m at low water springs but be careful as the bank may grow and/or move. Admiralty chart 3259 will be found useful and the water is crystal clear. Anchorage can be found in 5·5m just to seaward of the moorings, over weed and hard sand. There are rocks and a small offlying island, Anixa, at the east end of the bay.

There are no facilities other than a telephone kiosk behind the beach, half a dozen waterfront restaurants, and an oceanographic museum in Forte Arrábida on the western headland. Much of the surrounding area, including Anixa island, is a nature reserve.

Portinho de Arrábida seen from the southeast, with Ilha Anixa on the right and the Baixo do Alpertuche clearly visible in the foreground

CABO ESPICHEL TO CABO DE SÃO VICENTE

Setúbal, Tróia and the Rio Sado

Location
38°29'·22N 8°55'·9W (entrance)

Tides
Standard port Lisbon
Mean time differences
HW −0015 ±0005; LW 0000 ±0005
Heights in metres
MHWS	MHWN	MLWN	MLWS
3·4	2·7	1·3	0·5

Principal entrance lights
 Ldg Lts 040° *Front* **Fishing harbour E jetty** Iso.Y.6s13m22M
  Red and white striped metal structure 11m
Rear **Azêda** 1·7M from front Iso.Y.6s60m22M
  038·3°-vis-041·3° White tower, red bands 31m
Difficult to distinguish against the lights of the city
Lightbeacon No.2 Fl(2)R.10s13m9M
  Racon Mo 'B'(− · · ·)15M Red post, white lantern
Lightbeacon No.4 Fl.R.4s13m4M
  Red and white chequered column 5m
Forte de Outão Oc.R.6s33m12M
  Red hexagonal tower and lantern 9m
Lightbeacon No.5 Fl.G.4s13m4M
  Black post and platform 5m
Forte de Albarquel Iso.R.2s17m6M
  Red lantern on S corner of fort
Anunciada Iso.R.4s23m15M Red lantern
Algarve Exportador Oc.R.4s14m15M Red lantern

Warning
While entrance to the estuary should present no problems in light conditions and good visibility (when the leading lights will come into their own), it would be wise to await daylight before entering the marina

Communications
Administração dos Portos de Sesimbra e Setúbal
VHF Ch 11, 16 ☏ +351 265 542000
Email geral@portodeSetubal.pt
www.portodesetubal.pt (mainly concerned with commercial activity, and almost entirely in Portuguese)
Doca de Recreio das Fontainhas VHF Ch 16 but prior contact by telephone to check whether a berth is available is advised.
☏ +351 265 542 076,
Email docadasfontainhas@portodesetubal.pt
www.portodesetubal.pt (in Portuguese and some English).
Tróia Marina communications VHF Ch 9
☏ +351 265 499 333
Email (General) marina@troiaresort.pt
Email (Booking) marinabooking@troiaresort.pt
www.troiaresort.net (in Portuguese and English, click on Marina)

The Península de Tróia and entrance to the Rio Sado seen from the south-southwest over some of the extensive offlying sandbanks. The Setúbal waterfront is clearly visible beyond. The new Tróia marina is behind the high-rise building near the end of the peninsula

SETÚBAL

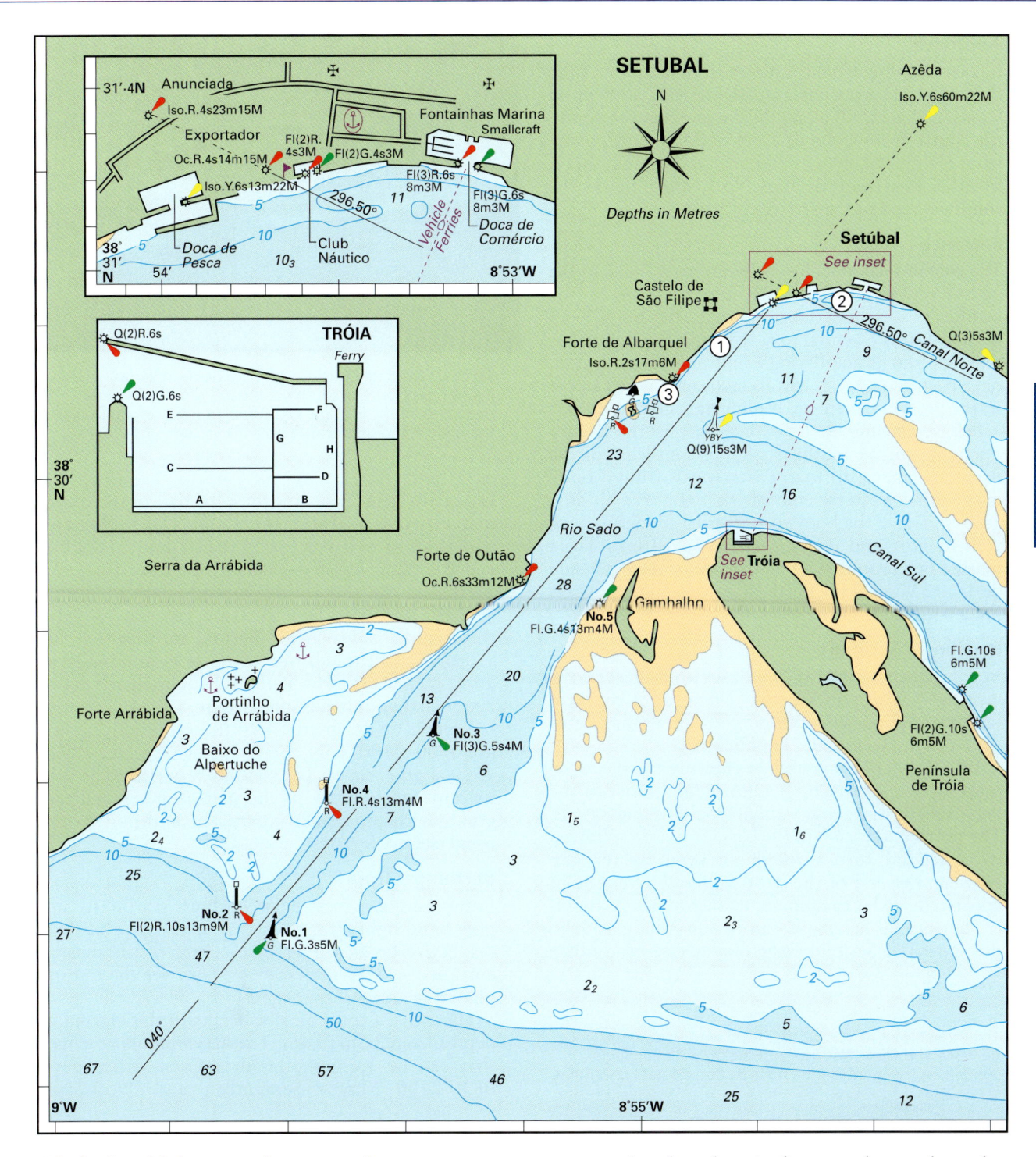

Rio Sado with improved space at the new marina at Tróia

Setúbal marina lies 3M from the entrance to the Rio Sado, and Tróia marina is just 1·5M in, on the end of the Tróia peninsula. The commercial port of Setúbal is the country's third largest and cannot claim to be attractive, though areas of the city have some charm. The beautifully sited pousada to the west of Setúbal lies within the walls of the Castelo de São Filipe built by Philip II of Spain to cow the local inhabitants and repel English pirates.

The entrance channel into the Rio Sado is narrow but well marked, although yachts are advised not to attempt it other than in fine weather and on the flood. The spring ebb can run at more than 3kn and with onshore winds of any strength should not be contemplated.

Of all the basins in Setúbal only the Doca de Comércio (commercial dock) containing the Doca de Recreio das Fontaínhas may have room for a visiting yacht. The Tróia marina on the peninsula is a better bet. It is possible to anchor throughout much of the estuary, and although large areas dry there is a navigable channel as far as Alcacer do Sal, 24M upstream, or at least to the railway bridge below it.

ATLANTIC SPAIN AND PORTUGAL 213

CABO ESPICHEL TO CABO DE SÃO VICENTE

Approach
If coastal sailing from the direction of Sesimbra, note that Cabo de Ares has an offlying rock so keep at least 0·5M clear all along the coast. From the south, the course from Cabo de Sines of 353° stands away from the unbroken low sand hills of the Tróia shore. In either case head for buoy No.2, which marks the southwest end of the approach channel.

Entrance
The entrance channel lies between buoy No.2 to the northwest and buoy No.1 about 600m to the southeast, widening out somewhat after buoy No.3 is passed. It is essential to stay within the channel as there are shoals and drying banks on either side and, once past buoy No.3, best to favour the north side if traffic permits. There are leading lights on 040°.

Before reaching the Forte de Albarquel the estuary opens up to the southeast. 800m southeast of the fort the Cabeça do João Farto west cardinal buoy marks the western end of an extensive middle ground. Leave the buoy to starboard for Setúbal, or well to port and turning to starboard into Tróia marina or to run down the east side of the Península de Tróia. Most of the north shore west of the town is lined with moorings.

Berthing – Setúbal
In Setúbal there is only one basin of interest to the visiting yachtsman at the Doca de Comércio (commercial dock) containing the small marina of the Doca de Recreio das Fontaínhas.

Take particular care when entering the basin, as meeting any of the car ferries plying between the Península de Tróia and Setúbal would be unpleasant. The port-hand turn into the basin is swiftly followed by a second turn through an even tighter gap between the end of the west wall and a very solid concrete ferry berth dolphin, neither of which are lit.

The Setúbal marina is run by the Administração dos Portos de Sesimbra e Setúbal whose head office

Setúbal's Doca de Comércio or Doca de Recreio das Fontaínhas from the south-southeast, with the marina pontoons on the left, the Península de Tróia ferry terminal in the middle and smallcraft moorings on the right

is nearby. It occupies the western half of the basin, and provides berthing for about 150 yachts and smallcraft as well as a few of the traditional double-ended trading vessels typical of the Sado estuary. All berths on the three long pontoons are alongside fingers and depths are said to be 3–3·5m throughout. Only three berths are reserved for visitors, and though one of these is nominally of 15m, if space is tight a smaller yacht clearly has a better chance of being squeezed in.

There is no designated arrivals berth. Office hours are 0900–2100 daily from May to October, 0900–1900 at other times. The staff are reported to be very helpful and security in the marina is particularly good, with uniformed guards in addition to the usual electronic gate.

Berthing – Tróia
Enter from the west between both starboard and port hand lights (range 3M) near the ends of their respective breakwaters. The centre of the marina entrance is 38°29'·652N 008°54'·173W. See the outline plan of the marina on page 213.

There are a total of 184 berths in the marina in depths from 2·5m to 4m. The maximum boat length that can be accommodated is 18m. Office open 0830-2100 May - September, and 0900-1800 October - April.

Formalities – Setúbal and Tróia
The *GNR–Brigada Fiscal* have a desk in the marinas' office buildings, with the *Alfândega* and *Polícia Marítima* nearby. Copies of the marina paperwork are circulated to all three, and it is no longer necessary for most skippers to visit them in person. The marina manager will advise if this is required – most probably due to non-EU yacht registration or crew.

The three basins at Setúbal are, from west to east, the Doca de Pesca, the Clube Nautico, and the Doca de Comércio containing the small marina Doca de Recreio das Fontainhas

SETÚBAL

Facilities – Setúbal

Boatyard The somewhat ramshackle boatyard at the west end of the town waterfront may be able to work on a yacht, but its marine railways would be unsuitable for hauling a deep-keeled yacht.

Travel-lift No travel-lift, though a mobile crane capable of lifting up to 40 tonnes is situated at the Doca de Recreio das Fontaínhas. There are no boatyard facilities on site and it should only be regarded as an emergency measure. The Clube Náutico de Setúbal (see below) has a 5-tonne crane.

Chandlery A branch of Contrafogo is at Rua da Saúde, 80, 2900-572 Setúbal. ☎ +351 265 534 014 www.contrafogo.pt
Email contrafogo.setebul@contrafogo.pt. Anything not in stock can be ordered from Lisbon.

Water On the marina pontoons.

Showers Shower block near the marina office, with card access (for which a deposit is required).

Launderette In the city.

Electricity On the marina pontoons.

Fuel Diesel and petrol pumps will be found on a pontoon in the eastern end of the basin beyond the ferry berths, open 0900–1200 and 1400–1800 in season. Payment must be made in cash. Small amounts of fuel can be bought from a filling station opposite the marina.

Bottled Gas The filling station above sells only Portuguese gas cylinders, though Camping Gaz is understood to be available elsewhere in the city.

Clube Náutico The Clube Náutico de Setúbal has premises overlooking the small basin west of the marina, with the usual bar and restaurant.

Weather forecast Displayed daily at the marina office.

Banks In the city.

Shops/provisioning Large supermarket one road inland from the Clube Náutico, and doubtless many others, as well as good general shopping in the city proper.

Produce market Fish and produce market adjacent to the supermarket above.

Cafés, restaurants and hotels Many throughout the city, including several waterside restaurants in the nearby public gardens.

Medical services In the city.

Facilities – Tróia

There is electricity and water on the pontoons, fuel, laundry service, showers and toilets, internet facilities and several restaurants. There is a supermarket within four minutes' walk of the marina. There is no travel-lift and probably no repair facilities or chandlery available.

The ferry terminal to Setúbal is adjacent to the marina.

Communications – Setúbal

Post office In the city.

Mailing address The marina office will hold mail for visiting yachts – c/o Administração do Porto de Setúbal, Doca de Recreio das Fontaínhas, Praça da República, 2904–508 Setúbal, Portugal. It is important that the envelope carries the name of the yacht in addition to that of the addressee.

Internet At least one cybercafé in the city, but at some distance from the marina.

Public telephones On the rear wall of the marina office.

Car hire/taxis In the city.

Buses and trains Services to Lisbon and elsewhere.

Ferries Shuttle service for foot passengers and vehicles to the Península de Tróia from inside the Doca de Recreio das Fontaínhas.

Air services Lisbon airport is some 35km distant.

Communications – Tróia

WiFi, phone and photocopiers are available in a 'business centre'.

Ferries Shuttle service for foot passengers and vehicles to the inside the Doca de Recreio das Fontaínhas from the Península de Tróia.

Adjacent anchorages

1. There is a designated fishing and smallcraft anchorage southeast of the conspicuous Castelo de São Felipe in 10–12m, but it is some distance from all facilities.
2. Alternatively it is possible to anchor off the Clube Náutico basin, convenient for shopping and where a dinghy can be left.
3. In the shallow bay west of Forte de Albarquel, if space can be found amongst the moorings. Beware the double rock, Arflor, to the west, though this is now buoyed.

    Anchorage is also possible along the eastern shore of the Península de Tróia, the northern 3M of which is quite steep-to, or among the rice fields on the upper Rio Sado, well beyond the commercial wharves and shipyards. A large-scale Portuguese chart, a reliable echo sounder and plenty of time are all essentials.

Tróia Marina looking west-southwest

CABO ESPICHEL TO CABO DE SÃO VICENTE

Sines

Location
37°55'·98N 8°52'·74W (entrance)

Tides
Standard port Lisbon
Mean time differences
HW −0040 ±0010; LW −0015 ±0005
Heights in metres

MHWS	MHWN	MLWN	MLWS
3·3	2·6	1·3	0·6

Principal harbour lights
Cabo de Sines Fl(2).15s55m26M
 001°-obscd-003° and 004°-obscd-007°
 White tower and building 28m
Note Numerous nearby red lights mark chimneys, radio masts etc
West breakwater Fl.3s20m12M
 White tower, red bands 8m
Note Lies about 500m SHORT of the breakwater end, which is marked by a buoy
Terminal Ldg Lts 358°
 Front Iso.G.6s17m10M Post 6m
 Rear 579m from front Oc.G.6s28m10M Post 20m

Fishing harbour (NW) mole Fl.R.6s6M
 White tower, red bands 4m
Marina (SE) mole Fl.G.4s4M
 White tower, green bands 5m
Southeast breakwater, NW corner LFl.G.8s16m6M
 Green column, white bands 7m
Other lights exist within the commercial harbour

Communications
 Administração do Porto do Sines ① +351 269 860 600
 Email geral@portodesines.pt
 www.portodesines.pt
 VHF Ch 12, 16 call *Sines Port Control* (24 hours)
 Marina de Sines ① +351 269 860 612
 Email portoderecreio@portodesines.pt
 Website as above, VHF Ch 09.
 Maritime radio station
 Atalaia (38°10'·3N 8°38'·6W)
 Remotely controlled from Lisbon
 Manual – VHF Ch 16, 23, 24, 25. *Autolink* – VHF Ch 85

Small but highly-praised marina in large commercial harbour complex

The town's history can be traced back to Roman times when it was called Sinus, and over the years it established good trading relations in the Mediterranean and thrived. Vasco da Gama was born in the castle here, and although until 1971 it was a relatively quiet fishing port, Sines (pronounced *cinch*) can now handle 500,000-tonne tankers and has heavy industry as well as petrochemicals supporting its economy. However, although it can be identified from well offshore by its many chimneys, many either lit or smoking, once in the anchorage or marina the industrial areas are masked behind the attractive old town and are soon forgotten. Sitting on a cliff overlooking a small sandy bay, there are still traces of heritage in the pleasant town centre. However, the only trace of da Gama in Sines these days is a statue in front of the Parish church.

The Marina de Sines, which lies behind a substantial stone mole southeast of the fishing harbour, has received a unanimous thumbs up from all who have reported on it since it opened in 1996 – an almost unique accolade.

Approach

Sines is most conveniently placed, being the only all-weather harbour between Lisbon, some 50M to the north, and Cabo de São Vicente, nearly 60M to the south.

For 35M north of Cabo de Sines the coast is an unbroken line of low sand hills – one long beach. The theoretical ranges of Cabo Espichel and Cabo de Sines lights overlap, but there are no other major lights in between. Cabo de Sines has offlying rocks and islands but 0·5M provides safe clearance.

From the south, the last major light is Cabo Sardão 13M distant, with a less powerful light Vila Nova de Milfontes. The coast between Cabo Sardão and Sines is rocky with cliffs, though there are sandy beaches around Vila Nova de Milfontes and Porto Covo (the latter about 7M southeast of Sines and identifiable by its water tower).

A considerable amount of commercial and fishing traffic should be anticipated on closing the coast, and watch kept accordingly.

The approaches are littered with pot buoys. Also keep a good lookout for commercial shipping entering and leaving the harbour.

Entrance

The entrance to the main harbour lies 1·5M south of Cabo de Sines and is protected by a long breakwater, the southern end of which has been in ruins for some years and is partially submerged – note that the breakwater light is situated almost 500m short of the breakwater end, which is marked by a (lit) red pillar buoy. Do not cut inside this buoy.

From the south the entrance is wide and should present no problems, though ships *en route* to the commercial terminals in the southeastern part of the harbour must be given ample space to manoeuvre.

Berthing

The small but welcoming Marina de Sines, run by the Administração do Porto do Sines, occupies the bight between the eastern inner breakwater and a steep rocky outcrop. Facilities include a hauling wharf, slipway, mobile crane, pontoons and fingers. It has capacity for 230 berths including two or three for more than 20m overall, and a hardstanding. A range of services is available including fresh water,

SINES

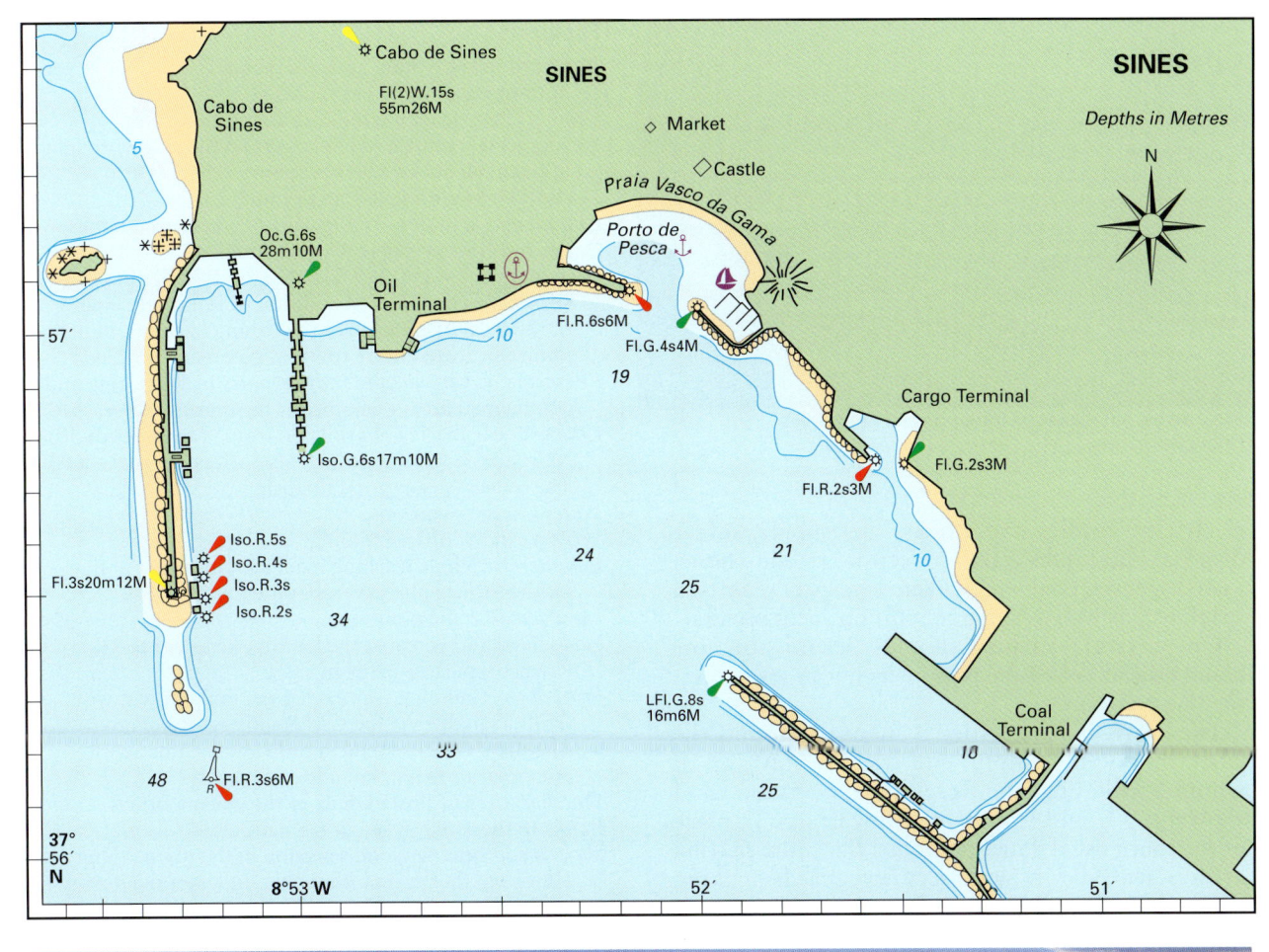

The inner harbour at Sines looking north. The Marina de Sines is on the right

ATLANTIC SPAIN AND PORTUGAL 217

CABO ESPICHEL TO CABO DE SÃO VICENTE

View across Sines Marina looking west northwest
Henry Buchanan

electricity, cradles and stocks, fuel supply, refuse disposal and liquid waste collection, public phone, cash dispenser, boat watch, meteorological reports, a snack bar, as well as some support on yacht repairs.

On arrival yachts should secure to the hammerhead below the rock, which also serves as a fuelling pontoon.

The smart marina office is manned around the clock by notably helpful and friendly staff, all of whom speak English. Reception is upstairs and showers, WC and laundry are downstairs. In place of the more usual gated pontoons the entire marina area is fenced off, with security guards making regular patrols.

Twenty eight berths are reserved for yachts in transit, normally on the northwestern pontoon (the approach to which can be exciting when the *nortada* is blowing). This is the first part of the marina to be affected by swell and storm surge, when visitors will be moved further in if space allows. Depths vary from 3–8m, with 5m or more throughout the visitors' area, and all berths are alongside finger pontoons.

Anchorage

Yachts are still permitted to anchor off the Praia Vasco da Gama, in 3–5m over sand and a little weed, provided they keep well clear of both fishing vessels and the marina approach. Being open to the southwest the anchorage is seldom without a slight roll, but the marina could not be closer should the wind shift onshore. Dinghies can be landed on the beach, which is cleaned and raked daily and is very popular with local residents.

There are charges for anchoring but only if marina facilities are used. Facilities include showers, launderette and the internet. Payment should be made at the marina office.

Facilities

Boatyard In the fishing and commercial areas, but as yet nothing specifically for yachts.
Cranes The marina has a 6·3-tonne static crane, supplemented by a much larger mobile crane brought in from the docks when necessary. There is also a slipway where yachts can dry out.
Chandlery Chandlery and marine business are on the ground floor of the new office building. Sinaútica ☏ +351 269 635 670, on Rua Teófila Braga, sells some chandlery in addition to inflatables and outboards. Also one near the fishing harbour, though naturally geared more towards commercial needs.
Engineers, electronic and radio repairs In the fishing and commercial areas – enquire at the marina office.
Charts Local charts are available from Nautisines on Rua Marquês de Pombal, which also offers internet access. The owner speaks good English.
Water On the pontoons.
Showers In the office building.
Launderette Single washing machine plus dryer at the marina office, plus several in the town.
Electricity On the pontoons.
Fuel Diesel and petrol at the hammerhead pontoon. Payment must be made in cash.
Bottled gas Camping Gaz exchanges in the town, with refills available via the GALP shop on Rua Pero de Alenquer. GALP claims to refill any cylinder with butane or propane, but allow three days.
Weather forecast Posted daily at the marina office.
Banks In the town. ATM in the marina.
Shops/provisioning Good selection in the town, about 2km from the marina (though a lot less if the dinghy is used, when nearly all the carrying will be downhill). No shops at all near the marina, though see Berthing, above.
Produce market Small but good open market in the old town.
Cafés, restaurants and hotels A snack bar next to the marina office, which may eventually expand. In the meantime the old town is well supplied with restaurants and hotels.
Medical services In the town.

Communications

Post office In the town.
Mailing address The marina office will hold mail for visiting yachts – c/o Administração do Porto do Sines, Porto de Recreio, Apartado 16, 7520–953 Sines, Portugal. It is important that the envelope carries the name of the yacht in addition to that of the addressee.
Internet Wireless broadband is available throughout the marina. Those berthed in the marina or paying to anchor can use one of the office computers for a small fee.
Public telephones At the marina office and in the town.
Car hire/taxis In the town, or can be arranged via the marina office.
Buses Local buses, with long distance services to Lisbon (just under three hours) and elsewhere from the bus station in the eastern part of the old town.
Trains Sines no longer has a passenger rail service.

VILA NOVA DE MILFONTES

Vila Nova de Milfontes

Location
37°42'·7N 8°48'·2W (entrance)

Tides
Standard port Lisbon
Mean time differences Milfontes
HW –0035 ±0005; LW No data
Heights in metres Milfontes
MHWS	MHWN	MLWN	MLWS
3·7	2·9	1·5	0·7

Principal lights
Milfontes (Rio Mira) Fl.3s22m10M
   White lantern on hut 5m

Warning
Night entry not possible under any circumstances – the bar calls for eyeball pilotage in good overhead light.

Beautiful, unspoilt river with challenging entrance

Reputedly used by Hannibal and once rich enough to be sacked by Algerian pirates, pretty little Vila Nova de Milfontes on the Rio Mira shows scant evidence of its former importance. Despite much recent holiday development, the white and tile village on the north bank has retained much of its character, and mercifully escaped the high-rise blocks which mar so many Portuguese resorts. There are superb beaches both inside and outside the entrance and the area's peace and tranquillity are a real treat – but first you must pick your way in.

Though viable for a keelboat in the right conditions the Rio Mira is shallow and, in common with many other Portuguese rivers, has a bar with a reported depth of no more than 1m at datum – considerably less if any swell is running. Once inside protection is excellent but flat weather, and particularly an absence of swell, are essential for both entry and departure. About a mile from the entrance there is a road bridge with a clearance of some 12m, but it is possible to explore the river by dinghy for many kilometres beyond.

Approach

The coast between Cabo de Sines to the north and Cabo Sardão to the south consists of rocky cliffs. There is a sandy beach at Porto Covo about 8M to the north, identifiable by its water tower.

Entrance

Since Vila Nova de Milfontes calls for careful eyeball pilotage, enter only in calm weather on a rising tide, preferably in the afternoon with the sun behind the boat. The entrance is marked by the Rio Mira light,

The shallow bar at Vila Nova de Milfontes, seen from the southwest. The challenge of entering the Rio Mira is exacerbated by the fact that no reliable chart is available

PORTUGAL – THE WEST COAST

ATLANTIC SPAIN AND PORTUGAL   219

CABO ESPICHEL TO CABO DE SÃO VICENTE

A panoramic shot taken from near the Rio Mira light, looking up upstream towards the town and bridge. Again, the V-shaped middle ground shows up as a pale, sandy shadow Anne Hammick

shown from the corner of a square white building with a tiled roof on the north side of the entrance.

Approach to about 600m with the light bearing 050° and, with luck, a local fisherman will lead the way across the bar (though this is considerably less likely now that most of the local smallcraft have moved the mile north to Portinho do Canal). Failing this, turn east and keep the reef which extends southwards from the light about 60m off on the port hand. Although part is exposed it extends for some distance underwater as a brownish–purple area – be guided by the colour of the water.

Just inside the entrance best water is found relatively close under the light, but further upstream there is an unmarked middle ground, drying at low water springs, below and downstream from the fort. Its shape – a wide V with the apex pointing downstream – makes it particularly dangerous and it would be only too easy to find oneself in a blind alley. It appears that a deep channel leads south of the middle ground (see photo), but minimum depths in this have not been ascertained. Fishing nets suspended from buoys are sometimes laid inside the river.

Anchorage

There is plenty of room to anchor in the river, either in the northwest bight just inside the mouth (depths are shallow), or further upstream off the fishermen's quay in 4m or more. The ebb tide runs at up to 3kn with the spring flood only marginally less, and it may be wise to set two anchors.

Formalities

The arrival of a foreign yacht in the river is a sufficiently rare event that it would almost certainly attract a visit from the authorities. Failing that there is a *GNR–Brigada Fiscal* office up the steps at the downstream end of the quay and, supposedly, a *Policía Marítima* office in the building supporting the single light.

Facilities

Quay with steps for dinghy landing, with a café/restaurant ashore and a public tap opposite. The town contains a range of shops from supermarkets to souvenirs, as well as banks, restaurants, a post office and several telephone kiosks. Buses run to Sines and elsewhere.

Looking out to sea from the Rio Mira light structure, with all kinds of rocks and reefs in the foreground Anne Hammick

ATLANTIC SPAIN AND PORTUGAL

VILA NOVA DE MILFONTES

Adjacent harbours and anchorages

1. **Porto Corvo, Portinho do Canal and Porto das Barcas** – if coastal sailing, the sharp-eyed may spot Porto Corvo at 37°51′N, Portinho do Canal at 37°44′·4N and/or Porto das Barcas at 37°33′·2N. Though all three are lit, to call any of them a 'port' is highly misleading and none could be entered by even the smallest yacht. Neither are there viable anchorages in their offings – sail on by.
2. **Arrifana**, this is a lovely anchorage in quiet, stable weather. The bay is surrounded by dramatic cliffs giving shelter from north and east, and lies 26M south of Vila Nova de Milfontes and 18M north of Cabo de São Vicente. Though isolated and remote it can be a useful passage anchorage, particularly if beating into the prevailing nortada. However, with any swell rolling in, the surfing community arrive in force – and they know where to find waves.

   The coast is rocky and steep-to with offlying stacks and islands. The ruins of an old fort stand on the cliff to the north with a cairn, Pedra da Agulha, to the south. Beneath both are rocky islets – those under the fort are lumpy while those under the cairn have needle-like angularity. Approaching from the southwest, the islets off the fort stand out from the land and the white cottages behind the sandy beach become plain. Anchor off the beach in 7m over sand, avoiding the northern area which is peppered with rocky shoals. Pots or net floats may be encountered anywhere in the bay.

   A miniature harbour, home to half-a-dozen small fishing boats, nestles amongst the rocks at the north end of the beach. However it has nothing to offer in terms of facilities – not even a water tap – and is considerably further from the village by road than is the beach. A café/restaurant overlooks the latter, with a public telephone about 50m up the steep cobbled road to the village. Other than dramatic views and a few more restaurants there is little to justify the climb.
3. **Carrapateira** (37°11′·3N 8°54′·8W), lying 6·5M south of Arrifana and 11M north of Cabo de São Vicente, may also suggest itself as a possible anchorage in northeasterly winds. However shelter is considerably poorer than at Arrifana and there are numerous rocks both in the approach and off the beach.

Arrifana: Looking NNW from the anchorage at 37°17′·56N 008°52·17W.
Note the fishing boat mooring buoys at approximately 37°17′·5N 8°52′·3W *Henry Buchanan*

The wide bay at Arrifana offers potential anchorage on the long haul between Sines and Cabo de São Vicente. Fully open to the west, however, it is also a popular spot with surfers *Anne Hammick*

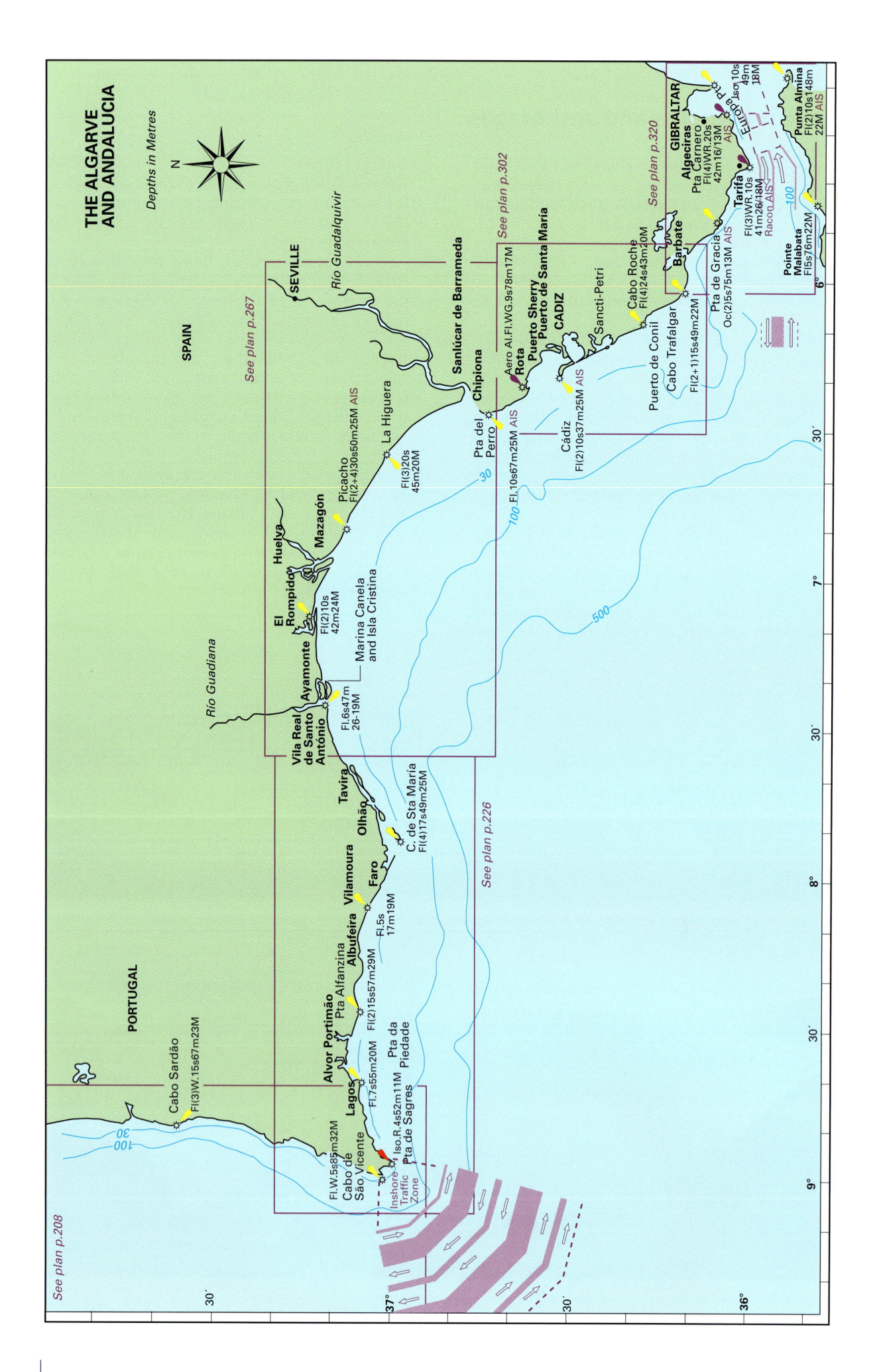

THE ALGARVE AND ANDALUCIA

Depths in Metres

PORTUGAL

- Cabo Sardão Fl(3)W.15s67m23M
- Cabo de São Vicente Fl.W.5s85m32M
- Pta de Sagres Iso.R.4s52m11M
- Lagos Fl.7s55m20M
- Pta da Piedade
- Alvor
- Portimão Fl(2)15s57m29M
- Pta Alfanzina
- Albufeira
- Vilamoura Fl.5s 17m19M
- Faro
- Olhão
- C. de Sta Maria Fl(4)17s49m25M
- Tavira
- Vila Real de Santo António
- Ayamonte Fl.6s47m 26-19M
- Marina Canela and Isla Cristina

SPAIN

- Rio Guadiana
- El Rompido Fl(2)10s 42m24M
- Huelva
- Mazagón
- Picacho Fl(2+4)30s50m25M AIS
- La Higuera Fl(3)20s 45m20M
- Rio Guadalquivir
- SEVILLE
- Sanlúcar de Barrameda
- Chipiona
- Pta del Perro Fl.10s67m25M AIS
- Rota Aero Al.Fl.WG.9s78m17M
- Puerto Sherry
- Puerto de Santa Maria
- CÁDIZ Fl(2)10s37m25M AIS
- Sancti-Petri
- Cabo Roche Fl(4)24s43m20M
- Puerto de Conil
- Cabo Trafalgar Fl(2+1)15s49m22M AIS
- Barbate
- Pta de Gracia Oc(2)5s75m13M AIS
- Tarifa Fl(3)WR.10s 41m26/18M Racon AIS
- Pointe Malabata Fl5s76m22M
- Algeciras Pta Carnero Fl(4)WR.20s 42m16/13M
- GIBRALTAR Europa Iso 10s 49m 18M AIS
- Punta Almina Fl(2)10s148m 22M AIS

See plan p.208
See plan p.226
See plan p.267
See plan p.302
See plan p.320

222 ATLANTIC SPAIN AND PORTUGAL

III. The Algarve and Andalucía

Cabo de São Vicente to Gibraltar

Cabo de São Vicente in the west *Henry Buchanan*

Gibraltar in the east *Alcaidesa Marina*

THE ALGARVE AND ANDALUCIA

Overview

Both ends of this stretch offer spectacular scenery with impressive cliffs. In the middle, these give way to sandy beaches often backed by lagoons – staging posts for migrant birds – including the Parque Natural de Ría Formosa around Faro and Olhão and the Parque Nacional de Doñana west of the Río Guadalquivir. The western Algarve has been intensively developed for the tourist and in places the shoreline is littered with high-rise blocks and time-share estates, though these decrease as one approaches the border. In Spain, the stretch east of Cádiz is the least developed piece of coast between Portugal and France. Human activity can be traced back for millennia, with Faro, Seville, Cádiz and other settlements dating back to Phoenician or Roman times. While on the Algarve see if you find any traces of the fish paste developed by the Phoenicians. This was a delicacy throughout the classical world and was major source of income for the people of the ancient Algarve.

In contrast to the west coast there are a number of good estuary and river anchorages, generally over good holding. From São Vicente to the Guadalquivir the bottom is sand. From Cádiz onwards it is usually mud, often glutinous, providing good holding but needing a deck pump (or mop and bucket) when the anchor is brought in. Anchoring off any beach is possible in fine, settled weather when there is no swell.

Hazards – tunny nets, fish cages and artificial reefs

Between March and early autumn *almadrabas* or tunny (tuna) nets tough enough to foul the screw of a freighter can be a considerable hazard, and may stretch several miles offshore. It is not advisable to sail over one, and officially vessels should not pass between the inner end of a net and the shore (though local fishermen habitually do so). Tunny nets can be found as far west as Fuzeta but are concentrated mainly in the 30M between Puerto de Conil and Tarifa. Further details of dates, locations and buoyage will be found under the notes for the nearest harbour, and annual positions are often displayed on marina notice boards. Note that the cardinal buoys used to mark the nets are frequently very undersized – sometimes less than 2m in height, including topmark – and should not be relied upon, particularly at night.

More prevalent though less worrying are the nets laid for other fish – less worrying because they generally lie too far beneath the surface to bother a yacht. When first laid they are inspected and must be correctly marked – two red or orange flags at the western end (anywhere from south-southwest to north) and a single green flag at the eastern end (north to south-southeast). In addition, white flags should be set at 1M intervals. At night each flag should be replaced by a yellow light (so two lights at the western end). However with the passage of time both lights and flags may disappear, to be replaced at random if at all.

In a few places floating fish cages may be encountered, and again details are included in the text. Most are indicated by yellow buoys and lights, and positions are indicated on current Admiralty and other charts. Finally, a number of artificial reefs have been constructed off the coast to provide fish havens, reducing the charted depth by up to 2·5m. However since these seldom lie in less than 10m and more often straddle the 20m line – and assuming that while yachtsmen may fish by line they seldom tow a trawl – they can safely be ignored.

Swell

Though less of a problem than along the west-facing coast, heavy swell can be produced either by an Atlantic disturbance or by a *levanter* blowing through the Strait of Gibraltar, and the shallower entrances should be avoided in such conditions.

Winds

In summer north and northeast winds predominate in the west, but the further offshore the more variable they become. Further east, the influence of the Portuguese trade winds gradually dies away. Like the Atlantic coast, the Algarve is also subject to stiff afternoon sea breezes. From early summer onwards these start to blow at around 1400, regularly reaching Force 6 and occasionally Force 7 (25 or 30kn) within an hour and continuing until sundown. Typically they pick up from the southwest, moving through west to west-northwest or northwest by evening.

East of Cádiz, the effect of the Strait becomes increasingly marked with 80% of winds in the Strait from either west (*poniente*) or east-northeast (*levante*). Gales are unlikely in the height of summer but *levanters* with winds of 50–60kn are not unknown, visibility dropping to 1M or less. They are not seasonal, generally last for two to three days, and blow up with little or no warning from the barometer – though sometimes a deep purple bank of haze in the morning or a sudden fast steep swell may give a clue. The *poniente* is generally less strong than the *levanter* but may last five days or more. Squalls can occur at any time in the Bay of Gibraltar if the wind is between northeast and southeast.

Visibility

Poor visibility, less than 2M, is more common (2–5%) in summer than in winter. Fog is infrequent but not unknown in the Algarve, while the Cádiz area has a reputation for fog in certain conditions associated with a *levanter*.

Shelter

In a *levanter* (easterly) shelter in the Strait is limited to the Cádiz complex, west of the Tarifa causeway, and Gibraltar. In a *poniente* (westerly) it is limited to the Cádiz complex, Tarifa itself, and Gibraltar.

OVERVIEW

Currents

Along the Algarve coast the set is predominantly east of southeast, running at about 0·5 knot. By the time it reaches the Strait it is running east at 1–1·5kn, compensating for water lost from the Mediterranean through evaporation. However this pattern can be upset by the wind – a southeasterly gale in the south of the area can produce a west-going stream along the coast as far as Cabo de São Vicente, while persistent strong westerlies, coupled with the regular current, can produce an easterly set of 4kn.

Tides

Tidal predictions for the Algarve use Lisbon as the Standard Port; those for Andalucía use either Lisbon, Cádiz or Gibraltar. When calculating Spanish tides using Lisbon data, note that allowance has already been made for the difference in time zones (Spanish time being UT+1, Portuguese time UT, both advanced one hour in summer – see page 4.) Volume 2 of the Admiralty *Tide Tables: The Atlantic and Indian Oceans including tidal stream predictions (NP 202)*, published annually, covers the entire coastline. Alternatively consult the UK Hydrographic Office's *EasyTide* programme at www.ukho.gov.uk/easytide which gives daily tidal data for all major harbours or the Imray Tides Planner app, which can be downloaded on the App Store or Google Play and used offline.

Tidal range decreases eastward, from 2·8m at springs and 1·2m at neaps at Lagos, to 0·9m and 0·4m respectively at Gibraltar – see individual harbours. There is no reliable information about tidal streams along the coast, though 2–3kn has been reported in some places, notably around Faro and Olhão. In the centre of the Straits the east-going stream starts shortly after HW Gibraltar and the west-going stream about six hours later, though the closer inshore, the earlier the change takes place – see diagrams page 322.

Cruising the Algarve is much more pleasant if it can be timed to coincide with morning and evening high tides (in practice a few days before neaps). Otherwise the typically shallow river entrances – which in many cases are dependant on at least half flood and good daylight – can complicate departure and arrival times.

Climate

Most rain falls between the end of October and the beginning of April with virtually none in July and August. Cool in winter, hot in summer, Lagos has a mean of 36°C in July with Gibraltar capable of 40°C in a *levanter*. Sea temperatures at Gibraltar range from 21°C in summer to 14°C in winter.

Maritime radio stations and weather/navigational services

Many Portuguese Maritime radio stations and those broadcasting weather and navigational information are situated between, rather than at, ports or harbours. Details will be found under the nearest harbour to the station. All are remotely controlled from Lisbon. In Andalucía, all Maritime radio stations are remotely controlled from Málaga. Broadcast times are quoted in UT, but all other times (office hours etc) are given in LT.

One of the hazards to navigation on this coast – the large fish conservation and tuna net area south of Fuzeta now marked by six large cardinal buoys (see page 262) *Martin Northey*

CABO DE SÃO VICENTE TO TAVIRA

Cabo de São Vicente to Tavira

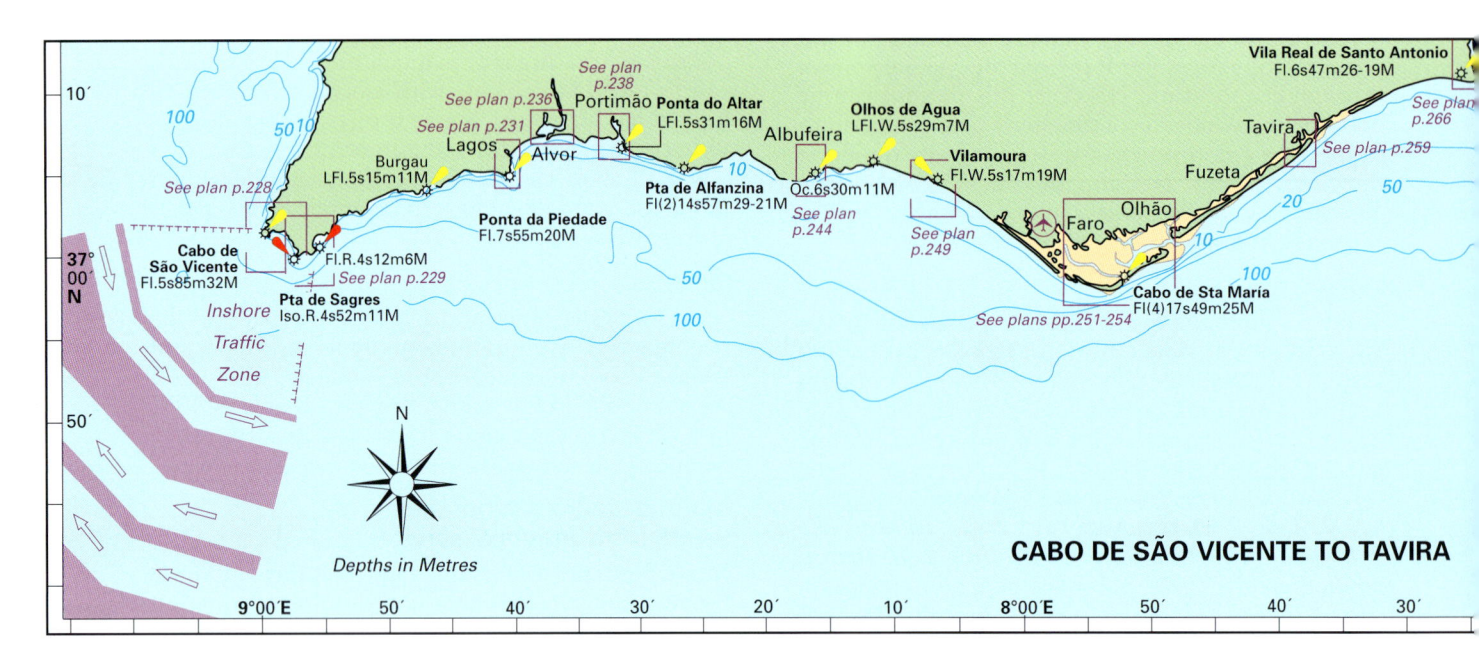

PRINCIPAL LIGHTS
Cabo de São Vicente Fl.5s85m32M Aero
   Off-white tower, red lantern, and building 28m
Ponta de Sagres Iso.R.4s52m11M
   Square white tower and building 13m
Ponta da Piedade Fl.7s55m20M
   Square yellow tower on building 5m
Ponta do Altar LFl.5s31m16M
   Square white tower and building 10m
Ponta de Alfanzina Fl(2)14s57m29-21M
   Square white tower and building 23m
Albufeira Oc.6s31m11M White column, red bands
Olhos de Agua LFl.5s29m7M
   White column, red bands
Cabo de Santa María Fl(4)17s49m25M Aero
   White tower and building 46m
Vila Real de Santo António Fl.6s47m26-19M
   White tower, narrow black rings, red lantern 46m

Fish are landed, cleaned, cooked and eaten on the quayside at Ferragudo, across the river from Portimão

Cabo de São Vicente from almost due south, with the lighthouse on the left and the Enseada de Belixe anchorage beneath the pale cliffs at centre right

226 ATLANTIC SPAIN AND PORTUGAL

CABO DE SÃO VICENTE

Cabo de São Vicente, Ponta de Sagres and Baleeira

Location
37°00'·71N 8°55'·15W (Baleeira entrance)

Tides *(at Enseada de Belixe)*
Standard port Lisbon
Mean time differences
HW −0040 ±0010; LW −0015 ±0005
Heights in metres
MHWS	MHWN	MLWN	MLWS
4·1	3·2	1·7	0·8

Principal lights
Cabo de São Vicente Fl.5s85m32M Aero
 Off-white tower, red lantern, and building 28m
Ponta de Sagres Iso.R.4s52m11M
 Square white tower and building 13m
Baleeira breakwater
 Fl.R.4s12m6M
 White tower, red bands 6m

Warning
Long surface nets, lit or unlit, may be laid throughout the area and particularly in the vicinity of Baleeira, in addition to shorter nets and individual fish pots
Night entry - All three anchorages can be approached after dark in the right conditions, but very careful watch must be kept for the nets mentioned above

Communications
Maritime radio station
Sagres – *Digital Selective Calling* (MF)
MMSI 002630400 (planned)
Foia (37°18'·9N 8°36'·3W)
Remotely controlled from Lisbon
Manual – VHF Ch 16, 23, 24, 28. *Autolink* – VHF Ch 27

Cabo de São Vicente and Sagres – the sacred promontory

Once the end of the known world and a springboard for the great Portuguese Discoveries, Cabo de São Vicente and Ponta de Sagres make a formidable pair, wild and windswept, sometimes seen for miles but, even in summer, sometimes heard before seen.

A few miles east of the headlands lies Baleeira, a relatively undeveloped harbour overlooked by a growing tourist resort. Its origins as a whaling centre are given away by its name and today a small fishing fleet still operates from the quay, along with a number of tourist boats. The beach close north of the harbour can be dirty, but Praia do Martinhal a little further east is well up to the Algarve's usual high standard.

Cabo de São Vicente and Ponta de Sagres – Approach

When coastal sailing from the north the last major light is Cabo Sardão and from the east it is Ponta de Piedade south of Lagos.

On passage southwards in the prevailing *nortada* both wind and waves are likely to increase noticeably on approaching Cabo de São Vicente, a combination of gusts off the cliffs and reflected swell. Both Cabo de São Vicente and Ponta de Sagres should be allowed a generous 2M clearance in these conditions, though much flatter water will generally be found east of Ponta de Baleeira. Equally, yachts heading west and north may expect to encounter rapidly deteriorating conditions on rounding Ponta de Baleeira, and should prepare accordingly. It may be necessary to stay 2M or more offshore until 5–6M north of Cabo de São Vicente in order to avoid the worst. By far the best time to make the passage is early in the morning before the *nortada* reaches its full strength, especially if heading north.

If making landfall from offshore, particular care must be taken whilst crossing the Traffic Separation Zone which rounds Cabo de São Vicente and Ponta de Sagres – in fact there is much to be said for avoiding it altogether. The zone is up to 22M in width, its inshore edge nowhere less than 14M from the coast.

Anchorages

Three anchorages can be useful if waiting for the usual strong afternoon *nortada* to die before heading north around Cabo de São Vicente, and though none give much protection from the south in these conditions most crews will, in any case, be wanting to press on.

Cabo de São Vicente and Ponta de Sagres – adjacent anchorages

1. **Enseada de Belixe** 37°01'·5N 8°59'W
   Wide open to the southwest and south, with straightforward entry day or night using the loom of Cabo de São Vicente light. If coming from the north, pass outside the tall rock off the headland and continue beyond the first, small, wedge-shaped bay until Enseada de Belixe opens up round Pontal dos Corval.

Coastline looking east from Ponta de Sagres (Baleeira)
Henry Buchanan

THE ALGARVE & ANDALUCIA

ATLANTIC SPAIN AND PORTUGAL

CABO DE SÃO VICENTE TO TAVIRA

ENSEADA DE BELIXE

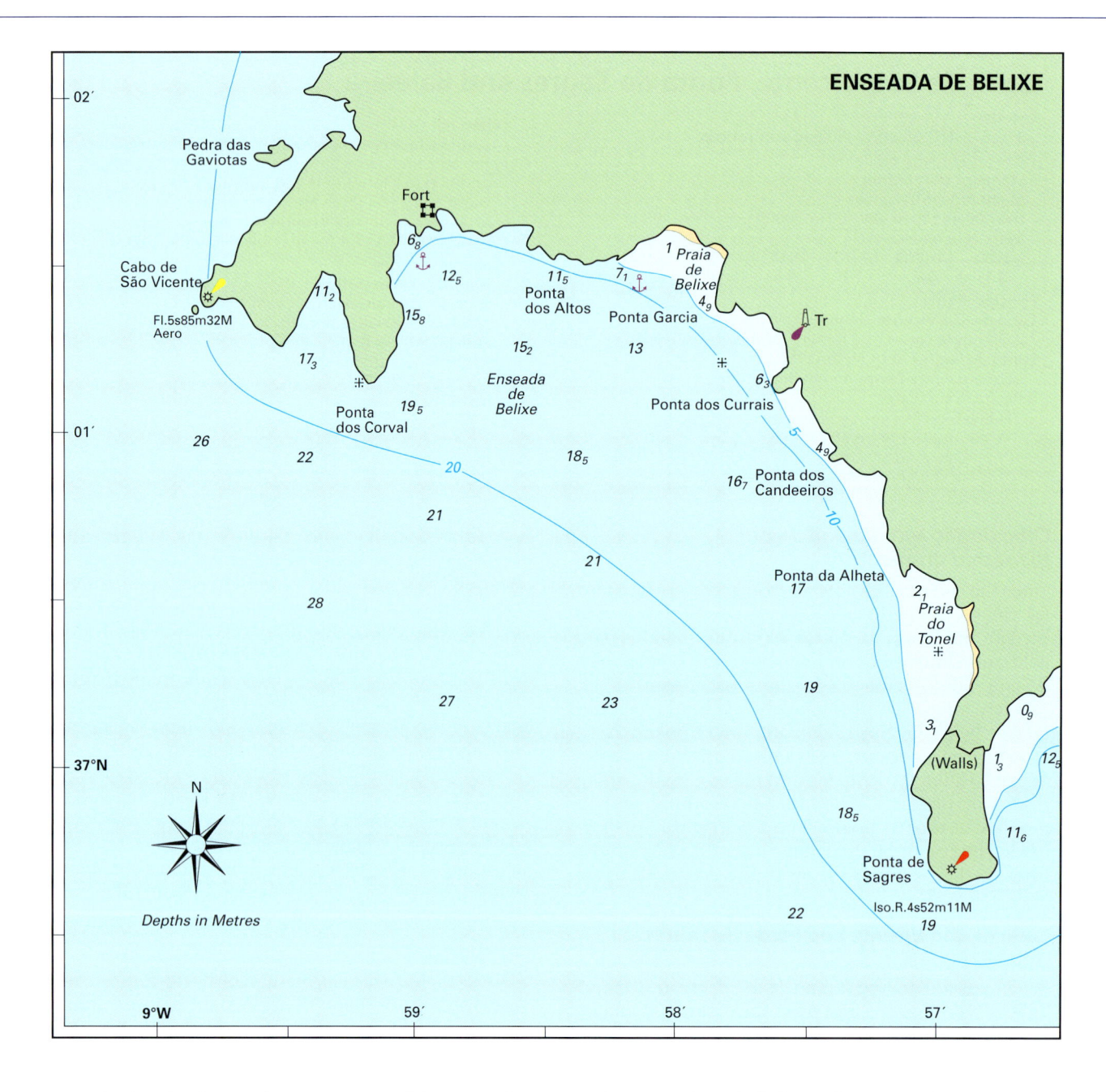

Anchor in the northwestern part of the Enseada de Belixe in 14m, or off the Praia de Belixe. Beware the rock some 200m south of the east end of the Praia de Belixe, which rises almost sheer out of 9m to show only at low water. The only realistic dinghy landing is on the beach at Praia de Belixe.

2. **Enseada de Sagres** (⊕150 – 37°00′·143N 008°56′·218W) is open to the southeast, with easy entry and excellent shelter from west through north to northeast. Anchor off the Praia da Marela or the Prainha Das Poças just north of the wall of the fort in 3·5m. There is good holding over sand at both positions. In Sagres at the top of the hill there are hotels (including Pousada), supermarkets, shops, banks and restaurants.

Anchorage at Enseada de Sagres from Sagres fortress
Henry Buchanan

228 ATLANTIC SPAIN AND PORTUGAL

BALEEIRA

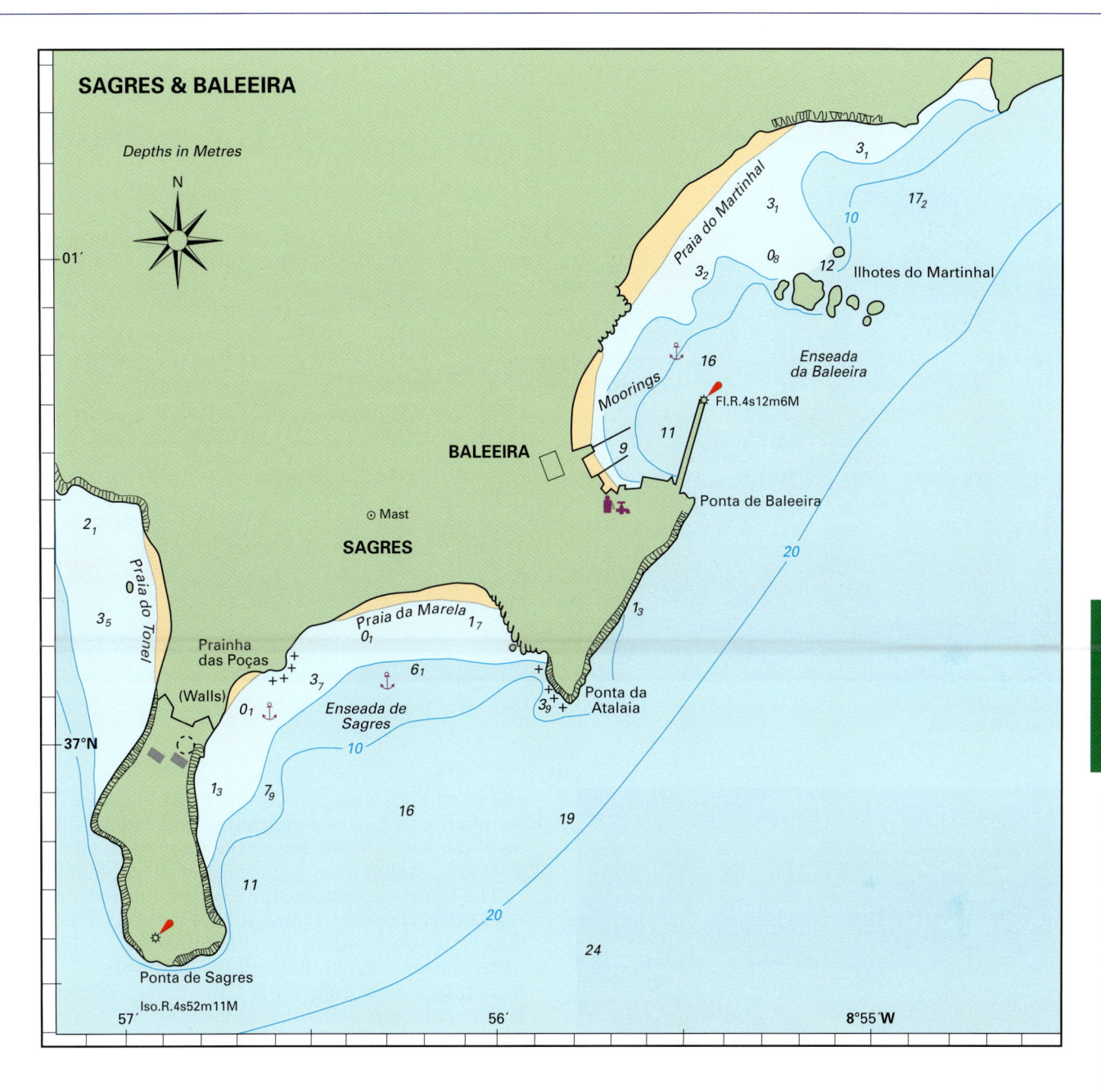

Baleeira – approach

Two fish farms lie northeast of Baleeira, a potential hazard if on passage to or from Lagos or beyond. One is marked by four yellow can buoys, all Fl.Y.14s4M, and is centred on 37°01'·1N 8°53'·5W, the other by four spherical yellow buoys, all Fl.Y.5s3M, and is centred on 37°01'·5N 8°52'·6W. In addition long nets may be set at an angle to the shore, normally indicated by lit yellow buoys (powered by solar panels) and supported by yellow floats. These nets are not connected to the shore and, with due care, yachts can pass on either side.

The harbour itself is sheltered by a high breakwater around 400m in length running northeast from Ponta de Baleeira, leaving it open to the east and with a fetch of nearly 1M to the northeast. The breakwater light is sectored, with its red area covering the Ilhotes do Martinhal, a group of large rocks about 500m to the northeast. Although it is possible to pass between the islands and the shore, the area is littered with rocks and strictly a case for eyeball navigation.

Baleeira – harbour and anchorage

The Baleeira anchorage gains some protection from the breakwater and is open only to the east. Anchor outside the moorings, northwest or north of the breakwater head, in 6–10m. Holding is patchy and the bottom is reported to be very foul – a tripline is recommended.

There are several ladders and a ramp convenient for landing, but if possible avoid going ashore at low water as the bottoms of the ladders are seriously dilapidated and the lower part of the ramp lethally slippery. The *Polícia Marítima* have an office in the Doca de Pesca building and may well intercept the

ATLANTIC SPAIN AND PORTUGAL

CABO DE SÃO VICENTE TO TAVIRA

Looking west across Baleeira harbour towards the Ponta de Sagres. The walls of Sagres fortress can be seen near the root of the long promontory

Baleeira harbour looking northeast *Henry Buchanan*

skipper and crew as they come ashore – bring ship's papers and passports, in case. The *GNR–Brigada Fiscal* are also likely to check on any foreign flag yacht.

Facilities in the harbour are limited to diesel and water on the fishermen's quay, and a telephone kiosk at the top of the steps up from the harbour. There is an old-style boatyard just north of the jetties where fishing boats are brought ashore for work, but the (elderly) cradle would not suit a deep-keeled yacht and in all but sinking condition it would be worth continuing to Lagos. Engineering and other skills may well be available, but again it would be much safer to head for a more yacht-orientated harbour.

The tourist development at the top of the steep road offers shops (including several supermarkets), banks, a post office and innumerable cafés, restaurants and hotels. Baleeira lies on the bus route from Lagos out to Sagres and Cabo de São Vicente, both popular tourist destinations.

Local interest
The inquisitive will wish to visit the site of the Sagres fortress on the peninsula at Ponta de Sagres. Although Henry the Navigator founded the town of Sagres to support ships sheltering in the bay, and built his Vila do Infante there, it is a myth that a school of navigation ever existed. There is what may be a 15th-century *rosa dos ventos* (wind compass) in the courtyard of the fortress, but with the exception of a small chapel and the northern wall, little else remains. Sir Francis Drake must take a share of the blame, although the final havoc was wrought by the 1755 earthquake which devastated much of the Algarve. An 'interpretative centre' has been set up within the vast Fortaleza, but inevitably the information presented (in several languages) is aimed at a very broad public and sadly the buildings are ugly and do not add to the general ambience.

LAGOS

Lagos

Location
37°05'·86N 8°39'·68W (entrance)

Tides
Standard port Lisbon
Mean time differences
HW –0025 ±0010; LW –0030 ±0005
Heights in metres

MHWS	MHWN	MLWN	MLWS
3·3	2·6	1·3	0·6

Principal lights
West breakwater Fl(2)R.6s5·5M
  White tower, red bands 7m
East breakwater Fl(2)G.6s6M
  White tower, green bands 6m

Warning
Long surface nets, lit or unlit, may be laid in the bay near the entrance to the harbour, in addition to shorter nets and individual fish pots
Night entry straightforward other than in strong onshore winds. The reception pontoon is not lit, but there is sufficient ambient light for all practical purposes.

Communications
Port Authority ☏ +351 282 762826
Marina de Lagos VHF 09, 16 (0800–2200 1/6–15/9, otherwise 0900–1800)
Weather information VHF Ch 12 at 1000 and 1600 daily from 16/7–31/8
☏ +351 282 770210
Email marina@marlagos.pt
www.marinadelagos.pt

A historic town with a large established marina

Lagos, a town of Roman origin situated on the banks of the Rio Bensafrim, was once the capital of Portugal. Together with Tavira, Lagos was coveted by Spain when it ruled Portugal. The two Atlantic ports were a major source of conflict between the two nations before Portugal finally gained its independence in the mid-17th century. It is a crowded and active trading, tourist and fishing town. The expedition to capture Ceuta set out from here in 1415. It was later favoured by Henry the Navigator, who founded a company here to trade with the newly discovered regions of Africa. The merchants of Lagos were assiduous in the search for gold and slaves and it was these merchants who played a major role in Portuguese economic expansion during the late medieval period. Under the arches of the old Custom House, there was once the only slave market in Portugal. Within the 5th-century walls the churches of São Sebastião, Santa Maria of Misericórdia, Santo António and the very old São João Hermitage (8th–9th centuries) are all worth a visit. There are many other notable buildings as well as an interesting museum and good nightlife. Its fairs, held in mid-August and mid-October, are lively events, especially Festa dos Descobrimentos, (Festival of the Discoveries) celebrating the town's links with Portugal's maritime history. It is notable for the processions in period costume through the town's streets.

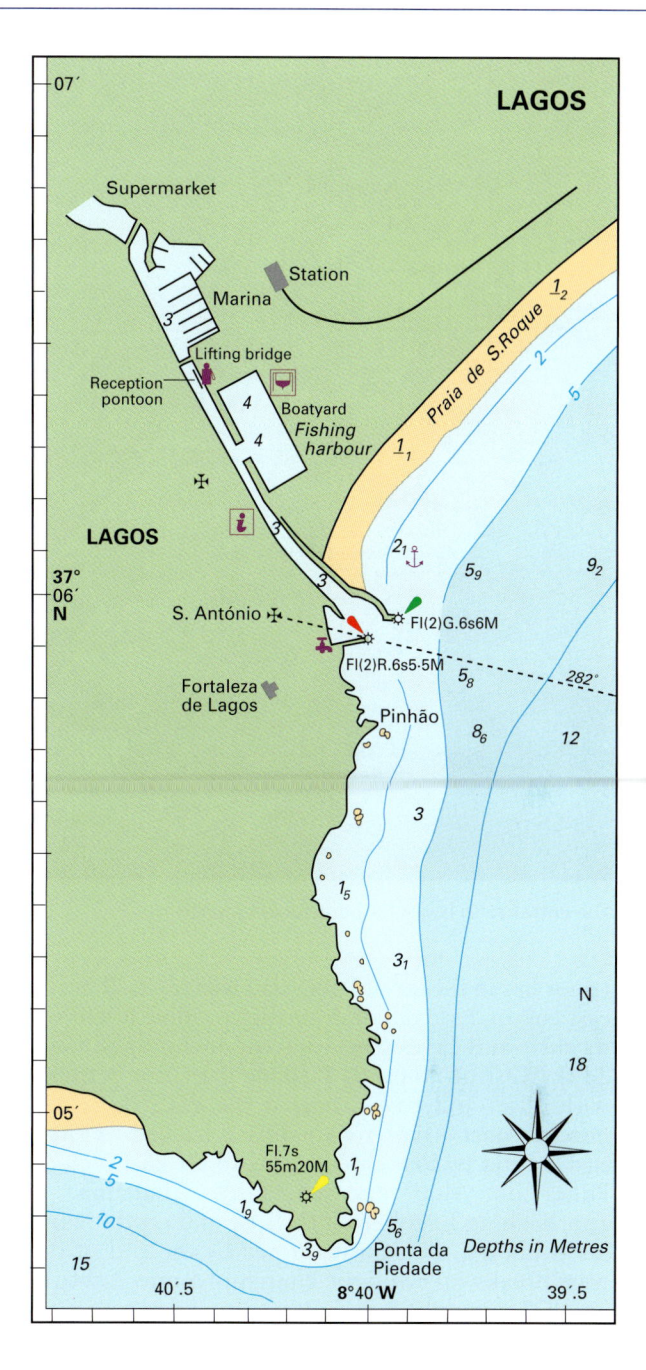

Approach

There is a fish farm to be avoided between Baleeira and Lagos. It is in a box shaped area orientated N/S E/W, 0·75M square with four yellow buoys at the corners, all with × topmark and a light.
The approximate positions of the northerly buoys are:

NE buoy: 37°04'·362N 008°41'·036W
NW buoy: 37°04'·223N 008°41'·7W

ATLANTIC SPAIN AND PORTUGAL

THE ALGARVE & ANDALUCIA

CABO DE SÃO VICENTE TO TAVIRA

The entrance to Lagos harbour, looking north

Lagos lies in the lee of Ponta da Piedade, itself at the east end of a stretch of dramatic coastline noted for its cliffs and caves (see Adjacent anchorages, page 234). West of Ponta da Piedade the coast is rocky with cliffs and caves, but to the east, there are beaches past Alvor to Portimão, backed at their eastern end by low cliffs. Lights to the east include Ponta do Altar and Ponta de Alfanzina. If approaching Lagos from the east and on the wind (as is likely), the transit formed by the end of the west breakwater and the church of Santo António on 282° is useful.

Entrance

Entrance between the twin breakwaters is straightforward, and though a bar periodically builds up southeast of the breakwater heads there is seldom less than 2·5m above datum. Even so, seas can build up in onshore winds. Once through the entrance the channel has a least depth of 3m, as does the marina. There is a 3kn speed limit in the entrance channel and throughout the marina.

Berthing

The marina lies about 0·7M inside the entrance. Secure to the 80m reception pontoon, close downstream of the lifting pedestrian bridge, to arrange a berth and complete formalities. Otherwise the bridge normally opens on demand (VHF Ch 09) during office hours (see page 231), seven days a week. When a train is due to depart or arrive – the station lies just behind the marina – the bridge remains closed for 15 minutes before or after, respectively. Multihull owners should note that the bridge has a limiting width of 11m.

The marina can take 462 yachts of up to 30m LOA, with room always found for visitors. All berths are alongside finger pontoons, with exceptionally large yachts occupying the seven hammerheads. The marina has been popular with British yachtsmen ever since it opened, and has a small but growing (and very loyal) band of long-term residents. It is also a frequent choice for owners wishing to over-winter in the Algarve, whether living aboard or returning home with occasional visits when the northern climate becomes too unpleasant.

Anchorage

Anchor northeast of the east breakwater in 5–6m over good holding in hard sand. The corridor off the beach a little further east, indicated by a number of small yellow buoys, serves the local windsurfing centre and should be left clear. The anchorage is very exposed to south and east, and a southwesterly swell may also work its way around Ponta da Piedade. Land on the beach near the Clube de Vela de Lagos or in the small harbour overlooked by the turreted Fortaleza. There is no possible anchorage inside the harbour itself – the large fishing boat basin may look tempting, but the authorities would not agree.

232 ATLANTIC SPAIN AND PORTUGAL

LAGOS

Formalities

The *GNR–Brigada Fiscal, Polícia Marítima* and *Alfândega* all have offices in the marina reception building – enquire on first arrival whether or not it is necessary to visit them. If anchored off, the skipper should call at all three offices with ship's papers, passports etc.

Facilities

Boatyards Yachtsmen are now well provided for by Sopromar Centro Nautico Lda, Estrada Sopromar , Estaleiro No 1, Lagos 37° 06′·00N 08° 40′·00W ☏ +351 282 763 889 +351 282 792 135 *Email* geral@sopromar.com www.sopromar.com Opening hours 0830-1200, 1300-1800 Mon-Sat, closed Sunday.

This is a family-run concern which has been highly praised by numerous owners. Yard hours are officially 0830–1200 and 1300–1800 Monday to Saturday, closed Sunday, but in practice at least one member of the Pereira family is nearly always onsite. English, French, German and Spanish are all spoken in addition to Portuguese. Many of the services offered – engineering, electronics, osmosis treatment with the Hotvac system, painting, rigging etc – are detailed below, but there is a very good chance that even if a particular service is not mentioned, Sopromar will be able to handle it.

Other services, including regular checking of unattended yachts left afloat in the marina, are offered by various long-term marina residents and local people – consult the noticeboard in marina reception.

Travel-lift 50-tonne capacity lift at Sopromar, with two waiting pontoons, a wide slipway and a scrubbing grid. The approach through the fishing boat harbour is said to carry adequate depths at all states of the tide and a 30m crane is available for mast removal.

Ashore there is secure lay-up space for at least 140 yachts plus 2,000m^2 of undercover workshops and storage. The hardstanding is well provided with water and electricity points, and ladders (or substantial steps for the less agile) can be borrowed. Owners are welcome to live aboard (there are immaculate toilets and showers on site), and to do their own work. 15 CCTV cameras monitor the area day and night.

Engineers Sopromar has an extensive engine repair shop, handles welding in all materials and is agent for Volvo Penta, Yanmar and Mercruiser. Pedragosa Engineering ☏ 282 688056, *Mobile* 96 7965 481 and 96 9018 894 *Email* mgsnook@bigfoot.com advertise their services for all types of work in stainless-steel and aluminium, including making one-off fittings from scratch. Finally Bluewater Yacht Services (though based mainly in Portimão, see page 239), still have engineers in Lagos who are happy to visit yachts in the marina. Their Lagos office, handling mainly brokerage, will be found on the first floor of the main commercial block.

Electronic and radio repairs At both Sopromar and Bluewater Yacht Services. In addition John Holloway, *Mobile* 91 4902 538 *Email* nojfairchild@hotmail.com handles all kinds of electrical and electronic work including radar etc.

Diver Francisco, *Mobile* 91 8287 551, will change anodes etc.

Sailmaker/sail repairs Fofovelas, ☏ 282 799425, *Mobile* 91 7550 960, *Email* fofovelas@sapo.pt, fofovelas@mail.pt, make and repair sails, as well as being agent for several well-known names.

Rigging Sopromar has a swage machine and stocks wire of all sizes.

Chandleries The chandlery at Sopromar – open 0900–1200 and 1430–1800 weekdays, 0900–1200 Saturdays – is one of the largest in Portugal, and items not in stock can generally be ordered within 48 hours. AlaRede, ☏282 792238 *Email* alarede@sapo.pt at the north end of the fishing boat basin carries some general chandlery in addition to fishing and diving equipment. There are several good ironmongery and hardware stores in the town.

Charts Local charts are available from both the marina office and AlaRede (see above). The latter will order Portuguese charts from Lisbon if required.

Water At all berths. Yachts anchored off may be able to get water in the small western harbour (but check depths in advance).

Pump out Available next to the fuel pontoon for black water only.

The Marina de Lagos looking northeast

THE ALGARVE & ANDALUCIA

ATLANTIC SPAIN AND PORTUGAL

CABO DE SÃO VICENTE TO TAVIRA

Showers Single block – but large and very well kept – at the north end of the marina's café/shops complex. Crews of yachts anchored off may be able to shower at the *clube de vela* (see below).

Launderette At the north end of the marina's café/shops complex. Tokens are available at the marina office.

Electricity At all berths, with a variety of voltages available.

Fuel Petrol and diesel pumps on the reception pontoon below the bridge, run by the marina and available during office hours only. Only American Express or cash accepted.

Bottled gas Sopromar do not arrange for gas cylinders to be refilled with butane or propane, but do have Camping Gaz. It is possible to refill a cylinder at the BP station on the road to Portimao, if you take your own adapter and are in a vehicle in which the bottle must remain. The full set of European gas refilling adapters are available from www.lpggpl.co.uk.

Clube náutico The Clube de Vela de Lagos ☎ +351 282 762 256 www.cvlagos.org *Email* mail@cvlagos.org has premises near the root of the west breakwater.

Weather forecast Posted daily at the marina reception and, during the high season, broadcast on VHF Ch 12 at 1000 and 1600.

Banks Several in the town, plus two cash dispensers in the marina complex.

Shops/provisioning Several large supermarkets, including an enormous Pingo Doce near the road bridge north of the marina (trolleys can be wheeled back and left at one of several designated 'trolley areas' for collection). Good general shopping in the older town on the west bank (direct access over the pedestrian bridge). Limited shopping in the marina complex – mostly tourist items and newspapers, including one supplying UK titles on day of issue.

Produce market Large produce and fish market on the west bank of the river (with great views from the roof terrace).

Cafés, restaurants and hotels Dozens if not hundreds, including several overlooking the marina itself.

Medical services LuzDoc ☎ 282 780700, a private medical clinic which also handles dental problems, has an office in the marina at Núcleo Gil Eanes 13 and a larger facility in the town, where there is also a public hospital.

Communications

Post office In the town.

Mailing address The marina office will hold mail for visiting yachts – c/o Marina de Lagos, Edificio da Administração, Sítio da Ponte, 8600–780 Lagos, Portugal. It is important that the envelope carries the name of the yacht in addition to that of the addressee.

Public telephones Several around the marina complex.

Internet Owners can connect their own laptop at the marina office, or use WiFi from on board (the necessary cards are on sale at reception). Alternatively there are public terminals at the Regatta Club Bar

Car hire/taxis Can be arranged via the marina office or in the town.

Trains Brand new station just behind the marina complex, the western end of the (distinctly slow) Algarve coastal line.

Air services Faro international airport is about 50 minutes by taxi or, at a fraction of the taxi fare, 90 minutes by train (though a taxi will still be needed between the station and the airport).

Adjacent anchorage

Off the beach at Praia da Luz (37°04′·82N 008°43′·61W), 3·5M west of Ponta da Piedade. Reported to be a pleasant anchorage in settled conditions off a small slipway, but fully exposed to the south.

Right and below Ponta de Piedade on the approach to Lagos. The limestone rocks have been sculpted into caves, arches and pillars and are a popular lunch stop *Jane Russell*

ALVOR

Alvor

Location
37°06'·87N 8°37'·06W (entrance)

Tides
Standard port Lisbon
Mean time differences
HW –0025 ±0010; LW –0030 ±0005
Heights in metres
MHWS	MHWN	MLWN	MLWS
3·3	2·6	1·3	0·6

Principal lights
West breakwater Fl.R.4s8m7M
  White tower, red bands 4m
East breakwater Fl.G.4s8m7M
  White tower, green bands 4m

Warning
Night entry not feasible due to shifting shoals which call for eyeball navigation. Any buoys encountered are likely to be unlit.

Attractive, windswept anchorage flanked by some tourist development

Although until relatively recently Alvor was little more than a small fishing village, it has a significant history, and its formidable fortress attracted the Crusaders in 1189. It is believed the Carthaginians founded Alvor, it was considered an important port by the Romans and it was allowed to issue its own money. Its importance is confirmed by the ruins of a wealthy Roman villa located slightly inland from the present village. After conquest by the Moors, it was finally recovered in 1250. Most of the original village and the castle were destroyed in the earthquakes of 1532 and 1755. Construction of twin breakwaters at the entrance during the early 1990s, allied to extensive dredging within, has opened the Rio Alvor to the cruising yachtsman. Even so, care is still required and the entrance should not be attempted at low water, when swell is running, in onshore winds, on the ebb tide or at night.

The town is touristy but attractive, with good shops, restaurants and cafés, and the anchorage a pleasant change from fishing harbours and marinas – and a paradise for birdwatchers.

Continuing pride in the area's maritime heritage is confirmed by the flawless condition in which the village's old rowing and sailing lifeboat is maintained. The red doors to her boathouse can hardly be missed, and now feature a glass panel through which she can be admired when they are closed.

The Alvor breakwaters and entrance from the south-southeast

THE ALGARVE & ANDALUCIA

ATLANTIC SPAIN AND PORTUGAL 235

CABO DE SÃO VICENTE TO TAVIRA

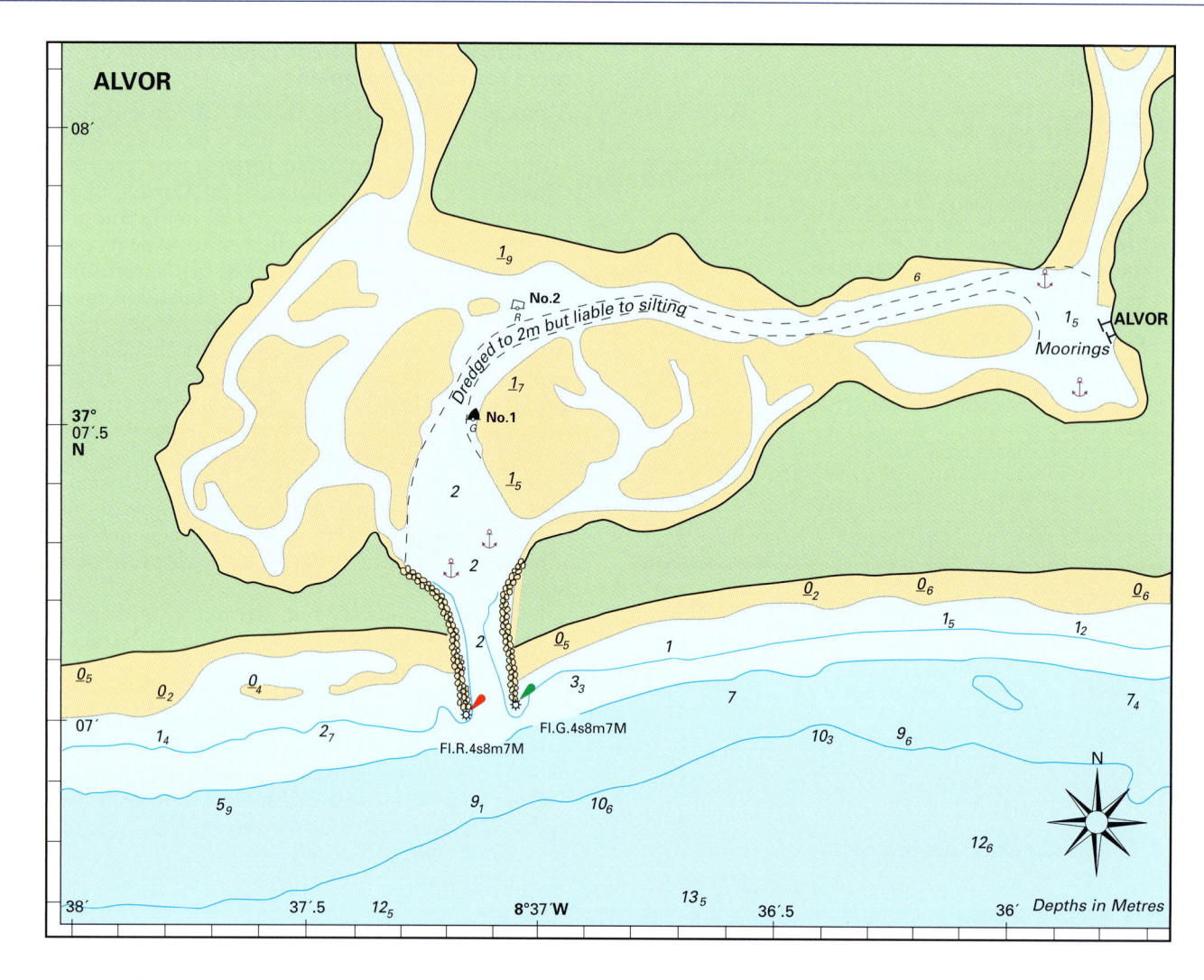

Approach
If coastal sailing, Alvor lies 2·3M east of Lagos and 4·3M west of Portimão, surrounded by sandy beaches – the Meia Praia, one of the Algarve's finest, stretches between Lagos and Alvor. The nearest major lights are Ponta da Piedade west of Lagos, and Ponta de Altar, close east of Portimão – Alvor no longer has a major light of its own, though both breakwaters are lit. High man-made sand dunes (created from dredged material) stand close each side of the entrance with conspicuous high-rise apartments further east.

Entrance
Parallel breakwaters bracket the entrance channel which, in common with other Rio estuaries, suffers from serious silting. Although dredged to a nominal 4m this can be reduced to 2m in some years. Enter on the half flood keeping to the middle of the narrow channel on a bearing of approximately 352°. Once inside, the estuary opens out and it is possible to anchor in the pool just inside the entrance, where at least 2m should be found at all times.

An added complication to navigation is that buoy positions inside in the Rio Alvor have been reported to be out of position on occasions over the years. In October 2017 for example the starboard hand green buoy No.1 was reported out of position at 37°07'·589N 8°37'·250W. Local guidance should be sought where possible.

The narrow, dredged channel leading up to the basin off the town is most easily followed below half tide on the flood when the fringing sandbanks are still uncovered. The channel should carry a nominal 2m at MLWS but it can be less. If in doubt the dinghy should be sent ahead to recce.

Anchorage
Anchor near the entrance, as described above, or off the village to the north of the moorings, an area which, in summer, may become very crowded. It is understood that holding in the river in the approach to the town, which is where visiting yachts have been seen anchored, is not good. Shelter in the basin is excellent and holding good over muddy sand. A small charge is sometimes made. The fairway leading to the fishermen's quay is no longer clearly defined by small craft moorings but must still not be impeded.

There are two pontoons with floating hammerheads, and though both are adorned with notices stating that it is 'Forbidden to place arts of

ALVOR

Looking northeast over the shallow lagoon at Alvor, backed by the channel leading to the anchorage off the town

fishing and to park any kind of boats', both are colonised by flotillas of dinghies. A long painter would clearly be an advantage.

A tidal lagoon just off the bottom left of the photo has been created for the conservation of the local wildlife habitat.

Facilities

Water by can from one of the waterfront cafés, with supermarkets, general shopping and a vast choice of restaurants in the town (the local shell fish is reputed to be particularly good). Services include a post office, public telephones, taxis and buses (at the roundabout), and Portimão station about 5·5km away.

The anchorage off Alvor town looking northwest

ATLANTIC SPAIN AND PORTUGAL   237

THE ALGARVE & ANDALUCIA

CABO DE SÃO VICENTE TO TAVIRA

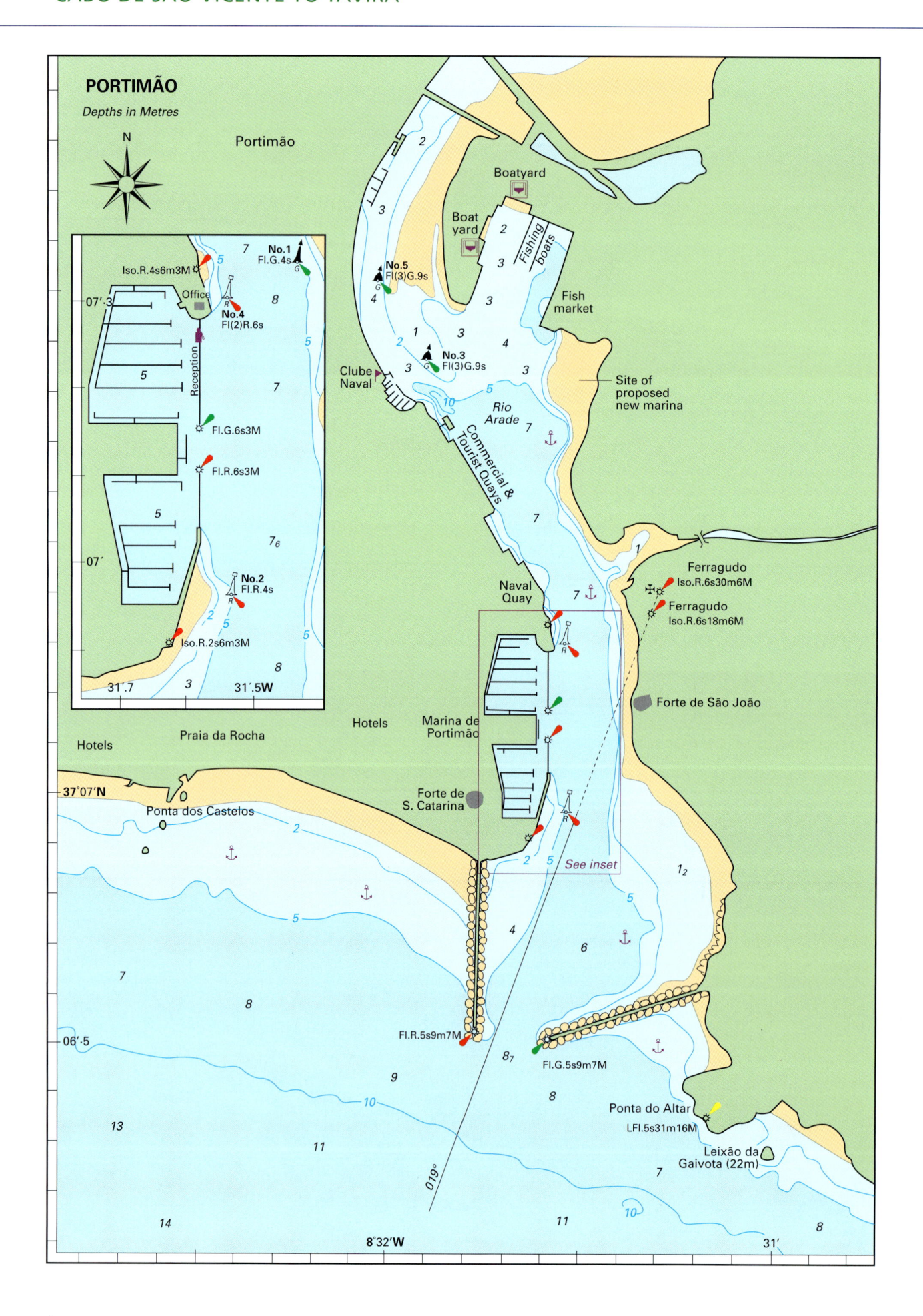

PORTIMÃO

Portimão

Location
37°06'·37N 8°31'·7W (entrance)

Tides
Standard port Lisbon
Mean time differences
HW −0025 ±0010; LW −0030 ±0005
Heights in metres
MHWS	MHWN	MLWN	MLWS
3·3	2·6	1·4	0·7

Principal lights
Ponta do Altar LFl.5s31m16M
   Square white tower and building 10m
Ldg Lts 019° *Front* **Ferragudo** Iso.R.6s18m6M
   White tower, red bands 4m
Rear 54m from front Iso.R.6s30m6M
   White tower, red bands 5m
West breakwater Fl.R.5s9m7M
   White tower, red bands 7m
East breakwater Fl.G.5s9m7M
   White tower, green bands 7m

Marina, southeast
   Iso.R.2s6m3M White column, red bands
Marina south pontoon head
   Fl.R.6s3M White column, red bands
Marina north pontoon head
   Fl.G.6s3M White column, green bands
Marina, northeast
   Iso.R.4s 6m3M White column, red bands

Communications
   Marina de Portimão
   VHF Ch 09, 16 (0830–2100 1 July–31 August, otherwise 0900–1800).
   Weather information in Portuguese and English
   VHF Ch 09 at 1000 daily from 1 July–31 August
   ☎ +351 282 400 680
   Email info@marinaportimao.com.pt
   www.marinadeportimao.com.pt

Portimão from the south. The anchorage can be seen inside the east breakwater

ATLANTIC SPAIN AND PORTUGAL

THE ALGARVE & ANDALUCIA

CABO DE SÃO VICENTE TO TAVIRA

All-weather entrance leading to a large, modern marina

Portimão on the Rio Arade has long been a busy fishing harbour, also handling small naval and commercial vessels. Since 2000, however, the waterfront on the west side near the entrance has been transformed with the opening of the large Marina de Portimão. Almost overnight Portimão began to rival Lagos and Vilamoura in its provision of berths and other services for visiting yachts. The marina staff speak English and their attitude is helpful and friendly.

The town of Portimão, on the west bank nearly 2M from the harbour mouth, is old and agreeable, but the beach resort of Praia da Rocha is somewhat brash. The region's undoubted gem is the waterside village of Ferragudo on the east side of the estuary. If settled in the marina, make the effort to launch the dinghy, cross the river, and enjoy a lunch of *sardinhas* grilled on a charcoal brazier on the tiny quay with seagulls wheeling overhead. A stroll through the village's steep cobbled alleys (mostly impassable to cars) will work off any resulting somnolence.

Approach

If inshore sailing, from Lagos to Portimão the coast consists of sandy beaches with a backdrop of hills. East of Portimão there are a few small sandy beaches but the shore is mainly rocky with cliffs. There are no off-lying hazards.

The anchorage and moorings off Ferragudo looking W towards the Naval Quay *Jane Russell*

Entrance

Entrance is safe in all but the heaviest onshore conditions, and should present no problems by day or night. The ends of the breakwaters are lit – these lights line up on 097° for those coming from Lagos. The charted leading line to enter the harbour itself is 019° (two red and white striped posts close east of Ferragudo church). However this leads close to a growing shoal around the head of the west breakwater, and about equidistant between the two heads offers better depths. From there leave buoy No.2 close to port before ducking through the marina entrance (both sides of which are lit) and securing to the inner side of the north pontoon.

If venturing further upstream, the buoyage is straightforward with a pair of lit buoys and then two unlit starboard hand buoys. The channel as far as Ponta São Francisco has a least depth of around 7m, but soundings shoal rapidly outside the buoyed channel.

Berthing

Nearly all the inner side of the marina's north pontoon is used for reception, though during office hours a yacht which makes contact via VHF or mobile phone may well be routed directly to a berth in the marina proper. Even when the tide is running at spring ebb it is claimed that the marina remains unaffected and securing is never a problem, though it has been reported that swell works into the north basin in southerly winds. Reception is housed in the circular orange building overlooking the pontoon

Looking across the river towards the Forte de São João, with port hand buoy No.4 in the foreground *Anne Hammick*

The anchorage inside the breakwater at Portimao looking SSW towards the entrance *Jane Russell*

240　ATLANTIC SPAIN AND PORTUGAL

PORTIMÃO

With little unused space near the marina, a sizeable boatyard has been established upriver in the old fishing harbour. The old centre of Portimão can be seen across the river at right, with the Clube Naval de Portimão and smallcraft basin (not open to visitors) at left

and operates 0830–2030 from 1 July to 31 August and 0900–1800 at other times.

Although having a total capacity of 620 berths including one 50m slot, nearly all in 5m or more depths, the marina has become crowded with the larger berths being particularly popular. Its only real downside, however, is its sheer size. Those berthed centrally face a lengthy walk to shops, toilets and showers (a bicycle would quickly prove its worth), while those in the south basin, though conveniently near most of the facilities, may be kept awake far into the night by music from the bars and karaoke joints. In compensation, there is an excellent beach nearby and swimming pool for hotel and marina users. Security throughout the marina is excellent, with two guards patrolling at all times in addition to card access gates and facilities.

There are no other visitors' berthing option on the Rio Arade. The upstream basin near the new Clube Naval building is reserved for local smallcraft, and visitors are no longer welcome on the old yacht pontoon just below the bridge. Rumours of a 'new marina' beyond the bridge relate to a private leisure club with a single, equally private, pontoon for small motorboats, limited by an air height of 5m beneath the old road bridge.

It is understood that plans to build a second yacht marina on the east side of the river just upstream of Ferragudo remain a pipe dream. A website gives an artist's impression at www.marinasdeferragudo.com (① +351 282 414 480). If this comes to fruition a further 330 berths for vessels of up to 50m and 5m draught would become available.

Anchorage

The anchorage inside the east breakwater is secure with good holding in sand, though sometimes affected by swell and/or wash. It would be a safe choice if arriving by night, but note that the bottom shelves steeply between the 5m and 2m contours. Alternatively, anchor off Ferragudo near the fishing boat moorings, in 3–4m over mud, but note that available space is very variable. Be sure to leave the marked channel clear as the fishing fleet appears to leave en masse in the hours before daybreak (if the throb of their engines does not wake you, their wash will).

To go ashore at Ferragudo, land your dinghy at the steps on the quay on top of which there is a stout iron ring. At low water, you will need a long line to reach the ring on the top of the quay. Also note that numerous taxi/ferry boats land passengers at the steps, so you should do your best to leave the dinghy out of their way.

No charge is made for anchoring in either spot.

A dinghy can safely be left at the marina, for a charge, but note that this can be substantial! A marina landing also involves a long walk into the town. Upstream possibilities are limited, though it would certainly be worth asking both at the smallcraft basin and at the *Clube Naval* de Portimão (where, if permission is granted, it would clearly be tactful to patronise the bar).

Formalities

All paperwork is carried out in the marina office with copies passed to the usual officials. None need to be seen, but non-EU registered yachts, or those carrying non-EU citizens, may be visited by one or more sets of officials in the days after arrival.

Facilities

Boatyard The marina's boatyard is some distance away in the old fishing harbour just short of the old road bridge (see plan page 238), with the compensation of almost unlimited lay-up area. Security is good, with high fences, gates locked overnight and regular patrols. Lockerage can be rented if required.

While lifting, pressure-hosing and chocking-up are carried out by marina employees, all other work is done by specialist contractors – see below. DIY is permitted, and owners may live aboard whilst ashore (the yacht area is provided with a single, rather basic, shower and toilet). There is a supermarket within walking distance.

ATLANTIC SPAIN AND PORTUGAL

Adjacent to the marina yard there is a complex that has several workshops and contractors' own yards. These may be cheaper and do deals for winter storage. All share the 50 or 300 tonne hoists. The commercial yard of Rosa Cabral & Soares LDA does metal bashing. Comprehensive workshops are available for most trades in the complex.

Travel-lift Choice of two at the boatyard, of 50-tonne and 300-tonne capacity respectively. The latter is believed to be the largest travel-hoist in mainland Portugal. Book at the marina office.

Engineers, electronics, and general maintenance Amongst the four or five contractors who regularly work in the yard, Bluewater Yacht Services, ☎ +351 282 432 405 *Email* info@bluewateralgarve.com www.bluewateralgarve.com, who also have an office near the marina's northern basin, appear to offer by far the widest range of services. Owner Paul Mallett is an engineer (as well as an Ocean Yachtmaster) and other members of the eight permanent staff can handle electrical work and electronics (installation and repair of water-makers and refrigeration are specialities), repairs in all materials, osmosis treatment (including slurry blasting and peeling), painting, in fact all disciplines necessary to keep yachts of up to 20m or so in good working order. Unattended yachts can be collected from and returned to the marina, and finally all work, or damage, should one be so unlucky, can be overseen/assessed by a fully qualified surveyor, recognised by Lloyds. Languages spoken currently include English, Portuguese, Spanish, German, Dutch and some French, and Paul and his team are happy to travel throughout southern Portugal and Spain to carry out work on boats in situ.

Sailmaker/sail repairs Marine Canvas, ☎ 967 084 927 *Email* marinecanvas@sapo.pt, in the boatyard area make covers, awnings etc, and can handle minor sail repairs. While not sailmakers themselves, Bluewater Yacht Services have contacts throughout the Algarve and can arrange for sails of almost any size to be made or repaired.

Rigging Bluewater Yacht Services can supply and fit all sizes of rigging, and have in the past replaced entire rigs on yachts in the 20m range.

Chandlery There is a good selection in the boatyard area at Aradenáutica Lda and also at Sopramar: *Email* portimao@sopromar.com ☎+351 282 425 173. The latter has its headquarters in Lagos.

Charts A stock of local charts is held by the marina office, while Portuguese charts for more distant waters can be ordered overnight from Lisbon.

Liferaft servicing Another item in the Bluewater Yacht Services portfolio

Water Throughout the marina, and in the boatyard.

Showers Two blocks in the marina complex, with card access, but quite a long walk from some berths.

Launderette Next to the marina office, with six washers and three dryers all token-operated, open 0900–1800. Again, a long walk from some berths.

Electricity Throughout the marina, and in the boatyard.

Fuel Two diesel and petrol pumps near the root of the north pontoon, operational during office hours. Fuel should be paid for in cash – though a credit card will be accepted in an emergency, a surcharge will be imposed (and note that it is a long walk from the fuel berth to the marina's single cash dispenser).

There is a second yacht fuelling berth just upstream of the *clube naval*, but operating times and other details are not known.

Bottled gas Camping Gaz is available in the town. The name of the BP filling station near Portimao has changed to RUBIS but note that it does not refill cylinders any more. There is, however, an LPG gas filling station for cars to the west of Boliqueime which is used by caravans. There are adapters for foreign bottles available and an 11kg bottle can be refilled in a minute. The station is to the west of Bouliqueime on the N270, a northern spur from the N125. Autocrew/ C.M.Pedro, EN270-8100-089 Boliqueime (Junto à En 125) ☎+351 289 360 767 37°12'·81N 8°15'·93W www.cmpedro.com *Email* cmpedroautoreparadoralda@gmail.com

Weather forecast Posted daily at the marina office and during the high season, broadcast on VHF Ch 09 at 1000.

Clube naval The Clube Naval de Portimão has smart new premises complete with their own pontoon on the Quai Vasco da Gama, just upriver of the smallcraft basin.

Banks In Praia da Rocha and Portimão, with a cash dispenser near the southwest corner of the marina's south basin.

Shops/provisioning In Praia da Rocha and Portimão, though considerably better (and cheaper) in the latter. See also under Buses, below.

There is a mini-market near the southwest corner of the marina, opposite the cash dispenser. Nearby are the usual range of tourist shops and newsagents. Limited shopping in Ferragudo.

Produce markets In Portimão and Ferragudo.

Cafés, restaurants and hotels Every second building in Praia da Rocha, if not even more, with a large hotel fronting much of the marina. The waterfront restaurant on the end of the central spur is said to be good.

Medical services In Praia da Rocha and Portimão – contact is best made via the marina office.

Communications

Post offices In Praia da Rocha and Portimão.

Mailing address The marina office will hold mail for visiting yachts – c/o Marina de Portimão, Edificio Administrativo, 8500 Portimão, Portugal. It is important that the envelope carries the name of the yacht in addition to that of the addressee.

Telephones Several kiosks around the marina complex, and in the town.

Internet WiFi is available throughout the marina, and there is a desk in the reception building with ethernet points for laptops. Failing this there is free internet access at the library in the old town, plus several cafés with WiFi in nearby Praia da Rocha.

Car hire/taxis No shortage. Both can be ordered via marina reception.

Buses Frequent if slow. A minibus runs daily from the reception area to the Modelo supermarket and the old town – enquire at the marina office for times.

Trains Station north of Portimão, and a convenient way to reach Faro airport.

Air services Faro International Airport is about 55km away.

Adjacent anchorage

Good anchorage in 5m is to be found 1·6M west of the west breakwater at Portimao at the west end of Praia da Rocha beach. It is well sheltered from a strong northwest wind and landing can be made on a small beach amid rocks and stacks before walking to the main beach. Beware a shoal patch carrying less than 2m extending 70m southeast from the southernmost of the two rocks off Ponta dos Castelos, itself 0·7M west of the breakwater. The anchorage is probably suitable for daytime use only, and open to the south.

ALBUFEIRA

Albufeira

Location
37°04'·82N 8°15'·24W (entrance)

Tides
Standard port Lisbon
Mean time differences
HW −0010 ±0025; LW 0000 ±0005
Heights in metres
MHWS	MHWN	MLWN	MLWS
3·6	2·8	1·5	0·7

Principal lights
Albufeira Oc.6s30m11M White column, red bands
North breakwater Fl(2)G.5s9m4M
   White column, three green bands 3m
South breakwater Fl(2)R.5s9m4M
   White column, two red bands 3m
Marina E Inner channel, north side Fl.G.2s4m1·5M
   White column, three green bands 3m
Marina W Inner channel, south side Fl.R.2s4m1·5M
   White column, three red bands 3m

Night entry
Though narrow, the entrance is well lit and should present no problems in normal conditions. However swells may build up outside in strong southerlies, making close approach in darkness unwise

Communications
Marina de Albufeira
VHF Ch 09 ☏ +351 289 510 180
Email info@marinaalbufeira.com
www.marinaalbufeira.com
(0900–2100 1 June-15 September, 0900–1800 1 November-31 March, 0900–1900 at other times)

The harbour and marina at Albufeira looking west-northwest

ATLANTIC SPAIN AND PORTUGAL

CABO DE SÃO VICENTE TO TAVIRA

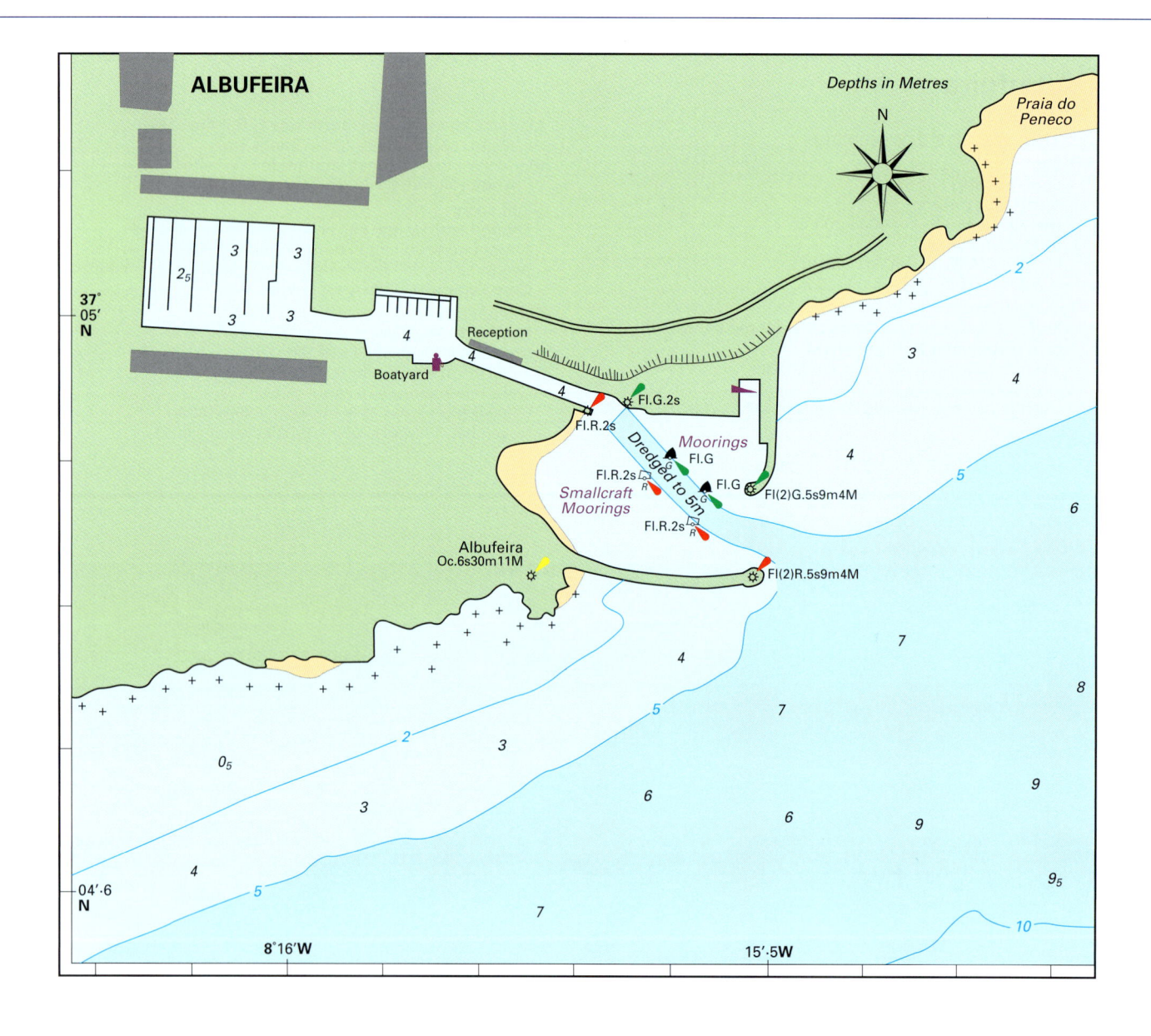

A marina distant from the main tourist centre

Berthed in the Marina de Albufeira it is hard to believe that the somewhat brash tourist resort of the same name is less than 2km away. Due at least in part to its position in a natural amphitheatre, the complex forms its own enclosed world, subtly emphasised by the quirky architecture and unusual colours of the surrounding buildings.

The inner basin is overlooked by apartments, villas, shops restaurants and bars, and is a lively spot.

Approach

The marina lies just under 15M east of Portimão and 5M west of Vilamoura. The approach is straightforward and without hazards, marked by Ponta Baleeira light on the cliffs close south in addition to the two breakwater lights. However by day the stone breakwaters may be difficult to pick out against the cliffs behind, particularly with an afternoon sun. Currently the marina lies at the southwest end of the considerable Albufeira conurbation, but it can only be a matter of time before this leapfrogs onto the ochre cliffs to the southwest. Several fishing floats were observed in the approach, a potential hazard to a yacht's propeller, particularly after dark.

Entrance

The marina's outer entrance is just over 100m wide and faces almost due east. Although this may well make entry in southerly winds more feasible than is the case with some of its neighbours, it should still be approached with caution in these conditions. The slightly angled channel through the outer harbour is indicated by four good-sized buoys, all of which are lit, and is dredged to 5m. Smallcraft lie to moorings on either side of the channel.

The long, relatively narrow cutting which gives access to the inner basin carries 4m along its length, as does the small intermediate basin where larger yachts are berthed. The long reception pontoon lies

244 ATLANTIC SPAIN AND PORTUGAL

ALBUFEIRA

on the starboard hand near the far end of this passage, with the marina office behind. Surge may affect the reception pontoon even in relatively light conditions making generous fendering wise.

Berthing
The Marina de Albufeira contains 475 berths, including one for a yacht of 30m or more, all alongside finger pontoons. Around 80 berths are reserved for visiting yachts in depths which decrease from 4m near the entrance to 2·5m in the western part of the basin. Once inside, shelter is excellent, though some surge may penetrate as far as the larger yacht berths. Security is also taken seriously, with CCTV and security patrols in addition to card access to the pontoon gates (most of which are, thoughtfully, provided with a small plan of the marina with essential services marked).

The office staff speak Spanish and some French in addition to English. Most unusually there is no weekly or monthly berthing rate, the shortest 'long term' it is possible to book for being nine months.

Formalities
None of the usual triumvirate of officials, the *GNR–Brigada Fiscal*, *Polícia Marítima* and *Alfândega*, have offices on site, though copies of the paperwork are circulated to them electronically. For skippers of EU-registered vessels with EU crews arriving from within Portugal, that is the end of the matter. Others might receive a visit from *Imigração* (immigration) or perhaps *Alfândega* (customs), though the onus was on the officials to visit the yacht rather than vice versa. Marina officials will advise.

Anchorage
Anchoring in the outer harbour is not permitted – in any case there would be no room to swing between the moored smallcraft – and though in theory one could drop a hook outside in the wide bay running east to Albufeira resort there is little protection.

Facilities
Boatyard Contractors operate within the boatyard area to the south of the intermediate basin. For services see below.

Travel-lift 70-tonne capacity lift plus 6·3-tonne crane – book at reception. The marina does not provide props, which are currently available only from boatyard contractors.

Engineers, electronics and maintenance Although PowerCool *Mobile* 91 7866 373 *Email* info@powercoolmarine.com www.powercool.org, specialises in generators and air-conditioning (Kohler and Dometic respectively), British owner Michael Killeen is cheerfully flexible and happy to handle anything from engineering (he spent 10 years working on large aircraft engines) through electronics to antifouling and polishing. They are also a Volvo Penta agent and service centre. Some spares are held in stock, while others can be ordered direct from the manufacturer or, failing that, fabricated locally. Should a task be outside PowerCool's scope, Michael will almost certainly 'know a man who can'.

Ben Smith (see *Chandlery*, below) is also an experienced marine engineer, formerly based in Vilamoura.

The marina basin at Albufeira. The reception pontoon can just be seen at the head of the narrow approach channel on the right

CABO DE SÃO VICENTE TO TAVIRA

Looking across the approach channel towards the reception pontoon, with a large ketch tucked in behind it *Anne Hammick*

General maintenance Riominho Náutica *Mobile* 96 8492 215 *Email* albufeira@riominho.com www.riominho.com handles yacht valeting and straightforward maintenance including painting/antifouling and minor GRP repairs. Alternatively Peter Heitman, *Mobile* 91 7262 359, offers carpentry services.
Diver Available via the marina office.
Sailmaker The boatyard buildings contain a purpose-built sail loft, but may not be operational. However Vilamoura is not far up the road…
Chandlery Tudo Marine Services Lda, *Mobile* 91 8608 809 and 91 2556 134, *Email* tudomarine@yahoo.co.uk, run by Ben Smith and Gavin Hawkins has premises in the boatyard area. Stock focuses on general chandlery and engine spares.
   Nearby is Santa María Artigos Náuticos, whose other shop overlooks the smallcraft marina at Faro. General chandlery, lifejackets and some clothes are likely to feature, with good English spoken.
Water At all berths.
Showers Temporarily housed in portacabins on the central spur, with two permanent shower blocks planned for the north side of the basin.
Launderette A launderette is likely to be built in due course, but in the meantime laundry can be left at the marina office to be done elsewhere.
Electricity At all berths.
Fuel Diesel and petrol pumps on a pontoon on the port side, opposite and slightly beyond the reception pontoon, open during office hours. Credit cards are accepted.
Holding tank pump-out At the fuel pontoon.
Bottled gas Camping Gaz exchanges at a filling station in the town, but no refills. It would also be worth enquiring at the chandlery.
Weather forecast Posted daily at the marina office.
Clube náutico Planned for the central spur.
Bank A cash dispenser is in the marina complex.

Shops, provisioning Mini-market in the marina complex, with other shops about 400m (most of it uphill) to the northeast.
Cafés, restaurants and hotels Several cafés and restaurants in the buildings overlooking the inner basin (some of which offer discounts to berth-holders and/or will deliver to yachts). A hotel is to be included in the second phase of the development.
Medical services First aid clinic in Albufeira and hospital in Faro – the office will be happy to advise.

Communications

Post office Planned, but not a priority. Several in Albufeira.
Mailing address The marina office will hold mail for visiting yachts – c/o Marina de Albufeira, Sítio da Orada, 8201-918 Albufeira, Portugal. Envelopes should give both the name of the yacht and that of the addressee.
Telephones Numerous kiosks dotted around the marina complex.
Internet Visitors can either use one of the office computers to check Email, or bring their own laptop to the reception building. WiFi may be installed in the longer term.
Fax service At the marina office.
Car hire/taxis Can be ordered via the marina office.
Buses Bus stop at the roundabout not far from the reception building.
Trains Station at Ferreiras, about 6km distant.
Air services Faro airport is 30km away – about 30 minutes by taxi.

Vilamoura

Location
37°04′N 8°07′·35W (entrance)

Tides
Standard port Lisbon
Mean time differences (at Albufeira)
HW −0010 ±0025; LW 0000 ±0005
Heights in metres
MHWS MHWN MLWN MLWS
3·6   2·8   1·5   0·7

Principal lights
Vilamoura Fl.5s17m19M
 Yellow tower on Navy control tower
Vilamoura marina
West breakwater Fl.R.4s13m5M
 White tower, red bands 6m
East breakwater Fl.G.4s13m5M
 White tower, green bands 7m
Quarteira (fishing) harbour
West mole Fl.R.3s13m6M
 White tower, red bands 6m
West mole spur Fl(2)R.4s8m3M
 White tower, red bands 4m
East mole Fl.G.3s12m6M
 White tower, green bands 6m

Notes
Night entry straightforward other than in strong southerlies.

Communications
Port Authority
☏ +351 289 313 214
Fax +351 289 310 580
Marina de Vilamoura
VHF Ch 09, 16 call *Vilamoura Radio* (24 hours)
Weather information in Portuguese and English:
VHF Ch 12 at 1000 daily.
☏ +351 289 310 560
Email marinavilamoura@lusort.com
www.marinadevilamoura.com

The approach to Vilamoura Marina with the reception pontoon in the centre, the boatyard on the left and the large basin behind

ATLANTIC SPAIN AND PORTUGAL   247

Large, well-established marina backed by vast tourist complex

The marina and its adjacent boatyard are surrounded by a large tourist complex which includes four golf courses, a casino and countless hotels, and offers a wide choice of open-air cafés, boutiques, souvenir shops etc. In contrast, a serious effort is being made to establish a 200 hectare Environmental Park just west of the marina to preserve the wetland home of many species of birds. There are also Roman ruins close by, together with a small museum or, for the less culturally inclined, an excellent beach within a short dinghy ride, or in walking distance if berthed on the west side of the basin. There is also a beach to the east of the entrance under the Tivoli hotel.

Vilamoura is a popular and secure place to leave a yacht, either long-term or for a few months – perhaps between a summer passage southwards and the late autumn passage to Madeira, the Canaries and beyond – in which case its proximity to Faro airport is an obvious advantage.

Approach

The coast on both sides of Vilamoura is low and rocky and the breakwaters may be difficult to pick out. The marina is surrounded by conspicuous tower blocks, particularly to the east where the 12 storey Tivoli hotel painted white with coloured balconies stands close to the entrance (the west end of the Tivoli can just be seen in the photograph). A small fishing harbour lies a few hundred metres east of the entrance, with the tower blocks of Quarteira beyond. There is no excuse for confusing the two entrances. Vilamoura to the west is considerably larger, and though the light characteristics of each breakwater pair are surprisingly similar the marina has its own major light close to the reception quay. Nevertheless more than one arriving yacht has managed to end up in the wrong place.

Entrance

The entrance is about 100m wide, between breakwaters which stretch a good 500m from the shore, and can be dangerous in strong southerly winds (true of most Algarve harbours). Previously congested with moored fishing boats the outer basin remains empty, but anchoring is not permitted.

Head for the 60m wide channel leading to the inner basin and secure to the long reception pontoon beneath the control tower and offices. Depths in the outer harbour are approximately 4m, decreasing to 3·3m off the reception pontoon and in the southern part of the basin and 2m in the northeast section. Although silting is an ongoing problem, particularly in the outer basin, periodic dredging has largely kept it at bay.

Berthing

The Marina de Vilamoura contains around 1,000 berths (the exact number appears to be flexible) and can take vessels of 60m or more. On arrival secure to

The inner basin at Vilamoura Marina seen from the southwest

VILAMOURA

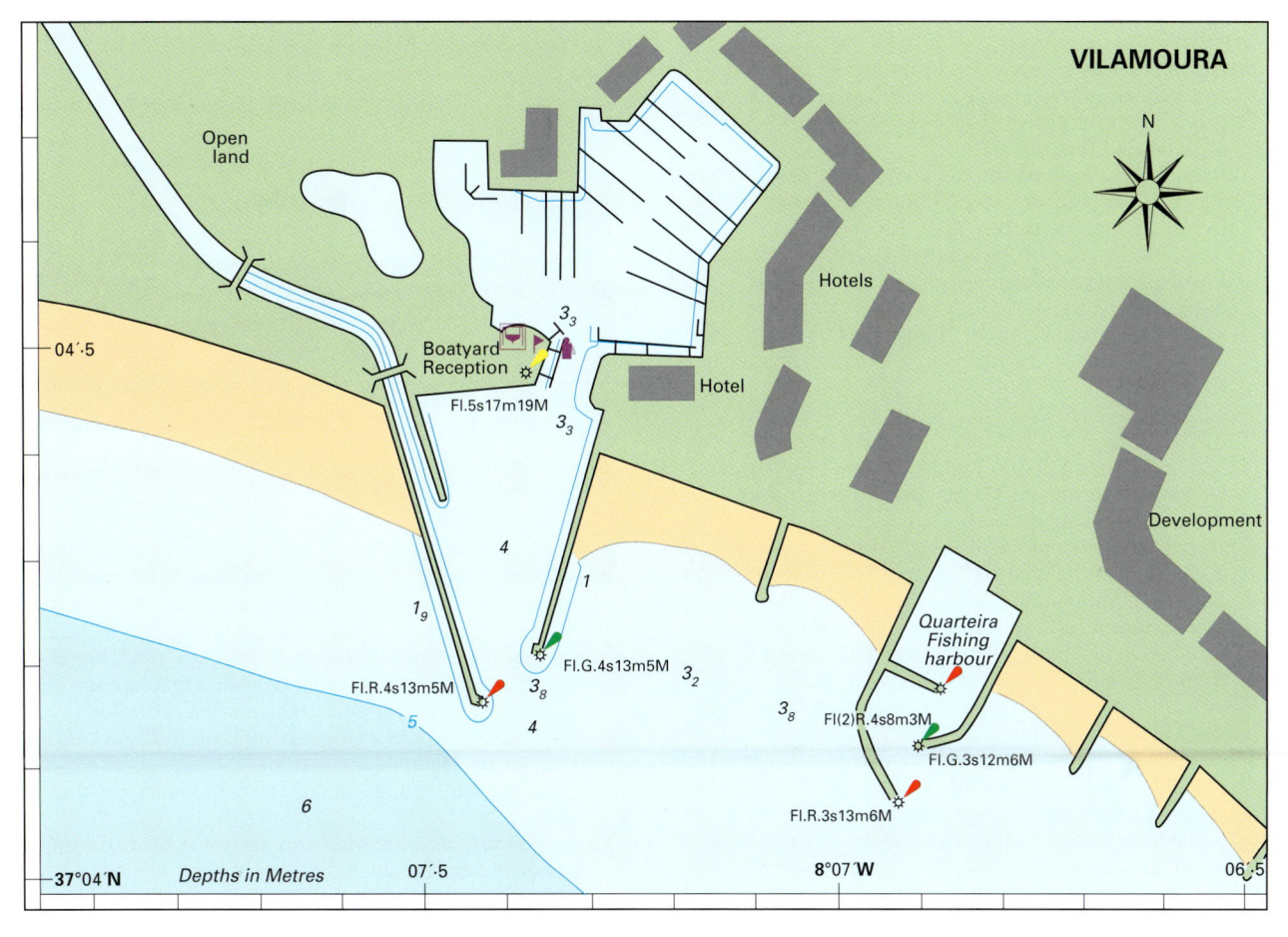

the reception pontoon until clearance procedures have been completed and a berth allocated. Office hours all year are 0830–1930 (1 April–31 May), to 2130 (1 June–15 September), to 1930 (16 September–3 October), and to 1830 (1 November–31 March). If arriving outside these times it will be necessary to remain at the reception pontoon until the offices open at 0830. Water and electricity are both available on the reception pontoon. Security throughout the marina is assured by CCTV, frequent patrols and pontoon gates operated by electronic cards.

Formalities

All paperwork (for which ship's papers, passports and evidence of insurance are required) is carried out in the marina office overlooking the reception pontoon. Where non-EU nationals and/or yachts are involved it is still necessary for the skipper to visit *Imigração*, while the *Alfândega* are most interested in yachts which have arrived from outside Portugal, and particularly from outside the EU. Both offices open seven days a week, maintaining the same hours as the marina office itself.

The outer breakwaters of Vilamoura Marina seen from the southwest with Quarteira fishing harbour in the background

ATLANTIC SPAIN AND PORTUGAL   249

CABO DE SÃO VICENTE TO TAVIRA

Facilities

Boatyard Services are provided by a range of different contractors, or owners can do their own work. Largest is probably BEB Carpentry Services, ☎ +351 289 302 797 *Mobile* +351 96 9097 580 *Email* bebcarpentry@hotmail.com run by Brian Brennan which can handle almost anything in timber or GRP. Others include Heitmann Yacht Services, ☎ +351 289 360 610; Technimarine, ☎ +351 289 301 070 *Email* tecni-marine@mail.telepac.pt; Lacomar Lda (osmosis experts), ☎ +351 289 312 470 *Mobile* 96 5089 867; and Emmanuel Bosch, *Mobile* +351 96 8959 359, who between them offer carpentry services, painting and GRP repairs.

Travel-lifts 30- and 60-tonne capacity hoists, plus two smaller cranes. The concreted hardstanding, which can take a maximum of 200 yachts, has good security, and DIY is not a problem. There is also a tidal grid for boats drawing less than 2m.

Engineers A number of engineering workshops are established in the boatyard area, including agents for Volvo and Yanmar and others specialising in welding and fabrication. A full list, including contact numbers, is included in the marina brochure (available on request from mid February onwards).

Electrical, electronic and radio repairs Janusz Oszczepalski, ☎ +351 289 322 615

Sailmaker/sail repairs The JP Velas-Doyle loft ☎ +351 289 314 827 *Email* j.p.velas@mail.telepac.pt will be found on the second floor of the reception building. Peter and Joanne Keeping, who together with their team speak seven languages, will build new sails from scratch, repair old ones, and handle canvaswork including spray hoods and biminis. They also supply roller furling gears and running rigging.

Chandlery A branch of Náutica Capitalcar, ☎ +351 289 314 764, overlooks the boatyard area – well-stocked and carrying a good range of maintenance materials. Open 0900–1200 and 1400–1800 weekdays, 0900–1230 Saturday. Other chandleries exist around the marina basin, but tending towards the decorative rather than the practical.

Charts Both Admiralty and Portuguese charts can be ordered from Lisbon via the marina office.

Water At all berths and the reception/fuel pontoon.

Showers Behind the marina office (effectively in the boatyard compound) plus two other blocks around the marina basin, all with card access.

Holding tank pump-out A very useful free service, though almost unique in this area, is the provision of a pump-out barge to empty a yacht's holding tank without the need for her to leave the berth. Arrange via marina reception.

Launderettes One on each side of the marina basin.

Electricity At all berths and the reception/fuel pontoon.

Fuel Diesel and petrol pumps will be found at the north end of the reception pontoon, open marina office hours and with credit cards accepted.

Bottled gas Camping Gaz cylinders can be exchanged at the chandlery, where it may also be possible to get other bottles refilled.

Clube náutico The Clube Náutico de Vilamoura has premises next to the marina office, overlooking the reception pontoon. Crews of visiting yachts are made welcome.

Weather forecast Posted daily at the marina office and broadcast on VHF Ch 12 at 1000.

Banks Several cash dispensers (ATMs) around the marina complex, with banks in the tourist area.

Alongside the reception / fuel berth in the entrance to Vilamoura Marina *Anne Hammick*

Shops/provisioning Several small supermarkets, mostly a street or two back from the marina, which meet daily needs (and will sometimes deliver) but are inadequate for serious passage provisioning. For serious stocking-up the best bet would be the big Modelo supermarket about 15 minutes away by car (ask at the marina office for directions). Dozens of tourist and general shops overlook the marina basin.

Produce market Well-stocked markets in Quarteira and Lidl.

Cafés, restaurants and hotels Dozens of the former right beside the marina (including one at the *clube náutico*), with lots more, plus several luxury hotels, within walking distance.

Medical services Medical centre (including dentists) in the tourist area, best contacted with the assistance of marina reception. Hospital in Faro.

Communications

Post Office In the tourist complex behind the marina.

Mailing address The marina office will hold mail for visiting yachts – c/o Marina de Vilamoura, 8125–409 Quarteira, Algarve, Portugal. It is important that the envelope carries the name of the yacht in addition to that of the addressee.

Public telephones Several around the marina complex, including one beside the reception quay and another in the boatyard compound.

Internet Free access via a computer in the marina office, plus an ethernet point for laptops. There is free WiFi in all marina berths for which the internet code/password will be given when checking-in at marina reception. Lastly, there are several cafés with WiFi in the tourist resort.

Taxis/car hire In the commercial area, or via the marina office. Note that sign-posting within the tourist complex is poor – allow for a few wrong turnings if hiring a car to catch or meet a plane etc.

Buses Bus service to Faro (about 40 minutes) and elsewhere, from stops in the tourist complex. Ask at the marina office for directions.

Air services Faro international airport is about 20 minutes by taxi, 40 minutes by bus (though a taxi will be needed from town to airport).

FARO AND OLHÃO

Faro and Olhão

Location
36°57'·55N 7°52'·25W (Cabo de Santa María, entrance)

Tides
Standard port Lisbon
Mean time differences (at Cabo de Santa María)
HW –0040 ±0010; LW –0010 ±0005
Heights in metres

MHWS	MHWN	MLWN	MLWS
3·4	2·6	1·3	0·6

Principal lights
Cabo de Santa María
  Fl(4)17s49m25M Aero
  White tower and building 46m
West breakwater Fl.R.4s9m6M
  White tower, three red bands 5m
East breakwater Fl.G.4s9m6M
  White tower, three green bands 5m
Ldg Lts on 021° *Front* **Barra Nova** Oc.4s8m6M
  White column, red stripes
Rear 512m from front **Cabo de Santa María** (above)
Ilha de Culatra, training wall
  Oc.G.5s6m3M Metal column on building 6m
Canal de Faro
First Ldg Lts 099° (a back bearing if entering)
  Front **Mar Santo** Oc.R.5s9m5M
  White column, red bands 5m
Rear 244m from front **Cabo de Santa María** (above)
Second Ldg Lts 328°
  Front **Casa Cubica (Fabrica Fritz)** Fl.R.3s11m6M
  Red post, white bands 6m
Rear 731m from front Oc.R.6s63m6M
  Lantern on church tower 21m
Canal de Olhão
Cais Farol Fl.G.3s7m6M Green metal column 5m
First Ldg Lts 220° (a back bearing if entering)
  Front **Golada** LFl.R.5s6m6M
  White over red cylinder on three white columns 6m
Rear 447m from front Oc.R.5s8m7M
  White over red cylinder on three white columns 7m
Ponte do Carvão, Ilha de Culatra
  Fl.5·5s5m6M Green column 4m
Ponte Cais, Ilha de Culatra
  Oc.G.4s6m5M Green column
Second Ldg Lts 125° (back bearing if entering)
  Front **Arraiais** Iso.G.1·5s6m5M
  Black and white striped column, ▲ topmark 5m
Rear 226m from front Oc.G.3s9m5M
  Black and white striped column, ▲ topmark 8m
Third Ldg Lts on 352° *Front* **Murtinas**
  LFl.R.5s7m7M Red column, white bands
Rear 301m from front Oc.R.5s13m7M
  Red column, white bands

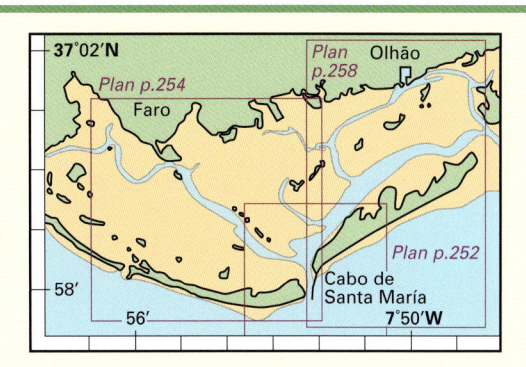

Fourth Ldg Lts 044° *Front* **Cais de Olhão**
  Iso.R.6s9m7M White column, red bands 7m
Rear **Igreja** 360m from front Oc.R.4s22m6M
  Church tower 12m
Doca de Olhao – west of dock entrance Fl.R.6s6M Post 5m
Many other lit buoys and beacons exist in the Canal de Faro, Canal de Olhão and Canal da Assetia. However, none should be relied upon implicitly, and any or all may be moved if the channels shift

Warning
  Night entry - the entrance is well lit, but tidal currents – and eddies – can be powerful. If unfamiliar with the channels it would be wise to anchor at the first opportunity and await daylight

Maritime radio station
  Estoi (37°06'·1N 7°49'·8W)
  Remotely controlled from Lisbon)
  Manual – VHF Ch 16, 24, 27, 28. *Autolink* – VHF Ch 86

Weather bulletins and navigational warnings
  Weather bulletins in Portuguese and English for Cabo Carvoerio to the Rio Guadiana within 20 miles offshore VHF Ch 11 at 0805, 2005 UT
  Navigational warnings in Portuguese and English within 200 miles offshore: VHF Ch 11at 0805, 2005 UT

Communications
  Faro – Port Authority
  VHF Ch 11, 16 (call *Postradfaro*) (24 hours)
  ☏ +351 289 803601 *Email* portfaro@mail.telepac.pt
  Olhão – Port Authority
  VHF Ch 11, 16 (call *Capimarolhão*) (0900–1230, 1400–1730 weekdays only)
  ☏ +351 289 703160
  Olhão – Marina
  ☏ +351 962 095 793 www.villagemarinaolhao.com
  Email enquiries@villagemarinaolhao.com

A single entrance leading to many anchorages and a marina at Olhão

Both Faro and Olhão (pronounced '*Oh-le-ow*') are sizeable towns, but for many the greater appeal lies with the tidal lagoons which run along the coast for some 30M between the mainland and the sea. The offlying islands, together with the coastal fringes, form the Parque Natural de Ría Formosa. Certain restrictions apply but the bird life, including storks and various waders, is abundant. To take full advantage of the geography a sailing dinghy or a shoal-draught boat able to take the ground is preferable, but there is water enough in the main channels for deep-draught yachts.

The entrance at Cabo de Santa María is well marked and the way through the sand defined by breakwaters. A stream of fishing boats may give a useful lead when they return with their catch in the early morning, but the bar, which is dredged from time to time, presents few problems in fine weather. Once inside, the channels are well buoyed, but if going to Olhão beware the wash of passing fishing boats. The ferries, too, are not over-considerate. Another potential problem throughout the area is the prevalence of floating weed, which tends to clog engine water filters, and small crustaceans which take up residence in log impellers. Both will need clearing regularly.

ATLANTIC SPAIN AND PORTUGAL   251

CABO DE SÃO VICENTE TO TAVIRA

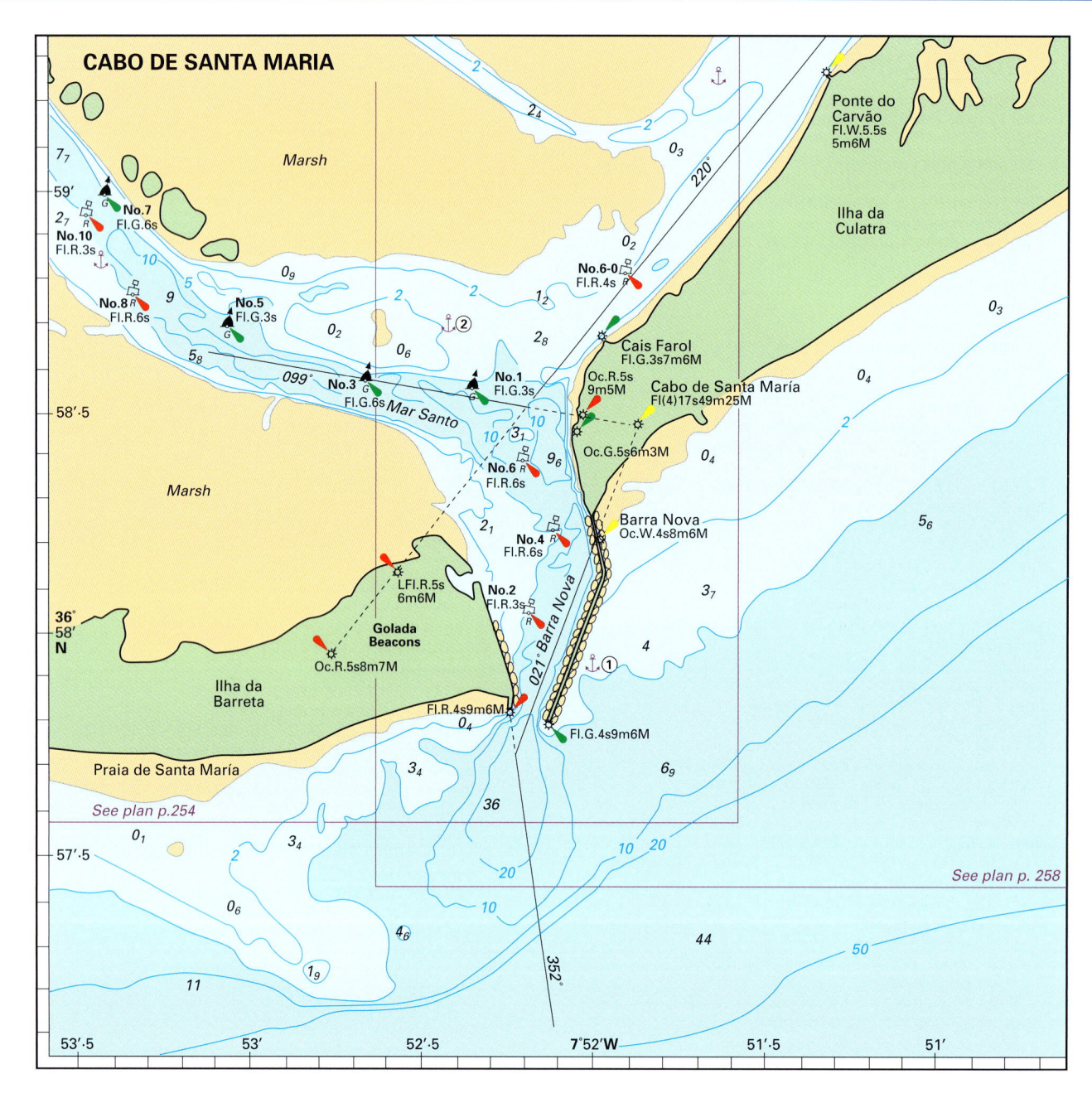

Approach

The coast is very low-lying and currents of up to 3kn may set along it. The 50m contour runs at 1M offshore at the point, further away on either side. The major light of Cabo de Santa María is on the sandspit about 1·3M northeast of the most southerly point of the cape and 0·7M north-northeast of the breakwaters. From a distance it looks like a needle on a sandy island.

Coming along the shore from the west, the beach starts a few miles east of Vilamoura and is backed by tourist villages. It becomes deserted to the southeast and 8M west from Santa María the lagoon starts, with an occasional shallow entrance across the sand, and Faro airport behind. The 5m line runs 600–700m offshore, except southwest of the entrance where it turns south to a point, very steep-to (shoaling from 30m down to 5m within 50m or less) more than 0·5M offshore. A short distance further west the 2m contour does much the same, forming a southwest facing bank over which the water shoals from 15m to 2m in little more than 100m. Either of these may cause a southwesterly swell to break. Remain at least 0·7M offshore until the west breakwater bears 352°.

Caution

There is an area of tuna nets south of Cabo de St Maria that is marked with a total of four special mark buoys and one south cardinal buoy as follows:

Special mark No.1: 36°56'·05N 007°56'·94W
Special mark No.2: 36°56'·90N 007°56'·63W
Special mark No.3: 36°56'·93N 007°55'·52W
Special mark No.4: 36°56'·08N 007°55'·17W
South Cardinal Buoy marked as S. Maria Sul near 36°55'·58N 007°55'·97W

252   ATLANTIC SPAIN AND PORTUGAL

CABO DE SANTA MARIA

On the Barra Nova transit 1 hour before HW Jane Russell

All five buoys are large (about 3m high) and lit and all are powered with solar panels.

To the east, the lagoon and its protecting banks extend 20M with some wide, but generally shallow, gaps. Opposite Fuzeta, 5M east of Olhão and identified by a distinctive church, the 50m line runs about 2M offshore. There is a network of tunny nets south of Fuzeta centered on 37°01'·20N 007°42'·80W that extends to a radius of ½M round that point. They are unusual, in that the nets are not in a long line extending for several miles, but instead are a complicated system of channels all in this one mile diameter. This area is well buoyed and lit and marked on all Portuguese charts as 'Armacoes do Atum'.

Looking north through the entrance to the Ría Formosa at Cabo de Santa Maria. Ilha da Barreta to port, Ilha da Culatra to starboard

Entrance

From a point at least 0·7M south of the entrance, steer 352° until the end of the east breakwater just opens to the east of a line with Santa María light. There can be a marked set across the entrance and it is important to remain on the leading line. Although there is adequate depth to enter at any state of the tide the spring ebb may run at 7kn through the entrance. In these circumstances hug the west mole – there is good water within 15m of it and the ebb will be reduced to about 4kn – but be ready for powerful eddies and keep a careful watch for fish-traps (often marked by black flags). There are three port-hand buoys before the channels to Faro and Olhão divide. Local yachtsmen frequently cut inside these, not least to escape the tide, but new arrivals may feel happier leaving them close to port.

Both channels are buoyed, and though in the past buoys were frequently reported to be out of position this is no longer common, particularly during the summer. A corrected copy of either Portuguese chart 26311 or Admiralty chart 83 is almost essential, but even so the banks shift continually and yachts have reported grounding well within the marked channel. As always, best water is to be found on the outsides of bends.

Note Vessels drawing more than 2·5m may not use the channel at night (not recommended for the visitor, in any case), and vessels are forbidden to cross each other's bows at the junction of the channels – those outward bound should remain outside the channel and let inward bound vessels pass.

THE ALGARVE & ANDALUCIA

ATLANTIC SPAIN AND PORTUGAL

CABO DE SÃO VICENTE TO TAVIRA

Anchorages near Cabo de Santa María

There are several possibilities in this area, most of them weather dependent and all requiring an anchor light to be displayed if remaining after dark. (Several yachts have been fined in this area in recent years for not displaying either an anchor ball or a light, as appropriate).

1. In settled northerlies yachts occasionally anchor outside, east of the east breakwater and south of Santa María light.
2. A useful anchorage for timing your entrance or exit will be found north-northwest of buoy No.1 (see plan below).

Faro

Location
37°00′·8N 7°56′·2W

This is a small marina for local fishing boats about 100m east of Ponte Cais pier.

Not to be confused with the tourist sprawl behind the beaches to the west of the city, Faro's walled Cidade Velha (old town) right next to the small Doca de Recreio should not be missed, providing welcome shade on a hot day and superb views over the estuary and town from the belltower of the Sé (cathedral). Pause to watch the storks on their untidy nests on the cathedral tower, above the Cidade Velha's neo-classical Arco de Vila, on lamp posts overhanging the city's streets… everywhere. Until recently they flew south to Morocco for the winter, but it seems that global warming has encouraged them to stay year-round.

Approach and anchorage

Again there is no option but to anchor, the favoured spot being the pool formed at the junction of the creeks in 3–4m, with the railway bridge covering the entrance to the Doca de Recreio bearing about 040°. Although now largely occupied by moorings it may be possible to find space in the channel leading southwest, where there is at least one deep pool, though two anchors (both from the bow and laid upstream and downstream respectively) may be required to limit swinging space.

When approaching the junction, favour the port side of the channel past buoys No.17 and No.21, switching to the starboard hand when the latter is 100m or so astern to avoid an extensive sand spit running out from the port bank (visible until mid-tide and marked by port hand buoy No.22). The deep channel here carries 4m or more depth but is a bare 15m wide.

Faro is famous for its storks – this pair have set up home on neo-classical Arco de Vila which gives access to the old city   Anne Hammick

A single-track railway links Faro to Vila Real de Santo Antonio in the east and Lagos in the west   Anne Hammick

Land either at the Doca de Recreio, passing under the railway bridge (about 1m clearance at high water), or at one of the three jetties outside (the northernmost is probably the best bet). If landing in the basin note that the pontoons are closed off by individual security gates, and that the entire east side is reserved for fishermen. The office of the Capitania – where the *Policía Marítima* are often to be found – overlooks the north end of the basin, sharing its premises with a small maritime museum (open 1430–1630). A weather forecast is posted outside.

Facilities and communications

Facilities include water from taps beside the slipway on the quay between the basin and the marshes, and the possibility of showers at the Ginásio Clube Navale next door (which also has a snack-bar and upstairs restaurant – the only thing it does not appear to have is much to do with sailing!). In the same building is Nautifaro, previously a chandlery but now specialising mainly in outboard engines and their needs.

Santa María Artigos Náuticos
① +351 289 804 805 www.santamarianautica.com
Email info@santamarianautica.com
Open 0900–1300 and 1500–1800 weekdays, 1000–1300 Saturday, a little way down the same quay has

CABO DE SÃO VICENTE TO TAVIRA

From Faro looking out across the Ría Formosa William Maltby

filled the gap. Good English is spoken and the helpful owner, a local yachtsman, is happy to order as necessary. Diesel is available by can from a filling station on the landward side of the basin, though there is nowhere that a yacht can fill tanks directly. Camping Gaz bottles can be exchanged at several hardware stores in the city, but it is not possible to get other cylinders refilled.

Faro is the regional capital and has facilities to match, including banks, shops of all kinds, wining and dining spots, and medical services. Communications include a post office and numerous telephone kiosks, several internet cafés, taxis, car hire, buses, trains (the station is close north of the smallcraft basin) and of course Faro International Airport, a couple of kilometres northwest as the egret flies, though rather more by road. Perhaps surprisingly, the aircraft noise is not intrusive and there appears to be little flying at night. In any case, any problems are more than offset by the proximity of the airport for crew changes and visiting friends.

Boatyard and storage ashore
If wishing to haul out for work or dry storage it would be well worth investigating the friendly Quinta do Progresso boatyard.
Mobile +351 919 317 171
Email jbotas@vodaphone.pt
This is an unpretentious but well-run concern some distance north northwest (approach channel approximately 37°01'·213N 007°56'·74W) of the Doca de Recreio. 'Bruce', the helpful Portuguese owner/manager, speaks English, French, Spanish and some German and Dutch, while engineer John grew up in the United States. There are onsite workshops for engineering, electronics, spars and rigging, GRP work and painting, though owners are welcome to do their own work, and stout metal cradles are available. Owners of yachts ashore are welcome to live aboard if they wish, with water and electricity throughout the yard and showers provided. Supermarkets and other shops are within walking distance.

Looking north-northeast over the anchorage at Faro to the Doca de Recreio and the boatyard beyond

ATLANTIC SPAIN AND PORTUGAL

Due to environmental concerns, as it is on the northern fringes of the Parque Natural de Ría Formosa, it took many years to obtain permission to dredge a channel up to the yard, but there should be at least 1·6m found at LWS and up to 4·4m at HWS. At the same time a massive 100-tonne capacity travel-lift should have replaced the slightly elderly 24-tonne lift of old.

There is a possibility of a small marina being built here with around 180 berths in 2m or so.

Anchorage at Ilha da Culatra

See (3) on plan on page 258

A very popular anchorage (more than 100 yachts in holiday periods) can be found along the length of Praça Larga north of Ilha da Culatra. Holding in both areas is good over sand, though wind against tide conditions can set up quite a chop and also cause yachts on single anchors to yaw considerably. Two anchors (both from the bow) may be wise if planning to stay for any length of time but take into account how yachts around you are anchored.

It is possible to enter or leave the Praça Larga from the east, via the Barra Grande (also known as the Barra Velha), but the shifting banks are not reliably buoyed and this route is not recommended without local knowledge.

There are reckoned to be around 3,000 permanent residents on Isla de Culatra, mostly in Culatra village though the village close to Cabo de Santa María (referred to locally as Farol, literally 'lighthouse'), is also growing at speed. There are no roads, and no cars, though a few tractors plough their way through the loose sand. But Ponte Cais is a popular holiday spot, particularly during the music festival held in August, so it has several shops including a small but surprisingly well-stocked supermarket, a cash point, numerous restaurants and bars, and both post and telephone offices. Ferries run between Ponte Cais, Farol and Olhão – two or three a day in winter and far more in summer.

Close east of Ponte Cais is a tidal lagoon which used to be a favourite wintering spot for both locals and liveaboard owners of multihulls and bilge-keelers, some of whom had been there for decades. The lagoon is now out of bounds, and piles/posts have been installed across the entrance to prevent access. Most boats have left but a few may remain from the clean-up programme the Authorities started in 2015. Many of the shacks and bungalows on Culatra and Armona were demolished sparking demonstrations.

There is a small marina for local fishing boats and fast skiffs only about 100m east of Ponte Cais pier.

Yachts anchored at the eastern end of Praca Larga. Olhão is beyond to the NNW Jane Russell

Looking east-southeast towards the Doca de Recreio at Faro and the yacht anchorage off to the right. The boatyard can be seen on the left

Praca Larga anchorage Ilha da Culatra looking NE from the marina breakwater Jane Russell

CABO DE SÃO VICENTE TO TAVIRA

CANAL DE OLHÃO

OLHÃO

Depths in Metres

ATLANTIC SPAIN AND PORTUGAL

OLHÃO

Olhão's marina and small craft harbour looking northwest, with the Grupo Naval's small basin and the much larger fishing dock on the right

Olhão

Location
37°01'·3N 07°50'·5W

There is reported to be little space for visitors at Olhão marina, and the minimum length of stay is one month. If intending to arrive by yacht, there is much to be said for first anchoring off Ponte Cais and taking the ferry over to Olhão to assess the current situation.

Olhão itself is a pleasant, non-touristy town with superb markets on the waterfront surrounded by public gardens and a small children's play area.

Saturday morning market in Olhão is full of entertaining distractions *Jane Russell*

Approach

Although it is perfectly possible to negotiate the channel (marked with withies) up to Olhão at low water, most skippers will feel happier at around half flood. From the Praça Larga turn northwest leaving Ponta da Lava and buoy No.8 to port, and either steer the courses indicated on the plan opposite or follow the buoyage as far as starboard hand No.5. Almost continuous dredging is required to keep this channel clear and yachts must not, under any circumstances, anchor in the fairway.

From a position close west of buoy No.5 steer directly for the hammer-head ferry pier, swinging west only just short of it to skirt the smallcraft pontoons and leave buoy No.2P well to port. Beyond it will be seen No.4P and, in the distance, No.6P. All are spherical red buoys with topmarks and are lit, though this is no place to be on the move after dark. Continue west, staying as close to the smallcraft pontoon as conditions allow, repeating the process past the marina proper. On no account err to the south, as the edge of the dredged channel is too steep to give any warning before impact (though too soft to do much damage). The marina is entered at its western end, as indicated on the inset plan.

Berthing

The marina comprises two separate sections, the eastern berthing local smallcraft on two long east/west pontoons, the western providing around 270 berths for yachts of up to 17m, in 3m depths. 250 of these berths are on the 11 inner pontoons, which run on a north/south axis from a single pontoon which parallels the shore. The remaining berths, and the only ones which may be accessible to a visitor, lie inside the long 'shelter' pontoon. It seems likely that this pontoon was never intended to provide more than short-term berthing as it is not provided with water and electricity points, though cleats are provided on the inner side. It is reported that, during strong southerlies, it becomes distinctly lively as soon as the rising tide covers the mudbanks to the south. A full-scale southerly gale has yet to be experienced.

On arrival, unless allocated a berth in advance, the best bet will probably be to raft alongside a yacht of suitable size on the inside of the long south pontoon. However this is frowned on by the authorities and the boat should not be left unattended even with the consent of those on the inside yacht. Security is via the usual card, and more necessary than in some areas, due to the traveller encampment to the west of the town.

Anchorage

It may be possible for two or three yachts to anchor in the western part of the gap between the two parts of the marina, though space is tight due to moored smallcraft. Holding is good in about 3m over mud.

Formalities

All formalities are currently handled at the office of the Instituto Portuário e dos Transportes Marítimos do Sul (IPTM), which overlooks the west side of the large fishing boat basin, open 0800–1200 and 1300–1630 weekdays. The *Capitania* and *Polícia Marítima* share an office on the corner opposite the Grupo Naval, easily distinguished by its array of radio aerials, with the *GNR–Brigada Fiscal* between the two.

Facilities

Boatyard The nearest boatyard to Olhão is the Marina Formosa located just up channel past the fishing harbour (**37°01′·518N 007°49′·670W**). Contact Dias and Sabino, Lda. Doca Nova de Pesca – Apartado 63 – 8700909 Olhão. ☏ +351 289 703 364. There is neither a website nor an email address for the boatyard. This is a working boat yard which carries out one-off and annual maintenance and repair work including lifting and craneage, boat cleaning, storage, polishing and antifouling and have specialists in mechanical and electrical engineering. There are also GRP services, yacht painting and traditional shipwright skills for the building and repair of all types of boats.

Also provided are dry berthing arrangements, a public slipway, drying out facilities, storage ashore and winter lay up, electricity ashore, shower and toilet facilities, and towing services within the Ría Formosa. The hydraulic trolley for lifting out, however, is really only suitable for fairly small boats (see photo opposite).

Engineers, mechanics, radio repairs At the fishing harbour.

Chandlery Sulcampo on the seafront road sells some general chandlery and electronics in addition to fishing tackle and diving equipment. Cabrita Lda, opposite the market buildings, is similar. The larger Sulnáutica, on the road behind the IPTM office, stocks outboards, batteries, inflatables, some chandlery and the inevitable fishing gear.

Looking north-northwest over the Olhão marina

OLHÃO

The narrow approach to Olhão marina, seen from the ferry pier to the east. It is essential to leave all three buoys to port Anne Hammick

Hydraulic trolley at Marina Formosa boatyard Olhão

Water No access to water on the outer pontoon of the marina, though supplied to the inner berths. Several public taps and water fountains nearby, however.
Showers Nothing at the marina, but several local *residencials* are willing to let yachtsmen use showers for a small fee.
Launderette Several in the town.
Electricity Not available on the outer pontoon.
Fuel By can from a filling station near the root of the ferry jetty.
Bottled gas Camping gas exchanges are done at Sulcampo, 200m west of the ferry pier on the seafront road.
Clube naval The Grupo Naval de Olhão has its own basin east of the ferry pier, but there is no space for visitors.
Banks In the town, with a cash dispenser almost opposite the market buildings.
Shops, provisioning Small supermarket up the road opposite the market buildings, plus a large Pingo Doce supermarket five minutes walk to the north of the pier at Olhão. Good general shopping in the town.
Produce market Excellent – and spotlessly clean – produce and fish markets virtually overlooking the marina. As always, at their best in the early morning.
Cafés, restaurants and hotels The usual wide variety, with some particularly good fish restaurants on the road behind the market buildings.
Medical services In the town.

Communications

Post office In the town, close to the church.
Telephones Several public kiosks near the market buildings with others in the town.
Internet Available in town.
Car hire In the town, or from Faro airport.
Taxis A few in the town.
Buses & trains To Faro, Tavira and beyond.
Ferries Regular ferries to Ilha Armona and Ilha de Culatra
Air services Major airport at Faro, about 10km to the west as the gull flies, though considerably further by land.

The inlet of Fuzeta, 15M east of Cabo de Santa María, might be described as a smaller version of Olhão, tucked behind broadly similar banks.

ATLANTIC SPAIN AND PORTUGAL 261

THE ALGARVE & ANDALUCIA

Fuzeta

Location
Entrance centre at 37°03'·03N 007°43'·75W

The small inlet at Fuzeta off the lagoon east of Olhão looking north-northwest. It can only be approached by shoal-draught yachts or multihulls, or perhaps by dinghy from larger yachts anchored further west

In February 2010 a storm caused a breach in the sand bank to the west of the original entrance to the tidal lagoon off Fuzeta. A new entrance was created to the west of the original entrance while the breach in the sandbank and the original entrance have been blocked with a very large quantity of sand. The centre of the new entrance to Fuzeta is at 37°03'·03N 007°43'·75W. Approach to this position should be made on a course of 282° and, for the deepest water, continue on this course toward a radio antenna and water tower in the centre of Fuzeta. Even this new entrance is extremely shallow and there is reported to be not much more than 1·5m at half tide. Approach with caution!

Though very appealing, it is feasible only for shoal-draught yachts or multihulls able to enlist local assistance for the approach. The inner banks appear to be largely of sand, rather than the mixture of mud and sand encountered further west, making drying out much more pleasant. The small town has all the usual facilities, including fuel at the fishermen's quay (up the narrow inlet, marked by prominent red/white and green/white banded towers), and nearby shops and produce market. A small and somewhat ramshackle boatyard lies near the head of the creek.

There is a large fish conservation and tunny net area south of Fuzeta marked by no less than six large (3m) cardinal buoys as follows:

1. North	NCB	037°01'·00N	007°44'·48W
2. Northeast	NCB	037°01'·94N	007°42'·20W
3. East	ECB	037°00'·88N	007°41'·57W
4. Southeast	SCB	037°00'·00N	007°44'·00W
5. South	SCB	036°59'·30N	007°46'·22W
6. West	WCB	037°00'·38N	007°45'·94W

There is a network of tunny nets within this area centred on 037°01'·20N 007°42'·80W that extends to a radius of about ½M around that point.

Additional tuna nets have been laid a little to the east of the nets mentioned above, marked by a south cardinal buoy at 37°01'·85N 007°39'·10W. About one mile to the north, the northern limit of the nets are marked by three special marks.

The eastern entrance to the lagoon off Fuzeta should not be tackled without local knowledge – and this is why...

TAVIRA

Tavira

Location
37°06'·38N 7°36'·63W (entrance)

Tides
Standard port Lisbon
Mean time differences (Portuguese time zone)
HW –0035 ±0020; LW –0020 ±0020
Heights in metres
MHWS	MHWN	MLWN	MLWS
3·2	2·5	1·3	0·5

Principal lights
Ldg Lts 326° *Front* Armação Fl.R.3s9m4M
  White post, red bands 5m
Rear 132m from front Fl.R.3s10m5M
  White post, red bands 5m
West breakwater Fl.R.2·5s7m6M
  White column, red bands 4m
East breakwater Fl.G.2·5s5m6M
  White column, green bands 4m

Warning
Though perfectly feasible, entry in darkness calls for settled conditions, a rising tide (half-flood or more) and considerable confidence.

Attractive and unspoilt river anchorage with limited facilities

A very old town, one of its bridges claims Roman origins, and the only Greek inscription to be found in Portugal was discovered in nearby Santa Luzia, Tavira is still heavily dependant on fishing and in spite of an ever-growing tourist trade has managed to retain much of its character. Some of its old walls and many of its tiled houses remain, with wrought iron balconies and original decoration, overlooked by floodlit churches and a ruined castle.

The anchorage is connected to the town by a 2km causeway flanked by salt pans and parking areas, and by the Rio Gilão which at high tide is navigable by dinghy. Once in the anchorage there is good protection from the sea, though little from the wind, and the current runs strongly. The area is part of the Parque Natural de Ría Formosa and the birdwatching possibilities are endless.

Approach

Between Cabo de Santa María and Tavira the coast comprises a low sandbank, broken east of Olhão and again off Fuzeta. A floating fish cage is positioned south of Fuzeta – see opposite – and at certain times of year tunny nets may be laid up to 1·5M offshore, but otherwise there are no natural hazards.

The entrance is dredged every few years, when 4m can be found along the leading line. It is not known, however, when this was last done and it would be prudent to assume some silting has taken place. The leading marks, a pair of red and white banded poles, can be difficult to identify – if in doubt err to the east, as a shoal extends beyond the end of the west breakwater.

Entrance

Do not enter before half flood or at all if the swell is heavy – if wind and/or swell are onshore conditions become rougher on the ebb. The best time for either entering or for leaving is about one hour before high water. When taking the sharp turn to port into the anchorage give the (unlit) tourist ferry quay and its offlying post a generous berth (floating lines may trail from it), and keep a sharp lookout for the small ferries, some of which move at surprising speed.

Looking northwest into the Ría Formosa entrance at Tavira

CABO DE SÃO VICENTE TO TAVIRA

Yachts anchored off the Quatro Aguas ferry jetty in the Ría Formosa.
The main channel – though not the ferry passage – is indicated by pairs of stout, lit posts

Anchorage

The channel west past Quatro Aguas ('four waters') towards Santa Luzia is indicated by pairs of very solid posts, all nominally lit, and though some local boats remain moored in what appears to be the fairway it would be most unwise to anchor in it. At the very least one would regularly be disturbed by wash from passing fishing boats. In summer it may be difficult to find sufficient space for a larger yacht to swing, in which case (and for all yachts at spring tides) it would be prudent to set two anchors, both from the bow and laid upstream and downstream respectively. The bottom is foul in places and a tripline is advised. Holding is good over sand, but the current runs strongly enough at springs for most yachts to remain tide-rode even in contrary winds of 20kn.

Shallow-draught vessels have the option of continuing southwest along the Ría Tavira towards Santa Lucia, again anchoring well clear of the fairway which is used by fishing boats day and night. The lower reaches are marked by lit posts.

Tavira with the Ría Formosa beyond Henry Buchanan

Formalities

There is a manned *GNR–Brigada Fiscal* office next to the ferry jetty, but Tavira is not a port of entry/exit and passports cannot be stamped for departure (which in any case should only be necessary in the case of non-EU citizens). The Capitania is located in the town, close west of the fishing quay.

Facilities and communications

At the anchorage water by can from the Clube Náutico de Tavira, which also has showers and a small bar (seek permission before helping oneself to either of the former, as a small fee may be charged), plus several other bars and restaurants but no shops. Fresh shellfish can be bought from a counter at the rear of wholesaler Tomé Mariscos, housed in a large yellow building west of the *clube náutico*.

A square concrete barge against which it is possible to dry out lies on the beach immediately opposite the ferry jetty. However it appears to be settling into the sand and now covers at high water springs. The smallcraft harbour on the west bank just inside the Rio Gilão is too small, shallow and crowded to be feasible for a visiting yacht, and landing by dinghy at the single pontoon is impractical due to a locked security gate. There is a lay-up area for local yachts (maximum about 8m) behind the *clube náutico*, and though there is no possibility of hauling a larger keel-yacht this would undoubtedly be the place to start enquiries if faced with a major problem.

There is a phone kiosk near the ferry jetty and the area is served by Tavira's 'land train' – popular with younger crewmembers as well as older ones encumbered with shopping. Heading in the other direction there is a passenger ferry to Ilha Tavira which operates on demand.

264 ATLANTIC SPAIN AND PORTUGAL

TAVIRA

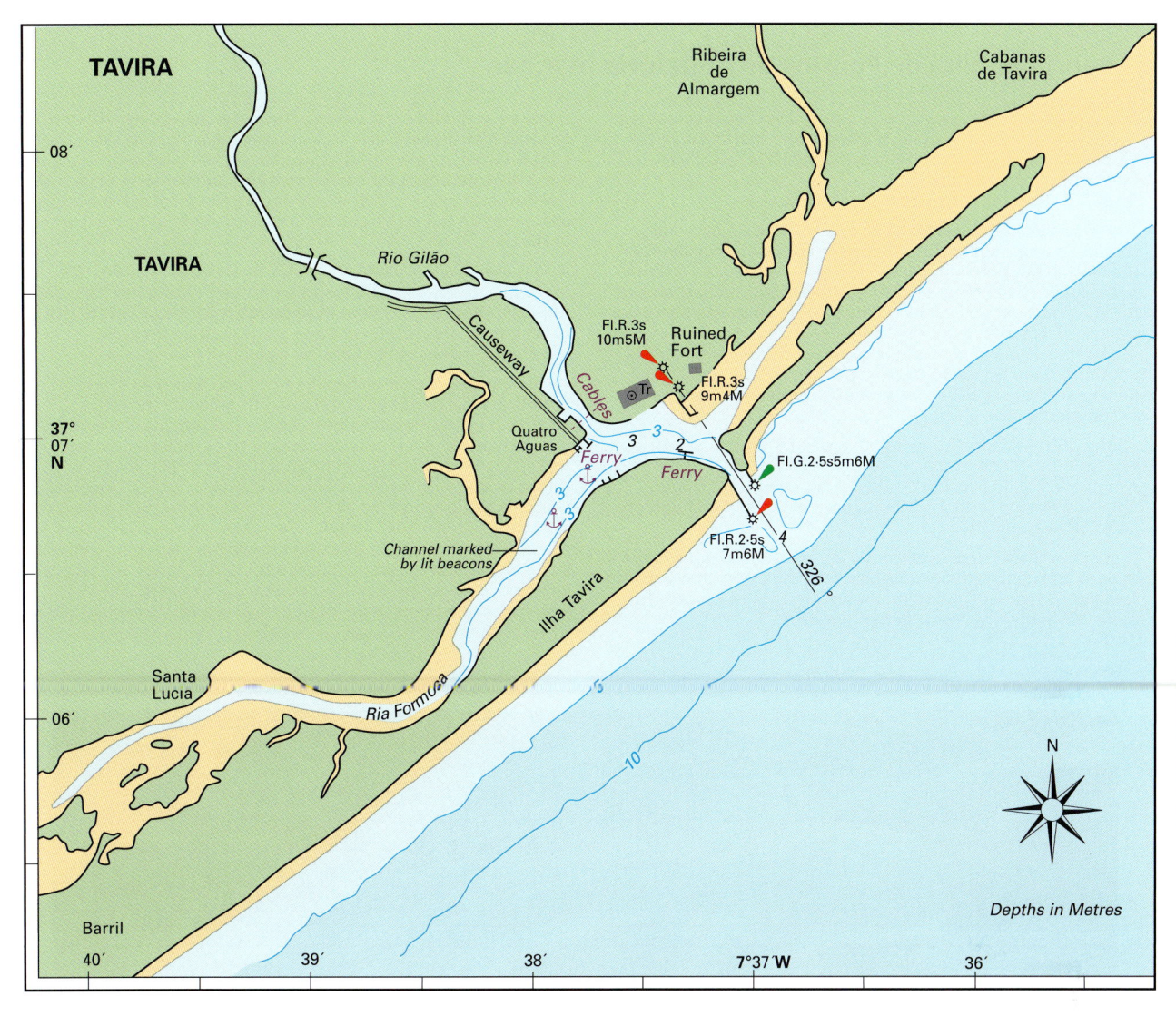

On Ilha Tavira campsite with several cafés and restaurants, a phone kiosk and a cash dispenser but, rather surprisingly, no shop.

In the town good shopping (including a vast Pingo Doce on the east bank near the new bridge), banks with cash dispensers, restaurants, hotels etc. Diesel can be transported by can from a waterside filling station just upstream of the new bridge (accessible by dinghy). There are several hardware stores at which Camping Gaz bottles can be exchanged (but not refilled), plus one near the east end of the cast-iron bridge which sells limited chandlery. Runabouts, outboards and inflatables are displayed in a showroom on the west bank near the filling station.

A post office, telephones and several cybercafés will be found (the latter including one on the east bank of the river between the two old bridges, which has 10 or 12 computers plus multiple sockets for laptop users). Transport options include taxis, buses (including the road train mentioned previously) and a station just north of the town. Faro airport is about 30km down the coast.

Dos and don'ts in the Parque Natural de Ría Formosa
Anne Hammick

ATLANTIC SPAIN AND PORTUGAL 265

RÍO GUADIANA TO RÍO GUADALQUIVIR

Agencia Pública de Puertos de Andalucía marinas

One cannot cruise for very long on the Andalucían coast without encountering the string of yacht marinas and sport fishing harbours financed, built and run by the Agencia Pública de Puertos de Andalucía.
①+34 955 00 72 00 *Email* comunicacion@eppa.es

The APPA website is at www.puertosdeandalucia.es/en/ and contains a wealth of useful information for yachtsmen. One of the most exciting developments has been provision of current bathymetric charts for the entrances to marinas and harbours to help with navigation in areas where shifting sands and bars are a worry. The Batimetría del Río Piedras (Febrero 2018), for example, showing depths and buoy positions can be downloaded for the entrance to the Rio de las Piédras (El Rompido) can be downloaded at www.puertosdeandalucia.es/en/documentation-en/batimetrias (see below).

APPA runs ten yacht marinas to the west of Gibraltar as well as several in the Mediterranean. From west to east these comprise: Ayamonte, Isla Canela, Isla Cristina, Punta Umbría, Mazagón, Chipiona, Rota, Puerto América (Cádiz), Sancti Petri and Barbate, only 35M west of Gibraltar.

Leaflets, available in several languages, feature aerial photograph of each marina together with a plan showing the location of facilities such as fuel, travel lift, showers etc. There is much the same information available in the website.

Prices are standard for the entire chain, despite widely differing facilities and appeal, but it appears that some discretion is allowed when it comes to charging for use of water and electricity. Multihulls are subject to a 50% surcharge. If a berth of the correct length is not available and a yacht is forced to occupy a larger berth this is charged for, irrespective of the actual length of the boat.

A 10% discount is available for a stay of a month or more, 15% for three months and 30% for six months (the latter not including July or August). All payment must be made in advance, with most major credit cards accepted. Evidence of insurance may be required, but does not need to be translated into Spanish.

All the marinas appear well maintained and nearly all offices include at least one English-speaker, often fluent. The office attitude is nearly always helpful. Where facilities include a travel-lift and hardstanding these also appear to be well-maintained and efficiently handled, with boats ashore normally placed in robust cradles with additional props. However, while owners are welcome to work on their own boats while ashore, living aboard, even for a single night, is totally forbidden. An inhabited yacht was blown over during a gale and though no one was injured it led to an existing rule being taken out, dusted down, and strictly enforced. Security gates are locked at night (usually 2200–0700) and in some harbours there may be no access at weekends. Check when booking.

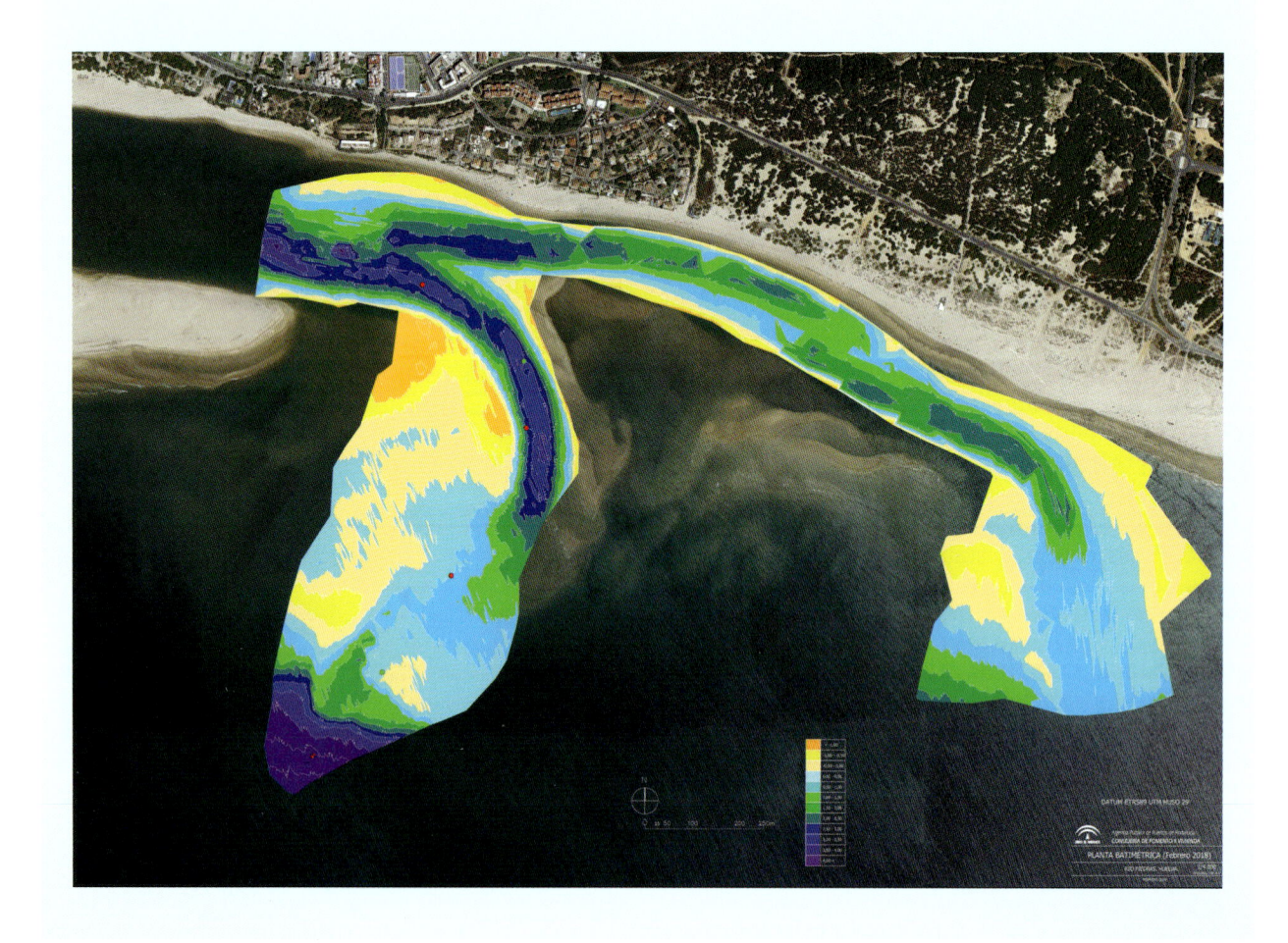

ATLANTIC SPAIN AND PORTUGAL

VILA REAL DE SANTO ANTONIO

Río Guadiana to Río Guadalquivir and Seville

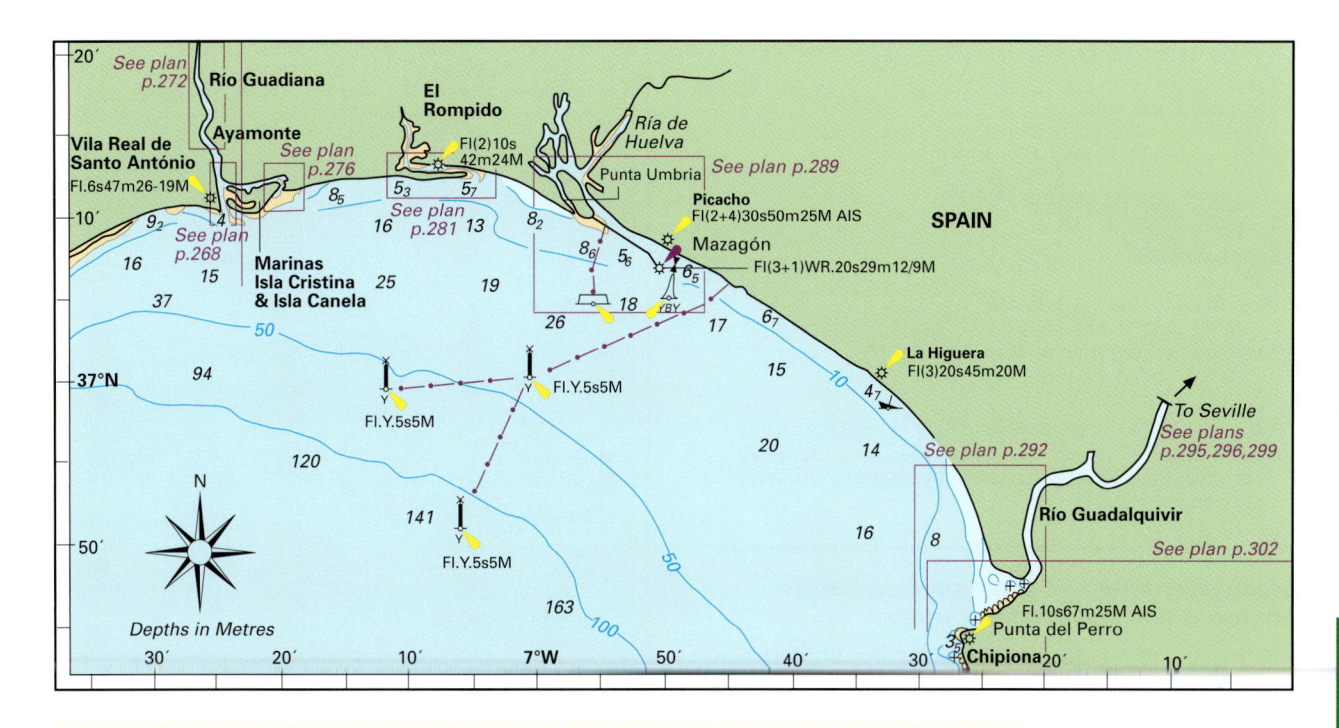

PRINCIPAL LIGHTS
Vila Real de Santo António Fl.6s47m26M-19M
  White tower, narrow black rings, red lantern 46m
El Rompido Fl(2)10s42m24M
  White tower, single red band 29m
Picacho Fl(2+4)30s50m25M AIS
  White tower with brick corners, as has building, 25m
Higuera Fl(3)20s45m20M
  White pyramidal structure, red band 24m
Punta del Perro (Chipiona) Fl.10s67m25M AIS
  Stone tower on building 60m

The mouth of the Río Guadiana looking north-northwest

ATLANTIC SPAIN AND PORTUGAL 267

RÍO GUADIANA TO RÍO GUADALQUIVIR

The Río Guadiana

Location
37°08'·15N 7°23'·83W (entrance)

Tides
Standard port Lisbon
Mean time differences (Portuguese time zone)
HW –0035 ±0020; LW –0020 ±0020
Heights in metres
MHWS	MHWN	MLWN	MLWS
3·2	2·5	1·3	0·5

Principal lights
Entrance
West breakwater Fl.R.3s9m4M
   White post, red bands 8m
East (submerged) training wall Fl(3)G.9s3M
   Black ┋ on black beacon, red band

Warning
Night entry perfectly feasible in light conditions on a flood tide, but nevertheless not advised unless familiar with the area. See also the warning regarding the ferry jetty on page 269

Scenic river with two small marinas, yacht pontoons and anchorages upstream

The Río Guadiana forms part of the border between Portugal and Spain. The river, which has strong currents, is navigable to Pomarão some 25M upstream and can make a pleasant change to seafaring. It has been reported that the upper valley of the Río Guadiana remains noticeably cooler than the surrounding areas even during the height of summer, possibly due to the chill of the river water which comes straight off the mountains inland.

There are small marinas at Vila Real de Santo António (Portugal) and Ayamonte (Spain). Some provision for yachts is also in place upriver, primarily at Alcoutim (Portugal) and Sanlúcar de Guadiana (Spain).

Approach

Either side of the Río Guadiana the coast consists of a low sandbank broken by gaps giving access to the lagoons which run from west of Cabo de Santa María to 2M east of the Río Guadiana. Further east the sand continues unbroken for another 12M. If coastal sailing, note that depths between the Río Guadiana and the Ría de la Higuerita are very shoal, with drying patches up to 1M offshore. The 5m line generally runs more than 1·5M offshore, making 2M a safe distance off. Fishing nets may be laid several miles offshore.

Approaching from the west, two conspicuous marks are the high-rise buildings of Monte Gordo 2M west of the entrance and the tall Vila Real light (white with narrow black bands). From the east, the tower blocks of Isla Cristina stand out. The twin pillars of the suspension bridge, about 4M upriver, can also be seen for many miles.

River entrance

The APPA bathymetric chart (Batimetría Canal del Guadiana) is at
www.puertosdeandalucia.es/en/documentation-en/batimetrias

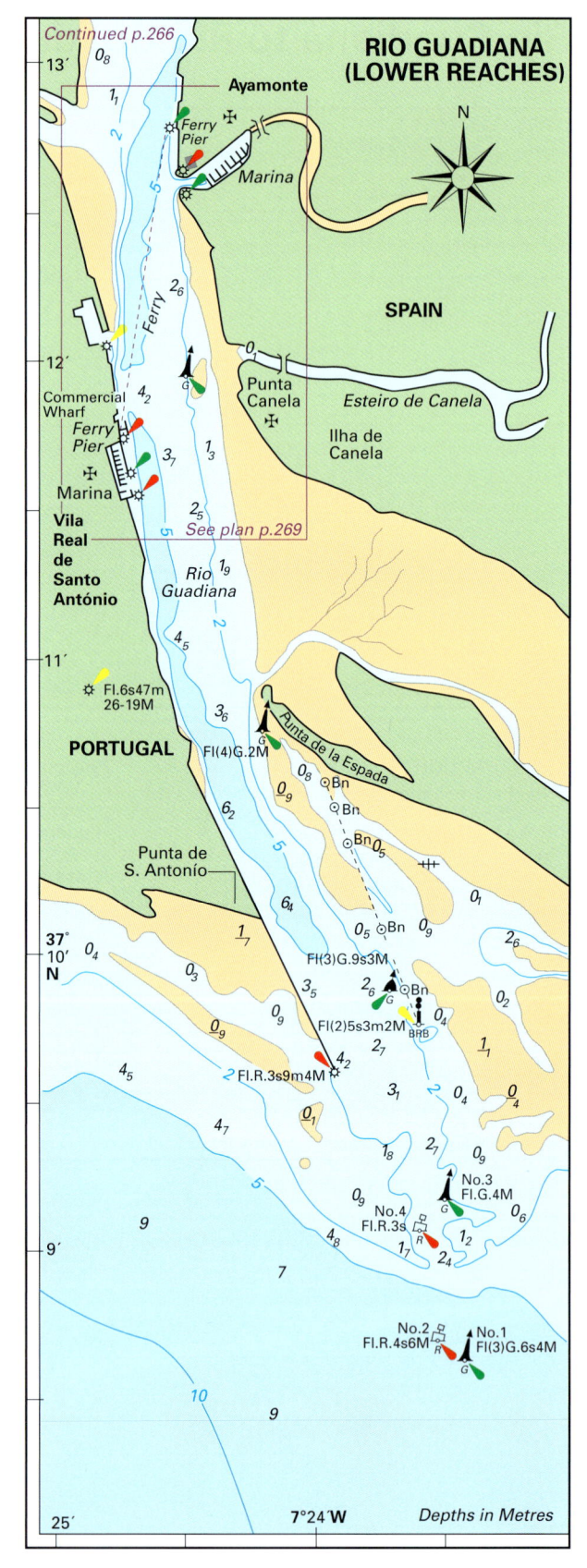

Do not attempt to enter other than at half flood or above and be especially careful if there is any swell.

The bar can be rough on the ebb, particularly if there is any swell running, and is hazardous in onshore weather. When planning departure, allow time to reach the bar before the ebb gathers speed.

268   ATLANTIC SPAIN AND PORTUGAL

VILA REAL DE SANTO ANTONIO

Vila Real de Santo António (Portugal)

Vila Real de Santo António (Portugal)
Marina south mole, angle Fl.R.3s2m2M Grey post 2m
Marina south mole, head Fl.R.3s3m2M Grey post 2m
Marina north mole, head Fl.G.3s2m2M Grey post 2m
Marina north mole, root Fl.R.3s1m2M Grey post 2m
Fishermen's quay Fl.Y.3s5m2M Yellow x on yellow post 4m
Communications
  Port authority
  VHF Ch 11, 16 call *Capimarvireal* (24 hours)
  ☏ +351 281 513 769 *Mobile* +351 911 509 011
  Email anguadiana@mail.telepac.pt
  Marina Guadiana
  VHF Ch 09, 12
  ☏ +351 281 541 571
  Email edmundo@marinaguadiana.com
  www.marinaguadiana.com

The town of Vila Real de Santo António was largely rebuilt in the 18th century, following destruction in the 1755 earthquake and tidal wave which decimated Lisbon as well as much of the Algarve. It follows a strict grid plan of wide avenues and open squares, often paved with black and white cobbles in intricate patterns. Even the much newer suburbs follow these lines – less interesting perhaps than the winding lanes of the older villages, but with considerably less scope for getting lost. A large part of the centre is a pedestrian area, making Vila Real de Santo António a very pleasant town in which to wander. As a final bonus it has, for some inexplicable but happy reason, been very largely overlooked by foreign tourists.

The Porto de Recreio do Guadiana contains about 360 berths for yachts of up to 20m, all against finger pontoons. A high proportion of these are nominally reserved for visitors, but the definition of 'visitor' is necessarily vague and the marina is frequently full in the high season. It is claimed that space will nearly always be found for new arrivals, but sometimes only for a single night. Even when the marina is full, yachts are not permitted to berth in the old Doca de Pesca about 0·5M upstream.

Approach

The river is canalised between a breakwater and a submerged training wall running 335°, their ends 550m apart and lit. Seaward of the walls are two pairs of port and starboard hand buoys, all lit (though the starboard hand buoys in particular have a reputation for unreliability and long periods off station).

Pass between the buoys and then head for the west breakwater, keeping it slightly open on the port bow. The east training wall is almost totally submerged, with a concrete tower marking its seaward end. Keep about 50m off the breakwater, remaining on the west side until off the town of Vila Real de Santo António.

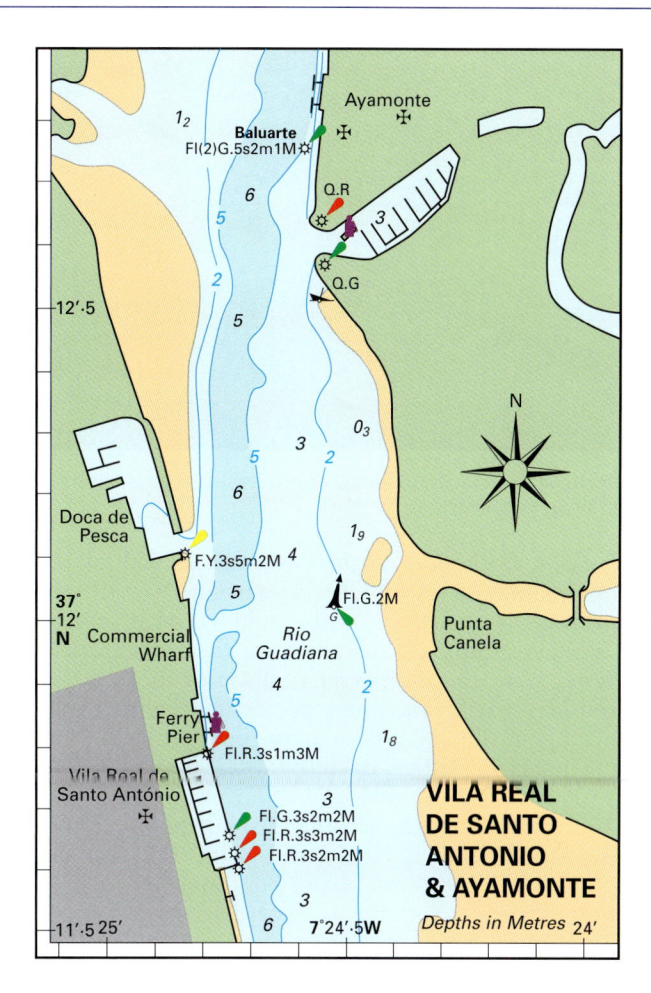

Entrance and berthing

If making for the marina (Porto de Recreio do Guadiana) at Vila Real de Santo António be aware that manoeuvring there is least traumatic at slack water.

The narrow marina entrance, which is less than 20m wide, is situated at its downstream end, with reception berths on the starboard hand alongside the inside of the long pontoon protecting the marina on its east flank. When this is occupied, the fuel pontoon, between the marina and the ferry pier to the north, may be pressed into service as a reception berth. At other times arriving yachts may be directed straight to a berth by marina staff. The staff cannot, of course, allow for the handling characteristics of individual craft, and at periods of strong tide it may occasionally be necessary to be deaf to directions and secure wherever possible until the flow diminishes. If planning to leave other than at slack water it would also be wise to turn the yacht in her berth in advance.

If manoeuvring in the river at night in the vicinity of the ferry jetty, note that although the pylons to which the ferry jetty is secured both carry lights, the jetty itself, which is painted matt black and projects a further 10m out into the stream, is totally unlit.

Both entrance and marina are subject to strong cross-currents. Flow in the river itself can reach 3kn on the ebb and 2kn on the flood making slack water by far the best time to manoeuvre. Once inside space

ATLANTIC SPAIN AND PORTUGAL   269

RÍO GUADIANA TO RÍO GUADALQUIVIR

Porto de Recreio do Guadiana at Vila Real de Santo Antonio looking northwest

is tight. Both sides of the entrance, as well as the upstream end of the fuel pontoon, are lit but movement at night is to be avoided as it will be difficult to estimate and allow for the cross-current. When new, the marina carried 4m or more in the southern part of the basin, decreasing slightly to the north, but silting has been an ongoing problem.

The marina office, open 0900–1230 and 1430 to 1800 (October–March), to 1900 (April–June) and to 2000 (July–August), occupies a smart portacabin at the north end of the basin with the services alongside. Both services and pontoons are secured by locked gates with the usual card access.

Formalities

If the yacht is registered in the EU, and all her crew are EU nationals, completion of the usual multi-part form in the marina office is sufficient. Otherwise it may be necessary to visit the offices of the *Polícia Marítima* and *Imigração* at the *Capitania*, about 50m south of the marina.

Facilities

Boatyard There is a boatyard, Marina Guadiana, downstream from the marina at 37°10′·9N 007°24′·7W, adjacent to the north side of the lifeboat station. Once a thriving, respected boatyard, management problems have clearly had an adverse effect on the capabilities of the yard. As of July 2018 the address remains Marina Guadiana Seca, Punta de Areia, Vila Real de Santo Antonio but apart from a poor website at www.marinaguadiana.com no other contact details are known. There is a large shed/workshop and tarmac yard with 40 boat spaces. In the past, boat owners have been allowed to live aboard. WC and shower block were open to all hours. Water and 230v power points were available for a small charge. Security was good with residents given a key to the gate.

There may well still be a 70-tonne travel-lift using a concrete ramp into the river at high water.

General repairs used to be carried out in most materials including GRP. Also, some engineering work, antifouling, and sand/shot blasting were available for yachts, fishing boats, and government craft.

Chandlery Nautiguadiana, opposite the marina, carries fishing tackle and some general chandlery. Marinautica, a little further down the road, stocks the above plus some electronics, stainless steel fittings, paint etc. The Boutique Náutica at the *clube naval* sells some chandlery in addition to clothing.

Water On the pontoons.

Showers In well-kept portacabins next to the marina office.

Launderette In the town – ask at the office for directions.

Electricity On the pontoons.

Fuel Diesel from a fuelling berth extending upstream from the marina, with petrol available by can from a pump ashore. Payment must be made in cash.

Bottled gas Camping Gaz refills are available from the shop opposite the filling station on the main road by the marina.

Weather forecast Posted daily outside the marina office and in the window overlooking the slipway.

Clube naval The Associação Naval do Guadiana, which now occupies a blue-tiled building at the south end of the marina basin, has a terrace bar and restaurant open to non-members.

Banks In the town, with a cash dispenser directly opposite the marina.

Shops/provisioning/produce market Good shopping of all kinds in the town, including a supermarket four blocks directly inland from the marina.

Cafés, restaurants and hotels An abundance of the former nearby, a good snack-bar restaurant on the quay (✆+351 281 511 836) and a comfortable if somewhat traditional hotel right opposite.

Medical services In the town.

Communications

Post office In the town.

Mailing address The marina office will hold mail for visiting yachts – c/o Associação Naval do Guadiana, Doca de Recreio, Apartado 40 Avenida da República, 8901-909 Vila Real de Santo António, Algarve, Portugal. It is important that the envelope carries the name of the yacht in addition to that of the addressee.

Public telephones Several nearby.

Internet Directly opposite the marina in the foyer of the Hotel Guadiana (small fee payable), at the public library (free, but often busy) and elsewhere.

Car hire/taxis In the town or via the marina office.

Buses Bus station beyond the ferry pier, itself next to the marina. Ten minutes ride northward is the attractive riverside village of Castro Marim, with two castles and a unusually imaginative children's playground.

Trains Vila Real is the eastern terminus of the Algarve coastal line, with a sleepy station close to the fishing harbour in the northern part of the town.

Ferries The diminutive passenger and car ferry departs every hour for Ayamonte, returning on the half hour.

Air services Faro International Airport is some 60km by road or rail.

The marina looking south *Henry Buchanan*

AYAMONTE

Ayamonte (Spain)

Lights
Ayamonte (Spain)
Marina basin south side
  Q.G.1s1M Green truncated conical tower
Marina basin north side
  Q.R.1s1M Red column
  Baluarte Fl(2)G.5s2m1M Green tower
Communications
  Puerto Deportivo del Ayamonte
  21400 - Ayamonte (Huelva)
  VHF Ch 09 ① +34 959 034 498 - *Mob* +34 600 149 140
  Email ayamonted@eppa.es
  www.puertosdeandalucia.es

Ayamonte, a village of Greek origin, is, in its way, just as attractive as its Portuguese rival and certainly as historic. The parador here has extensive views of the town and river. Parts of the original 16th-century walls are still visible, there are several old and interesting churches, and all the generations gather for the evening *paseo* in the exuberantly tiled squares. With fewer tourists than the Algarve, the shops are better stocked with practical, everyday items and the cafés are thronged with local people.

This old fishermen's basin contains the westernmost of the string of yacht marinas and sport fishing harbours run by the Agencia Pública de Puertos de Andalucía – see page 266. There are now nine pontoons with finger berths in the marina with a reported capacity of around 317 berths (mostly for yachts 18–20m in length), 25 percent of which are nominally reserved for yachts in transit. It is believed that the entire basin has been dredged to a minimum of 3m.

Entrance and berthing

The marina suffers badly from silting. The last dredging operation to restore 3m depths was completed in 2016. The entrance to the basin is some 60m wide and subject to strong cross-currents, but complete protection is gained once inside. Both sides are lit, and arrival at night is feasible, but call on VHF Ch 09 before entering the basin. Failing the quick allocation of a berth, secure to the westernmost hammerhead or, failing that, choose a suitable berth on the westernmost pontoon.

Weekday office hours are 0930–1330 and 1600–1700, closed Saturday and Sunday afternoons in winter. There is 24 hour security in addition to electronic pontoon access gates, toilets/showers, water, electricity, and used oil disposal.

Formalities

As is usual in Spain, formalities are very relaxed. After completing the usual paperwork in the marina office it is possible that an official may visit the yacht, though this is unlikely in the case of an EU yacht and crew.

Facilities

Boatyard Fishermen's yard near the ferry pier, but nothing for yachts.
Engineers Some mechanical skills available – enquire at the marina office.
Chandlery AYAMAR yacht chandlers: John & Diane PEER have their shop on the main road opposite the marina roundabout. Av. de Andalucia 31, 21400 Ayamonte, Huelva. ①+34 959 470 814 *Mob* +34 677 600 590 *Email* centronautico@aol.com. The chandlery is well stocked and they offer a laundry service.
Electricity and water Available on the pontoons. Water and electricity is always charged, even if there is no consumption when the boat is locked up and the owner goes home.
Showers In a portacabin next to the marina office.
Fuel A 'fuel pontoon' has been in position near the entrance to the basin on the port side for many years completely bereft of pumps or even shore access. It is a real hazard to yachts entering after dark being grey, low-lying, and totally unlit.
Bottled gas Exchanges of Camping Gaz available at the CEPSA shop at the west end of the market building just in from the river.
Weather forecast Posted daily outside the marina office.
Banks In the town.
Shops/provisioning Good shopping in the town, plus a supermarket one block to the east of the marina basin.
Produce market In the town.
Cafés, restaurants and hotels Plenty in the town, but nothing at the marina itself.
Medical services In the town.

Communications

Post office In the town.
Mailing address The marina office will hold mail for visiting yachts – c/o Puerto Deportivo Ayamonte, 21400 Ayamonte, Huelva, España. It is important that the envelope carries the name of the yacht in addition to that of the addressee.
Internet Most use the Cafeteria de Fuenta (part of a hotel) adjoining the SuperSol supermarket, 250m east of the marina office. Also, TodoAPC that is 30m from the northwest corner of the main square nearest the ferry in Calle de Jose Perez Barroso. The technicians have 3 computer terminals and do repairs.
Car hire/taxis/buses In the town.
Ferries Small but frequent passenger and car ferry to Vila Real de Santo António.
Air services Faro International Airport is some 65km distant by road, Seville approximately twice as far.

Puerto Deportivo de Ayamonte looking south *APPA*

ATLANTIC SPAIN AND PORTUGAL   271

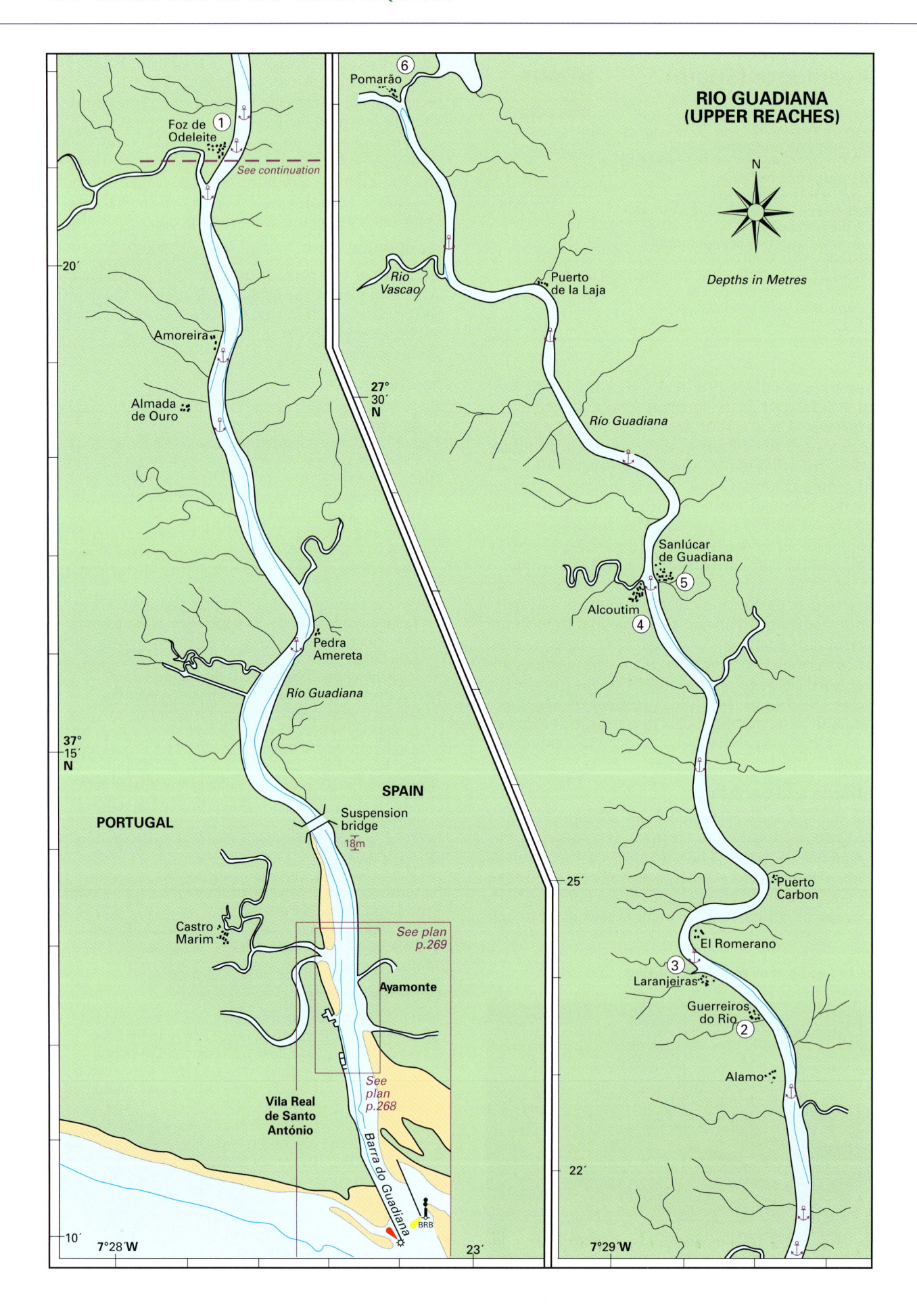

RÍO GUADIANA TO RÍO GUADALQUIVIR

RIO GUADIANA (UPPER REACHES)

Depths in Metres

272　ATLANTIC SPAIN AND PORTUGAL

THE RÍO GUADIANA

Río Guardiana

There is general agreement that the upper reaches of the Río Guadiana are not to be missed, particularly by birdwatchers. White storks can often be seen on the lower reaches of the river above Ayamonte, along with other interesting birds. These include cattle egrets, black-winged stilts and kingfishers. Red-rumped swallows, hoopoes, golden orioles and bee-eaters may be seen further upriver, and a flock of azure-winged magpies live close upstream of Alcoutim/Sanlúcar.

If heading upriver, leave at low water, favouring the starboard side while passing Ayamonte to avoid the muddy shoal which extends nearly halfway across the river north of Vila Real. There is relatively little traffic other than regular ferries, excursion boats in summer and a few fishing vessels.

After passing under the rather elegant suspension bridge (note that the clearance given on Portuguese charts is 18m but that this is referenced to Mean Sea Level.) the Río Guadiana is quiet, pretty and deep but has a current to be reckoned with – approaching 2kn on the flood and 3kn on the ebb. With the aid of the former it is possible to make the 20M or so up to Portuguese Alcoutim and Spanish Sanlúcar de Guadiana on one tide. A minimum of 3·5m, and a maximum of 20m, may to be found as far as Alcoutim/Sanlúcar even at dead low water.

About 50 red and 50 green fixed beacons (steel posts) have been installed over the 15 miles from the suspension bridge to Alcoutim/Sanlúcar. Each is a painted vertical post piled into the river bed with the appropriate small topmark (red can or green triangle) and solar powered light. The positioning seems a bit random being sometimes right at the edge of the river and widely separated, and occasionally placed singly to mark the shallows at the inside of a bend. The 6 posts at Alcoutim itself are strangely positioned, including 2 red ones unnecessarily close to the pontoon. The need for these navigation aids is uncertain as yachts have gone happily up and down river with the tide keeping to the stronger stream and deeper water on the outside of each bend. Perhaps tripper boats from Vila Real intend to use the river at night.

The second pontoon lies off the Portuguese village of Guerreiros do Rio (2), where there is a small river museum
Anne Hammick

Anchorages/pontoons

Straight stretches usually offer the best anchorages, with 6–8m depths and good holding over mud. Boats anchor on both sides of the river, but experience has shown that wind against tide make for an uncomfortable berth. Also, there have been instances of local fishermen setting nets around anchored boats. In one case this led to a light ramming and demands for money to repair nets. Others simply reported torrents of abuse.

High water at Alcoutim/Sanlúcar occurs about 2hrs after Vila Real, high water at Pomarão about 2·5 hours later. In both cases tidal range is marginally reduced compared to the entrance.

Avoid venturing upstream immediately after heavy rain further inland which, as well as adding to the already strong current, can send large items of floating debris such as branches, bamboo canes etc careering downstream.

The Spanish side is sparsely inhabited as far as Sanlúcar, but there are several small villages on the Portuguese bank, including Foz de Odeleite

The pontoon at Foz de Odeleite (1), the first settlement one passes when venturing up the Río Guadiana Anne Hammick

The third Portuguese village to have its own pontoon is Laranjeiras (3), where there is also a good anchorage
Anne Hammick

ATLANTIC SPAIN AND PORTUGAL

THE ALGARVE & ANDALUCIA

RÍO GUADIANA TO RÍO GUADALQUIVIR

The town of Alcoutim (4) on the Portuguese bank, which has three pontoons (one reserved for commercial craft) and is a favourite spot for over-wintering *Anne Hammick*

(37°21'·22N 7°26'·46W), Guerreiros do Río (37°23'·85N 7°26'·8W) and Laranjeiras (37°24'·23N 7°27'·48W). All three have short pontoons, also used by tourist boats running day excursions up the river from Vila Real, to which yachts can secure for no more than three nights. All three pontoons are nominally equipped with water and electricity but may not be operational. Depths alongside have not been verified, but appear generous. Although it was reported some years ago that visitors moorings were to be laid off the villages, there is little evidence of this. None has much in the way of shoreside facilities beyond a bar or two, though a van selling bread and basic foodstuffs makes regular visits, but all are served by the bus which runs north from Vila Real to Alcoutim and beyond. A 'river museum' can be visited at Guerreiros do Río, while a Roman villa is being excavated near Laranjeiras (yachts too large for the pontoon will find good anchorage opposite the village in 4–5m).

Portuguese Alcoutim (37°28'·29N 7°28'·25W) and Spanish Sanlúcar de Guadiana (37°28'·37N 7°28'·11W), linked by pedestrian ferry, are an entirely different matter to the villages downstream.

Both towns have cafés, restaurants, limited shopping (including pharmacies), banks with cash dispensers and public telephones. Alcoutim also has a small hospital and internet access in the public library (2 terminals, booking advised). Camping Gaz can be found in the hardware shop.

Squat stone castles peer at each other across the river, but most would agree that the Castelo de San Marcos on the Spanish side, with origins dating back to the 13th century, has the visual edge over its Portuguese rival, though the latter contains a small museum. Younger crew members will enjoy the praia fluvial (river beach) on a narrow tributary just north of Alcoutim, complete with sand, safe paddling/swimming, and a nearby play area. On the Portuguese side buses run to south to Vila Real and north (twice weekly) as far as Mértola, an old walled town complete with obligatory castle and museums.

Berthing at Sanlúcar and Alcoutim

Both towns have good pontoons, three on the Portuguese side and a single long one on the Spanish, all with functioning water and electricity.

Sanlúcar There is a small flat fee for all yachts lying alongside overnight, though lying to a buoy is understood to be free, as is anchoring. Nominally a maximum of two weeks alongside is allowed but seldom enforced. Adjacent to the Sanlúcar pontoon are purpose-built showers and toilets for the use of berth-holders (key from the nearby *capitania*).

Alcoutim There is a daily charge for the first 7 nights that doubles for the next 7 nights, and after 2 weeks the space has to be vacated. There is space for 2, maybe 3, yachts on the north pontoon and 4 on the south pontoon. Alcoutim's central pontoon is intended for tourist boats rather than yachts.

At least two dozen visitors of all nationalities choose to winter at Alcoutim/Sanlúcar, five or six alongside, a few on moorings and the majority at

Opposite Alcoutim is the Spanish town of Spanish Sanlúcar de Guadiana (5), dominated by its hilltop castle. A pedestrian ferry plies between the two towns *Anne Hammick*

THE RÍO GUADIANA

Pomarão (6), on the Portuguese bank, is as far up the Río Guadiana as most yachts can penetrate, though care is needed on the approach *Anne Hammick*

anchor. If planning to stay at anchor for any length of time it would be wise to lay two, the heaviest upstream and a second, more than a kedge, downstream, secured together at a point deep enough for the yacht to swing.

Upper reaches of the river

Hand drawn charts of the upper reaches of the river can be obtained from the library in Alcoutim for a minimal copying fee. They are obviously only basic aids, but seem reasonably accurate, and might be useful to anyone going up as far as Pomarao.

During May there is a fishery for spawning fish in the upper reaches. The fish is only taken for its roe, the carcass being ditched, but overfishing has led to licensing of the fisherman. This has led to 'gentlemen of the night' taking the law into their own hands and several illegal nets being set at night, some very close to established anchorages (e.g. just around the corner above Alcoutim). Nets have appeared after dark and sunken nets have fouled anchors. Apparently the fishermen simply drop the net at dawn so they are not evident, and recover them again after dark with the aid of grapnel.

There are a number of sizeable boats that look to be abandoned up the river anchored with considerable amounts of chain veered. They are a menace in squally weather, taking up most of the swinging room around them.

A muddy shoal runs out from the west bank just north of Alcoutim and local advice is to keep well to starboard of the line of mooring buoys if heading upriver. With persistence most yachts can get as far as Pomarão (37°33'·28N 7°31'·57W), on the Portuguese side about 7M upstream of Alcoutim. This takes one past disused mine workings and derelict piers once used by sizeable ore-carriers, but the river narrows and has silted in places (the best water will generally be found on the eastern side). Particular caution should be exercised in the approach to Pomarão, which has numerous offlying rocks and boulders. Two short pontoons, both provided with water and electricity, lie beneath the village, which has a seasonal café but little else. There is a short pontoon on the south side but nothing whatsoever ashore. Some road maps show a bridge at Pomarão, but it has long gone if it ever existed at all, and there is no sign of supports or other remains. If anchoring in the vicinity of Pomarão it is best to avoid the area off the old ore-loading jetty immediately west of the pontoons, which is reported to be fouled with chains. Continue about 200m upstream before dropping. Even so a trip line would be adviseable.

Intrepid explorers may wish to continue beyond Pomarão towards Mertola (Portuguese) although a sand and shingle bar halts yachts a few miles downstream of Mertola (not even allowing sufficient depth to proceed by dinghy).

Please note that a hand drawn plan of the river beyond Pomerao is essential and it is a risky trip. There is a report of 3 yachts that have done it, one of which sank in the attempt.

This last stretch of the river runs between stony cliffs and is totally undeveloped. However rocks and sandbanks abound, the latter most often around the mouths of small tributary creeks, and navigation is strictly visual. The water comes straight off the mountains and is clear but very cold.

THE ALGARVE & ANDALUCIA

RÍO GUADIANA TO RÍO GUADALQUIVIR

Islas Canela and Cristina (Ría de la Higuerita)

Location
37°10'·45N 7°18'·93W (entrance)

Tides
Standard port Lisbon
Mean time differences (Portuguese time zone)
HW −0035 ±0020; LW −0020 ±0020
Heights in metres

MHWS	MHWN	MLWN	MLWS
3·2	2·5	1·3	0·5

Principal entrance lights
West breakwater VQ(2)R.5s8m4M
  Red framework tower 4m
Pantalán del Moral, head Fl(2)R.7s4m3M
  Red ■ on red post 3m
Note The tall white building on Punta del Caimán is NOT a light structure but an apartment block

Warning
As with the (much wider) Río Guadiana, while night entry is perfectly possible in the right conditions it is best avoided by those unfamiliar with the area

Communications
VHF Ch 09 (see also marinas, pages 278 and 279).

Dredger off Isla Cristina

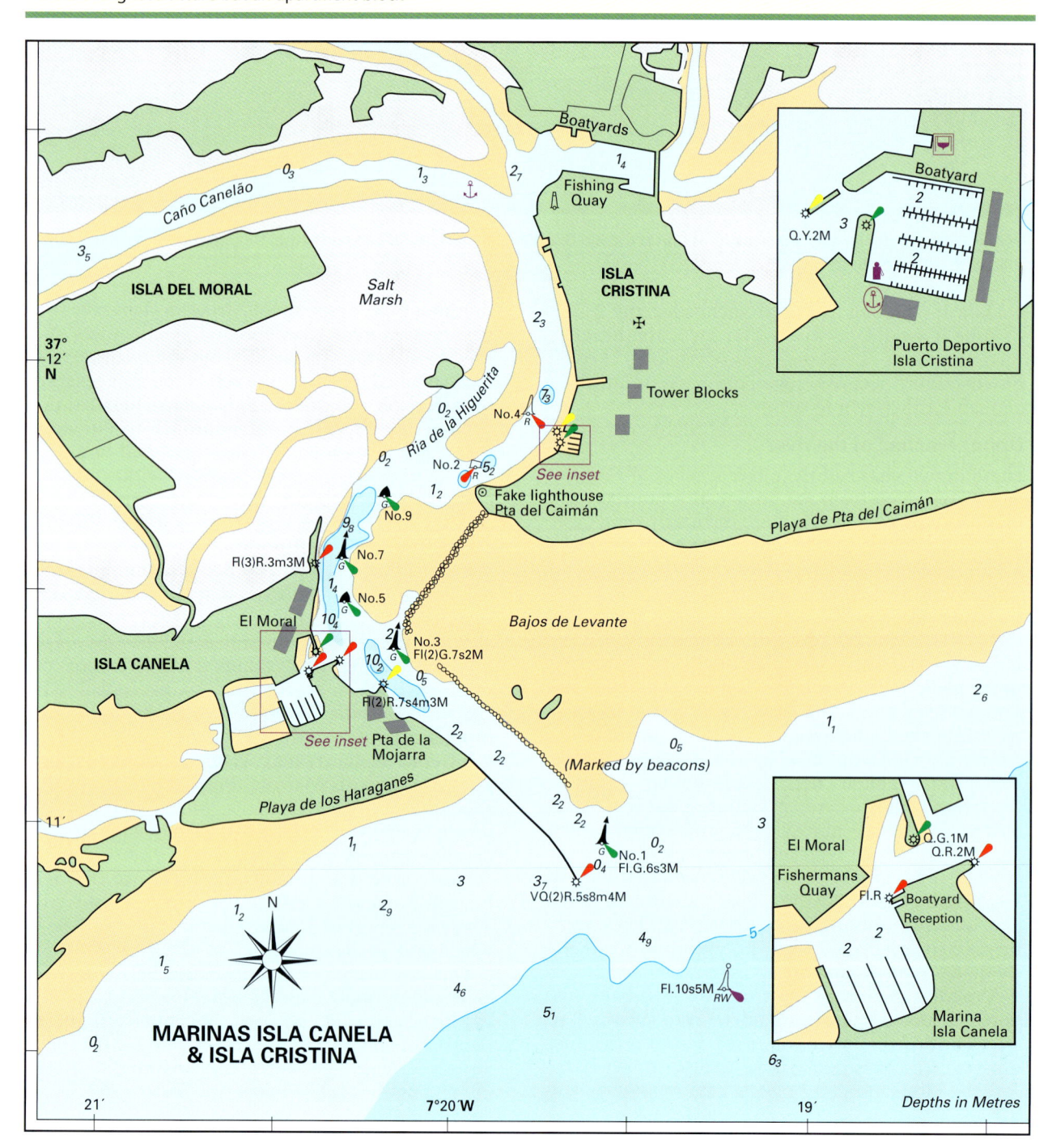

276 ATLANTIC SPAIN AND PORTUGAL

ISLAS CANELA AND CRISTINA

Two well-run marinas surrounded by windswept salt marsh

Marina Isla Canela and the Puerto Deportivo Isla Cristina represent very contrasting styles of Spanish marina development. The former is of the 'marina village' style and while quiet and secure lacks any shoreside atmosphere. However it is only a short walk to a superb beach.

In contrast Isla Cristina, on its long sand spit to the east of the Ría de la Higuerita, is one of the most important fishing ports in Andalucía with a thriving fishing harbour and bustling market. Tourism, much of it Spanish, is a growing industry here and the old town a short walk away is attractive. An illustrated notice in three languages gives some explanation for the visitor.

Approach

If coastal sailing, note that depths between the Río Guadiana and the Ría de la Higuerita are very shoal, with drying patches up to 1M offshore. The 5m line generally runs more than 1·5M offshore.

A fish haven lies 2M offshore, and a fish farm marked by yellow pillar buoys with × topmarks, both lit Q.Y, centred on 37°07'·63N 7°17'·56W, lies 3·7M offshore.

Although the shore on either side of the entrance is low-lying, the development at Punta de la Mojarra (generally referred to as Isla Canela) and the long, pale buildings at Isla Cristina show up well from seaward. Near the southwest corner of Punta del Caimán will be seen a tall beige building complete with domed superstructure, looking for all the world like a rather fancy lighthouse. In fact it is yet another apartment block, but a fine daymark. An older tower, the Torre Catalán, lies halfway between Isla Cristina and El Rompido.

Looking SW into Marina Isla Canela entrance from main channel Jane Russell

Entrance

To aid navigation the APPA bathymetric chart (Puerto de Isla Cristina) for the entrance and well into the Ría de la Higuerita can be found at www.puertosdeandalucia.es/en/documentation-en/batimetrias.

Approach from the south, preferably at between half and three-quarter flood, and turn in to run parallel with the west breakwater. The deeper water is on the western side of the channel.

Upriver

Above the marinas and fishing wharves the channel becomes sinuous and shoal, flanked by salt marsh and ancient, abandoned hulks. The Caño Canelão is marked on the north side with withies and then two prominent wrecks. It is possible to anchor a little way up Caño Canelão, but be aware that the current can run very strongly. Upstream, this is an area to be explored by dinghy, and with an eye to the tide-tables.

The mouth of the Ría de la Higuerita looking northwest, with Marina Isla Canela and its associated development on the left and Isla Cristina further upstream on the right. The distinctive 'fake lighthouse' stands just to the right of centre

ATLANTIC SPAIN AND PORTUGAL   277

RÍO GUADIANA TO RÍO GUADALQUIVIR

Marina Isla Canela

Principal lights
Pantalán del Moral, head Fl(2)R.7s4m3M
South mole Q.R.2M Red post 2m
North mole Q.G.1M Green post
Travel-hoist dock Fl.R.1M Red post

Communications
VHF Ch 09 ① +34 959 479000
Email marina@islacanel.es
www.marina-islacanela.com

Marina village development

Marina Isla Canela is of the 'marina village' type. The surrounding buildings have a distinctly North African character, perhaps related to the fact that *canela* means cinnamon. The old fishermen's quarter at El Moral on the north side of the basin is being swallowed up by new development. Much of the area to the south, while rather attractive with Moorish architecture atop old castle walls in well-kept grounds, is emphatically private.

Entrance

The entrance is well marked and is lit to port, but the triangular green base on the starboard hand has been reported without lens or light. The reception berth requires a second turn to port, lying just beyond the travel-lift and crane and below the blue and white marina office. The four pontoons lie beyond, well sheltered from fishing boat wash and other disturbance, with the largest yachts to the southwest and smallest to the northeast.

Berthing

There are 231 berths in minimum depths of 2·5m. Only 24 of these can take yachts of more than 11m overall including three hammerheads, each rated for 24m. There is room for expansion to the west, where dredging will one day create space for a further 305 berths. The Office is open 24 hours and check-outs can be made at any time.

Multihulls pay a 50% surcharge, water is included but electricity is metred and charged in addition. Discounts are available for longer stays if paid in advance. Most major credit cards are accepted.

Formalities

Whether arriving from Spain or Portugal a single-sheet form is completed at the marina office, a copy of which is automatically passed to the authorities.

Facilities

Boatyard Generous (7200m²), if slightly exposed, area of secure, concreted hardstanding on which yachts are propped but not in cradles. Several contractors are authorized to work in the Marina Marina Umbría, S.L. ①+34 959 313 165 Email info@marinaumbria.es www.marinaumbria.es
Náutica Avante, S.L. ①+34 959 541 306
Email info@nauticavante.com
www.nautica-avante.com
Talleres Mecánicos El Terrón, S.A. ①+34 959 381 527

Marina Isla Canela looking northeast *APPA*

Email recambios@talleresterron.es
www.talleresterron.es
DIY work is permitted, but this is restricted to office hours, and owners are not allowed to live aboard a yacht while ashore.
Travel-lift 32-tonne capacity lift in the boatyard. Also a 2-tonne crane.
Security 24hr. Access by the usual electronic card.
Engineers, electronic and radio repairs Some facilities In the boatyard.
Chandlery Náutiva Avante (see above) operate a small chandlery in the commercial centre but it is almost totally given over to fishing tackle.
Water/ electricity On the pontoons.
Showers In the blue and white reception building.
Launderette Neither available nor planned.
Fuel: Diesel and petrol available 24 hours a day from pumps near the office.
Bottled gas Not available.
Weather forecast Posted daily at the marina office.
Bank No bank, but at least one cash dispenser in the commercial area.
Shops, provisioning Two small supermarkets in the commercial area. For more serious shopping it would be necessary to visit either Ayamonte or Isla Cristina.
Cafés, restaurants and hotels A wide choice in the commercial centre, with a few more in the old town to the north.
Medical services Can be summoned from Ayamonte via the marina office.

Communications

Post office Not as such, not even a post box! The supermarket sells stamps and mail for despatch can be left at the marina office.
Mailing address The marina office will hold mail for visiting yachts – c/o Marina Isla Canela, 21409 Isla Canela, Ayamonte, Huelva, España. It is important that the envelope carries the name of the yacht in addition to that of the addressee.
Internet Internet café in the commercial centre.
Car hire At least one agency in the commercial centre.
Taxis Order via the marina office.
Buses Bus stop a little way down the road.
Air services International airports at Faro (Portugal) and Seville (Spain).

ISLAS CANELA AND CRISTINA

Puerto Deportivo Isla Cristina

Principal lights
South mole Q.G.5m2M Green column 2m
Wavebreak pontoon Q.Y.2M Post 2m

Communications
VHF Ch 09 ⏰ +34 959 077 613, +34 600 149 130
Email islacristinad@puertosdeandalucia.es
www.puertosdeandalucia.es

Puerto Deportivo Isla Cristina looking south APPA

The first APPA marina built

The Puerto Deportivo Isla Cristina was one of the first built by the Agencia Pública de Puertos de Andalucía (APPA - see page 266) and is best suited to smaller yachts, being relatively shallow and with few berths able to accommodate more than 10m overall.

Entrance and berthing

Shortly after passing the entrance to Marina Isla Canela the channel bends to starboard around a drying middle ground marked by several starboard hand buoys (do not be tempted to emulate local craft which may take a short cut across the shallows). A port-hand buoy opposite the 'lighthouse' and a second almost opposite the marina entrance mark a second shoal. A 90m wavebreak pontoon has been laid off the marina entrance in a partially successful attempt to deflect the considerable wash from passing fishing boats, few of which take any notice of the 4kn speed limit.

The relatively narrow entrance to Puerto Deportivo Isla Cristina lies inside the shelter pontoon. Although it is lit, particular care should be taken if entering after dark. Depth in the entrance is 2·5m, decreasing to 2m inside. Secure to the reception/fuel pontoon immediately to starboard to be allocated a berth, preferably having already called up on VHF Ch 09 – a wise precaution in any case, since only 20 of the marina's 203 berths are able to take yachts of more than 10m overall. These are all on the northernmost pontoon, with all berths now alongside finger pontoons.

Office hours vary from summer to winter, being 0800–2000 daily in summer, 0930–1330 and 1600–1730 in winter, closed weekend afternoons. Berthing staff are on duty from 0700–2200 and there is 24 hour security, as well as electronic gates to individual pontoons and the boatyard area.

Formalities

Whether arriving from Spain or Portugal a single-sheet form is completed at the marina office, a copy of which is automatically passed to the authorities. Nothing further needs to be done, even if arriving from outside the EU, though occasionally the *Guardia Civil* may visit the yacht in her berth.

Facilities

Boatyard An area of gated hardstanding near the travel-lift enables owners to do their own maintenance or to call in one of the contractors in the area. Yachts are placed in cradles with additional shores.
It would appear that Náutica Levante SYS have stopped trading or changed its name, so the authorised contractors described for Marina Isla Canela should be contacted as required.
Travel-lift 32-tonne capacity lift, fixed crane, 5 tonne.
Engineers, electronics and radio repairs Some facilities in the boatyard.
Sail repairs Can be arranged through contractors in the boatyard.
Chandlery There is a well-stocked chandlery in the commercial block.
Water/electricity On the pontoons.
Showers At the rear of the commercial block.
Launderette At the rear of the commercial block.
Fuel Diesel and petrol available at the fuel/reception berth, open 0700–1900 daily. Exact payment must be made in cash. No change is given.
Bottled gas Camping Gaz available in the town, but no refills.
Weather forecast Posted daily at the marina office.
Banks In the town.
Shops/provisioning All usual shops in the town, a short walk from the marina, but no food shops on site.
Cafés, restaurants and hotels Small café overlooking the marina, but no restaurant. However both are to be found in the older part of the town, with hotels mainly centred in the newer beachside areas.
Medical services In the town.

Communications

Post office In the town.
Mailing address The marina office will hold mail for visiting yachts – c/o Puerto Deportivo Isla Cristina, Officina del Puerto, Bda Punta del Caiman s/n, 21410 Isla Cristina, Huelva, España. It is important that the envelope carries the name of the yacht in addition to that of the addressee.
Internet Several places in the town, including a cybercafé on the ground floor of the 'lighthouse' building.
Car hire/taxis Available in the town or via the marina office.
Buses To Ayamonte, Huelva and beyond.
Air services International airports at Faro (Portugal) and Seville (Spain).

ATLANTIC SPAIN AND PORTUGAL   279

RÍO GUADIANA TO RÍO GUADALQUIVIR

Rio de las Piédras

Location
37°11'·667N 7°03'·356W (Fairway Buoy 2018, but varies)

Tides
Standard port Lisbon
Mean time differences (at Huelva bar)
HW +0010 ±0010; LW +0035 ±0005
(allowing for one hour difference in time zones)
Heights in metres

MHWS	MHWN	MLWN	MLWS
3·2	2·5	1·2	0·4

Principal lights
Rompido de Cartaya Fl(2)10s42m24M
White tower, red band 29m
Fairway buoy No.1 LFl.10s5M
Red and white vertical striped pillar buoy, • topmark
Note At least a dozen further buoys should indicate the channel (see plan).

Warning
Both the position of the bar and the depths over it alter frequently. In an initiative to reduce the risk of grounding on entry, APPA and the Puerto Marina El Rompido provide information on their respective websites:
APPA www.puertosdeandalucia.es/en/documentation-en/batimetrias. This includes a Bathymetry Chart of the entrance to the Rio de las Piédras (see example page 266)

www.puertoelrompido.com/index.php/es/inicio/97-riopiedras/213-balizamiento This shows the latest positions of buoyage which they are responsible for moving several times a year. Puerto Marina El Rompido is always ready to provide advice see details below.

Night entry
Unsuitable for night entry by a keel yacht under any circumstances.

Communications
Puerto Marina El Rompido VHF Ch 71 ☎ +34 959 399 614 and +34 607 456 480 *Mob* +34 695 589 510
Email info@puertoelrompido.com
fran@puertoelrompido.com
www.puertoelrompido.com
Club Náutico Río Piedras VHF Ch 09 ☎+34 959 504 270 or +34 663 928 666
Email gerencia@cnriopedras.es www.cnriopedras.es
Asociatión Deportiva Nautica Sān Miguel ☎ +34 959 399 070 info@adnsanmiguel.es www.adnsanmiguel.es
Asociación Deportiva Nautica Nuevo Portil Marina Nuevo Portil ☎ +34 959 504 100 adnnportil@yahoo.es www.adnnuevoportil.es

Río de las Piédras looking east. Punta Umbría in the distance *APPA*

280   ATLANTIC SPAIN AND PORTUGAL

RIO DE LAS PIÉDRAS

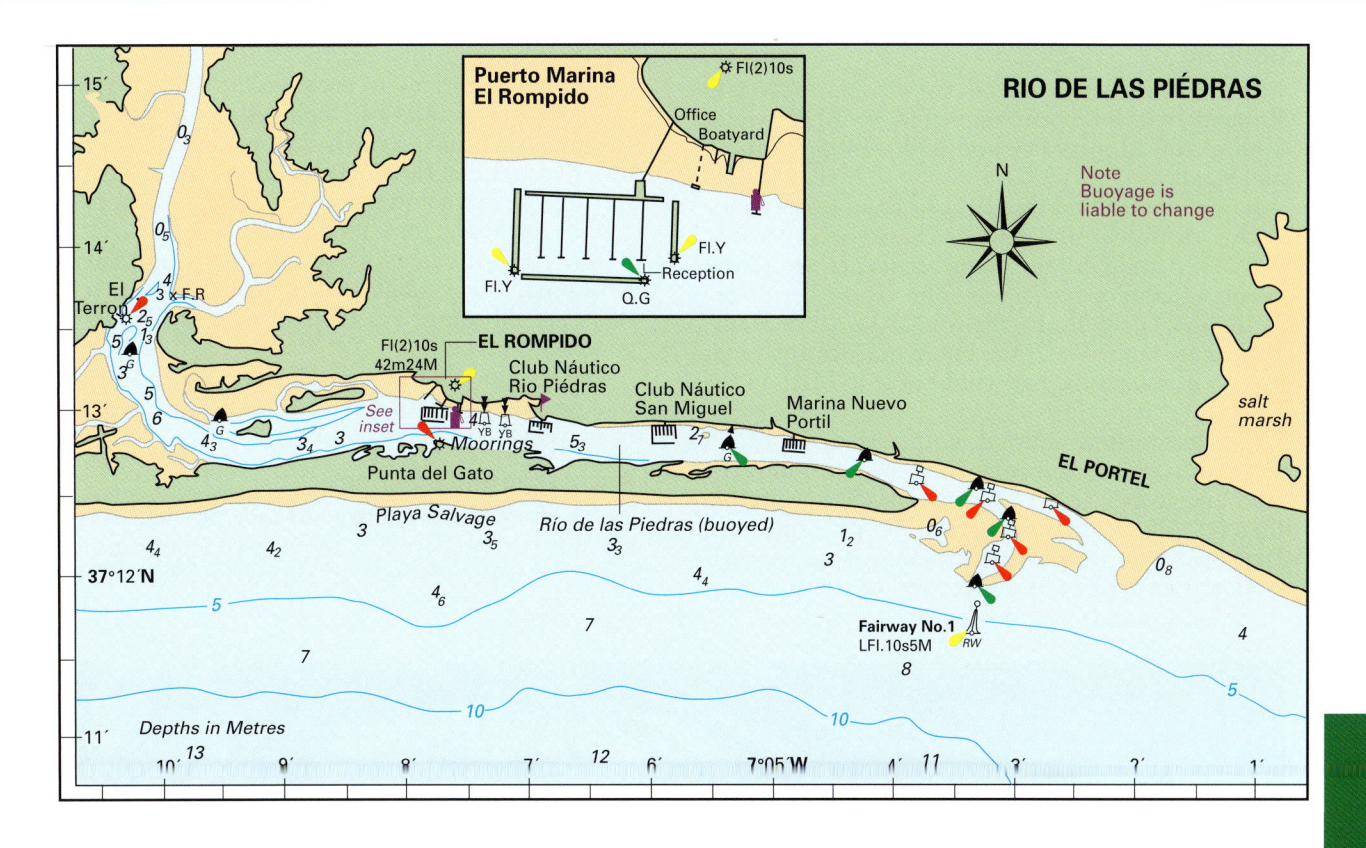

Shallow, challenging entrance leading into a coastal lagoon-like river

Most cruising yachtsmen would agree that the Rio de las Piédras is one of the most attractive spots along this stretch of the coast. That it has been inhabited since pre-Roman times comes as no surprise, the long sandspit of the Punta del Gato (rompeolas = breakwater) making the protected waters of the Río Piedras seem more like a lagoon than a river. However, before gaining its tranquil interior, a difficult, twisting bar must be negotiated.

Considerable change has taken place in the Río de la Piédras in recent years with the creation of three new marinas. El Rompido itself has been developed as a seasonal holiday resort for Spaniards from Seville and elsewhere. Out of season there is a distinct lack of life, except on sunny Sundays when the restaurants fill up with visitors coming to dine on the shellfish and seafood.

The river is well protected but has strong tides. Locals fish from dinghies and small boats on moorings, and harvest shellfish and oysters from the shallows. Some decked fishing boats are based upstream at El Terrón.

In season, a road train links the hotels with the village, and ferries ply across the lagoon to the sandspit, for beach access to the Atlantic.

Approach

From the west, the shoreline is unbroken between Isla Cristina and the entrance to the Rio de las Piédras with a daymark, the Torre Catalán, on the higher dunes west of the point where the Río de las Piédras turns inland past El Terrón. To the east, the beach is backed by dunes rising up to 40m and topped by umbrella pines.

If conditions are less than perfect on arrival at the Fairway No.1 buoy, decide whether it is safe to press on or whether it would be more prudent to turn west for Portugal or east for Mazagón and beyond.

Entrance

Daylight and no significant swell are basic prerequisites for entry into the Río de la Piédras. When planning an entry the advice and support provided by both APPA and the Puerto Marina El Rompido in their respective websites should be consulted (see Warning on page 280). The bar alters continuously in both shape and charted depth, and buoys are moved several times a year to reflect this. The bar has only about 0·5m at MLWS but with a spring range of 3·7m (and neap range of 2m) most cruising yachts should be able to enter with reasonable care. Enter near high water, on the flood. It is well worth the effort.

It should be noted that with easterly winds in the Straits of Gibraltar tide levels can rise by up to 20 cm above the predictions. Conversely a strong west wind will produce a drop in tidal height.

From the fairway buoy the first buoy to the north is a green buoy to starboard, then further up a red buoy to port. The buoyage then leads through to where the curves round to the west into deeper water in the lagoon where there is plenty of depth.

There are two large and distinctive floats further upriver opposite the village. Both are marked as Southerly Cardinal Buoys, to keep traffic away from the small boat moorings on the north shore.

RÍO GUADIANA TO RÍO GUADALQUIVIR

Berthing

Most visiting yachts head to the marina at El Rompido which is open: summer 0730–2230; winter 1000–1200 Mon to Fri, and 0900–1400 Saturday and Sunday.

It contains 331 berths, 20% of them reserved for yachts in transit and half of these for short-stay visitors. Although long-term berths are limited to yachts of 20m or less, a few 30m visitor berths are available. There are berths for 10-15 catamarans. Depths are limited at 2-3m, but in practice any yacht able to negotiate the bar will be able to berth in the marina.

The structure is unusual, with a single pontoon secured by piles projecting some distance into the river and giving access to the marina's five projecting fingers. All berths are against finger pontoons. Detached floating wavebreaks made from recycled tyres are secured up and downstream, with a third (concrete) pontoon to the south. These will obviously do nothing to decrease the tidal flow, and newcomers would be well advised to avoid manoeuvring during the height of the ebb or, to a lesser extent the flood, particularly at springs. At springs, the current in the river can reach 3 knots for a while, including through the marina berths.

Marina staff can assist with berthing and have a workboat, but if conditions are particularly adverse there are moorings available to wait until suitable conditions pertain.

The reception berth is on the hammerhead of the 2nd pontoon (No 4). The office is ashore, near the head of the long access pontoon.

Anchorage and moorings

There is now little room to anchor downstream of the marina but space may be found immediately upstream but well out in the river, clear of the

Puerto Marina El Rompido looking North *APPA*

Puerto Marina El Rompido looking southwest *APPA*

282   ATLANTIC SPAIN AND PORTUGAL

RIO DE LAS PIÉDRAS

shallows. A problem is the lack of a landing by dinghy, with the ferry and fuel jetties out of bounds. The Puerto Marina El Rompido will provide a swipe card for access, and permission to tie up a dinghy for a fee.

Multihulls and other shoal draught vessels may be able to work upstream as far as El Terrón, where there is a busy fishermen's quay and a shallow pontoon for local smallcraft. Holding is said to be good over mud. Water, telephones, restaurants and basic shopping will be found ashore, and fuel is available at the quay. There are information boards about the *Paraje Natural 'Marismas del Río Piedras y Flecha de El Rompido'*, an area covering the Punta del Gato sand spit and much of the Río Piédras estuary. For those with yachts already on a secure mooring it would make an interesting dinghy excursion.

Facilities

Boatyard, engineers, electronic and radio repairs Nautica Portil Varadero ✆ +34 959 369 026 at Puerto de El Rompido S/N (antiguo varadero Río Piedra) 21459 - El Rompido - Cartaya - Huelva (España) *Email* astillero@varaderospalmas.com www.varaderospalmas.com The owner, Francisco Palma (2017), is expected to continue the yard's excellent reputation for helpfulness and efficiency. The yard is tucked between the long hammerhead jetty and the marina, almost directly below the lighthouse.

Employees or subcontractors can handle repairs in timber, GRP and metals including stainless steel and aluminium. Alternatively owners can do their own work. There are on-site mechanical and electronics workshops, plus an agency for Volvo, Nautech and Lewmar. The yard would be an excellent place for winter lay-up, though space is limited.

Travel-lift The boatyard's marine railway can handle vessels of up to 50 tonnes and 6m beam.

Sailmaker Olivier Plisson of Vop Sails, ✆ +34 959 399025 *Email* info@vopsails.com www.vopsails.com who has premises just outside the Varadero Río Piedras, makes and repairs sails and will handle canvas work of all kinds.

Chandlery Small chandlery at the boatyard, with further items ordered as required.

Water Available on the marina pontoons, or by can from the boatyard or the Club Náutico Río Piedras (where there is a coin-operated tap on the pontoon).

Launderette and showers Excellent and modern in a building close by the marina office that issues electronic cards for access. Also tokens for the washing machine and dryer. Showers otherwise at the boatyard or the Club Náutico, both of which make a small charge.

Camping gas Exchanges can be made through the marina office.

Security Electronic card and very watchful marineros (good CCTV).

Shops/provisioning The El Faro Commercial Centre by the lighthouse has a large El Jamon supermarket. Fashion boutiques in season.

Cafés, restaurants Available in the marina complex with excellent views of the lagoon.

Communications

Post office Backing onto the church.

Mailing address: The marina office will hold mail for visiting yachts – c/o Puerto El Rompido, s/n 21459 – El Rompido (Huelva) España. It is important that the envelope carries the name of the yacht in addition to that of the addressee.

Internet WiFi is available throughout the marina, with additional connection facilities in the office.

Taxis Best ordered by phone.

Coaches From Huelva to Seville 14/day (2 hour journey time) arrive at the Plaza de Armas bus station where the Airport bus leaves every ½ hour (allow ¾ hour journey time).

Air services International airports at Faro (Portugal) and Seville (Spain).

From fuel pontoon over ferry pontoon to boatyard and lighthouse Henry Buchanan

THE ALGARVE & ANDALUCIA

ATLANTIC SPAIN AND PORTUGAL

RÍO GUADIANA TO RÍO GUADALQUIVIR

Canal de Punta Umbría

Location
37°08'·71N 6°56'·91W (entrance)

Tides
Standard port Lisbon
Mean time differences (at Huelva bar)
HW +0010 ±0010; LW +0035 ±0005
(allowing for one hour difference in time zones)
Heights in metres
MHWS	MHWN	MLWN	MLWS
3·2	2·5	1·2	0·4

Principal lights
Breakwater head VQ(6)+LFl.10s10m5M
Black ▼ on tower with black base 4m

Warning
Though well lit, in view of depths at the bar night entry is not recommended for those unfamiliar with the area

Harbour communications
Real Club Marítimo y Tennis de Punta Umbría
VHF Ch 09, 16 ☎ +34 959 3118 99 (Secy) or +34 959 315 677 (Capt)
Email rcmtpu@rcmtpu.com
www.rcmtpu.com
Puerto Deportivo de Punta Umbría
VHF Ch 09 ☎ +34 959 314 304 or +34 959 314 298
Club Deportivo Náutico Punta Umbría
VHF Ch 09 ☎ +34 959 314 401 *Mob* +34 659 506 303 / 649 871 337
Email info@cdnpuntaumbria.es
www.cdnpuntaumbria.es
APPA www.puertosdeandalucia.es/en/documentation-en/batimetrias.

Attractive channel in the Ría de Huelva

Punta Umbría on the west bank of the Canal de Punta Umbría has developed from being a small fishing village to a thriving tourist resort, thanks largely to its excellent beaches. The reconstructed Real Club Marítimo y Tennis de Punta Umbría (RCMTPU) provides space for larger yachts to now berth in the channel.

It was on the beach at La Bota that the corpse of *The Man Who Never Was* and the disinformation contained with the body was found by local fishermen. It had been launched from the submarine HMS Seraph and the 'intelligence' reached the Punta Umbría police, found its way to Berlin and formed the first stage of the plot to deceive Hitler over Allied intentions for the landings on Sicily later in 1943. The body of Glyndwr Michael is now buried in the cemetery of Nuestra Senora de la Soledad in Huelva (Grave No. 1886).

In the Ría de Huelva, the marshlands and the natural park of Las Marismas de Odiel are major attractions with the World Biosphere Reserve providing a habitat for over 200 species of birds.

Approach

From the west Low, sandy, pine-topped cliffs stretch from the lighthouse at El Rompido all the way to Punta Umbría. There is a line of tower blocks to the west of Punta Umbría. Beyond Punta Umbría, the most prominent coastal feature is the refinery on the Canal del Padre Santo (Mazagón Huelva Canal), further east again.

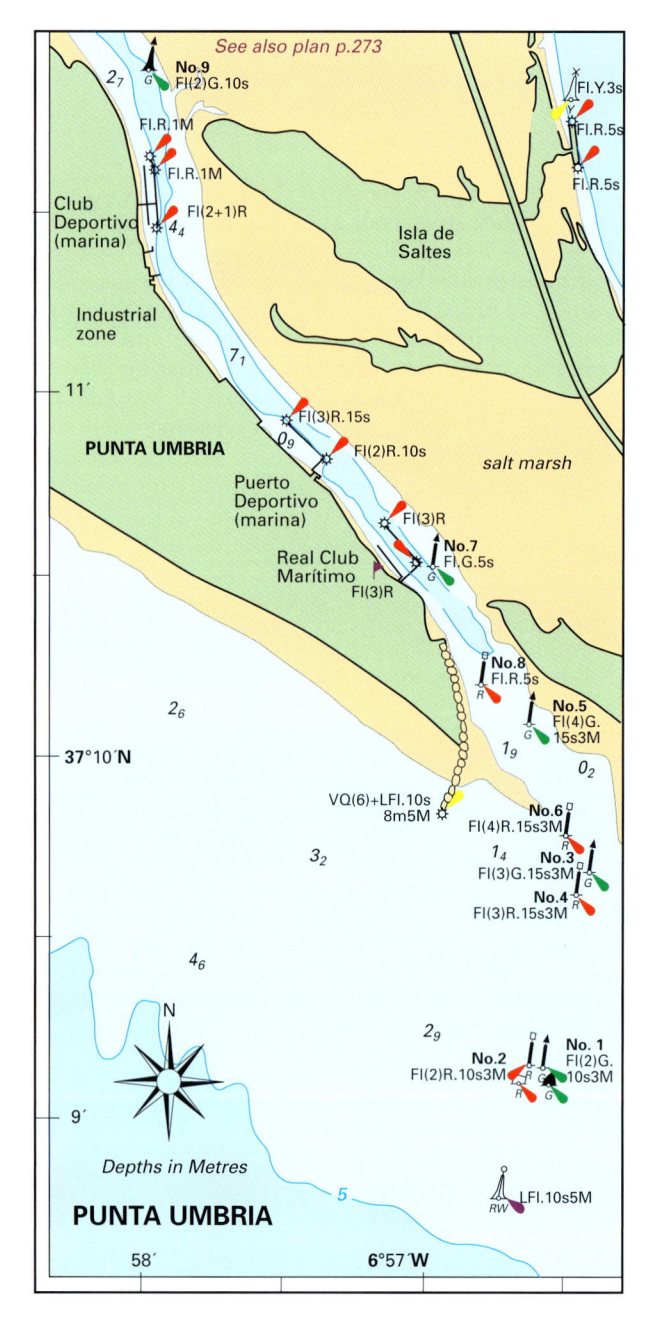

From the east The coast from Matalascañas as far as Mazagón is backed by sand dunes while the final 7M from Mazagón is formed almost entirely of the impressive Juan Carlos I breakwater. Against this a low-lying sandy beach, the Playa de Espigón, has formed.

Entrance

The breakwater into the Canal de Punta Umbría is about 0·5M in length, though much of this is masked from the west by an accretion of sand against it that has allowed the beach to form. During storms from the westerly sector, sand is blown over the breakwater forming a bank out into the channel.

The extent of the sand bank and thus the position of the entrance channel varies, especially after

284 ATLANTIC SPAIN AND PORTUGAL

CANAL DE PUNTA UMBRÍA

The entrance looking south and the Real Club Marítimo y Tennis de Punta Umbría in the foreground *APPA*

westerly storms. In an initiative to reduce the risk of grounding on entry, APPA provides information on their website. This includes a Bathymetry Chart of the entrance to the Puerto de Punta Umbría, see page 266.

Depths at the bar are no more than 1m at chart datum (4·2m at MHWS or 3·5m at MHWN). Local advice is to err towards the east side of the channel which is marked by 8 buoys. With so much traffic in the channel there is an excellent chance of following a local vessel in, though allowance must be made for the probable difference in draught.

Once past the root of the mole the channel begins to deepen, after which 5m or more should be found about 100m from the western bank.

View up-channel along the wavebreaker pontoon at the Real Cub Maritimo y Tennis de Punta Umbría
Henry Buchanan

Berthing and moorings

There are three berthing possibilities in the Canal de Punta Umbria:

1. The **Real Club Marítimo y Tennis de Punta Umbría** (RCMTU) has enjoyed a major reconstruction offering 260 berths, of which 25% are reserved for transit yachts. It can take yachts up to 22m (2 or 3 berths), and the breakwater system pioneered in Spain allows an impressive reduction in noise and any movement caused by wash from passing fishing boats.

Available services include electricity, water and 24 hour assistance and security. In addition there is WiFi covering the entire marina area.

2. The **Puerto Deportivo de Punta Umbría** is one of APPA's smallest in all senses of the word. It also lacks many of the shoreside facilities found at its larger peers. Even though depth is not an issue, with a minimum of 2·5m throughout, only a dozen of the 197 berths can take vessels of more than 10m, and the vast majority are occupied by diminutive runabouts. At first glance the long outer pontoon appears spacious and tempting, but any direction to secure to it should be resisted strenuously. A detached wave-break pontoon is positioned downstream of the marina, but the outer pontoon receives no protection whatsoever from the wash of speeding fishing boats. The entire marina heaves and groans alarmingly as each one passes, and few fishermen appear to pay even lip service to the 5kn speed limit. When several boats follow each other in close succession and their washes combine, damage may occur.

ATLANTIC SPAIN AND PORTUGAL 285

THE ALGARVE & ANDALUCIA

RÍO GUADIANA TO RÍO GUADALQUIVIR

Looking northeast at Punta Umbría showing the marinas from left to right –
Club Deportivo Náutico Punta Umbría, Puerto Deportivo de Punta Umbría and Real Club Marítimo y Tennis de Punta Umbría.
The Huelva channel is beyond.

The marina office is open from 1000–1330 and 1630–2000 daily in summer, closing at 1730 during the winter (when it is also shut on weekend afternoons). Water and electricity are available on the pontoons, with showers ashore (but no launderette). A weather forecast is posted daily, and fuel is available nearby (see Facilities, below), but little else appears to be on offer. Surprisingly, despite jutting much further into the channel than any of the other jetties, the southeast corner of the marina is unlit.

3. The **Club Deportivo Náutico Punta Umbría**, upstream of the fishermen's quay, is by far the most peaceful. Although private and normally full of members' boats, space for a visiting yacht of up to 10m can usually be found alongside the long outer pontoon in depths of 5-6m, if only for a night or two. The club also controls a number of moorings able to take up to 12m. In both cases it would be wise to make contact before arrival.

The club has extensive grounds and a sizeable clubhouse featuring the usual bar and restaurant. The secretary's office will be found upstairs, having entered at the rear of the building, and is open 1100–1400 and 1600–2000 Monday to Saturday inclusive. Water and electricity are available on the pontoons, including the outer one, and there are showers in the clubhouse, but there are no other facilities on site. However, it is only a short walk into the town, and even shorter to the supermarket in the industrial zone.

Anchorage

The channel is too narrow and full of moorings to anchor opposite the town, and the lower reaches and are at the mercy of the busy fishing fleet. Continue past the Club Deportivo Náutico Punta Umbría, beyond the moorings, and anchor either side of the channel where depth allows. Though most fishing boats go no further than the wharf just upstream of the Puerto Deportivo, tripper boats ply to and fro to Huelva via the connecting channels and the fairway must be left clear. An anchor light should be displayed at night. In all cases allow for the strength of the ebb tide, which may reach 4–5kn at springs even close in to the shore.

View out across the Canal from the CDN Punta Umbría *CDN Punta Umbría*

286   ATLANTIC SPAIN AND PORTUGAL

CANAL DE PUNTA UMBRÍA

The Náuticas Punta Umbría marine railway facility
Henry Buchanan

Puerto Deportivo de Punta Umbría looking west *APPA*

Facilities

Boatyard Náuticas Punta Umbría SA ✆+34 959 310 700
  Email nauticaspuntaumbria@hotmail.com
  www.geocities.com/nauticaspuntaumbria. This is a large, gated boatyard in the industrial area north of the Puerto Deportivo and the fishing wharf, where many local yachts are wintered ashore. Although served by a good-sized marine railway, the maximum size appears to be around 10m.
  The Varadero boat services facility is alongside the boatyard at:
    Antigua Zona Industrial, C/ Varaderos S/N, 21100 - Punta Umbría - Huelva (España)
    www.varaderospalmas.com
    Email astillero@varaderospalmas.com
    ✆ +34 959 311 901
  Varadero run the boatyard at El Rompido also.
Travel-lift None (though see above).
Engineers, electronics Náuticas Punta Umbría SA is able to handle most types of yacht and engine maintenance.
Sailmaker/sail repairs Shanty Sails, ✆ +34 959 310700, close to Náuticas Punta Umbría in the industrial zone, make and repair sails and handle general canvas work.
Chandlery Náuticas Punta Umbría SA (open 1000–1330, 1630–2030, closed Saturday afternoon and all day Sunday) has a well-stocked chandlery adjacent to its boatyard.
Water On all three sets of pontoons.
Showers At all three clubhouses/offices.

Puerto Deportivo de Punta Umbría marina looking up-channel (N) *Henry Buchanan*

Launderette In the town.
Electricity On all three sets of pontoons.
Fuel Diesel and petrol from a pontoon between the Puerto Deportivo and the fishermen's quay. Hours are not specified.
Bottled gas Camping Gaz exchanges available in the town, but no refills.
Weather forecast At all three clubhouses/offices.
Clube Náuticos The long-established Real Club Marítimo y Tennis de Punta Umbría, and the much newer Club Deportivo Náutico Punta Umbría. See under Berthing, above.
Banks In the town, with cash dispensers.
Shops/provisioning Large and cavernous supermarket (the Spanish equivalent of a cash and carry) one block in from the boatyard mentioned above. General shopping of all kinds in the town.
Cafés, restaurants and hotels At the two Clube Náuticos, with dozens more throughout the town.
Medical services In the town.

Communications

Post office In the town.
Mailing address Use the following addresses as appropriate:
  Real Club Marítimo y Tennis de Punta Umbría, Av. Alm. Pérez Guzmán nº 20, 21100 Punta Umbría, Huelva, España
  Puerto Deportivo de Punta Umbría, Prolongac. Av. de Marina, S/N, 21110 Punta Umbría, Huelva, España
  Club Deportivo Náutico Punta Umbría, Prolongación Avenida de la Marina, s/n, 21100 Punta Umbría, Huelva, España.
  They will hold mail for visiting yachts by prior arrangement only. In all cases it is important that the envelope carries the name of the yacht in addition to that of the addressee.
Car hire Several offices in the town.
Taxis In the town, or order via the office(s).
Buses In the town, connecting with trains at Huelva.
Dinghies It is possible to take the dinghy through the east arm of the channel under a causeway bridge to the main Huelva channel. This comes out opposite the power station and Columbus statue with La Rabida opposite, beyond another causeway bridge, to secure the dinghy.
Air services About equidistant between Faro (Portugal) and Seville (Spain).

RÍO GUADIANA TO RÍO GUADALQUIVIR

Mazagón Huelva Channel (Canal del Padre Santo)

Location
37°05'·25N 6°49'W (entrance)

Tides
Standard port Lisbon
Mean time differences (at Huelva bar)
HW +0010 ±0010; LW +0035 ±0005
(allowing for one hour difference in time zones)
Heights in metres

MHWS	MHWN	MLWN	MLWS
3·2	2·5	1·2	0·4

Principal lights
River entrance
Juan Carlos I. Breakwater head Fl(3+1)WR.20s29m12/9M
165°-W-100°-R-125° Racon Mo 'K'(–·–)12M AIS
White tower, red band 27m
Dir Lt 339° DirWRG.59m8M
337·2°-G-337·8°-Oc.G-338·3°-WG-338·9°-Oc.W-339·1°-WR-339·7°-R-340·2°-R-340·7° White tower 15m
Note The deep channel shifts from time to time and buoys are moved accordingly.
Marina
Southwest breakwater head Q.G.7m2M
Grey framework on green base 4m
Northeast breakwater head Q.R.5m2M
Grey framework on red base 4m
T-breakwater Fl.G.5s3m1M
Grey framework on green base 4m
Reception quay Fl.R.5s3m1M
Grey framework on red base 3m

Communications
Puerto Deportivo de Mazagón
VHF Ch 09, 16 ① +34 959 070 071 - 671 539 702
Email mazagon@eppa.es www.puertosdeandalucia.es
Coast radio station
Huelva *Digital Selective Calling*
MMSI 002241012
VHF Ch 10, 16, 26
Weather bulletins and navigational warnings
Weather bulletins and navigational warnings in Spanish and English: VHF Ch 10 at 0415, 0815, 1215, 1615, 2015 UT

One of the Columbus ships at La Rabida *Jane Russell*

Modern, purpose-built yacht marina with good facilities, little character but local interest

Another of the new harbours built and run by the Agencia Pública de Puertos de Andalucía, Puerto Deportivo Mazagón is somewhat larger than most. It contains 647 berths, including 25 reserved for visiting yachts. The marina is also home to various 'official' craft including the smaller Huelva pilot boats, fishery protection vessels and a Guardia Civil RIB.

There is an excellent beach right next to the marina, with the quiet and leafy town a steepish walk up the road, worth the effort for some friendly local colour and good restaurants.

Mazagón is a good base for exploring links with Columbus at Palos de la Frontera and La Rábida monastery. The pronouncement that the voyage would go ahead was made in the church of St George at Palos de la Frontera. Many of the crew for the ships came from here, and it was from here that Columbus finally set sail. The replica Columbus Ships at La Rabida are worth the walk down from the monastery.

Approach

From the west The Juan Carlos I breakwater, one of the longest in Europe, has its southern point at the entrance to the Mazagón Huelva Channel (Canal del Padre Santo). A restricted area containing a tanker loading berth and associated pipeline extends almost 5M offshore about 4·5M west of the breakwater. Anchoring and fishing are banned in its vicinity, but vessels may pass inside or between the buoys.

From the east The coast from Matalascañas, with its prominent radio aerials, as far as Mazagón, is backed by sand dunes. A gas pipeline nearly 25M in length and fed by at least two production wells comes ashore about 4M southeast of Mazagón. Two yellow buoys with topmarks, both Fl.Y.5s5M, indicate its western and southern extremes at 36°59'·5N 7°11'·4W and 36°51'N 7°05'·3W respectively. A further two buoys, identical to the above, mark the junction at 37°09'·9N 6°59'·7W. Anchoring and mooring are prohibited in the vicinity, but there are no restrictions on sailing over it.

Once in the channel, Mazagón marina will be seen on the starboard hand about 1·5M inside the breakwater end.

Entrance

The bathymetric chart for the Puerto Deportivo de Mazagón and its immediate approach can be found on the APPA website www.puertosdeandalucia.es/en/documentation-en/batimetrias > 'Batimetría Puerto de Mazagón'.

The entrance, which is lit, carries at least 4·5m as far as the reception pontoon, which is on the port hand below the prominent tower housing the marina office.

Berthing

Secure to the long reception pontoon, which doubles as a fuelling berth (avoid securing in the centre for this reason). If arriving outside office hours (1000–1300, 1600–1730 daily in winter, rather longer in summer), security staff will allocate a berth, or leave the yacht where she is if no berth is available. A total of 11 pontoons (all with fingers) take yachts of up to

ATLANTIC SPAIN AND PORTUGAL

RÍA DE HUELVA

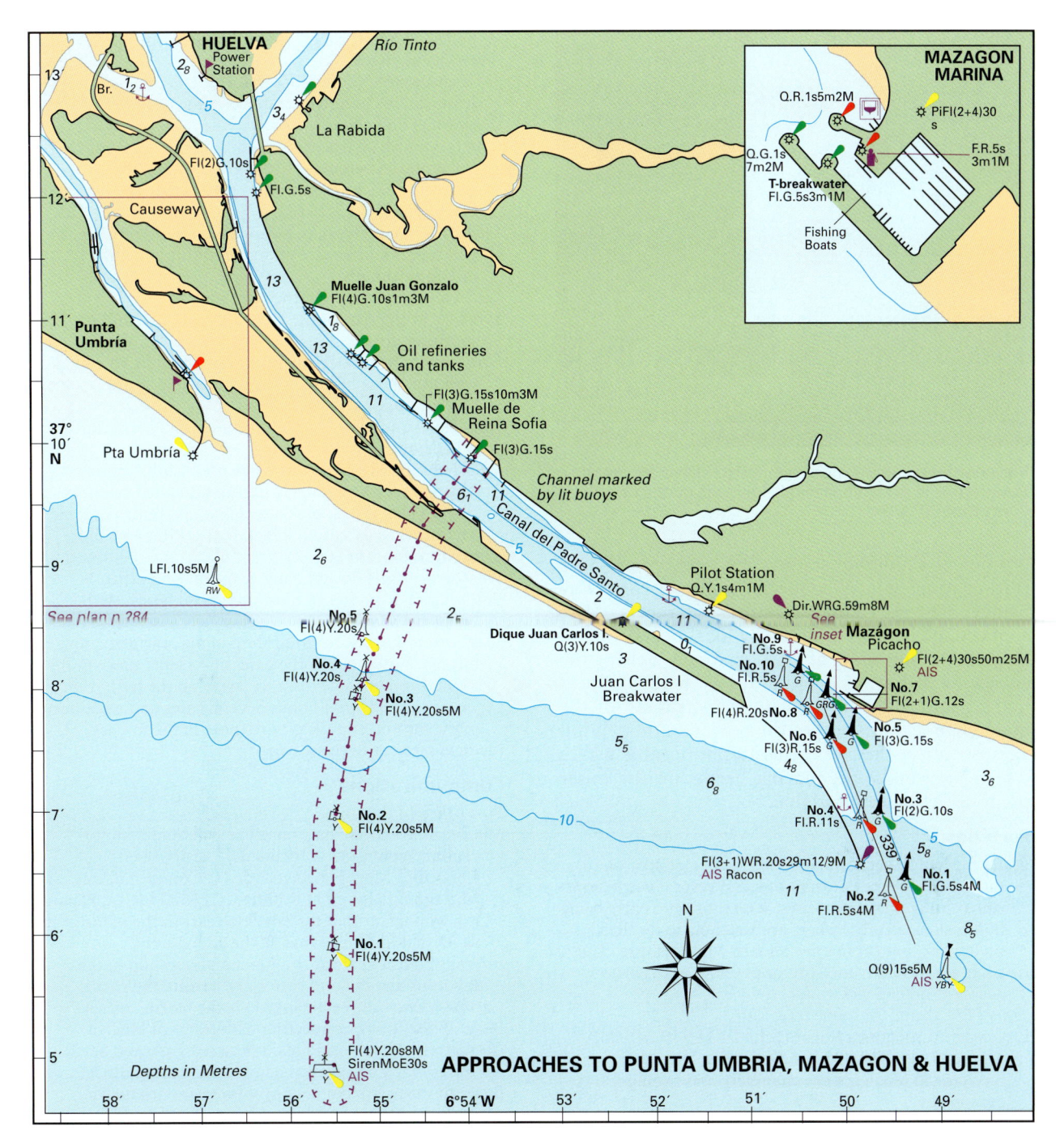

20m in 4m depths throughout. Yachts of more than 20m are normally berthed alongside the southwest breakwater. Visitors over 12m are put on pontoons in the southeast corner. Wind funnelling through the harbour entrance can make it uncomfortable here.

Anchorages

Anchoring in the Mazagón Huelva Canal is possible but not encouraged. The tide runs strongly, heavy ground tackle is required, and it is essential to display a riding light as there is considerable fishing boat traffic at night as well as large freighters which pass each other in the channel.

In southwesterly winds yachts have successfully anchored close north of the breakwater, about 400m in from the end. Considerable wash from passing traffic should be anticipated and this is a distinctly short-term solution. In all but strong southerlies, a better bet would be either off the beach northwest of the marina (taking care to avoid the sewage outfall, marked by an unlit yellow post with an × topmark), or about 1M further up the channel beyond the pilot station. Both offer good holding over sand, but again may be uncomfortable due to wash. It is essential to keep well clear of the channel itself.

Finally, yachts occasionally venture up the Huelva channel and anchor off the port side of the channel. The best spot is southwest of the main channel port hand marker to the west of the power station and

ATLANTIC SPAIN AND PORTUGAL   289

RÍO GUADIANA TO RÍO GUADALQUIVIR

View northwest up the main channel to Huelva: Mazagón foreground, Punta Umbría middle distance on the Canal de Punta Umbría *APPA*

prominent Columbus statue. This anchorage is in a side channel which connects, under a causeway bridge, to the Punta Umbría channels. The connecting channels are used by local boats, so find a spot to one side of this channel, below the causeway bridge, as depth allows. There is a local marina and mooring area on the east side of the main channel, adjacent to the power station. Wind against tide in the river generates noticeable waves which may make the marina berths on the outer pontoon very uncomfortable.

Facilities

Boatyard Not as such, though there is a large area of rather windswept hardstanding and several workshops run as individual enterprises, with more currently being built. Alternatively owners are welcome to do their own work, but cannot live aboard whilst ashore. The gates are locked from 2100 until 0900, with card access at other times.

Travel-lift 32 and 75 tonne travel-lifts.

Engineers Autonautica Raggio S.L. ①+34 959 249 849 Mob +34 609 814 805 handles engine and other mechanical repairs, some chandlery and fishing equipment.

Electronic and radio repairs Alfamar ①+34 959 377 825 who have premises in the commercial block near the marina office, are agents for Simrad, Furuno, Trepat, Raymarine etc, and handle repairs.

Sailmaker/sail repairs The marina office will contact Shanty Sails, ①+34 959 310 700, in Punta Umbría.

Chandlery An unexpected variety, all in the commercial block on the northwest side of the marina and all quite small. In alphabetical order:
Autonautica Raggio S.L. (see above) sells fishing equipment and some chandlery.
Broker de Servicios Náuticos S.L. ①+34 959 376221, sells general chandlery and clothes in addition to yacht brokerage.
Idamar Náutica ①+34 959 536 160,
Email nautica@grupo-idamar.com stocks general chandlery and fishing equipment. A branch of the much larger Idamar Group, they are also agents for Bénéteau and for RFD inflatables (see also liferaft servicing, below).
Titulaciones Náuticas, ①+34 959 376 292, is a Jeanneau agent and also stocks some chandlery, clothing and shoes.

Charts Spanish charts are available in Huelva from Valnáutica SL–Idamar SA ①+34 959 250 999 at Avenida Enlace 16, and from the Instituto Geográfico Nacional ①+34 959 281 967 at Vázquez López 12.

Liferaft servicing Idamar Náutica is agent for RFD but will repair and service all makes of liferaft and inflatable dinghy.

Water and electricity On the pontoons.

Showers At the rear of the commercial block, and on the southeast mole.

Launderette In a block on the southeast mole, so a long walk for those berthed near the marina office. Access by electronic card.

Fuel Diesel and petrol at the reception/fuel berth during office hours.

Club Náutico The blue and white tiled Club Náutico de Mazagón looks strangely like an up-ended swimming pool (which it has, plus a tennis court, both available to visitors for a nominal fee). It also offers the more usual restaurant etc.

Weather forecast Posted daily at the marina office.

Banks Cash dispenser in the commercial block, with banks in the town.

Shops/provisioning No food shop in the marina complex, but one close outside the gates and plenty more in the town (though some distance away up the hill).

Cafés, restaurants and hotels Several cafés and restaurants in the marina complex, with more in the town.

Medical services In the town.

Communications

Post office In the town.

Mailing address The marina office will hold mail for visiting yachts – c/o Oficina del Puerto, Puerto Deportivo Mazagón, Avda. de los Conquistadores, s/n, Mazagón, Palos de la Frontera, 21130 Huelva, España. It is important that the envelope carries the name of the yacht in addition to that of the addressee.

Internet Internet café at the Amena phoneshop in the town (up the hill and turn right beyond the park).

Car hire/taxis Can be arranged via the marina office.

Buses In the town, connecting with trains at Huelva.

Air services About equidistant between Faro and Seville.

Car hire/taxis Can be arranged via the marina office.

Buses In the town, connecting with trains at Huelva.

Air services About equidistant between Faro and Seville.

Entrance to Chipiona from reception pontoon
Henry Buchanan

CHIPIONA

Chipiona

Location
36°45'·2N 6°26'·2W (entrance)

Tides
Standard port Lisbon
Mean time differences (at Río Guadalquivir bar)
HW 0000 ±0005; LW +0025 ±0005
(allowing for one hour difference in time zones)
Heights in metres

MHWS	MHWN	MLWN	MLWS
3·2	2·5	1·3	0·4

Or refer to EasyTide at www.ukho.gov.uk/easytide or the Imray Tides Planner app

Principal lights
Punta del Perro (Chipiona) Fl.10s67m25M AIS
   Stone tower on building 60m
Breakwater head Fl(2)G.7s4m5M Green tower 5m
East mole Fl(4)R.11s2m3M Red tower 3m
Breakwater spur Fl(3)G.9s2m1M Green tower 3m

Night entry
Not recommended for those unfamiliar with the area, due to shoals near the entrance.

Communications
Puerto Deportivo Chipiona
VHF Ch 09 ☎ +34 856 109 711 or 600 143 522
Email chipiona@eppa.es
www.puertosdeandalucia.es

An efficient and friendly marina backed by a pleasant holiday town

Chipiona is an obvious place to wait for a fair tide up the Río Guadalquivir, as well as to top up with fuel.

The town is pleasant and shady with many restaurants, supermarkets and shopping precincts, and is well worth exploring. Punta del Perro lighthouse, built in 1867, is particularly worth a visit as the lower floors are sometimes open to the public. The low cliffs between the lighthouse and Chipiona feature a number of restaurants and cafés, nearly all with local seafood on the menu.

If intending to venture up the Río Guadalquivir, note the paragraph on page 294 regarding Ricardo Franco's *La Navegación de Recreo por el Río de Sevilla* (Leisure Navigation on the River of Seville). Though now out of print, a copy of this impressive work can be consulted at the marina office.

Approach – Chipiona and the Río Guadalquivir

From the north If coastal sailing towards the Río Guadalquivir from Mazagón the first 20M is backed by sand dunes, but southeast of Matalascañas the coastline flattens. A firing range exists inshore from about 5M southeast of Mazagón almost as far as Matalascañas. When active, a Range Safety Vessel will call up any craft straying into the area on VHF Ch 16 with instructions to keep clear.

In good visibility a course can be shaped directly for No.2 WCB guarding Bajo Pichaco rock and a wreck stuck on it. Though the buoy is sometimes difficult to see against the land, the wreck is still prominent.

From the south From Bahía de Cádiz and other points south, the 10m contour lies up to 1·75M from the coast between Rota and Punta del Perro. Off the latter lies the dangerous Bajo Salmedina, extending almost 1·6M offshore and marked by a west cardinal tower, plus several wrecks. If in doubt keep 3M offshore.

Having rounded Bajo Salmedina, remain a minimum of 0·5M offshore while working northeast for Chipiona, as multiple obstructions, some natural, some artificial, extend at least 600m out from the shore for most of the distance. Do not turn in for Chipiona until the marina entrance bears at least 110°.

Looking northeast into the mouth of the Río Guadalquivir. Punta del Perro lighthouse is in the foreground, with the Puerto Deportivo Chipiona directly behind

ATLANTIC SPAIN AND PORTUGAL

RÍO GUADIANA TO RÍO GUADALQUIVIR

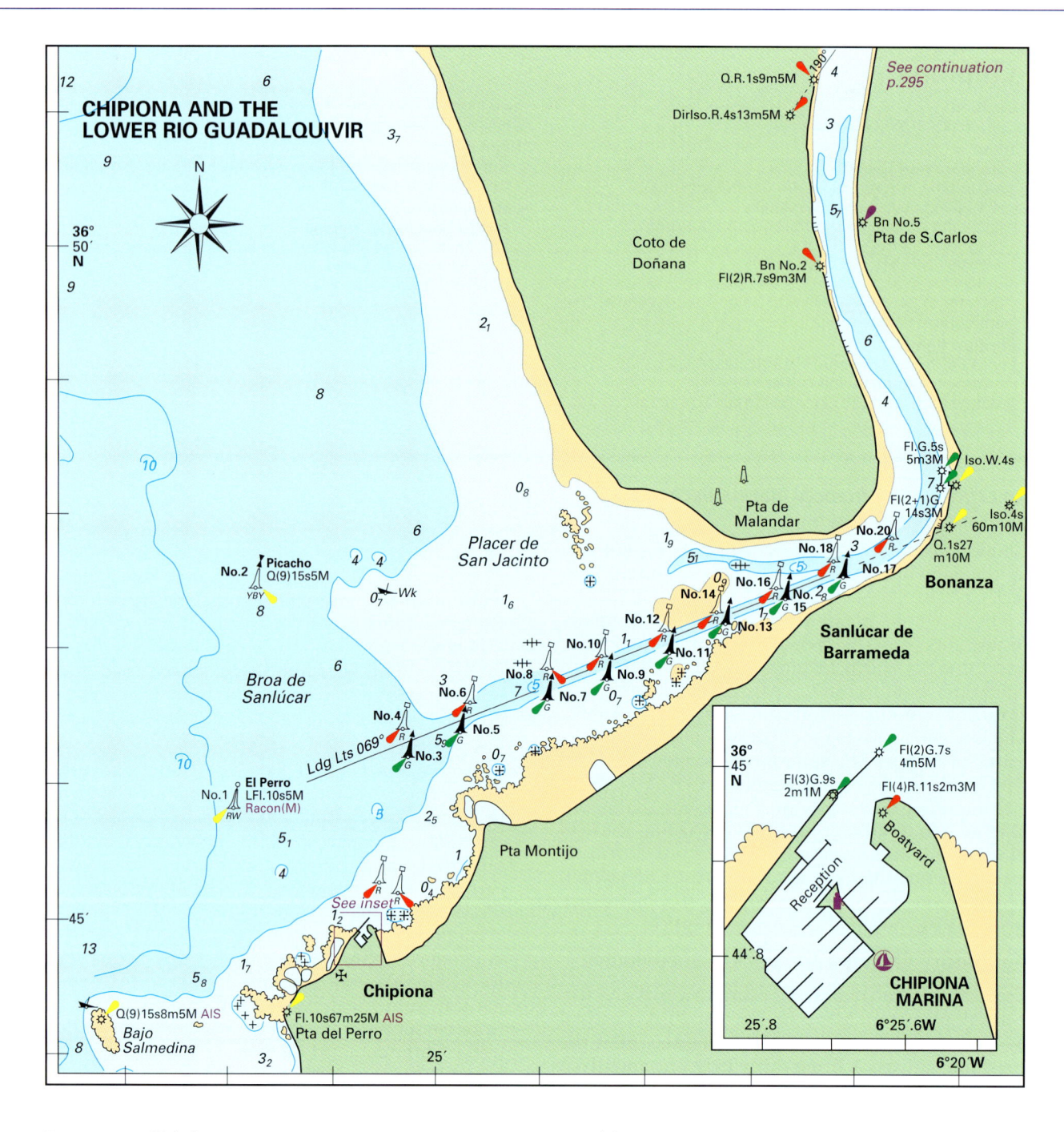

Entrance – Chipiona

The bathymetric chart for the Puerto Deportivo Chipiona and its immediate approach can be found on the APPA website.

If approaching from any point west of north the entrance is hidden until very close in. Make for the breakwater head with its bright green tower, leaving the two smallish red pillar buoys to port, finally swinging southwest to enter. After dredging a minimum of 3·5m should be found at all times.
APPA www.puertosdeandalucia.es/en/
documentation-en/batimetrias > 'Batimetría Puerto de Chipiona'.

Berthing

Secure to the long reception pontoon at the head of the central mole, the Muelle de Espera, directly beneath the marina office. The northeast basin (dredged to 4m) is largely occupied by larger yachts and visitors in transit, with local boats in the south basin and fishing vessels along the breakwater. There are finger pontoons throughout. One or two seriously large yachts, up to 40m, can lie alongside the west side of the outer pontoon, but it is essential to contact the marina office well in advance. All the marina's 412 berths are often full in the high season, though a smaller visitor may be found space in the south basin among the locals in 2·5-3m depths.

Weekdays office hours are 1000-1330 and 1600-1730 in winter, closed Saturday and Sunday

292   ATLANTIC SPAIN AND PORTUGAL

Reception and Fuel pontoon looking southeast. Office behind *Henry Buchanan*

afternoons, but remaining open later in summer with no weekend closing. There is 24 hour security, with card-operated gates to the pontoons.

Anchorage

An anchorage can be found to the east of the marina entrance, but it is exposed to the northwest.

Facilities

Boatyard On the northeast arm, with a generous area of concreted hardstanding behind a high security fence. Yachts from several nations over-winter there, all generously propped, essential when there is so little protection from the wind. The gates are locked from 2200 until 0700 and living onboard is forbidden.

Travel-lift 45 tonne capacity lift in the boatyard area. Book at the marina office.

Engineers, electronic and radio repairs Volvo/Honda at Servicios Nauticos J.A Moreta. www.jamoreta.es Email info@jamoreta.es ☏+34 956 371 514. *Mobile* +34 670 211 941. Also, Nautica Gusty (Yamaha) www.nauticagusty.com Email info@nauticagusty.com ☏+34 956 371 802. Carretera Chipiona, Sanlucar km. 2,700, Pista Montijo Nave 2, CP: 11550. Chipiona (Cádiz)

Chandleries Fernando Medina Náutica, ☏+34 956 374 772, *Mobile* +34 670 594 451 and +34 607 833 237 opposite the southeast corner of the south basin, open 0930–1400 and 1630–1900 weekdays, closed Saturday afternoon and Sunday.

Water/electricity On the pontoons.

Showers The shower block is on the south side of the basin, with access via electronic card.

Launderette Near the marina office.

Fuel Diesel and petrol at the reception pontoon, 0800–1300 and 1630–1930 weekdays, 0830–1400 weekends.

Bottled gas Camping Gaz exchanges are available in the town, but no refills.

Weather forecast Posted daily at the marina office.

Banks In the town, but no cash dispenser at the marina.

Shops/provisioning Small general shop in the block overlooking the north basin, otherwise the nearest food shop is a supermarket some 300m distant, with plenty more in the town proper. The *lonja* (fish market) at the southwest corner of the basin also sells retail, and is well worth a visit.

Cafés, restaurants and hotels A good range. Chipiona has long been a popular holiday resort among Spaniards. Several small café/restaurants overlook the north basin.

Medical services In the town.

Communications

Post office In the town.

Mailing address The marina office will hold mail for visiting yachts – c/o Oficina del Puerto, Puerto Deportivo Chipiona, Avda Rocío Jurado s/n, 11550 Chipiona, Cádiz, España. It is important that the envelope carries the name of the yacht in addition to that of the addressee.

Internet There is WiFi in the bar but not in the marina.

Car hire/taxis Best organised via the marina office.

Buses To Rota, Seville (about 2 hours) etc.

Air services International airport at Seville, national airport at Jerez for connections to Madrid etc.

Looking north over Chipiona Marina *APPA*

RÍO GUADIANA TO RÍO GUADALQUIVIR

Río Guadalquivir and Seville

Location
36°46′N 6°28′W (outer approach)

Tides
Standard port Lisbon
Mean time differences (at Río Guadalquivir bar)
(allowing for one hour difference in time zones)
HW 0000 ±005; LW +0025 ±0005
Heights in metres

MHWS	MHWN	MLWN	MLWS
3·2	2·5	1·3	0·4

Mean time differences (at Bonanza)
HW +0030 ±0010; LW +0070 ±0010
(allowing for one hour difference in time zones)
Heights in metres

MHWS	MHWN	MLWN	MLWS
3·0	2·4	1·1	0·5

Mean time differences (at Seville)
HW +0415 ±0015; LW +0530 ±0020
(allowing for one hour difference in time zones)
Heights in metres

MHWS	MHWN	MLWN	MLWS
2·1	1·8	0·9	0·5

Principal lights
Entrance
Ldg Lts 069° *Front* Q.1s27m10M
  Yellow ■ on metal tower
  Rear Iso.4s60m10M Yellow ■ on metal tower
Eight pairs of lit pillar buoys, plus one extra port-hand buoy, mark the channel as far as Bonanza
Bonanza
Bonanza Iso.W.4s21m3M
  Red tower, cupola and building 20m
Detached breakwater, S end Fl(2+1)G.14·5s5m3M Green column, red band, 2m
Detached breakwater, N end Fl.G.5s5m3M
  Green post 2m
  Many other lit buoys and beacons mark the Río Guadalquivir up to Seville – see plans opposite, and on pages 296 and 299

Communications
See page 298.

Entrance and fuel pontoon, Chipiona *Henry Buchanan*

Historic city with a lengthy river approach of 55M

Seville is one of the foremost cities of Spain, steeped in history and with something unexpected around every corner. The old part appears to have far more than its fair share of monuments and historic buildings, including a stunning cathedral and several royal palaces. A guide book and street plan are almost necessities. A yacht provides a most convenient base for exploration, but as summer temperatures can rise above 40°C (102°F) the best time to visit is in spring or autumn, though Seville is also becoming an increasingly popular place to winter on board for many nationalities. Highlights of the year are the Easter processions of Semana Santa and the vast *feria* which is held two weeks later on a site adjacent to the Club Náutico Sevilla.

In common with most large cities, Seville has a reputation for petty crime, including pickpockets. But a purposeful air, valuables tucked away out of sight and avoidance of secluded areas after dark should give reasonable protection. It is not a place to hire a car as traffic is frequently grid-locked and parking next to impossible. Several (brave) yachtsmen and women have recommended bicycles as a practical means of transport. A stout chain is recommended.

The approach up the Río Guadalquivir (from the *Arabic Wadi-al-Kabir* or 'big river'), while tedious at times, is not without interest. In particular, the *Parque Nacional de Doñana* on the west bank is world famous for its birds and other wildlife and it is usually possible to spot some of its residents. In 1998 the park suffered an ecological disaster when the failure of a major dam upstream released nearly seven million cubic metres of lead-zinc slurry into the river system, killing most of the fish and many of the birds which depended on them. It has been estimated that it will take up to 50 years for the region to recover fully, but in the meantime much of the wildlife has already made a remarkable comeback.

If spending a few days in Chipiona prior to tackling the river, ask marina officials for a chance to study their copy of *La Navegación de Recreo por el Río de Sevilla* (Leisure Navigation on the River of Seville). This fascinating volume, first published in 1981 and revised in 1998 by master mariner and Guadalquivir pilot Ricardo Franco, is already out of print but a copy can be obtained from:
Flores Imprenta y Papeleria, Avda. De la Raza S/N, Ed. Elcano 41012 – Sevilla ☏ +34 954 617 257
Email floresdesantis@telefonica.net.

It is beautifully presented in a dark blue box cover, profusely illustrated by aerial photographs and detailed charts, and with detailed and authoritative text in English as well as Spanish, it would well repay study with a notebook and the current chart to hand. While in the marina office it would also be worth confirming that the lock and bridge-opening times given over the next few pages are still current. The helpful Chipiona staff should have all the details to hand.

294 ATLANTIC SPAIN AND PORTUGAL

RÍO GUADALQUIVIR AND SEVILLE

The wide mouth of the Río Guadalquivir looking northeast. Sanlúcar de Barrameda is on the right, with the long breakwater off Bonanza in the distance

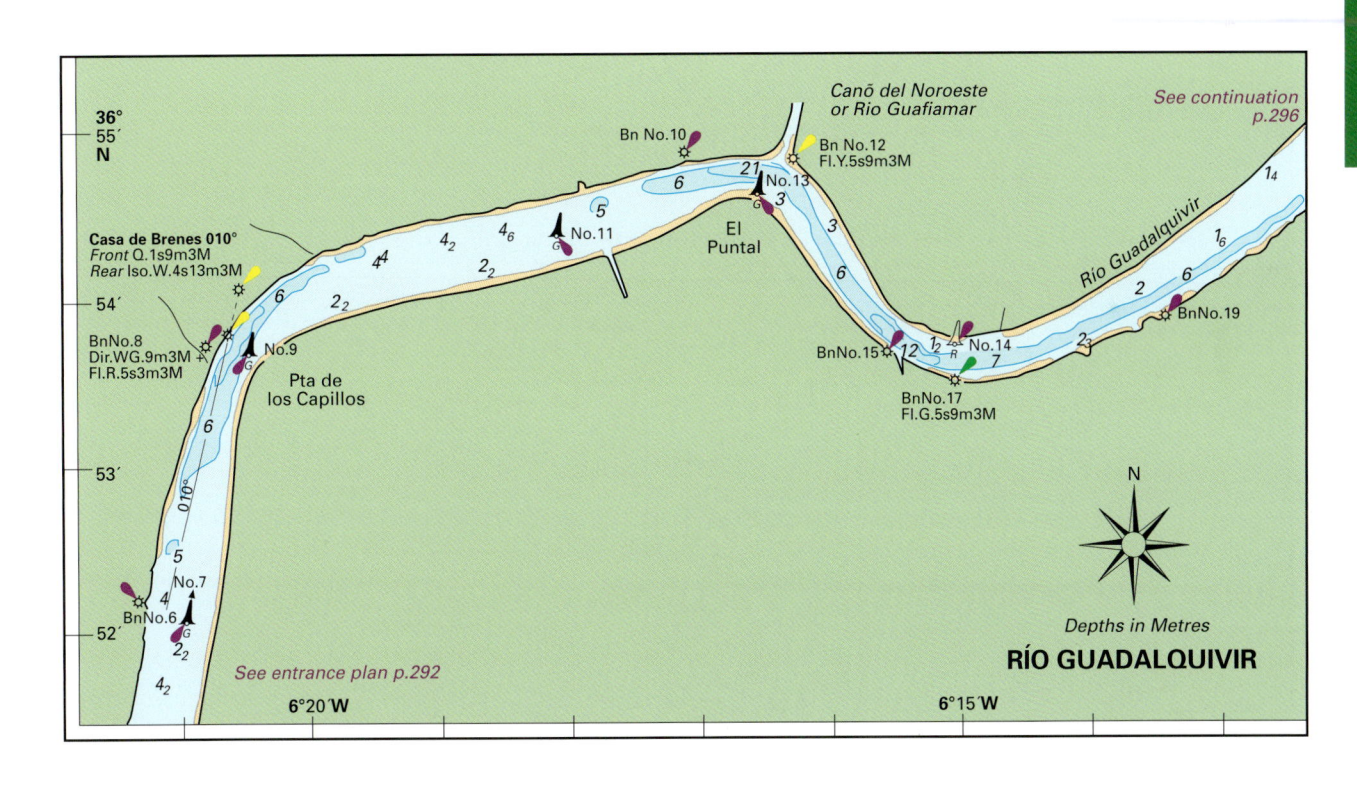

RÍO GUADALQUIVIR

Depths in Metres

See entrance plan p.292

See continuation p.296

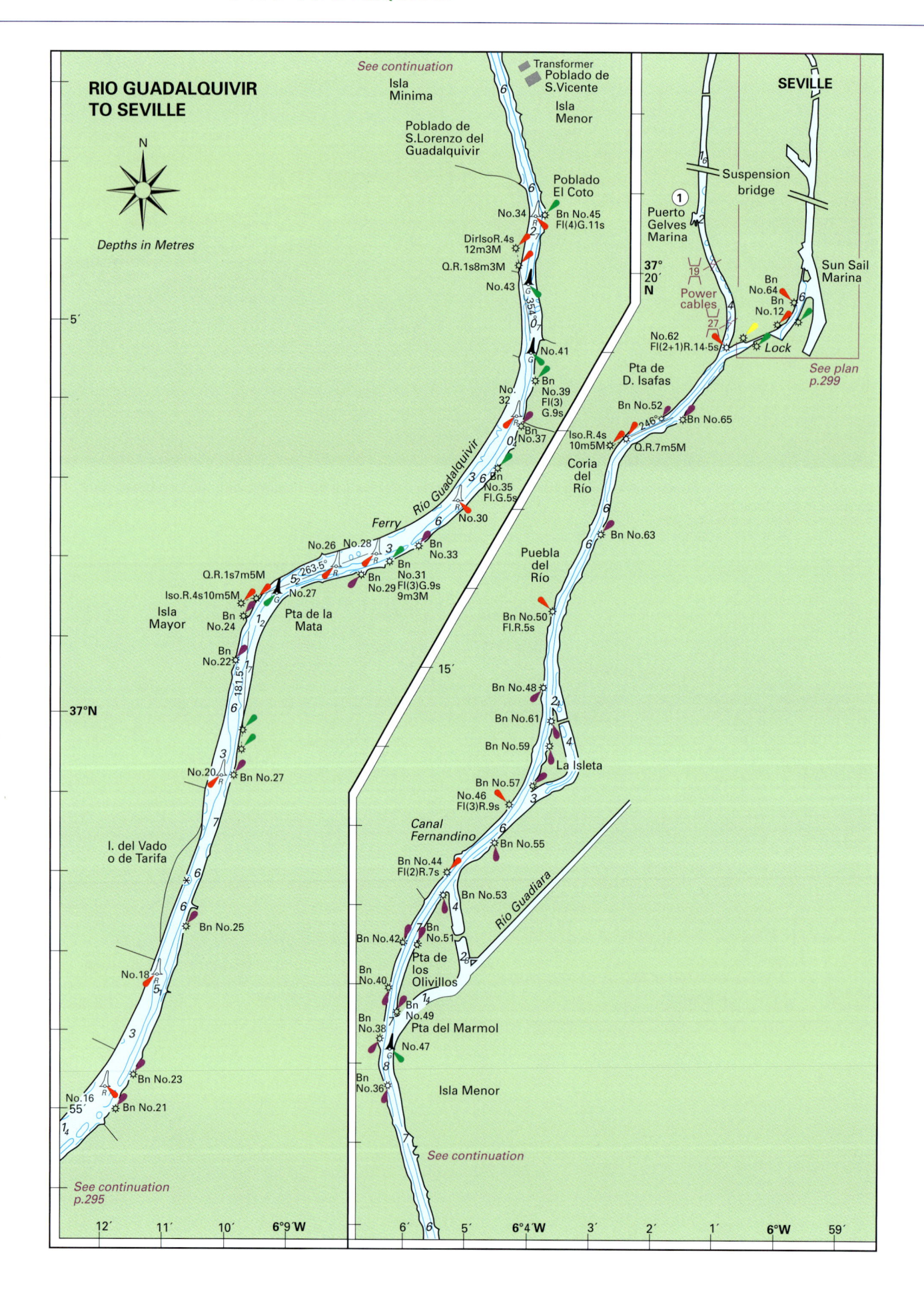

RÍO GUADIANA TO RÍO GUADALQUIVIR

RÍO GUADALQUIVIR

Approach

The approach to Chipiona at the mouth of the Río Guadalquivir is described on page 291 where the chartlet also shows the buoyed approach to the river. The channel close to the mouth is wide, but can become dangerously rough when strong west or southwest winds oppose the spring ebb and cause short steep seas to build. The 'service centre' for the Río Guadalquivir's buoyage is at Bonanza and, perhaps as a result, maintenance is generally excellent.

The river

It is about 55M from the mouth of the Río Guadalquivir to Seville. Starting an hour or so before the beginning of the flood (which a yacht can ride upriver for at least 9hrs – see *Tides* above) most yachts will be able to make it on one tide.

It has become essential today, however, to plan carefully with the marina in Seville one intends using at the end of the river passage. To this end it is recommended (perhaps essential) that before heading upriver a stop in the marina at Chipiona for advice, and to top up with fuel, be made. There is only one marina, Puerto Gelves, that is on the river but even this gets busy and should be contacted. The other two marinas, Sun Sail Marina and Club Náutico Sevilla are in the Canal de Alfonso XIII (see below) with pleasure craft having first to cross the hurdle of the reconstructed Seville Lock (set of gates at either end), and if going on to the Club Náutico Sevilla, the Puente de las Delicias lifting bridge.

Both the lock and lifting bridge are primarily operated for commercial reasons and this must be respected. Unfortunately, yachts and pleasure craft have a very low priority and opening times in recent years have become severely limited. It is no longer a call-up and get-in arrangement which makes planning ahead essential.

The request for opening with the promise of a confirmed berth must come from either the Sun Sail Marina or Club Náutico Sevilla 24 hours in advance of going through the new lock and lifting bridge in Seville, and even then a set opening time has to be met. Again, the marina at Chipiona can assist with planning and liaising with the marinas.

It is possible to anchor off Sanlúcar de Barrameda (the home of Manzanilla wine), where there is a large and stylish yacht club, a superb beach and, perhaps of greatest interest, the visitors' centre for the *Parque Nacional de Doñana* housed in the old ice factory. Itself worth a visit for its imaginative tilework. In 1519 Sanlúcar de Barrameda was the departure point for Magellan's fleet and the port to which, three years later, the 18 survivors returned.

Little more than 1M further upriver lies Bonanza, where a yacht may be able to secure temporarily to the inside of the long detached concrete breakwater (quite unmistakable with its downstream end painted in diagonal red and green stripes) while the fishing fleet is at sea. Other possibilities are to anchor north of the moorings well out of the powerful current, or on the west bank around the corner 1M above Bonanza, again well out of both the fairway and the current. Even at neaps the ebb may run at 3kn in the centre of the channel, and is considerably stronger at springs. The flood never attains anything like the same rates. It is said that owners of wooden vessels should avoid Bonanza due to its reputation for shipworm, said to breed in the old hulks which litter the surrounding shores.

Above Bonanza

After passing the tall, shining heaps of locally-produced salt just upstream of Bonanza the river winds through flat and somewhat featureless countryside, a passage described with feeling as 'very long and boring', until close to Seville, progress best being marked by simply ticking off the buoys and beacons as they are passed. There is good water the whole way (6,000-tonne freighters visit the city) but the channel is not always in the centre of the river. Where beacons run down one side they indicate the main channel, seldom less than 5m though down to 4m on the reach north of Bonanza (where the channel follows the west side) and above the first starboard turn (where the channel is to the north). A few red and green buoys also give guidance. The river carries such a heavy load of silt that echo-sounders are generally unable to cope. Typical performance is to give no sensible reading for tens of minutes, then briefly read the correct depth for a minute or two, and then go haywire again. Probably of more concern is the commercial traffic, with ships apparently maintaining full speed both day and night.

There are several possible anchorages to be found out of the fairway, but none are very convenient and the current can be strong.

Returning downstream, unless one can make at least 7kn the passage will take more than one tide. Low water at Bonanza occurs nearly 4·5 hours earlier than at Seville, so for every mile made downstream the ebb will finish that much earlier. Leave Seville about three hours before local high water, and after about two hours of foul tide pick up the ebb. If unable to make 7kn it will be necessary either to push against the flood, though this seldom exceeds 2kn even at springs, or to anchor en-route.

RÍO GUADIANA TO RÍO GUADALQUIVIR

Seville

Communications
Port Authority VHF Ch 12 (24 hours)
🕾 +34 954 247 300
Email sevilla@apsevilla.com
www.apsevilla.com
Puerto Gelves VHF Ch 09, 16
🕾 +34 955 761 212
Email info@puertogelves.com
www.puertogelves.es
Sunsail marina 🕾 +34 954 230 326
Club Náutico Sevilla VHF Ch 09
🕾 +34 954 454 777
Email nauticosevilla@nauticosevilla.com
www.nauticosevilla.com
Seville lock VHF Ch 12 🕾 +34 954 247 332
Puente de las Delicias lifting bridge
VHF Ch 12 🕾 +34 954 454 984

Puerto Gelves marina from the north. The amount of suspended silt in the river water is very apparent

The Río Guadalquivir divides on the southern outskirts of the city to form an island, the two branches rejoining some 6M further upstream. The tidal western branch which contains the Puerto Gelves marina is in fact artificial, and was created to enable the eastern, commercial branch to be canalised.

Air height to both branches is determined by power cables. The single set which cross the eastern arm carry 44m so are unlikely to trouble any yacht, but the northern of the two sets which cross the western channel to Gelves carry only 19m at high water. This has on occasion inconvenienced larger yachts, which may have to pass under at low water and then anchor before catching the ebb downstream, but this is rare. The cables encountered about 0·6M further downstream on the same channel carry a more generous 27m.

1. **Puerto Gelves** (37°20'·4N 6°01'·4W)
   VHF Ch 09, 16   🕾+34 955 761 212 C/ Rafael Zamora, 10 41120 Gelves I Sevilla.
   Email info@puertogelves.com www.puertogelves.es

   The marina was the centrepiece of a small marina village, planned in conjunction with EXPO '92 and is situated in the tidal part of the river. There is 4-5m depth except very close to the banks, but the marina is effectively the limit of navigation for sailing yachts as several low road and rail bridges cross the river less than a mile upstream.

   The marina claims to have 133 berths for yachts of up to 16m plus many more small craft 'dry-sailed' from the boatyard area. The depth is declared to be 3m in the marina, but sad to report in recent years the marina has suffered from chronic silting which has reduced low water depths in the basin to less than 2m (though the underlying mud is extremely soft). Contact the marina well before arrival but entry around HW is advisable noting that a power line charted at 19m clearance is over the approach.

   Boats of any size have decamped to a long pontoon (with electricity and water) on the riverbank outside the marina. The pontoon on the river can take about 12 boats (but mainly long term ones in the winter) and there are buoys on the opposite bank in season. On arrival it may be necessary to anchor and enquire at the office.

   Normally, one would secure to the reception pontoon on the starboard side of the entrance and call at the portacabin office at the root of the north wall. The entrance is lit, with appropriately painted beacons on either side, but navigating in the river after dark would be unwise. The marineros used to be quick off the mark to spot new arrivals but their number has been much reduced since its heyday. The office is open weekdays only 0900–1400. A 'port tax' (www.apsevilla.com; click on Tasas y Tarifas) is included in the charges. Puerto Gelves offers free transport between the marina and Gelves.

   There is one shower/WC for ladies and one for gents, plus a washing machine and dryer. But these get crowded when the marina puts camper vans (up to 15) on the site.

   A haul out here was reported to have been carried out very professionally. In 2014/15 the new marina manager stopped owners living on board.

   Other facilities at and around Puerto Gelves are included in the *Facilities* section below.

- **Adjacent anchorage at Gelves** It is possible to anchor in the river just upstream of the marina entrance, where maximum tidal range is 1·6m and holding generally good in soft mud, but note that after heavy rain inland the current has been known to attain 8kns! On payment of a small fee, those at anchor can use the marina's showers, launderette, etc.

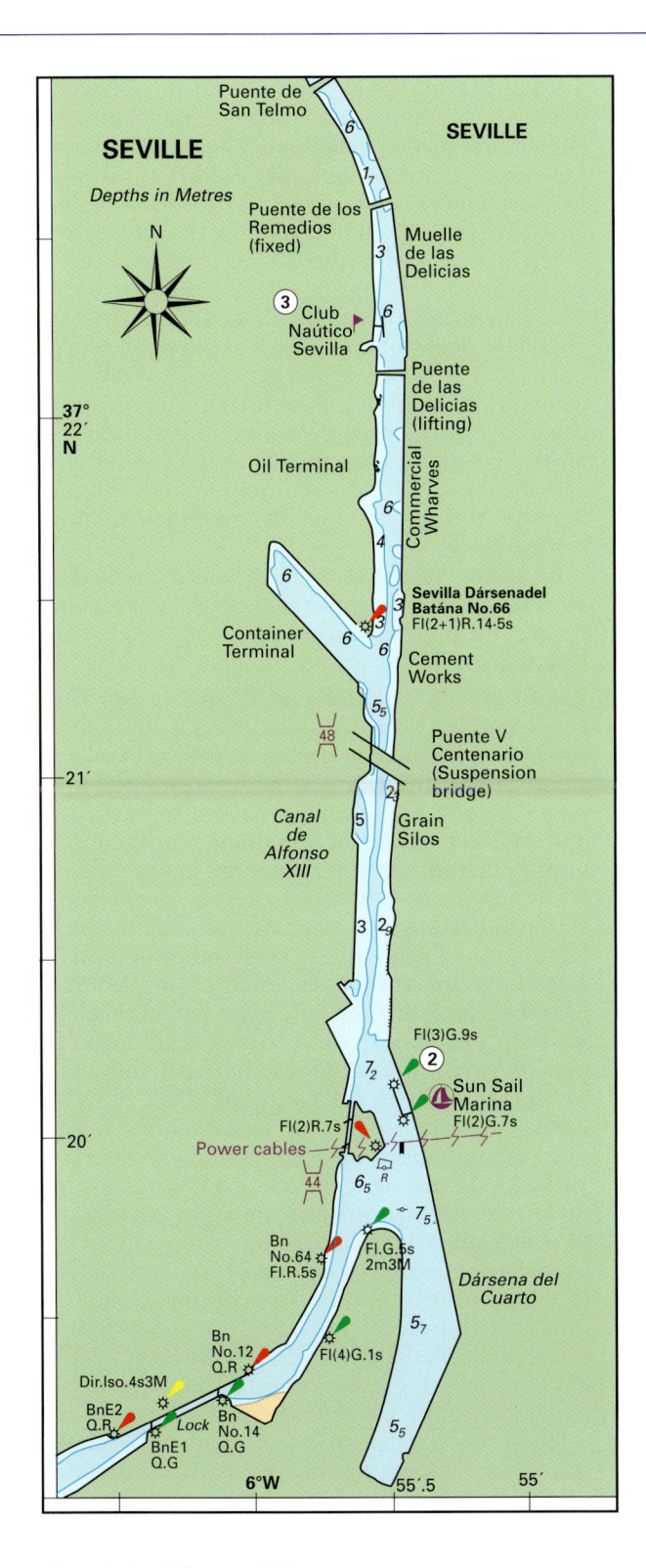

SEVILLE

The view upstream towards the Puente V Centenario suspension bridge (48m clearance), with the Puente de las Delicias lifting bridge beyond Anne Hammick

The Seville lock

Check the up-to-date opening schedule for the passage of pleasure craft at http://portal.apsevilla.com:

Summer						
Mon	Tue	Wed	Thur	Fri	Sat	Sun
0900	0900	0900	0900	0900	0900	0900
2100	2100	2100	2100	2100	2100	2100
2400		2400		2400		
Winter						
Mon	Tue	Wed	Thur	Fri	Sat	Sun
1000	1000	1000	1000	1000	1000	1000
1900	1900	1900	1900	1900	1900	1900
2400		2400		2400		

Signals

A red and green traffic light system operates. Boats lock outbound first. The lock-keepers monitor VHF Ch 12.

However, a call to the lock keeper on spec is likely to be answered by a security guard. A request for its opening, with the promise of a confirmed berth, must come from either the Sunsail Marina or Club Náutico Sevilla 24 hours in advance. The marinas at both Chipiona or Mazagón can assist with this planning.

Rebuilt lock system at Seville giving access to the canal Ocean Cruising Club

Canal de Alfonso XIII

The depth of water in the Canal de Alfonso XIII is controlled by a lock which is primarily operated for commercial reasons. For yachts, it is no longer a call-up and get-in arrangement which makes passage timing up the river less flexible. Planning ahead is essential.

ATLANTIC SPAIN AND PORTUGAL

RÍO GUADIANA TO RÍO GUADALQUIVIR

If it all becomes too difficult follow the river to Puerto Gelves instead. There is a very frequent and cheap bus service to Seville from the Puerto Gelves marina (see above).

2. **Sunsail Marina** (37°20'N 5°59'·5W) ☎ +34 954 230 326 This used to be known as Marina Yachting Seville and is situated just north of the 44m power cables and opposite the old lock. This is likely to be the only place to wait for the Puente de las Delicias lifting bridge further up the canal, which now only opens once a day.

The Puente de las Delicias lifting bridge

Check for updates on http://portal.apsevilla.com for the opening schedule for the passage of pleasure craft:

Summer							
Mon	Tue	Wed	Thur	Fri	Sat	Sun	Fest'l
2200		2200		2200	0800	0800	0800
Winter							
Mon	Tue	Wed	Thur	Fri	Sat	Sun	Fest'l
2200		2200		2200	0900	0900	0900

Signals

Slow flashing red
Passage for boats that can clear the suspension bridge downstream (48m).

Fast flashing red
All traffic prohibited.

Fast flashing red-green
Bridge opening/closing. Passage forbidden to all traffic.

Slow flashing green
Large ship traffic allowed in the direction indicated by this.

Sun Sail Marina, just N of the powerlines *APPA*

Sunsail Marina is set amidst rural if somewhat bleak surroundings and is some 3·5km from the city centre, tucked behind an industrial area and far from either shops or public transport. However, there is no reason why the enterprising crew should not commute into the city by dinghy.

The marina comprises a single pontoon with yachts berthed alongside. Depths range from 3-6m. Secure in any available space, and if an attendant does not appear call at the small office, open 0930-1900 weekdays, closed weekends (though with 24 hour security). Charges are calculated on a length x breadth basis and do not alter throughout the year. Water and electricity are included. Other facilities at and around Sunsail Marina are included in the *Facilities* section below.

It is now essential to have made contact in advance because a confirmed berth is necessary before the Sunsail Marina can notify the Seville lock that a yacht is making passage.

3. The **Club Náutico Sevilla** (37°22'·2N 5°59'·6W) This Club unquestionably offers by far the most convenient berthing in the city as well as excellent shoreside facilities. It lies on the west bank just upstream of a lifting bridge, backed by extensive and well-kept grounds containing tennis courts, mini-golf and several swimming pools, all of which may be used by visiting crews. To reach the club it is necessary to negotiate not only the lock but also the Puente de las Delicias lifting bridge (see above for opening times etc). The Sun Sail Marina is probably the only place to secure while waiting. The majority of berthing is stern-to off one of two long pontoons (haul-off lines are provided, tailed to the pontoon). That furthest upriver is reserved for club members, the lower one is mainly used for visitors and can take 27 yachts of 12m or less, including a few against its inner side. Further downstream again is a section of wall against which can be fitted a maximum of 14 yachts of between 12m and 24m overall (fewer if a high proportion are very beamy), lying to their own bower anchors. At least 4m is found throughout. Perhaps surprisingly, space is nearly always available other than during the April Feria, when for a few days the prices treble.

However, it is now essential to have made contact in advance because a confirmed berth is necessary before the Club Náutico Sevilla can notify the Seville lock that a yacht is making passage. The club office is to be found upstairs in the main building, open 0900–1900 weekdays, 0900–1300 Saturday, closed Sunday. Charges are calculated on a length x breadth basis and do not alter throughout the year, other than at the time of Seville's great April *Feria*. Water, electricity, IVA and 'port tax' (www.apsevilla.com; click on Tasas y Tarifas) are all included.

Facilities at and around the Club Náutico Sevilla are listed in the following pages.

300 ATLANTIC SPAIN AND PORTUGAL

SEVILLE

Club Náutico Sevilla *APPA*

Facilities

Boatyard Repair services at Puerto Gelves are available but since Astilleros Magallanes (✆ +34 955 760 545 *Mobile* +34 610 829 297) closed down it is not know who is providing them. The travel lift is backed by a generous area of hardstanding where owners are welcome to do their own work, but living aboard on the hard is no longer permitted.

Travel-lift 25-tonne capacity hoist at Puerto Gelves, booked via the marina office,

Engineers, electronics and radio repairs Náutica Vergara has a workshop either on site or nearby. Albea, a short distance up the road, deals mainly with cars but will handle boat electrics and is a good source for 12 volt batteries. Ask at the marina office if in search of less usual items or services, such as a company to re-galvanise anchor chain.

There is a well-equipped engineering workshop at Sunsail Marina in the Seville canal ✆+34 954 230 208, while the office at the Club Náutico Sevilla will call in mechanics and other specialists as necessary.

Sail repairs and canvaswork Sunsail has premises near Puerto Gelves at Carretera del Copero s/ (Zona Portuaria), Sevilla, 41012 Sevilla, Spain. ✆ +34 954 184 848. Open in summer 0800–2000 but initial contact is best made via the marina office. Reported to be a very helpful outfit.

Chandlery Náutica Vergara at Puerto Gelves ✆+34 955 761 063.

Email nauticavergara@vianwe.com, holds limited stock and recommends local DIY/household stores in Gelves which are excellent.

Didier Boat Broker (✆+34 955 761 792 *Mobile* +34 654 800 256 *Email* info@didierboatbroker.com www.didierboatbroker.com) whose range tended towards spares and hardware used to be based at Puerto Gelves but may have closed down.

NáutiSevilla SL (see *Charts*, below) occupies premises in the city itself where limited stocks are held. Hours are 1000–1330, 1630–2000 weekdays, 1000–1330 Saturday.

Charts NáutiSevilla SL, ✆+34 954 414 832 at Calle Recaredo 14, and the Instituto Geográfico Nacional ✆ +34 955 569 324 at Avenida San Francisco Javier 9, No.8, mod 7, both stock Spanish charts.

Water/ electricity On the pontoons at all three marinas. The Club Náutico Sevilla has separate taps for drinking water and for boat washing – do not confuse them!

Showers At all three marinas.

Launderette Washing machines next to the shower block at Puerto Gelves, but no laundry facilities at the Club Náutico Sevilla (though the office can arrange for it to be done elsewhere).

Bottled gas Camping Gaz exchanges at most hardware stores, including one almost opposite the Puerto Gelves entrance, but little chance of getting other cylinders refilled.

Club Náutico The Club Náutico Sevilla is worth a visit even if not staying on its pontoons. A reasonable standard of dress is expected in the clubhouse.

Weather forecast Posted at the Puerto Gelves office at weekends (during the week it is necessary to ask). Daily at the Club Náutico Sevilla.

Banks Throughout the city and at Gelves.

Shops/provisioning Excellent in the city, as one would expect, but no shops anywhere near Sunsail Marina, and some distance to walk from the Club Náutico Sevilla (fortunately, several of the larger city supermarkets have delivery services). Puerto Gelves boasts a handy mini-market just around the corner from the marina bar, with more shops within walking distance. A hypermarket is 2km distant.

Produce markets Near the river north of the bullring and on Calle Alfarería in the Triana district (about 20 minutes' walk from the Club Náutico Sevilla), plus a weekly market at Gelves.

Cafés, restaurants and hotels Thousands, at all price levels, with only the Sunsail Marina apparently lacking. The Club Náutico Sevilla has a particularly pleasant terrace bar overlooking its yacht pontoons.

Medical services All aspects including major hospitals. Doctor and dentist at Gelves.

Communications

Post office Throughout the city and at Gelves.

Mailing address All three marina offices will hold mail for visiting yachts:
c/o Puerto Gelves, Autovía Sevilla–Coria, km 3·5, 41120 Gelves, Sevilla, España;
c/o Sun Sail Marina, Carretara del Copero s/n, Punta del Verde, 41012 Sevilla, España;
c/o Club Náutico Sevilla, Avda Sanlúcar de Barrameda s/n, Apartado de Correos 1003, 41011 Sevilla, España.

It is important that the envelope carries the name of the yacht in addition to that of the addressee.

Internet Numerous possibilities throughout the city, with Sevilla@Internet almost opposite the Cathedral particularly recommended. It is reasonably quiet and, being on the first floor, generally quite cool and airy.

Compustation, near Puerto Gelves, does not offer internet access but does handle computer repairs as well as selling consumables such as inkjets.

Car hire/taxis The office staff at all three marinas are happy to telephone for taxis.

Buses Run every 20 minutes from just outside Puerto Gelves into the centre of Seville (about 15 minutes), and from near the Club Náutico Sevilla.

Trains Good services throughout Spain (e.g. 2·5 hours to Madrid). Seville's metro line features a stop little more than 1km from Puerto Gelves which provides a handy link with the city centre.

Air services International airport 20km just outside the city.

THE ALGARVE & ANDALUCIA

ATLANTIC SPAIN AND PORTUGAL

Río Guadalquivir to Cabo Trafalgar

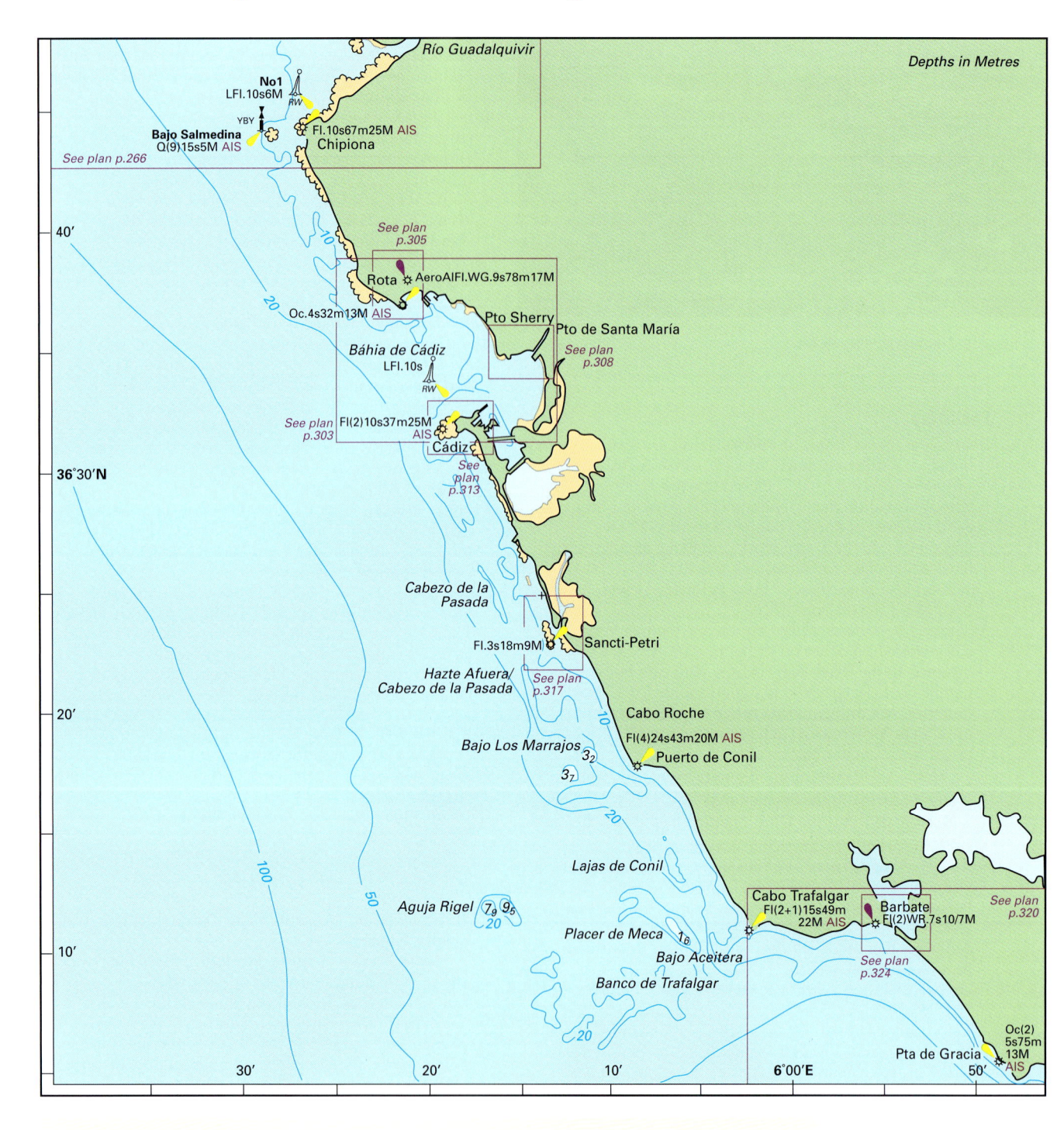

PRINCIPAL LIGHTS
Punta del Perro (Chipiona) Fl.10s67m25M AIS
  Stone tower on building 60m
Bajo Salmedina Q(9)15s8m5M AIS
  West cardinal tower, X topmark
Rota Aeromarine Aero AlFl.WG.9s78m17M
  Red and white chequered spherical tank 49m
Cádiz, Castillo de San Sebastián
  Fl(2)10s37m25M AIS
  Aluminium tower on castle 37m
Castillo de Sancti-Petri Fl.3s18m9M
  Square tower 16m
Cabo Roche Fl(4)24s43m20M AIS
  Brown square tower 20m
Cabo Trafalgar Fl(2+1)15s49m22M
  White conical tower and building 34

BAHÍA DE CÁDIZ

Bahía de Cádiz (Cádiz Bay)
Approaches to Rota, Puerto Sherry, Santa María and Cádiz

Principal lights
Rota old lighthouse Oc.4s32m13M AIS
  Off-white tower, red band 28m
Rota Aeromarine Aero AlFl.WG.9s78m17M
  Red and white chequered spherical tank 49m
Cádiz, Castillo de San Sebastián Fl(2)10s37m25M AIS
  Aluminium tower on castle 37m
Harbours and marinas – listed individually.

Communications
  Coast radio station
  Cádiz (remotely controlled from Málaga)
  Digital Selective Calling MMSI 002241011
  VHF Ch 16, 26, 74

Weather bulletins and navigational warnings
Weather bulletins in Spanish and English: VHF Ch 74 at 0315, 0715, 1115, 1515, 1915, 2315 UT
Navigational warnings in Spanish and English: on receipt

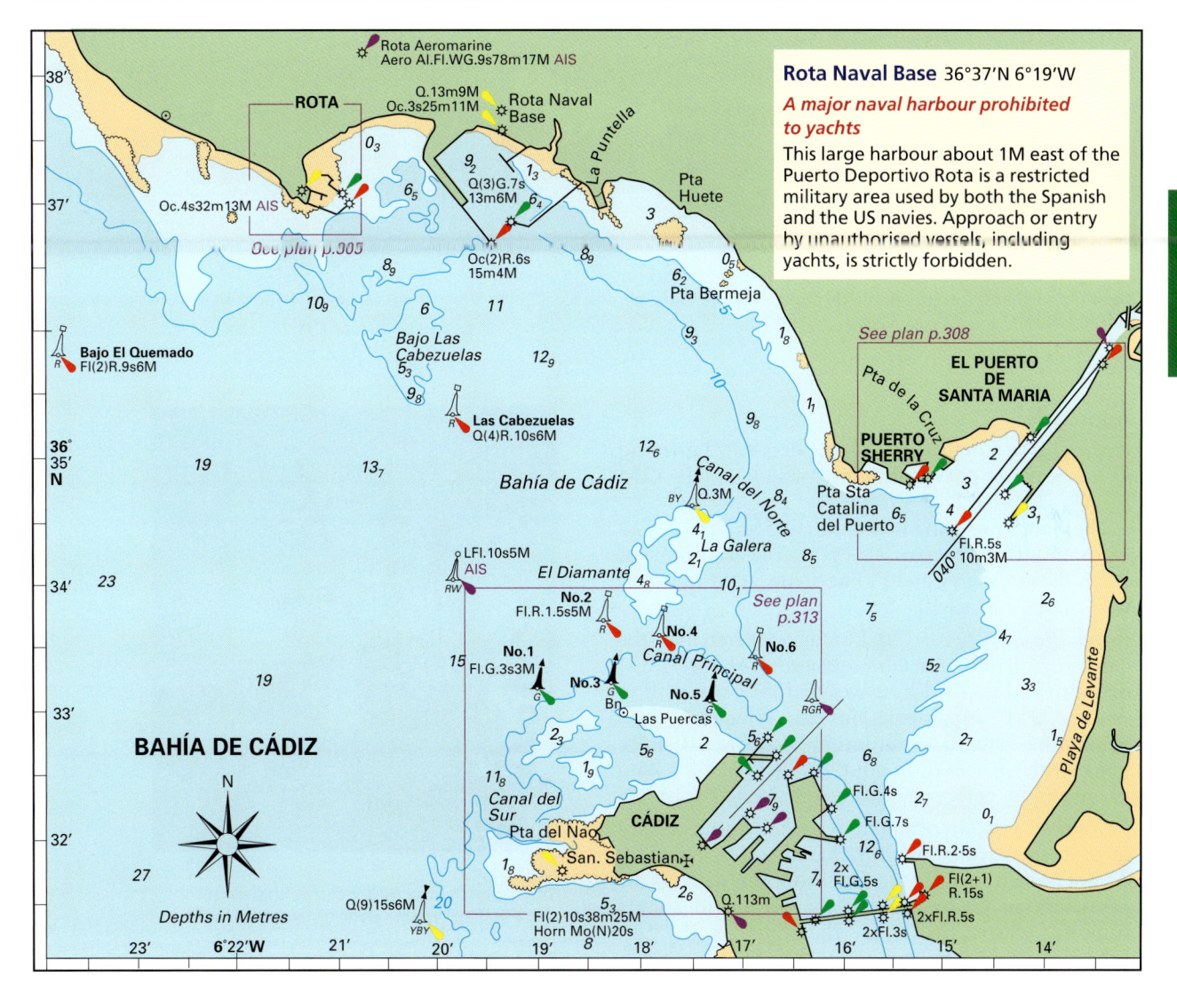

Rota Naval Base 36°37′N 6°19′W
A major naval harbour prohibited to yachts

This large harbour about 1M east of the Puerto Deportivo Rota is a restricted military area used by both the Spanish and the US navies. Approach or entry by unauthorised vessels, including yachts, is strictly forbidden.

ATLANTIC SPAIN AND PORTUGAL 303

RÍO GUADALQUIVIR TO CABO TRAFALGAR

Looking northeast into the Bahía de Cádiz over the Cádiz peninsular. Puerto Sherry marina, and the Santa Maria breakwater are visible top left.

Approach
It should be noted that fishing nets can be found as far out as the 100m line which is 10–12M from Cadiz.

The Bahía de Cádiz is more than 5M wide across at its mouth and gives access to the harbours of Rota, Puerto Sherry and El Puerto de Santa María as well as to Cádiz itself.

From the northwest Off Punta del Perro lies the dangerous Bajo Salmedina, extending almost 1·6M offshore and marked by a west cardinal tower. If in doubt, 3M offshore. Having rounded Bajo Salmedina remain a minimum of 1·3M offshore until south of 36°36′N. In poor weather head for Bajo El Quemado, before shaping a course into the bay.

From the south, an offing of at least 2M is necessary to clear the various offshore hazards. In particular, do not be tempted to take any short cuts around the peninsula of Cádiz itself – the reefs and shoals running westwards from the Castillo de San Sebastián have claimed many vessels over the years. Unless very confident it would be wise to come in on the west cardinal buoy about 1M southwest of the Castillo, from there shaping a course northwards to Rota or on 030° for Los Cochinos buoy No.1 and so entering the Canal Principal.

Further information on the final approaches to each harbour will be found in that harbour information following.

The replica of the Nao Victoria, a Spanish carrack. The only survivor of five ships in the Magellan - Elcano circumnavigation of 1519-1522, sailed from these shores (see page 297)
Henry Buchanan

ATLANTIC SPAIN AND PORTUGAL

Rota

Location
36°36'·78N 6°20'·76W (entrance)

Tides
Standard port Cádiz
Mean time differences
HW –0010; LW –0015 ±0005
Heights in metres
MHWS	MHWN	MLWN	MLWS
3·1	2·4	1·1	0·4

Principal lights
Rota old lighthouse Oc.4s32m13M AIS
  Off-white tower, red band 28m
Southwest breakwater Fl(3)R.10s8m3M Red post on towered hut 3m
Northeast breakwater Q(6)G.12s3M Green metal post (Close to floodlit statue of the Virgin and Child)

Communications
Puerto Deportivo Rota VHF Ch 09 ☏+34 856 104 011 and +34 600 141558 and +34 600 141 558
Email rota@eppa.es www.puertosdeandalucia.es
Club Nautico de Rota ☏ +34 956 813 821
Email clubnauticorota@telefonica.net
www.clubnauticorota.com

A well-kept, expanding marina close to an interesting old town

The northwesternmost of the Bahía de Cádiz harbours, Rota is an attractive old town with strong Moorish influences, not least in the massive stone archways which span its narrow streets. Like many Spanish towns it is best explored on foot. Excellent beaches fringe its harbour on both sides, and the tall slim lighthouse with its single red band which stands near the root of the south breakwater makes identification certain by day or night. Rota is becoming an increasingly popular place for liveaboards to winter afloat.

The Corrales de Rota reserve extends along the beach to the northwest from the old town. The corrales are a system of fish pens dating back to Roman times. Fish, cuttlefish and octopi were brought into the pens by the tide and then harvested. The dune system backing the beach is part of the reserve, accessed by a wooden walkway, and is home to Spain's largest population of chamaeleons. Spot one if you can!

Like a number of other harbours run by the Agencia Pública de Puertos de Andalucía, Rota combines the functions of yacht and fishing harbour, though the latter have now been banished to the southwest breakwater. It is occasionally referred to as Puerto Astaroth, but is more normally known by the less romantic but much more descriptive title of Puerto Deportivo Rota. It should on no account be confused with the much larger Rota Naval Base which lies about 1M further east.

Major development ashore has provided restaurants, bars, shops and *Club Náutico de Rota*. There are ferries from the marina across the bay to Cadiz.

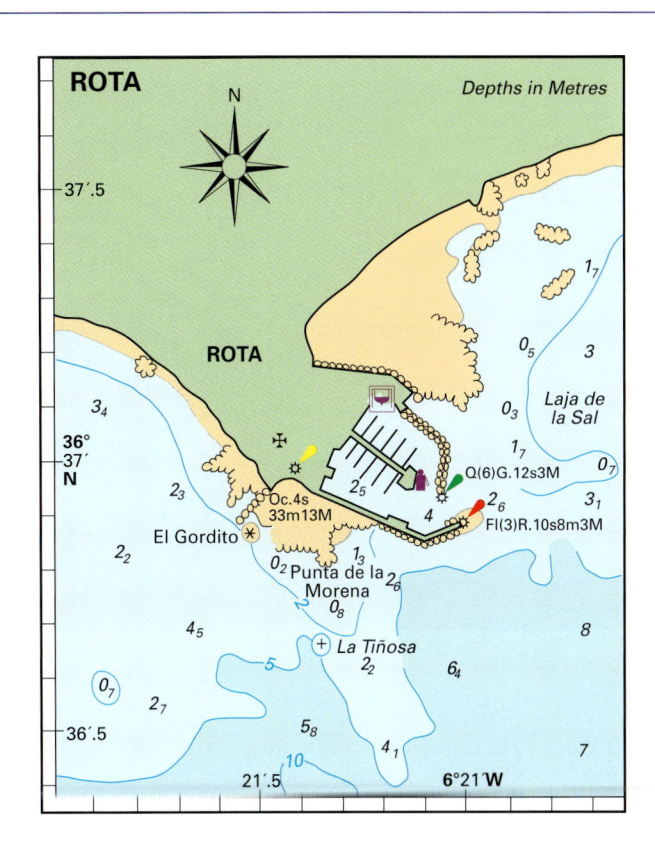

Approach and entrance

The bathymetric chart for the Puerto Deportivo Rota and its immediate approach can be found at the APPA website www.puertosdeandalucia.es/en/documentation-en/batimetrias > select Batimetría Puerto de Rota.

Allow generous clearance around the breakwater as sand has built up beyond the light. The north breakwater will open up behind. For maximum protection the entrance was built facing northeast with the prominent white statue of the Virgin and Child close to its end. From the south or southeast the breakwater head can be approached directly. The entrance forms a dogleg and is relatively narrow, but otherwise presents no problems.

Berthing

The reception/fuel pontoon lies directly opposite the entrance under the end of the central mole, with the marina office above. With a total of 509 berths on eleven pontoons, 144 of them able to take yachts of 12m or more, space for a visitor can nearly always be found, if only for a couple of nights (though note APPA's policy that if a berth of the correct length is not available and a yacht occupies a larger berth this will be charged for, irrespective of the actual length of the boat). If staying long-term and offered a choice, the northeast basin is considerably more protected than that to the southwest which, during gales, suffers both from surf breaking over the breakwater and swell from the entrance. Depths shoal gradually from 4m near the mole end to 2·5m along the northwest perimeter.

RÍO GUADALQUIVIR TO CABO TRAFALGAR

Puerto de Rota looking east of north *APPA*

Weekdays in winter, office hours are 1000–1330 and 1600–1730, closed Saturday and Sunday afternoons. The office remains open later in summer with no weekend closing. The staff are particularly helpful, and there is 24 hour security with card-operated gates to the pontoons.

Facilities

Boatyard On the north side of the marina, with a large area of secure (but somewhat windy) hard standing. All larger boats occupy cradles with additional shores. Laying-up ashore in Rota is becoming increasingly popular.

Travel-lift 50-tonne capacity lift at the boatyard.

Engineers, electronic and radio repairs Available at or via the boatyard. For more major jobs specialists may be called in from Puerto Sherry.

Chandlery There is Nautica Vergara (Yamaha) ☎+34 956 846 362. *Email* nauticavergararota@hotmail.com.

Water/electricity On the pontoons.

Showers On the hammerhead (in the building which also houses the fuel berth office), and in an anonymous cream building with grey doors near the root of the central mole, both well-kept.

Launderette In the anonymous cream building.

Fuel Diesel and petrol at the reception pontoon on the central hammerhead, 0800–1400 and 1500–1900.

Bottled gas Camping Gaz in the town, but no refills.

Weather forecast Posted daily outside the marina office.

Club Náutico In premises overlooking the marina.

Banks In the town, with cash dispensers.

Shops/provisioning Good shopping in the town only a short walk from the marina.

Produce market Directly opposite the marina.

Cafés, restaurants and hotels Mina Street is a lively, fun area at night with several reasonable restaurants.

Medical services In the town.

Communications

Post office In the town.

Mailing address The marina office will hold mail for visiting yachts – Glorieta José Pemán, 1 11520 Rota (Cádiz) España. It is important that the envelope carries the name of the yacht in addition to that of the addressee.

Internet There is one internet pay terminal in the café at the root of the central jetty. There are other places in town, and free access in the library.

Car hire/taxis Can be organised via the marina office.

Ferry There is a small ferry terminal in the same building as the marina office. A fast catamaran runs seven to eight times daily to Cadiz (three times on Sat and Sun). This berths in the southeast corner of the main commercial basin in the centre of Cadiz, next to the train and bus stations. In bad weather, a bus replaces the ferry keeping to the same schedule.

Buses To Chipiona, El Puerto de Santa María, Seville etc.

Air services International airports at Seville and Jerez.

A caravel statue in old Rota *Jane Russell*

Jerez de la Frontera, the home of sherry *Martin Craven*

306 ATLANTIC SPAIN AND PORTUGAL

PUERTO SHERRY

Puerto Sherry

Location
36°34'·5N 6°15'·2W (entrance)

Tides
Standard port Cádiz
Mean time differences
HW –0005 ±0010; LW –0005 ±0010
Heights in metres

MHWS	MHWN	MLWN	MLWS
3·2	2·6	1·1	0·4

Principal lights
Santa María, West training wall, head
  Fl.R.5s9m3M Red metal tower 4m
South breakwater Oc.R.4s5M
  White truncated conical tower
East mole, SE corner Oc.G.5s3M Green tower
Inner harbour, E side Q.G.1M
  Squat Green tower 2m

Warning/Notes
Night entry straightforward but narrow. Swing wide and head up the centre to avoid shallows to port and an unlit concrete spur opposite

Communications
Puerto Sherry VHF Ch 09 (24 hours)
② +34 956 870 103 and +34 956 850 202
Email puertosherry@puertosherry.com
recepcionpuerto@puertosherry.com
www.puertosherry.com/en/

Large, purpose-built marina with a good onsite boatyard but functional surroundings

Puerto Sherry is by far the largest, oldest and, in some ways, best equipped marina on the Atlantic coast of Andalucía. Planned as a true 'marina village' with construction begun in 1985, many of the buildings still remain unfinished today although many apartments and a hotel have been completed. There is no true village ashore, the marina complex being backed by carefully landscaped villas and golf courses.

The overall impression is still that of a building site, with some of the completed buildings already beginning to peel. It would be fair to say that few cruising yachtsmen spend time in Puerto Sherry for pleasure, but more than one has found its well-equipped boatyard and concentration of specialised skills to be a veritable lifesaver in time of need.

To visit Cadiz it is necessary to take a taxi, or walk (45 minutes), to the ferry terminal at Santa Maria (see plan page 308) and take the ferry from there.

Approach

For outer approaches from the northwest and southeast refer to Bahía de Cádiz, page 304.

Once in the bay, from north of west approach via Las Cabezuelas buoy and the Canal del Norte, passing no more than 1M off Punta Santa Catalina del Puerto in order to avoid the La Galera and El Diamante banks which shoal to 2–1m. From south of west, follow the directions for Cádiz – page 313 – diverging from the Canal Principal after passing El Diamante port hand buoy No.4. From there a direct course of 063° leads to the marina entrance.

From all directions the cream 'lighthouse' building at the end of the south breakwater, which houses the marina office, makes a conspicuous daymark.

Entrance

The 100m wide entrance faces slightly south of east and is well sheltered, but care must be taken of a shoal, at one time described as extensive, around and inside the end of the south breakwater. This has been marked by pink buoys, some in clusters, none of which are lit. The intention of building a training wall to mitigate this problem between Puerto Sherry and Rota has not been realised.

Rounding the south breakwater light enter the harbour on a course of 289°. A minimum of 3m at low water is claimed in the centre of the entrance.

The reception pontoon is on the inside of the south breakwater close to the marina control tower opposite an unlit concrete spur, which juts out from the wall opposite.

Berthing

Puerto Sherry contains 842 berths for craft of up to 60m (provided they can cope with the 3m depths) in totally sheltered conditions, and it would be rare for space not to be available for a visitor. All pontoons are equipped with fingers. Those immediately overlooked by the two hotels are somewhat public, those to the south are quieter but entail longer walks. In fact the size of the complex is such that, if berthed on one of the western pontoons and needing to visit the boatyard area, it might well be worth launching the dinghy.

The marina staff are efficient and welcoming, and have been seen helping to moor a boat at the reception pontoon at 0200 in the morning. Security is excellent with gates to each pontoon and CCTV monitoring. The office is open 0800–2100 from 1/6-30/9 otherwise 0800-2000.

Looking northeast over Puerto Sherry Marina *APPA*

ATLANTIC SPAIN AND PORTUGAL

RÍO GUADALQUIVIR TO CABO TRAFALGAR

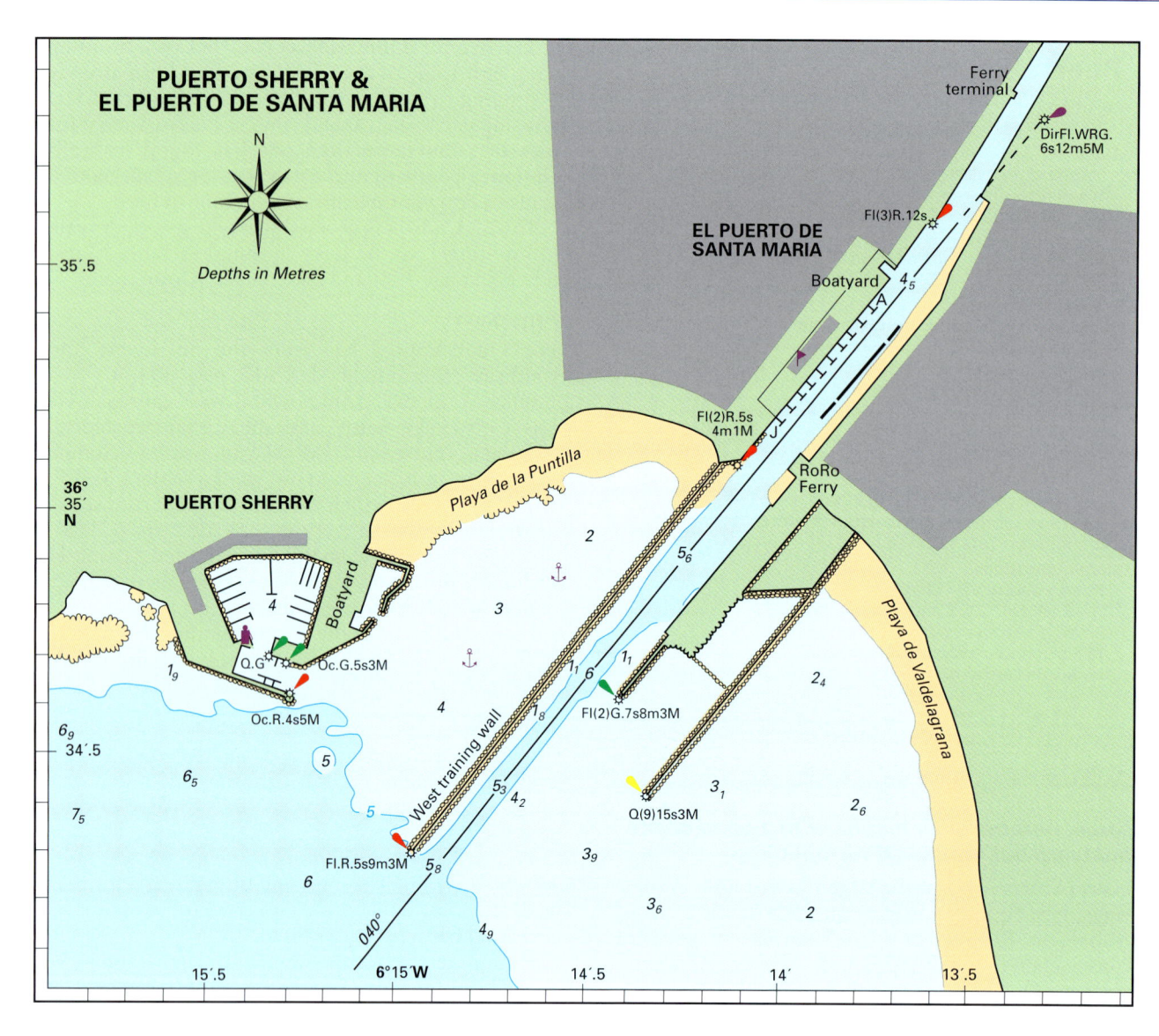

Facilities

Boatyard There is a large area of gated hardstanding (22,000m^2) on the wide east mole where a number of companies offer their services. Security is relaxed during the day, but doubtless better at night. DIY work is permitted, but owners cannot live aboard yachts that are ashore.

Travel-lift 200 tonne and 50 tonne capacity lifts for which bookings must be made at the marina office. No shortage of shores and some cradles.

Engineers, electronic and radio repairs Industria Náutica del Sur SL: Puerto Sherry, s/n. 11500 Cádiz ☎+34 956 874 000, www.industrianauticadelsur.com which handles hull and engine maintenance and repairs, osmosis treatment, painting etc. There are other companies on site that have a range of expertise.

Sailmaker/sail repairs Velas Climent SL, ☎/*Fax* +34 956 870 539, occupies a rather anonymous white building with blue trim in the boatyard area. They are experienced sailmakers, as well as handling repairs and general canvas work.

Rigging Industria Náutica del Sur handles rigging, with a specialist brought in from Valencia if necessary.

Chandleries Industria Náutica del Sur SL (see above) runs a chandlery in the complex.

Water On the pontoons.

Puerto Sherry marina control tower and reception pontoon
Puerto Sherry Marina

Showers Several shower blocks around the marina complex reported to be kept impeccably clean.

Launderette On the west quay of the marina.

Electricity On the pontoons. However large, non-standard adapter plugs are necessary and the marina office does not always have enough to lend or rent to visitors.

ATLANTIC SPAIN AND PORTUGAL

PUERTO SHERRY

Entrance to Puerto Sherry marina from the welcome pontoon
Jane Russell

Fuel Petrol and diesel pumps on the west side of the entrance to the inner harbour. In theory fuel can be bought at any time of the day or night, and credit cards are accepted.
Bottled gas Not available.
Weather forecast Posted daily at the marina office.
Bank Not only no bank, but no card machine in the entire complex. Berthing can be paid for by credit card, but not an ice-cream or a cup of coffee.
Shops/provisioning Small supermarket on the west side of the inner basin, though it would be necessary to go into El Puerto de Santa María (and take a taxi back) for serious storing up.
Cafés, restaurants and hotels Several cafés and restaurants along the west side of the inner basin, with a large hotel to the north, but no longer a café in the boatyard area.
Medical services First aid point in the marina, with more serious facilities in nearby Puerto de Santa María.

Communications
Post office In El Puerto de Santa María.
Mailing address The marina office will hold mail for visiting yachts – c/o Puerto Sherry, Av. de la Libertad, S/N, 11500 El Puerto de Sta María, Cádiz, España. It is important that the envelope carries the name of the yacht in addition to that of the addressee.
Internet WiFi is free but described as tortuous to use. Laptops can be connected via a metered socket in the hotel.
Car hire/taxis Can be arranged via the marina office. The walk along the beach to El Puerto de Santa María takes about half an hour.
Air services International airports at Seville and Jerez.

Adjacent anchorage

Yachts of modest draught can anchor off Playa de la Puntilla, east of Puerto Sherry marina and north of the Puerto de Santa María training wall, sheltered from all directions other than southwest when a nasty swell can roll in from the bay to the anchorage. The beach shoals gently and fairly evenly, though there are a few shallower patches, with holding good over sand and mud.

The anchoring area outside Puerto Sherry is this side of the long breakwater and can become quite crowded at weekends. This is looking S from Playa Puntilla at low water
Jane Russell

ATLANTIC SPAIN AND PORTUGAL

THE ALGARVE & ANDALUCIA

RÍO GUADALQUIVIR TO CABO TRAFALGAR

El Puerto de Santa María

Location
36°34'N 6°15'·15W (entrance channel)

Tides
Standard port Cádiz
Mean time differences
HW –0005 ±0010; LW –0005 ±0010
Heights in metres
MHWS	MHWN	MLWN	MLWS
3·2	2·6	1·1	0·4

Principal lights
Ldg Line 040° Dir.Fl.WRG.6s12m5M
  Round metal tower
West training wall, head Fl.R.5s9m3M
  Red tower 6m
East outer breakwater Q(9)15s3M
  West cardinal tower 3m
East inner breakwater Fl(2)G.7s8m3M
  Green tower 4m
West training wall, root Q.R.5m2M Red tower 3m

Warning
Night entry not recommended in a strong southwesterly, otherwise well lit and without hazards

Communications
Real Club Náutico de Santa María
VHF Ch 09 (0830–2130, not Sunday)
☎ +34 956 852 527
Email rcnpuerto@rcnpsm.es
www.rcnpsm.com

Small, club-run marina on a busy river

El Puerto de Santa María is a pleasant town and a very old port which formerly handled all the produce of Jerez, brought down the Río Guadalete on barges. Whitewashed sherry *bodegas* (warehouses) still line parts of the river and most producers offer tours – check with the tourist office. In Elizabethan times, at least one planned attack on Cádiz went awry when English sailors on forays ashore discovered the stored liquor and drank themselves to a standstill.

The Real Club Náutico de El Puerto de Santa María prides itself on its friendly atmosphere for members, but they take priority when busy at the height of the season when visitors can be treated as a nuisance. In common with many Spanish yacht clubs it has a small but attractive garden and sports facilities including a gymnasium, tennis courts and open-air swimming pool, which visiting yachtsmen are welcome to use for a small fee.

The river, which is relatively narrow, still carries some commercial traffic as well as fishing and ferry boats, and there is no space to anchor.

Approach and entrance

For outer approaches from the northwest and southeast refer to Bahía de Cádiz, page 304.

Once in the bay, from north of west approach via Las Cabezuelas buoy and the Canal del Norte, passing no more than 1M off Punta Santa Catalina del Puerto in order to avoid the La Galera and El Diamante banks which shoal to 2·1m. From south of west, follow the directions for Cádiz – page 313 – diverging from the Canal Principal after passing El Diamante port hand buoy No.4. From there a direct course of 073° leads into the entrance channel, which itself runs 040°, parallel to the training west wall.

Berthing

The Real Club Náutico, founded in 1920, administers an ageing marina facility in need of a refit. It is capable of berthing around 175 yachts and smallcraft, including a few vessels of up to 25m. Other than at the innermost berths, depths are generous at 5m or more. Shelter from wind and waves is good, but wash from fishing boats and ferry boats that do not respect the 3kn speed limit are a problem and currents in the river can reach 2·5kn at springs. Think twice before leaving a boat here, especially on a hammerhead. About 20 berths are normally reserved for visitors, all of them on the 10 hammerhead pontoons approached from the northwest bank. The three detached pontoons on the southeast side of the channel are reserved for club members. Regattas are held during August, at which time the pontoons are likely to be full and visitors given a low priority. A visiting yacht can nearly always be found space at other times.

It is highly recommended that contact is made 24 to 48 hours before arrival to secure a berth. Otherwise call on VHF Ch 09 on the approach and hope for the best. It has been reported that communications can be difficult depending on who is on duty in the office (at least one of the office staff speaks excellent English), in which case secure to any hammerhead and enquire at the white control tower or the office (near the road gate and turnstile) for a berth. The office is open 0830–2130 Monday to Saturday and does not close for siesta. Security is good, with a uniformed guard when the office is closed and card-operated turnstiles into the grounds. The club's *marineros* will keep an eye on any unattended yacht.

Facilities

Boatyard Small boatyard at the upstream end of the premises with limited hardstanding mostly occupied by members' yachts.
Travel-lift There is a 25-tonne travel-lift in the Club Nautico enclosure but rather typical of the marina infrastructure it is in need of refurbishment.
Engineers Some mechanical capabilities at the boatyard. For serious problems it may be necessary to go to Puerto Sherry.
Chandlery There are no chandlers in Santa Maria but they can be found in Puerto Sherry or Cádiz.
Water On the pontoons.
Showers In the Real Club Náutico building next to the tennis court.
Laundry/launderette Available in the Club Nautico building, otherwise there are launderettes in the town.
Electricity On the pontoons but cabinets in poor condition and earth leakage significant.
Fuel Fuel is not available.
Bottled gas Camping Gaz available at hardware stores in the town, but no refills.
Weather forecast Available at the office on request.
Banks In the town, with cash dispensers.
Shops/provisioning/produce market Good shopping of all

EL PUERTO DE SANTA MARÍA

The Real Club Náutico de Santa María looking southeast *APPA*

kinds in the town 15 minutes away, with a busy market a few blocks west of the Real Club Náutico.
Cafés, restaurants and hotels Very pleasant restaurants at the Real Club Náutico, both terrace and indoor (the latter more formal), with plenty more in the town and along the beach.
Medical services In the town.

Communications

Post office In the town.
Mailing address The Real Club Náutico will hold mail for visiting yachts – c/o Real Club Náutico de El Puerto de Santa María, Av. de la Bajamar, 13, 11500 El Puerto de Sta María, Cádiz, España. It is important that the envelope carries the name of the yacht in addition to that of the addressee.
Internet In the Real Club Náutico. There are reported to be several cybercafés in the town, as well as free connection at the library.
Car hire/taxis In the town, or can be arranged via the office.
Buses and trains To Cádiz, Jerez, Seville (about an hour) and elsewhere.
Ferries Passenger ferries to Cádiz (and not a bad way to visit that city).
Air services International airports at Seville and Jerez.

Looking down the Río Guadalete over the pontoons of the Real Club Náutico de El Puerto de Santa María
Anne Hammick

ATLANTIC SPAIN AND PORTUGAL

RÍO GUADALQUIVIR TO CABO TRAFALGAR

Cádiz

Location
36°33'·57N 6°18'·42W (entrance)

Tides
Standard port Cádiz
Heights in metres
MHWS	MHWN	MLWN	MLWS
3·3	2·5	1·2	0·5

Principal lights
Cádiz, Castillo de San Sebastián Fl(2)10s37m25M
  Round metal tower on castle 37m
Dique Mar de Levante Fl(4)G.10s10m3M
  Green post suspended from semicircular structure
North breakwater Fl.G.3s9m5M
  Green triangular column 6m
East breakwater Fl.R.2s10m5M
  Red triangular column 5m
Marina southeast breakwater Fl(4)G.16s1M
  Green post 2m
Marina northwest mole Fl(4)R.16s1M Red post 2m
Plus many other lights in the commercial harbour

Harbour communications
Port Authority VHF Ch 16, 74
☏ +34 956 240 400
Email cadiz@puertocadiz.com www.puertocadiz.com
Marina Puerto América VHF Ch 09
☏ +34 856 580 002 - 600 148 523.
Email puertoamerica@eppa.es www.puertosdeandalucia.es
Real Club Náutico de Cádiz VHF Ch 09
☏ +34 956 213 262 *Fax* +34 956 228 701
rcncadiz@infocadiz.com
Centro Náutico Elcano VHF Ch 09 ☏ +34 956 264 008 and +34 956 290 012
Email scnelcano@deportedecadiz.com
Puerto de Gallineras ☏ +34 956 486 259
Email cngallineras@telefonica.net www.cngallineras.es

Puerto América in the foreground, Real Club Náutico de Cádiz just beyond *APPA*

312 ATLANTIC SPAIN AND PORTUGAL

CÁDIZ

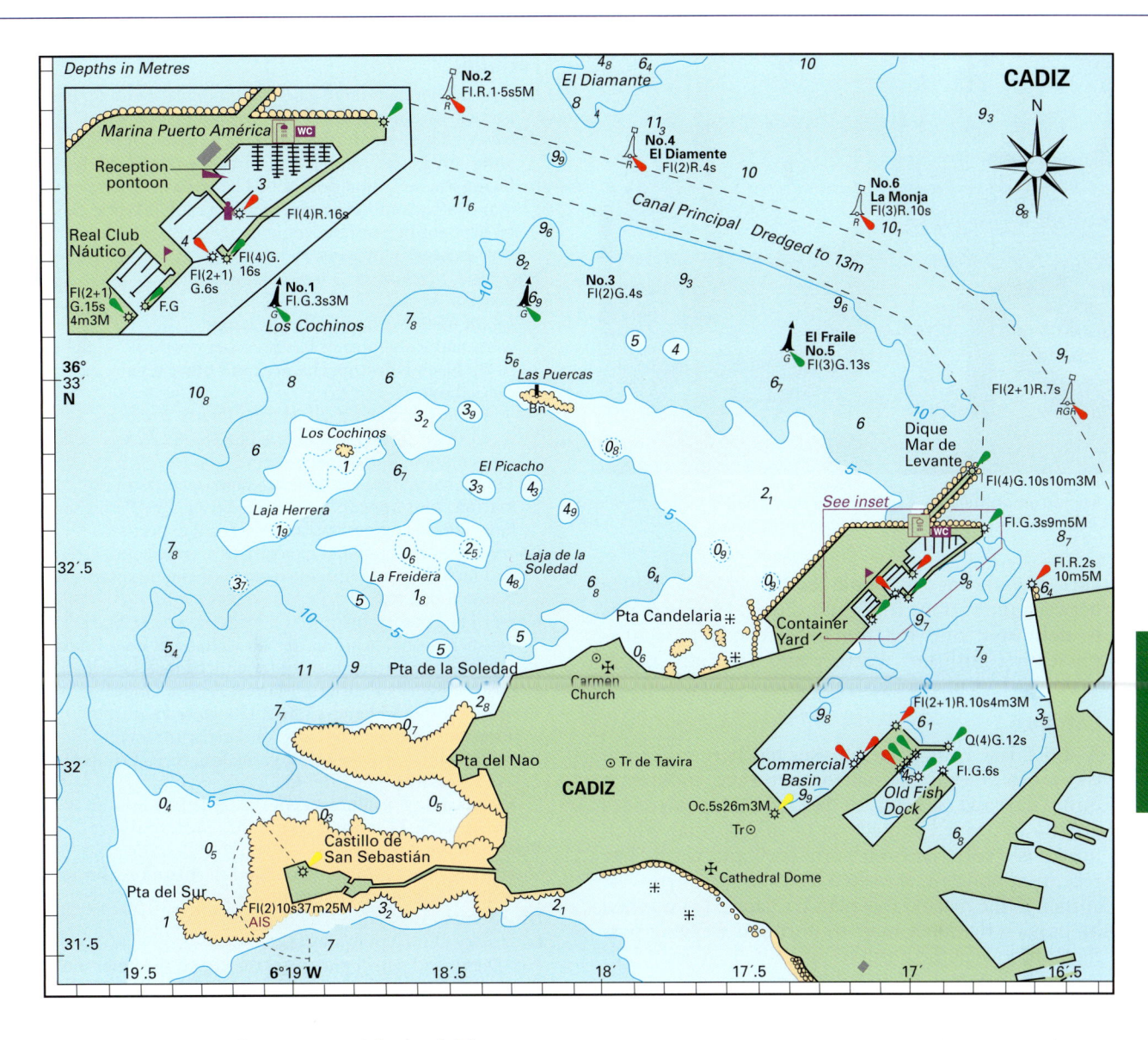

A well-run marina (Puerto América) within walking distance of one of Spain's oldest cities

Cádiz is an ancient and fascinating city, founded by the Phoenicians over 3,000 years ago, settled by Romans and Moors, and today discovering its archaeological heritage and presenting it to the world. It has long been a major port, with a fine defensive position and good shelter, and for many years handled nearly all the lucrative trade with the New World. This led to great wealth, the results of which can still be seen in the scale of its public and private buildings, many of which date back to the 18th century. The commercial area extends along the peninsula to the southeast, less impressive architecturally but containing good shopping, restaurants and hotels.

Until the early 1990s Cádiz was a difficult city to visit by yacht, the docks devoted to fishing and commercial use and the pontoons in the Real Club Náutico de Cádiz basin packed with local craft. The opening of the Marina Puerto América overcame this problem, and though set amidst bleak surroundings nearly a kilometre from the old city walls it offers good shelter and security for the yacht whilst the crew explore the area.

Approach

For outer approaches from the northwest and southeast refer to Bahía de Cádiz, page 304.

The final approach is best made via the Canal Principal, which is well buoyed and lit and may safely be used by day or night. After identifying Los Cochinos buoy No.1, in normal weather it is safe to make direct for buoy No.5 (starboard hand) on 094°, passing close south of buoy No.3 in a least depth of 5m. Do not, however, be tempted to cut much south of buoy No.1 for fear of the unmarked Los Cochinos shoal. From buoy No.5 a course of 115° leads well clear of the end of the Dique Mar de Levante, around which the north breakwater head, will be seen. In heavy weather, or when a large swell is running, it would be wise to remain in the Canal Principal which has a dredged depth of 13m.

Fishermen may be seen using a passage close northwest of the peninsula, which uses bearings on

ATLANTIC SPAIN AND PORTUGAL 313

RÍO GUADALQUIVIR TO CABO TRAFALGAR

Roman amphitheatre, Cadiz Henry Buchanan

various buildings in Cádiz itself to plot a course between the various rocks and shoals. However, this is definitely one for the experienced navigator possessing both fair weather and a current large-scale chart or, of course, detailed local knowledge.

Entrance
A short, low lying wave breaker has been laid from the south side of the marina entrance, making it quite narrow (see photo below). This provides greatly improved protection in the marina, which previously suffered from both swell and wash. The reception pontoon is tucked away in the northwest corner of the marina (see plan on page 313) reached by passing the inner mole to port and weaving past the pontoons in the north basin.

Berthing
The marina's capacity is now 175 berths with many of the new slots able to take yachts of 12m or more up to a maximum of 15m. All berths are alongside individual fingers. The marina is becoming popular so it is best to make contact by phone in advance, calling on VHF Ch 09 on closer approach.

Office hours are 0930–1300 and 1700–2000 daily in summer, 1000–1330 and 1600–1730 in winter, remaining closed in the afternoon on Wednesday, Saturday and Sunday. The marina manager is helpful and pleasant and speaks excellent English. His somewhat elderly portacabin office is near the root of the inner mole. Security is good with guards outside office hours and individual card-operated gates to pontoons and services. In common with other marinas in the area, the night time guards may not take over immediately after the office closes but are friendly and helpful if ships papers, passports etc. are taken to them as soon as possible after a late arrival.

Facilities
Boatyard There is a large gated area of hardstanding, but no boatyard as such.
Travel-lift There is not thought to be a travel-lift in situ although a large ramp has been built in the north basin facing the reception pontoon. There is a 10-tonne crane onsite, and in an emergency a mobile crane can be brought in from the commercial docks which is a very expensive process.
Engineers, mechanics, general maintenance
Náutica Benítez ☏ +34 956 220244
Email nautica@nautica.benitez.com
www.nauticabenitez.es has premises overlooking the south basin where mechanical and other repairs are carried out.
   An outfit calling itself Marina Puerto América ☏ +34 956 211 091 *Mobile* +34 638 082 528
www.marinapuertoamerica.com
Email marina@puertoamerica.com operates in the marina. This appears to be a brokerage but claims to have repair, engineering and electrical expertise.
Chandlery Some chandlery, mostly of a practical nature and including an impressive range of engine spares, at Náutica Benítez.
Charts The Spanish Instituto Hidrográfico de la Marina has its national headquarters in Cádiz, but does not sell direct to the public. Instead try either Libreria 'Alfa 2' (also known as Papelería Manuel Pereira González, open 0930–1330 and 1730–2030, closed Saturday afternoon and Sunday) at Calle Pelota 14, in a pedestrian area close to the cathedral; or JL Gándara y Cia SA ☏ +34 956 270443
Email cadiz@gandara-sa.com at Calle La Línea de la Concepción 11 in the Zona Franca industrial area.
Water On the pontoons.
Showers A smart shower block is on the main breakwater overlooking the north basin.
Launderette Adjacent to the shower block.
Electricity On the pontoons.
Fuel Diesel and petrol pumps on the end of the inner mole.
Bottled gas Camping Gaz available in the city, but no refills.
Club náutico The Real Club Náutico de Cádiz, close south of the marina, welcomes reasonably tidy visitors to its terrace bar and restaurant.

Puerto America – From the inner mole looking southwest showing a yacht entering the marina between the breakwater and low-lying wavebreaker Henry Buchanan

ATLANTIC SPAIN AND PORTUGAL

CÁDIZ

View across the western basin to the entrance *Henry Buchanan*

Weather forecast Posted daily in the marina office, as are warnings of firing exercises.
Banks Many in the city, but no cash dispenser at the marina.
Shops/provisioning/market Excellent shopping and a good produce market in the city, but all at some distance from the marina. It is hoped that in due course a supermarket and other shops will open on the large empty space nearby.
Cafés, restaurants and hotels Snack bar next to the marina office plus a small restaurant at the Real Club Náutico. For those with transport (or happy to walk) there is a wide choice in the old city.
Medical services In the city.

Communications

Post office In the city. Stamped mail can be left at the office for posting.
Mailing address The marina office will hold mail for visiting yachts – c/o Puerto América, Punta de San Felipe s/n, 11004 - Cádiz, España. It is important that the envelope carries the name of the yacht in addition to that of the addressee.
Public telephone Next to the marina office, otherwise a booth at the Real Club Náutico plus many in the city.
Internet At the Real Club Náutico, plus several cybercafés in the city – ask for directions at the office. Informática Gaditana SA on the road behind the ferry basin sells computers and consumables such as inkjets.
Car hire/taxis There is a car hire/taxi office in the marina.
Buses and trains Links to Jerez, Seville etc from the city, but no public transport near the marina.
Ferries Passenger ferries to El Puerto de Santa María – and to the Canaries!
Air services Airports at Seville and Jerez, both served by Ryanair among others.

Other berthing in the Cádiz area

The following are included largely for interest and to dispel any possible hopes, since none have much to offer a visiting yacht.

1. **The Real Club Náutico de Cádiz** lies next to Puerto América (though threatened with displacement to make way for a container park), where it has a 182-berth basin packed with member's own vessels. Visitors are welcome to visit the bar and waterside restaurant.
2. **The Centro Náutico Elcano** (36°30'·0N 6°15'·67W) is a private marina situated just north of the main (bascule) bridge. Depths are less than 2m and maximum length 9m, though most craft berthed there are considerably smaller. No provision is made for visitors and it is doubtful whether space could be found for an overnight stay.
3. **Puerto de Gallineras** (36°26'·4N 6°12'·2W) is a somewhat ambitious name for the single pontoon run by the Club Náutico de Gallineras to which a number of smallcraft are secured. It is on the shallow waterway which links Cádiz with Sancti-Petri, and there are several bridges if approached from the north. It may be possible to make an interesting dinghy trip from Sancti-Petri (distance 2·5M).

Slipway and reception pontoon looking northeast. Shower block centre right. Marina office centre left *Henry Buchanan*

ATLANTIC SPAIN AND PORTUGAL

RÍO GUADALQUIVIR TO CABO TRAFALGAR

Sancti-Petri

Location
36°22'·3N 6°13·16W (entrance)

Tides
Standard port Cádiz
Mean time differences
HW –0010; LW –0015 ±0005
Heights in metres
MHWS	MHWN	MLWN	MLWS
3·1	2·4	1·1	0·4

Principal lights
Punta del Arrecife Q(9)15s7m3M
   West cardinal beacon, ⌶ topmark
Castillo de Sancti-Petri Fl.3s18m9M
   Square tower 16m
Bajo de Poniente Fl.R.5s7m2M Red pillar
Piedra Larga Fl.G.5s7m2M Green pillar

Warning
Night entry not recommended under any circumstances. However in light conditions it would be possible to anchor close south of the outer buoys and await daylight

Communications
Puerto Deportivo Sancti-Petri VHF Ch 09 ☏ +34 856 101 096 and 600 141 564
Email sanctipetri@eppa.es www.puertosdeandalucia.es
Club Náutico de Sancti-Petri VHF Ch 09 ☏ +34 956 495 428 and 956 494 565
Email clubnauticosanctipetri@gmail.com
Puerto de Gallineras (36°26'·4N 6°12'·2W)
☏ +34 956 486 259
Email cngallineras@telefonica.net www.cngallineras.es

Attractive harbour with marina berths for visitors unlikely, but some moorings and anchorages

The sandy and windswept lagoon at Sancti-Petri provides a peaceful port of call for those confident of their pilotage. The peninsula to the east has become a recreational boating centre with an active Club Náutico, a small APPA marina and cafés. The old village buildings have either fallen into ruin or been demolished, but the little church has been restored. Street lamps run down the cobbled streets and benches recline in the shade of palm trees around the square. A *paseo* and fishermen's quay has been constructed along the southeast side of the peninsula.

Facilities for yachts have improved, though it is highly unlikely that a cruising yacht will be able to find a slot in either of the marinas. A mooring is a possibility, though many visitors prefer to lie to their own anchors. The stone quay is used by fishing vessels and ferries which ply out to the tiny, rocky Isla de Sancti-Petri, which has been inhabited since prehistoric times. It is claimed that the remains of a temple to Hercules can still be seen, along with more recent fortifications and the square-sided lighthouse.

Alternatively explore further up the estuary, and the channel to the Puerto de Gallineras, where the bird life is superb, particularly during the winter when large flocks of flamingoes are to be seen.

Approach (see plan opposite)

Coastal sailing towards Sancti-Petri from Cádiz or other points north, the coastline appears low and somewhat featureless, consisting of marshes and saltpans. Remain outside the 10m line in order to avoid a small, unmarked, isolated rock about 2M north of Punta del Arrecife, at the north end of the reef which extends more than 1M north from the Isla de Sancti-Petri. Punta del Arrecife is marked by a lit west cardinal column with topmark – on no account attempt to cut inside it, but instead give the island generous clearance until able to pick up the outer pair of buoys.

Coming from the south, beware the long, rocky shoal which runs southwest from Cabo Trafalgar, culminating in the dangerous Bajo Aceitera more than 1·5M offshore. In heavy weather the Placer de Meca bank, 3·2M to the west, may break and should also be avoided. A race can form up to 8M offshore in these conditions, particularly when east-going current and tidal stream oppose the *levanter*. North of the cape a direct course for Sancti-Petri takes one uncomfortably close to the 1·2m shoal of Lajas de Conil – keep a good 2·5M offshore until approaching Cabo Roche. Once past the headland with its square lighthouse there are no hazards other than the isolated Laja Bermeja about 1M south of the entrance. Remain outside the 10m line until able to pick up the outer pair of buoys.

Care must be taken to avoid the Hazte Afuera/Cabezo de la Pasada bank, a long narrow ledge which shoals to 3·1m in places. The bank, which lies parallel to the coast about 2·5M off, extends for more than 3M from end to end.

In onshore swell the offshore banks may break, in which case any thoughts of entering Sancti-Petri should be forgotten.

Entrance

Though protection once inside is good, the entrance should only be attempted on a rising tide, in fair weather and in good visibility. If in doubt wait for a local vessel to give a lead in.

The bathymetric chart for the Puerto de Sancti Petri covers the entry channel from buoys No. 1 and No.2 to buoys No. 6 and No.7 on the final approach to the Sancti Petri marinas.
www.puertosdeandalucia.es/en/documentation-en/batimetrias, select Batimetría Canal de Acceso a Sancti Petri.

The bar is believed to carry at least 2m at MLWS, but an onshore swell can create very dangerous conditions and the surrounding sandbanks shift with every gale. The current runs strongly, with a good

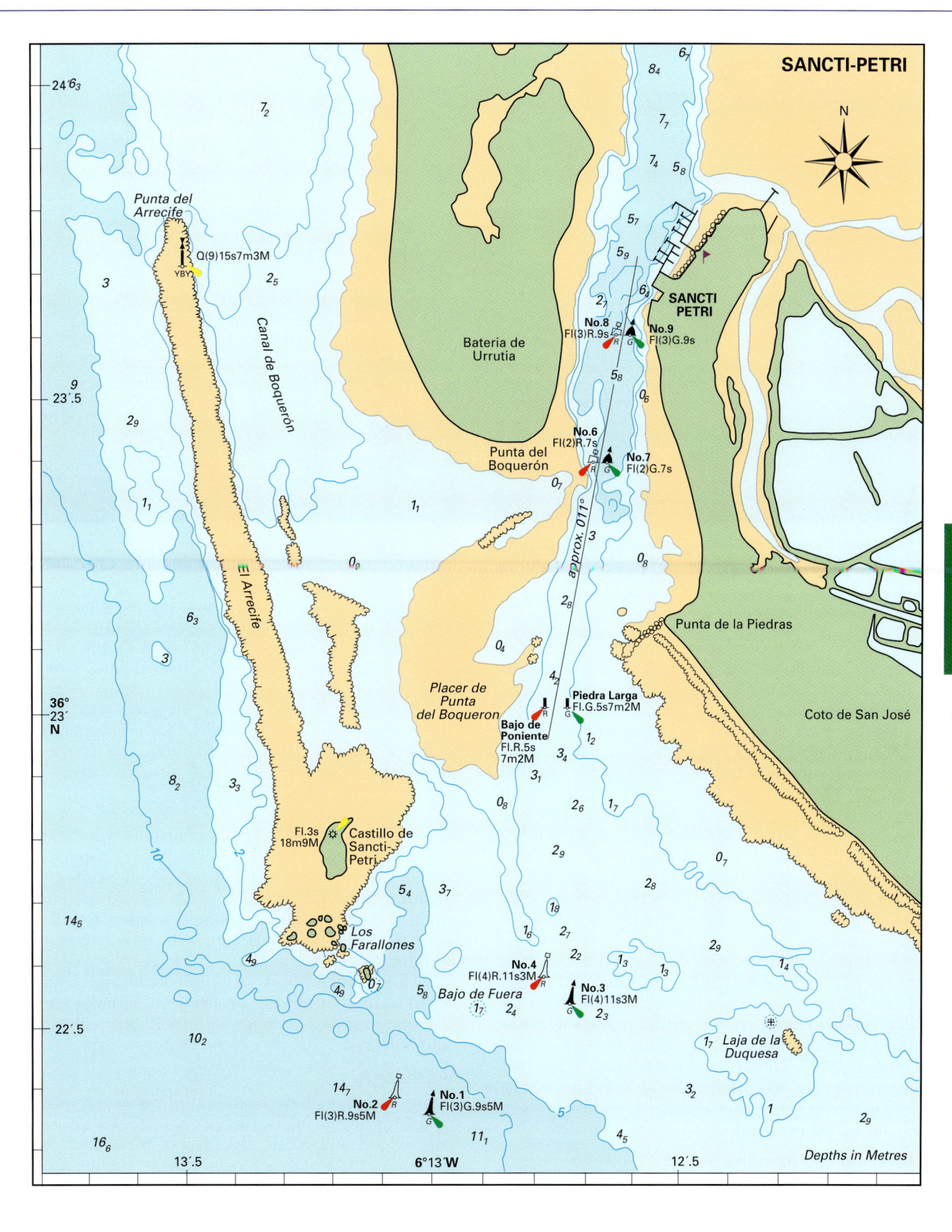

SANCTI-PETRI

RÍO GUADALQUIVIR TO CABO TRAFALGAR

Sancti-Petri entrance from south-southwest. The island castle stands on the left, from which the Los Farallones reef runs out towards the pair of entrance buoys. At near low water the Placer de Punta del Boqueron sandbank shows clearly, with Sancti-Petri village behind

2kn on the flood and more on the ebb. Night approach should not be contemplated, even though the entrance is lit.

Having made a position southwest of the Castillo de Sancti-Petri as described above, pass between the outer pair of buoys at the start of the buoyed channel. The channel shifts from time to time, and if the buoys do not agree exactly with the chart it is probably best to trust the former, but see the latest APPA bathymetric chart. Although the first two pairs of buoys are officially listed as being pillars with topmarks, they have been reported as being much smaller and without topmarks, though of the correct colour.

Continue on approx. 346° until about 100m short of the gate formed by Bajo de Poniente and Piedra Larga (identical red and green columns with lattice baskets surrounding their lights), turning slightly to starboard through the gap. Continue upriver on approx. 011°, favouring the starboard side. Two extra sets of port/starboard hand buoys have been laid in the final approach channel where a minimum of 3m should be found.

Berthing and mooring

There are two sets of pontoons at Sancti-Petri. The downstream set form the APPA Puerto Deportivo Sancti-Petri, and the upstream set, together with the many moorings, are administered by the Club Náutico de Sancti-Petri.

The Puerto Deportivo Sancti-Petri contains 92 berths for boats of up to 12m, but of the 25 nominally reserved for visitors only one can take a yacht of more than 10m. Depths of 5m are claimed for the three hammerheads, where it may be possible to lie for a short period to fill water tanks etc. The marina office is located in a building on the quay, open 1000-1330 and 1600-1830 weekdays, 1000-1330 weekends, and some English is spoken. Access to the marina is via an electronic gate, making it unsuitable for landing by dinghy. However it may be possible for crews at anchor to obtain, on payment of a small fee, a card which will also give access to the immaculate toilets and showers.

The Club Náutico de Sancti-Petri no longer accepts visiting yachts on its pontoons, which are full to capacity with locally-owned boats, though it may be possible to rent a mooring out of season. Again, pontoon access is via an electronic gate, limiting dinghy landing possibilities unless a card is forthcoming. The club occupies the only two story building on the waterfront which also houses the bar/café. Office hours are 0900-1400 and 1600-1930 daily, but closing at 1900 on Monday and Tuesday, and not opening until 0930 on weekends and holidays.

Anchorage

Many moorings have been laid in the estuary and space for anchoring is, therefore, restricted. In the absence of a card to give access to one of the pontoons, the best prospect for dinghy landing is on the muddy beach at the head of the peninsula, also used by local fishermen. Watch out for numerous underwater obstructions if coming in using an outboard motor.

There is more room beyond the moorings and in the channel to the APPA marina at Puerto de Gallineras (2·5M). This is a somewhat ambitious name for the single pontoon run by the *Club Náutico de Gallineras* to which a number of

SANCTI-PETRI

smallcraft are secured. It could make an interesting dinghy trip.

Note that the ebb can run at 3kn or more, but holding is excellent over sand and mud. It may be necessary to pick a buoy for which a charge will be made.

Facilities
Boatyard The *Club Náutico* has a walled compound near the quay where members lay up yachts to 11m or so. However a crane must be brought in for the purpose as there is no travel-lift or marine railway.
Engineers Enquire at the *Club Náutico*.
Chandlery Nautime Jet ☏+34 956 495 975, has premises on the quay, mainly concerned with jet skis but also selling a limited range of general chandlery, clothes and electronics.
Water On both sets of pontoons – yachts on moorings may be able to lie alongside briefly to fill tanks.
Showers On the quay for *Puerto Deportivo* users, or in the *Club Náutico*.
Electricity On both sets of pontoons.
Fuel: There is no fuel facility.
Club Náutico A small and friendly club with few facilities but helpful members.
Weather forecast Posted daily outside both offices.
Banks Several in Chiclana de la Frontera about 7km inland, and at least one cash dispenser in Costa Sancti-Petri about 2km away.
Shops/provisioning/market Other than a kiosk selling cold drinks and ice-creams there is no shop in Sancti-Petri of any kind. The nearest serious shopping is in Chiclana de la Frontera, though basic needs can be met in Costa Sancti–Petri.

Cafés, restaurants and hotels There is a bar/café at the *Club Náutico* with restaurants on either side, plus other cafés and restaurants on the east side of the peninsula.
Medical services Red Cross post operational in summer only, otherwise in Chiclana de la Frontera.

Communications
Post office In Chiclana de la Frontera. There is no box either though harbour staff may be willing to post stamped mail for visitors. Alternatively hand to the postman on his daily visit.
Mailing address Both offices will hold mail for visiting yachts:
    c/o Oficina del Puerto, Puerto Deportivo Sancti-Petri, Poblado de Sancti Petri 11139 - Chiclana de la Frontera (Cádiz), España or,
    c/o Club Náutico de Sancti-Petri, Calleja, 1 Poblado de Sancti Petri, 11139 - Chiclana de la Frontera (Cádiz), España. It is important that the envelope carries the name of the yacht in addition to that of the addressee.
Internet In Chiclana de la Frontera and understood to be available in Costa Sancti–Petri, though this has not been verified.
Taxis Organise via either office.
Buses About every two hours from a stop near the quay (check the return timetable before departure).

Looking southeast over Sancti-Petri. Most visitors must anchor, as both the APPA-run Puerto Deportivo Sancti-Petri and the pontoons of the Club Náutico de Sancti-Petri are generally full

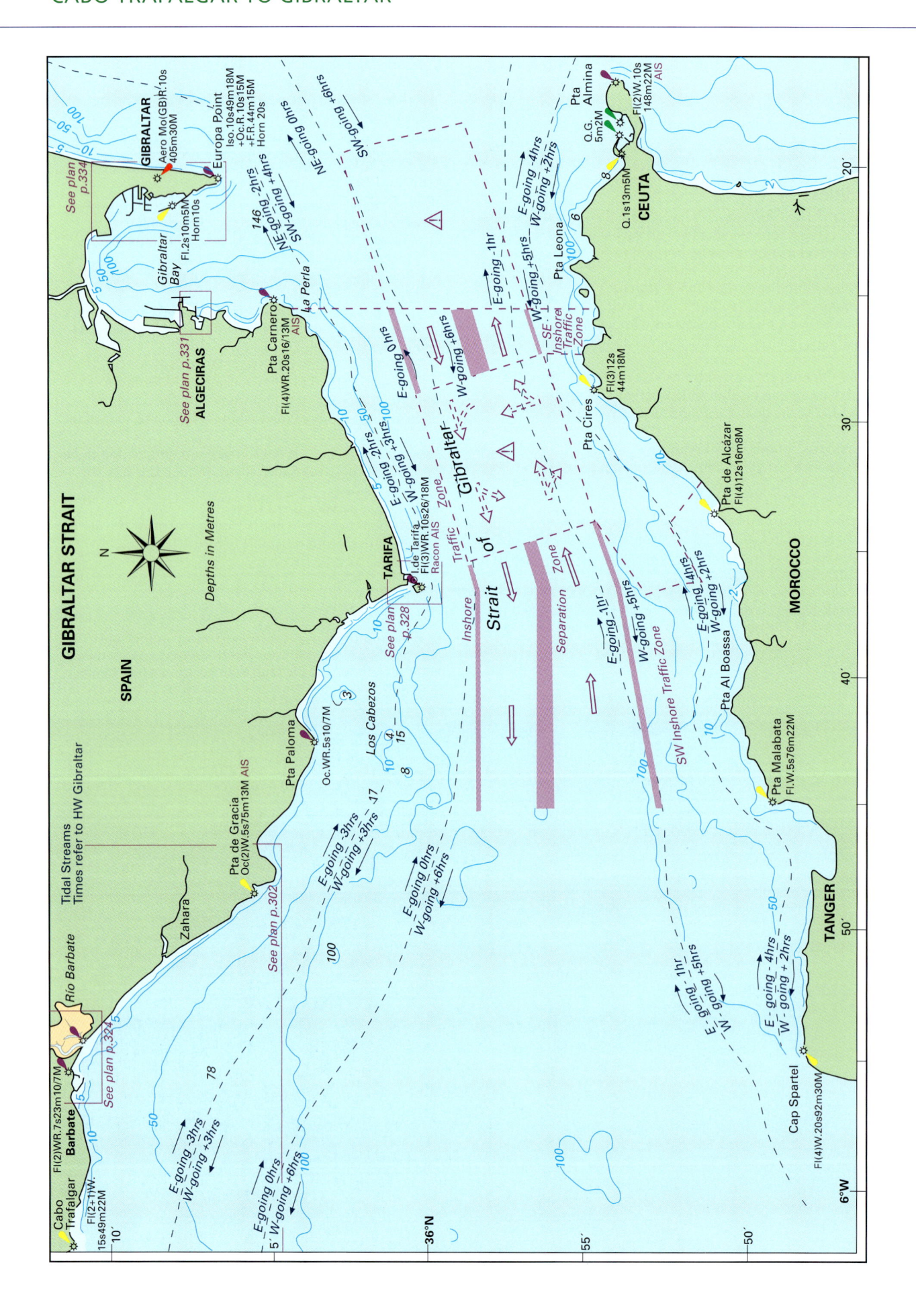

CABO TRAFALGAR TO GIBRALTAR

320 ATLANTIC SPAIN AND PORTUGAL

Cabo Trafalgar to Gibraltar

PRINCIPAL LIGHTS
Europe
Cabo Trafalgar Fl(2+1)15s49m22M White conical tower and building 34m
Punta de Gracia (Punta Camarinal) Oc(2)5s75m13M AIS
Round masonry tower 20m
Punta Paloma Oc.WR.5s44m10/7M
010°-W-340°-R-010° (over Bajo de Los Cabezos)
Two-storey building 5m
Tarifa Fl(3)WR.10s40m26/18M
089°-R-113°-W-089° (over Bajo de Los Cabezos)
Racon Mo 'C'(—·—·)20M AIS White round tower 33m
Punta Carnero Fl(4)WR.20s41m16/13M AIS
018°-W-325°-R-018° (Red sector covers La Perla and Las Bajas shoals)
Round masonry tower and white building 19m
Great Europa Point, Gibraltar
Iso.10s49m18M 197°-vis-042°, 067°-vis-125°
White tower, red band 19m
South mole Gibraltar Fl.W.2s10m5M
White column 7m
Africa
Cabo Espartel Fl(4)20s95m30M
Yellow square stone tower
Pta Malabata Fl.5s76m22M
White square tower on white dwelling
Ksar es Srhir Fl(4)12s16m8M
Column on metal framework tower
Pta Cires Fl(3)10s44m18M
Brown truncated conical tower
Pta Almina Fl(2)10s148m22M
White round tower on white building

Traffic Separation Zone
There is a Traffic Separation Zone in the Strait of Gibraltar between 5°25'·5W and 5°45'W – see plan opposite. The Inshore Traffic Zone to the north is nowhere less than 1·7M wide (off the Isla de Tarifa) and generally more than 2M. Tarifa Traffic monitors VHF Ch 16 and 10 and vessels are advised to maintain a listening watch whilst in the area. Weather and visibility information for an area including the Traffic Separation Zone is broadcast on VHF Ch 10 and 67 as detailed over.

Migrant boat people in distress
Telephone numbers for relevant authorities:
MRCC Tarifa ☏+34 956 684 740
MRSC Algeciras ☏+34 956 580 930
MRCC Madrid ☏+34 917 559 132 or +34 917 559 133
ARCC Madrid ☏+34 916 771 718 or +34 916 785 271

Surface flow in the Strait of Gibraltar

Surface water flow through the Strait is the product of a combination of current and tidal stream, the former dominant for at least eight hours out of the twelve.

A permanent, east-going current sets through the Strait, compensating for water lost from the Mediterranean through evaporation. Strength varies from 1kn close to the northern shore to approaching 2kn in the centre and southern part of the channel, with a decrease to 1·5kn or less near the Moroccan shore. However this pattern can be upset by the wind, and persistent strong westerlies, coupled with the regular current, can produce an easterly set of up to 4kn. Conversely, the entire flow may reverse after prolonged easterly winds, though in practice this seldom happens.

Tidal streams, though capable of exceeding 3kn at springs and more off the major headlands, must be worked carefully if attempting to make progress westwards – riding the stream eastwards is generally not a problem unless faced with a strong *levanter*. Streams turn earlier near the coast – see plan on page 321 – but bear in mind that even then the current may prove stronger than the tide for a considerable part of the cycle. In the middle, the tidal stream runs directly through the Strait, but inshore it tends to follow the coastline. Where the boundary between east and west-moving water lies with a west-going tide depends on the relative strengths of the two forces, and in stronger winds may be readily detectable by the sea state. Tidal races may form off Cabo Trafalgar, the Bajo de Los Cabezos west of Tarifa, and Isla de Tarifa itself, typically when east-going current and tidal stream oppose the *levanter*.

Over the course of the passage, particularly in a slower yacht or if beating, it may be possible to extend the duration of favourable tide available by moving from one tidal band into another. For example: leaving Gibraltar at HW+0300 to head west, using the west-going stream inshore until it turns east at HW–0300, then moving offshore to gain a further three hours of west-going stream until HW Gibraltar (though it should be noted that this tactic will take a yacht from the Inshore Traffic Zone into the main west-going shipping channel). *See also overleaf*.

Warning
If enjoying a fine spinnaker run into the Straits from the west be aware that winds in excess of 30kn are said to blow at Tarifa for 300 days of the year.

Battle of Trafalgar

In October 1805 Napoleon's dream of invading Great Britain with the Grande Armée was thwarted after the destruction by Admiral Nelson of the combined Fleets of France and Spain at the Battle of Trafalgar. The battle took place 5·5M west of Barbate off Cabo Trafalgar.

Two hundred years after the battle, British Royal Navy, French Marine Nationale and Spanish Armada Española ships formed a substantial part of an international Fleet that gathered in the Solent off Portsmouth (England) in 2005. This was to commemorate the battle in a spirit of reconciliation, and to honour the heroism and loss of life on all sides in this greatest of sea battles.

CABO TRAFALGAR TO GIBRALTAR

5 HOURS BEFORE HW GIBRALTAR

4 HOURS BEFORE HW GIBRALTAR

3 HOURS BEFORE HW GIBRALTAR

2 HOURS BEFORE HW GIBRALTAR

1 HOUR BEFORE HW GIBRALTAR

HW GIBRALTAR

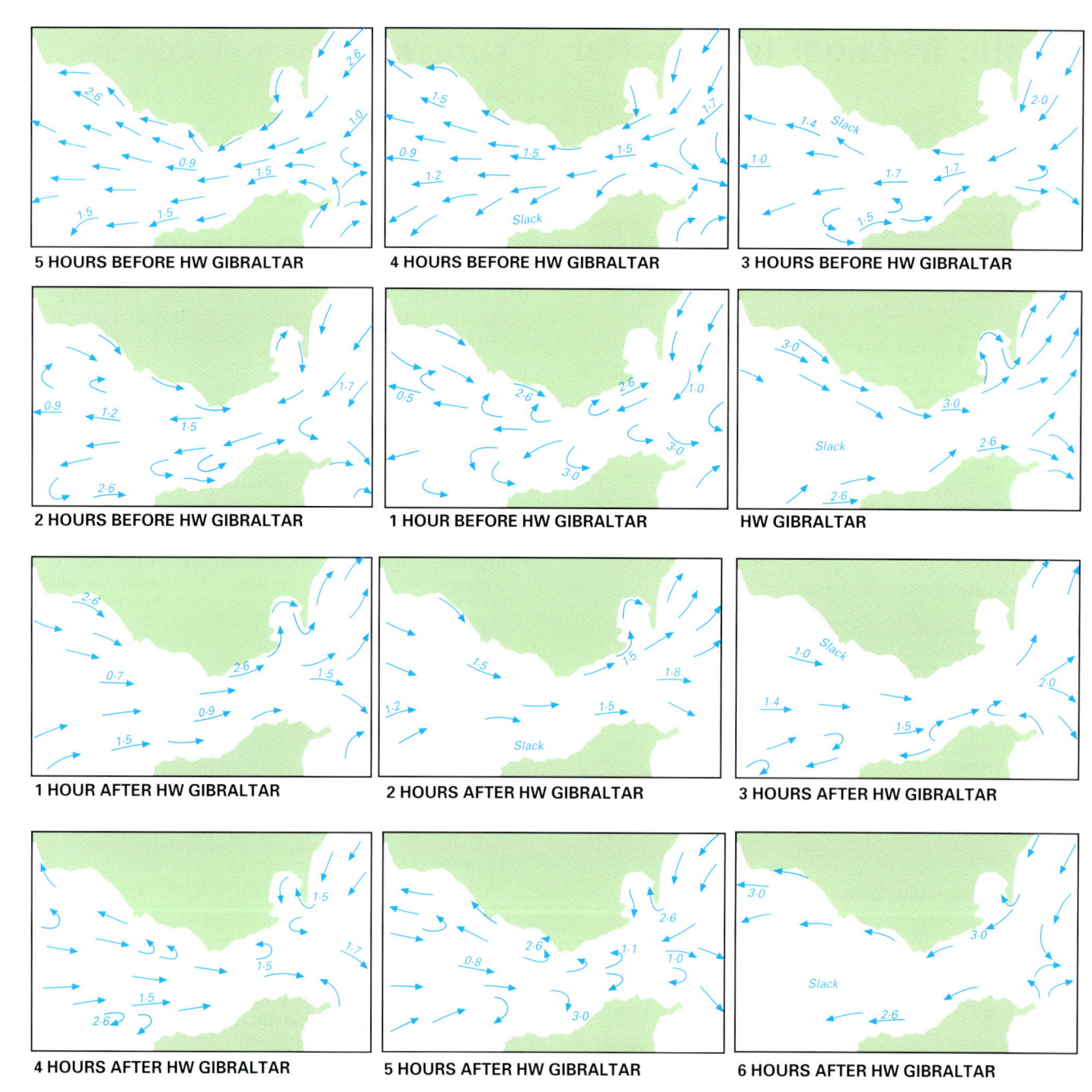

1 HOUR AFTER HW GIBRALTAR

2 HOURS AFTER HW GIBRALTAR

3 HOURS AFTER HW GIBRALTAR

4 HOURS AFTER HW GIBRALTAR

5 HOURS AFTER HW GIBRALTAR

6 HOURS AFTER HW GIBRALTAR

These diagrams are published with the kind permission of Dr M Sloma, editor of *Yacht Scene*. Under no circumstances will *Yacht Scene* or the RCC Pilotage Foundation be liable for any accident or injury which may occur to vessels or persons whilst using the above current predictions.

Strait of Gibraltar

Graham Hutt, author of *North Africa* (Imray), who knows the Strait well, offers the following strategy:

Eastbound vessels

For yachts entering the Strait from the west, there is no real problem going eastwards, unless there is a strong easterly wind, in which case passage will be rough, especially around Tarifa, where winds often reach 40kn. If strong winds are forecast, stay in Barbate (or Tanger) until it drops or anchor in the lee of Tarifa or Cabo de Gracia if strong east winds are encountered once on passage. The best time to depart for the trip east is soon after LW.

Westbound vessels

In strong westerlies it is almost impossible to make progress west, due to the combined east-going current that can, with unfavourable tide, reach 6kn or more – with steep swell and overfalls off Tarifa, Ceuta Point and Punta Malabata.

In good conditions, to make use of the favourable current, set off from Gibraltar two hours after HW. Keeping close inshore, a foul current of around a knot will be experienced off Punta Carnero. A favourable west-going current four hours after HW will assist passage during springs, although this is weak and east-going at neaps. If heading south out of Gibraltar for Tanger, it is usually wise to use the engine to cross from Tarifa making a fast passage to counter the increasing east-going current – or anchor in the shelter of Tarifa and wait for the next favourable tide, around LW, to make the crossing.

322 ATLANTIC SPAIN AND PORTUGAL

BARBATE

Barbate

Location
36°10'·56N 5°55'·8W (entrance)

Tides
Standard port Cádiz
Mean time differences
HW +0005 ±0000; LW +0015 ±0000
Heights in metres
MHWS	MHWN	MLWN	MLWS
1·9	1·5	1·0	0·6

Principal lights
Barbate Fl(2)WR.7s23m10/7M 281°-W-015°-R-095° White round tower, dark red bands 18m
Outer south breakwater Fl.R.4s12m5M Red truncated conical tower 2m
Inner breakwater head Fl.G.3s8m2M Green truncated conical tower 2m
Inner breakwater W elbow Fl(3)G.15s1M Green post 3m
Wave barrier SE end Fl(2+1)R.21s2M Red post, green bands
Wave barier 7 Fl(4)Y.20s
Marina, south mole Fl.R.2M Red column 3m
Marina, north mole Fl(2)G.2M Green post 3m

Notes
Night entry straightforward in normal conditions, taking care to avoid both the tunny nets detailed below and the low-lying anti-swell barrier inside the harbour itself (see plan)

Communications
Puerto Deportivo Barbate VHF Ch 09
☏ +34 856 108 399 and +34 600 140 312
Email barbated@eppa.es
www.puertosdeandalucia.es

The large harbour at Barbate looking east-northeast. The marina basins are at the lower left of the photograph

ATLANTIC SPAIN AND PORTUGAL

CABO TRAFALGAR TO GIBRALTAR

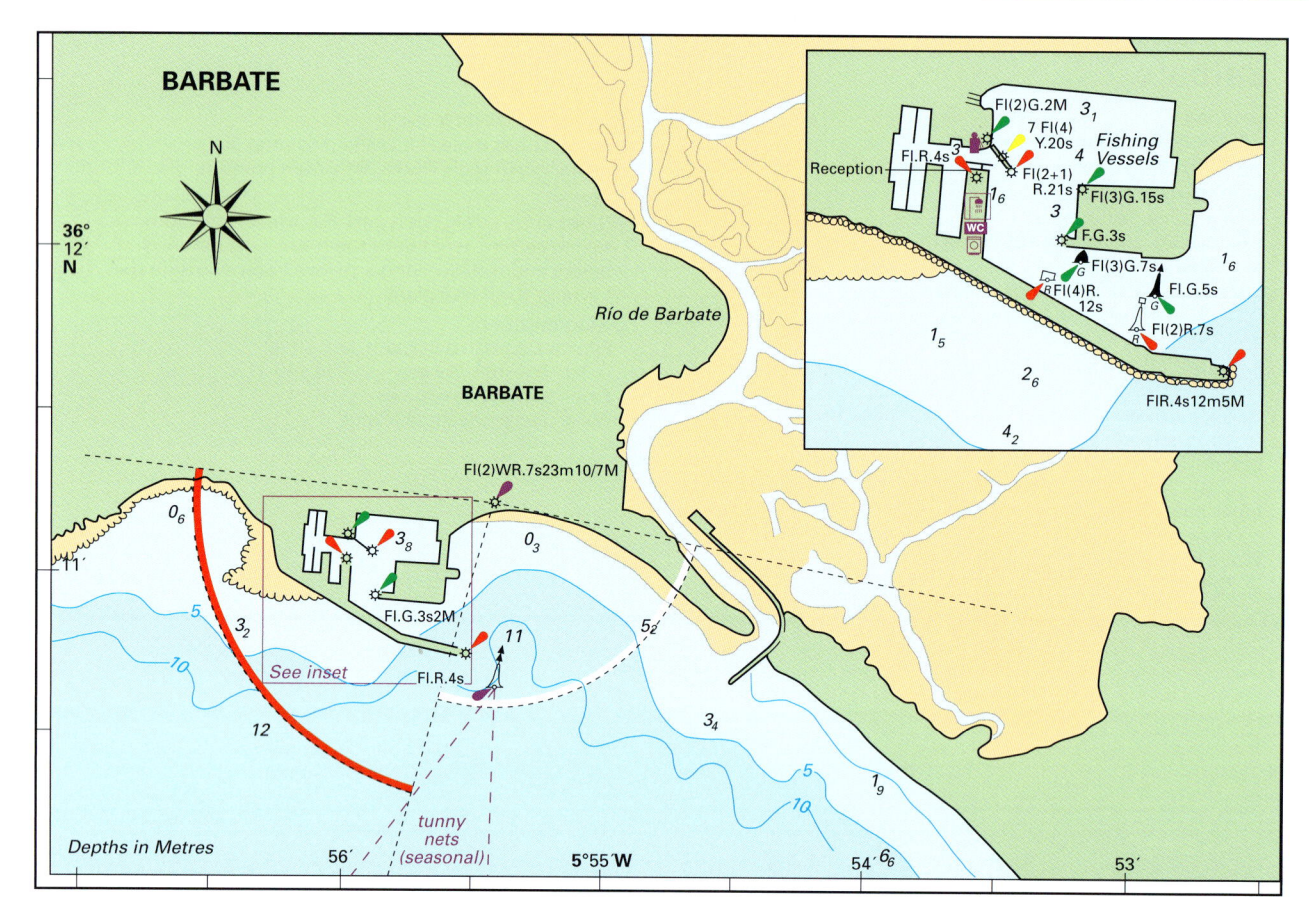

The nearest marina west of the Gibraltar Straits. Very useful when poised to transit the Straits

The old fishing town of Barbate has been swallowed up by new development but has much to offer the visiting yachtsman in terms of recreational facilities. The town is charming and filled with good shops and restaurants offering fresh tuna. The market is excellent and only 0·5km from the marina. The beaches are delightful as is the nature park behind the marina.

The marina itself is rather soulless but is useful as a refuge from the strong winds characteristic of the Straits, and as a stepping-off point when conditions permit. The harbour, in which fishing boats berth to the east and yachts to the west, covers a large area.

The shallow Río de Barbate about 0·4M to the east is used by local boats, but the entrance is difficult and depths within are less than 2·5m.

Approach

If inshore sailing from the west, swing wide around Cabo Trafalgar to clear the dangerous rocky shoal which runs southwest from the Cape to Bajo Aceitera more than 1·5M offshore. Cabo Trafalgar, only about 20m high, appears low-lying compared to the hills 2km to the northeast. In heavy weather the Placer de Meca bank, 3·2M to the west, may break and should also be avoided. A race can form up to 8M offshore in these conditions, particularly when east-going current and tidal stream oppose the *levanter*. An inside passage is used by fishermen, but it should not be attempted without local knowledge.

From the southeast, Punta Camariñal cuts the direct line from Tarifa (off which a race may also form). Note also the dangerous Bajo de Los Cabezos shoal, 5M west of Tarifa and 2M south of Punta Paloma, on which waves break even in calm weather. Between Punta Camariñal and Barbate the coast is relatively steep-to. In either case take care to avoid the two tunny nets laid in the area each year – see below.

Caution

Three *almadrabas* or tunny (tuna) nets are laid annually in the vicinity of Barbate.

The Ensenada de Barbate net is laid from March to September each year very close to the harbour entrance – it is stated that vessels should not pass between the inner end of the net and the shore, but local fishermen habitually do so. It remains in roughly the same position each year and is marked by four lit cardinal buoys:

North Cardinal buoy 36°10'·75N 5°55'·4W
(about 200m SE of the south breakwater head)
Q.3M
West Cardinal buoy 36°09'·18N 5°56'·00W
V.Q(9)10s3M
South Cardinal buoys
36°08'·85N 5°57'·09W (March to June)
36°08'·08N 5°55'·08W (June to September)
V.Q(6)(1)+LFl.12s3M
East Cardinal buoy 36°09'·90N 5°55'·39W
Q(3)10s3M

324 ATLANTIC SPAIN AND PORTUGAL

BARBATE

Cabo Trafalgar on the western approach to Barbate

Between September and February the Ensenada de Barbate net is replaced by a floating fish cage some 270m by 60m, marked by two lit buoys:

West Cardinal buoy 36°09'·18N 5°56'·00W
V.Q(9)10s3M
East Cardinal buoy 36°09'·90N 5°55'·39W
Q(3)10s3M

The Cabo Plato tunny net is laid from March to August each year off the small village of Zahara some 4·5M southeast of Barbate. Again it appears to maintain much the same position, and is marked by three lit cardinal buoys:

West Cardinal buoy 36°07'·53N 5°52'·07W
Q(9)15s3M
West Cardinal buoy 36°06'·38N 5°52'·07W
Q(9)15s3M
South Cardinal buoy 36°06'·33N 5°50'·58W
Q(6)(1)+LFl.15s3M

Finally, and a more recent addition, the Ensenada de Bolonia net is laid about halfway between Barbate and Tarifa off the village of that name (worth visiting for its Roman ruins). It is also marked by three lit cardinal buoys:

West Cardinal buoy 36°04'·15N 5°46'·29W
Q(9)15s3M
South Cardinal buoy 36°03'·73N 5°47'·05W
V.Q(6)+LFl.15s3M
East Cardinal buoy 36°04'·07N 5°45'·76W
Q(3)10s3M

Entrance

The entrance is straightforward although a shoal can build up around the head of the south breakwater which must be given a generous clearance. Two pairs of lateral buoys should then be seen, though the starboard hand inner buoy is seldom on station. A minimum of 2m should be found in the channel at MLWS. The bathymetric chart for the Puerto de Barbate approach and entry shows this clearly. The chart can be found on the APPA website at: www.puertosdeandalucia.es/en/documentation-en/batimetrias, and then selecting *Batimetría Puerto de Barbate*.

Berthing

The marina is reached through a narrow entrance leading almost due west from the main harbour, with a reception pontoon on the port hand under the office building and a fuel facility opposite. A low yellow and black anti-swell barrier runs out from the northern side – see plan. The weakish red light on its end is said to be unreliable so particular care must be taken at night.

The marina consists of two separate and almost completely enclosed basins, one leading out of the other, with pontoons laid around their perimeters and down the centre of the larger, western basin. There is at least 3m depth throughout. There are 314 berths in total, 120 of them able to take yachts of more than 11m and 18 for more than 15m. There is always room for visitors, who are usually berthed near the marina office. Hours are 0800-1430 and 1530-2130 from 1/6-30/9, and 0830-1430 and 1530-1900 from 1/10-31/5.

Facilities

Boatyard, engineers, electronic and radio repairs Talleres Gonzalez-Guerra: Calle del Puerto, 11160 Barbate, Cádiz, Spain ☎+34 956 431 903, *Mobile* +34 666 400 677 www.gonzalezguerra.com Email through the website. General manufacturing and repair in stainless steel and aluminum from premises just outside the boatyard on the north side of the marina. Also marine engine repairs and servicing.

CABO TRAFALGAR TO GIBRALTAR

Reception pontoon Barbate *Henry Buchanan*

Nautica Trafalgar For engines' servicing and some chandlery. Puerto deportivo de Barbate 11160, Barbate (Cádiz). ☎+34 956 434 265 www.nauticatrafalgar.com
Email almacen@nauticatrafalgar.com for workshop services, administración@nauticatrafalgar.com for administration, billings etc. oficinatecnica@nauticatrafalgar.com for technical queries.
Travel-lift 45 tonne and 150 tonne capacity lifts handling both yachts and fishing boats, with a large area of fenced (but windy) hardstanding. Book at the marina office.
Chandlery A good range of general chandlery at Talleres Gonzalez-Guerra, open 0900–1400 and 1530–1830 weekdays, 0900–1330 Saturday. They are happy to order if necessary.
Water/electricity On the pontoons.
Showers In the office building.
Launderette In the office building.

Fuel Available during office hours at the fuelling pontoon on the north side of the entrance.
Bottled gas Camping Gaz available in the town about 2km distant.
Club Náutico Near the fishing harbour.
Weather forecast Posted daily at the marina office.
Bank In the town.
Shops/provisioning Good supermarket on the road behind the harbour, with more shops in the town.
Produce market The market is excellent, and only 0·5km from the marina.
Cafés, restaurants and hotels The town offers hotels and nice restaurants offering fresh tuna, but the financial crisis of 2008 closed the café and restaurant in the harbour, and also the Fairplay Beach and Yacht Club.
Medical services In the town.

Communications
Post office In the town.
Mailing address The marina office will hold mail for visiting yachts – c/o Puerto Deportivo Barbate, Avenida del Mar, s/n 11160 - Barbate (Cádiz), España. It is important that the envelope carries the name of the yacht in addition to that of the addressee.
Internet WiFi at the café/bar in the marina. At least one internet café in the town.
Car hire/taxis Book via the office.
Buses Bus service to Cádiz, Algeciras and La Línea.
Air services International airport at Gibraltar, a short walk across the border from La Línea. Alternatively, Jerez or Seville.

Fuel pontoon and boatyard Barbate looking N
Henry Buchanan

326 ATLANTIC SPAIN AND PORTUGAL

Tarifa

Location
36°00'·24N 5°36'·14W (entrance)

Tides
Standard port Gibraltar
Mean time differences
HW –0040; LW –0040
Heights in metres

MHWS	MHWN	MLWN	MLWS
1·4	1·0	0·6	0·3

Principal lights
Isla de Tarifa Fl(3)WR.10s41m26/18M
  089°-R-113°-W-089° (over Bajo de Los Cabezos)
  Racon Mo 'C'(–·–·)20M AIS White round tower 33m
Isla de Tarifa East side Fl.R.5s12m5M
  Red ■ on red 4-sided tower 2m
East breakwater Fl.G.5s11m5M 249°-vis-045°
  Green ▲ on green metal framework tower
  (Dwarfed by square stone pillar surmounted by
  Breakwater elbow Q(3)10s11m3M
  255°-vis-045° Easterly cardinal column,
  east topmark, 2m
Inner Mole east end Fl(2)R.7s7m1M
Red ■ on corner of white hut 4m

Warning
Night entry not advised, at least until an area in the harbour is designated for visiting yachts.

Navtex
Tarifa Identification letters 'G' and 'T'
Transmits 518kHz in English; 490 in Spanish
Weather bulletins for Cabo de São Vicente to Gibraltar and the Western Mediterranean within 450 miles of the coast: English – 0900, 2100; Spanish – 0710, 1910
Navigational warnings for the Rio Guadiana to Gibraltar: English – 0100, 0500, 1300, 1700; Spanish – 0310, 0710, 1110, 1510, 1910, 2310

Coast radio station
Tarifa (remotely controlled from Málaga)
Digital Selective Calling MMSI 002240994
MF Transmits/receives: 2182kHz
VHF Ch 10, 16, 67, 74
Weather bulletins and navigational warnings
Weather bulletins and visibility (fog) warnings in Spanish and English for Bahía de Cádiz, Strait of Gibraltar and Alborán: VHF Ch 10, 67 at 0015, 0215, 0415, 0615, 0815, 1015, 1215, 1415, 1615, 1815, 2015, 2215 UT
Navigational warnings in Spanish and English for the Strait of Gibraltar: VHF Ch 10, 67 on receipt

Commercial and fishing harbour with little provision for yachts

Tarifa is the most southerly city of mainland Europe and, at barely 8M distant, considerably closer to North Africa than is Gibraltar. It is famous for its frequent strong winds, which together with excellent beaches have made it the boardsailing capital of Europe.

It is reputedly where the Moors landed on their European invasion, and the older part of the town still shows a strong North African influence, particularly in the well preserved streets around the harbour. It has an active tourist industry and consequently is well provided with shops, restaurants and hotels. Unfortunately the Isla de Tarifa is a military area and closed to the public, as is the handsome old Castillo de Santa Catalina to the northwest, but the road between Tarifa and Algeciras is worth traversing if possible for its dramatic views of both Gibraltar and the Strait.

Looking north over Isla de Tarifa, with the busy fishing and ferry harbour on the right

CABO TRAFALGAR TO GIBRALTAR

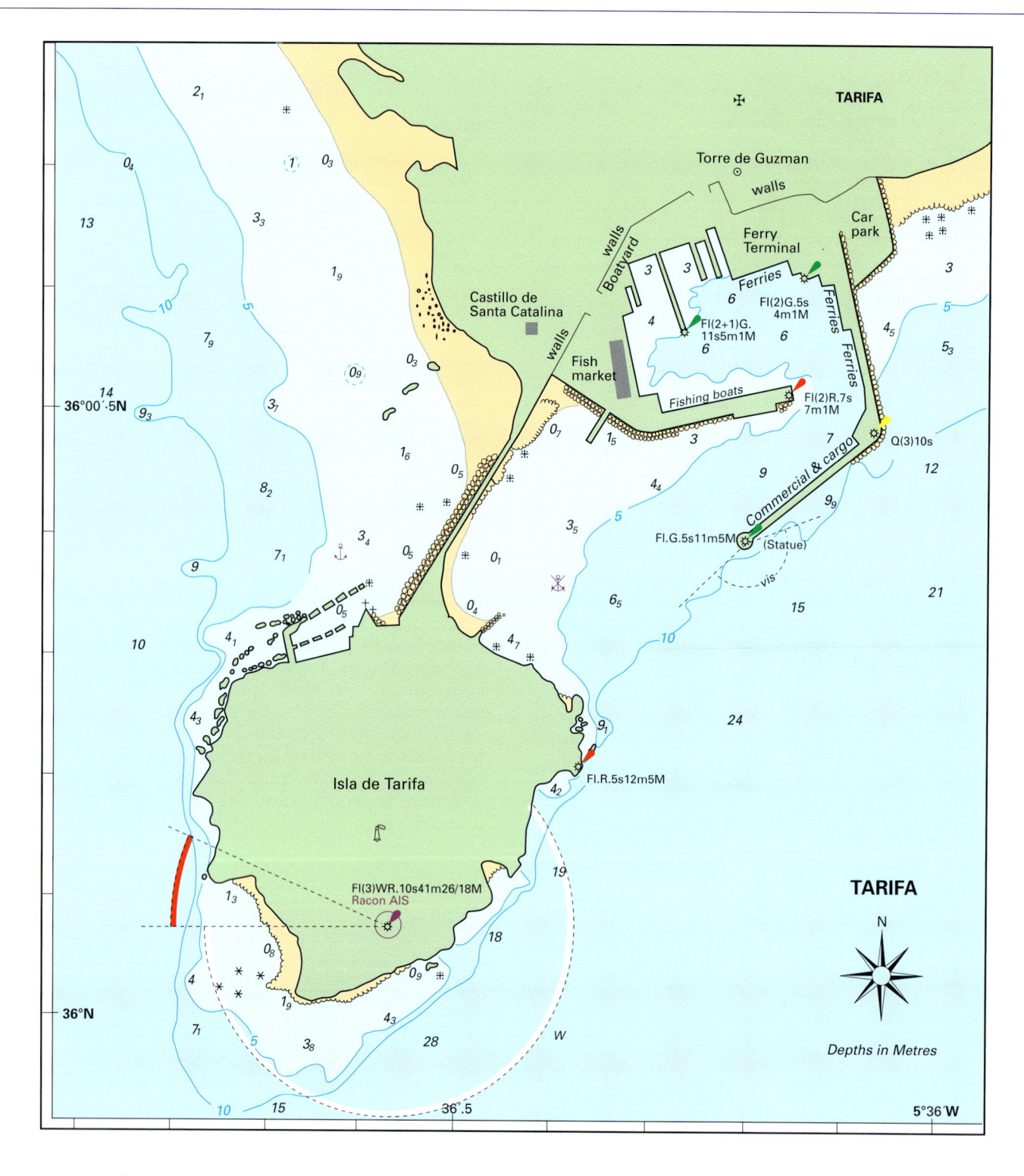

Approach

If coastal sailing from the west, Tarifa light stands high on its promontory clear of the land. Chief danger is the Bajo de los Cabezos, 5M west of Tarifa and 3M south of Punta Paloma. The bank is marked by broken water even in calm weather, and several wrecks are reputed to lie close to the surface. From the east, there are dangers up to 1M offshore between Punta Carnero and Punta de Cala Arenas, but once west of the latter the shore is generally steep to. There is a prominent wind farm on the hills northeast of the town.

A race may form off Isla de Tarifa when east-going current and tidal stream oppose the *levanter*.

TARIFA

Considerably nearer to North Africa than Algeciras or Gibraltar, Tarifa is primarily a commercial harbour with, as yet, no provision for yachts

Caution

An *almadraba* or tunny (tuna) net known as *Lances de Tarifa* is laid between March and July each year northwest of Isla de Tarifa. It remains in much the same position each year, and is marked by three lit cardinal buoys:

Northwest – West Cardinal buoy 36°01'·15N 5°38'·26W
  Q(9)15s3M
Southwest – West Cardinal buoy 36°00'·90N 5°38'·11W
  Q(9)5s3M
South Cardinal buoy 36°00'·70N 5°37'·61W
  Q(6)+LFl.15s3M

Entrance

The harbour entrance faces southwest towards the Isla de Tarifa and its connecting causeway. Head for the conspicuous statue at the end of the east breakwater, before making the dogleg into the harbour.

Note In a *levanter* this approach becomes a lee shore and it may be wiser to use the second of the anchorages mentioned below – or to press on for Barbate or beyond.

Berthing

Tarifa is far from yacht-orientated and there is no designated spot where visiting yachts may berth, though the best bet would almost certainly be amongst the local craft which lie bow or stern-to the concrete moles to the northwest. Some command of Spanish would be a major advantage.

The east wall is no longer viable, being entirely taken up with ferries and small cargo vessels. Constant comings and goings by the fishing fleet make for almost continuous movement.

Formalities

The *Policía* and *Inmigración* both have offices in the ferry terminal (*Estación Maritima*) at the root of the east breakwater and should be visited if arriving from outside Spain. Foreign yachts are also a sufficient rarity that the Capitania is likely to visit. A charge is levied for an overnight visit despite the almost total lack of facilities.

Facilities

Virtually nothing, other than a few water taps. There is no yacht fuel and no possibility of getting electricity aboard. The small boatyard (with marine railway) in the northwest corner of the harbour is geared to fishing boats but could doubtless carry out minor yacht repairs if necessary.

A café/bar will be found on the southwest arm, otherwise the town has shops of all kinds, a produce market, banks, restaurants and hotels.

Communications

Post office in the old part of town, with telephones around the harbour etc. Several internet cafés, one (slightly northwest of the harbour) combining operations with a launderette! Taxis in surprising numbers. Buses to Cádiz, Algeciras and La Línea, from which it is a short walk to the international airport at Gibraltar.

Adjacent anchorages

A *Parque Natural* has been established along the coast between Punta de Gracia in the west and Punta Carnero in the east, extending more than 1M offshore. However although some fishing and diving activities are prohibited there appears to be no ban on anchoring in the area.

There is now only one anchorage allowed at Tarifa which is just north of a derelict mole on the northwest side of Isla de Tarifa, with shelter from easterly seas (though not the wind) given by the causeway. Good holding over sand in 3–4m. Anchoring northeast of the Isla de Tarifa is no longer permitted, and a harbour launch may impose this restriction. This is because the fast catamarans to Tangier manoeuvre in this area.

Isla de Tarifa. Beware the high-speed ferries
Henry Buchanan

ATLANTIC SPAIN AND PORTUGAL

CABO TRAFALGAR TO GIBRALTAR

Algeciras

Location
36°06'·95N 5°25'·43W (entrance)

Tides
Standard port Gibraltar
Mean time differences
HW –0010; LW –0010
Heights in metres

MHWS	MHWN	MLWN	MLWS
1·1	0·9	0·4	0·2

Principal lights
Commercial Harbour
NE breakwater Fl.R.5s11m7M
 Red round tower 6m
Dársena del Saladillo (yacht basin)
Light buoy Fl(3)R.9s3M

Warning
Night entry not advised, since all three marinas in the Dársena del Saladillo are private and anchoring is forbidden.

Harbour communications
Port Authority
VHF Ch 08, 13, 16, 68, 74 (call *Algeciras Tráfico*)
☎ +34 956 585400
Email apba@apba.es www.apba.es
Club Náutico Deportivo el Saladillo ☎ +34 856 020 041
info@cdnauticosaladillo.es www.cdnauticosaladillo.es
Coast radio station
Algeciras *Digital Selective Calling*
MMSI 002241001 VHF Ch 16, 74
Weather bulletins and navigational warnings
Weather bulletins in Spanish and English: VHF Ch 74 at 0315, 0515, 0715, 1115, 1515, 1915, 2315 UT
Navigational warnings in Spanish and English: on request

Major commercial harbour, with three private marinas in a separate basin

Algeciras is primarily an industrial and ferry port, through which passes many of the guest-workers returning to Africa with roof racks bending under their loads.

Yachts have their own basin – the Dársena del Saladillo – south of the main harbour, where three separate clubs run three separate marinas. Sadly none welcome visiting yachts (See *Berthing*). The following approach and entrance instructions are given for the Dársena del Saladillo in the hope that this situation may one day change.

Approach

The approaches to Algeciras are extremely busy with commercial traffic of all sizes. In particular, a sharp watch needs to be kept for the many high-speed ferries, including hydrofoils, which run between Algeciras and Morocco. These are notorious for maintaining their course and speed at all times, presumably adhering to the 'might is right' principle.

Coming from the west, there are dangers up to 1M offshore between Punta de Cala Arenas and Punta Carnero. On rounding this headland the city and harbour will be seen some 3M to the north behind a mile-long breakwater terminating with a light. Various ledges run out from the headlands between Punta Carnero and the entrance to the Dársena del Saladillo (also lit).

If approaching from Gibraltar or other points east, the entrance to the Dársena del Saladillo should be easily seen south of the oil tanks on the commercial quay and it can be approached directly.

Note that a N – S breakwater has been constructed off Algeciras in recent years with its southern extremity at: 36°07'·00N 5°25'·05W (see plan page 331).

Entrance

The dogleg entrance to the Dársena del Saladillo has been very well designed, such that when visited in a 30 knot easterly wind no swell at all was entering. As noted above, three buoys mark the final approach, after which the entrance itself is straightforward.

Berthing

As stated above none of the three marinas in the Dársena del Saladillo accept visitors. Taken clockwise on entry these are the Real Club Náutico de Algeciras, which previously had premises in the main harbour, the Club Náutico Saladillo and the Club Deportivo El Pargo. The first (southern) marina is also the largest by a considerable margin, and would undoubtedly be the best one to try in an emergency. It is also the club where some English is most likely to be spoken, and visitors are also welcome to dine in the Real Club Náutico's restaurant.

Facilities

The Real Club Náutico marina is provided with all the usual facilities, including a fuel berth on the end of the breakwater which forms its eastern limit.

The west side of the basin is home to Astilleros y Varaderos 'El Rodeo', ☎ +34 956 600511, a shipyard primarily engaged with work on steel fishing vessels and other commercial craft, although a steel yacht ashore has been seen there. Almost opposite, across the busy harbourside road, will be found Náutica Iberia, where a limited range of chandlery is on sale in addition to smallcraft and jet-skis. Spanish charts may be obtained either from SUISCA SL ☎ +34 902 220007, *Email* admiraltycharts@suiscasl.com or in the Centro Blas Infante; or from Valnáutica SL ☎ +34 956 570677 at Avenida 28 de Febrero 33.

All the usual shops, banks, restaurants and hotels are to be found in the city, but at some distance, together with a post office, telephones, car hire and taxis. Trains run to many destinations including Madrid, and buses to La Línea, from which it is a short walk to the international airport at Gibraltar.

ALGECIRAS

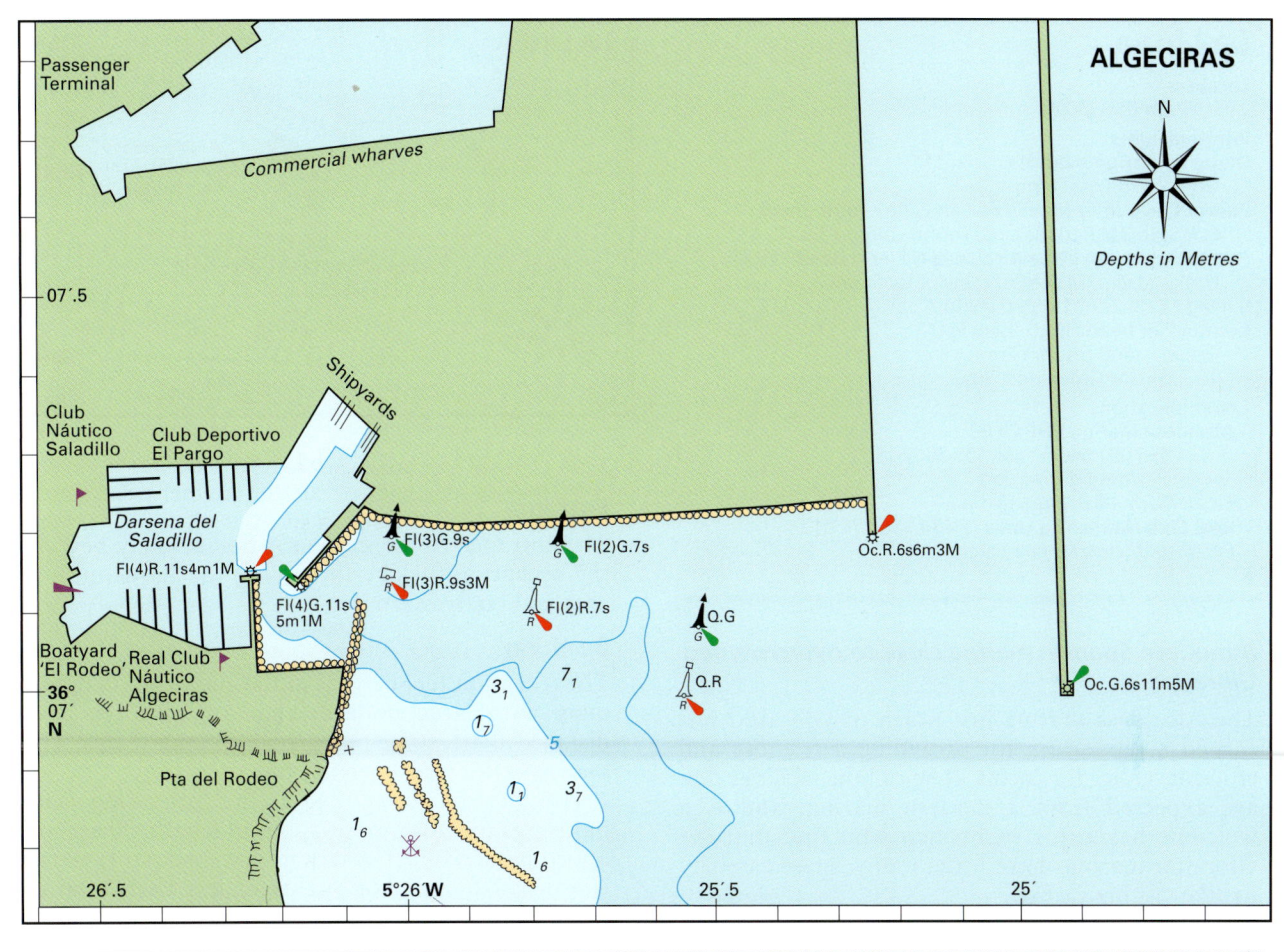

The Dársena del Saladillo at Algeciras, seen from east-southeast. Although the Real Club Náutico de Algeciras, the Club Náutico Saladillo and the Club Deportivo El Pargo all have pontoons in the harbour, none currently accept visitors

ATLANTIC SPAIN AND PORTUGAL

CABO TRAFALGAR TO GIBRALTAR

La Línea

Location
36°09'·5N 05°22'·2W

Principal lights
Dique de Abrigo head Fl.G.5s8m5M
  Green ▲ on green post 3m
Puerto Chico Jetty Muelle de San Felipe south head
  Fl.R.5s5m3M Red ■ on red round column 3m
Puerto Deportivo de La Alcaidesa N Pier N head
  Fl(4)G.11s5m1M Green round column 3m
S head Fl(2)R.7s5m1M Red column 3m
Central Pier head Fl(3)G.9s5m1M
  Green round column 2m
Fl(2)G.7s5m3M Green post 3m

Communications
Alcaidesa Marina VHF Ch 09
 ☏ +34 956 021 660 or +34 639 365 613
 www.alcaidesamarina.com
 Email marina@alcaidesa.com
Real Club Nautico La Línea ☏ +34 956 171 017
 Email contacto@rcnlalinea.es

A modern Spanish marina close to overcrowded Gibraltar

The Alcaidesa marina just north of Gibraltar has earned a reputation for providing a friendly and efficient service for yachts. It has all the facilities that are expected from a modern marina, and is a welcome haven for yachtsmen who find that the Gibraltar marinas have little, if any, spare capacity to take visiting yachts.

Approach

The approach through Gibraltar Bay is straightforward, although many anchored ships will be encountered to the west of the rock. Round the end of the Dique de Abrigo and head for the reception/fuel berth at the end of the concrete quay running northwest/southeast.

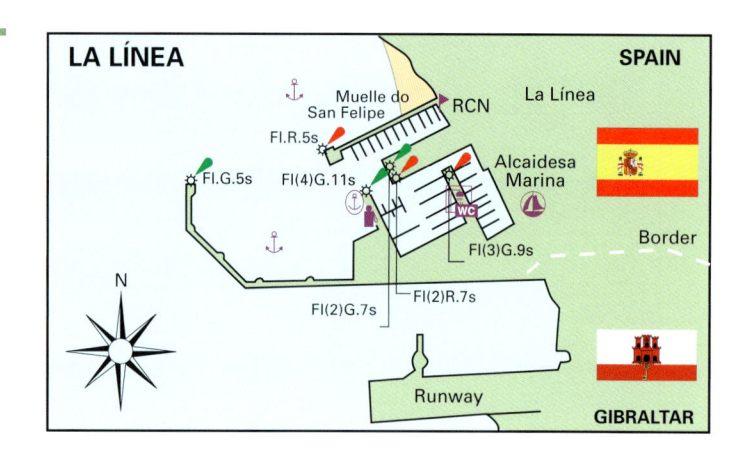

Entrance

The entrance to the marina is immediately beyond the reception/fuel berth leaving the hardstanding area and boatyard to port.

Berthing

The reception/fuel berth is at the end of the concrete quay with large bollards that are rather a long distance apart, so be prepared with long warps. The marina office is just behind this.

The marina has 624 berths providing safe moorings for boats of 8–100m in length. There are approximately 170 spaces in dry stack storage for lengths of 6–8m. For yachts of less than 30m in length, the jetties are floating with finger pontoons. For larger yachts the jetties are fixed concrete jetties with vehicular access.

It is a long walk from the furthest pontoons to the marina office but a golf cart service is available.

Office hours are 0900-1900. Annual berthing for catamarans is at monohull rates.

Alcaidesa Marina (La Linea) and the Rock of Gibraltar. Africa in the distance *Alcaidesa Marina*

ATLANTIC SPAIN AND PORTUGAL

LA LÍNEA

Anchoring east of the Dique de Abrigo
The anchorage immediately outside the marina entrance, sheltered by the Dique de Abrigo, is not controlled by the marina. Many of the yachts using this anchorage use the RCN La Línea and dinghy ashore. The yacht club make a small charge per day for their facilities including showers, WiFi, etc. as well as safe dinghy dockage. The understanding is that the anchorage area is under local authority/port authority control. It's possible that at some point the authorities will decide that they don't want yachts to anchor, but so far there seems to have been no problem in this area.

Facilities
Showers and WC These are in the northeast corner of the marina.

Laundry A coin operated laundry service (washing machine and tumble drier) is located in the same building as the showers and WC.

Water and Electricity Supplied to all berths.

Boatyard The boatyard has a 75-tonne boat hoist and storage areas. There is a hard standing of 17,000m² for the repair of every kind of vessel. ☎ +34 956 021660 *Email* tovaradero@alcaidesa.com. A full workshop facility is operated by Elias Blanco S.L. (Volvo agent) ☎ +34 956 90 90 49.

Dry Dock Storage For boats from 6–8m on a rental basis for winter usage.

Chandlers In town or in Gibraltar.

Parking Facilities More than 1,000 parking bays are provided, both in the area reserved for marina clients, for whom access is available through a security checkpoint, and in the recreational and leisure areas.

Security Closed circuit television system and security surveillance and control. Access to the jetties is through automatic gates.

Fuel There is fuel at the reception berth and Calor gas is available.

RCN La Línea The RCN yacht club is near the root of the Muelle do San Felipe (Puerto Chico jetty) at the north side of the marina area. This has 11 pontoons but it is strictly private with no space for visitors. The restaurant is open for visiting yachtsmen.

Shops/Provisioning There is good shopping, including a large supermarket and an excellent produce market in La Línea. Gibraltar is well within walking distance but passports are necessary to cross the border.

A misty Gibraltar from Alcaidesa Marina *Henry Buchanan*

Cafés, restaurants and hotels The original concept of bars, shops and restaurants has not yet been realised in the wake of the 2008 financial crisis. However, the marina has opened a cafeteria/snack bar, the 'Alcaidesa Lounge'. The cafeteria is situated near the entrance to the marina adjoining Pontoon 9 where Sergio the landlord offers his specialty tapas.

Communications
WiFi Since November 2016 WiFi has been free to all boat owners who have a berthing contract with the Alcaidesa Marina. Otherwise access can be expensive.

Post office In La Linea.

Mailing address Alcaidesa Marina, Marina office, Avda. Príncipe de Asturias s/n, 11.300 La Línea, Cádiz, Spain.

Transport Gibraltar airport is a short distance away across the border. Bicycle hire is available in the marina. There are buses into Gibraltar from the Gibraltar side of the border. There are taxi offices close by in La Línea.

La Línea tourist train During the summer months the train includes the Alcaidesa Marina on its route. It makes stops outside the Alcaidesa Lounge Bar for those who wish to make use of the service provided.

Looking north to La Linea from the Rock, Gibraltar *Henry Buchanan*

CABO TRAFALGAR TO GIBRALTAR

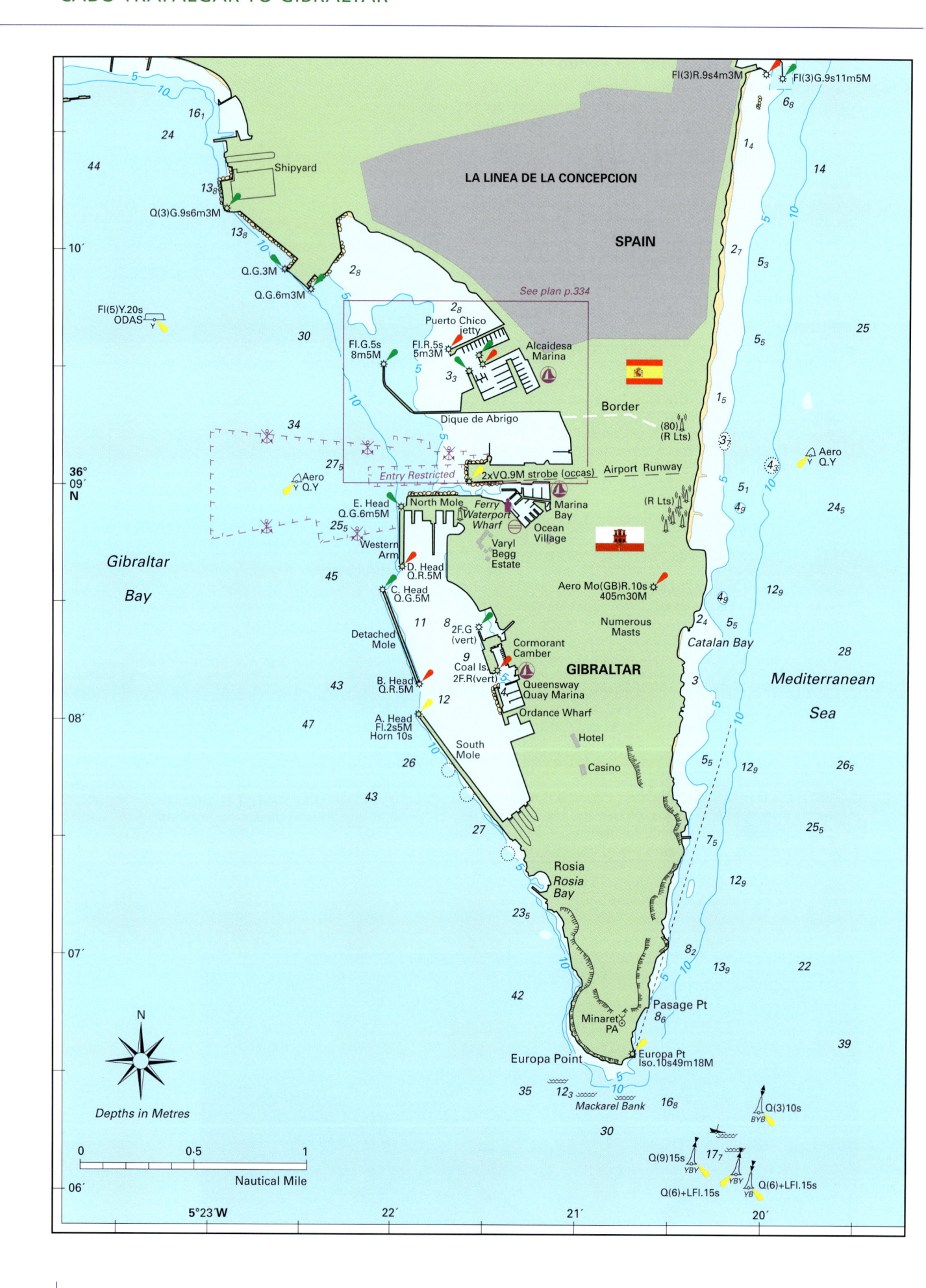

334 ATLANTIC SPAIN AND PORTUGAL

GIBRALTAR

Gibraltar

Location
36°08′N 5°22′·3W (South Gap, for Queensway Quay)
36°08′·98N 5°22′·35W (North mole, for Marina Bay)

Tides
Gibraltar is a standard port.
Heights in metres
MHWS	MHWN	MLWN	MLWS
1·0	0·7	0·3	0·1

Principal Lights
Approach
Punta Carnero Fl(4)WR.20s42m16/13M
   018°-W-325°-R-018°
   (Red sector covers La Perla and Las Bajas shoals)
   Round masonry tower and white building 19m
Gibraltar Aeromarine 36°08′·6N 05°20′·6W
   Mo(GB)R.I0s405m30M
   Obscured on westerly bearings within 2M
Great Europa Point, Gibraltar Iso.10s49m19M
   197°-W-125° White tower, red band 19m
Harbour
South mole, north end (A head) Fl.W.2s10m5M Horn 10s
   White column 7m
Detached mole, south end (B head) Q.R.9m5M Metal structure on concrete building 11m
Detached mole, north end (C head) Q.G.10m5M Metal structure on concrete building 11m
North mole, western arm (D head) Q.R.18m5M Black 8-sided metal framework tower 17m
North breakwater, northwest elbow (E head) Q.G.6m5M
   Tower Plus other lights in the interior of the harbour and to the north

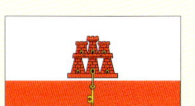

Communications
Radio
Gibraltar Port Control VHF Ch 16, 6, 12, 13, 14 (24 hours)
Lloyds radio VHF Ch 8, 12, 14, 16 (24 hours)
Queens Harbourmaster VHF Ch 8 (0800–1600 Monday to Friday) All marinas VHF Ch 71 (0830–2030, later in summer)
Telephone and email
Port Captain ☎ +350 200772 54
Port Operations Room ☎ +350 20078134/ 20077004
Queensway Quay ☎ +350 20044700,
   Email qqmarina@gibnet.gi
Marina Bay Office ☎ +350 20073300,
   Email pieroffice@marinabay.gi www.marinabay.gi
Sheppards Marina Repair facilities
   ☎ +350 200768 95, Chandlery ☎ +350 200771 83
Ocean Village ☎ +350 200400 48
   Email info@oceanvillage.gi www.oceanvillage.gi

View south over La Linea and Gibraltar *Alcaidesa Marina*

CABO TRAFALGAR TO GIBRALTAR

The 'gateway to the Mediterranean', with excellent facilities for yachts but very crowded

Gibraltar is a safe and convenient stopping point for yachts entering or leaving the Mediterranean, as well as being a duty-free port. All facilities are available for repairs and general maintenance, and both general and ship's stores of every kind can be obtained in Gibraltar or by air from England (for some items it may be cheaper, if more effort, to arrange for delivery from England marked 'For Yacht – in Transit' and therefore duty free, rather than to buy off the shelf once there). Both the pound sterling and the Gibraltar pound (at parity) are legal tender.

There are three marinas on the eastern side of the Bay of Gibraltar (known as the Bay of Algeciras to the Spanish). The existing Queensway Quay Marina, the new Ocean Village Marina that is to combine with the existing Marina Bay Marina, and a third marina in La Línea, Spain, across the border to the north (page 332). There has been something of a hiatus as new marina construction has taken place and the 7-deck cruise liner *Sunborn* sunk in position between Ocean Village Marina and Marina Bay. This has exacerbated the cronic shortage of available yacht berths in Gibraltar making it essential to book ahead.

A tour of the Rock itself is recommended, as is a visit to the museum, with displays of Gibraltar in prehistoric, Phoenician and Roman times. The WWII tunnels are testament to the most extraordinary feats of mining and engineering. Crossing the border into Spain is quick and easy on foot, though a passport should be carried. Making the crossing by car is another matter entirely. It is normal to queue in either direction, but while the wait to come in seldom exceeds 10 minutes it is not unusual to queue for an hour or more to leave – considerably longer during the rush hour. A phonecall ☎ 42777 will give the current outward waiting time. If telephoning from Spain, or by mobile phone in either country, include the Spanish access code ☎ 9567.

Approach

By day Gibraltar Rock, rising to 406m, is clearly visible except in fog, which is rare, though more frequent in summer, It is safe to enter the Bay of Gibraltar (Algeciras Bay) in almost any conditions but beware of squalls near the Rock once in the bay, particularly during strong easterlies, when strong downdraughts occur off the Rock. From the south and east, Europa point is prominent, with its lighthouse at the end. A short distance further up the point, the minaret of a new mosque will be observed. Strong currents and overfalls occur around the tip of the point when wind is against tide. From the west, Punta Carnero light lies at the southwest entrance to the bay, near an old whaling station. The coast is fringed with wrecks from all eras, many popular as dive sites – any vessel flying International Code Flag 'A' (white with a blue swallowtail) should be given a generous clearance. Yachts must also give way to naval and commercial vessels at all times.

By night The west side of the Rock is well illuminated by the town; and to the east by the bright red lights marking the radio antennas on the north face; which is itself illuminated by spotlights. This can be confusing even in good visibility and makes lights difficult to identify. The most conspicuous are likely to be those on the south mole's A head and north mole's D head. To the south is the lighthouse on Europa Point, easily seen from north-northeast clockwise to north-northwest, with a small red sector indicating the dangerous rocky shoreline to the west between Punta del Acebuche and Punta Carnero, which must be given a wide berth. If approaching in poor visibility beware the amount of traffic in the vicinity.

Gibraltar weather forecasts

Radio Gibraltar (GBC) and British Forces Radio (BFBS) broadcast local weather forecasts (see table below). The marinas post weather faxes on their notice boards daily. See also www.bbc.co.uk/weather/coast/pressure/ and http://meteonet.nl/aktueel/brackall.htm for five day forecasts. Sites www.sto-p.com/atol and www.accuweather.com give complete hour-by-hour predictions over 16 hours and general forecasts up to 15 days.

Tarifa Radio broadcasts area weather on Channel 16 at regular intervals, in Spanish and English.

Gibraltar weather forecasts

LT	BFBS 1 Mon-Fri	Sat	Sun	BFBS2 Mon-Fri	Gibraltar BC Mon-Fri	Sat	Sun
0530					X	X	
0630					X	X	X
0730					X	X	X
0745	X						
0845	X	X	X				
0945		X	X				
1005	X						
1030					X		
1200				X			
1202		X	X				
1230					X	X	X
1602			X				
1605	X						

Also storm warnings on receipt
93·5 FM 89·4 FM   1438 AM
97·8 FM 99·5 FM   91·3 FM
                   92·6 FM
Includes high and low water times   100·5 FM

Entry formalities

Whereas in the past all yachts calling at Gibraltar first proceeded to the customs and immigration offices opposite Marina Bay, this no longer applies. Proceed to any marina where paper formalities are part of the check-in process carried out by marina staff.

Gibraltar, like the UK, is not party to the Shengen agreement, which has different visa requirements to Spain. Check for latest information from the Gibraltar government website www.gibraltar.gov.gi or contact the immigration department ☎ +350 20046411 *Email* rgpimm@gibynex.gi.

GIBRALTAR

Queensway Quay (centre) with Coaling Island (right) and the military base (left) *Graham Hutt*

Crew intending to remain ashore, or obtain work in Gibraltar should inform Immigration Authorities of their intention and supply an address.

Anchoring in the Bay
Anchorage is possible (although not encouraged) north of the runway in 4–6m sand, with good holding. As this area is British territory it is first necessary to clear Customs and Immigration, which may create a problem now that these are handled only by the Gibraltar marinas.

Otherwise, there continues to be considerable uncertainty as to what is allowed and what is not allowed concerning anchoring in the Bay. Sometimes the Spanish Guardia come around and clear out the yachts, telling them to go into the Alcaidesa marina. At other times they leave them alone. Most of the time, they are just taking notes of who is there for future reference. As these yachts are clearly in Spanish waters, there is a theoretical tax liability after six months if the owners are living aboard. This is of course in addition to VAT if unpaid. Most yachtsmen think that because they are not tied up in a marina, they are considered as being at sea. Not so according to the tax authorities!

For safety reasons yachts are prohibited from anchoring close to the runway or on the flight path anywhere west of the runway.

Queensway Quay Marina

Location
36°08'·1N 05°21'·3W

The Marina
This is the closest marina to Europa Point, but was reconstructed during 2005/2006 due to initial design faults which allowed unacceptable surging, with resulting damage to yachts. The Queensway Quay Development includes luxury apartments, a restaurant and many business enterprises around the marina. Queensway Quay Marina has the advantage of being some distance from the airport, with all the noise, and is close to the largest supermarket, Morrisons, and Main Street, which is also within walking distance. It provides 150 berths. Some of which will have been allocated to the owners of the houses built on the new 'island' that forms the western breakwater of the marina.

Entry formalities
Both marina and entry formalities are now completed at the marina office.

Approach
The marina is approached through the main harbour via either of the two entrances, continuing towards the gap between Coaling Island and the new 'island' which forms the western breakwater of the marina. On passing through this gap the entrance lies immediately to starboard. The buildings overlooking the marina are floodlit.

Berthing
Visitors' berths are few and it's best to call ahead on VHF Ch 71 to ask if one is available. Mooring is stern, or bows-to, on floating pontoons. A limited

ATLANTIC SPAIN AND PORTUGAL   *337*

THE ALGARVE & ANDALUCIA

number of deepwater berths varying from 3–7m in depth at LWS, with power points and metered water, are available along the southern wall of the marina. Berth at the reception pontoon on the east side of the new entrance on first arrival. The marina office is to be relocated to overlook the area but in the meantime is situated near the root of the north mole. Hours are 0830–2200 daily in summer. 0830–2100 in winter. During the renovations the marina was dredged to 4m throughout.

Facilities

Berth Services Every berth has access to a Service Module, with electricity, water, intercom and telephone.
Security Access to the floating pontoons is by coded lockable gates and security is excellent.
Car park By the Marina Control Centre (MCC).
Office facilities Available in the MCC include fax and photocopying, book swap and restaurant.
Repairs Only available at Sheppard's ☏ +350 20076895.
Showers and WC Situated in the MCC. Facilities available for the disabled. Bath available for a charge. These amenities close 30 minutes earlier than the rest of the establishment.
Toilets For after-hours use can be found along the Main Quayside to the rear of the large anchor. Lock code available from Reception.
Laundry Incorporating a dry cleaners in the MCC. Others in the town.
Weather Daily reports are posted in the office. A weather station is on view at the MCC.
Transport Local buses from the bus station. No.3 bus to the frontier from Line Wall Road.

Ocean Village Marina

This marina complex is on the site of Sheppard's old piers, just south of Marina Bay Marina with which it is going to combine. With a depth of 4·5m and over 200 berths, Ocean Village Marina can accommodate most vessels including super yachts. Each berth has new facility points for water, power, telephone, fax and satellite TV. New shower and toilet facilities, including those for the disabled, are available at the pier office building. Ocean Village is a vibrant new waterfront area with a variety of international stores and a range of restaurants and bars to suit all tastes. The Leisure Island complex will feature a casino, nightclub, champagne bar and much more. An artist's impression of the development can be seen at www.oceanvillage.gi

Ship Hotel *Sunborn*

A huge 7-deck cruise liner, the *Sunborn*, which is a luxury hotel, has been moved into the 'slot' between the Ocean Village Marina and Marina Bay. The ship is a permanent fixture, being sunk in position alongside the casino. It has meant the removal of many yacht pontoons, greatly reducing the capacity for yachts in a country where there are no spare visitors' berths available in the summer months. Fortunately for the yachting community, the Alcaidesa Marina (see above) less than a mile away has plenty of room and is an attractive and cheaper alternative to Gibraltar.

Looking west over Marina Bay with the permanently moored *Sunborn* on the left and airport runway to the right *Motorboat and Yachting/Ocean Village*

GIBRALTAR

Looking eastwards, the entrance to Marina Bay is just S (to the right) of the airport runway. Note the restricted navigation zone off the end of the runway (shown on plan p.334)

The Rock from Marina Bay *Jane Russell*

Marina Bay
Location
36°08'·9N 05°21'·4W

The Marina
Just south of the runway, Marina Bay is an excellent location from which to visit Gibraltar or Spain if they have berths available. The ground tackle which fell into disrepair has been replaced and facilities are excellent. The marina can take over 200 yachts up to 70m or 4·5m draught. The nearby bars and restaurants along the quay and in Neptune House provide excellent food and a good social atmosphere, as well as providing protection form the east winds.

Approach
The marina is 0·5M east of the north mole, and is approached by rounding the north mole's northwest corner. At night a row of red lights at the end of the airport runway mark the north side of the channel. Note that yachts may not move in the vicinity while the runway lights are flashing, there is also a height restriction of 23m.

Berthing
Call the marina office on Ch 71 for berth allocation. Note: Depths in the marina are around 4·5m but some areas are less. Make sure the berthing master knows your draught to ensure the correct location in the marina. If staff are not around, berth alongside the office, towards the outer end of the main pier or find an empty mooring. Hours are 0820–2200 daily in summer, 0830–2030 in winter. Berthing is Mediterranean-style – bow or stern-to with a buoy and lazy-line provided to the pontoon.

Facilities
Water Available at every berth charged at 1p per litre.
Electricity Available at every berth charged at 15p/Kwh.
Repairs Mechanics can be brought to the yacht.
Showers and WC On ground floor under Pier Office building. Facilities for the handicapped.
Launderette In the marina.
Dentist Mr C. Linale, Neptune House Marina Bay.
Security Security guards 24hr ✆ +350 20040477.
Weather Daily bulletins are posted at the Pier Office, BFBS Radio ✆ +350 20053416.
Eating out Enjoy the relaxed atmosphere of the waterfront restaurants within the marina complexes or the many restaurants, pubs and fast-food houses in the town, particularly in Main Street. A full list may be obtained from the tourist board.
Transport The No. 9 bus from the frontier to the bus station stops in Winston Churchill Avenue in front of the tower blocks at the northern end of Glacis Road, but it is only a 10 minute walk to the bus station and city centre.

General facilities
Gas Camping gaz can only be obtained from Sheppard's (closes 1300 on Saturdays). It is not stocked by the fuel stations in Marina Bay. Otherwise gas is available from the 'New Harbours' commercial area ✆ +350 2007026.
Fuel Diesel (and water) is obtainable at the Shell or BP stations opposite Marina Bay. Shell ✆ +350 20048232, BP ✆ +350 20072261.

THE ALGARVE & ANDALUCIA

ATLANTIC SPAIN AND PORTUGAL

CABO TRAFALGAR TO GIBRALTAR

Provisions Morrisons supermarket is a short walk from Queensway Quay and not far from Marina Bay. It is on the No. 4 and 10 bus route (see below), fresh fruit and vegetables are best obtained from La Línea market, just across the border in Spain, on Wednesday mornings, Duty-free stores are available via Albor Ltd ☎ +350 20073283, at Marina Bay – which doubles as a newsagent, bookshop and internet cafe – where almost anything in almost any quantity for a yacht in transit can be purchased.

Charts Available from the Gibraltar Chart Agency, Irish Town ☎ +350 20076293.

Chandlery Most items available at Sheppard's (temporarily at the old marina site ☎ +350 20077183 www.sheppard.gi which has the best range of yacht chandlery here. **However,** do be aware that with all the changes – including a move of the Sheppard's chandlery shop – several yachtsmen have complained that availability of 'just about anything' no longer applies. There are also smaller chandlers located at Marina Bay.

Repair facilities The old Sheppard's Marina has been developed as part of the Ocean Village project. Sheppard's is continuing to offer haul-outs (max 4·5 T/9m) at the container berth and most repairs from their workshop facilities at Coaling Island (near Queensway Quay Marina). Sheppard's chandlery remains open in the building adjacent to Ocean Village. M. Sheppard & Co Ltd. Chandlery ☎ 200 75148/ 77183. Repairs ☎ 200 76895
Email admin@sheppard.gi or yachtrep@gibraltar.gi www.sheppard.gi
The nearest alternative boatyard and travel-hoist facility is just N at the Alcaidesa Marina (see page 333).

Engineers Sheppard's can handle light engineering, welding, engine servicing and repairs to most makes and are Volvo Penta agents. Also-Marine Maintenance Ltd ☎ +350 20078954
Email fred@gibnet.gi (Perkins and Yanmar) at Marina Bay, and Medmarine Ltd ☎ +350 20048888 (Yamaha) at Queensway Quay, Tempco Marine Engineering ☎ +350 20074657
specialise in refrigeration.

Electronics and radio repairs Sheppard's workshops (as above) or Electromed ☎ +350 20077077
*em*ail mail@electro-med.com www.eletro-med.com at Queensway Quay, who can supply and repair equipment from most major manufacturers.

Sailmaker/sail repairs Sail makers, ☎ +350 20041469 in South Pavilion Road, who also handle general canvaswork and upholstery. Alternatively Magnusson Sails ☎ +350 952 791241, about 35 miles away in Estepona, who may be willing to deliver/collect. Canvas work and sprayhood (but not true sailmaking) is also undertaken by ME Balloqui & Sons ☎ +350 20078105, at 3941 City Mill Lane.

Rigging Sheppard's workshops, as above.

Liferaft servicing GV Undery & Son +350 20073107 Email compass@gibtelecom.net (who are also compass adjusters)

Money The UK Pound Sterling is legal tender, along with the Gibraltar pound and of equal value, but only in Gibraltar. Beware of trying to exchange excess Gibraltar currency in the UK, as it is worth very little there. Euros can also be used in most shops but not in the Post Office where only sterling is accepted. There are several Bureaux de Change agencies in Main Street. Visa, Switch, American Express, Mastercard etc, are accepted almost everywhere, though not the post office and some government offices. ATMs at Barclays Bank in Main Street and Morrisons supermarket.

Banks Gibraltar has well established banking services for both offshore and local customers with a full range of international banks, including several UK institutions, Banking hours are generally between 0900–1530 Monday to Friday.

Crossing the border Crossing the border into Spain is quick and easy on foot but another matter by car. In both cases a passport must be carried. By car, it is normal to queue in either direction, but while the queue to come into Gibraltar seldom exceeds ten minutes, it is not unusual to queue for up to an hour to leave during rush hour. Long queues also result when planes take off and land. There is a very reasonably priced airport carpark opposite the airport, near the border which charges about 50p an hour short term and £4 for 24 hour parking.

International travel Gibraltar airport is located close to the frontier for daily flights to the UK and onward connections ☎ +350 20073026. Málaga airport is a little an over an hour's drive up the coast (A7 or AP7 *peaje* toll road) for more destinations. Taxis are expensive.

Approaching the Rock from the northeast *Henry Buchanan*

The Barbary Ape. Wild guardians of Gibraltar *Henry Buchanan*

Appendix

I. Charts and books

Obtaining charts

Up-to-date information on British Admiralty chart coverage for North Africa is available at
www.ukho.gov.uk
where full details of chart schemes, titles and scales are given.

The catalogue of Spanish charts may be seen at
www.armada.mde.es

Up-to-date lists of sales agents for Portugal and IHM (Spain) are available on the websites.

The catalogue of Portuguese charts may be seen at
www.hidrografico.pt

Imray Laurie Norie and Wilson are sales agents for UKHO charts and publications which may be ordered through www.imray.com

Imrays are able to help with enquiries and supply Spanish and Portuguese charts.

Chart agents

Before departure

British Admiralty and Spanish charts from
Imray Laurie Norie & Wilson Ltd,
Wych House, The Broadway, St Ives,
Cambs PE27 5BT
☎ 01480 462114
www.imray.com

However in the case of Spanish charts, stocks held are limited and it may take some time to fill an order. It may be simpler to order directly with a credit card from

Instituto Hidrográfico de la Marina,
Pl. San Severiano, 3, DP 11007 Cádiz
☎ (956) 59 94 12

Gibraltar

Gibraltar Chart Agency,
4th Floor, Leon House I
☎ +350-200-76293
Email gibchartag@gibtelecom.net
www.gibraltarchartagency.com

Spain (Algeciras)

SUISCA SL
Avda. Blas Infante, Centro Blas Local 1, 11201 Algeciras, Cádiz
☎ +34 902 220007
Email barcelona@suiscasl.com
www.suiscasl.com

Portugal

J. Garraio & C.ª, Lda
Avenida 24 de Julho, 2, 1200-478 Lisboa, Portugal
☎ +351 213473081
www.jgarraio.pt

Imray charts

Chart Title   *Scale*

- **C18** Western Approaches to the English Channel and Biscay WGS 84   1:1,000,000
- **C19** Portuguese Coast Passage Chart Cabo Finisterre to Gibraltar WGS 84   825,000
  Plans A Coruña, Baiona, Leixões, Lisboa Approaches, Cascais, Sines, Lagos, Bahía de Cádiz, Rota, Strait of Gibraltar, Gibraltar
- **C48** La Coruña to Porto WGS 84   1:350,000
  Plans A Coruña, Ría de Corme e Laxe, Ría de Camariñas, Ría de Muros, Approaches to Ría de Arousa, Ría de Arousa, Cabo de Cruz, Vilagarcía, Illa de Arousa to Cambados, Ría de Pontevedra, Ría de Vigo, Baiona, Viana do Castelo, Leixões, Barra do Rio Douro
- **C49** Ría de Aveiro to Sines WGS 84   1:350,000
  Plans Figueira da Foz, Nazaré, Porto de Peniche, Cascais, Lisboa Approaches, Lisboa (Lisbon), Sesimbra, Entrance to Rio Sado (Setúbal), Setúbal, Sines
- **C50** Sines to Gibraltar WGS 84   1:350,000
  Plans Sines, Lagos, Portimão, Vilamoura, Vila Real de Santo António, Isla Cristina, Mazagón, Chipiona, Rota, Bahía de Cádiz, Puerto Sherry, Sancti-Petri, Barbate, Tarifa, Gibraltar, Strait of Gibraltar
- **M10** Western Mediterranean – Gibraltar to the Ionian Sea WGS 84   1:2,750,000
- **M11** Mediterranean Spain – Gibraltar to Cabo de Gata & Morocco WGS 84   1:440,000
  Plans Strait of Gibraltar, Gibraltar, Estepona, Puerto de Almerimar, Almería, Ceuta

IMRAY DIGITAL CHARTS
Mobile downloads
Imray Navigator app

Full details at
www.imray.com

APPENDIX

II. Waypoints

Any numbered waypoints are shown in safe-water positions. In most cases this is on an approach line to a port, harbour or anchorage to indicate where pilotage may take over from GPS navigation. Waypoints and tracks between them should always be plotted and checked on an up-to-date chart before being used for navigation. Users are reminded that they are offered as an aid to navigation. All should be cross-checked against other sources of information and used in conjunction with eyeball navigation.

Positions

Although a few official charts of this area have yet to be converted from Datum ED50, skippers should note that all positions in this book are to WGS84. All were derived using C-Map electronic charts and Admiralty charts, and in some cases handheld GPS ashore.

III. Useful addresses

Spanish embassies and consulates

London (Embassy) 39 Chesham Place, London SW1X 8SB
  www.spain.embassyhomepage.com
  ☎ +4420 7235 5555
London (Consulate) 20 Draycott Place
  London SW3 2RZ. ☎ 020 7589 8989
  Manchester (Consulate) Brook House,
  64-72 Spring Gardens, Manchester M2 2BQ
  ☎ +44907 018 0023
Edinburgh (Consulate) 57 Castle Street
  Edinburgh, EH2 3HT ☎ +44131 220 1843
Washington DC (Embassy) 2375 Pennsylvania Ave,
  NW Washington DC 20037
  ☎ +1 202 452 0100 & +1 202 728 2340
  Email emb.washington@maec.es
New York (Consulate) 150 East 58th St, 30th Floor
  NY 10155, New York, USA
  ☎ +1 212 355 40480
  Email cog.nuevayork@maec.es

Portuguese embassies

London 11 Belgrave Square, London SW1X 8PP
  ☎ +4420 7235531
  Email londres@mne.pt
  www.portuguese-embassy.co.uk
Washington DC 2310 2012 Massachusetts Ave
  NW Washington DC 20036
  ☎ +1 202 328 8610
  Email embassyportugal-us.org

British and American embassies and consulates

In Spain
British Embassy Madrid Torre Espacio, Paseo de la
  Castellana 259D 28046 Madrid, Spain
  Email (Consular enquiries): Info.consulate@fco.gov.uk
  ☎ +34 917 146 300
British Consulate General Madrid Torre Espacio,
  Paseo de la Castellana 259D, 28046 Madrid
  ☎ +34 91 334 2194
  Email enquiries.madrid@fco.gov.uk
Embassy of the United States Spain
  Serrano 75 28006 Madrid, Spain
  ☎ +34 91 587 2200
United States Consulate General Barcelona Paseo Reina
  Elisenda de Montcada, 23 08034 Barcelona, España
  ☎ +34 93 280 22 27
  Email barcelonaacs@state.gov

In Portugal
British Embassy Lisbon Rua de São Bernardo 33,
  1249-082 Lisbon , Portugal
  Email ppa.lisbon@fco.gov.uk
  ☎ +351 21 392 40 00
  Email portugal.consulate@fco.gov.uk
British Consulate Lisbon Rua de São Bernardo 33,
  1249-082 Lisboa, Portugal
  Email portugal.consulate@fco.gov.uk
  ☎ 808 20 35 37 *(if calling from Portugal)*
  ☎ +351 21 392 4082 *(if calling from overseas)*
United States Embassy Lisbon Avenida das Forças
  Armadas, 1600-081 Lisboa
  or Apartado 43033 1601-301 Lisboa
  ☎ + 351-21-727-3300 or +351-21-094-2000
  Email lisbonweb@state.gov

Spanish national tourist offices

London 6th Floor 64 North Row, London W1K 7DE
  ☎ +442073172011
  www.spain.info/en_gb/
New York 60 East 42nd Street-Suite 5300 (53rd Floor),
  New York NY 10165-0039
  www.spain.info/en_us

Portuguese national tourist offices

London 11, Belgrave Square, London, SW1X 8PP
  ☎ 020 7201 6666
  Email tourism.london@portugalglobal.pt
  www.visitportugal.com
New York 590 Fifth Avenue, 4th Floor, New York,
  NY 10036-4704
  ☎ +1 212 354 4403

IV. Regulations, tax and VAT

(The information below should not be considered definitive. Skippers of non-VAT paid boats and those planning to stay for more than 183 days in a years are strongly advised to verify the regulations which will be applicable to them.)

Personal documentation

Spain – Currently EU nationals – including UK citizens – may visit for up to 90 days, for which a national identity card or passport is required but no visa. American, Canadian and New Zealand citizens may also stay for up to 90 days without a visa, though Australians need one for more than 30 days. EU citizens wishing to remain in Spain may apply for a *permiso de residencia* once in the country; non-EU nationals can apply for a single 90-day extension, or otherwise obtain a long-term visa from a Spanish embassy or consulate before leaving home. The website www.graysworld.co.uk/spanish-property/resident-tourist provides advice on this matter.

Certificate of competence
1. Given below is a transcription of a statement made by the Counsellor for Transport at the Spanish Embassy, London in March 1996. It is directed towards citizens of the UK but doubtless the principles apply to other EU citizens. One implication is that in a particular circumstance (paragraph 2a below) a UK citizen does not need a Certificate of Competence during the first 90 days of his visit.
2. a. British citizens visiting Spain in charge of a UK registered pleasure boat flying the UK flag need only fulfil UK law.

b. British citizens visiting Spain in charge of a Spanish registered pleasure boat flying the Spanish flag have one of two options:
  i. To obtain a Certificate of Competence issued by the Spanish authorities. See *Normas reguladore para la obtención de titulos para el gobierno de embarcaciones de recreo* issued by the Ministerio de Obras Publicas, Transportes y Medio Ambiente.
  ii. To have the Spanish equivalent of a UK certificate issued. The following equivalencies are used by the Spanish Maritime Administration:
  Yachtmaster Ocean *Capitan de Yate*
  Yachtmaster Offshore *Patron de Yate de altura*
  Coastal Skipper *Patron de Yate*
  Day Skipper *Patron de Yate embarcaciones de recreo*
  Helmsman Overseas* *Patron de embarcaciones de recreo restringido a motor*

  *The Spanish authorities have been informed that this certificate has been replaced by the International Certificate of Competence.

3. The catch to para 2(a) above is that, in common with other EU citizens, after 90 days a UK citizen is technically no longer a visitor, must apply for a *permiso de residencia* and must equip his boat to Spanish rules and licensing requirements.

   In practice the requirement to apply for a *permiso de residencia* does not appear to be enforced in the case of cruising yachtsmen who live aboard rather than ashore and are frequently on the move. By the same token, the requirement for a British skipper in charge of a UK registered pleasure boat flying the UK flag to carry a Certificate of Competence after their first 90 days in Spanish waters also appears to be waived. Many yachtsmen have reported cruising Spanish waters for extended periods with no documentation beyond that normally carried in the UK.

4. The RYA suggests the following technique to obtain an equivalent Spanish certificate:
   a. Obtain two photocopies of your passport
   b. Have them notarised by a Spanish notary
   c. Obtain a copy of the UK Certificate of Competence and send it to the Consular Department, The Foreign and Commonwealth Office, Clive House, Petty France, London SW1H 9DH, with a request that it be stamped with the Hague Stamp (this apparently validates the document). The FCO will probably charge a fee so it would be best to call the office first ☎ 020 7270 3000.
   d. Have the stamped copy notarized by a UK notary.
   e. Send the lot to the Spanish Merchant Marine for the issue of the Spanish equivalent.

It may be both quicker and easier to take the Spanish examination.

Tax

Although the tax rules appear not to be applied evenly across Spain the following is offered as general advice to help individuals consider whether to seek more formal advice regarding their particular situation. The Spanish operate a self assessment system and can reclaim tax back for five years. Three types of taxes may apply specifically to yacht owners:

Tarifa G-5 This is broadly a port tax levied to help maintain the port. Its application appears to vary from harbour to harbour and province to province. It is likely to form part of a marina fee for short stays. If staying for long periods or over-wintering it would be wise to ensure that a contract with the marina is inclusive of all taxes,

Wealth tax This is a national tax but may be applied differently from region to region. A person staying in Spain for less than 6 months is not liable to wealth tax. However, if the 183 day limit is exceeded the rules of residency may apply and trigger a demand for the tax. It is the individual's time in Spain which is relevant, not the location of the boat.

Other taxes If staying beyond 183 days the full Spanish Legislation and tax rules apply – and could include such matters as income tax, property tax, local town tax.

Portugal Currently EU nationals need only a national identity card or passport to enter Portugal and can then stay indefinitely. American and Canadian citizens can remain for up to 60 days without a visa, Australians and New Zealanders for up to 90 days. Extensions are issued by the Sevico de Estrangeiros which has a branch in most major towns, or failing that by the local police. At least one week's notice is required.

VAT and temporary import

A boat registered in the EU and on which VAT has been paid in an EU country, or which was launched before 1 January 1985 and is therefore exempt on the grounds of age (and has the documents to prove it), can stay indefinitely in any other EU country without further VAT liability.

The time limit for which relief from customs duty and VAT is available to non-EU registered yachts visiting the EU is 18 months. The period for which a yacht must remain outside the EU before starting another 18 month period is not specified. Those affected are recommended to check current regulations which may be found on HM Customs and Excise website www.hmce.gov.uk Search 'Pleasure craft'.

Spain A VAT paid (exempt) yacht may normally remain in the country almost indefinitely provided a '*Permiso Aduanero*' is first obtained, but may not be used commercially (i.e. for chartering).

Portugal There is no limitation on length of stay for a VAT paid or exempt yacht. An annual tax is levied on all yachts kept for long periods (over 183 days) in Portuguese waters irrespective of their VAT status, see page 132.

Gibraltar As Gibraltar is not a part of the EU, VAT does not apply.

V. Portugal and Andalucía online

Portugal
www.cp.pt Comboios de Portugal (the national railway system), in Portuguese and English. Routes, timetables, fares and online booking in an impressively user-friendly layout.
www.flytap.com the national airline, TAP Portugal. In most major languages with schedules, fares and online booking. Fast and user-friendly.
www.hidrografico.pt the Portuguese Hydrographic Institute, with full chart catalogue. In Portuguese only, but easy enough to follow. No online sales, but links to two Lisbon chart agents
www.portugal-info.net a well-organised site carrying information on and/or links to pretty well every town of any size in the entire country. Useful maps, current weather conditions, telephone numbers etc. English language only.
www.portugalvirtual.pt another general site worth

APPENDIX

investigating. A little more commercially-orientated than some, but if you want a plan of the Lisbon metro or opening times for the Palácio Nacional de Ajuda, it's all here. In Portuguese and English.

www.theportugalnews.com online edition of The Portugal News, an English-language national daily paper.

www.travel-images.com thousands of downloadable pictures of the entire world, including Portugal and Spain, but with little accompanying text. Check the Utilities section for some quirky lists.

www.visitportugal.com Portugal's official tourism website, in six languages including English. Well constructed and illustrated, and updated regularly with details of forthcoming events. Several short video clips. Recommended.

Andalucia

www.andalucia.com commercial (and some might say superficial) site mainly slanted towards the Mediterranean part of the province.

www.andalucia.org official website of the Andalucían Tourist Office, covering all the usual aspects plus (via the Sports Activities button) an unusually full and accurate list of the province's marinas and yacht harbours. In good English, with a useful search facility.

www.armada.mde.es the Spanish Hydrographic Institute, with full chart catalogue as well as Avisos a los Navegants (Notices to Mariners). In Spanish only, but relatively easy to follow.

www.puertosdeandalucia.es the Agencia Pública de Puertos de Andalucía which runs the majority of marinas in Andalucía. Other, non-APPA marinas are also included. In Spanish and English, though not all pages are fully translated.

www.iberia.com the Iberia website, in numerous languages (the United Kingdom is Reino Unido) and with all the usual bells and whistles.

www.idealspain.com perhaps the most appealing of the Andalucían tourist sites, with maps and well-illustrated notes about many places of interest. Includes an image library and message board. English only.

www.renfe.es fast but slightly forbidding site of RENFE, the Spanish rail network, in four languages including English.

VI. Glossary

A more complete glossary is given in the *Yachtsman's Ten Language Dictionary* compiled by Barbara Webb and Michael Manton with the Cruising Association (Adlard Coles Nautical). Terms related to meteorology and sea state follow at the end of each section.

General and chartwork terms

English	Spanish	Portuguese
anchor, to	fondear	fundear
anchorage	fondeadero, ancladero	fundeadouro, ancoradouro
basin, dock	dársena	doca
bay	bahía, ensenada	baía, enseada
beach	playa	praia
beacon	baliza	baliza
beam	manga	largura, boca
berth	atracar	atracar
black	negro	preto
blue	azul	azul
boatbuilder	astillero	estaleiro
bottled gas	cilindro de gas, carga de gas	cilindro de gás, bilha de gás
breakwater	rompeolas, muelle	quebra-mar, molhe
buoy	boya	bóia
bus	autobús	autocarro
cape	cabo	cabo
car hire	aquilar coche	alugar automóvel
chandlery (shop)	efectos navales, apetrachamento	fornecedor de barcos, aprestos
channel	canal	canal
charts	cartas náuticas	cartas hidrográficas
church	iglesia	igreja
crane	grua	guindaste
creek	estero	esteiro
Customs	Aduana	Alfândega
deep	profundo	profundo
depth	sonda, profundidad	profundidade
diesel	gasoil	gasoleo
draught	calado	calado
dredged	dragado	dragado
dyke, pier	dique	dique
east	este	este
eastern	levante, oriental	levante, do este
electricity	electricidad	electricidade
engineer, mechanic	ingeniero, mecánico	engenheiro, técnico
entrance	boca, entrada	bôca, entrada
factory	fábrica	fábrica
foul, dirty	sucio	sujo
gravel	cascajo	burgau
green	verde	verde
harbourmaster	diretor do porto	capitán de puerto
height, clearance	altura	altura
high tide	pleamar, marea alta	preia-mar, maré alta
high	alto/a	alto/a
ice	hielo	gelo
inlet, cove	ensenada	enseada
island	isla	ilha, ilhéu
islet, skerry	islote	ilhota
isthmus	istmo	istmo
jetty, pier	malecón	quebra-mar

English	Spanish	Portuguese
knots	nudos	nós
lake	lago	lago
laundry, launderette	lavandería, automática	lavanderia, automática
leading line, transit	enfilación	enfiamento
leeward	sotavento	sotavento
length overall	eslora total	comprimento
lighthouse	faro	farol
lock	esclusa	esclusa
low tide	bajamar, marea baja	baixa-mar, maré baixa
mailing address	dirección de correo	endereço para correio
marina, yacht harbour	puerto deportivo, dársena de yates	porto desportivo, doca de recreio
medical services	servicios médiocos	serviços médicas
mud	fango	lôdo
mussel rafts	viveros	viveiros
narrows	estrecho	estreito
north	norte	norte
orange	anaranjado	alaranjado
owner	propietario	propietário
paraffin	parafina	petróleo para iluminação

344 ATLANTIC SPAIN AND PORTUGAL

GLOSSARY

English	Spanish	Portuguese
petrol	gasolina	gasolina
pier, quay, dock	muelle	molhe
point	punta	ponta
pontoon	pantalán	pontão
port (side)	babor	bombordo
Port of Registry	Puerto de Matrícula	Porto de Registo
port office	capitanía	capitania
post office	oficina de correos	agência do correio
quay	muelle	molhe, cais
ramp	rampa	rampa
range (tidal)	repunte	amplitude
red	rojo	vermelho
reef	arrecife	recife
reef, spit	restinga	restinga
registration number	matricula	número registo
repairs	reparacións	reparações
rock, stone	roca, piedra	laxe, pedra
root (eg. of mole)	raíz	raiz
sailing boat	barca de vela	barco à vela
sailmaker, sail repairs	velero, reparacións velas	veleiro, reparações velas
saltpans	salinas	salinas
sand	arena	areia
sea	mar	mar
seal, to	precintar	fechar
shoal, low	bajo	baixo
shops	tiendas, almacéns	lojas
shore, edge	orilla	margem
showers (washing)	duchas	duches
slab, flat rock	laja	laje
slack water, tidal stand	repunte	águas paradas
slipway	varadero	rampa
small	pequeño	pequeno
south	sur	sul
southern	meridional	do sul
starboard	estribor	estibordo
strait	estrecho	estreito
supermarket	supermercado	supermercado
tower	torre	tôrre
travel-lift	grua giratoria, pórtico elevador	e pórtico, pórtico elevador, içar
water (drinking)	agua potable	água potável
weather forecast	prevision/boletin metereológico	previsão de tempo, boletim meteorológico
weed	alga	alga
weight	peso	pêso
west	oeste	oeste
western	occidental	do oeste
white	blanco	branco
windward	barlovento	barlavento
works (building)	obras	obras
yacht (sailing)	barca de vela	barco à vela
yacht club	club náutico	clube náutico, clube naval
yellow	amarillo	amarelo

Meteorology and sea state

English	Spanish	Portuguese
calm (Force 0, 0–1kns)	calma	calma
light airs (Force 1, 1–3kns)	ventolina	aragem
light breeze (Force 2, 4–6kns)	flojito	vento fraco, brisa
gentle breeze (Force 3, 7–10kns)	flojo	vento bonançoso, brisa suave
moderate breeze (Force 4, 11–16kns)	bonancible	vento moderado, brisa moderado
fresh breeze (Force 5, 17–21kns)	fresquito	vento fresco, brisa fresca
strong breeze (Force 6, 22–27kns)	fresco	vento muito fresco, brisa forte
near gale (Force 7, 28–33kns)	frescachón, ventania moderada	vento forte,
gale (Force 8, 34–40kns)	duro	vento muito forte, ventania fresca
severe gale (Force 9, 41–47kns)	muy duro	vento tempestuoso, ventania forte
storm (Force 10, 48–55kns)	temporal	temporal, ventania total
violent storm (Force 11, 56–63kns)	borrasca, tempestad	temporal desfieto, tempestade
hurricane (Force 12, +64kns)	huracán	furacão, ciclone
breakers	rompientes	arrebentação
cloudy	nubloso	nublado
depression (low)	depresión	depressão
fog	niebla	nevoeiro
gust	racha	rajada
hail	granizada	saraiva
mist	neblina	neblina
overfalls, tide race	escarceos	bailadeiras
rain	lluvia	chuva
ridge (high)	dorsal	crista
rough sea	mar gruesa	mar bravo
short, steep sea	mar corta	mar cavado
shower	aguacero	aguaceiro
slight sea	marejadilla	mar chão
squall	turbonada	borrasca
swell	mar de leva	ondulação
thunderstorm	tempestad	trovoada

General and chartwork terms

Spanish	English	Portuguese
Aduana	Customs	Alfândega
agua potable	water (drinking)	água potável
alga	weed	alga
almacéns	shops	lojas
alto/a	high	alto/a
altura	height, clearance	altura
amarillo	yellow	amarelo
anaranjado	orange	alaranjado
ancladero	anchorage	fundeadouro, ancoradouro
apetrachamento	chandlery (shop)	fornecedore de barcos, aprestos
aquilar coche	car hire	alugar automóvel
arena	sand	areia
arrecife	reef	recife
astillero	boatbuilder	estaleiro
atracar	berth	atracar
autobús	bus	autocarro
azul	blue	azul
babor	port (side)	bombordo
bahía	bay	baía, enseada
bajamar	low tide	baixa-mar, maré baixa

ATLANTIC SPAIN AND PORTUGAL   **345**

APPENDIX

Spanish	English	Portuguese
bajo	shoal, low	baixo
baliza	beacon	baliza
barca de vela	sailing boat, yacht	barco à vela
barlovento	windward	barlavento
blanco	white	branco
boca	entrance	bôca, entrada
boya	buoy	bóia
cabo	cape	cabo
calado	draught	calado
canal	channel	canal
capitanía	port office	capitania
carga de gas	bottled gas	cilindro de gás, bilha de gás
cartas náuticas	charts	cartas hidrográficas
cascajo	gravel	burgau
cilindro de gas	bottled gas	cilindro de gás, bilha de gás
club náutico	yacht club	clube náutico, clube naval
dársena de yates	marina, yacht harbour	porto desportivo, doca de recreio
dársena	basin, dock	doca
dique	dyke, pier	dique
dirección de correo	mailing address	endereço para correio
diretor do porto	harbourmaster	capitán de puerto
dragado	dredged	dragado
duchas	showers (washing)	duches
efectos navales	chandlery (shop)	fornecedor de barcos, aprestos
electricidad	electricity	electricidade
enfilación	leading line, transit	enfiamento
ensenada	bay, inlet, cove	baía, enseada
entrada	entrance	bôca, entrada
esclusa	lock	esclusa
eslora total	length overall	comprimento
este	east	este
estero	creek	esteiro
estrecho	narrows, strait	estreito
estribor	starboard	estibordo

Spanish	English	Portuguese
fábrica	factory	fábrica
fango	mud	lôdo
faro	lighthouse	farol
fondeadero	anchorage	fundeadouro, ancoradouro
fondear	anchor, to	fundear
gasoil	diesel	gasoleo
gasolina	petrol	gasolina
grua giratoria	travel-lift	e pórtico, pórtico elevador, içar
grua	crane	guindaste
hielo	ice	gelo
iglesia	church	igreja
ingeniero, mecánico	engineer, mechanic	engenheiro, técnico
isla	island	ilha, ilhéu
islote	islet, skerry	ilhota
istmo	isthmus	istmo
lago	lake	lago
laja	slab, flat rock	laje
lavandería, l. automática	laundry, launderette	lavanderia, l.automática
levante	eastern	levante, do este
malecón	jetty, pier	quebra-mar
manga	beam	largura, boca

Spanish	English	Portuguese
mar	sea	mar
marea alta	high tide	preia-mar, maré alta
marea baja	low tide	baixa-mar, maré baixa
matricula	registration number	número registo
meridional	southern	do sul
muelle	breakwater, pier, quay, dock	quebra-mar, molhe, cais
negro	black	preto
norte	north	norte
nudos	knots	nós
obras	works (building)	obras
occidental	western	do oeste
oeste	west	oeste
oficina de correos	post office	agência do correio
oriental	eastern	levante, do este
orilla	shore, edge	margem
pantalán	pontoon	pontão
parafina	paraffin	petróleo para iluminaçao
pequeño	small	pequeno
peso	weight	pêso
piedra	rock, stone	pedra
playa	beach	praia
pleamar	high tide	preia-mar, maré alta
pórtico elevador	travel-lift	e pórtico, pórtico elevador, içar
precintar	seal, to	fechar
previsión/boletin metereológico	weather forecast	previsão de tempo, boletim meteorológico
profundidad	depth	profundidade
profundo	deep	profundo
propietario	owner	propietário
Puerto de Matrícula	Port of Registry	Porto de Registo
puerto deportivo	marina, yacht harbour	porto desportivo, doca de recreio

Spanish	English	Portuguese
punta	point	ponta
raíz	root (eg. of mole)	raiz
rampa	ramp	rampa
reparacións	repairs	reparações
repunte	tidal range, stand, slack water	águas paradas, amplitude
restinga	reef, spit	restinga
roca	rock	laxe
rojo	red	vermelho
rompeolas	breakwater	quebra-mar, molhe
salinas	saltpans	salinas
servicios médicos	medical services	serviços médicas
sonda	depth	profundidade
sotavento	leeward	sotavento
sucio	foul, dirty	sujo
supermercado	supermarket	supermercado
sur	south	sul
tiendas	shops	lojas
torre	tower	tôrre
varadero	slipway	rampa
velero, reparacións velas	sailmaker, sail repairs	veleiro, reparações velas
verde	green	verde
viveros	mussel rafts	viveiros

ATLANTIC SPAIN AND PORTUGAL

GLOSSARY

Meteorology and sea state

Spanish	English	Portuguese
calma	calm (Force 0, 0–1kns)	calma
ventolina	light airs (Force 1, 1–3kns)	aragem
flojito	light breeze (Force 2, 4–6kns)	vento fraco, brisa
flojo	gentle breeze (Force 3, 7–10kns)	vento bonançoso, brisa suave
bonancible	moderate breeze (Force 4, 11–16kns)	vento moderado, brisa moderado
fresquito	fresh breeze (Force 5, 17–21kns)	vento frêsco, brisa fresca
frêsco	strong breeze (Force 6, 22–27kns)	vento muito fresco, brisa forte
frescachón	near gale (Force 7, 28–33kns)	vento forte, ventania moderada
duro	gale (Force 8, 34–40kns)	vento muito forte, ventania fresca
muy duro	severe gale (Force 9, 41–47kns)	vento tempestuoso, ventania forte
temporal	storm (Force 10, 48–55kns)	temporal, ventania total
borrasca, tempestad	violent storm (Force 11, 56–63kns)	temporal desfeito, tempestade
huracán	hurricane (Force 12, 64+kns)	furacão, ciclone
aguacero	shower	aguaceiro
depresión	depression (low)	depressão
dorsal	ridge (high)	crista
escarceos	overfalls, tiderace	bailadeiras
granizada	hail	saraiva
lluvia	rain	chuva
mar corta	short, steep sea	mar cavado
mar de leva	swell	ondulação
mar gruesa	rough sea	mar bravo
marejadilla	slight sea	mar chão
neblina	mist	neblina

Spanish	English	Portuguese
niebla	fog	nevoeiro
nubloso	cloudy	nublado
racha	gust	rajada
rompientes	breakers	arrebentação
tempestad	thunderstorm	trovoada
turbonada	squall	borrasca

General and chartwork terms

Portuguese	English	Spanish
agência do correio	post office	oficina de correos
água potável	water (drinking)	agua potable
águas paradas, amplitude	tidal range, stand, slack water	repunte, repute
alaranjado	orange	anaranjado
alfândega	customs	aduana
alga	weed	alga
alto/a	high	alto/a
altura	height, clearance	altura
alugar automóvel	car hire	aquilar coche
amarelo	yellow	amarillo
areia	sand	arena
atracar	berth	atracar
autocarro	bus	autobús
azul	blue	azul
baía, enseada	bay, inlet, cove	bahía, ensenada
baixo	shoal, low	bajo
baliza	beacon	baliza
barco à vela	sailing boat, yacht	barca de vela
barlavento	windward	barlovento
bôca, entrada	entrance	boca, entrada
bóia	buoy	boya
bombordo	port (side)	babor
branco	white	blanco
burgau	gravel	cascajo
cabo	cape	cabo
calado	draught	calado
canal	channel	canal
capitán de puerto	harbourmaster	diretor do porto
capitania	port office	capitanía
cartas hidrográficas	charts	cartas náuticas
cilindro de gás, bilha de gás	bottled gas	carga de gas, cilindro de gas
clube náutico	yacht club	club náutico
clube naval		
comprimento	length overall	eslora total
dique	dyke, pier	dique
do oeste	western	occidental
do sul	southern	meridional
doca	basin, dock	dársena
dragado	dredged	dragado
duches	showers (washing)	duchas
e pórtico, pórtico elevador, içar	travel-lift	grua giratoria, pórtico elevador
electricidade	electricity	electricidad
endereço para correo	mailing address	dirección de correio
enfiamento	leading line, transit	enfilación
engenheiro, técnico	engineer, mechanic	ingeniero, mecánico
esclusa	lock	esclusa
estaleiro	boatbuilder	astillero

Portuguese	English	Spanish
este	east	este
esteiro	creek	estero
estibordo	starboard	estribor
estreito	narrows, strait	estrecho
fábrica	factory	fábrica
farol	lighthouse	faro
fechar	seal, to	precintar
fornecedor de barcos, aprestos	chandlery (shop)	apetrachamento, efectos navales
fundeadouro, ancoradouro	anchorage	fondeadero, ancladero
fundear	anchor, to	fondear
gasoleo	diesel	gasoil
gasolina	petrol	gasolina
gelo	ice	hielo
guindaste	crane	grua
igreja	church	iglesia
ilha, ilhéu	island	isla
ilhota	islet, skerry	islote
istmo	isthmus	istmo
lago	lake	lago
laje	slab, flat rock	laja
largura, boca	beam	manga
lavanderia, l. automática	laundry, launderette	lavandería, l. automática
laxe	rock	roca
levante, do este	eastern	levante, oriental
lôdo	mud	fango
lojas	shops	almacéns, tiendas
mar	sea	mar

ATLANTIC SPAIN AND PORTUGAL 347

APPENDIX

Portuguese	English	Spanish
margem	shore, edge	orilla
norte	north	norte
nós	knots	nudos
número registo	registration number	matricula
obras	works (building)	obras
oeste	west	oeste
pedra	rock, stone	piedra
pequeno	small	pequeño
pêso	weight	peso
petróleo para iluminação	paraffin	parafina
ponta	point	punta
pontão	pontoon	pantalán
Porto de Registo	Port of Registry	Puerto de Matrícula
porto desportivo, doca de recreio	marina, yacht harbour	puerto deportivo, dársena de yates
praia	beach	playa
preia-mar, maré alta	high tide	pleamar, marea alta
preto	black	negro
previsão de tempo, boletim meteorológico	weather forecast	previsión/boletin metereológico
profundidade	depth	profundidad, sonda
profundo	deep	profundo
propietário	owner	propietario
quebra-mar	jetty, pier	malecón
quebra-mar, molhe, cais	breakwater, pier, quay, dock	muelle, rompeolas
raiz	root (eg. of mole)	raíz
rampa	ramp, slipway	rampa, varadero
recife	reef	arrecife
reparações	repairs	reparacións
restinga	reef, spit	restinga

Portuguese	English	Spanish
salinas	saltpans	salinas
serviços médicas	medical services	servicios médicos
sotavento	leeward	sotavento
sujo	foul, dirty	sucio
sul	south	sur
supermercado	supermarket	supermercado
tôrre	tower	torre
veleiro, reparações velas	sailmaker, sail repairs	velero, reparacións velas
verde	green	verde
vermelho	red	rojo
viveiros	mussel rafts	viveros

Meteorology and sea state

Portuguese	English	Spanish
calma	calm (Force 0, 0–1kns)	calma
aragem	light airs (Force 1, 1–3kns)	ventolina
vento fraco, brisa	light breeze (Force 2, 4–6kns)	flojito
vento bonançoso, brisa suave	gentle breeze (Force 3, 7–10kns)	flojo
vento moderado, brisa moderado	moderate breeze (Force 4, 11–16kns)	bonancible
vento fresco, brisa fresca	fresh breeze (Force 5, 17–21kns)	fresquito
vento muito fresco, brisa forte	strong breeze (Force 6, 22–27kns)	fresco
vento forte, ventania moderada	near gale (Force 7, 28–33kns)	frescachón
vento muito forte, ventania fresca	gale (Force 8, 34–40kns)	duro
vento tempestuoso, ventania forte	severe gale (Force 9, 41–47kns)	muy duro
temporal, ventania total	storm (Force 10, 48–55kns)	temporal
temporal desfieto, tempestade	violent storm (Force 11, 56–63kns)	borrasca, tempestad
furacão, ciclone	hurricane (Force 12, 64+kns)	huracán
aguaceiro	shower	aguacero
arrebentação	breakers	rompientes
bailadeiras	overfalls, tide race	escarceos
borrasca	squall	turbonada
chuva	rain	lluvia
crista	ridge (high)	dorsal
depressão	depression (low)	depresión
mar bravo	rough sea	mar gruesa
mar cavado	short, steep sea	mar corta
mar chão	slight sea	marejadilla
neblina	mist	neblina
nevoeiro	fog	niebla
nublado	cloudy	nubloso
ondulação	swell	mar de leva
rajada	gust	racha
saraiva	hail	granizada
trovoada	thunderstorm	tempestad

VII. Abbreviations used on charts

Spanish	Portuguese	Meaning
F.	F.	Fixed
D.	Rl.	Flashing
Gp.D.	Rl.Agr.	Group flashing
F.D.	F.Rl.	Fixed and flashing
F.Gp.D.	F.Rl.Agr.	Fixed and group flashing
Ct.	Ct	Quick flashing
Gp.Ct.	Ct int	Interrupted quick flashing
Oc.	Oc.	Occulting
Gp.Oc.	Oc.Agr.	Group occulting
Iso	Is.	Isophase
Mo.	Morse	Morse

Colours

am.	am.	Yellow
az.	azul	Blue
b.	br.	White
n.	pr.	Black
r.	vm.	Red
v.	vd.	Green

Seabed

A	A.	Sand
Al	Alg	Weed
R.	R.	Rock
F	L.	Mud
Co.	B.	Gravel

Index

A Coruña (La Coruña), 23, 30-35
A Pobra do Caramiñal, 77, 80-81
abbreviations used on charts, 349
Acebuche, Punta del, 336
addresses & websites, 4, 6, 8, 9, 342-4, *see also start of each chapter*
Adra/Agra, Playa Arena de, 105
Aguete, 109
Aguiera, Punta, 63
Aguillons (Cabo Ortegal), 11, 12
Aguiño, 71, 72, 75
Alandra, 203
Albufeira, 243-6
Alcaidesa Marina (La Línea), 332-3, 334, 337
Alcântara, Doca de (Lisbon), 198, 199-200
Alcobaça, 171
Alcoutim, 268, 273, 274-5
Aldan, Ría de, 111
Algarve, 2, 222, 223-70, 343-4
Algeciras, 327, 330-31
Algeciras, Bay of (Bay of Gibraltar), 336
Algés, Centro Náutico de (Lisbon), 203
Almacén, 99
almadrabas see tunny nets
Alva, Barca de, 157
Alvor, 235-7
América, Playa de (Baiona), 127
América, Puerto (Cádiz), 266, 313-15
anchor lights, 7
Ancora, 138
Andalucía, 2, 5, 222-5, 266, 271-333, 334, 344
APL marinas (Lisbon), 196-200
APPA marinas (Andalucia), 266
Arade, Rio, 238, 240-41
Arena, Playa de (I. Cíes), 113
Arena de Adra/Agra, Playa, 105
Arena das Rodas, Playa, 113
Arenas, Punta de Cala, 328, 330
Ares, Cabo de, 211
Ares, Ría de, 23, 27
Ares Marina, 26-7
Arousa, Isla de, 89-91
Arousa, Ría de, 11, 70-97
Arousa, Villagarcía de (Vilagarcia), 86-7
Arrábida, Portinho de, 211
Arrifana, 221
Artabo, Golfo, 23-35
Astaroth, Puerto *see* Rota
Astilleros Lagos Boatyard (Vigo), 118
Atlantic National Parks (Galicia), 15-17
Atlântico, Porto (Leixoes), 150, 151
Aveiro, Ria de, 158-63
AVELA Club Marina, 162, 163
Ayamonte, 266, 268, 271, 273

Bahía de Cádiz, 303-315
Baía de São Jacinto, 161, 162, 163
Baiona (Bayona), 125-7
Baiona, Ensenada de, 124-7
Baiona Sports Harbour, 127
Bairro dos Pescadores, 183

Baleeira, 227, 229-30
banks, 9
Barbate, 266, 323-6
Barca de Alva, 157
Barcas, Porto das, 221
Barizo, Ensenada de, 39
Barra, Ensenada de, 115
Barra de Aveiro, 159
Barrana, Playa (Escarabote), 83
Batalha, 171, 176
bateas, 12
Battle of Trafalgar, 321
Bay of Gibraltar/Algeciras, 336
Bayona (Baiona), 125-7
BBC Radio 4, 6
Belém, Doca de (Lisbon), 196-7, 199-200
Belixe, Enseada de, 227-8
Beluso, 110
Bensafrim, Rio, 231-2
Berlenga, Ilha da, 177, 180, 182
berthing costs, 8, *see also start of each chapter*
Betanzos, Ría de, 23, 27
BOAT Marina Shop (Nazaré), 171, 173
boat people, 321
Bolonia, Ensenada de, 325
Bom Sucesso, Doca de (Lisbon), 196, 199-200
Bonanza, 297
Bornalle, Ensenada de, 63
bottled gas, 8
Brexit, 6
Bueu, 110
buoyage, 3
Burgo, Playa del, 35

Caballo, Punta, 11, 90
Cabeiro, Punta, 68
Cabo de Ares, 211
Cabo Carvoeiro, 180
Cabo Corrubedo, 71
Cabo Cruz, 82, 83
Cabo Espichel, 184, 185, 208, 210
Cabo Finisterre (Fisterra), 11, 12, 44, 45, 51-4
Cabo de Gracia, 322
Cabo Mondego, 159, 165
Cabo Ortegal, 11, 12
Cabo Plato tunny net, 325
Cabo Prior, 22
Cabo da Roca, 180, 183, 184, 185
Cabo de Santa María, 251, 252, 254, 257
Cabo de São Vicente, 2, 208, 221, 222, 223, 226, 228
Cabo Silleiro, 128, 129
Cabo Toriñana, 45, 47
Cabo Trafalgar, 302, 316, 320-22
Cabo de Udra, 111
Cabo Villano, 47
Cádiz, 303, 304, 312-15
Cádiz, Bahía de (Cádiz Bay), 303-315
Caion, 37
Cala Arenas, Punta de, 328, 330

Caldas da Rainha, 171
Camariñal, Punta, 324
Camariñas, 45, 46, 47, 48, 49
Camariñas, Ría de, 45, 46-9
Cambados (Puerto de Tragove), 91, 92
Camelle, 45
Caminha, 137, 138
Camino de Santiago see Santiago de Compostela
Canal, Portinho do, 220, 221
Canal do Judeo (Seixal), 203
Canal do Montijo, 203, 207
Canal de Padre Santo (Mazagón), 288-90
Canal de Punta Umbría, 284-7
Canal de Sagres, 71, 72, 73
Canela, Isla, 266, 276-8
Cangas, 116
Caño Canelao, 277
Cape St Vincent *see* Cabo de São Vicente
Caramiñal, 77, 80-81
Cariño, Ensenada de (El Ferrol), 24
Carnero, Punta, 322, 328, 330, 336
Carrapateira, 221
Carregeros, Playa de, 83
Carreiro da Fortaleza, 182, 183
Carreiro do Mosteiro, 182, 183
Carril, 87
Carvoeiro, Cabo, 180
Cascais, 186-9
Cávado, Rio, 142
Cedeira, Ría de, 19-21
Cée, 56, 57
Centro Náutico de Algés (Lisbon), 203
Centro Náutico Elcano (Cádiz), 315
certificates of competence, 6, 7, 342-3
Ceuta Point, 322
chandlery, 7
chart datum, 4
charts & chart agents, 3-4, 341
Chipiona, 266, 291-3, 294, 297, 299
Cíes, Islas, 11, 16, 17, 112, 113
Cirro, Ensenada de, 29
climate see weather & forecasts
Club Nautico de Cobres (Vigo), 123
Club Náutico Sevilla, 297, 299, 300, 301
Clube Naval da Nazaré, 172-3
coast radio stations, 4, *see also start of each chapter*
Cobres, Club Nautico de (Vigo), 123
Coimbra, 161, 165
Columbus, 285
Combarro, 106-7
consulates, 342
Corcubión, Ría de, 53, 56-8
Corme, 42
Corme y Laxe (Lage), Ría de, 40-43
Coroso, Isolote, 79
Corrubedo, 69
Corrubedo, Cabo, 71
Cortegada, Islas, 16, 17, 87
Corvo, Porto, 221
Costa da Morte (Coast of Death), 12, 36-45

ATLANTIC SPAIN AND PORTUGAL **349**

INDEX

Costa Nova, Marina da (Canal Mira), 162
Costa de Prata (Silver Coast), 159
Couso, Punta, 111
Cova do Sono, 183
Crebra, Isla, 63
crime, 7, 8
Cristina, Isla, 266, 276, 277, 279
cruising grounds, 1-2
Cruz, Cabo, 82, 83
Cruz, Puerto de, 82-3
Cubelo, Porto, 57, 58
Culatra, Ilha da, 257
currency, 9
currents, 2, *see also start of each chapter*

Davila Sport (Vigo), 119
day signals, 7
Deutscher Wetterdienst (DWD), 4, 5
diesel, 7
Doca de Pedroucous (Lisbon), 198
documentation, 6-7, 342-3
Doñana National Park (Parque Nacional de Doñana), 294, 297
Douro, Rio, 152-7
drinking water, 8
drugs, 7
Dunes National Park, 69

El Ferrol, 23, 24-5
El Puerto de Santa María, 303, 304, 310-311
El Rompido, 280-83
El Son (Puerto del Son), 68
El Terrón, 283
Elcano, Centro Náutico (Cádiz), 315
electricity, 8
email, 9
embassies, 342
Enseada de Belixe, 227
Enseada da Nazaré, 172
Enseada de Sagres, 228
Ensenada de Baiona, 124-7
Ensenada de Barbate tunny net, 324-5, 329
Ensenada de Barizo, 39
Ensenada de Barra, 115
Ensenada de Bolonia tunny net, 325
Ensenada de Bornalle, 63
Ensenada de Cariño (El Ferrol), 24
Ensenada de Cirro, 29
Ensenada de Esteiro, 63
Ensenada de Ezaro, 57, 58
Ensenada de La Lanzada, 96
Ensenada de Limens, 115
Ensenada de Llagosteira, 53, 54
Ensenada de Mera, 35
Ensenada Norte de San Xulian (San Julian), 90
Ensenada de Palmeira, 79
Ensenada de San Francisco, 63
Ensenada de San Simón, 115, 122-3
Ensenada del Sardiñeiro, 55
Ensenada Sur de San Xulian (San Julian), 90-91
entry & regulations, 6-7
Ericeira, 183
Escarabote, 83
Esmoriz, Lagoa de, 157
Esordi, Playa, 55
Espichel, Cabo, 184, 185, 210
Espigón, Playa de, 284

Espinho, 157, 159
Esposende, 142, 144
Esteiro, Ensenada de, 63
Estuario de Tejo, 201-2
EU regulations, 6-7, 342-3
Euro, 9
Europa Point, 334, 336
European Health Insurance Card (EHIC), 9
Ezaro, Ensenada de, 57, 58

facilities, 7-9, *see also start of each chapter*
Farilhões, Ilhéus dos, 183
Faro, 251, 255-7
Faro, Isla del (I. Cíes), 113
Farol (Culatra), 257
Fatima, 171
fax, 9
Ferragudo, 241
Ferrol, Ría de, 23-5
fiestas, 9
Figueira da Foz, 164-7
Fisterre (Finisterra), Cabo, 11, 12, 44, 45, 51-4
Finisterre (Fisterra), Puerto, 53, 54
Finisterre Vessel Traffic Services, 45
fish & fishing, *see tunny nets*; *viveros and start of each chapter*
flags, vii, 6, 7, 336, 342-3
fog, 1, 2, 4
Fontán, 28-9
forecast areas, 4, 5
formalities, 6-7, 342-3
Formosa, Ría (Parque Natural), 251, 256-7, 263
Fortaleza, Carreiro da, 182, 183
Foz, Figueira da, 164-7
Foz do Minho, 134-8
Foz de Odeleite, 273-4
Freixo (Freijo), 63, 64-5
Frouxeira, Punta del, 22
fuels, 7-8
Fuzeta, 253, 262, 263

gales, 2
Galicia, 1, 2, 5, 10-129
Galicia Day, 97
Gallineras, Puerto de (Cádiz), 315, 316, 318-19
gas, 8
Gelves, Puerto, 297, 298, 300, 301
Gibraltar, 1, 2, 6, 7, 334-40, 343
Gibraltar Bay (Bay of Algeciras), 336
Gibraltar Strait, 2, 321-2
Gilão, Rio, 263-4
glossary, 344-8
Golfo Artabo, 23-35
Google Earth/Google Maps, 4
Gracia, Cabo de, 322
GRIB files, 4, 5
Grove, San Martin del (Puerto O Grove), 91, 92
Guadalquivir, Río, 294-301
Guadiana, Río, 267-75
Guerreiros do Río, 273, 274
Gures, Playa, 57, 58

harbour signals, vii, 4, 133 *see also marinas and start of each chapter*
hazards, 1, 2, *see also tunny nets*; *viveros, and start of each chapter*

health matters, 8-9
Higuerita, Ría de la, 276-9
holding tanks, 8
holidays, national, 9
Huelva, Ría de, 284-7

Ilha da Berlenga, 177, 180, 182
Ilha da Culatra, 257
Ilhéus dos Farilhões, 183
Ilhotes do Martinhal, 229-30
Inmarsat, 5
Inshore Traffic Zones, 4
Insua Nova, 136, 137
insurance, 6-7
internet, 4, 5, 6, 8, 9, 342, 343-4
Isla de Arousa, 89-91
Isla Canela, 266-7, 276-8
Isla Cortegarda, 16, 17, 87
Isla Crebra, 63
Isla Cristina, 266, 276, 277, 279
Isla del Faro (I. Cíes), 113
Isla del Norte (I. Cíes), 113
Isla Ons National Park, 16, 17, 98, 99, 100
Isla de San Martín (I. Cíes), 113
Isla Tambo, 105, 106, 108
Isla de Tarifa, 327, 328, 329
Isla Toxa Grande, 91, 92
Isla Viños, 113
Islas Cíes National Park, 11, 16, 17, 112, 113
Islas Cortegada National Park, 16, 17, 87
Islas Sagres, 71, 72, 73
Islas Sálvoras National Park, 16, 17, 71, 72, 74
Islas Sisargas, 36, 39
Islote Jidoiro Arenoso, 91
Islote Ostreira, 80
Isolote Coroso, 79

Jerez, 310
Jidoiro Arenoso, Islote, 91
Judeo, Canal do (Seixal), 203

La Bota, 284
La Coruña *see* A Coruña
La Graña (El Ferrol), 25
La Guardia, 128-9
La Lanzada, Ensenada de, 96
La Línea, 1, 332-3, 335, 336
La Passage (Foz do Minho), 137, 138
Ladeiro do Chazo, 83
Lage (Laxe), 43
Lagoa, Punta (Vigo), 121
Lagoa de Esmoriz, 157
Lagoa de Obidos, 176
Lagos, 231-4
Lances de Tarifa tunny net, 329
Langosteira, Punta, 36
languages, 1, 14, 344-8
Laranjeiras, 274
Las Marismas de Odiel, 284
Las Piédras, Río de, 266, 280-83
Laxe (Lage), 43
laying up, 7
Leixões, 148-51
Lerez, Río, 108
levante, 2
Liceo Maritimo (Vigo), 119
lights & light dues, 3, 7
Lima, Rio, 139-42

Index

Limens, Ensenada de, 115
Lisbon, 184, 185, 191, 194-203
Llagosteira, Ensenada de, 53, 54
Lobeiro Grande, Playa de, 83
Luz, Praia da, 234

mail, 9
Malabata, Punta, 322
Malpica, 36, 37-8
The Man Who Never Was, 284
Mandeo, Rio, 27
Mañons, 83
maps, 4
Mar de Palha (Lisbon), 203
Marela, Praia da, 228
Marin, 105, 108
Marina Bay (Gibraltar), 336, 339-40
Marina da Costa Nova (Canal Mira), 162
Marina Playa de Mugardo (El Ferrol), 25
marinas, 6, 7, 8, 14, 196-8, 266, see also start of each chapter
Las Marismas de Odiel, 284
Martinhal, Ilhotes do, 229-30
Martinhal, Praia do, 227
Matalascañas, 284, 288, 291
Mau, Rio, 143
Mazagón, 266
Mazagón Huelva Channel, 284, 288-90, 299
medical matters, 8-9
Meia Praia, 236
Melide, Playa de, 99
Meloxo (Melojo), Porto de, 95
Mera, Ensenada de, 35
Mértola, 274, 275
migrant boat people, 321
Milfontes, Vila Nova de, 219-21
Minho (Miño), Rio, 135-8
Miño (Ría de Betanzos), 27
Mira, Rio, 219-21
Moaña, 117
Mojarra, Punta de la, 277
Mondego, Cabo, 159, 165
Mondego, Rio, 165, 166
money, 9
Monte Real Club de Yates (Baiona), 126, 127
Montijo, Canal do, 203, 207
Mosteiro, Carreiro do, 182, 183
Mugardo, Marina Playa de (El Ferrol), 25
Mugia (Muxía), 47, 50
Muros, 61-3
Muros, Ría de, 58-69
Muxía (Mugia), 47, 50

national holidays, 9
national parks, 15-17, 69, 72, 87, 99, 113, 294, 297, see also *Parques Natural*
Navegador (Seixal), 207
navigation, 2-4
navigational warnings, 4, 5
Navtex, 4-5
Nazaré, 169-74
Noia (Noya), 63, 64, 65
nomenclature, 4
nordeste pardo, 2
nortada, 132
Norte, Isla del (I. Cíes), 113
Northwood (RN), 5
Noya (Noia), 63, 64, 65

O Grove, Puerto (San Martin del Grove), 91, 92
O Sitio, 171, 173, 174
O Xufre, Porto, 90
Obidos, 171
Obidos, Lagoa de, 176
Ocean Village Marina (Gibraltar), 336, 338
Odiel, Las Marismas de, 284
Oeiras, 190, 191, 192-3
Olhão, 251, 258, 259-61
Ons, Isla, 16, 17, 98, 99, 100
Oporto *see* Porto
Ortegal, Cabo, 11, 12
Ostreira, Islote, 80

Padre Santo, Canal de (Mazagón), 288-90
Palha, Mar de (Lisbon), 203
Palmeira, Ensenada de, 79
Palmeira, Puerto, 79
Panjón (Panxón), 127
paperwork, 6-7, 342-3
paraffin, 8
Parque das Nações Marina (Lisbon), 196, 200, 201-2
Parques Natural, 251, 256-7, 329
passage planning, 1-2
passports, 6, 7, 342-3
Pedras Negras, Porto, 96
Pedroucous, Doca de (Lisbon), 198
Peniche, 177, 178, 179-83
Peniche do Cima, 181
permiso aduana, 343
permiso de residencia, 342, 343
petrol, 7
Piedra Borron, 113
Las Piédras, Río de, 266, 280-83
Pindo, Porto del, 57, 58
place names, 1
Placere, Playa, 108
plans (key to symbols used), 9
Plato, Cabo, 325
Playa de América, 127
Playa de Arena (I. Cíes), 113
Playa Arena de Adra/Agra, 105
Playa Arena das Rodas, 113
Playa Barrana (Escarabote), 83
Playa del Burgo, 35
Playa de Cangas, 116
Playa de Carregeros, 83
Playa Esordi, 55
Playa de Espigón, 284
Playa Gures, 57, 58
Playa Lobeiro Grande, 83
Playa de Melide, 99
Playa de Mugardo, Marina (El Ferrol), 25
Playa Placere, 108
Playa de la Puntilla, 309
Playa de Quenje, 56
Playa de San Martín (I. Cíes), 113
Playa Sardiñeiro, 55
Playa de Seaya, 39
Playa de Silgar, 102
Pobra do Caramiñal, 77, 80-81
Pomarão, 268, 273, 275
poniente, 2
Ponta de Sagres, 227-8, 230
Ponte Cais (Faro), 255, 257, 258
Pontevedra, 108
Pontevedra, Ría de, 98-110
Portimão, 238, 239-42

Portinho de Arrábida, 211
Portinho do Canal, 220, 221
Porto (Oporto), 152-7
Porto Atlântico (Leixoes), 150
Porto das Barcas, 221
Porto Corvo, 221
Porto Cubelo, 57, 58
Porto de Meloxo (Melojo), 95
Porto Novo (Ría de Pontevedra), 101, 102, 103
Porto O Xufre, 90
Porto Pedras Negras, 96
Porto del Pindo, 57, 58
Portosin, 66-7
positions, 4, 10
postal services, 9
Póvoa de Varzim, 143-5
Praça Larga, 257, 259
practicalities, 6-8
Praia, Meia, 236
Praia de Belixe, 228
Praia da Luz, 234
Praia da Marela, 228
Praia do Martinhal, 227
Praia da Rocha, 240, 242
Prainha Das Poças, 228
precipitation, 2
Prior, Cabo, 22
public holidays, 9
public transport, 9
Puente del Puerto, Río de, 47
Puerto América (Cádiz), 266, 313-15
Puerto Astaroth *see* Rota
Puerto Deportivo de Baiona, 127
Puerto de Cruz, 82-3
Puerto de Finisterre (Fisterra), 53, 54
Puerto del Gallineras (Cádiz), 315, 316, 318-19
Puerto Gelves, 297, 298, 300, 301
Puerto Deportivo Isla Cristina, 266-7, 277, 279
Puerto Marina El Rompido, 280-83
Puerto Deportivo de Muxía, 50
Puerto O Grove (San Martin del Grove), 91, 92
Puerto Palmeira, 79
Puerto Deportivo Punta Lagoa, 121
Puerto Deportivo San Adrián, 122-3
Puerto Deportivo Sancti-Petri, 318, 319
El Puerto de Santa María, 303, 310-311
Puerto Sherry, 303, 304, 307-9
Puerto del Son (El Son), 68
Puerto de Tragove (Cambados), 91, 92
Punta Aguiera, 63
Punta Caballo, 11, 90
Punta Cabeiro, 68
Punta de Cala Arenas, 328, 330
Punta Camariñal, 324
Punta Carnero, 322, 328, 330, 336
Punta Couso, 111
Punta del Acebuche, 336
Punta del Frouxeira, 22
Punta de la Mojarra, 277
Punta Lagoa (Vigo), 121
Punta Langosteira, 36
Punta Malabata, 322
Punta Umbría, 266, 284-7
Puntadueme, 27
Puntilla, Playa de la, 309

ATLANTIC SPAIN AND PORTUGAL 351

INDEX

Queensway Quay Marina (Gibraltar), 336, 337-8
Quenje, Playa de, 56

Radio France International, 6
Radio Nacional de España, 6
radio stations, 4, 5, 6, *see also start of each chapter*
radio weather forecasts, 5, 6
Radiodifusão Portuguesa, 6
rainfall, 2
Rates, 143
Raxó, 105
Real Club Náutico de Vigo, 120
regulations, 6-7, 342-3
repairs, 7
Ría de A Coruña, 23, 30-35
Ría de Aldan, 111
Ría de Ares, 23, 27
Ría de Arousa, 11, 70-97
Ria de Aveiro, 158-63
Ría de Betanzos, 23, 27
Ría de Camariñas, 45, 46-9
Ría de Cedeira, 12, 19-21
Ría de Corcubión, 56-8
Ría de Corme y Laxe (Lage), 40-43
Ría de Ferrol, 23-5
Ría Formosa, Parque Natural de, 251, 256-7, 263
Ría de Huelva, 284-7
Ría de la Higuerita, 276-9
Ría de Muros, 58-69
Ría de Pontevedra, 98-110
Ría de Vigo, 114, 115-23
Rianxo (Rianjo), 84-5
Rías Altas & Bajas, 1, 12
Ribeira (Riveira), Santa Uxia de, 77, 78-9
Rio Arade, 238, 240-41
Río de Barbate, 324
Rio Bensafrim, 231-2
Rio Cávado, 142
Río del Puente del Puerto, 47
Rio Douro, 152-7
Rio Gilão, 263-4
Río Guadalquivir, 294-301
Río Guadiana, 267-75
Río de las Piédras, 266, 280-83
Río Lerez, 108
Rio Lima, 139-42
Rio Mandeo, 27
Rio Mau, 143
Rio Minho (Río Miño), 135-8
Rio Mira, 219-21
Rio Mondego, 165, 166
Rio Sado, 212-15
Rio Tejo, 184, 185, 190-207
Riveira (Ribeira), Santa Uxia de, 77, 78-9
Roca, Cabo da, 180, 183, 184, 185
Rocha, Praia da, 240, 242
Rodas, Playa Arena de, 113
El Rompido, 280-83
Rota, 266, 303, 304, 305-6
Rota Naval Base, 303
Royal Cruising Club Pilotage Foundation, vi
Royal Yachting Association, 7
RTTY, 4, 5

Sada Marina, 28-9
Sado, Rio, 212-15
Sagres, Enseada de, 228
Sagres, Islas, 71, 72

Sagres, Ponta de, 227-8, 230
sailing & navigation, 2-4
Sálvoras, Islas, 16, 17, 71, 72, 74
San Adrián, 122-3
San Francisco, Ensenada de, 63
San Julian (San Xulian), 89, 90-91
San Martín, Isla (& Playa) de (I. Ciés), 113
San Martin del Grove (Puerto O Grove), 91, 92
San Simón, Ensenada de, 115, 122-3
San Vicente del Mar, 96
San Xulian (San Julian), 89, 90-91
Sancti-Petri, 266, 316-19
Sangengo (Sanxenxo), 101, 102, 104-5
Sanlúcar de Barrameda, 295, 297
Sanlúcar de Guadiana, 268, 273, 274-5
Santa Luzia, 263, 264
Santa María, Cabo de, 251, 252, 254, 257
Santa María, El Puerto de, 303, 304, 310-311
Santa Uxia de Riveira (Ribeira), 77, 78-9
Santiago de Compostela, 31, 54, 66, 86, 97
Santo Amaro, Doca de (Lisbon), 196, 197, 198, 199-200
Santo António, Vila Real de, 268, 269-70, 272, 273, 274
Sanxenxo (Sangengo), 101, 102, 104-5
São Jacinto, Baía de, 161, 162, 163
São Martinho do Porto, 175-6
São Vicente, Cabo de, 2, 208, 221, 222, 223, 226, 228
Sardiñeiro, Ensenada del, 55
Sardiñeiro, Playa, 55
Schengen Agreement, 336
sea temperatures, 2
Seaya, Playa de, 39
security, 7, 8
Seixal, 203, 204, 205-7
Seno de Corcubión, 56-8
services, 7-9, *see also start of each chapter*
Sesimbra, 209-211
Sétubal, 212, 213-15
Seville, 294, 297, 298-301
sewage discharge, 8
Sheppard's (Gibraltar), 338, 339, 340
Sherry, Puerto, 303, 304, 307-9
Ship Hotel (Sunborn), 336, 338
shipping forecasts (BBC), 6
ship's papers, 6, 7
siesta period, 8
signals, 4, 7
Silgar, Playa de, 102
Silleiro, Cabo, 128, 129
Sines, 216-18
Sisargas, Islas, 36, 39
Sitio, 171, 173, 174
smuggling, 6
Sociedad España de Radio, 6
Son, Puerto del (El Son), 68
Sono, Cova do, 183
Southern Bay (Isla Ons), 99
Strait of Gibraltar, 2, 321-2
Sun Sail Marina (Seville), 297, 299, 300, 301
Sunborn (Ship Hotel), 336, 338
swell, vii, 1, 2, *see also start of each chapter*
symbols used on plans, 9

Tagus Yacht Center (Seixal), 203, 205, 206-7
Tambo, Isla, 105, 106, 108
Tanger, 322
Tarifa, 2, 322, 327-9
Tarifa, Isla de, 327, 328, 329
Tarifa G-5 port tax, 343
Tavira, 263-5
taxes, 7, 133, 343
Tejo, Rio, 184, 185, 190-207
telephones, 9
temporary import, 343
El Terrón, 283
The Man Who Never Was, 284
tides, 2-3, *see also start of each chapter*
time, 4
Toja (Isla Toxa Grande), 91, 92
Tomar, 171
Toriñana, Cabo, 45, 47
tourist offices, 342
Toxa Grande, Isla, 91, 92
Trafalgar, Cabo, 302, 316, 320-22
Traffic Separation Zones, 3, 4
Tragove, Puerto de (Cambados), 91, 92
transport & travel, 9
Trinity House, vii
Tróia, 212, 213-15
tunny nets (almadrabas), 2, 324-5, 329

Udra, Cabo de, 111
Umbría, Punta, 266, 284-7

Varadoiro do Xufre Boatyard, 89
VAT, 7, 343
vendavale, 2
Viana do Castelo, 139-42
Vigo, 118-20
Vigo, Ría de, 114, 115-23
Vila do Conde, 146-7
Vila Nova de Milfontes, 219-21
Vila Real de Santo António, 268, 269-70, 272, 273
Vilagarcía, 77, 86-7
Vilamoura, 247-50
Vilanova Marina, 88
Vilaxoan (Villajuan), 87
Villagarcía de Arousa, 77, 86-7
Villano,, 47
Viños, Isla, 113
visas, 342-3
visibility, 1, 2, 4, *see also start of each chapter*
viveros (shellfish rafts), 12, 14, 76, 80

Walk on Wind (chandlery), 151
warnings, navigational, 4, 5
water supplies, 8
waypoints, 10, 342
weather & forecasts, 1, 2, 4-6, *see also start of each chapter*
Weatherfax, 5
websites & addresses, 4, 6, 8, 9, 342-4, *see also start of each chapter*
Wi-Fi, 9
winds, 1, 2, *see also start of each chapter*
World Biosphere Reserve, 284

Xufre, Porto O, 90

Yate Clube de Porto, 150

Zahara, 325